D0787130

The Order of Evils

The Order of Evils

Toward an Ontology of Morals

Adi Ophir

Translated by Rela Mazali and Havi Carel

ZONE BOOKS · NEW YORK

2005

© 2005 Adi Ophir
ZONE BOOKS
1226 Prospect Avenue
Brooklyn, NY 11218

Originally published in Hebrew © 2000 Am Oved
Publishers, Tel Aviv.

Printed in the United States of America.

Distributed by The MIT Press,
Cambridge, Massachusetts, and London, England

Library of Congress Cataloging-in-Publication Data

Ophir, Adi.
    [Lashon la-ra'. English]
    The order of evils : toward an ontology of morals / Adi
Ophir ; translated by Rela Mazali and Havi Carel.
        p. cm.
    Includes biographical references (p.) and index.
    ISBN 1-890951-51-X
    1. Ethics. 2. Philosophy, Moral. 3. Good and evil.
4. Philosophy, Modern – 20th century. 5. Holocaust, Jewish
(1939–1945) – Moral and ethical aspects. I. Title.

BJ1401.06413 2005
170–dc22   2004050121

There is an evil which I have seen under the sun, and it is common among men.

—Ecclesiastes 6.1

Contents

Preface

This treatise seeks to give Evil a tongue.* It seeks an idiom that will enable one to express Evil as part of reality, a quotidian, routine, and ordered part: not as a diabolical element that transcends reality and not as a meaningless and unreal absence of good, but as part of what is. Instead of confronting the source of Evil, that which allegedly lies at the essence of man's body or soul or of the political regime, this treatise examines the unnecessary social and historical production of evil. Rather than discussing the evil urge (*yetzer hara*), it investigates the production of evils — the evil things that make people's lives bad: pain, suffering, loss, humiliation, damage, terror, alienation, and ennui. To assume that the social production of evils has more or less ordered patterns, which can be exposed and changed, is to attempt to develop a more or less ordered and systematic moral discourse: ordered, but not closed; a systematic effort of the kind that lays its own foundations without presuming in advance to know how secure those foundations are.

This work provides a general outline and the central themes of a moral theory based on a new interpretation of Evil. This theory arises from one simple insight: people cause other people many evils — intentionally and unintentionally, knowingly and unknowingly, alone and in company with others. A large proportion of

---

* Throughout the text, "evil" designates two different things. The uppercase "Evil" refers to the general and abstract noun, whereas the lowercase "evil" refers to specific, concrete cases of a "bad thing," injury, harm, or wrong. The Hebrew word that the lower-case "evil" translates is *raah* (רעה), which may connote both the event of being harmed, harm as an object, and a sense of injustice related to this event's occurrence or this object's coming into being. This distinction between Evil and evils follows (to a certain extent) Heidegger's distincion between Being and being. See p. 14. — Trans.

11

these evils is not accidental; their cause has its own pattern and order. In other words, one can talk about the production and distribution of evils in the same manner one talks about the production and distribution of goods or merchandise. One can look for their production patterns, production relations, and modes of production, the patterns of distribution and exchange, and even the patterns of consumption.[1] Some of these evils are superfluous; some are preventable, and if they are not preventable then at least the suffering and damage they cause can be reduced. Superfluous evils that can be prevented or reduced should be prevented or reduced. Evil is the order of superfluous evils in a society.

This conception of Evil develops here gradually, through an analysis of the two main types of evils — suffering and loss — and by combining a phenomenological investigation of the experience of evil with a structural investigation of the social aspects of its production and distribution. This interpretation of Evil results in a transformation of the moral discourse, a new demarcation of the moral domain, a new definition of what is "morally proper," and an account of the historical moment in which this transformation of moral discourse occurs.

When someone is indifferent to superfluous evils, he expresses an immoral attitude, and perhaps performs an improper act — improper from a moral perspective of course. But one can also say just that he lacks any moral interest at all.[2] Indifference to someone who suffers superfluous evils is the end of moral interest and of the moral matter, and the limit of the moral as a domain within culture: just as indifference to deceit and error excludes one from the scientific domain, indifference to superfluous suffering and loss excludes one from the moral domain. No scientific study can be conducted in an atmosphere of indifference to deceptions and errors; no moral judgment can be properly enacted and no moral act can be properly conducted in an atmosphere of indifference to superfluous evils. This indifference is not a mental trait but a mode of relating, a threshold of sensibility, a type of blindness, structured by a fairly organized field of vision, speech, and action. Overcoming this indifference does not necessarily entail a mental transformation. To change a few characteristics of the discursive or cultural field will suffice. These characteristics, which determine the threshold of moral sensibility and vary culturally and historically, are what I analyze extensively in the course of this study.

Generally speaking, moral interest is here presented as care for the other. To be "inside the moral" is to have an interest in the superfluous evils others suffer from, but also an interest in the production and distribution of these evils. A moral action is dead set on disrupting these orders so as to lessen the evils and reduce their harm. The order of superfluous evils and its treatment in all relevant fields of knowledge and spheres of action should be positioned at the center of any moral system. It should interpret what evil is before it determines what the good, the just, or the proper are. It should position Evil as a top priority in its contemplative hierarchy, but it should also understand that Evil is a result of concrete historical and social conditions, whose investigation and interpretation become an inseparable part of its agenda.

The moral theory presented here develops out of a very mundane, secular answer to an old, mainly theological, question: what is Evil and what is its source? Evil, I argue, has no meaning other than the ever-changing, open-ended ensemble of superfluous evils and the order of their social production. Satan and the evil urge, original sin and the breaking of the tablets, all disappear at once. This answer displaces the center of debate from theology (how could Evil exist in a world created by an omnipotent, benevolent God?) and psychology (is man born evil? precisely where does Evil reside in man?) to sociology, political economy, political science, geography, and ecology. This displacement is another step in the secularization process of Western thought that began with modernity. The quest here is to rid the question of Evil not only of the shadow of theodicy but also of the last remnants of transcendence that have characterized Western moral thought, in particular the disciples of Kant and of Lévinas. This treatise aims to position Evil in human history, in historical forms of social existence, and to attribute to human beings full responsibility for what they do to other human beings, without letting them escape to heaven or hell, but also without letting them retreat from the historicity of social existence to the depths of the human soul and its mysterious, unchangeable nature, or to the enigma of human freedom.

Moreover, this answer stubbornly attempts to redefine "the morally proper" as the right action in the face of superfluous evils, and to discover the proper through a morally motivated interpretation of the historical reality producing these superfluous evils. The moral "ought" is not presented here as the opposite of the "is." Rather, it is the opposite of a certain possibility of the being of Being — the being of a superfluous excess, which is precisely the being that ought to be abolished. For one to understand what is proper (that is, what ought to be done[3]), there is no need for a moral law that allegedly floats above reality or is somehow intuited

13

or uncovered beyond it. It is enough to understand superfluous evil, those unnecessary evils that could have been prevented or reduced but were not.

Using Heideggerian jargon, but in a way that goes directly against Heidegger's explicit understanding of ethics and morality, one may say that values, rights, and duties are but particular forms of letting the superfluous appear.[4] There may be others: virtuous dispositions, moral sensibilities, sympathy, and the very experience and display of suffering. Whatever these forms, they are formations of "the moral," for the moral is a certain discourse, point of view, and type of concern — all three together — that let Evil appear or — it comes to the same thing — let a certain excess of being appear as that which should not have been.

Evil never appears as such; it is always already "enframed" by one of these formations. Only evils appear, in the plural, as particular entities, "existents" with certain objective and certain subjective features. The manifold of evils relate to Evil in the same way that the manifold of beings relate to Being in Heidegger's thought: making it present and concealing it at one and the same time, articulating it in and through language (that names and describes this and that particular being, or evil), and making one forget the persistence of the yet, or forever, inexpressible Evil and the possibility of different kinds of enframing it. Kinds of ethics, moral systems, and normative codes see no Evil; they can only designate (refer to, show, put on display, remind and commemorate, predict and warn against) and interpret series of occurrences of suffering and pain, losses, damages, and ruin that should not have taken place.

The problem is to understand the being of the moral, the modus of its existence, in order to understand the moral way of being. It is necessary to understand what is a moral matter (*res morale*) in order to understand what a moral interest is. Moral matters determine moral interests. The question of moral judgment that has dominated moral discourse since Kant, at least, will here be demoted to second place. Instead, the discussion focuses on moral matters: on things, superfluous evils; and on intentionality and interest, the attempt to disrupt the order of production and distribution of these evils. In this sense, this is a moral ontology, a discussion of the moral as part of what there is. The moral theory this treatise aims to develop may thus be named an ontology of morals.

Despite the implications of discovering (but not deducing) an "ought" within what is, this ontology of morals opposes the attempt to reduce the moral to another, more fundamental dimension of human reality. Such a reduction is a familiar move in modern Western thought, and it is identified more than anything with its three great "interpreters," Marx, Nietzsche, and Freud, who offered, each in his own way, a reduction of the moral to something else: the economic (the relations of production), life or the force pulsing in it (the will to power), or the erotic (libidinal drives). In opposition to this reductionism, the moral must be envisioned as a relatively autonomous domain and as a moment of intention, thought, and action that cannot be reduced to any other element that allegedly predates and conditions it. The moral "ought" will be impossible to deduce from any amoral interest. Explicating and corroborating this claim will reaffirm and reinterpret a central element in Kant's moral theory: the absolute independence of the moral imperative from any other consideration. But this independence would not imply or presuppose the radical separation that Kant introduces between the phenomenal realm of suffering and loss and the noumenal realm of freedom and the goodwill that guides moral judgment. The gap between "what really is" and "what ought to be" remains in the midst of the real, and out of this real an "ought" is extracted. This gap appears every time someone is in distress, suffers, experiences loss, cries for help — and can be assisted without unbearably increasing the suffering and loss of others. However, the transcendental moment is not completely erased. It reveals itself through the appeal of others in distress. This distress is shown as a type of presence that positions those confronting it as beings with moral interest and entreats them to transcend the "is" toward an "ought." The deliberation guiding the response to this call unfolds before our eyes because particular attention is paid to the complex ensemble of existing and putative causes and conditions — all of which compose the experiences of individuals with moral interest. The very existence of that call and the concrete possibility of the response is interpreted as another stage in the secularization of the transcendent characterizing Western thought from its very inception.

Moral interest is an interest in an other who is (or might be) in distress, in his suffering and welfare. This definition strongly resembles the moral philosophy of the Jewish-French thinker Emmanuel Lévinas, to whom I am more indebted than my footnotes might suggest. But my distance from Lévinas is no less important. Lévinas speaks of the traces of otherness, which has no content or form and appears through the face of a concrete other, and of absolute transcendence beyond Being, which the other testifies to without being able to represent (or presence) it. I, on the other hand, insist on speaking about concrete others and their concrete or possible plight only. If a trace of transcendence still haunts my thinking, it is transcendence beyond the "is" to an "ought" that is completely within the world of human experience. My discussion belongs to a branch of ontology and not to a separate philosophical discourse that precedes and excludes it, as Lévinas's ethics aims to do. Moreover, in opposition to Lévinas, and to Derrida, who also takes up this same question, it is not the "otherness" of the other that is the basis or source of moral interest. Otherness is not morally relevant, only concrete others are, and they are morally relevant only because, and to the extent that, they are vulnerable, prone to suffering and already suffering concrete evils. What guides moral knowledge (or practical reason, *phronesis*) is the interest in superfluous evils that befall particular and concrete others or threaten them. What guides moral judgment and the intention of a moral act is the care for those others whom evil befalls. The care of the self, with all it entails, from self-love and nurturing to self-preservation, is, by definition, outside the domain of moral interest.

This leads to some far-reaching conclusions — only a few of which will be mentioned in this preface — concerning the character of the moral domain, its principle of demarcation, and the main questions at stake in it, its relation to other domains of theory and practice, of knowledge and power. This also, I repeat, entails a new agenda for moral theory. The main values in the ethical and moral tradition, such as justice, the good, happiness, freedom, and equality, are to be reinterpreted in light of the ontological interpretation of the concept of Evil. Questions such as what justice is, how to found a coherent theory of justice, and how to reconcile freedom and equality are marginalized, if not discarded altogether. Not because the ontology of morals has no interest in values like justice and equality, but because its interest focuses on modes of being and the cultural existence of values with special attention to their contribution to the order of superfluous evils in society. Values should preoccupy moral theory and discourse according to their contribution to the order of superfluous evils, since values are the creations every particular discourse — legal, political, ideological, or religious — that serve as instruments whose function is more or less defined in a given culture, and that serve this or another regime of evils and this or other forms of opposition and resistance to this regime. Values are that which should be judged and not what is used as a basis or guide for judgment. Proper values enable one to reduce the superfluous evils in a given society and to disrupt the order of their production and distribution.

This moves, of course, toward a relativist interpretation of the concept of value in general and of each and every specific and relevant value — justice, freedom, and equality included — but it will not entail moral relativism. In every given moment, there is only one true answer to the question which value, which normative conception, and which discursive strategy, of those possible in a given situation, more effectively reduce "the accumulative volume of superfluous evils." Certainly, there is no final, positive answer to this question, at least not one available to humans, since no human being can grasp the multitude and simultaneous occurrences of evils in their entirety, let alone predict all evils that would result from a certain course of action. And yet, given that different answers have different effects on the volume of superfluous evils, it is impossible that different answers to the same question will be equivalent, or similarly valuable or invaluable. Therefore, the fact that the answer to the (originally Nietzschean) question of the value of values has only a probable answer and cannot be answered with certainty, and the fact that no one can answer that question without being involved and interested in the answer, that there is no one to judge objectively and disinterestedly between competing answers, and the fact that one has to keep asking who is the one asking about the value of values and for whom is the value of each value measured — all these facts will not turn the moral theory presented here into a relativist theory. They will only make any situation in which moral deliberation takes place highly complex.

The complexity increases when one takes into account how fuzzy and problematic, indeed absurd, the notion of "the accumulative volume of superfluous evils" is. How can we compare one form of suffering with another, one loss with another, and how can we quantify suffering and loss? The solution presented here (particularly in Chapters Three and Six, in the discussions of damage and suffering) will be not to abandon any attempt to estimate and assess what increases Evil and what reduces it, but to single out certain components in familiar social situations that tend to impair the situation of people, and other components that tend to give them better protection from superfluous evils. Here's one example: situations and institutions that clearly separate the inside from the outside, where the cost of entering and existing is high (prison, for instance, but marriage or group travel as well), tend to have a greater volume of evils than situations that feature a low exit or entrance price. This happens because one entrapped in such a situation prefers exposure to evils over paying the exit price, and because relief from the outside is either too expensive or too hard to get.

Even more generally, we can expect a more reasonable answer to the question of "the accumulative volume of superfluous evils" the further we look and the larger the chunk of social and historical reality observed. In this sense, moral theory is no different from economics: it is highly difficult to explain the price of a single product in an insular economic interaction; it is much easier to explain patterns of price rises and drops over a relatively long time and large space. It is difficult to estimate the personal use value of someone's property (because one must take into account the sentimental value of objects, or the personal use value of different things); it is easier to estimate the property of a financial firm (which completely erases the personal use value) or of an individual taken merely as an economic subject. The same is true for physics: it is the difference between predicting the place and motion of a single particle in a gas chamber and predicting the pressure and temperature of the gas in that same chamber. Hence special attention must be paid to paradigmatic situations and institutions in which the logic of the production and distribution of evils becomes manifest — for example, a concentration camp, an army base, a regime of occupation, a state of war, a disintegrating family.

It is reasonable to assume that the ontological moral theory presented here will be interpreted as a version of utilitarianism: the concept of Evil replaces utility or happiness as the basis for determining what ought to be done and for evaluating values, institutions, and actions; the aspiration to reduce the volume of evils is nothing but a negative formulation of the aspiration to maximize general happiness or utility. And without a doubt, gain and loss, profit and damage, increase of enjoyment and reduction of suffering will be crucial to our thinking about moral judgment. Furthermore, the principles from which, allegedly, proper behavior is deduced will be examined by the amount of evils they cause or prevent. But this ontology of morals will nonetheless differ from most utilitarian conceptions on at least two main issues: first, in opposition to classical theories of utilitarianism, it does not presume an "external," objective, and disinterested point of view from which principles for the calculation of profit and damage, happiness and misery, can be proposed. This concession is not trivial; it forces us to redefine the limits and possibilities of moral discussion, to consider the patterns of competition for the authorized, knowledgeable representation of superfluous evils in different cultural sectors and to pay attention to social struggles over the calculation of the accumulation and dissemination of evils.

Second, in opposition to classical and contemporary utilitarian conceptions, the utility, damage, pleasure, and suffering at stake are those that were caused or might be caused to concrete, particular, and identifiable others. In the moral domain, the calculus of profit and loss is never selfish. The care for the other, and only that kind of care, is the determining factor. Also, the object of care will never be some indistinct collective — like "us," "our family," "the nation," or "society" — that also includes the utilitarian speaker, who conceives of it as an extended self, identifies with that self, and appoints himself as its spokesman or as the guardian of its welfare and well-being. Concern for the other, and this alone, is the determining factor.

It therefore follows that the moral act is not limited by the conditions of a just exchange system or just distribution. Responding to the call of others entails giving up and giving gratuitously. In the classical utilitarian conception, "general well-being" or "maximum utility or happiness to the maximum number of people" are concepts that mediate between the giving self and the benefiting self. Eventually, through the utility calculus, the loss involved in giving and sacrificing turns into profit through the increase in the general utility, in which the giver partakes as well. But according to the conception of negative utility offered here — minimizing evils for the maximum number of people — the self is taken out of the equation; the profit or damage he might incur as a result of the improvement in the condition of others is not taken into account. What renders giving its moral meaning, lets it appear as a moral act, is always the situation of the other in need, who is the object and the addressee of moral care, not the situation of the one who cares for the other. The moral (*hamusari*) is nothing but a type of giving (*mesira*) and a form of devotion or self-giving (*hitmasrut*). That is why matters such as compassion and solidarity, gift and sacrifice, will be emphasized in this treatise (especially in Chapters Five, Six, and Eight), at the expense of other moral categories such as justice, fairness, equality, or autonomy.

These last ideas echo Nietzsche's and Bataille's thoughts on expenditure and self-overcoming; moreover, they reveal, again, the influence of Emmanuel Lévinas's ethics, in particular its development by the French philosophers Jacques Derrida and Jean-François Lyotard. Sections of this treatise, and not only those dealing with sacrifice and giving, were written as a sympathetic

yet critical dialogue with the work of the latter two, especially
with Lyotard's interpretation of the victim and of moral obligation in *The Differend*. My affinity with these two thinkers is interwoven throughout this treatise, although I do not systematically
attempt to present or interpret their philosophical "doctrines"
(or those of any other philosopher for that matter). Through its
critical dialogue with and selective reading of Lévinas, Lyotard,
and Derrida, this treatise situates itself in the context of the ethical turn in contemporary Continental philosophy. The thrust of
this turn is to apply to moral theory several ideas from the radical critique of modern philosophy characterizing French thought
since the mid-1960s. This criticism borrows from Nietzsche and
Marx, Freud and Lacan, from structuralism, semiotics, and the
analysis of language, and perhaps above all from Heidegger. It
places any discourse — scientific, literary, aesthetic, legal, ideological, religious, and in particular philosophical — under suspicion.
Almost all of these suspicions acknowledge the material, embodied, and practical reality of reason and of the discourse that
articulates it. Radical critique recognizes discursive practices as a
type of action, even when discourse posits itself as the opposite of
action, as pure and disinterested deliberation, and it tries to trace
the mediating function of discourse in every act of consciousness.

French philosophy has developed this radical criticism in
several directions, two of which have substantially influenced
philosophical discourse as well as the social sciences and the humanities outside of France. One direction, identified mainly with
the early work of Jacques Derrida, continues to deconstruct discourse, trying to extend deconstruction to all spheres of knowledge and culture. Philosophical discourse is transformed here into
some kind of literary criticism of philosophical (or legal, political,
scientific, or aesthetic) texts, which actually erases the borders
between argument and rhetoric, philosophy and literature. The
other direction, primarily associated with the work of Michel Foucault, emphasizes the historicized and constructed nature of different discursive regimes and tries to uncover the template of their
relationships with other layers of social reality, and to reconstruct
the genealogy of their creation, institutionalization, and transformations. Philosophical discourse evolves in this framework into a
special type of cultural history of discursive regimes. Despite clear
differences between these two directions, both distance themselves from traditional philosophical discourse and blur the boundaries between philosophy and other forms of discourse. In both
directions, the awareness of the loss of a stable reference point of

scientific cognition, aesthetic taste, and moral deliberation is both exaggerated and nuanced. If one acknowledges the lack of a common criterion for the different "systems of values," "language games," or competing "discursive regimes," and between different views on what is morally proper, then one can envision this dead end as a departure point for a new form of thought.

Those accustomed to thinking with labels will quickly identify here some of the familiar trademarks of postmodernism in philosophy. This treatise's affinity with the so-called "French postmodern" philosophers is explicit and pronounced. Nonetheless, the topics surrounding the insipid debate about postmodernism in philosophy and in culture in general will barely find a place here.[5] The almost-popular debate about postmodernism usually omits the most interesting and important aspect of contemporary French post-structuralist philosophy, the very aspect that inspired this treatise and to which it is most deeply indebted: namely, philosophical thought as an attempt to understand the historical present ("our times," *l'actualité*), and the limitations and possibilities of reflexive and critical thought in the present historical conditions. More than being postmodern in spirit or style, the French post-structuralists are postmodern because they willingly take on the challenge presented by a postmodern world, which mocks the pretensions of modern philosophy to trace the limits of reason and language and guide our use of them, to lay the groundwork for moral and aesthetic judgment (or for the proper use of concepts, or the legitimate performance of speech acts), and to guarantee the existence of one philosophical or scientific idiom that can faithfully describe multiple dimensions of reality and translate correctly and unambiguously into "one language and one speech" what is said and expressed in all languages and dialects spoken.

This is a philosophy that never ceases to think its place in a world after Auschwitz and Hiroshima, a world haunted by terrorism and the threat of nuclear and/or ecological catastrophe, a world whose every corner connects to a capitalist global market, entwined in those global networks of information that feed it and to which it is exposed, a world where it is almost impossible to think a thought without an immediate economic, practical, or informative value. In this world, at this time, this philosophy strives to develop modes of thought and discursive practices that "make a difference," that are not immediately measured by market values or by their conformity with the existing social order and its prevalent discourse and not even by the criteria of the academic institution, at least not when the latter is run in close affinity with — and usually in subjection to — both the market and the state. Several of the philosophers who partook or are partaking in this discourse also try explicitly to restore to this world a moral point of view and give a critical account of it. While doing this, they assume a radical critique of the foundations of modern philosophy and do not, as many others persist in doing, defend their moral point of view from this criticism. This treatise is likewise preoccupied with the historical present characterizing postmodern philosophical discourse. It recognizes its debt to that very nonhomogeneous group of French philosophers that includes not only Emmanuel Lévinas, Jean-François Lyotard, Jacques Derrida, and Michel Foucault, but also Jean-Luc Nancy and Etienne Balibar.

Having said all this, perhaps I should boldly state that this is not a treatise about French philosophy or in French philosophy. If Israeli philosophy existed, this work would be part of it. It was thought and written in Hebrew, and it is activated and limited by the temporal conditions of this place and by the spatial conditions of this time, by what could be called "the Israeli condition" (which is always also, and has been since 1948, "the Palestinian condition"). The Israeli condition constantly remains on the horizon of the discussion presented here. This is so even when there is a conscious and explicit attempt to be liberated from the limitations of the dejecting prism that the Israeli context forces on the systematic effort to think the moral matter and to interpret moral categories (such as loss, suffering, indifference). These limitations are first and foremost relevant to the meaning of the Holocaust in Israeli culture and the status of "Auschwitz" as a synonym of "absolute" or "radical" Evil, a criterion for every possible evil, and an exemplary model for every future evil. Let me exaggerate the stakes: this work was born from an attempt to find a way to talk about Auschwitz without presupposing any meaning of "Auschwitz" and without positing Auschwitz as an absolute negative pole that any discussion of Evil must lead to and stop at. I wanted to think Evil outside the halo of the name "Auschwitz," in a way that would be liberated, as much as possible, from the shadow of this halo. I wanted to do that, among other things, in order to better understand Auschwitz as well as the present era that unwillingly finds its symbol and exemplar in it (I discuss this in the first half of Chapter Nine). But equally important was my desire to think about Evil outside the shadow of Auschwitz, free from the imperative to place any other catastrophe on the scale of Evil that Auschwitz created by becoming the paradigm of absolute Evil. I

wanted to clear a space — in Hebrew, in Israeli culture — for thinking about other catastrophic events that may be less horrible than
Auschwitz, perhaps, but whose call upon thought is much more
urgent. More urgent also because they involve an evil that is produced now, in conditions that can still be amended, or a future
evil that could still be prevented. More urgent also because such a
thought touches on my own responsibility, and that of my Israeli
readers, for the catastrophic conditions created in the territories
under Israeli occupation.

I refuse to accept the semireligious imperative, so prevalent in
Israeli culture, that forbids any comparison between Auschwitz
and other sites of Evil and that believes that such a comparison is
blasphemous. I looked for a responsible, deliberate, justified way,
rooted in a systematic moral theory, to restore a conceptual continuum that allows for a comparison between the Evil that took
place in Auschwitz and the Evil that the descendants of the victims and their inheritors create for the people they have turned
into refugees, foreigners, and noncitizens in their own country,
subjects of a military regime and freedom fighters in an anticolo-
nial struggle, terrorists, murderers. But just as much, I tried not
to presuppose my prejudice about the Israeli occupation in the
West Bank and Gaza and the relationship between Jews and Palestinians in Israel. The Israeli occupation initially turned my philosophical interest to the question of Evil, and in that context I
have found some of the clearest examples of the conditions under
which superfluous evils are produced. But here, too, I tried to
restore a conceptual continuum between everyday life under
occupation and everyday life in an allegedly democratic state,
whose citizens enjoy full civil rights, in order to compare the conditions of the production and distribution of evils, as well as various venues to oppose or resist the order of evils in different social
contexts and different historical situations. In general, Israeli reality at this time delineates the horizon of this treatise and provides
one of its motivations. This implies, among other things, a conscious and deliberate attempt to find in the moral theory developed here the means to crack the contemporary Zionist ideology
that dominates moral discourse in Israel today and to overcome
the limitation it imposes on thinking.

This work has two parallel beginnings, which could, in principle,
be presented in the reverse order. The parallel movements they
open will coincide at a certain point of the discussion, when the
notion of evil(s) appears and commences a third movement that

continues both simultaneously. The entire treatise is therefore divided into three parts according to the three movements of the discussion. Every part contains three chapters, all in all nine chapters that create a kind of *Aeneid*.

One starting point, which initiates the discussion in Part One, is disappearance — a simple, abstract category of experience. On the basis of the analysis of disappearance (in Chapter One), the categories of loss (Chapter Two) and damage (Chapter Three) are examined. A second starting point, which initiates the discussion in Part Two, is presence (Chapter Four), which is interpreted here as another abstract category of experience, on the basis of which the categories of excitation (Chapter Five) and suffering (Chapter Six) are explored. The discussion in each of the six chapters of the first two parts unfolds around one category of experience. Different aspects of experience associated with that category are examined, related, and juxtaposed. As mentioned above, this is done from two points of view, which, for the sake of convenience, I have called phenomenological and sociological. The former seeks to examine the limits and scope of discernible forms of experience, from which Evil will finally emerge as a specific mode of intensification; the latter looks for the social conditions of these forms of experience, which define the environment where evils are produced and distributed. From a methodological point of view, the phenomenological description of the subjective experience (of suffering, loss, and so on) is closer to the existentialist phenomenology of Sartre and Lévinas, and to the ontological phenomenology of Heidegger, than to the work of the other philosophers mentioned earlier. But the phenomenological analysis does not claim independence or primacy. It proceeds simultaneously with, leads to, and relies on a series of structural analyses of the objective conditions of experience, of different aspects of its existence as a being among beings, a sequence of events that take part in a complex web of social relations of power and exchange, of production and consumption.

The transition from one category to another results from an addition, accumulation, acceleration, and intensification of the simpler, more abstract experience, and its more general conditions: an intensified presence becomes an excitation, an intensified excitation becomes suffering; a disappearance to which an interested person is added is a loss; a loss whose value is estimated in terms of a certain exchange system is a damage. Suffering that is not prevented or relieved is an evil; damage that is not prevented or compensated for is an evil; when evil can be prevented but is not, can be relieved but isn't, it is a superfluous evil. This is where the third movement begins, the one dealing directly with Evil.

The discussion in the first two parts of the book is relatively abstract and unfolds as an analysis of a series of conceptual and experiential "simples," from disappearance to suffering. The aim of this analysis, however, is not to extract a new foundation for morality, to ground the discussion of Evil in a transcendental realm, or to look for its ultimate presuppositions. The aim is, rather, to develop and propose a new repertoire of concepts that will play, at one and the same time, in the existential-experiential realm and in the sociopolitical realm, and will be morally relevant without being drawn from — or necessarily being part of — a language of rights, duties, or values that idealizes "Man" and dehistoricizes his nature.

In the jargon of phenomenology, this means an attempt to coordinate (but not to confuse or bring into fusion) two "ontological regions" (the experiential and the social) in order to delineate morality itself as a sui generis ontological region. Evil will emerge as the central figure and focal point of this region, playing the role of God in religion, of the state in politics, or of truth in science. A whole new geography of the moral region ("the moral domain," in my own jargon) will be open at this point, and its articulation will become possible with the help of these concepts that claim to designate "moral entities" or, more precisely, entities susceptible to becoming morally loaded. In other words, my assumption has been that morality does not need new foundations; it needs a renewed language, a language that would bring it closer to social and existential reality, to the minute experiences of everyday life as much as to the most tragic upheavals of history.

In modern philosophical ethical jargon, the same project means a conscious and systematic disregard of the so-called natural fallacy that derives "ought" from "is." Since evil(s), and the moral interest in evil(s), are part of what is, it is necessary to understand the being of evil(s) before discussing the values, duties, or obligations associated with the elimination or prevention of evil(s). And since obligations, duties, and values are foundationless, embedded, historicized, and always given to interpretation according to the nature of the evil(s) that endow them with their meaning and form, it is worthwhile to endeavor to understand how these normative, prescriptive concepts emerge from the reality they are supposed to guide. This is one task of the book's third part.

Part Three takes up about half the treatise. It is more historically oriented, especially in its two last chapters. It engages extensively some episodes in the philosophical history of Evil, from Plato to Lévinas, and other episodes in the modern, political history of Evil, paying special but by no means exclusive attention to the extermination of the Jews in Europe. In style, cadence, and tone, this part differs significantly from the more schematic discussions of the two earlier ones. To a certain extent, this is because the moral language sought in the earlier chapters is already at hand. This language is now put to use.

Chapter Seven presents the central idea of the treatise — the existence of a traceable social order of the production and distribution of superfluous evils — and derives from it a series of consequences. It is in this context that the concepts of justice, wrong, and tort are redefined, the moral interest (in the double meaning of this word mentioned above[6]) is extensively discussed, principles are set for the demarcation of morality as a theoretical and practical domain, and several new categories appear as essential to completing the first sketch of an ontological moral theory: moral sensibility and its particular and rather selective thresholds in different social and cultural settings, cruelty and responsibility, urgency and deferment. It is the moral responsibility of the intellectual to be attentive to what is most urgent, and what is most urgent for anyone capable of thinking is to understand the "moral condition" of a society. These are the conditions for the production, distribution, and reproduction of superfluous, unbearable evils. A critique of any discourse that justifies, naturalizes, or conceals these evils and their social order entails the same responsibility. Ever since Marx, Nietzsche, and Freud reduced morality to real power relations and understood the critique of morality as systematically undermining it, critical theory (regardless of its genre, from Marxism to deconstruction) has conceived of itself as a substitute for or displacement of moral philosophy. In contradistinction to this conception, the theoretical perspective proposed here portrays critical theory as a necessary extension of moral philosophy, a supplement that the latter cannot do without.

One could also argue that although one can do the right thing only on the basis of a certain "enframing" of Evil, no ethics, moral code, or political discourse can exhaust evil; at any particular moment, discourse — any discourse — enframes only some of the existing evils and lets only some of its victims come into presence and assume their own voice. Because such a discourse is inherently structured and is embodied in a limited point of view and a particular kind of care, its indifference to other kinds of evils is inherent and structured. In this context critical theory is not a methodology or a set of axioms about the limits of knowledge or its constructedness; it is, rather, the attempt to keep open the perspective of "the moral." "The moral" is an attitude that subsists on the margin of any particular ethics and political discourse, nurtured from their sources but aspiring to transcend their limits and always maintaining a residual openness to that Evil which escapes articulation within these particular discourses. The moral is attentive to that Evil which ethics or a dominating political discourse has made one forget; it allows occurrences of Evil to come into presence and to appear as evils. The moral is care for the victims to whom a prevailing discourse is blind; it is a willingness to call into question the limit of that discourse and the means it employs in order to objectify evils.

Chapter Eight presents a systematic interpretation of the concept of Evil as the order of superfluous evils in society. This interpretation emerges while following a small group of canonical philosophical texts (mainly Plato, Leibniz, Spinoza, Kant, and Nietzsche). This reading takes place in a discussion of central categories of moral theory that were traditionally related to Evil: the Good, which thought has often understood, naively, as the simple negation of Evil; necessity and chance, two concepts Evil has traditionally been identified or at least associated with; and freedom, often conceived as the root of Evil as well as the condition of its overcoming. At this stage of the work, I offer a redefinition of the moral domain; ethics is distinguished from moral theory according to the distinction between self and others, and utilitarian moral theory (as it is commonly understood) becomes inoperative once the interest in self-interest is removed from the moral domain. The self, if it exists, is morally relevant as a source of spending and dispensing, on the one hand, and as a limit set on giving and forgiving, on the other hand. An entire tradition of moral philosophy that focuses on moral character and its virtues is marginalized here; it is subjected to the contingent constraints and demands of proper giving.

The other precedes the self not only because it is the object of moral concern but also because its plight is what prompts moral interest and determines its propriety. What counts are the needs of others, always in the plural, without reifying any Other, and those others count only insofar as they (might) suffer superfluous evils. The superfluity of evils is Evil's mode of being. It is the way in which an evil is suffered, experienced, assigned expression or compensation; the way it addresses a call, invites response, opens up a gap in someone's existence, institutes duties, and creates obligations. Superfluity is the manner of Evil's situatedness and embodiment in a concrete field of social relations. Superfluity is Evil's way of being-there, as a being placed within an individual, an injured victim, and at the same time as being shared by all those others harmed when an individual is hurt and being common to (and for) all those whose actions and missed actions help bring it into existence and cause it to appear as anything less than a scandal — what should not have taken place.

The eruption of Evil is the negation of the "should not have taken place." Evil is a superfluous excess of Being that should not have come into being. Evil is the being of beings stamped by a negated negation. This double negation is more general and fundamental than the negation implied by the "ought"; it is not opposed to "is" but inheres in Being itself, for it is an excess of Being — not its lack — that is at stake here, both theoretically and politically. There is nothing mysterious about this excess. It is produced, distributed, and administered by men and women, by the innocent and the malicious, by "professional" perpetrators, but also by the victims and their heirs.

With this understanding, the discussion finally turns to the paradigm of Evil in contemporary Western culture, the Holocaust. Chapter Nine builds on the analysis of the production and distribution of Evil and of the nature of moral interest, as well as on some insights drawn from Hannah Arendt's work on totalitarianism and Michel Foucault's work on "the disciplined society," two thinkers who are at the background of this discussion from the beginning, in order to think the event called Auschwitz. One of this chapter's aims is to liberate the thinking of Auschwitz from the dogma of uniqueness and, as already stated, to restore and explore several conceptual continua that will enable one to better position it within the geography and history of contemporary Evil. On the one hand, Auschwitz is interpreted in relation to the dispersion of evils in everyday life and to common situations of disaster, occupation, and domination, in closed institutions as well as in an open society. On the other hand, Auschwitz is thought in relation to other cases of genocide, in relation to familiar catastrophes and those that can only be imagined, and finally in relation to the real possibility of a catastrophe that will bring an end to the world.

More generally, the final chapter strives to relate the thinking of Evil to the philosophical task of interpreting the historical present. Critically drawing on Foucault and Lyotard, whose readings of Kant's short historical essays were an occasion to articulate a critical, philosophical interest in the historical present, this chapter attempts to position the entire project in a tradition of thought that insists on what Foucault called "an ontology of the present." This tradition questions "what is really going on" and what place we hold in what goes on, which means asking what the historical-epistemological conditions are for philosophically questioning the historical present. It also means asking who "we" are, and who those "we" are who are capable of asking this question, and at the same time placing themselves (ourselves) as its addressees. The questions about "us," about our era, and about our contemporary forms of Evil appear as inseparable in Chapter Nine.

From this moral perspective, our era is differentiated and defined neither by its own self-understanding or self-constitution nor by what distinguishes it from its past, but rather by what distinguishes it from the future threatening to bring it — and the entire history of humanity with it — to an end. Auschwitz and Hiroshima are not only epitomes of Evil. They are also events in which the human destruction of the human world appeared as a real historical possibility. The end of the world is no longer merely a popular theme of apocalyptic writings. It is now present as an event "in the making," a possible result of a network of global processes of domination, armament, technological and biotechnological developments, capitalization, and mediatization. The traces of this event are already visible everywhere, in scientific conferences and diplomatic congresses and on the evening news.

In our era, the end of the world is present within the world, and every attempt at historical self-understanding calls for an anticipation of the various forms in which human history may become a truly universal history at the very moment of its end. This possibility signals a point where the distinction between human and non-human forms of life blurs and the difference between care of the self and care for others is overcome. It announces radical otherness whose very appearance on the historical horizon captures moral giving along with self-centered investments within one closed economy of threat and hope. "We" who seek to represent this era are doomed to work within this closed economy, no matter how much we work against it.

The historicity of the present era is a historicity of coming to an end. This end is a common one and should be — in fact, already is — the basis of a new communality. The finitude that constitutes this end is not one that separates individuals and marks their singularity but rather an active force that lays their common ground. A globalizing force, one might have said, except that it has been materialized first and foremost within the antiglobalization movement. Chapter Nine examines this and related phenomena, like the new forms of humanitarian action, only in passing; the task itself falls outside the scope of this work. The final chapter merely prepares the ground for such a study and for its incorporation within moral philosophy.[7]

Moral philosophy that accounts for the moral call arising from a humanity approaching the finish line converges with an ontology of the present that concerns itself with the new forms of Evil that have appeared in Auschwitz and Hiroshima, in the Gulag, Cambodia, and Rwanda... This means that the historical present must be thought from the standpoint of these new forms of Evil. Thinking the present means responding to the challenge that the humanity of the "extremes," generating, carrying, and suffering these forms of Evil in practice, poses to thought. Our thought, made possible by certain conditions of human existence, is caught in "the middle," a progeny of the terror spread from this or that extreme, but also a deferment of that extreme that is placed at some point on a continuum that might lead via this or that slippery slope to the end of the world. Thought must never stop measuring the distance from the end, assuming that it is already in the making; action must never tire of efforts to extend that distance.

Throughout this book, the discussion proceeds in fragmented, sometimes hesitant, steps. Every section is numbered, but the numbering is not continuous from beginning to end. Every chapter has six sections, and every section has several subsections (six at the most), which in turn break into more subsections (again, six at the most). The number of a subsection indicates the chapter (the digit to the left of the decimal point), the section (first digit to the right of the decimal point), the subsection (second digit to the right of the decimal point), and the sub-subsection (third digit to the right of the decimal point). The digit 0 is used to indicate the first section, subsection, or sub-subsection. This numeric marking tries to indicate the logical structure of the progress of phenomenological description as well as its incomplete ends. The descriptions are discrete and accumulative and move from one matter to another with leaps that appear necessary by the nature of what accumulates through the description, but also break off and reassemble through the distributive logic of species and genus. The text never forgets its origin as a peregrination in writing; it does not pretend to trace a dialectical journey and does not hide the fact that systematization came at the end.

Occasional sections in the book deal relatively extensively yet in a non-orderly manner with philosophical texts. Most of these texts come from the canon of philosophy, both ancient and modern, some from the shelves of contemporary European philosophy — and discuss the positions presented in them. But the discussion does not evolve and unfold as an interpretation of or an argument for any one of these positions. The focus on the interpretation and critique of these philosophical texts is restricted to the particular issue at stake. Philosophical texts are used here as familiar places to stay for a while. They are usually mentioned like an acquaintance you accidentally meet, greet with a slight nod, and talk of to the person walking next to you. Thus, the texts gradually come to create a familiar philosophical environment — one familiar to me — and are supposed to function in this way, as close and remote surroundings that have homely familiarity together with certain alienation, open spaces, closed horizons, hurdles, tarmac roads, and muddy paths, waste to be removed, spaces that should be nurtured, a place to leave, a place to live in, a place to travel to. Surroundings are not a collection of arguments, a theory, or a systematic body of knowledge. Surroundings are a habitat, an atmosphere, work conditions, an invitation for a walk. The sections dedicated to readings of classical texts try to signify the intellectual surroundings within which the thought invested in this treatise and the writing that carries it travel. Those sections do not pretend to document the surroundings or systematically report them, but to turn the readers' attention to them, not let them be ignored. They try to leave the philosophical surroundings as a background to the movement of the thought itself without turning them into its objects. Readers who are uncomfortable in these surroundings need not acclimatize themselves to them; they are invited to skip over the "intra-philosophical" parts. Either way, the thought that here unfolds is now in their hands. If the writing was successful and if their reading was fruitful, they will take it from there to their own habitat or surroundings.

The writing of this book started more than ten years ago and lasted almost seven years. I presented its main arguments in three lectures that I delivered at the Van Leer Jerusalem Institute, whose generous support also allowed publication of the original Hebrew version. The English translation required a lot of rewriting, and the English edition differs, sometimes significantly, from the Hebrew one in numerous scattered places. But I have not changed the book's basic arguments and structure and was not able to keep pace with numerous relevant publications that have

31

appeared or come to my attention since the manuscript was handed to the publisher. I especially regret not being able to learn from and come to terms with Giorgio Agamben's treatise on Auschwitz, and with the entire trilogy of which it is a part.[8]

Work on the English edition was supported by a grant from the Israeli Science Foundation. Rela Mazali and Havi Carel, my judicious translators, were always responsive to my language, my questions, and my never-ending insistence on rewriting what had seemed to be completed. The intellectual and friendly ambience at the Shalom Hartman Institute in Jerusalem, where part of this work was undertaken, turned the agony of editing and rewriting into a rewarding experience. Traces of the continuous dialogue with my first reader, Ariella Azoulay, are scattered throughout the entire work. Even if I were able to identify and note all of them, it would still fall short of expressing her contribution to the creation of this book. Hannan Hever assisted the birth of the first ideas that eventually became the book, encouraged me to undertake it, and has accompanied it in a still-ongoing discussion. A short sabbatical at the University of Human Sciences in Strasbourg, and the wonderful company and inspiration of two philosophers, Jean-Luc Nancy and Philippe Lacoue-Labarthe, helped me formulate the third part of the work. In addition, I am deeply indebted to those friends and colleagues who offered significant comments — to Yemima Ben-Menahem and Elhanan Yakira for responses to parts of Chapter Eight, to Michal Ben-Naftali for words of criticism and encouragement after reading an early version of Chapter Nine, and to Ran Sigad, my teacher, for a probing critique, following his reading of the whole work. I would like to extend special gratitude to my students Abed Azzam and Tal Arbel for endless patience and wise, efficient assistance with completion of the footnotes and index.

PART ONE

That Which Was and Is No Longer

First Curve

0.100   What is Evil? For the moment, it is a question of definitions: Evil is the collection of evils and their order.

0.101   To propose a definition is to invite a recursive move to prior definitions, regressing to the point where definition is no longer possible. From that point, one can begin over again, progressively moving toward description and clarification, gradually extricating one meaning from the other. When I begin over again, I know where I want to go — that is, to the last definition in the series, the opening definition. But the last definition, which is the first definition, presupposes the entire process of description and all the claims it involves. In a philosophical treatise (perhaps in any scientific treatise), the reader always starts from the place where the writer has concluded.

0.110   Evil is the collection of evils and their order. What is an evil? An evil is any injury irreparably worsening someone's condition. Evil is a regularity in the production of evils and their distribution among all those injured by them, and the systematic reproduction of this order. Consequently, Evil is not a negative value. Neither is it the lack of a positive value, or a feature of various states of affairs, human beings, or acts, which may possess other features and exist, equally, without evil. Evil is part of that which is; Evil belongs to the order of things and existents.

0.111   A discursive series of definitions follows: an evil is an injury worsening someone's condition so that no compensation is possible. Compensation assumes the existence of a system of exchange whose terms make it possible to assess the value of the injury. An injury involving losses that are expressible in terms of a system of exchange amounts to damage. Damage is a loss whose value is assessable. Loss is an irreversible disappearance of some irreplaceable thing. A disappearance is the transition of some thing from "is there" to "is not there."

35

0.20 And what is "is there"? And "is not there"? Can one define "is there" and "is not there" without recourse to being and nothingness? And not only due to the precise meaning of the terms one wishes to define but because definition, the act itself, requires an assertion of being and its negation. In order to define some X, I must know something about being and not being X, and give meaning (or assume an already-given meaning) to being and nonbeing.

0.21 Since the beginning of philosophy, that which is has been stripped of all its traits, save its very being, and viewed as "an entity," while the being of "entities" was viewed as an abstract substance, Being. "Manifestly you have long been aware of what you mean when you use the expression '*being*'" — Heidegger quotes Plato's *Sophist* at the beginning of *Being and Time* — "We, however, who used to think we understood it, have now become perplexed."[1] Prior to our rethinking anything else, Heidegger sends us to rethink Being (*Sein*), which is revealed in every present entity but also goes beyond every presence, hidden in its very revelation. Unlike the readers of Plato and Heidegger, "we" do not imagine that we know what being is or that we know how to define it. Plato's questions, like those of Heidegger, embarrass us, not because we find out we don't know what we wrongly thought we knew, but because we don't know how to go on thinking their questions or how to think with them without assigning some meaning to the concept at stake from the outset. It's an embarrassment that doesn't make us stop and think "being" itself, not even the very being-there in that which is there, apart from that which is. We know, however, that being can be thought only through some thing which is there, which is present, even if its presence is immediately questioned; "is there" and "is not there" always belong to some thing, some entity, or some existent which is or is not.[2] They are always mediated by the language that allows this or that thought and that, moreover, allows it to be thought as distinct from some other thought.

0.22 We know we operate the phrases "is there" and "is not there" while thinking, speaking, and writing about everything that may be thought, spoken, and written of, and that there is no thinking without them even when they themselves are thought. Therefore, even without thinking being itself, we will try to show below that Evil is there, that it exists in actuality, and that all the negations it involves, and most of all the negation of "being," unfailingly leave something that is still there, something that, even if devoid of substance, is evil by virtue of its very presence. If we understand, in

36

the end, that Evil is part of "what there is," we will add something to the understanding of is-there-ness or, more generally, to the possibilities of being. If it turns out that evil is there, like a rock or a mountain, like the wind or the forest, like a mine field or a magnetic field, like extreme exhaustion or burning desire or horrible pain, and that it is there in a way that is also different from all of these, this will mean that being consists of more than many have formerly believed and that Evil possibly consists of less than previously believed.

0.23 These understandings will materialize, if at all, only in the last part of this treatise. The first stage assumes that we know enough about what it means "to be there" and "not to be there," and it will begin with the transition between "is there" and "is not there." This transition is disappearance.

0.30 Evil is part of what there is. There is Evil whose birth is the disappearance of some thing, but not all Evil is of this kind. There is Evil whose birth is not in disappearance but rather in the presence of some thing. A progressively intensifying disappearance must constitute a continuous presence in order for it to cause Evil, but the emergence of Evil may also result from a presence that has become intensified. Both that which has disappeared and that which appears can engender evil only to the extent that they constitute a continuous presence of some kind. Disappearance and presence are not opposites; they are two separate categories denoting two disparate states of affairs. Therefore, there are two ways to speak of Evil: one in terms of the progressively intensifying transition from "is there" to "is not there," and the other in terms of the progressively intensifying presence of what is there. These ways, initially distinct, eventually converge. They create the three-part structure of this work. Its first two parts study each of these two distinct ways separately: growing disappearance and progressively intensifying presence. The third part studies the common ground shared by these two ways: the order of the production and distribution of evils.

0.31 The transition from "is there" to "is not there" will be a point of departure. A line drawn from it will run through six categories: disappearance, loss, damage, injustice, wrong, and evil. The transition from category to category will be accompanied by the accumulation and dissipation of presence. Loss will appear with the appearance of one who has an interest (inyan) in that which has disappeared — the presence of disappearance will then grow more intense. Damage will appear with the appearance of relations of exchange — the presence of the loss will then grow less intense.

Injustice will appear when the damage or loss is perceived as superfluous, unnecessary, preventable; wrong will appear when there is no possibility of demanding the restoration of what has been lost, or when the damage remains without expression or compensation. The presence of damage will intensify in the case of injustice and blur in the case of wrong. The presence of loss will intensify in both cases. Evil will be the systematic pattern in the appearance of injustice and wrong; Evil is an order of superfluous being and of being that is unexpressed. Injustice and wrong intensify the presence of loss, each in its own way, in a focused, singular manner, while they do not always intensify the presence of damage. Evil is an effect of the orderly, systematic intensification of both loss and damage. Evil can be expressed as a transition between "is there" and "is not there" that has intensified progressively, grown more and more powerful, until the presence and the superfluity of loss and damage, and the impossibility of expressing loss and of being compensated for damage, have become increasingly complex and orderly, ordered, to the point of dwelling at the heart of the order of things.

0.32 Every category will be examined in relation to its opposite: disappearance opposed to appearance, loss opposed to possession, damage opposed to benefit, injustice opposed to distributive justice, wrong opposed to reparative justice, Evil opposed to good. But these oppositions will be of limited and conditional interest only. The line connecting opposing concepts grows increasingly fragmented and faint the more closely it approaches the Good. There will be no need of it.

0.33 The second way, to be discussed in the second part of this work, will reveal a continuous curve of growing presence. It will connect another series of categories: presence, excitation,[3] suffering, injustice, wrong, and evil. Along this curve, too, every category will be examined in relation to its opposite: absence opposed to presence, indifference opposed to excitation, pleasure opposed to suffering. Here, too, the line running through the opposing concepts becomes more and more fragmented the closer it comes to the Good, and it will not be needed. In fact, it is one and the same line. The two curves begin from different points but converge at the place where suffering, loss, or damage exceeds itself — in the form of injustice or wrong. The categories of injustice and wrong are shared by the two separate ways leading to Evil. The joint section of the two curves, including injustice, wrong, and evil, will, as stated, be studied in the third part of the book.

0.40 Additional categories that may be part of the concept of Evil, or to which this concept is connected in the tradition of the philosophical discussion of ethics — such as cruelty, humiliation, sin, absence, lust, self-love, or arrogance (hubris) — will not be examined here in or of themselves. They are interesting to this discussion only to the extent that they are describable in terms of suffering and loss. There exists no need to study them independently. I will not try to prove this claim, but I will attempt to corroborate it through the negation of several possible claims about other ostensibly necessary categories (7.0). However, even if it turns out that progress from "is there" and "is not there" to Evil can be achieved through alternative routes, one must begin somewhere. I propose to begin at the transition from "is there" to "is not there," to begin with the moment when something disappears.

0.41 This highly condensed overview will be clarified at length below.

Chapter One

Disappearance

1.0 *Giving Names*

1.000 Disappearance is a transition from "some thing, this or that, is there" to "the same thing is not there." Disappearance is the opposite not of being or of presence but of appearance (not in the sense of an outer appearance or image, but in the sense of an occurrence, an appearing, a birth, an apparition). Appearance is a transition in the opposite direction, from "is not there" to "is there." When something disappears, there is disappearance. Disappearance is there. When someone is faced with it, it is present (see also 1.223–1.224).

1.001 Disappearance is always of some thing. Some thing that was and is no longer. Just as every experience is always an experience of some thing. Disappearance is a kind of occurrence, at the beginning of which some thing is present and at the end of which it is absent. There's no experience of disappearance per se, only the disappearance of some thing, this or that specific thing.

1.002 In the same vein, we may add that one cannot experience being as such, only what is, what exists, this or that thing; one cannot know nonbeing as such, only the nonbeing of some thing. "Being" and "Nothingness" are totally abstract concepts, perhaps, as Hegel maintained, the most abstract concepts of thought, devoid of experience. "Present" and "absent," which always refer to some thing, are the most abstract concepts of experience, themselves situated on the borderline of the experiential. It is possible to experience the being or nonbeing of some thing only in relation to other things that are present and are not absent, which appear and disappear, in relation to what is happening, to occurrences.

1.010 Disappearance is not a negation (of the form "man is not woman") or an absence (of the form "a man is incapable of nursing"), although it includes a negation (what disappears is no longer present) and an absence or lack (something missing, something absent from the place where what disappeared was formerly present). In addition to negation and absence, disappearance includes a transition from being to nonbeing. This is always a transition of that thing which was there (present) and is no longer. That which undergoes the transition is that which goes away. Disappearance is something that happens to some thing that goes or passes away; it is an occurrence, and it can be experienced as such. A situation in which some thing or some one undergoes something, or a situation in which some thing or some one experiences something, or, more generally, a situation in which something simply goes on and the going on itself has presence is an occurrence. Thus disappearance is a kind of occurrence.

1.011　Experience is always an experience of an occurrence, which itself constitutes an occurrence. Experience is an occurrence framed in time and space. When someone experiences, his experience is an occurrence, and what he experiences is an occurrence.[1] Something takes place in an occurrence, even if no actual place is occupied; something happens, some thing that was not present appears, some thing else that was present disappears. "Disappearance" is a term describing a concrete occurrence, but it is also an element in every occurrence. Like, and along with, appearance, it is a simple term, perhaps the simplest of all, and the most abstract of all, within a series of terms referring to experience as an experience of occurrence. The fact that the present discussion places it at the beginning of this series does not mean that it should be taken for granted or that it is an "immediate" given, introduced as is, even if it seems somehow closer to "the things themselves."

1.012　Disappearance as an occurrence, as a transition, is something that is there, even if momentarily, but that is also destined to disappear. Disappearance is the occurrence of an end; its finitude is its very essence.

1.013　Everything that is there can disappear, but not everything that disappears leaves behind it a wake of disappearance. Disappearance itself may disappear without a trace (see 1.200), without being something for someone, even momentarily.

1.014　What disappears is not there, is gone, at least from the viewpoint of someone from whom what was there has disappeared. Even if what was there is present somewhere else, or for someone else, when that thing disappears, something is gone, even if it is only this: that-there-was-something-there-for-someone.

1.020　Some things disappear along with their disappearance. What disappears without having its disappearance disappear has at least a name or an epithet, even if it is only "that there," or at least might have a name, in some language. Only what is already "en-tongued" can disappear thus.[2] What is en-tongued, christened into language, comes to bear a name, and in the same instant is christened as present either potentially or actually. What is en-tongued is what was present, or what could have been present, in the past, or what could be present, in the future, in some possible world ("possible world" is a common space populated by the named referents of statements mentioning things by their names). Possessing a name means being in danger of disappearing. What has no name, either now or after the fact, cannot disappear without the disappearance of its disappearance. If it is not given a name, even after the fact, its disappearance will be an undifferentiated instant in the annihilation or the creation of something other than it — a nameless and pointless instant for the one who has not identified it by name.

1.021　A name is not necessarily a first name, and there is no need of a family name. An index will suffice — "here, this, down there." The eye and the hand are enlisted for pointing, for the act of en-tonguing. They extend the nonlinguistic horizon of the linguistic act, but they do not transcend it.

1.022　Something that loses its name loses its ability to leave traces of its disappearance. A name is a necessary condition for inscribing disappearance, including a future or a past disappearance. A name allows something to be that which has now disappeared, even if this thing was never present and no one was there to behold it, like the ancient gods, or the heroes from the world of "the mighty men ... of old, men of renown," or the awful *Carcharodontosaurus* and the *Sinosauropteryx* with its primitive feathers. Language and its speakers are responsible for a thing's ability to be something that has disappeared, even if it was never something that appeared. And vice versa. Things that disappear (like things that appear) are responsible for the ability of speakers to identify things, to give names.

1.023　Name giving and disappearance do not necessarily occur at the same time. What has disappeared can be identified as "it," "the disappeared," that is, by the traces it has left. It can be named, and the time of its disappearance can be estimated as an hour, a year, centuries, or aeons earlier.

1.030 Disappearance (like appearance) is an occurrence in which language cuts across the space of things. And vice versa: an occurrence in which the space of things cuts across language. Disappearance (like appearance) is an occurrence of en-tonguing. Language en-tongues being. The one who en-tongues, the en-tonguer, brings being into his tongue and his tongue into being. The en-tonguer betrays being, revealing what or who was hidden, causes what is there to appear. But what was hidden is not necessarily concealed behind a screen or buried. It was there all the time, in plain sight, but we didn't know it was such, that it was this and that. The en-tonguer allows the identification of who or what is there as such and such; he reveals the (real?) identity of what has been en-tongued. He allows a fit between the pointing that gives a name and the pointing that indicates "that there," between the seen and the spoken.

1.031 En-tonguing is a betrayal of being, but it does not ensure apprehending and capturing. En-tonguing allows apprehension of what is elusive in language alone, not its actual capture. Capturing in language means forgetting the myriad possibilities of the en-tongued to continue eluding. In fact, the en-tonguer forces being to appear as what-is, and nothingness to appear as what-is-not, some thing that is such and such.

1.032 Nothing exists for us as something that has not been en-tongued, whether or not it is present. Can you show me anything like that? Or point to it or tell about it? If so, that will obviously be en-tonguing, and you will be the one who has en-tongued, who has betrayed being, who sentenced, who framed something in language.

1.033 And the one who en-tongues is complicit in the game of hide-and-seek. Who is the en-tonguer? Who is it that betrays being? Who is "Deep Throat"?[3] The throat of the en-tonguer is unfathomably deep. En-tonguing has no end. Every en-tonguing that closes a single gap between the thing and its essence, between what is seen and what is spoken, between being and its representation, between temporality and presence, opens up other gaps in other places. En-tonguing makes us forget being as absence, or as concealment, or as undifferentiated flux, or as the possibility of another appearance, re-created by each representation.[4]

1.034 There is always more being than there are representations of being, more being than en-tongued being. And this "more" cannot be banished, not only due to the finiteness of human beings, or the limitations of consciousness, but because this excess belongs to the being of what is there. Being consists of unlimited possibilities of appearing as that which is such and such; every appearance, every disappearance, every coming into presence, every departure from presence simply reorganizes the relation of what is present to what is absent, of what is there to what is not there, of what is en-tongued to what has not yet been en-tongued. Philosophy, poetry, and the visual arts make a consistent effort to en-tongue what has not yet been en-tongued, what is still — or forever — ineffable.[5] But clearly the phrases "what has not yet been en-tongued" and "what cannot be en-tongued" are, themselves, a general kind of en-tonguing.

1.035 What is present for all eternity, in or out of which nothing has appeared, in or out of which nothing has disappeared, is the ultimate nameless, and therefore perhaps, precisely due to this, it is named *hashem* (the Name) (that is not to be taken in vain). *Hashem* occupies the space that no language can traverse. Therefore, that which is present for all time is also that which is absent for all time. Always on the verge of treason or hoax, all attempts to en-tongue the Name are doomed to fail. Nevertheless, from the instant that what is present for all time appeared on the horizon of language, attempts to en-tongue it have not abated, whether to use language as a vehicle for escaping language or to come to terms with what is beyond language, to domesticate it, to open up gaps in its disappearance, marking its traces, making them identifiable, signifiable.

1.040 Disappearance opens up a gap in what is there, a gap between "was there" (before) and "is not there" (now). In disappearance, what is there emerges as temporary, and temporariness emerges as something that is there. What disappears temporalizes what is there while at the same time making present the flow of time. In other words, disappearance is one way that being is temporalized and time is made present. Disappearance is the opening of a gap in being, the departure of some thing from being to nothingness. Disappearance (as well as appearance) is the instant when an occurrence emanates from presence, the instant when the character of presence as an occurrence becomes clear (see 1.221).

1.041 Disappearance is not extinction and is not the opposite of becoming. What disappears is not "there" any longer, but may be somewhere else. It may be an unknown present, which is not in the process of becoming anything, and which is immutable, but which is hidden from sight (from the sight of all, or the sight of someone). Both becoming and extinction situate being and nothingness relative to time, but without turning presence into an occurrence. Extinction, like becoming, operates at the heart of presence or behind its back, hypothesized or presupposed as a necessary background for every presence, a reason known in advance for every disappearance. In contrast to extinction, disappearance situates being and nothingness relative to someone who recognizes disappearance while being present at its very occurrence, or at the appearance of its traces, and who, at the same time, is made aware of the presence of time through recognizing its occurrence or its traces, someone who recognizes time through disappearance while presupposing the flux of time in order to let disappearance appear.

1.042 From the outset, speaking of disappearance assumes that something is left, that something is still there, even after the disappearance, and that there is someone who recognizes the thing that is there and, through it, recognizes that something was there and is not there anymore. There is someone who distinguishes between before and now, for whom there was something there that is not there. Speaking of disappearance assumes that there is, or was, a witness.

1.050 Is it necessary to assume that the testimony is reliable? To assume that the testimony was given at all? Or that it could, in principle, have been given? Giving testimony is a communicative-social event. But in order for someone to witness something (as opposed to "stand witness" or "testify" — which is always before others), communication between the witness and what appears or disappears is sufficient. Disappearance (like appearance) can be a private experience. The witness can become that all alone. Like a person walking along a street on his own when a cat flashes by at a leap, or a child discovering with wonder that a thing or a person he or she has learned to know and identify has disappeared, or a prophet witnessing a divine revelation and its vanishment. But is even this necessary? Isn't an infant witness to the disappearance of some thing that an adult identifies as its mother? Of some thing that an adult identifies as a ball or doll, or calls "zephyrs of light"?[6] Doesn't an animal witness the disappearance of its prey?

1.051 That something has disappeared may be a private matter, but not what has disappeared, for this involves language, which is never private. However, if the infant and the animal can witness disappearance, what disappears may nevertheless be nameless. I am the one identifying the infant or the animal as the one identifying that some thing has disappeared, and I am identifying what has disappeared as that which has disappeared for the infant or the animal (see 1.210–1.211). My language has crossed or traversed the world of things in their stead. I have given them the names they lack and ascribed to them an extremely simple cognitive mechanism that performs the same work for them which naming performs for me: a mechanism identifying what recurs and what disappears (or appears) as the same thing, or the same kind of thing, erasing differences that do not make a difference and strengthening differences that make a difference.

1.052 When the doll disappears, the infant cries. The doll's name isn't "waaaah," but I assume the cry to be evidence of the identification of disappearance, of the ability to distinguish between figure and background, of the infant's ability to identify the repetition (and failure to recur) of "the same" figure, and its ability to connect part of the figure, its particular configuration or its shadow, with the entire figure, that is, to connect signifier and signified. What is identified in the repetition — and later in the disappearance — is not necessarily the "doll." Something along the lines of "that thing whose figure is familiar and that feels nice to the touch" will suffice, and in fact, of course, not even this, but some wordless substitute for it. Obviously, the linguistic mechanism of identification doesn't equal a nonlinguistic mechanism of identification, but clearly we are unable to think of it without seeing it as a proto-tongue of sorts: figure and background, repetition and difference, signifier and signified. The fact that we are unable to think of proto-linguistic identification without attributing it to a quasi-linguistic mechanism does not entail either an assumption that identification is truly linguistic or an assumption that language evolves from it. Similarly, it isn't necessary to agree with the infant and the animal on the identification of what has disappeared in order to ascribe discernment of the disappearance to either of them. From our point of view — that is, from the point of view which isn't that of the infant or the animal — this discernment means that what has disappeared has a name. A nameless name. Of course, we can only *ascribe* discernment to the animal and the baby, making them witnesses, possessors of proto-linguistic or quasi-linguistic competence. But, in the relevant instances, is there any way in which we cannot ascribe it?

1.1 *Time*

1.100 Disappearance is not a beginning; it assumes a prior presence, and it assumes that someone is there to witness it. The presence of what is there is not necessarily a beginning either. It may be that no one witnesses what is there (what is there is not present before any witness; it is devoid of the relational aspect of presence) until that thing disappears. Neither are being and nothingness, or time and idle is-there-ness (such as Lévinas's "il-y-a"), the beginning.

Every description of a "primordial" experience (Lévinas's dark night, devoid of distinctions and replete with being; Heidegger's anxiety of Nothingness) is at best a metaphoric and rather idiosyncratic description of an extreme experience, to which someone attempts to grant special rights on the basis of presuppositions to be interpreted later as if they were entailed by this very attempt.[7] In a stricter sense, if there is a beginning point, it can be not "inside" experience but, at most, at its margin. Every attempt to conceptualize the categories on the threshold of experience in and of themselves immediately situates someone who conceptualizes them within the framework of a more or less definitive discourse and within a conceptual web preceding his or her attempt. Concepts are embedded in a web with no single point of beginning, only endless anchor points. An attempt to conceptualize the threshold of experience is itself, necessarily, part of experience.

1.101 Like, for instance, the attempt to conceptualize death, the end of all experience. Death is disappearance with a capital *D*. And my own death is a paradox of disappearance. Here is the most important, most terrible disappearance, and I won't be able to witness it. Epicurus said of this, "If you are, it is not; if it is, you are not." If you can be a witness, you are still alive; if you have died, you cannot be a witness. Lévinas quotes Epicurus but claims the latter has entirely missed the paradox of death, "for it effaces our relationship with death, which is a unique relationship with the future."[8] Lévinas is imprecise here. Epicurus's aphorism is misleading not only because he doesn't perceive death as a present future or as the presence of a future absence but also because he ignores the disappearance, the transition from "you are" to "you are not," from "I am" to that "I am not" which I will never be able to say.

1.102 An interest in death follows not only from the temporalizing presence of certain yet delayed death but also from the enraging certainty of the transition from one who is to one who is no longer, a transition generating what is (at least for me) an impossible combination between the end of my personal time and the indifferent continuance of others' time. Epicurus attempts to eliminate death as the problem of the individual who is going to die and therefore eliminates it as disappearance. But, of course, whenever I become conscious of my personal time, the time I still have, the time already passed, and the time that is passing, I am conscious that my disappearance is already in progress. Though I know for certain that I am in the process of disappearing, I will never witness my own complete disappearance. My complete disappearance is always my problem, although, and perhaps precisely

48

because, I will never be able to bear testimony to it. My death will necessarily be a disappearance (or a group of disappearances) for someone else, not for me. But it is my problem at every instant when I'm capable of — or incapable of not — imagining it, forerunning it, representing it to myself (whether "authentically" so or not). My death is the disappearance of the sole witness to my personal time and to the entire experience that this temporariness engenders. Every time I imagine my own death, I am inventing the witness that I will never be. Just like Epicurus, who wishes to soothe me, I ignore the disappearance, the transition itself.

1.103 There is fear of death that is a fear of nothingness, and there is fear of death that is a fear of becoming nothing. One day I will no longer be. Then one day the people who were witnesses to my death will disappear as well. Then one day there will be no more witnesses. The future will bring total nothingness, an eternal void, a time of the disappearance of the last disappearance and the disappearance of the traces left by the disappearance of this last disappearance, which will never occur as a real disappearance, because it will have no witness. All this, however, has nothing to do with what will happen to me when I disappear, first to me and then to others around me, if there are others around, with how my disappearance will take place, how the witness within me will be gathered into the gradually or abruptly disappearing thing.

1.110 After a disappearance, in a new order of things, after the transition and because of it, a negation and an absence that were not previously there can be identified. But the relation between the former and the present situation is only created due to the disappearance. The piece of now stain-free clothing *is not* the stained piece of clothing (negation); it has *no stains* (absence); I learn this because I was witness earlier to the stains that disappeared and later to the disappearance of the stains. Between "earlier" and "later," the time that was, of course, there all the time appears, acquires presence. Presence, absence, disappearance (and appearance), are always already within time. Disappearance (like appearance) gives presence to time.

1.111 *Disappearance is both presupposed and denied in the transition from Being to Nothingness at the beginning of Hegel's* Logic. *The transition for Hegel does not involve time; it is purely conceptual, and yet it yields a temporal concept, Becoming, which was actually presupposed in the movement of thought from one concept to the other.*[9] *Becoming cannot be derived from the combination of being and nothingness without presupposing a third concept of time. On the one hand, being*

49

is what is present, nothingness is what is as yet, or already, not pre-
sent, and this presence of being (which is absent in nothingness) is
conceived as that which is, at present, even if it counts "outside of
time," as it were, as something immune to the "tooth of time," or, in
other words, as a double negation of both the future (because it is
already here) and the past (because it stands and does not pass). On
the other hand, the transition from being to nothingness, like every
transition, always involves a passing into the past and assumes a gap
of time, time being always already given in what passes. The tempo-
rariness that appears in transition as what was presupposed by it is the
temporariness of being; being that appears in transition as what has
always already been temporalized is always also the being of time.[10]

1.120 I write "being" and "is-there-ness" as opposed to "entity" and
"substance," which might imply an atemporal or hyper-temporal
existence of the permanent and hidden infrastructure of reality
that time cannot overcome.[11] "Being-there" — whatever what is
there is, innate or conscious, or even virtual — is always already
permeated by time, exists alongside other things "inside" time,
and imprisons within itself "its own" time. One should assume
here, following Heidegger, the difference between a particular
entity, this or that thing is (*Seiende*), and being (*Sein*), which
appears, but is also hidden, through that which is.[12] The intentional strangeness arising from the addition of "-ness" attempts to
avoid enhancing or determining the being that is in what is, and
to imply its relation to time. Being-there is the general way to talk
about what is as what is temporalized, not given within time as
within some external vessel but temporalized, simultaneously
both given as that which is and ushering in time in the way it
came about, endures, and is about to pass away. But unlike Heidegger, I assume that the temporalization of being is not exclusive to the being of the one who experiences being (Heidegger's
Dasein) but is always already implied in the way any object is
given to experience.

1.121 Temporalization is both the mode of given-ness of being, the way
in which it is given (or discovered, or appears, or shines forth, or
happens, or is disastrously encountered), and the form in which
being is taken away (or disappeared, or lost).

1.122 For instance, Grandfather's stopped cuckoo clock. There it is on
the wall from the time of my earliest memories, or, in other
words, it was here before I was, but Grandfather is dead, and
tomorrow we're clearing out his apartment, and it won't be here
any longer, it won't stay on here after me. That is the clock's time

alongside other things, a time of before and after. And the clock has a time "of its own," the time of the cuckoo stuck in its nest, of the rusted pendulum, erosion time. On the one hand, the disappearance of the clock from the wall to which it has lent character and charm, a predictable, sudden disappearance; on the other hand, the gradual disappearance that accompanies the process of erosion. Two kinds of disappearances and two kinds of temporalizations that have no need of a clock in order to differ from each other. And there is the clock, gradually eroding (but still standing) and still there (but only until tomorrow). The clock's being-there involves its predicted disappearance and its gradually accumulating disappearance, and the two types of temporalizations these involve. Its being-there is the way in which it makes present or foreruns or conceals its own disappearance and that of other things relating to it (for instance, Grandfather's passing away, the departure of the wall's charm).

1.123 Similar things can be said about appearance, too, transition in the opposite direction. But this will not concern me here. And just as disappearance (like appearance) temporalizes is-there-ness, it spatializes it as well. Some thing is alongside others in a spatial environment; some thing imprisons a spatial environment within the limits that determine it as that same thing. Its being-there is that double spatialization: of "this alongside that" and of "this within that." Disappearance is always a disturbance of some familiar order of things, one alongside the other and one within the other, a disturbance that opens up a gap (1.040).

1.130 Disappearance is a transition combining being, nothingness, and time as three that were always already there. It might be said that in this transition, time joins being with nothingness; but it might equally be said (along with Sartre) that nothingness joins being with time. In any case, two oppositions are mutually projected on each other: being and nothingness, previously and now (or before and after). But even these cannot be isolated and combined as atomistic units, for there is something there after what has disappeared is gone (the traces on the ground, in one's memory), and what-is-there-now is present as what it is by virtue of what-was-there-before. Disappearance is a difference that entails or makes present — and is also always already within — a web of differences in an environment where a gap has opened up. A single witness will suffice in order to speak of disappearance, but what is there must already contain a multiplicity.

1.131 A multiplicity exists because there is a difference (one is enough, but there are differences), because someone can witness the difference. Differences can be bracketed, ignored, but they cannot be forced to disappear entirely. Instead of these, there will always be others. It is impossible to reduce disappearance to a single opposition: some thing that is there versus some thing that was there and is no more. For a single opposition to appear as a "differentiating difference" (was there and is no more), the entire web must be operated.

1.2 *Traces*

1.200 Operating the web means, first of all, identifying traces. In every case of disappearance, traces of something must remain, some being-there that was and is not, that is no longer. Some thing that has disappeared without leaving any traces whatsoever — no traces anywhere — is tantamount to what never was. There must have been many such things, surely more than those that did leave traces, but their hypothetical existence doesn't add or subtract a thing. At least not until some thing is revealed that owes its existence, or its disappearance, to that which disappeared before, some thing in which the disappeared left traces. Some thing has to remain present "to this day," and first and foremost here and now, in order to testify to what has disappeared. The dinosaurs disappeared but left traces. That which caused their disappearance apparently disappeared without leaving (almost) any (clearly identifiable) traces. But their disappearance is testimony to (a trace of) some thing that operated in their environment. Disappearance to the second degree; the gradually diminishing presence of the traces, the gradually depleting identity of what disappeared, to the point where all that can be said is: "There was some thing there" (that led to the disappearance of the dinosaurs, for example). And sometimes, even before one can say that, or after even that can be said no more, all that is left is a vague sensation, a sort of affect, that only in hindsight, and always hesitantly, with no certainty at all, could be said to be a trace of some-thing-that-was-there.

1.201 At this moment, too, the sensation has a name, as does that whose disappearance it indicates, even if all that remains of the name is "it" or "some thing" or "that." And the name itself is a trace of what has disappeared, a trace in the memory of the speaker — and there it is: the thing in question already has several traces.

1.202 A trace is the presence of some thing that refers to another presence, which is already gone. There are prints in the sand and in the soul. Every instance of excitation can be the trace of the exciting thing, every sensation of the thing that is sensed. Someone in love wishes to preserve the excitement that has overcome him, even the very longing, for the excitement is a substitute for the disappeared beloved. For an excitation to be a trace of what was but is no more, it must, before its very positioning, be distinct from other sensations, already placed, just like the footprint in the sand, within a web of differences. The denser the web, the more distinct and precisely characterized what-was-there-and-is-no-longer will be. A dense enough web means there is a language, that what is or was there has already been en-tongued, enmeshed in language. But dissolving traces may be enmeshed in a progressively looser web. At the end of the continuum lies a being that leaves no traces, an is-there-ness that is not at all grasped in language, not even in loose *a posteriori* images. Such a being has no signifier, and it cannot disappear. Its end will leave no traces. Nearby it, only barely held in a loose web of distinctions and differences, are excitations that trace what-was-and-is-no-more. Here it becomes difficult to discern between the exciting positing of what-was-and-is-no-more and excitation as a last trace of that same thing, or between the name of the trace and the name as a trace.

1.203 *Lyotard, who interprets and "reworks" Kant on this matter, draws a definite line from positing a sensation or an affect as a trace, which already amounts to capturing it in language, to the wordless presence of the sensation itself, which can always only be designated retrospectively. The difference lies between the presence (of the sensation) and its representation, between presentation and re-representation, when representation is unfailingly retrospective, in language or quasi language, and which — as an act that can be posited in the ensuing representation — itself possesses presence.* [13] *Sartre tried to say something very similar about the relation between an "unreflected consciousness" or a "pre-reflective consciousness" and a "reflective consciousness."* [14] *For Sartre and Lyotard — and on this issue both are Kantians — there is a quantum leap between presence and positioning in a representation, or between pre-reflective excitation and the object of reflective consciousness. I prefer, both here and elsewhere, to speak of continua; the quantum leap is merely the effect of appearance or disappearance from the point of view of some witness after a certain threshold of accumulation or diminution of traces has been crossed.*

1.210 Traces are a kind of sign. As happens with all relations of signification, the signifier testifies both to the signified and to itself, to the fact that it is a signifier. The trace simultaneously testifies that "what-is-present is a remainder of something else that is no longer there" and that "there was something else here, which is absent now." The trace gives double testimony about what is present: about the presence of what-is-there as a remainder of presence, and about the presence of all the rest as what-is-absent. But a trace also gives double testimony about the absence itself: about the fact that some thing was, and is no longer, present, and about the fact that at some point in time, between the presence of that thing and the presence of what remains of it, a disappearance took place. The witness imagines some witness to that which perhaps never had a witness. He imagines a witness both to the thing that was, and is not, there and to its disappearance. Those things-that-are-there are paved with traces. Things that are studded with traces, that are flecked with dead and unborn souls, testify to the presence of what was there and disappeared and left traces.[15]

1.211　If so, is the infant truly capable of witnessing a disappearance? Yes, but it is still incapable of positing it, of identifying a trace as "a trace of that," of naming "that which has disappeared." The instant disappearance is posited, witnesses multiply indefinitely: those who were and those who will be and those who currently share with me the occurrence in the course of which I am witnessing something disappear gradually or disappear in a flash. No wonder, for the act of positing is already an act of en-tonguing. There is private witnessing (an individual recognition of some present thing), but testimony cannot be given as a private matter, for there is no private language and no truly private identification of some thing as this and this.[16]

1.212　There are traces of what no one ever witnessed and traces of what no one could ever witness, of what cannot be remembered, of what is always only present as what was there. These are traces of things that cannot be recalled and cannot, or can hardly, or should never, be forgotten. Cannot be recalled, because there is nothing to recall, because the witness never witnessed the presence that disappeared; cannot be forgotten, not only because the traces themselves persist, accompanying the witness like a ghost, a shadow not to be shaken off, but first and foremost because only what was present can be forgotten. The traces can be forgotten, not that which left them, which was never present, never reached the point of presence. The presence of these traces is the presence of the essential failure to recall, and actually of every inscription of history, if history is understood as a reconstruction of presence. Every already-written history, every history being written, is entirely and only a continuing testimony to disappearances, including the disappearance of the ability to recall, testimony that knows not what it testifies to. There is little writing of history, literature, or art that knows, and attempts to testify to, precisely this, to what cannot be testified to.[17]

1.220 Do I, in these formulations, assign precedence to presence? I don't think so. What is present refers to what is absent, and what is absent has disappeared, is being disappeared; if disappearance is present, that is only because the presence of something is fading, something is departing; disappearance is an occurrence that is there, but what is present through it is permeated by the gaps of absence; the present witness refers to other witnesses who may never have lived but who were possible in principle and who, be this as it may, are disappeared.

1.221 In any case, witness and presence are mutually dependent and inseparable. This relation is embedded in the ambiguity of the concept of presence itself. Every presence contains what is present and who it is that is both present at and recognizes what is present, as well as the traces of something disappeared (or appeared), through which the witness has recognized, and has been present at, what is present.[18] As stated, disappearance (like appearance) is the instant when an occurrence emanates from presence, and also the moment when the character of presence as an occurrence becomes clear (1.10). Presence is an occurrence (I'm leapfrogging ahead here); it is not a condition of being, and it is not a condition of consciousness. It is the encounter between a witness and something whose disappearance (or appearance) has left him with traces (4.1–4.3).

1.222 Permanent, unchanging presence, from which all traces of disappearance (or appearance) have been erased, is an empty presence, like a white wall, or white noise, or a black backdrop encompassing one's entire field of sight. At such a moment, the witness stops sensing what stands before him, his attention turns inward, sensations that originate within him appear and disappear. There is no longer someone who recognizes the permanent presence facing him, which is now a presence that no one recognizes (a contradiction). The one who recognizes some thing is the one who distinguishes figure from background, before from after, being-there from not being there. Disappearance and appearance are inseparably intertwined; neither one takes precedence. Disappearance was chosen as my point of departure because departure has to start from some point. The choice of a point of departure is a rhetorical or a political matter, and the point of departure will change eventually. It's possible to start from another point, to rearrange the order.

1.223 *In Platonic philosophy, the presence of the phenomenon refers to the presence of the Idea: what is here and now as a phenomenon with a witness is but a pale shadow of what is for all time, but will never have a witness for all time (that is, up to the boundary line between this world here and the world beyond, where the pure, fortunate soul will behold it). Plato assigns precedence to presence, that which has a witness and is like a passing shadow (the phenomenon) and that which has no witness and exists beyond time (the Idea). Without the former, the witness would be unable to imagine the latter, or even just recognize its existence (what it is, he may never know); without the latter, the former would not exist, could not be recognized as what it is, could not persist as such, even for the fleeting moment allotted to it. This precedence is metaphysical; it is nothing but a promise and a suspension. The promise is threefold: that certain things exist unchanging for all time; that what is for all time can be envisioned in the mind's eye; that this vision can be represented in words that are true to the original. The suspension is threefold in keeping with the three promises: the words are still untrue (the inscription is unsuccessful, and in fact so is speech—not here, not now, not with you, Socrates's interlocutors or the dialogues' readers); conditions are not yet right for the vision (one should still learn more, be further enlightened, purified, transcend even higher); we still have no conclusive, unshakable proof of the actual existence of those entities that are beyond hypothesis. Both the promise and the postponement of its fulfillment are effects of the philosophical discourse. Platonic discourse places presence first, but always in another position as well. The witnesses capable of bearing testimony in the philosophical discourse are only capable of promising that one day they will be witness to a presence in which there is neither disappearance nor appearance; in the meantime, they can only recognize what is present between appearance and disappearance, or the presence of both.*

1.224 *The presence of the phenomenon in Kantian philosophy refers to the presence of the witness: what is there, here and now (in space and time), as a phenomenon results from an encounter between a witness and that which has no witness except an omnipotent god (in his archetypal mind)—the thing itself. However, the outcome of such an encounter testifies to the witness, to the conditions allowing the encounter, to "the transcendental structure of consciousness" that forms the constructing principle of witnessing in general, prior to and determining any particular testimony. Kant assigns precedence to the witness and to the construct of witnessing. The witnessing to which the critic of pure reason is witness, and from which he learns the conditions that enable witnessing in general, is the witness's testimony to*

56

the presence of phenomena in time and space. In Kantian discourse, presence is assigned epistemological precedence, on the grounds that the critique presumes to offer a narrative of the presence of reason to itself. And indeed this is a narrative of presence; that is, this self-presence with such a universal claim doesn't exist except in the particular Kantian narrative, an effect of his philosophical discourse, unfolding over time, caught in the web of differences and traces, of appearances and disappearances of the language of German philosophy at the end of the eighteenth century.

1.230 The witness who catches some thing at the moment of its occurrence[19] is not a witness for whom the moment of occurrence is present, for the moment of occurrence itself is never present as such — neither at the moment of occurrence nor afterward (it isn't the object we refer to when we speak of some thing's presence). But the time of the occurrence leaves traces. Sometimes it is the condition of the witness who witnessed the disappearance. The disappearance itself is not present; what is present are only "what has disappeared," the traces of the disappeared, and the traces of the disappearance. The witness who witnesses all these also bears part of the traces or all of them. But sometimes it is possible to witness the disappearance itself; to look into the face of a dying person giving up his or her soul; to listen to a failing sound receding to the point of silence; to chase a stolen car until one's lungs are bursting after having interrupted the thief in action, and then to watch it disappear around the corner. When disappearance is witnessed thus, is it — disappearance — present?

1.231 This depends on where the production line is interrupted, how the stills (the utterances) are selected from the video recording (the event), whether the point of focus is the object (its gradual blurring makes disappearance present) or the movement (the chase after the disappearing object, after its transition from "is there" to "is not there"). It depends on which differences are focused on and which are erased. It depends on how language cuts across the space of things, how the appearing world is entongued. The presence of the trace, the presence of the traces of disappearance, dismantles the field of presence as a monolithic, atemporal field of being-there and introduces into it differences, multiplicity, and temporality. Is-there-ness splits and scatters, expands and contracts in many ways at once, in time and space; witnesses multiply, and with them points of view and channels of sensation and excitation. Within this conceptual web, presence has no precedence, even if, at times, due to linguistic habit or intellectual laziness, it is still more convenient to hold on to it when one sets out to reconstruct the fabric.

1.240   In the trace, the signifier testifies not only to what it signifies but also to the type of signifier it is: it signifies that the tie connecting it with its signified is a causative-ontological tie, and that the gap between it and its signified is first and foremost a gap of time, between the presence of that which has disappeared and the presence of its traces.

1.241   The time gap is bridged by an ontological relation between the signifier and the signified. The two occurrences of presence are connected by a relation that bridges the time gap, for both were enclosed in the same space, were part of the same body or the same system, or existed in the presence of the same witness, or — in the absence of all these — were connected through some other mediating concatenation ensuring ontological contiguity between the trace and what disappeared. The time gap assumes the unity of space, the unity of the witness, or the continuity of mediation. If no ontological relation is assumed, even implicitly, between what-was-there-and-is-no-more and what-is-present and testifies to what-is-no-more, then what-is-present will not be perceived as a trace of what-is-absent. Without such a mediating, concatenating relation, as indirect or multiphased as it may be, the sign is not a trace.

1.242   *Platonic phenomena are not traces of ideas, though certain metaphors (describing the phenomenon as "taking part in" an idea, as its "shadow," or as its "reflection") indicate an ontological relation: from the viewpoint of the witness who is chained to the world of the senses, the idea is never present, and all the more so "before" the phenomenon; from the viewpoint of the witness who already envisions ideas in his mind, the idea is forever present, and all the more so when simultaneous with the phenomenon.*

1.243   In the trace, the signified, too, has a double role or existence: it is simultaneously some thing that disappears and the disappearance of some thing. Or perhaps more precisely: every signified, signified as what has disappeared, can in turn signify disappearance, and every signified, signified as disappearance, in turn signifies some thing that has disappeared. But this precision is analytic, after the fact. What is present is studded with traces of what is gone and of disappearances of things that were there and are no more. These testify to those, and those reveal these, all in keeping with the manner in which the signifiers are isolated from the web in which they are held, while some are foregrounded on the operating table of the witness who interprets them and others are relegated to the background and swallowed in its murmur. Ideas multiply the perceived world; hidden essences lend it depth. The perceived world, when perceived as studded with traces, is a world of surface. What is now hidden from sight or heart once occurred, too, and appeared on the surface of things, and may occur or appear yet again.

1.244 In *The Ash Wednesday Supper* (1584), Giordano Bruno wrote, in a postmodernist moment, before the final disappearance of the medieval world and the appearance of the self-consciousness of modernity:

> The succession of cold and heat causes growth and diminution, which follows the sun and its course, [and] by means of which the parts of the earth acquire diverse forms and properties. So some watery places persist for a certain period and then dry up and grow old, while others spring to life again and some parts accordingly become watery. So we see springs vanish; rivers now small become large, those now large become small and finally dry up. And from the disappearance of the rivers, it follows of necessity that ponds disappear and the seas change. But, since all this occurs successively all around the earth and at long and slow intervals, we can hardly notice these transformations in our lifetimes or in those of our fathers. Thus it happens that the age and the memory of all peoples fades, and great corruptions and transformations come by desolation and abandonment, by wars, by plagues and by deluges, by changes in languages and writing, by migrations, and by places becoming barren; so that we do not remember these transformations, which have been happening from the beginning through the long, changeable and turbulent centuries.... Sufficient evidence of these great transformations is given by the remains of ancient Egypt, at the mouths of the Nile ... by the houses of the city of Memphis, and by Argos and Mycenae.... Now, the same thing that happens to such small places, happens also to larger places and to entire regions. So we see that many places, once watery, are now continents, while the sea has covered many others. We see that these transformations take place little by little ... as is shown to us by the corrosion of very high mountains, very far from the sea, on which the marks of violent waves seem almost fresh.[20]

1.245 These are the words of saint Bruno, the first anti-Platonic thinker of modern times, the man who declared the infinity of the universe, canceled the boundaries between text and nature, and saw traces of everything everywhere. Saint Bruno was the postmodern forerunner of modernity. Giordano Bruno, who lived in the sixteenth century, was a kind of prophet of a world that would, at the end of the twentieth century, be conceived of as a world of traces. *The Ash Wednesday Supper* is not a treatise on geography, geology, or archaeology. Memory disappears as well; wars and human migrations are also causes of disappearance. Bruno is speaking of the disappearance of things alongside the disappearance of memory, and the disappearance of traces of whatever has disappeared, and at the same time of the signs of all these disappearances, scattered all about. Indeed, for Bruno, only the wise man, the magus, who himself is not supposed to witness a thing, for he never wastes time on observation, knows how to decipher the testimonies and truly understand what others are seeing, although anyone can testify more or less accurately to what appears and disappears.[21] However, if we behead the arch-magus, erasing the traces of Renaissance images of knowledge, and if we read "Theophilos" and the god the wise man loves as rhetorical patterns whose role is analogous to the acknowledgments conventionally introducing an academic work, the end result will be none other than the contemporary war of interpretations.[22]

1.250   Disappearance is not only an occurrence that took place in the past, a signifier that has left traces. Disappearance is an actual occurrence, the presence of the very transition from being to nothingness. To know what amounts to a trace, one needs to witness this transition, to be one who has already experienced disappearance, one who has experienced, at least once, an occurrence in which something turns from "is there" to "is not there" and from "present" to "absent." The field of perception, a transient, ever-changing assembly of what is present, is not only full of traces of what is gone but also full of occurrences of trace-leaving. For an occurrence to be perceived as a disappearance, someone must perceive both what still is and the traces it leaves behind after it disappears. A synthesis is needed between what is present (in the meantime) only to the senses, and to the mind that entongues it while positing it as some thing, and what is present (still) as an excitation (not yet posited) or as a memory (which is posited, as yet, as a pictorial image or, already, in words), and which is usually in some vague process of transition from excitation to pictorial image or from image to word.

1.251   The talk of synthesis, too, is imprecise, because only through an analysis after the fact can disappearance be isolated from the flow of the experiencing consciousness and a single synthesizing act be extricated from the flow of language prompting what is experienced. By the same token, only reflection after the fact, or a particular interest in disappearance or in what has disappeared, can focus the occurrence as disappearance and isolate it from its other facets: the appearance of what appears, the presence of what is present, the repetitions, the differences.

1.3 *Some One and Some Thing*

1.300 For a disappearance to be perceived as an occurrence, some one must synthesize what is present to the senses and what is present as an excitation or a memory, an image or a concept; for disappearance to be interpreted as a signified, a witness must interpret signs. Disappearance is always disappearance for someone, with regard to his excitation, memory (pictorial or linguistic), gaze, and expression, given that his speech or drawing or photograph or, in short, means of representation allows things to appear and disappear. For a disappearance to be discovered and become the object of a language attempting to describe and explain it, there must be a speaking observer, an observing speaker, an interpreting observer. (An animal discovers its prey has disappeared, but this is revealed only to the eyes of an observing speaker, someone who can express what he has seen, who can connect expression and gaze [1.052].) When some thing appears as what has disappeared (but not necessarily when it in fact disappears; there may be a gap of millions of years in between), some one appears who is capable of recognizing that there was some thing there and that it is there no longer.

1.301 "Who is" and "what is," "some one" and "some thing," serve here to express an open, transient, unstable identity, caught in speech and writing as in adhesive tape, no more. Thus "the witness" is merely "the one who is present at and recognizes that," "the one who observes," and not "the observer" with any determinant capital O, the one who is observing at this moment; and at this very moment, he is also the one who is doing or isn't doing many other things, not to speak of who he was a moment earlier or who he will be a moment later, and only language, through naming and the use of indexicals, can relate them all to a single subject and also distinguish between them. Therefore, language will always offer the question that dismantles the unity of this subject, "who," and the unity of the objects to which the subject relates, "what," and the cohesive power that restores this unity, "one." Every time this discussion reads "some one" or "someone" or "one who does such and such," it implies a cluster of questions about who is speaking, who that someone is, who-he-has-already-been, who-he-may-yet-be, and what-he-can-still-do. Every time the discussion reads "some thing," it implies a cluster of questions about "that" thing which cannot remain that thing: What is that thing? What-has-it-already-been? What-can-it-still be?[23] "Who" and "what" are the way I attempt to designate the seepage of time (already and still) and of difference (change, otherness) into the being of what is and who is, a seepage which is not a process that started at some point and will end at some other point, but is, rather, the state of being-there, of everything that is there, which is always already "s(t)eeped" in time and difference. The transient identity of "that something" (which already was, which is yet to be) is a necessity of language or of consciousness, but its substantiality and its unity are not. The relative openness of the phrases "the one who" or "the thing that" and also of "some one" or "some thing" is a temporary dodging mechanism used in thinking that wishes to push language to its limits, to avoid objectifying actions and freezing objects within names.[24]

1.302   The identity of some thing is no more set or stable than the identity of some one, but the former seems to depend on the latter. The identity of some one is no less set or stable than the identity of some thing, but it sometimes seems to approximate permanence and stability ("grant perfect rest").[25] The difference expressed by this dependence and this approximation is one aspect of the modern philosophical distinction between object and subject, between the object of cognition, which has been perceived since Kant as what is constituted or posited by the subject, and the subject or bearer of cognition, who has been perceived since Kant as the one constituting or positing objects, his own self included. This matter invites a digression from the main course of investigation, one that will occupy the rest of the present section. The reader can skip from this point (and move directly to subsection 1.421), but he's invited to return to this digression in the course of the following chapters, on encountering references to the discussion presented below.

1.303   The ability to identify an object and to maintain its identification as such and such results from an integration of gaze, expression, and touch (or contact, or instrumental operation, or manipulation). An object is something that someone posits as such and such in an act that combines expression with gaze (as well as listening and — more rarely — taste and smell) and contact or touch.[26] These combinations vary and change, of course, in keeping with the object and with the circumstances in which something is posited as an object by he who posits it as such. So, for instance, the ultimate philosophical object, the desk, is described by Bertrand Russell as follows:

> It seems to me that I am now sitting in a chair, at a table of a certain shape, on which I see sheets of paper with writing or print.... I believe that, if any other normal person comes into my room, he will see the same chairs and tables and books and papers as I see, and that the table which I see is the same as the table which I feel pressing against my arm.... To the eye it is oblong, brown, and shiny, to the touch it is smooth and cool and hard; when I tap it, it gives out a wooden sound. Any one else who sees and feels and hears the table will agree with this description, so that it might seem as if no difficulty would arise; but as soon as we try to be more precise our troubles begin.[27]

"Our troubles begin," for among the users of the desk, or those interested in it, something went wrong with the coordination of gaze, contact, and expression. The viewpoints of different people looking at the desk cause them to see it in different forms and colors and therefore to describe it differently. These troubles grow even stronger when the multiple configurations and descriptions of the desk encourage those with philosophical leanings to determine, once and for all, what the desk is, in and of itself. Amid all this, and regardless of whether it is possible to determine what the desk is, in and of itself, each participant in this imaginary conversation will have to relate what he sees, feels, and describes to the same desk. Usually, with regard to objects such as desks, the pattern of integration and coordination among touch, gaze, and expression is shared by many and allows unhindered communication. When the expert in antique English furniture arrives, he will surely see, feel, and know how to describe things that the philosopher, as well as other users of the desk, overlook or cannot discern. But the expert's integration pattern will nevertheless include a degree of commonality sufficient to allow the expert and the others to speak of the same desk. When the physicist arrives and proposes a view of the desk as an agglomeration of molecules, made up of atoms, made, in turn, of subatomic particles, the difference will be more dramatic. The physicist will in fact propose the replacement of one pattern of integrating what is seen, what is tangible, and what is described with a different integration pattern.

1.304   Gazing (as well as hearing and smelling) involves a distance between the gazer and that which is gazed at. Touch (and taste)
eliminates the distance between the one or the thing touching
and that which is touched. Speech posits a distance between the
one who speaks and that which is spoken about. The person
touching can touch himself, but when touched (through an offen-
sive name, through searching and poignant words, in a caress),
even the self is posited as an object and is accordingly gazed at
or spoken of. Someone touching himself is touched himself,
but the touch, the sensation, is either present rather than posited
or posited and no longer present (see Chapter Five). There is an
unbridgeable gap between someone present to himself in a gaze,
or present to himself when being touched, and someone who
posits this self as an object (in this or that integration of expression-gaze-touch). The posited self is always just a trace of that self
which was present and has disappeared. Consequently, every confession is a series of traces of a disappeared presence, even when it
is no more than a series of erasures, conscious or unconscious, of
present traces.

1.305   The self may be posited as an object, but the very act of positing,
of referring to an object through expression-gaze-touch, doesn't
necessarily entail the assumption of a pole of selfhood that stays
constant beyond the positing act, or of the identity of the one
doing the positing — as philosophers from Descartes through
Husserl held.[28] Without the assumption of a placeless, bodiless
synthesis of expression, gaze, and contact, they claimed, it was
impossible to posit the posited object, to define its essence, to
determine its boundaries. But the pole of self-identity they assumed is no more than an imaginary, ideal point of convergence
of the one who speaks, the one who gazes at, and the one who
touches/is touched by. The pole of this convergence stems from
an idealized image and an unspoken projection. *An idealized
image*: there is always a concrete act of positing that allows seeing,
touching, and speech, and it is anchored in a definite space and
time, in a social and cultural environment, from which someone
can see, touch, speak. In modern philosophy, the image of this
positing has undergone idealization; it has been detached from its
concrete time and place and perceived as unified and void (seeing,
touching, and speaking occur at and from this placeless place).
Thus the physicist's consciousness stands in for physics as a discourse and a discipline, and the mundane consciousness of other
desk users replaces the form of social community that allows the
practice of proper communication between them. *An unspoken*

projection: the coordination of gaze, touch, and speech, by virtue of which the object is perceived as singular, is projected on the person who is gazing, touching, and speaking, and the three are perceived as one. This brings in the physicist, who produces a mathematical description of a physical object, not as one who takes a position in the discourse of physics but rather as one who somehow sees the traces of the desk material's molecular structure, upon which he or she is able to act. In the language of modern philosophy, this imagined-projected pole of unity is termed a subject. Modern philosophers have set it both as the limit of experience and what makes experience possible, but also as a structure with a peculiar existence of its own, an existence that is not in space and in some cases not even in time.

1.310 It is not that there is no limit to experience or that there are no enabling conditions. But regarding the identity of the positing self, these limits and conditions are not transcendental; they result from a concrete position occupied by the person speaking, gazing, and touching, which is culturally and historically determined. My wish is not to give up the concept of the subject entirely but to ground it in a cognitive and changing position, placed in a structured cultural field of practices of gazing, speaking, and touching. Such a position enables and delimits the positing of objects within a given area, grants and limits the authority to speak of them, to gaze at, scrutinize, and touch them, and it always maintains power relations and mutual relations of exchange with other standpoints in, and outside of, the same field (see 1.322 and 1.331).[29] A subject is one who positions something, including his body, his sensations, his soul, or "himself" (his identity), in speech-gaze-touch. The subject who wishes to situate or position himself once and for all, "who wishes to be pitiless stone,"[30] seeks for himself the identity of a thing; but even the solid identity of a thing is mere illusion — an illusion of the senses, of language, usually of both. Things do not have permanent identities or definite meanings outside the discourse that names and describes them, and the difference distinguishing one thing from another, one thing from that which is no longer that thing, is repeatedly reinstated just like the thing itself. A thing is always some thing, and the "some" depends on an entire network of positing acts by those authorized to gaze at, speak of, touch the thing (and also by those prohibited from seeing, speaking, touching it).

1.311 Some thing is not an object until some one posits it through speech, gaze, and touch; and some one does not take the position of subject until he posits something through speech, gaze, and touch. An object is always that which is posited; a subject is he who posits. The object can be real (the book you are holding right now, the moon that Galileo spoke of, watched) or not (the next book I'll write, the Little Prince's planet); the subject cannot, by definition, be anything but ideal, imagined. The subject is the structured entirety of ideal characteristics of one who occupies a position from which some things may be posited as objects. Therefore, the subject cannot be acted upon. A person's body, even his soul, can be acted upon, but always and only as some thing, some thing that only a subject can identify as his if he first posits himself as possessing a body, possessing property, possessing a horizon of expectations and hopes and comparable things that can be acted upon and damaged, injured, or destroyed.

1.312 An object and a subject are poles of identity. The traditional terms are worth retaining only when one speaks of a relatively constant identity. For the time being, the following is a minimal interpretation of the concept "subject": one who can simultaneously be the same one speaking of, gazing at, and touching or being touched by the selfsame thing. "Can simultaneously be": meaning, recognized by others as able and authorized to speak, gaze, and touch in this way. "The selfsame thing," the object, acquires its identity because a community of subjects agrees on the more or less constant relations between what is seen (or touched, heard, or sensed in some other way) and what is said about what is seen (or sensed). And vice versa: individuals take or hold subject positions after having been trained and qualified by a community of individuals holding similar positions to identify the said objects, that is, to speak, gaze at, and touch the same things in similar ways — instruments, physical particles, body parts, heavenly bodies, texts, works of art, legal testimonies, and so forth.

1.313 In contradiction to the idea seemingly implied by Kant's famous sentence — "It must be possible for the 'I think' to accompany all my representations" — someone's appearance as a subject (to himself and others) is conditional on granting identity to an object rather than the opposite.[31] This could be phrased, more or less, as "It must be possible that some thing must, necessarily, be there to be grasped as that thing itself in order for me to identify myself as the subject who recognizes it." The subject is a delayed rebound effect, as it were, of the object's positioning, a positioning that positions itself as the selfsame thing. The subject who posits himself is always also already an object. In addition, the very act

66

of positing is an effect of practices of expression, gaze, and touch, of the daily use of various things that were not necessarily positioned as objects of a scrutinizing consciousness,[32] of patterns of association and communication with other position-taking subjects, and so forth. In other words, both the posited object and the positing subject are products of more or less structured practices, which are maintained at least until the object can be identified as such and such and the subject can be identified as able and authorized to identify the object as that same object.

1.314 This identity itself is not static, but is, rather, a process in which the possibility of being different and being another is maintained at all times and is repeatedly eliminated or blocked or abandoned anew. The identity of what is posited, like the identity of the one positing, is incessantly re-created, like the way the Cartesian god re-creates the world. The subject is an idealization of he who takes a position (from which something can be seen, spoken of, and touched) but who may also transcend it, of he who takes a place but who can also evacuate it. The subject differs from an object — and this difference is part of its very essence — precisely because he is capable of transforming his identity and transgressing the boundary of its position. An object is that which is posited in a determinate place in the order of things, an object of speech, observation, and action from particular positions that depends on the stability of these positions. The subject's transcendence of his own position, his extension "beyond himself," poses a permanent threat to the identity of the subject but also to the order of things: when a doctor "forgets himself" and falls in love with a patient, her paleness turns from a symptom into a seductive expression, and the treated body appears in an erotic unity, of which the diseased or damaged member was never a part. A redescription of what is there is a threat to the order of things but also to the identity of the subjects acting, and acted upon, within this order — gazing, speaking, touching, and being touched. A map of Israel showing four hundred Palestinian villages, abandoned and destroyed in the war of 1948, threatens to dismantle and complicate not only the landscape, which has become spectral, burdened with the repressed memory that re-floods consciousness, but also the position of the Jewish-Israeli subject hiking through the homeland, which is suddenly shared with a multitude of present absentees.

1.315 In general, an object's identity will be preserved within a given order of things; a subject's identity will be preserved within a given field of positions from which one may speak, see, touch

67

(and act). When the order of things is undermined, when the field is ruptured, when some thing exceeds its boundaries, when some one deviates from the stand assigned him, there is no point in talking about subject versus object any longer. In such circumstances, both the subject and the object are no-longer-what-they-were (and perhaps they-are-already-what-they-still-aren't, because they have not yet been posited as possessing such and such identity, as currently being-what-they-are).

Below, I will distinguish between the moment of relatively set identity and the moment of deviation: the subject positions and the objects posited relative to them will only be worth discussing based on a more or less stable field of positions and relations among positions, and things and relations among things. To designate ruptured identities, or the moment of deviation from identity, I will resort to speaking of "some thing" (or "that which") and "some one" (or "he who"). Like lightning in the negative of a photograph, a flash of darkness in a sea of light — as happens at a blinding moment, one cannot see what is present, while what was there, what was vaguely, absentmindedly viewed just a moment ago, becomes clear and stable in memory alone. At the moment of transgression, a disappearance posits itself, positions itself relative to itself; identity is present as what-was-there-and-is-no-more, and what is there, is present as still devoid of identity, what has not yet been posited as this and this.

1.320 — It would seem that "some one" is simply a distorted translation of Heidegger's *Dasein*, the entity that transcends any identity by virtue of its very existence, the entity that "in its very Being that Being is an issue for it."[33] (The mark — indicates an internal dialogue.) It would also seem that "some thing" is a cramped translation of what Heidegger termed *zuhanden*, "at hand, ready for use," the being given to use in the broadest sense, which does not yet determine such and such a thing,[34] and which Heidegger attempts to employ for preserving the indefiniteness of the Greek ον or τοδε τι.[35] Is that so?
— Heidegger's influence cannot be denied. But in the present text, "some one" and "some thing" are considered in order to address not the question of Being in general, of Being in all its forms, but only the question of the being of Evil, and particularly of its being-there, its is-there-ness. The Heideggerian residue is borne by a philosophical language that rejects any attempt to clear ontology of moral questions and from which nothing could be more remote than succumbing to the large-scale politics of

"destiny," or the people's "historical vocation," or to any order-building and order-destroying power intimating the historical possibility that conditions are supposedly right for a reopening "toward" Being. This discussion conceives of "some one" and "some thing" for the purpose of performing the opposite move exactly: in order to restore morality to ontology, to allow the thinking of what is there as what, properly, should or shouldn't be there. To begin with, what interests me here is not being but disappearance, not Being (*Sein*), as distinct from anything else which is there as this or that thing (*Seiende*), but the practices of determining the differences between this or that thing, of determining identities and deconstructing them. The phenomenological analysis that follows the movement of differentiation and identification, their reproduction and deconstruction, makes it necessary to identify and differentiate between the enabling conditions of identifying and differentiating and he who identifies and differentiates, or between the subject position and some one capable of taking upon himself the conditions of this position (and who then, too, will never be one with it) or of transcending its mold.

1.321 The subject position, just like the very someone who acts and is activated from within it and who can transcend it, precedes any distinction of kind or type, group or class, and first and foremost any gender distinction. Some one may be posited as male or female, man or woman, precisely because the subject position itself is prior to gender divergence and because such a divergence is one of its (not inevitable) possibilities. The subject is perhaps the projection of a grammatical pattern onto the analysis (phenomenological or otherwise) of experience, but it is an empty template, just like the grammatical subject; its identity as a template is maintained only by the grammatical structure. Therefore, when speaking of a subject position, or of some one who deviates from it, one might appropriately opt for neutral pronouns. The English language provides one such pronoun, but it refers only to objects. Therefore, in this discussion I've chosen to use gendered pronouns for the length of an entire chapter and to alternate them between chapters.

1.322 A subject position is not a role, though it may be embedded in institutional differentiation of roles and division of labor (see 1.343). A subject position determines a range of possible modes of integrating expression, gaze, and touch; it limits and enables modes of speech and action. Subject positions differ from each other in keeping with the possibilities for action that they construct within a given sphere. The possible in this context should be understood as the legitimate, the authorized, and more generally the "not impossible."

1.323 Subjectivity will not be understood here as consciousness, and definitely not as self-consciousness. Neither will it be understood as the transcendental structure of experience. Subjectivity is a differential function within a given field of practices in which experience assembles and organizes. Being a subject means producing with bodily acts, with gaze, and with speech, but in a manner always limited by and conditional on the subject position, gaps in what is there. An acting subject causes things to appear and disappear, to come into being and to end; he temporalizes what is there and en-tongues what-is-there and what-is-not-there, what-appears and what-disappears, what-was-there-and-is-no-more, what-is-there-but-will-disappear (or what should properly disappear, or whose disappearance is desired), what-is-not-there-but-is-expected-to-appear (or should properly appear, or whose appearance is desired). The acts of positing, through speech, gaze, and touch, are carried out relative to an ideal point at which the one-who-is-speaking-gazing-touching-feeling is supposed to be placed and from which he is supposed to carry out the synthesis that allows the identification of some thing as an object within a given order of objects. This point is a product of a synthesis after the fact, of an abstraction from concrete acts performed from the subject position, and of an idealization of the structural constraints of this position.

1.324 The subject position is always permeated by an ambiguity created by the irreconcilable tension between the "immanence" and "worldliness" of the concrete practices of speech, gaze, and touch, on the one hand, and the transcendentalism of the viewpoint and the source of speech to which the positing-identifying-differentiating synthesis is ascribed, on the other. The concrete practices always depend on the material, linguistic, and cultural contexts; the synthetic-ideal point is supposed to ensure complete independence of context. Such a tangential point, bordering on the space of action but never falling within it, is implied in every case where someone claims to know some thing and, more broadly, to judge some thing as right or proper. Kantian critique attempted to formulate and anchor the formal, universal limiting conditions of the point of synthesis once and for all, for all future experience. Since Hegel, and particularly since Marx, Nietzsche, and Freud, the main schools of critical thought have attempted to reveal the contextual conditions (historical, social, linguistic, or psychological) of practices that enable and delimit the idealization of this synthesis. The ancient debate between realism and relativism is rooted in the fundamental structure of the subject position itself.

1.330 In modern times, subject positions are instituted in disparate spheres of action (in economics, law, art, science, or religion, for instance), in which they receive highly developed and explicit expression. When some one acts as a subject, he is already placed within a more or less disciplined field of practices of speech about and speech to, of communication and association, of gazing at and acting on. There are many such fields, and each of them constructs subject positions that differ within the same field and across fields. Constructing the subject position means constructing and limiting the options of the one who occupies a position to speak (or use other means of expression), to look (or use other senses), and to touch (and see 1.303), but also to occupy other subject positions (the nurse isn't authorized to occupy the doctor's position, and the student isn't authorized to teach; but the doctor may, in some circumstances, occupy the position of the nurse, and the teacher is authorized, is obliged perhaps, to go on learning). In the field of possibilities in which the subject position is placed, other subject positions operate in cooperation, in competition, and in a struggle over the ways of differentiating and temporalizing what is there and of making time present. The mutual relations between these are always permeated by inconsistencies, permanently present, though they change in dimension, between experiences of disappearance and appearance of what is there and the articulation of these experiences in colloquial language or specialized discourse. In this field, there are also always "lines of flight,"[36] fissures, and ruptures through which one can escape, at varying degrees of risk, into other spaces of action, stealing into other subject positions, reshaping the boundaries of the expressible, visible, and touchable.

1.331 In the modern era, the institution of subject positions in different fields of discourse and action is connected to the development of two types of cultural mechanisms: those designed to constitute objects by determining who is authorized to speak of them, see them, touch them; and those designed to constitute subjects by determining the objects that they are supposed to posit and observe, to interpret and analyze, to sanctify or destroy. These mechanisms are at work in courts, in the press, in the laboratory, in the museum, at the archaeological site, and at other locations throughout social space.[37] The history of the modern subject is the history of the differing fields of discourse and of the mechanisms for mutual stabilization of the identities of the subject and object acting within them, the mechanisms for constituting, presenting, and representing objects, and the mechanisms training and approving the occupiers of subject positions. But the subject is not only the holder of a position in a field: one who faces, one who undertakes negotiations with, one who interprets and judges, one who exchanges with, and so on. From the beginning of the modern era, this subject was also the object of specific fields of discourse — the linguistic discourse, the medical discourse, the discourse of psychotherapy, of criminology, of sexology, and other fields of discourse in other areas of the humanities. Some of these fields of discourse grew out of various disciplinary institutions (the medical hospital, the psychiatric hospital, the school, the prison), nurtured them, and combined with them in a complete weave of knowledge and power relations that allowed the simultaneous creation of distinct and general subject positions and the individuation of the individuals who occupied them. This is but a thumbnail sketch of one of the general claims presented by Foucault in his works on the disciplinary practices and institutions of modern times.[38]

1.332 — The modern subject may have a history, but the general form of the subject position is presented as a transcendental condition of experience. Doesn't "the fundamental structure of the subject position" (1.324) have a history of its own?
— Major chapters in the history of philosophy may be reconstructed as different articulations of the same general form. Plato and Aristotle didn't have a concept of subject, of course. Neither did Thomas Aquinas or Maimonides. Nevertheless, their theories of knowledge and affection can be described, in hindsight, in terms of subject positions and of the ability to transcend them. Degrees of knowledge in the work of Plato or Spinoza are different subject positions, involving different practices of situating the known object (observation, measurement, dialectical discourse) and various capabilities of synthesis allowing its identification and the presumption of "knowing" it. The philosophical Eros leading the soul higher and higher up the ladder of knowledge is a description of transcendence; the discussion of Eros in the *Symposium* is a discussion of the structure of transcendence itself.[39] The soul's wish to free itself from the body is a wish to transcend any subject position, to free itself from the very positioning of the knowing subject. No wonder that the apex of knowing, knowing the Good, is supposed to be the knowledge of that which is "still

beyond being, exceeding it in dignity and power."[40] However, this is an imagined subject position; it doesn't describe the position taken by the philosopher who founded the Academy. There is a huge gap between the subject position implied by Plato's theory of knowledge and the position of the philosopher in public discourse, or of the "intellectual" in Athens (which is portrayed, criticized, and deconstructed in the earlier dialogues).

— But in both cases, the general form of the subject position is reaffirmed: a position that "determines a range of possible modes of integrating expression, gaze, and touch; it limits and enables modes of speech and action" (1.322). Isn't the claim about the subject position a transcendental claim, a popular, disguised form of Kantianism?

— Kant gets a hand from Heidegger here (the condition of "touch-ability," of that which is given to manipulation, and so on), his transcendental aesthetic is given a Foucauldian twist, and his universal understanding is incarnated in a multiplicity of languages and forms of discourse. Moreover, when consciousness is replaced with a position in a field of social relations, the transcendental itself is incarnated in society, historicized, and spatialized.

— But you still aspire to give a general form to this social incarnation, historicization, spatialization. Aren't you prepared to give up this residue of transcendentalism?

— No, although I keep in mind that this attempt to generalize and abduct universal forms from changing historical conditions is both made possible by and seen as necessary due to a certain subject position, that of a philosopher of a certain brand, which I am trying to occupy.

1.333 Different types of discourse assign the subject position a coherent structure, a foundation of legitimacy, and mainly — the common denominator it shares with positions in other fields — the option of moving from one field to another. Every field witnesses the evolution of its own habits, expectations, tendencies to respond in particular patterns, gestures, and body positions — in short, what Bourdieu, following Aristotle, has called "habitus." Each field has a *habitus* of its own, and each of these is distinct from the *habitus* of daily life, in which individuals function as relatives, friends, consumers.

Perhaps the problem of the identity of self is so sharply posed in modern times because of the separation of these distinct fields, on the one hand, and the possibility that the same someone may occupy different subject positions in different fields while different individuals may occupy the same subject position, on the other. Who is that someone and who can vouch for his identity when he comes and goes through different fields of discourse and action, wandering among different subject positions? The philosophy of the subject, from Descartes to Sartre, through Kant, Husserl, and (the early) Heidegger, is preoccupied with this question, which it strives to answer once and for all (Kant, Hegel, Husserl), or whose very presentation it strives to construe as absurd (Sartre), or every attempted answer to which, it strives to demonstrate, necessarily involves forgetfulness and concealment (Heidegger). However, all these thinkers, including Heidegger and Sartre, propose a universal structure, which in turn makes possible uniqueness and singularity. Consciousness, or the transcendental I, the spirit, consciousness as freedom and nothingness, or *Dasein* and its *existentialia*, all purport to somehow anchor the singular in the universal and to provide a coherent structure of possibilities within which the same someone can take different subject positions, can institute changing identities for himself, but meanwhile, as well, tell himself a tale of one identity that embraces all of these.

1.334 This identity, which seems to protect the said someone from splitting into different subject positions, was given explicit expression in the modern era within the framework of a wide variety of cultural practices. Since the eighteenth century, the public sphere has appeared as the locus of the "net" subjectivity, underlying and common to the structures of subjectivity in various fields, and allowing passage from one field to another.[41] The public sphere is the place where everyone can, supposedly, appear, introduce and represent himself, sound his voice, and be viewed, like everyone else, as an individual with rights and with essentially equal access to various spheres of action. The unifying identity of that someone who may take different subject positions in separate fields of action and discourse is the identity of the citizen.[42] The public sphere has a close relation to real sites within the social space — the city square, the market, the street, the café, the theater, the museum, and similar public meeting places — but it also has its virtual sites, such as the newspaper, the magazine, the radio or television program. Modern literature, first and foremost the novel, offers another virtual space, which serves as a laboratory of sorts for the construction and examination of self-identity. (And parallel to this, almost since the time of its birth, from Sterne [*Tristram Shandy*] through Joyce to Carver, it has also offered the table on which this identity is dissected.)

1.335 The public sphere presupposes a general and homogeneous iden-

74

tity whose individuation is accomplished by giving names, titles, and a few more external distinguishing marks. Various literary genres imagine a singular, private identity, and they unfold memory through social space where literary characters travel in search of their identity. Meanwhile, the various genres of psychoanalytic discourse offer memory itself as the space out of which self-identity is designed through various practices of remembering, questioning, interviewing, dialogue, and narrative. Psychoanalytic narrative constructs the subject as that interiority which remains one even if it is split and torn and which encounters different subject positions as external to it, attempting to mold them according to its own projected image. But this story can be told only by one who takes the position of patient, and only with the aid of the mediating knowledge creating the subject of psychoanalytic discourse, and through the power exerted by this knowledge.

1.340 Some one doesn't always act as a subject, not even when he's awake, not even when he takes a subject position. In other words, an individual can be awake (and not just in the hovering half-sleep experienced by the insomniac and described by Lévinas[43]), and can even take a subject position, without positing any object and without relating to any of the objects that act upon him (see 4.300). On the other hand, there may also be superior primates, dolphins, or angels who operate as subjects, while we are incapable of knowing this. Subjectivity can be ascribed to an animal, and one may relate to the animal accordingly, but it is impossible to know what its subjectivity is. This is not because we cannot understand its language but because we ourselves, in principle, cannot occupy the subject position that we ascribe to it and cannot imagine a real world in which it would occupy a subject position such as ours.

1.341 We are capable of grasping an imaginary world where both these things occur, as demonstrated by unending legends and fables. But in all of these tales, the animal has no subject position peculiar to it. Animal fables project human subject positions on the community of animals, and animals on human subject positions. At times, they include descriptions of subject positions that only an animal could take (because no human being is as perfectly innocent and honest, or as perfectly sly, or as farsighted as any speaking animal). All these fables simply bring out more forcefully the problematic distinction between humans and animals as they create an unbridgeable gap between the humanized animal and the animal — or the human — familiar from daily life.

1.342   He whose subjectivity is recognized is he who is capable of taking this or that subject position. If he doesn't take one for the moment, this may be ascribed to obstacles created by education, class, gender, ethnic affiliation, age, and so forth. There are cultural-political circumstances in which such obstacles are insurmountable: in certain cultures, a woman cannot take a man's subject position and vice versa, and the same holds for slave and master, white and black, civilized and savage. The subjectivity of a woman, a slave, a black man, a savage, is questioned by those in power — usually white men — who control access to various subject positions.

1.343   A subject position is a function of discourse. I'm using the term "discourse" in the thick sense introduced by Foucault, denoting not only a regime of discourse or communicative practices within a given realm of words and things but also a regime that determines the conditions of visibility and manipulability of objects in the same realm.[44] As noted above (1.322), it is impossible to establish a subject position on a role that is a function of an institution. There are intersections and partial overlaps between a subject position and a role, as there are between an institution and a discourse, but they are not fully equivalent or compatible. People fulfilling the same role may take different subject positions (the outgoing faculty dean is internationally known as an eminent researcher and an authority in his field; the incoming dean is well versed and agile in matters of academic politics), and two people who take similar subject positions may fulfill different roles (one expert cardiologist may head a hospital department; his colleague may be content with managing a private clinic). In addition, a position should not be identified with a subject, for not every position is a subject position and not everyone who takes a position in a field of discourse (as a speaker and as an observer) is a subject in the full sense of the term. A doctor, an intern, and a nurse take different positions, and only the doctor is a complete subject of medical discourse; the nurse takes a subject position in the discourse of the clinic as a place where patients get treatment, but not as a place of that knowledge presupposed by this treatment and by the very notion of a patient. The defendant takes a subject position in the economic field that allows the exchange between him and the counsel for the defense; in legal discourse, the defendant is only a subject in the investigation room and on the witness stand, and he reaches these two positions involuntarily; he cannot determine of his own accord whether he will maintain, or be cut off from, them. The defendant is a subject only with regard to giving testimony, to the facts, but not with regard to the trial itself, to the ruling and the sentence, to determining the motive and the offense. Being a subject means taking a position, but not everyone who takes a position is a subject (the patient takes a position but is not a subject in medical discourse).

1.344 Someone enters the department, passes by employees and visitors who do not recognize him, meets a colleague from a neighboring department and two familiar nurses, and nods hello. He walks into his office, takes off his coat, and puts on a white gown. Lying on his desk are the morning paper and some medical files of the patients he will be seeing today. The head nurse enters and greets him. She has some urgent matter to deal with, but she will be back immediately to coordinate the department's schedule for the morning. He glances at the newspaper absentmindedly, phones the bank to arrange something, takes a few papers out of his briefcase, switches his glasses, and looks vacantly at the files lying in front of him. For as long as possible, he delays his entry into the position of the medical subject. He will take it only when he must, when the first problem presents itself. The head nurse returns; he asks how she is, and they exchange a few inane morning phrases. But at nine o'clock, the doctor's rounds begin in the department, and he opens the first file. How did he do last night? he asks. This question was already uttered from his subject position. His intonation is enough to indicate to the head nurse that the friendly interest he has just expressed in her well-being has now been replaced by a professional interest in the condition of the patient first on the list. The information she provides will be given in keeping with the rules of medical discourse. It will join an entire web of knowledge, information, and practices of gaze, expression, and touch that will lead the doctor to his next question. His immediate problem is reconfirming the dosage of medication prescribed for the patient in question. He needs to redetermine the relations between several objects, all of which are more or less controllable through an integration of touch, gaze, and speech: blood-pressure and blood-sugar levels, time elapsed since surgery, healing rate of the incision, the patient's age, previous medical events, the graph of relations between the recommended dosage of the medication and a series of other medical parameters, and so on.

1.345 Readers can tell analogous stories about a lawyer at her law firm, a teacher in his classroom, a biologist in her lab, a psychologist in his clinic, a writer in front of her computer screen. You can also illustrate the limited subject positions of the auto mechanic, the waitress, your domestic help, and also your children. But it's worth noting that a limited subject position is not identical with the limitation of liberty. The liberty of the student to fall in love with his teacher is greater than that of the teacher to fall in love with her student. The sentry has more free time and more liberty to fantasize, flirt, and read than do the managers in the office building he guards.

1.350 A subject position is in no way identical with private experience or with the consciousness of subjectivity. A subject position constructs the form of the individual experience and the formation of individual identity in accordance with its placement in a given field of discourse and activity, and in keeping with the options open to it within that field. It does so in a manner that constructs even what is private and singular or unique in general and communicable patterns, allowing association and communication between similars and limiting them between dissimilars. However, at the same time, it also marks areas of a completely incommunicable singularity. What is beyond the possibility of expression, what is represented as ineffable, what is spoken of along with the lack of means for its expression, what it is that one longs to "reach" while regretting the impossibility of sharing it with others, result from the same discursive conditions that make expression possible.

1.351 One who takes a subject position may be conscious of his subjectivity, that is, of the way in which his subject position allows and limits his experience. This consciousness of subjectivity is always limited. What is there, in the subject position (the conditions, the constraints, the possibilities), always exceeds what consciousness reflects; the reflecting consciousness is always lacking relative to the being that it is supposed to reflect. Overcoming this lack is, according to Hegel, the aim and the apex of the dialectical journey of reason. But we have no evidence to show that a process of overcoming this lack is possible, that it progresses in a dialectical manner, or that it progresses at all. Reflection on the subject position is limited by the conditions of the position from which it is performed (whether this is another or the same subject position).

1.352 What-is-there but is hidden from the eyes of the subject seeking to know his subject position isn't hidden as a result of a disappearance, because it has never appeared and because it doesn't reveal itself through traces testifying to its disappearance. That is, except for a possible affect conveying that "there-is-something-else-there." That something else may appear at the moment of transgression, or following a leap to another subject position, when self-identity is articulated anew, and what was too close, un-reflected, taken for granted, is now en-tongued explicitly.

1.353 In order to take action as a subject (to act from a subject position), one need not thematize self-identity. Thematization of self-identity ("know thyself" in its various modes and transformations) is an action of a subject seeking to locate gaps in the existence of the subject itself, to call the subject into presence, to temporalize its being-there, to posit it as an object, and to identify appearance and disappearance in the field of subjective being-there.

1.354 Sometimes some one is summoned to a subject position when a problem arises; sometimes entry into a subject position creates the problem or allows its manifestation. The difference between one who takes a subject position and one who doesn't is roughly as follows: the former has a more or less orderly, organized social route, anchored in institutional cultural practices, for handling problems he cares about; the latter lacks such a route and depends, when such problems burden him, on the goodwill of others capable of taking a subject position. Beckett's Molloy comes to mind, for instance: a no man of sorts, a cluster of problems, all wounds and bruises and putrefying sores, who cannot take any kind of subject position and who has no means for dealing in an orderly or logical way with any of his problems.[45]

1.4 Problems

1.400 A subject position is always actualized vis-à-vis a problem encountered by the one who holds it. A problem means disturbance in the order of things that demands attention, treatment, action, speech, or the expectation of such a disturbance, or the apprehension that it may arise. The disturbance can be caused by the disappearance of some thing or by the appearance of some thing, immediately manifested as lack or excess in the presence of some thing (in the doctor's instance: blood pressure, the quantity of sugar in the blood, the pulse rate, the trajectory of the graph on the ECG machine, and so on [see 2.312]). A person acting from a subject position identifies and creates problems. Is there a possibility of a subjectivity devoid of reference to a problem — whether theoretical or practical? It would seem that a perfect world has no place for subjectivity — the final solution with which all problems are solved is the end of the game — and no need of objects: perfect reason, "archetypal," in Kant's terms, does not posit anything but perceives through its direct gaze things as they are, leaves them as they are, longs for nothing, and seeks to change nothing. Subjectivity is unfailingly realized in the face of a gap between what has disappeared and what remains, what appears and what is truly there, what is there and what is desired or proper, what is desired and what is possible, what might be and what is desirable.

1.401 A subject position structures the way problems are experienced; it makes it possible to identify problems and their treatment. But it also creates problems through the gaps it opens up between what appears and what is truly there, what is there and what is desired, and so on. At times, the first problem of one who takes up a subject position is to safeguard a source of problems that sustain the subject position, that delay the end of the game.

1.402 A problem is a necessary correlate of a subject position. The opposite, however, is not the case: not everyone who has a problem necessarily takes a subject position. Children repeatedly encounter problems that they handle without taking a subject position. Sometimes this involves disappointment, lack, or pain, and the complaint is immediately referred to an adult who is expected to take care of it as an expert. Adults take many more subject positions from children's point of view than they take in practice, chiefly due to the main subject position occupied by adults from the point of view of children: that of parent (or teacher, or guide).

1.410 Sometimes, though, it is merely a game. The game constructs a subject position for the child that is valid within the boundaries of the game. This is so whether the child invents the game himself or learns it from others, whether he plays it himself or along with others. The more structured the game is, the more highly structured the position is. And it can also be said that a structured field of discourse and action is a grown-ups' game. But grown-ups have other games, too, "real" games. Adults play in order to "rid themselves" of and to "flee" and to "free themselves" from problems, and sometimes also from subject positions that are joined by such problems, or in order to take up, or at times even to make up, subject positions for themselves and to take pleasure in the ability to deal with the problems that adjoin them (and even to take pleasure in the invention of such problems).

1.411 What is the difference between real games and games of the real? Nothing that can be stated *a priori*, or analytically. A structured field of action and discourse isn't a "real" game just because it is perceived as real, and because what is at stake in it seems more valuable than what is at stake in other games. A game isn't "real" precisely because it is perceived as "a real game" and what is at stake in it seems insignificant in comparison to what one risks oneself for in the "true" game of life. The differentiating difference is not between what is real and what is merely a playful act within the realm of the game but between the more structured and the less structured game.

1.412 The professional basketball player (for whom the game is real business, personal identity, social status, and career) differs from the amateur (for whom it is "just a game") mainly because the former has a contract and a yearly income and cannot take a leave as he pleases without severe penalties, while the latter has little to lose if he stops playing in the midst of a boring game. For the professional, the game is an endless source of problems; for the amateur, it is the time and space of a leisurely leave of absence from constantly surmounting problems. And this difference, too, is as fluid as the rules of the game in question.

1.420 There are many reasons why some one might seek to deal with problems outside of existing subject positions. Perhaps he is denied access to the relevant subject positions; perhaps he encounters his subject position as his own problem; perhaps he is very tired. Individuals don't always act in relation to a structured field of relations within the framework of a given discourse and do not continuously occupy the subject positions open to them. Subject positions and their problematic correlates in the order of things can always be avoided, escaped, betrayed; each subject position offers its own "lines of flight."

1.421 A problem is the area in some order of things in which someone has an interest. An interest (or engagement) is someone's attitude to a problem. I am referring here not to the general interest that someone has in, say, literature or modern painting but to the interest involved in seeking some thing that is lacking or excessive, that is wished for or apprehended, that one wishes to advance or prevent, to maintain and continue or to stop immediately, some thing whose expected appearance, or current presence, one makes efforts to change. When Kant wrote about aesthetic judgment that "the mere representation of the object is accompanied with satisfaction in me, however indifferent I might be [with regard to the existence of the object of this representation]," he meant precisely this: an image that is without any lack or excess, that one has no wish to change either in its expected appearance or in its current one, that one neither apprehends nor longs for, with the obvious exception of the interest of an observer in the very presence of this image involving no interest and in the continuance of this presence.[46]

1.43 But a problem, by its very nature, is an elusive matter, its identity hard to stabilize. Every attempt to define a problem is already part of the solution of the problem and therefore a change in the nature of the problem itself. Problems transcend attempts to posit some thing within a given order of things; a problem is the impossibility of bringing to completion the positing of some thing. Accordingly, a problem is the impossibility of stabilizing the identity of some one as the one who posits (observes, speaks) some thing. Therefore, the problem is a permanent locus of self-identity formation. The project of attributing a self-identity always requires an unsolved problem in relation to which identity forms (who am I, what do I know, who is entitled to this or that, who is a Jew, what is a woman, what is happening to us, what should I do now). A problem is the paradigmatic locus where being exceeds what has already appeared as observable, touchable, or sayable, and all the more so exceeds what has already been observed, touched, or said. A problem calls on the subject in order to restore this excess of being to its invisible place, to clear a space for it in the order of things and in the order of discourse, to change this order greatly or slightly so as to contain it.

1.440 In every problem, some thing is concealed, but this does not necessarily mean that some thing disappears. Disappearance is a particular kind of problem. Disappearance is a problem in which someone has an interest in what was there and is there no longer, in what was present and has ceased appearing, and he is interested in it precisely because it was previously there and is no longer.

1.441 The problem of disappearance has at least two facets: either what disappears is absent, its lack is someone's problem, and the disappearance as a kind of occurrence is part of it; or the disappearance is an event that has presence or traces of presence, and this presence is someone's problem (which may also lead him to trace what has disappeared). In other words, disappearance is a problem because what has disappeared is missing and its traces are experienced as the presencing of a lack; or because someone seeks to know where it is, why it disappeared and how; and also, sometimes, when only traces of the disappearance are left, because someone seeks to know what it was exactly that disappeared — the traces are an excessive presence, as it were, that can't be gotten rid of.

1.45   A unique type of disappearance takes place as the result of a loss of access to a subject position. Nothing is left from which to follow the traces of such a disappearance. Such a disappearance is a problem around which no interested subject is capable of stabilizing his self-identity. The traces of the disappearance left for the one who was a subject, those that nearly only the body still remembers, fade increasingly, for it is impossible to posit them and it is impossible to stabilize their identity. And along with these traces, the problem that was the disappearance gradually disappears as well.

1.5   *Equivalence and Reversibility*

1.500   Disappearance belongs to the realm of facts and states of affairs; it is designated (or referred to) by an existential statement. The expression (articulation) of a disappearance in discourse determines it as an occurrence, and as such it is an object of speech, description, interpretation, and analysis. Occurrence is the object of existential statements and of probability statements. As such, disappearance is at stake in different types of "truth games" within various fields of discourse.[47] In various types of scientific discourse and in many other kinds of discourse based on scientific discourse and its procedures of corroboration, consent, and refutation, disappearance is not a unique occurrence but part of the field of phenomena to which discourse refers and which it articulates. The phenomenal space that is the correlate of statements within a given discourse includes, as a matter of course, recurring disappearance alongside recurrences of appearance and continuing presence.[48]

1.501   At times, disappearance and appearance are reversible and equivalent processes. The disappearance cancels out what has appeared; the appearance restores what has disappeared. Such a situation is familiar in the phenomena described, for instance, by the discourse of physics or chemistry: the appearance and disappearance of a substance, a motion, or a material structure. This may also be the case in economics, sociology, or psychology: the appearance and disappearance of demand in the stock market, of social gaps, of emotional tensions. And there is an equivalence between appearance and disappearance in child's play, too — the repeated wonder and amusement of the child confronted with the disappearance and reappearance of someone or something.

1.502   When claims are made for the equivalence of disappearance and appearance, it is assumed that some thing that has disappeared returns as the same thing, that the differences between what has disappeared and what has reappeared have been erased or can be ignored. A child whose doll has disappeared, only to reappear later under a pile of toys, will disregard the dust it has accumulated and immediately identify it as the selfsame doll. The sources of demands that reappear on the capital market may be ignored, as may the internal structure of the investment portfolios involved in the demands. When a particular substance reappears, the chemist ignores the question whether these are the selfsame molecules, sufficiently satisfied that this is "the same substance." When a patient loses blood, it is enough to know the blood type in order to restore what he has lost. Usually, the question whether the same kind of thing or matter has reappeared, or whether it is the selfsame piece of matter, is the detective's question, not the chemist's, the pathologist's, or the doctor's. And in any case, in order for what has disappeared to reappear as the selfsame thing, we must ignore what has disappeared or appeared between its disappearance and appearance.

1.503　When claims are made for the equivalence of disappearance and appearance, it is possible, in principle, to locate or reconstruct what has disappeared and to cause it to reappear. One need only know the details about what has disappeared, and sometimes the circumstances of the disappearance. When a stone is thrown into the water and disappears in the depths, it is possible to send a diver down equipped with enough of the stone's distinctive features in order for him to bring it back. When footprints disappear in the sand, they can easily be restored, given the knowledge of who made them. But when a person is thrown into the depths, only a body can be brought up out of the water, and when it is not known who made the footprints, all that can be restored is the imprint they made in memory.

1.504　It is possible to construct a scale of uniqueness as follows: what has disappeared and can be restored in the form of a substitute exactly like it; what has disappeared, can be restored, and will, when it reappears, be what it was, but can have no substitute if it is not restored; what has disappeared and will never again, even if restored, be what it once was.

1.510　All types of historical discourse share a study of irreversible disappearances. Astrophysicists study the disappearance (the "death") of stars; geologists study the disappearance of land formations, aided by the traces of disappeared organisms; evolutionary biologists study species and subspecies that have disappeared; anthropologists study human species that have disappeared or species that are in the process of disappearing; and historians study cultural and social formations that have disappeared. All these disappearances are irreversible, and not all of them can be reconstructed (and none of them can be fully reconstructed). At a certain point between the geologist and the historian a disappearance of a unique character emerges: the one-of-a-kind disappearance which is sui generis, that is, which differs from any classification as a species, subspecies, type.

1.511 History was not always perceived as the tale of irreversible disappearances. The *historia naturalia* of the seventeenth century placed disappearance in the margins of the phenomena being studied: only the monsters had disappeared, and this disappearance, too, was doubtful; other kinds of subspecies and species stayed as constant as the rows and columns of the table in which they were classified.[49] The cyclic conception of history sought to cancel the irreversible character of historical processes, or at least some of them. The "nomothetic" conception of history sees disappearances as occurrences in the physical or chemical vein, results of the same constellations of circumstances; only the particular tokens disappear, while the range of types and traits remains unchanged. The same is true of economic relations in the paradigm reigning in current economic discourse. Capital appears, accumulates, and is stored in one place and disappears in another, but the range of economic relations and the mechanisms of the market remain intact. In contradistinction, when the phenomena under study are conceived as phenomena whose essence is historicity, most disappearances are viewed as irreversible (capital accumulation and bankruptcy, for instance), and more irreversible disappearances are posited as objects of study, to be described and explained. Or vice versa: when irreversible disappearance is posited as an object of study, when it is problematized and given thematic expression, the phenomena studied in a given area undergo historicization.

1.512 Historicization is not necessarily the lot of what is unique and singular. Historicity can be possessed by man as a member of his species, by meaning as a member of its kind. But then there is need of a description in which the entire species or the whole genre is perceived as unique or singular.

1.520 A disappearance that is part of a multifaceted process or occurrence can seemingly be described in terms of the appearance of something else, some contrasting substitute (the disappearance of spots from the test tube, from the screen, from the face of the sun, is an appearance of a more homogeneous surface; the disappearance of organized crime is the stabilization of orderly, lawful social life and a rise in the number of non-organized crimes; the disappearance of ozone is the appearance of an added amount of other gases). But the seeming equivalence between the expression of an occurrence as a series of appearances and its expression as a series of disappearances is always misleading. It is an equivalence between types of things, effects, idioms of description, that always misses both the thing itself, what has disappeared, and the disappearance as an occurrence in itself. It misses the thing itself in the sense that the whole, the thing that has disappeared (or appeared), is not equal to the sum of its parts. But it misses it, first and foremost, in the sense in which every combination of the same factors — forces, processes, and matter of the same kind, in the same quantities, in the same proportions, in the same mutual relations — will create the same effect, will create a thing of the same type, but not the same thing itself, which has appeared or disappeared in the previous occurrence. In other words, this equivalence misses the uniqueness of what has disappeared, misses what has disappeared as what can never return.

1.521 In a more precise manner, following Deleuze: only the unique and singular can truly return, it, itself, and none of its substitutes; when the unique and singular disappears, it is impossible to establish in its place a replacement, anything that resembles it. The demand for return is a demand for the elimination of all difference, the elimination of the gap between the similar (a member of the species) and the same (it, itself).[50]

1.522 A description of a birth cannot be equivalent to a description of a series of disappearances; a description of a death cannot be equivalent to a description of a series of appearances (for example, of processes of organic disintegration); and so forth concerning the extinction of animal species or the disappearance of all the manuscripts of Aristotle's treatise on comedy. Think, for instance, of the erasure of an entire file from a computer's hard disk. There is no backup file, and the text that was on it (or the text that was it) has disappeared. No traces are left on the screen of the computer; if there are traces, they are in the memory of the author and the memories of some readers of the text, if there were any. In such a case, there is no possibility of identifying an appearance or a series of appearances with any connection to the disappeared text. And of course it is impossible to identify a series of appearances whose description will be equivalent to the disappearance. Anyone who insists on identifying such a series at the level of the diskette's hardware (and this itself seems dubious) will not be able to cross back from hardware to software (to the disappeared text).

1.523 When disappearance is the problem of someone who is interested in what has disappeared and in the fact of its disappearance (1.440), and when the disappeared has no substitute and cannot be restored, this is a loss.

Chapter Two

Loss

2.0 *Irreplaceable*

2.000 Loss is a singular type of disappearance: the irreversible disappearance of some irreplaceable thing. Whenever the disappeared is not replaceable, and as long as it has no replacement, it is a loss. The singular is the irreplaceable par excellence: it is that which is distinct from anything similar to it and from anything that aspires or pretends to replace it. The singular cannot be expressed in terms of what appeared when it disappeared; its disappearance is a loss. But this does not apply only to the disappearance of the singular. Even the disappearance of a banknote, which is by definition replaceable and is the prototype of the replaceable, is a loss as long as no replacement has been found.

2.001 A loss is perceived as irreplaceable from the viewpoint of an interested person. Loss is a disappearance that is "for someone," not only in its occurrence, but also in the way it is present in someone's world as irreplaceable (at least for the time being).

2.002 A child loses a doll the likes of which can be found at any shop. Father buys her a new doll, identical with the first. But the new doll lacks the old doll's smell and the tooth marks on its legs, and its hair is still intact. The child refuses to be consoled, the old doll has no replacement, the loss has not been recovered. After a while, the lost doll is found, or another doll that the child, who has by now forgotten, takes to be the lost doll. The loss is annulled, erased. What is not erased is the disappearance itself as an occurrence, and the experience of loss that remains in the child's memory. A child loses a ball time and again. Every time the ball is lost the worried parent rushes to buy a new one for the child, similar to or nicer than the previous one. For the child, loss becomes disappearance, and disappearance becomes a game.

2.003 The difference between what is lost and what disappears can be expressed in terms of what one expects to get back. The one who has lost some thing expects to get back the exact same thing; the one for whom some thing has disappeared is willing to make do with a replacement. The gap between expecting "the exact same thing" and the prospect that it will be returned causes the pain that usually accompanies loss. The relative lack of interest in disappearance, which enables us to turn disappearance into a game with relative ease, stems from the disappeared thing's replaceable character. Similarly, exchange is a type of relation in which we are able to tolerate disappearance because it acquires the status of a moment in a game; that is, exchange presupposes a guaranteed compensation. This applies to all institutionalized exchange systems, starting with children's swapping games. This is how Lyotard states the rule of the genre of economic discourse: "The cession of that thing ought to annul the cession of this thing.... Sense is not the sense of the exchange objects, exchange is the sense."[1] Gambling is based on the illusion that what has disappeared has a chance of returning "big time"; the wheel of fortune camouflages the deepening loss of the gambler as a moment in the game of disappearances. The addicted gambler is seduced by an illusion. If she is unlucky, her loss will be unbearable when she sobers up.

2.010   Either the interest in what has disappeared removes the disappeared from an exchange cycle and positions it as what was lost to the interested party, or the impossibility of entering into an exchange cycle and restoring the disappeared turns someone into an interested party and the disappeared into her lost thing. Someone's interest in the disappeared and her impossibility of entering into an exchange relationship in order to restore it are interrelated in every case of loss, although not always in the same way. Each one of these on its own is a necessary but insufficient condition for something to appear as lost. An interest in what has disappeared is insufficient; the disappeared must also be irreplaceable. At the same time, it is not enough for replacement to be impossible; a person must also be interested in the irreplaceable.

2.011   Hence there are two ways to annul a loss. One is to return what was lost to a framework of exchange relations, to reduce it to the exchange value in some sort of exchange economy. The other way is to give up the interest. Giving up is the easy way, well known to parents: distracting, tantalizing, redirecting the interest from one object to another, from one problem to another. In fact, that is how second-order exchange relations are created: not between one object of value and another, but between one object of interest and another. In return for the new interest created, what was lost is no longer represented or is no longer represented as something that has any interest, or its disappearance is no longer a problem. This is an economy of forgetting. The one who forgets loses the loss.

2.012 To lose means to remember; the continuous presence of the loss depends on a constant effort of remembering. To lose is to preserve in another place, to displace something from one level of existence to another. This is a displacement from the level of things directly present to the eye and touch to the level of things one can no longer touch but only represent. But this is not the only kind of displacement, because not every lost thing is something one can see or touch to begin with. This is the case when, for example, a person loses her vision (she does not see her own seeing) or a memory, or the chance of winning the lottery, or, more generally, an ability, capacity, or possibility. These had no presence to begin with other than that through which they are represented — an action, a feeling, a lottery ticket, and so on. Losing them means displacing them from one level of representation to another, the one we call in a general and imprecise way memory (see 2.110).

2.013 Institutions of preservation — libraries, museums, archives — preserve what is left to enable their visitors to experience the disappeared as lost. They turn the representation of the disappeared into an exhibit that testifies to itself as being nothing but a substitute for what is really irreplaceable. This is also the function of "the thing itself" when it becomes an exhibit (a chamber in the royal palace, or an artist's studio) — to represent a complete life-world it was a part of that is now irrevocably lost. Through the exhibit, the preserving institution asks the visitor to become interested in the disappearance itself and in what has disappeared as something irreplaceable.[2]

2.014 The preserving institution aims to make something present in order to make those not interested in it renew the work of mourning for what no longer exists. But the purpose of mourning is precisely the opposite: to displace what was lost from living memory to the museum of memory and to place the loss itself in the soul's archive.

2.015 If the loss depends on an effort of remembrance, the one who is interested is partially responsible for the loss. By merely being interested in what has disappeared, and as long as she remains interested, she is responsible. This is the case also if what was lost is replaceable but is not replaced because the interested party is prevented from entering an exchange relationship. Entrance to the exchange relationship is barred and beyond her control, but her continued interest in what is exchanged there does not stop being within her responsibility. She can stop desiring it or find replacements for its replacements; that is, she can try to replace not only the disappeared thing but also the exchange system itself. And she can train herself to stoically overcome any loss. When a thief stole Epictetus's iron lantern, he said to himself: "Tomorrow ... you shall find a clay lantern; one can only lose what one has."[3] And for most of what one has, one is responsible to some extent (see 2.220 on).

2.020 An owner's interest in a lost thing, the discourse about it, the memory of its tangible presence, the attempt to revive its vision from memory, the investigation into the circumstances of its disappearance and the possibility of its return, the refusal to ignore the difference between the thing and its possible replacements — all these are done from the position of a subject, with its conditions of speech, gaze, and action.

2.021 The subject is responsible for identifying what has disappeared as singular or replaceable. The subject determines the differentiating difference (the difference that *makes* the difference, so to speak) for her and differentiates the singular from what resembles it. She does not do this totally by herself, of course, but within a complex network of differentiation and exchange that offers her, through mechanisms of rarefaction, assessment, and displacement, tools for identifying the singular and the replaceable. But as the father who rushed to the toy shop to buy his child "the exact same doll" realized, the interested child alone is ultimately responsible for determining the difference that makes the difference and consecrating something as singular, irreproducible. The doll may be a distinct product of the "age of mechanical reproduction," but in order to turn it into a singular thing, no aura is necessary; a slight stench that has always enveloped the old chewed doll is enough. And vice versa: any art dealer knows that under suitable conditions, even the rarest artwork can be replaced — the taste of consumers, experts, and amateurs alike is flexible enough.

2.022 The child who lost the doll refuses any substitute. She may not have the words to express the doll's singularity, but her power of observation is developed enough to recognize unfit replacements, and her expression is sufficient — a whimper or a cry will do — to protest when they are offered to her. In the relationship between the parents, who are losing their patience, and the stubborn child, the child has already taken the position of a subject. The parents' attempts to calm her down, distract her attention from the lost thing, or convince her that the thing in the colorful wrapping is a replacement for what has disappeared — in other words, the whole negotiation between the child and her parents that develops around the loss — testifies to that. But in the toy shop, the saleslady is impatient. To her mind, the value of each doll is exactly the same as its exchange value, that is, its retail price. The only meaning the child's ability to distinguish and protest takes on for her is "not this" and "not that." After a moment or two in which she tries to understand the child, she will turn to the parents and continue negotiating with them. This is a negotiation between economic subjects. To her mind, the complaining, stubborn child is not a subject but an intruder who causes a loss of time and customers.

2.023   The ability to identify what was lost, to take an interest in it, and to express that interest is a principal component in the constitution of subjectivity. The crying baby who is not yet capable of saying "the doll that Grandmother once brought me" but already knows how to protest when it is not *it* takes up a limited subject position in the family system but is declined such a position in the economic system. As the abilities to identify, take, and express an interest grow, so grows the range within which the subject position is open in the family system, and so grows also the ability to take up the subject position outside it. In a few years, this crying baby will be able to go to the toy shop and buy herself a replacement for what was lost.

2.024   Meanwhile, the gap between the ability to recognize what was lost and the ability to express the loss and demand its rectification from a given subject position is an endless source of sorrow, disappointment, frustration, and rage. A deliberate widening of this gap is a type of abuse.

2.030   In general, the interested subject is responsible for every positioning of a singular object in the way she is responsible for any historicization. Here is an example that relates loss and historicization. At the end of the 1980s and the beginning of the 1990s, the Israeli artist David Reeve painted, according to the interpretation of Ariella Azoulay, "the Israeli viewer's loss of collective vision."[4] Rather than painting on the basis of photographs, mainly media photos, as he used to do, Reeve painted the margins of the developed films (the contact sheets) and turned them into a web in which an abstract painting is woven. The painted contact

sheets were left empty. The crying Palestinian child, the soldier
ordering the removal of graffiti, and the jeep driving through an
alley in which all the shops are shut are not seen anymore. You
can no longer see the power relations and the suffering, the
sorrow and the shame. All that can be seen is the margins of a
film, but the scenes imprinted on it have no trace. Reeve, argues
Azoulay, paints those who can no longer see, those who, even if
they wanted to, could not see. See the evils of the Israeli occupation, of course. Some saw the Reeve abstracts and said, "The
image has disappeared," and then analyzed combinations of colors
and forms. They had no particular interest in the image that had
disappeared; they were only interested in what was present. For
them, nothing was lost; only styles had changed, one thing disappeared and another appeared. Some saw the Reeve abstracts and
said, "The image has disappeared. Why did it disappear, where is
it now, and from where precisely does Reeve paint and paint until
the image disappears?" These viewers were interested in the disappeared. For them, what is present bears witness to what is gone
and, perhaps more than that, bears witness to those who are present, as those who can no longer see what has disappeared. For
these viewers, something was lost in Reeve's paintings; he is a
painter of loss. Together with Reeve and through him, they became subjects interested in that loss. When you understand that
Reeve paints the loss of vision of the Israeli viewer who looks at
the occupation and sees abstraction, sees canvas, sees a web, sees
stripes and colors, when you understand all this, you acknowledge the historicality of the gaze, the artistic gaze included.

2.031 Acknowledging the historicality of cultural forms, of the meaning
of an artwork or a text, of social or political structures, means
acknowledging their immanent loss, the impossibility of reconstructing their previous forms (not to mention the impossibility
of reconstructing what they are "in themselves") out of their
traces in the cultural archive and out of their presence in different
fields of contemporary culture. At the same time, this means taking responsibility for the loss, that is, conceiving the act of representation as the only mode of existence of what was lost. On the
other hand, to deprive cultural forms of historicality is to declare
the possibility of returning to the same forms themselves and
reconstructing the same meaning itself by the absolutely isomor-
phic substitutions of their forms and meanings in various means
of representation. To deprive the cultural forms of historicality
means to shake off responsibility for what has disappeared and not
to give the act of representation a role in presencing the traces of

what has disappeared. The first position is fundamentally Nietz-schean. Only those who acknowledge the historicality of man can declare the appearance of the superman (or anticipate the loss of man, who will disappear like a face drawn in sand at the edge of the sea, as Foucault promised in the conclusion of *The Order of Things*[5]). The second position is Platonic. The forms are always present through their substitutes, phenomena. Some cannot see the forms, but they will never truly disappear. The form is what cannot, in principle, disappear. Mourning for what is lost is one reason the poet, whose forte is lamenting, is banished from the ideal city.[6]

2.1 *Movement*

2.100   The interest in the disappeared that turns disappearance into a loss does not necessarily presuppose a relationship of ownership. The extinction of a rare species is a loss without anyone (a zoolo-gist, the World Wildlife Fund, "man") owning the extinct species. It is enough for someone to have an interest in the lost thing. If someone does have such an interest, you cannot translate an utterance claiming the loss of something into an utterance claim-ing the disappearance of something (let alone translating an utter-ance like that into an utterance about an appearance of something else). To utter loss means to posit an interested subject; to posit an interested subject means to point to an immanent loss. When someone becomes interested, she becomes vulnerable, someone who can experience the loss of something. From this point on, it is only a question of time.[7]

2.101   A representation of loss is a form of temporalizing what there is and someone who is interested in it. The displayed loss presences what there is as what no longer is and someone who is interested in it as someone who no longer has it. The displayed loss is a way of presencing the past in the present, and the introduction of a scale to gauge the present with. But at the same time, presencing, the act of display, wishes to cancel the present and continuous temporalizing of the displayed, to erase the traces of what it was and the signs testifying to what it will be in order to maintain its unified, unchanging identity in a continuous present. When the loss is displayed as having a fixed identity, the past and the future remain at a constant, safe distance from the continuous present.

2.110   The identity of what was lost, the stability of its presence as a continuous being, depends on the discourse that represents it and on the way in which the interested subject participates in this discourse. To stabilize the identity of what was lost, one must undergo a prolonged mourning, or yearning, or hoping for its return. Even these are not enough. In all these practices of representation, what was lost is an absent signified that has no presence, whose signified are its replacements and placeholders, for now or forever. What would guarantee the identity of the signified and its unity? More practices of representation, of course, this time those that represent the discourse itself as dealing with the thing that was lost as that same thing, that point to the repeated element in the different and changing references to what was lost, and so distance attempts to undermine the one identity, to bifurcate it, to invest it with plurality, or to exchange it for another. Like praying for Jerusalem, every year "in the coming year," always for the same Jerusalem, or like longing for the lost plot of land in Palestine that, even if years go by and the refugee camp dries up the mind, wounds the skin, and cracks the memory, remains the same plot of land. And so the mourning for the dead lover, the obsessive return to an old letter, to a yellowing photograph, and that certain surprise awaiting the mourner when she suddenly remembers that only death guards the dead lover from the teeth of time, from aging, and from another death.

2.111 Sometimes a whole archive gathers around the one who was lost, and suddenly new aspects of him — unknown, denied, or forgotten — are discovered. The readiness to admit the principal instability of what was lost or the one who was lost, the dependence of the loss on the work of remembering and on the regime of forgetting, the laborious collection of facts, and the indolence of memory latching on to the familiar, this readiness is the genesis of redemption from the tyranny of what was lost. This is also the moment in which history begins to be an advantage to life, or at least stops being a disadvantage.

2.112 The intense presence of what (or who) was lost is the contracting of the past into the present, and the extending of a present that the interested subject fixes herself in. During the days of mourning, nothing happens, what happens does not change anything, things seem to remain in place, frozen where the one who was lost left them, morning and evening come and go, the passing days go by like an exterior cover that does not touch the one who temporalizes, the one who is interested (see 5.234). And maybe the temporalizing subject tries to stop time from passing, to leave everything in the place where the one who was lost left it. This is a way of preserving the only possible presence of the one who was lost, the presence in the traces, but also a way of preserving the presence of the loss itself, and with it the pain. The constant presence of the loss, the unstopping pain, becomes a new pole of identity for the subject who wishes to permanently be what she is now. Family and friends try to give the interested subject her old identity back, so they enclose the mourning in predefined days and dates and classify the one who fixates on the loss as an "abnormal" and "anomalous" case that needs to be "treated." Mourning fixation could subvert the social order, could challenge what is culturally self-evident.[8]

2.113 And so the opposite: the presence of the loss that becomes increasingly vague contracts the present and extends the past.

> And the years were compressed and dense and quicker than us,
> People came in and out of them
> With speed,
> Said something and disappeared.
> In the closet there remained things
> And clothes of those who are no longer with us,
> The heart is tired of them
> Some sometimes saw this as evidence.
> It was impossible to understand anything.
> There was time for nothing. It was impossible to hold
> Anything. But we behaved as though we were "immortal"
> And as though there is time for everything. And for the lack,
> Or the kind word, or the silence.[9]

When the past extends, it is no longer possible to forcefully remember the smell of the man who was lost, his walk, the way he filled the space of the room. When it is no longer possible to remember the body that he was, the remembering body realizes its own loss. The subject that temporalizes her loss in this way turns herself from someone who has lost something to someone who is losing herself. Gradually she becomes the source of the loss, as well as the site where the loss occurs. Something similar to this happens every time nostalgia erupts; another kind of narcissism.

2.120 What happens if no one is interested in the lost thing, no one for whom the disappearance is a problem? The lost is reducible to the disappeared, which is often expressible in terms of appearance. Think about a changing fashion. The interest disappears, no one loses anything, the old style disappears, a new style appears. Or the disappearance of dinosaurs — the scientists' problem is the presence of their traces, their remains, their lack of presence, and the reason for their disappearance. But the fact that dinosaurs are irrevocably gone is not a problem for science. It is just that lately a passing fashion in children's culture has created a new interest. Children who learned to be interested in dinosaurs discovered that the disappearance of the dinosaurs and the appearance of their replacements are their problem. Some of them experience this disappearance as a loss; for others, stuffed animals shaped like miniature dinosaurs make new objects of loss. The dinosaurs have disappeared, no one can lose them anymore, but little people now lose little dinosaur replacements, a totally predictable loss from the perspective of the observing adult.

2.121 If fashion, advertising, or propaganda can raise an interest in what was lost and distribute its representations, it is obvious that loss can be distributed using relatively simple means and, allegedly, without causing any substantial change in the situation. Thus the loss strangely moves from someone who was supposed to lose to what is supposed to be lost. The nationalist discourse, for example, demands sovereignty and ownership over areas inhabited or ruled by foreigners. Places that never belonged to those enchanted by the nationalist discourse acquire an aura of loss; the abstract concept of sovereignty, which never existed, is reincarnated in gestures, rituals, and sacraments, which are all imagined as lost signs of the presence of a lost sovereignty. The expansion of the nationalist discourse in literature, media, political speeches, and textbooks is the wind that carries the movement of loss from the national subject, who acquires a loss together with national subjectivity, to objects and presences in the social space, which acquire the status of traces of what was lost. The nationalist discourse baptizes the loss and makes it a legitimate citizen of the national ensemble. And so with religious discourse, particularly in times of religious zeal or the appearance of a new mass religion, and also with revolutionary, or "redemptive," discourse, which uncovers the future of the subjugated — their possibility of being different from what they are, of living differently from how they live — as what was taken away from them by the existing social order. The revolutionary movement presents the loss of the future of the oppressed, and only then promises to return the loss to its owner, to give the oppressed the future they deserve. In all these cases, there will be a movement of "consciousness-raising."

2.122 A loss is also spread through other means — a plague, an outbreak of thefts, vermin. Loss is produced and distributed by directly targeting what is lost and in itself becomes a core of the distribution of loss. New technologies produce new possibilities for the movement of loss. The speed of the spread of loss, the range of movement, and its character — these can be functions of extermination technology. Spraying vast areas of a forest is preferable to cutting down tree after tree; the tribe that lives in the forest (as well as the thousands of species) loses its living space in an instant. A grueling trench war, stagnant, lasting almost four years, is preferable in this sense to quick, face-to-face, decisive battle; the loss front is very wide and prolonged. Some kinds of losses move relatively slowly, but this movement encompasses a huge population. Nail bombs are preferable to ordinary bombs, a chemical warhead is preferable to an ordinary one, an ordered train movement to gas extermination is preferable to the extermination units of the *Einsatzgruppen* (it is more efficient to bring the object of extermination to the exterminating facilities than the other way around). In general, there is no doubt that primitive societies are (objectively and unequivocally) inferior to more developed societies in their loss-production capacities: their ability to create a swift and wide-ranging loss movement and their ability to control it.

2.130 The movement of loss can be imagined as a wave movement: water particles or light shards appear and disappear, but the movement is not theirs; it does not belong to any one particle. What moves is not any single particle that materializes and disappears but the very transition from appearance to disappearance between one particle and another. A movement of loss can pass from father to son, from generation to generation, from one borough to another, from close counties to remote ones. If it were possible to freeze a passing moment of this movement, it would turn out that in every moment something else disappears; what is lost at the beginning of the movement is not what is lost at its end. But when you look again at the movement, it seems like the loss itself is moving from one moment to another, from one place to another, like a low-pressure area, like the eye of a storm, and in every place it passes, it leaves behind pits of longing, of sorrow, and of mourning.

2.131 This movement of loss can be imaginary (as, for example, between the dinosaurs and the children playing with their images) or real (as, for example, between the children who learn the interest in dinosaurs from one another, or between one plague-stricken or unemployment-stricken town and the villages near it). Plague and bankruptcy are real movements of loss.

2.132 The loss itself is always real, even when the movement is imaginary. At the ends, the loss seems sharp and clear: the father imagines the movement of loss from the child he was to the child his
son now is to the child he will lose when this child grows up. The
veterinarian describes the movement of the spread of rabies, at
the end of which almost all the village people will have lost their
dogs. But between the direct distribution of loss and the imaginary relations people find between cases of loss that have no
proven connection (evil eye, family fate), there is a whole scope
of what is perhaps a movement, perhaps an imaginary movement.
Think of cases where there is a loss of collective memory: when a
society shakes off its past, or when a dysfunctional family loses the
capacity to love. Does the movement of loss exist even if no one
wishes to reconstruct it in order to rehabilitate what was lost, to
return the repressed to memory, or to teach herself to love again?

2.133 A loss can move in a linear chain movement, as when the news of
someone's death is whispered from one person to another, or in
a wave movement, as when a contagious disease spreads out, and
it can spread out in a bang like an earthquake or in a combined
form in which there are breakdown and shock waves, like a stock-
market collapse. When an unexpected disaster occurs, the loss
spreads quickly in concentric circles. The bigger the disaster
radius, the wider the circles. This on the condition that the disaster does not extinguish the interested persons as well (see 2.230),
or that the ratio between the disappearance of the interested persons and the appearance of new ones feeling the loss is maintained. In opposition to the concentric circles of disaster, lying,
stealing, or deceit could cause the loss to spread in a chain movement. There is also a chain movement of deferred loss, as in the
case of stealing equipment in an army base or when returning
equipment at the end of a reserve military service. In these cases,
a chain of exchange develops called in military slang "completing
your gear," where every soldier steals a missing bit of gear from
another, who steals from another, and so on, and one party is
always forced to participate in the exchange relations (the one
from whom the article was stolen) and one party is always invisible (the one who stole). The stolen object has a replacement, the
loss is distanced in the chain of thefts from one soldier to another,
like an empty hole in a game of patience, and it never remains
anywhere once any single thief has had his turn. The loss will
position itself in the social space only when the chain is stopped;
sometimes the movement continues throughout several recruit-
ment cycles.

2.134 Impoverishment is a spiral movement, spreading out in a chain going in expanding circles around one or several centers. We can perhaps learn something about this matter from geologists who follow the spread of a shock from the center of an earthquake, or from explosives experts who know the pattern in which shock waves spread out during an explosion. It is usually difficult to follow a real movement of loss. The physics and geography of loss are not even sciences in their germinal stage. The distinctions presented here might at most hint at possible directions of inquiry in these fields.

2.135 Whoever understands the movement of loss can control it, at least partially. Placing a plague-stricken town under quarantine is a familiar way to control the movement of loss. A person who uses such means pretends to know something about the movement patterns of the loss or of its causes. In the case of plague, quarantine is a practice that much predated the understanding of how plague is spread. Since Antiquity, the authorities imposing quarantines knew very little about the causes of a plague — viruses or bacteria — but knew much about the movement patterns of the loss that the plague spread. Sometimes it seems like this is the situation that authorities face today when they deal with spreading terrorist action. There is much talk of a "wave of terrorist actions," although there is nothing more foreign to the terrorist than a wave movement. The terrorist emerges and vanishes; the wave movement is the movement of loss. The clearest thing about terrorism is the way in which it is distributed and the way that the loss spreads from the moment of the terrorist attack. It is a lot less clear how the carriers of terrorism move and spread. It is possible that all the security measures and the rituals that accompany them help today's "fight against terrorism" in the same way that a quarantine of a town infected with pestilence, and the rituals that went along with it, helped prevent the spread of plague in medieval and early-modern times. Understanding the loss movement and being able to partially control it enable one to intervene in the social patterns of the distribution of evils that the loss movement brings about (on this, see Chapter Seven).

2.140 As was said (2.121), the loss movement could continue and the loss could continue spreading in social space through representations of loss, because the representation of what has disappeared can turn someone into an interested party and turn something into a lost thing. We can imagine a scale that measures representations according to their ability to create loss. Not a feeling of loss, but real loss, because the disappeared becomes lost from the moment an interested person appears and identifies the disappeared as singular, irreplaceable. Like that trip to the cabin in the mountains. One can return to the cabin time and again, walk on the same trail, recognize the burned tree trunk and the rabbit hole, but one cannot bring back the scents and sensations of that first journey long ago. This is the nature of nostalgia, to create a longing for what no longer is, to posit it as lost and bring out in it the thing that is irrevocably gone.[10] A song, a book, a film, can turn a past period into something that was lost (see 2.230).

2.141　Does the feeling of loss diminish when the interest moves from the lost thing that no longer is to the present representation of what was lost to the production of the representation and its reception? Maybe a nostalgic representation (of loss) is a borderline case of representation in which you can no longer distinguish the interest in the lost thing from the interest in the replacement that represents it as lost. That is, isn't any nostalgic representation a kind of simulation? Nostalgic representation is similar in this sense to seduction, in which the difference between the artificial and the authentic is also erased and "one cannot distinguish between reality and its models, there being no other reality than that secreted by the simulative models."[11] And maybe seduction is a private case of nostalgia for something that was lost. You don't know what it is, but you already know that you have lost it.[12]

2.142　The loss itself, at least the one with captivating presence — like seductive femininity in Baudrillard, but in a more radical and general sense — does it not "simultaneously provide radical evidence of simulation and the only possibility of its overcoming"?[13] Seduction is a distracting presence, inviting and unattainable, that contains nothing but what is present, what disappears and appears, but nonetheless cannot be determined as that thing that has appeared and is present. Nostalgia is an interest in a distracting disappearance of what was attainable and no longer is, which has nothing but the play of the traces of what is gone and yet cannot be determined as this thing that has disappeared. In seduction, as in nostalgia, the gap between signifier and signified is erased for the benefit of the play of signifiers or traces that suddenly acquire, within the signifying act itself, an unexpected reality, which takes over the entire field of presence and transgresses the representable (see 4.530–4.543).

2.143　If nostalgia is similar to seduction, then the event in which disappearance is perceived as loss for an interested person is similar to the moment in which the seducing object is caught and the seduction is lost. Like seduction, nostalgia is caught in a game of simulation, with no ability or interest in signifying the difference between the real and the imaginary or out of an interest in deferring that signifying moment; at the moment of loss, the erasure of the difference is the most real. The moment a loss occurs (or when someone grasps a loss that has occurred), all the simulations that aimed — in anxious or resolute anticipation — to precede the moment of disappearance come true. From this moment on, a movement of representations begins, similar in structure to the one activated in seduction but reversed in its direction. In seduction as in loss, the moment in which the object of interest is captured is deferred, and this deferral is the condition of interest — whether as seduction or as a sense of loss. In some kinds of loss and seduction, the deferral can be canceled, the seductive or lost object can be caught, and the seduction or loss can be annulled; in other kinds, this is impossible — that which seduces will not be captured, that which is lost will not be returned. But in seduction the crucial moment is always in the future, and deferral is a source of pleasure, whereas in loss the crucial moment is in the past, and deferral is a source of pain.

2.144　A necessary and insufficient condition of nostalgia is the waning acuteness of the loss. Nostalgia does not appear every time the acuteness wanes; sometimes it is simply forgetting or another form of losing interest. Nostalgia is a mental intention and cultural practice that maintains the interest in what was lost when it is no longer possible to distinguish the representations of what was lost as it really was from its other representations. Loss only becomes painfully present when nostalgia is impossible, when it is impossible to ignore or blur the difference between the real and the imaginary, when the difference is at its most acute for the interested person. This difference is clearest because at that moment the interested person has no interest in representations, truthful or false, of what was lost — except a representation of what was lost as what is gone. She has no interest in knowing what or who the thing was; her whole interest is focused on the fact that the thing was and is no more. The sharper the feeling of loss, the longer it takes to renew interest in the lost thing or person, and the more delayed is the moment in which truthful or false representations mix with simulations again.

2.2　Reality and Absence

2.20　The moment of loss is an event in which the subject comes closest to an unmediated encounter with a firm, definite reality; the real

is always experienced at the moment of grasping the loss as something or someone that was. Lyotard says that the real — what can
be named, shown, and given meaning — is an uncertain matter,
open to future proofs.[14] Tomorrow it may transpire that this was a
case of mistaken identity, of misinterpreted data, of a miscalculation, that the theory according to which something was determined to be really present, or to be really such and such, is not
true. That something that has been christened into reality may
always return to old or new domains of imagination or reality:
this is not Troy, that is not "Ivan the Terrible" of Treblinka, these
are not traces of quark, these are not symptoms of leukemia, the
stock market did not crash, the man did not die. Someday we will
find Troy or Atlantis, maybe these were aliens after all, I am afraid
that it is leukemia. But that is not so in the case of loss. Loss blocks
the way for future proofs in at least one sense. At the moment of
loss, even if I was wrong about everything I knew about what was
lost, and even if I was wrong about the fact of loss itself (as in the
case of a mistaken death announcement), I cannot be mistaken
about the reality of what or who was lost, even if it is only allegedly lost and even if it has been lost only as what it was for me.
That is why the relativist or the skeptic loses in this argument, or
withdraws from it the moment the realist forces her to talk about
the absoluteness of the absence of someone who died.

2.210   I lose, therefore I am. But if I lose, something or someone other
than myself existed. I lose, therefore something besides me is. I
cannot be mistaken about the fact that it was something real,
something that was, for me, although I might be mistaken about
the question of what exactly the thing was that was lost. What it
was — that is a matter for "future proofs," for cognitive phrases
that will never bridge the gap between what the thing itself was
and the representations that give it and its traces meaning, which
can still be shown. But that it was, that something was — that is
indubitable; otherwise, it would be impossible to explain the
sense of loss. The sense of loss is the best guarantee for external
reality, when I need such a guarantee, or if I needed it.

2.211   But a person could be delusional, could believe she has what she
never owned — money, a kingdom, or a lover — and then experience the loss as a terrible pain. And perhaps the good God or a
malicious demon deceives me into thinking I have lost something
or someone, and plants a sense of loss in me without my having
really lost what I feel I have lost; perhaps he impregnates me with
a sense of loss without my having something or someone real to

lose. How does Descartes rescue himself from his radical doubt? With the help of a benevolent God, who guarantees the existence of the external world, outside the cogito of the skeptic, a world that does not depend on his consciousness. How does the Cartesian skeptic know that the good God exists? From understanding his own finitude as the one who doubts (a finitude that is analytically deduced from his skepticism), he deduces a concept of perfect infinity (whose name is God) whose existence is included in his essence — it is impossible that perfect infinity would lack anything, and surely not its own existence.[15] My skeptic, too, could rescue herself in the same way from her radical doubt, if she insisted on entering the same dead end to begin with: there is nothing like the sense of loss to testify to finitude and to enable one to imagine a perfect being that does not lose anything, the being about which it is said, "And He was, and He is, and He will be in splendor." (But what interest could such a being have in what is outside it? Will there be anything outside it? And how could it rescue the radical skeptic?)

2.212 It seems that the best way to rescue oneself from Cartesian doubt is to not cast it in a radical form to begin with. It is enough for me to reveal myself as an interested party who has lost what and whom he is interested in. I cannot imagine an argument that will convince me that I never had what I lost without supplying me with something else, external and real, to be interested in instead as the source of my feeling of loss. The Cartesian philosopher would suggest the benevolent God at this point, but for the sense of loss the malicious demon will do. I will never know with absolute certainty in what way exactly I had what I lost, or what it precisely was, and I may discover that what I thought I had never existed but was a fantasy or an illusion. But every such discovery entails a new loss — of the illusion of reality — and a new acquisition of something that is liable to be lost as well, without which I could not be convinced that the thing I attributed reality to was nothing but an illusion. The sense of loss is a possible cure for skepticism that has deviated from its normal course and become too radical.

2.213 This is not a response to radical skepticism, in the form of Descartes's malicious demon, or to the skepticism madness raises with respect to the reality of the illusion, or love with respect to how real the lover and her qualities are. But the moral is not that even loss can be doubted, because the doubt depends on the reality of the object of interest, not on the reality of the experience of loss. The madwoman sobering up from her delusion may discover that she has lost nothing, or that she never had what she claims to have lost. The lover sobering up from his drunken love may discover that the woman who has deserted him was not lovable after all. The sobering up that confirms the doubt does not necessarily erase the sense of loss; it might increase it when the loss of the illusion is discovered.

2.214 The reality of the object of interest is a secondary matter in the case of loss. It may preoccupy friends trying to offer solace, the therapist, the insurance agent, or the policeman. The reality of the loss is the reality of an experience that cannot be abolished as long as the lost thing, whether imaginary or real, has no substitute, imaginary or real. The difference between the loss of something imaginary and the loss of something real is crucial, of course, but only in a practical context — of finding a substitute, compensation, or the consolation in establishing who is responsible for returning what was lost (see 2.320 and 6.232). This difference has nothing in common with the reality of the loss as long as the substitute has not been found, as long as the memory has not been silenced.

2.220 Loss is possible because someone has an interest in what and who is around her and within her, regardless of whether the object of interest is there at all and whether it is, in some sense, "owned" by the interested party. The only thing the interested party has to "own" is the interest itself, but this is an ownership with no property, that is, only this relation of "mineness"; it is the interest of someone, her matter. "Interest," like care (*Sorge*) in Heidegger's lexicon, is the most general concept of relating to what and who is different from the interested person, the interested party. The difference between the one who is interested and the object of her interest is maintained even when someone is interested in her body, or her soul, or the figments of her imagination. Loss is the moment in which the interest someone has in something or in someone is conceived with apodictic certainty.

2.221 Sometimes we differentiate between what someone has but could have not had, on the one hand, and what is "part of her" and without which she is not "the same person," on the other. "My commitment and belonging to the Palestinian people, the pride I feel in the achievements of my people and my deep pain for their losses [in the Palestinian-Israeli struggle] — these are things no one can take away from me," said Edward Said in response to the accusation that from his comfortable home in the United States he could not experience the suffering of his people.[16] No one could take away from Said the sense of identification with his people, but Said could get up one day and deny this identification himself. When someone feels that she cannot lose something unless she gives it up herself, she not only defines herself as an interested party but also defines the interested I, and thus determines a realm of inalienable selfhood. And when she determines herself as who she is, she also determines herself as responsible for what she is.

2.222 "Things no one can take away from me" — that is how a person in a capitalist society defines what one can call her "internality." She knows that thieves or bailiffs may take away her TV set, but not the horrific pictures burned into her memory during the last documentary she watched. The difference between the private sphere, which state authorities may violently invade with a repossession injunction, and the sphere of internality that the private sphere is supposed to protect is the difference between two kinds of "things" an individual has: those that can be taken away from her and those that cannot. This is a conception that projects the logic of private property on the soul and ignores the countless ways in which social institutions sow in the garden of internality what the individual "cannot lose" or uproot from it what "no one can take away" from her.

2.223 The private sphere. The concept of right in the liberal tradition can be interpreted as an attempt to mark a realm of selfhood around what the individual has that cannot be expropriated: private property, opinions and feelings and the possibility of expressing them, freedom of movement, and so on. The right is the duty of the state or the political regime to protect the individual from an expected loss of what is within that realm of inalienable selfhood. The state cannot cause such a loss on its own unless there are special reasons that justify its invasion of selfhood, and it is supposed to prevent others from doing so. The realm of selfhood simultaneously defines the external sphere within which the state is allowed, in principle, to cause loss and the private sphere and the condition under which the individual is free but also abandoned, free to lose everything she has. What is the realm of selfhood? That which is culturally conceived as such, and this conception has changed tremendously since the evolution of the notion of the individual in the Middle Ages, through the development of the distinction between private and public spheres in the early-modern age, to the recent changes in the perception of body and space in our times. My interest here is not in the details of this history but in pointing to the historicity of the concepts of self and right and to the fact that they mirror a sociocultural state rather than fundamental, irreducible, and non-assailable attributes that belong to each person by definition, as part of her nature.[17]

2.224 By the same logic, it is also possible to delineate a difference between what belongs to someone that no one can take away from her but that she can renounce or give up, and what even she cannot give up without losing herself. Some kinds of losses bring about a loss of self: for example, a complete loss of interest in what was lost, the loss of the ability to be an interested party, as in apathy or autism, or the exact opposite, complete amnesia, the loss of the ability to retain anything, living in a constant sense of loss (anyone who has seen a sclerotic patient at an advanced stage of his illness will understand).

2.230 After the loss, the representation of what was lost or who was lost produces new interested parties. The new interested parties could "acquire" in retrospect what was lost and join the circle of those who lose. A terrible loss could be produced by creating new interested parties. Differences among cases of genocide, for example, are always also differences among types of interested parties. (Who is interested in the Armenian genocide besides the Armenians? Who is interested in the genocide of the Tutsi in Rwanda besides the Tutsi? And who in Europe or the United States dares to say publicly that she is not interested in the genocide of the Jews?)

2.231 The collective patterns of remembrance that immortalize loss in the culture of a particular community are, among other things, a means to preserve the interest in what was lost, that is, to produce new interested parties. Hence, the biggest loss is the loss of interested parties. A complete annihilation wishes to annihilate the movement of loss along with what is being lost: a loss multiplied, the loss of the ability of the disappeared to become lost, to exist as someone's problem. When the Nazis established the Jewish Museum in Prague, were they interested in the loss of the Jews? Did they wish to preserve the traces of the Jews like the traces of cultural dinosaurs? Or did they betray the project of the final solution?[18]

2.232 The paradox of loss: when the interested parties are lost, the loss is simultaneously the largest and the smallest. There is no one to testify to the loss, there is no one to mourn it, the position of the disappeared as lost is canceled, the loss itself is lost. This is absolute loss. In the loss of the interested parties, the largest destruction merges with the smallest destruction in the space in which all differentiation has been annulled.[19] When all interest in the loss ceases, all that is left is the logical relation of absence.

2.233 Like a question without an answer; like a meaningless sound; like a sign without a signified, a non-deciphered hint, an opaque meaning; like a landscape with no signposts; like a strange instrument with no user manual; like a being with no identity. As in all of these cases, in loss absence is present as a problem. But not exactly, because this is not merely an absence but a disappearance, the very passage from "being here" to "gone," from present to absent. That is why it should be like an instrument whose user manual has been lost, like a landscape with uprooted signposts, like the meaning of a word in a forgotten language — but then the loss is already included in what is supposed to explain it (and the metaphors that are supposed to demonstrate by analogy turn out to be synecdoches that illuminate by illustration). Loss can be present as a problem even without the moment of disappearance (as we shall presently see). Loss cannot be perceived as someone's problem (that is, there is no loss) if it does not contain a presence of absence (see 4.140) that is always a presence for someone (see 4.030). Loss is a kind of present absence for an interested party.

2.240 Absence is always present through what there is. Something in what there is (present) testifies to what is not — but could have been. The present, that which is and appears, signifies simultaneously what was and is no longer and the fact of its disappearance. And in the loss, what is added to this testimony, which is a semiotic relation in which presence points to absence, is a direct presence of the loss itself. What is signifies simultaneously what was and is no longer and its passing away, but — as opposed to disappearance — this passing away is present, and is present even after the thing has disappeared. It is not only an absent signified but a present signifier. It is present as a problem for someone.

2.241 The semiotic relation characterizing loss is one of a double trace: the trace points both to what or who imprinted it, which was and is now gone, and to its continuing deletion. And also to whoever is following it. The one who identifies traces of something lost, the one who remembers the loss or discovers it through identifying the traces of something lost, identifies at once the lost thing and herself as an interested party that carries on despite its deletion. Identifying the traces is part of the process by which the interested party acquires her identity as a subject.

2.250 But the subject who perceives the loss and the subject whose loss it is are not necessarily the same. The daughter realizes that her aging mother is gradually losing her hearing and tries, to no avail, to turn her mother's attention to that. The daughter and the mother both have a problem related to the mother's loss of hearing, but it is not the same problem. In the beginning, the daughter attributes to the mother a problem that the mother does not recognize as her problem: the mother does not notice the disappearance, or does not see it as a loss. The daughter's problem is doubled: the disappearance of her mother's hearing (the mother's problem) and the fact that the mother does not acknowledge her problem (nonrecognition as a problem). But even when the mother recognizes her problem, the mother and the daughter have different problems. The mother will experience her loss of hearing, and with it a loss of confidence and spatial orientation and an increase of shame and discomfort, which in turn cause the loss of acquaintances and friends. The daughter will experience the loss of the healthy, lively mother she once had. Every subject is located differently in the order of things, has a different perspective and a different horizon of expectations from someone else, even if that someone has a position similar to hers. Positions in a field can be similar in kind but must be different in location; they cannot occupy the same space and time. That is why two subjects cannot have exactly the same problem.

2.251 Identification between subjects is expressed in the attempt to create an overlap in the horizon of expectations, when the problem of whoever is the object of identification serves as an intentional axis, and a common grid. Like transparent paper being shifted on top of a map, a little here and a little there, according to an emphasized line or raised coordinates, until it overlaps perfectly. A full overlap in identification between subjects can be no more than a regulative idea, because no subject can completely cancel the difference between her point of view and that of an other and also because every subject has many problems that do not necessarily cohere, and they create a bustle of different intentional axes on the map.[20]

2.3 *Patients*

2.30 Someone has a problem when a gap in her horizon of expectations is created, a space in the order of things in which and from which she acts (see 1.400). Sometimes the mother does not answer the phone. The worried daughter thinks she is at home and suspects the mother does not answer the phone because she cannot hear it ringing. The mother is unaware of her loss of hearing and is worried that so few people call her; even her devoted daughter forgets her all too often. Two unfulfilled expectations make up two different problems, and make present two different kinds of losses.

2.310 In order to identify a problem, an interested party should be posited, there should be someone who can grasp this problem, talk about it, see it or its signs and show them to others, pay attention to it, do something about it. When these actions are more or less structured, when they have a measure of interdependence, consistency, and coherence, the one who has a problem already occupies a subject position, and her dealing with the problem is an important part of her shaping as a subject. Otherwise, the problem attributed to her is the problem of an other who identifies a problem with her: a worried parent facing a sick baby, or a teacher facing a difficult pupil. The baby dozes off, helpless, but her illness is not the parent's problem. The pupil nervously shrinks every time the teacher speaks to her, or every time her "friends" make fun of her, but the "psychomotor adequacy problem" is not her problem; it is attributed to her by the teacher, who sees her as "abnormal." People attribute problems to other people, to animals, to social institutions, to nature (the "hole" in the ozone layer), but only from a subject position can they represent themselves consistently as those who have a problem.

2.311 A dog whines when it is wounded or hungry. A baby whimpers when she is hungry or bored. Both the animal and the baby are already directing themselves toward some lack, are showing or sounding something, calling for help. Can we attribute to them the capacity to identify a problem or an intention to call for help? Why not, really? Why not treat their entrance into a communicative situation as a sign that they occupy a subject position, "premature," "embryonic," simple, and lacking as it might be? It is true that "not everyone who has a problem necessarily takes a subject position" (1.402), and there is no reason to presuppose that if someone attributes a problem to a dog or a baby, it already takes up a subject position. Consistency in the behavior of the dog or the baby when facing a problem may indicate traces of identity formation and a potential for a certain diluted subject position. However, a subject position does not hatch out of an egg into the world and grow with the growing baby or the developing animal. It is constituted only out of its interpretation from those traces, completely dependent on the recognition of others who interpret. "The dog is man's best friend" if there is a man who recognizes it as a friend, that is, as someone who takes up a subject position in the familiar relationship that often develops between a man and his dog.

2.312 In medical discourse, the patient is not a subject. In what sense can the physician who identifies a disappearance or a phenomenon related to a disappearance (calcium deficiency, a drop in blood pressure) treat these as a loss, that is, as a problem of a subject? First, in order to function as a physician, she does not have to do so. The problematic phenomenon is a problem of the physician as a subject in medical discourse, a problem the physician is supposed to deal with instrumentally — to find the most efficient means that will achieve the aim — by solving and removing the problem at the lowest cost. The sick body is a malfunctioning object and has to be repaired so it will function normally again. The sick body is a faulty machine. The expectation that the physician will not act only as a technician and that the hospital will not look like a service station is linked to a certain image of medicine in certain cultures and historical periods. It is also linked to the perception of the mind-body relationship and to the status of physicians among other specialized experts and the status of medicine among other care professions, and these, as well, are variables that depend on changing cultural and historical contexts. Second, if the physician treats the loss as the patient's problem (whether the patient is aware of her problem or not; whether the physician wants to turn her attention to the problem or not), she posits the patient, and sometimes herself, too, as a subject in another field, not the medical field.

2.313 I can see myself taking the subject position of the teacher, but not of the baby or the dog. This is a limitation of my conception of the other, not necessarily of the capabilities or characteristics of the baby or the dog (see 1.340 and 1.341). Children give a subject position more easily to animals, and not just in play (or without distinguishing "play" and "reality"). This is because they are capable of imagining such an exchange of positions, and more generally because in the field of discourse and action within which they themselves take up subject positions that allow such recognition, there are not enough constraints to prevent it. As these fields are differentiated and their structure becomes complex, it becomes difficult to take up a subject position within them, and the number of the expelled increases.

In principle, someone's inability to take up a subject position is a limitation of the field within which such positions are constituted. This could, for example, be a limitation of the field of teaching, within which the teacher takes up a subject position but the pupil is expelled, and the same goes for the relationship between judge and defendant, sovereign and subject (who is always perceived as *subjectus* but not necessarily as a subject). When someone has a problem and she cannot take up a subject position from which she could express her problem, the responsibility lies on the field within which such a position is possible but prohibited in principle. The dog, the baby, the pupil, the patient, the defendant, or the subject — each of these could, in principle, have won recognition as someone who is expressing her problem, but in a certain field of discourse and action this possibility is prohibited in principle. Very often this is the situation in therapeutic professions that have developed in modern times.

2.314 When someone steps outside her subject position in such a therapeutic field, there is a larger chance that she may not only attribute a problem to her "patient" but also recognize him as someone who has a problem, which he recognizes himself, articulates in his own discourse, looks at and shows to others, and in general deals with himself, pays attention to. Loss is a problem that begs such a stepping out of subject positions. When loss is at hand, it is easier to recognize and identify someone who has a problem. However, perhaps precisely because of that, different discourses, especially within the "therapeutic" professions, cultivate objectification mechanisms that cancel expected effects of identification with whoever has a problem and distinguish between someone who has a problem that she can define and treat appropriately and someone whose problem defines her.

2.315 The one defined by a problem is still a subject, even if only a subject that has been posited as an object. A thing is defined not by problems but by other things. Only a person can be defined by a problem. A "patient" within this context is someone defined by her problems.

2.320 A caretaker (therapist, physician, social worker, teacher) in this context is the one who wishes to rearrange the experience of loss for the patient so that the patient will lose the interest that made the disappearance of something his problem, all of it or some of it. Psychoanalysis aims to activate a movement of loss between changing objects that will continue until the patient is able to cope with the loss of analysis, and with the loss of the therapist. In this sense, therapy is the opposite of pity: in therapy, there is a tendency to cancel the matter responsible for the loss; pity is a relation to the other that tends to adopt the loss as the interest of the one who pities.

2.321 Perhaps more than other troubles and agonies, a loss that has been presenced allows or invites empathy, identification, stepping out of a subject position that defines a problem that defines someone and stepping toward a position of a subject facing her own problem. The capacity to perform this transformation creates a sense of solidarity, fraternity, or civil responsibility, but sometimes it turns out to be no more than compassion (see 5.332–5.334).

2.322 Sometimes the problem is how to raise consciousness about something. The socialist shows the workers the freedom they have lost, what they lost of their creativity and humanity when their work became a commodity, what they lost of their relationship to their wives and children when they became enslaved to their workplaces. The feminist shows women their lost freedoms, the opportunities stolen from them, the joy in sex, and the liveliness they have been denied. The nationalist shows his fellow people what other nations who rule over them take away from them on a daily basis. Where was what was lost before it was discovered as a problem for the one who lost it? Identification with the other as a member of the same class, gender, nation, or minority group enables me to turn the other's loss into my problem. The conscious one (the one who becomes class-, gender-, or nationality-minded) attributes to someone else a problem that defines her but also suggests a way to turn that problem into *her* problem, to be the one who defines herself through that problem, through acquiring that loss. As a rule, self-consciousness, identity, and self-definition are always acquired through the mediation of someone else, whose consciousness or identity or definition is not hers, even if she seems to be its origin, or at least it is not hers in the same way that it belongs to the one who acquires it now. This mediation and acquisition are always accompanied by the creation of new circles of loss (see 7.343–7.354).

2.323 Modern liberation movements develop complex mechanisms of loss acquisition. Allegedly, the loss is not produced; it appears as what exists anyway, imprinted in the conditions of the subjected group. But in fact it is acquired through the development of true (or less distorted) representations of these real conditions (see 2.431 on). But can we really distinguish the representation of the conditions from the production of loss that they entail? And does someone have reason enough to choose, if she could, between the "state of loss" before the "consciousness-raising" and the "state of loss" after it? Not to mention the losses caused by the liberation struggle itself.

2.324 Does this mean that we should give up in advance all liberation struggles? Not necessarily. But we should better understand the physics, geography, and typography (that is, the set of representations) of loss that are tied with every struggle for liberation. And there are, of course, different types of struggle and of liberation. We should bear in mind the terrible cost of some well-known liberation struggles in modern times, but also the fact that not all of them had such a cost. It is also worth remembering that certain liberation struggles occur in a very narrow arena — the home, the family, the workplace — whereas others encompass the whole of society and should be judged differently.

2.325 And yet the size of the loss entailed by the struggle is a yardstick (although not the only one, because we have to take into account the suffering as well) that we should use to measure every struggle for liberation in order to determine not only if it is worthwhile but also if it is proper. How one measures the loss I still cannot say; it is doubtful that I will be able to. But I can anticipate a point that I will argue later (see Chapter Eight): loss is the measure for the promised freedom in the liberation struggle and not the other way around; the promised freedom cannot justify any loss; the experienced and expected loss can be part of what justifies sacrifice in the liberation struggle, and sacrifice always means loss. The struggle for liberation presupposes a loss that must be restored, in the same way that the interpreter presupposes a meaning that must be deciphered — a circular presupposition. An estimate carried out through the prism of loss will judge the liberation struggle according to the "loss situation" before, during, and after the struggle. This estimate is always wrong and should always be open to rectification. But it does not presuppose that there is a loss to restore and there is something to be liberated. That is what must be proved. (And yet, it is true, one must be free enough to prove, that is, to have some control over the means of representation.)

2.330 Matters get more complicated because we always also lose things that have never been. Loss is not necessarily linked to the past. There can be a loss of what is not yet, of a potential to do something or to become something. The lost potential was in the past, but in what sense does a potential exist? Only as a mark of what might be, of a future that is not. That is, potential is a future that is not, which is present in the present as such. The loss can be a loss of something in the future (which had a past) just as much as it can be a loss of something from the past (which had a future).

2.331 The one hurt in an accident loses a predicted income from work. Courts and insurance companies take for granted this loss of something that has never been and is only a representation of a chance. In such a case, what was the thing that was lost without the capacity to conceptualize it through statistical tables of earning capacity calculated by age, gender, education, and status (see 2.52 and 3.0–3.1)? Is there a difference, in this sense, between the loss of this chance and the loss of freedom and the chances of "doing things" entailed by a state of oppression or deprivation? In both cases, what is lost depends completely on the representation mechanisms of the loss; the one who lost something cannot turn this loss into her problem until she acquires a certain level of control over these mechanisms.

2.332 But the contingent accident that caused someone to lose her expected income for a year or a lifetime is a result of bad luck, and in this sense it is deeply different from structural conditions within which a continuous under-privileging of a minority produces an original loss of the chance to eat well, live well, acquire education and a profession, move to a new house, and love and die in peace. But maybe the difference is less deep if an accident is less of a contingency than it seems at first, whereas social and historical forms that create waves of loss are more contingent. Maybe in order to prevent the accident or lessen its chances of happening, organized social action is needed, which is not different, in principle, from that required to gain what is lost through social oppression.

2.4 *Loss of Subject*

2.400 We cannot identify or talk about loss without presupposing something that was there before. But something can be represented as lost, as missing, in order to help one imagine what was there before. Different kinds of discourses, language games, and daily situations that stabilize the order of things allow the identification of loss in different ways, creating different types of passages from being to nothingness in relation to a subject and constituting differently the temporality of being as a problem of a subject. Across these variations among discourses, the disappearance constituted and perceived as a loss always has a double relation to a subject, for whom the disappearance is a problem, and to a more or less defined phenomenal field within which the gaps and passages between being and nothingness take place. The objective field is not stable; it is often turbulent and subject to transformations because its border is determined in relation to a problem of a subject, and hence to the way she perceives and experiences disappearance as her problem (even when she has never owned or experienced that which has disappeared).

2.401 When I lost a wallet with a little money and a few documents in it, I experienced this loss in terms of time and money, a missed meeting, a note I kept as a memento and a dear memory that will be lost with it. But when the wallet was lost, I found the time to buy a new one, to update my photo, which appears in different documents, and an excuse not to pay a certain bill, to avoid a certain meeting. The different things that disappear with the loss and the different possibilities that appear with it are not necessarily distinguished, and certainly are not placed in a clear hierarchy or order. The fact that loss opens new possibilities and that the one who loses may gain different kinds of utility and pleasure from the loss further complicates the link between loss and liberation struggles that are intended to cancel conditions seen as responsible for the loss, and primarily responsible for the loss of chances and opportunities.

2.410 The subjectivity of the subject for whom a certain loss is a problem does not diminish as a result of the loss. Sometimes it is the other way around. The lost object becomes a pole of identification, and its commemoration is a common way to construct a subject position. In certain cases, the capacity to experience loss, to perceive disappearance as a problem, is a test of subjectivity. The capacity to lose is the hallmark of the universal subject.

2.411 The loss of subjectivity is a matter of all or nothing. Subjectivity cannot be lost like calcium, spread like the hole in the ozone layer, spill like blood, evaporate like a puddle in the desert. Everything that was and is gone, every being that has been identified as lost, and something that was and no longer is, becomes an object, even if it belonged to the subject in the most intimate manner — feeling, memory, idea, enthusiasm, hope, and so on. The subject can lose more and more of what belongs to her, she may even lose everything that belongs to her but her shackles, without damaging her subjectivity. The subject position can be narrowed down increasingly, constraints can be put on it through seduction or compulsion, its gaze blinkered like that of a horse, its hands handcuffed, its mouth shut, and none of these will erase subjectivity; on the contrary, all these limitations presuppose it.

2.420 Subject and object appear in a double sense here: on the one hand, the subject has problems; the disappeared object causes them. On the other hand, the object was capable of disappearing; the subject is capable of identifying and expressing disappearance as someone's problem, and she can witness the loss.

2.421 A theological idea: every loss has a witness, and God witnesses every loss. But if a subject is someone who has problems, then God, the perfect witness, cannot be a subject. And neither can he be an object, of course, because God is what cannot disappear, whether because he has never appeared or because "he is hidden from all." Hegel, who perceived God as the totality of the actual, wanted to see in him a perfect amalgamation and *Aufhebung* of absolute subject and infinite object, and lost both the object and the subject.

2.422 On the one hand, the loss of the subject herself is the appearance of the subject as object. As was said, subjectivity disappears not in bits but at once, as in death, or in turning the subject into an object in a discourse that fixates her (the doctor who becomes a patient, the king who loses his mind, the servant who is ignored from time to time and is talked about in her presence). The disappearance of one subject as a problem of another subject is the prototype of loss. A disappearance of a subject that does not pose a problem to any subject is the complete reification of the subject, returning the subject to the order of things. The Fascist regime in Argentina, where in the 1970s "disappearance" became a code name for a system of political assassinations, presented the loss of the individual who had been murdered as a problem of the family and her disappearance as a citizen as a nonproblem of the government, and completely separated the private interest of the family from the interest of the regime. The disappeared citizen was no longer a judicial subject; she was a subject that became a *subjectus* that became an object. The Nazis, who wanted to exterminate all the Jews, wanted the disappearance of the last Jew not to be a problem for any subject (see 9.130 on).

2.423 On the other hand, the subject might lose many of "her" objects, but no object lost will in itself prevent her from taking the same subject position and will not necessarily create a change in that subject position. The loss could be an axis in the constitution of self-identity from that same subject position and throughout a transformation of this identity (2.221–2.322), but not necessarily; every such constitution depends on the active participation of the subject interested in what is lost. Turning the disappeared into something lost is not enough to change the subject; disappearance, let alone loss, is enough to change the object. Even if what was lost is preserved unharmed somewhere, it is no longer "hers" or "in her possession." The relation of ownership, which makes something "mine," already presupposes the two poles — a subject who can "have" things and an object that can "belong" to someone.

2.424 A subject who posits herself as witness to the loss taking place "inside" her — who identifies a disappearance of something that was "hers" as her problem — is, in fact, preoccupied with her own objectification. Something of "hers" has been fixed as something that was and is now gone; something of hers is identified as a thing. That is, self-consciousness is an instrument of reification, even when it is recruited to struggles of liberation. But at the same time, that subject is also busy with her design of her own self, with auto-subjectification. Every time something that disappears becomes her problem, a space opens up for disputing the taken-for-granted status of her link to the world that is perceived as objective and for presenting both what is perceived as objective and the objectivity of what is perceived as a problem. That is, in self-consciousness there is a moment of transcendence, even when it is recruited to oppressive projects.

2.430 The identification of loss, and mainly its reification, are a common and vital mechanism in the construction of a group as an imaginary subject: a people that lost its freedom, a congregation of believers that lost a spiritual leader or faith itself, the class that has nothing to lose but its chains. Usually, the loss is not simply represented but expressed in a rich narrative with a more or less determined structure: the tragedy that led to the loss; the heroic struggle, destined to fail, to prevent the loss; the heroic struggle to preserve a few ashes of what was lost, ashes that will enable the story of loss, its "passing down to the next generation," making it an anchor in the construction of group identity. In order to become part of the group, the individual is supposed to identify the group loss as her problem, to construct herself as interested in what was lost. One would be considered alienated (from her family, her people, her class) when she stops (or dodges or becomes free from) problematizing the loss, when she ceases to see the lost thing as her problem. The imaginary subjectification of the group is tied to the reification of what was lost and the reification of the group's identity in terms of what was lost. The imaginary subjectification of the group and the reification of its identity are two sides of the same coin (see also 3.340).

2.431 A group that has lost nothing is almost incapable of appearing to be a subject. The loss guarantees the group an identity, stretching from the past to the present, a presence of the past in the present, and even a horizon of future action — to return what was lost (honor, freedom, land, money) or at least receive compensation for it. The group recruits the individuals who are supposed to belong to it by passing on the loss, "implanting it in their souls," "inscribing it in their consciousness." The loss guarantees the particular identity of the group and the group as particular.

2.432　The loss that passes on in the group, from first-comers to new-comers, from generation to generation, is in fact multiple: the loss as an event that once took place and an object that once was and is no longer; the loss as an absent object whose enduring presence one constantly witnesses and experiences; and the loss as an obligation and vocation to commemorate forever, which secure a lasting future for the lost object.

2.440　One can suggest a taxonomy of a group according to the way in which the group constitutes the loss that constitutes it, and according to the way in which the relationship to the loss constitutes the group's self-identity — a typology of loss communities.[21] An organization of those harmed by disaster or bankruptcy constitutes itself directly around the axis of loss (for example, survivors of concentration camps; an organization of bereaved parents; an organization of people hurt in road accidents; residents of an area hit by natural disaster, or of a green neighborhood that is about to be split by a highway). A family could reconstitute its identity as a group in a period of mourning in direct relation to the loss, the memory of the dead, the struggles about her representation, and the competition over control of the archive collected around the one who was lost.

2.441　Several branches of Jewish rabbinical discourse, first and foremost prayer, and — in different ways — some forms of Zionist discourse, have generated the destruction of the Temple in Jerusalem as a constitutive loss. The Diaspora spreads out as a continuous presence of this primal loss, which gathers all the previous losses and all those that come after it, until this day. The expression and function of this primal loss in rabbinical ultraorthodox discourse are very different from those of mainstream Zionist discourse, and these differences are arresting.[22] Here is one of the main differences in their relation to an event that epitomizes Jewish Loss — the Holocaust. In Zionist discourse, which tries to bring back what was lost with the creation of Jewish Diaspora, the Holocaust is often expressed as a horrible, albeit inevitable, apex in the logic of loss that has been imposed by the situation of Diaspora. The

Holocaust becomes the prototypical expression of the state of Diaspora. And Jewish sovereignty in the land of Israel, which is supposed to cancel the previous state of Diaspora, is perceived as the prototypical expression of the response to the Holocaust. On the other hand, in Jewish ultraorthodox discourse, within which the Diaspora is seen as the existential and historical condition of the Jewish people, there are almost no institutionalized cultural means that facilitate and articulate the loss that is gathered under the name of "the Holocaust." The Holocaust joins the list of disasters the Diaspora brought on the Jewish people without its having any substantial influence over the way rabbinical discourses cope with the unprecedented magnitude of the loss.

2.450   When a loss constitutes a social association or when it is a central axis in its constitution, this association, or at least its ideology, is directly opposed to the logic of capitalist market society. The capitalist market is characterized by sophisticated mechanisms that introduce every loss into a cycle of exchange relations and do not allow it to be preserved as a problem for too long. Everything that represents loss is exchanged as a commodity in the cultural market; even nostalgia is produced as a commodity, and the lost things that it represents can always be replaced by other things. Capitalist society is characterized by a fluid loss that cannot be fixed and thus cannot be used to organize a group identity around it. When individuals in a market society mourn what they have lost and constitute their self-consciousness around this loss, that is their private business. While the state nationalizes some losses and forces others to be shared, the market privatizes all losses, and this privatization is the condition for justifying all other privatizations.

2.451   If the privatization of loss really characterizes a capitalist market society, this could add something to our understanding of the breakdown of communities and the appearance of *Homo economicus* as an abstract subject, with rights and property but with no particular belonging. It could also add something to our understanding of one of the basic oppositions between modern liberation movements and capitalist society: liberation movements try to fix, represent, put on display, and distribute the loss for which the market tries to determine an exchange value. Liberation movements try to constitute an identity around the loss, whereas the market offers countless substitutes to fill the hole that the loss bores. The market might incessantly commodify the constituted loss of the group (sand from the Holy Land, water from the Jordan River, tourist packages for pilgrims); the group may incessantly try to command its loss over the market (to recruit all the re-sources in order to return what was lost; to declare lost territory that has been recovered as nonsalable).

2.452 There once was a group, a very general group, that lost everything as a result of its position in the market economy and had nothing to lose but its chains. Therefore, it tried to cancel the market economy itself. Even if this Marxist legend is true, the group that is discussed, the proletariat, never was a universal group. But there were many small groups that crystallized around whoever was assumed to represent the universal group that never was and give it the identity, images, and self-consciousness that emerged from the consciousness of the loss.

2.453 Many social struggles can be redescribed and explained in terms of a struggle for the authority to represent the loss of a group sub-ject. The authority to represent the loss in the group is always a central object of struggle, because the representation of loss has a crucial part in legitimizing relations of domination in the group and is constitutive of the group ideology. Hence the interest of the state in controlling various memorial projects, or of family members in controlling the commemoration of their beloved (and the conflict between the two groups that becomes inevitable from the moment family members stop representing their loss in the idiom offered to them by the state).

2.5 *Facts*

2.500 Loss, like disappearance, belongs to the realm of facts. It is the object of existential statements (was or was not) and of probabil-ity statements (will or will not be, it is impossible for it to happen, it cannot be prevented from happening). But unlike with disap-pearance, it is not enough to determine the mere occurrence of the change from presence to absence and from being to nothing-ness. One must also fix the interest of the interested party in what has disappeared and is irreplaceable. The interest that makes dis-appearance into a loss is a fact, just like the disappearance that turns a party interested in what is into a party interested in what was. That is, loss is a double-faced fact, or two separate facts that someone joins together: something has disappeared and has no substitute or replacement; someone is interested in what has dis-appeared and has no replacement and is interested in it precisely because it is irreplaceable, and for as long as it has no replacement.

2.501 Who is authorized to call a disappearance a loss? Sometimes it is possible to determine the disappearance of something as a loss in the same way a physician determines death, or a restoration ex-

pert in a museum determines that a work of art has been so cor-
rupted it can no longer be restored. Loss is placed on a scale and
used as an object for struggle in different discourses and "truth
games" (1.500). Often the loss belongs to scientific discourse and
its branches, to pseudoscientific discourse, or to a discourse that
tends to base some of its factual claims on scientific discourse (the
legal or bureaucratic discourse, for example). The margins of the
unique halo of what has disappeared are never well defined;
sometimes there are institutionalized types of discourse to determine and stabilize them, and sometimes there are not. Only the
expert is authorized to determine that the painting is a fake and
therefore cannot be a replacement for the lost artwork. Only the
child who lost the doll (2.002) can determine whether any of the
dolls offered to her as a substitute will do.

2.502   A continuum can be noticed here between cases of loss that can
easily be posited as facts in an institutionalized discourse (the
destruction of a work of art or the death of a beloved person, for
example) and cases of loss that are subject to the idiosyncratic
judgment of an interested individual. It is relatively difficult to
dispute cases of the first kind (not death itself is disputed but the
fact that this death is a loss); it is difficult, but not impossible:
the losses of the enemy are "our" advantage, and if the enemy is
declared "the enemy of mankind," no one could lose from his
losses. It is relatively easy to dismiss cases of the second kind (not
that the doll is lost, but that it has no replacement); it is easy, but
not always: when idiosyncratic loss judgments become the trade-
mark of someone whose obstinacy has no limits, when a culture
develops a mechanism that backs up this obstinacy and rewards
the whims of those who demand the exclusive right to determine
the margins of loss.

2.503   Who is authorized to determine the interest of the interested party
as a fact? Who is authorized to determine that someone has an
interest in what was lost? Is it enough for the interested party to
testify that for her the thing that was lost is irreplaceable? Of
course the individual could have the authority to determine what
is replaceable when taken away from her; but to determine the
interest? Interestedness can be produced (2.121) and can be extinguished or repressed (in the same way that an appetite can be
extinguished, or a child's desire to ask a question about a dubious
relative who has disappeared, or mental patient's obsessions or
nightmares through the administration of drugs or electric shocks).
But interestedness cannot be denied when it is expressed. At
most, one can accuse the interested party of merely pretending.

But how can you tell the difference between real interest and simulated interest? Only within a police discourse of some kind — interrogating and looking deep into one's soul — that can, allegedly, tell the difference between "real" intentions and pretense. Every time one denies or ignores an expressed interest in a lost object, the danger of a violent intervention looms.

2.504 The opposite case, when an interest is attributed by others, is more complicated and not always violent. Others may attribute to someone an interest in a disappeared object or call her attention to it when she expresses no interest, but they may do it gently and for her own sake. When my daughter's dog disappears, I fear for it because I fear for her, although at the moment she is not showing any interest in the dog. I want to call my mother's attention to her loss of hearing, although she denies this fact and pretends she has no interest in it. But when the Israeli right-wing politicians present handing the Palestinian city of Hebron over to the Palestinian Authority as a terrible loss and mark me as an interested party in what is lost in this handing over (in the best-case scenario), or as someone who has lost his "Zionist identity" and his "Jewish roots" and therefore lost at least some of his authority in the political debate (in a worse case), I quickly lose my patience. The way in which they make me join them as an interested party suffocates me; the way in which they try to exclude me from the political discourse is exasperating. In both cases, this is a coercive intervention in the discourse in which I, too, am a legitimate speaker. This intervention is intended to legitimize the continuation of violence in the Palestinian city while ignoring its occupation by the Israelis as a powerful mechanism for producing loss among the Palestinian residents. The interest I may have in the loss these residents suffer is silenced together with the direct voice that may express it — the voice of the Palestinians.

2.510 Assessing the dimensions of the loss is also tied to "if only" judgments: what would happen if only a certain disappearance would not take place, what would not be lost as a result of the initial loss? What would the torso look like if only it had not lost its head, how would the patient's body function if only she had not lost so much blood, what would the army's level of preparedness be if only it had not spent so many days controlling the uprising in the occupied territories? What would life here look like if only war had not broken out? These judgments cannot be put to an empirical test, and the testimony of interested parties is insufficient. They rely solely on appraisals, on estimates of probability.

2.511 Some losses occur in chains: a man lost the code to his safe → the access to his money → the possibility of completing the purchase of a flat for which he was supposed to pay a large lump sum on that day → the down payment he has already paid according to a contract. The subsequent loss could have a much larger effect and assume more significance than the initial one: a man lost the code to his safe → and the possibility of participating in an auction of a rare work of art he had a great interest in; the army lost hundreds of days of training → the army lost its military capabilities → the army might lose the war.

2.52 The physics of loss is not even in its infancy (2.134), but many types of loss accounting are flourishing. Different kinds of losses have different experts: expert physicians estimate the level of disability, appraisers determine the value loss, military experts and military historians assess the number of losses in the battlefield, restoration experts estimate loss in works of art and precious trinkets, and so on. In case of a disagreement, one can always subject the estimate to the usual competence tests of phrases in a scientific discourse, but not necessarily to the empirical tests that this discourse structures (this holds for most of the "if only" sentences). This was not always the case, and it is not always the case nowadays. Loss judgments require truth games, but not necessarily a scientific discourse. The prophet estimated what the people had lost: the loss of faith and fear, the loss of obedience, and even the loss of the ability to fight. Many other types of losses are not up for judgment in a scientific discourse, and still they belong to this or that truth game, and their determination is a matter of fact and of estimate — the loss of trust, or love, or motivation, or the will to live.

2.530 Usually, loss is perceived as an event with a negative meaning, an occurrence that makes the condition of the one who lost worse. But not every loss is harmful (a week after the purchase of the flat was supposed to take place and didn't because of the loss of money [2.511], the flat is destroyed in an earthquake). Some cases of loss are neither here nor there, or are sometimes one way and sometimes the other (loss of patience, loss of exclusivity, loss of documents, loss of part of the text). Some losses make things better, at least from certain perspectives (weight loss, loss of virginity, loss of fear and repression). The weight that was lost as a result of a diet cannot be reduced to the appearance of the alternative thing — a slim body, a good feeling, freshness — and nonetheless, from

the point of view of someone interested, the loss is not a depreciation but a gain.

2.531　From the point of view of someone interested, a loss that causes
depreciation is harmful. Harmful losses may be assessed and measured in terms of the gains that may cancel them within a certain
exchange system. When a harmful loss can be expressed, assessed,
and measured in terms of an exchange system, it is damage.

Chapter Three

Damage

3.0 *Exchange*

3.000 Damage is a harmful loss that is assessed as depreciation in terms of an exchange system. Every assessment of damage includes an assessment of the depreciation caused by a loss, but not every loss causes depreciation or damage. As stated, some cases of loss don't add or detract, others do either this or that at different times, and still others improve conditions (2.530).

3.001 Damage can be suffered by anyone whose loss of some thing is expressible in an exchange system. An exchange system that allows the expression of a given depreciation is not sufficient for the purposes of determining who can incur damage. There must also be a discourse that identifies someone as having a losable thing. The presence of such discourse can never be taken for granted. Many struggles — political, economic, legal, and others — are waged over the question of who can or cannot be damaged and what counts as expressible depreciation. At stake in such discourse is always more than the question presents explicitly.

3.002 Is a people or a nation capable of incurring depreciation? If so, what are the things that a people may lose that cannot incur depreciation to it? And what about a state? And a public company? Or "the environment"? Not everyone who loses a memory also suffers consequent depreciation; a loss of "self-identity" does not always mean depreciation for the self to whom identity is ascribed. For a loss to result in depreciation, an exchange system whose values enable the expression of such a loss must be in place.

3.003 Can an injured animal incur depreciation? Lyotard says that "the animal is a paradigm of the victim," for it lacks the ability to testify to the damage caused it and to prove that such damage in fact occurred.[1] Lyotard ascribes this inability to the animal's exclusion, in principle, from human discourse. I wish to sharpen this claim and to ascribe the animal's victim condition to the fact that it cannot incur depreciation; that is, there is no exchange system in which the animal's loss can be translated into terms of depreciation. One who cannot incur depreciation cannot count as damaged and, for precisely this reason, is a victim. He or she or it is a victim not only because it cannot testify to the damage caused it but also because it cannot express the loss it has suffered in terms of depreciation (and no one can do this in its stead). The *différend* creating the condition of victim exists between the discourse describing loss in unassessable terms and the discourse describing "the same" loss in assessable terms.

3.010 Damage can always be attributed to a loss that results from some occurrence: someone trips and loses a bill he was holding, someone is robbed and loses an object he possessed, someone is hurt in an accident and loses a limb or some capacity, someone is fired and loses his livelihood, someone is deserted and loses the support of an intimate other. In all these cases, someone incurs depreciation as a result of an occurrence leading to loss. Can there be damage that is not expressible in terms of loss? I can't imagine such a case, although many kinds of damages are also expressible in terms of the addition of some thing, of excess, such as overeating, a cancerous growth, a bad neighbor, or a competing business.

3.011 The condition of one who suffers damage is always worse than it was before the damage — worse, not in moral terms or in absolute terms, but in terms of that order of things within which the damage was caused: the economic order, or the physiological one, or the psychological one, or the moral one, or some combination of these. When loss causes damage, the deterioration in conditions is measured in terms of the order of things within which the lost thing was expressed and assigned value. The depreciation incurred through the loss of an asset is measured in economic values. The depreciation incurred through the loss of a limb is measured in values of function, appearance, and self-image. The depreciation incurred through the loss of a reputation is measured in values of prestige, social contacts, and economics. The depreciation incurred through the loss of authority is measured in terms of values of power and symbolic capital. Each of these is also measured in terms of economic values. The loss of a dear one is measured in terms of all these values together and more. And the same holds for lost time. This "more" is what distinguishes damage from loss.

3.012 One who suffers economic damage may gain attention and sympathy as a result of the loss, and one who suffers damage to his reputation may gain a lot of money. The assessment of depreciation will not include these; it is limited to the order of things within which the loss occurred.

3.020　Different kinds of discourse — economic, medical, psychological, national, and suchlike — specialize in the representation of different kinds of losses. Within the more or less accepted framework of a given discourse, loss can be represented, and its occurrence proved, with relative ease. It is also possible to describe a chain of losses and secondary losses stemming from a single "primary loss." Such a discourse allows assessment of the investment gone to waste due to the damage and the investment now required in order to restore or substitute what was lost.

3.021　Damage is an assessment of the depreciation resulting from a loss. Depreciation is the result of one of two gaps, and sometimes of both: the gap between what was there and what is there; the gap between what could have been and what is there. Conjoining these gaps with the investment gone to waste and with the required investment produces at least three possible axes for assessing depreciation: the condition of the person damaged when he was still in possession of what was lost versus his present condition; the condition of the person damaged if he were still in possession of what was lost versus his present condition; the condition of the person damaged if there were no need to make the effort of obtaining substitutes for what was lost. The degree of damage to a person who lost a hundred dollars depends on what transactions with this sum were denied him as a result of its loss: the resulting damage to a rich person would be negligible; the resulting damage to a poor person might be enormous. The damage suffered by a person who has lost about 20 percent of his hearing varies in accordance with his occupation and his hobbies: a musician will incur far more damage in such a case than the operator of a tractor, and an opera lover will incur more damage than a football fan. All this is self-evident and trivial.

3.022　The assessment of someone's depreciation in terms of the gap between what was there and what is currently there, and what is currently there as opposed to what could have been there, determines the damage between two poles: prevention and compensation. The expression of a loss is inserted into an exchange system in order to assess the extent to which the damage may have been preventable and to assess what is required in order to mend it (see 3.401). A calculation of the damage as depreciation caused by the loss assumes that the gap between what was there before and what is there now could have been decreased in advance, or that the gap between what is there now and what might have been there can be decreased at present, or that both gaps can be decreased.

3.023 In other words, for a loss to turn into damage through the mediation of an exchange system, it is necessary to discern in the loss what was inevitable and what was preventable, and to distinguish between what can never be replaced and what can still be mended. Inevitable loss and irreversible loss adorned the damage as the margins of an aura that cannot be rendered in words — the words of the mediating exchange system, of course.

3.030 Loss is damage only if it has resulted from some more or less definite occurrence. Every natural process, first and foremost maturing and aging, can be described as a damage-causing occurrence. But usually, this doesn't hold for the process itself, because that stays out of the exchange system. It is possible to stop or slow down the loss of hearing or sight in the course of aging. It is even possible to slow down the aging process itself. But (at least given the present condition of knowledge) it is impossible to cancel or stop the process entirely. For every case in which a series of factors can be isolated, and the loss they are causing indicated, it is possible to speak of damage if it is possible in principle to indicate other factors that might have prevented the loss. Damage is loss that worsens someone's condition as a result of an occurrence that could, in principle, have been prevented.

3.031 A complaint regarding damage entails indicating the conditions in which the damage would not have occurred and indicating someone's responsibility for the fact that these conditions did not hold. Therefore, a person who has lost his youth cannot present a complaint regarding damages. A good-looking woman who has lost her looks can present such a complaint if there exists a treatment capable of amending what time has destroyed, even slightly, to which she has been denied access.

3.032 The preventability of a given loss is a necessary condition for the existence of damage; knowing the details of the occurrence of a loss and its causes is not. I don't need to know how or when my car was broken into and my car radio stolen; I just need to know that there was a break-in and that the car radio was removed. I don't need to know how, when, or why the refugees were uprooted, I don't need to know whether this uprooting was a result of war or an earthquake, and I certainly don't need to know anything about the intentions of the people who brought about this uprooting, if indeed it was brought about by people. It is enough to know that the event can, in principle, be prevented or that people can be protected from when it occurs, and that after it has occurred, it can, in principle, be repaired, even if only to a limited extent. If I know this, I will understand that the losses the refugees have experienced since the time of their expulsion were preventable, and I can assess the cumulative damages.

3.1 *Signifier and Signified*

3.100 When damage is determined, the damage signifies a loss. But an assessment of damage doesn't signify any specific loss, and loss does not necessarily signify damage. These are asymmetrical semiotic relations (see 3.311). A statement expressing damage implies a claim expressing the existence of some loss (and it can therefore be said to signify an existential statement). These are semiotic relations between statements and not between things in the world. Determining damage requires establishing a causal relation between what has happened (disappearance and loss) and what could have happened (the ability to prevent the loss and what might have happened if it hadn't occurred).

3.101 Loss is expressed (perceived, interpreted) in terms of the depreciation it involves, and the latter is assessed in the values of an exchange system. The assessment of depreciation can be reconstructed in two statements. The first statement presents the loss as a sign of the damage, similar to a seismograph presenting a series of lines as a sign of an earthquake: the event — the occurrence of a loss, the earthquake — takes the position of an addresser, while the one interpreting its meaning — the extent of the damage, the intensity of the earthquake — takes the position of an addressee. In the second statement, an addresser determines the extent of the damage, the intensity of the earthquake, and the addressee — possibly even the same person — listens and interprets the meaning of the existential statement. In the first statement, the addresser's position is virtual and may remain vacant, while the addressee's position is real and necessary; in the second statement, the addressee's position is virtual and may remain vacant, while the addresser is real and necessary. In both the first and the second statement, the signified is the value of the depreciation (or the magnitude of the earthquake), while what was lost is the signifier; it holds the same position in this semiotic relation as the series of lines on the seismograph paper.[2]

3.102 The damage is a sign whose signifier is what was lost and whose signified the value of the depreciation. In Saussure's conception of the sign, signifier and signified are joined like the two sides of a page, while totally dependent for this relationship on the contingent conventions of the system of signs.[3] The same holds for damage: what was lost and the value of the depreciation are joined, but depend completely on the contingent conventions of the exchange system.

3.103 What is *a* without an alphabet? What is *a* without the English language? What is a poster of Madonna without the economy of rock stars? What are a hundred shekels without the Israeli economy? Someone who loses a poster of Madonna or a hundred-shekel bill will incur depreciation amounting to the value of the lost object in terms of the exchange system that gives it value in the first place (for the moment I'm ignoring indirect depreciation). But the analogy is still imprecise. An *a* without an alphabet is a dead character, a graphic form that signifies nothing, that doesn't function as more than what it is, a curved line drawn on some background. A bill without the economy that christened it as a legal form of currency remains just a scrap of paper. But the rag doll a child has lost is not a rag, even if the toy market is annihilated. It may be worth just a few cents at a yard sale, but the child will only agree to such an exchange when he has lost his childhood. In that sense, it is unlike a mere linguistic sign; it is more like a sign functioning at one and the same time within and outside language. Like an arabesque, for instance: it is, of course, a transcription that can be read, but only an observer who has lost aesthetic interest will agree to accept a substitute in writing.

3.104 Damage cuts across the loss and erases within it what exists outside the language in which depreciation is expressed, the language of the exchange system. Assessing the loss as damage causes the loss of part of the loss. As long as one remains within the language of a certain exchange system, this loss cannot be, and is not, assessed.

3.110 Semiotic relations between a signifier and a signified always hold through a medium and within a context, and in relation to an addresser and an addressee, whether virtual or actual. If the value of the depreciation is the signified, its context is the possible prevention and the possibilities prevented; the order of things within which depreciation is measured (physical, economic, and so on) is its medium (or vehicle). As said above (3.101), in the first statement of damage it is possible to describe the event causing the loss as an addresser, and the person assessing the damage as the addressee of that event. By analogy to the conventional representation of the general semiotic relation as a relation between six instances:

$$\text{addresser} \rightarrow \frac{\text{signifier}}{\text{signified}} \rightarrow \frac{\text{medium}}{\text{context}} \rightarrow \text{addressee}$$

the following relation can be presented:

$$\frac{\text{the event}}{\text{of loss}} \rightarrow \frac{\text{what was lost}}{\text{depreciation}} \rightarrow \frac{\text{the order of things}}{\text{possibilities of prevention}} \rightarrow \frac{\text{assessor of}}{\text{the damage}}$$

The flexibility of the context, which no description can determine completely and without which no deciphering of meaning is possible, is similar to the flexibility of the conditions of prevention and the possibilities prevented: no description can determine them in a final, conclusive manner, and no determination of damage is possible without such a description. The medium can be described as an environment through which the signifier moves; the order of things in which the loss occurs can be described as the environment surrounding the movement of the dyad of what was lost and depreciation. Finally, the excess of the signifier — what was lost — belongs in principle to the semiotic form of the damage (3.104).

3.111 The fundamental non-closure of the context in which an act of signifying takes place ensures the fundamental instability of every sign system and the inexhaustible options for creating new meanings out of "the same" signifiers. When the traces of what was lost are the signifier, and what was lost, or the loss itself, is the signified, the representation of what was lost (or of the event of loss as present [2.110]) is fundamentally unstable. The semiotic relation of the loss is substituted by a signifier, which signifies what was lost but erases the event of loss. In the case of damage, this signifier is joined with the value of the loss, the depreciation, which it signifies. When the relations between what was lost and the depreciation are in question, the issue is the fundamental non-closure of the description of the conditions of prevention. Changes in this description entail reassessment of the damage. In order to institutionalize the assessment of damages, one must agree on the description of the conditions of prevention and the prevented possibilities; in order to challenge the assessment of damage, one must merely cast doubt on the agreed-on description.

3.112 At times, new studies or new data indicate that the damage could have been prevented if certain measures had been taken beforehand. The critical question then is whether the one capable of preventing the damage was in possession of this knowledge and whether the one in possession of this knowledge was also capable of preventing the damage. The conditions of prevention are always a combination of knowledge and access to the means of prevention, or at least to the means of alert. Someone damaged by the authorities, for instance, will seek to prove that the authority in question had sufficient data to know, and sufficient means to act, in a manner that would have prevented the damage. The accused authority will usually seek to prove that it lacked either the information or the means or both. Was the authority responsible for obtaining additional information about the possibilities of prevention or for obtaining additional means of prevention? When authorities are sued for damages, all other aspects of a case may be agreed on, and the charges pertain to the issue of this responsibility. Sometimes the authority declares itself exempt from such responsibility in advance. A plaintiff unable to prove such responsibility on the part of the authority will be in the same situation as someone who has suffered damages that he cannot express (see 3.544). He cannot prove that the damage he has suffered was preventable, or that someone is responsible for the damage and failed to prevent it.

3.113 Even when all the information is available and the means are accessible, prevention may still be avoided due to exorbitant costs. In such a case, the prevention of damage incurred to one party is damage to another party. Accordingly, establishing that abstention from prevention was justified necessitates a comparison of damages. We shall postpone the question of justifiable and justified damage until later (3.432, 7.2, 7.5).

3.120 When damages are sued for, the damaged person, or his representative, takes the position of the addresser, as the one who represents the event of loss (the second statement of damage [3.101]). In the position of the addressee he places the party being sued, or his representative. He supplements the dyad of what was lost/depreciation with the dyad of damage/compensation. Compensation is a substitution and a supplement, a substitution for what was lost and a supplement to the signification of what was lost as having value. For its part, the damage, as an assessment of depreciation, functions as a mediator between loss and compensation. The compensation sought, which defines the value of what was lost, completes the process of signification, concludes the testimony to what was lost, ends the semiotic chain, and usually represses whatever is left without compensation. If the damaged person agrees to the compensation, this cancels the mediating role and the semiotic value of the damage. What is left is what was lost, the compensation, and what was lost and has no compensation — the aura left by the loss.

3.121   The more sophisticated the exchange system, the smaller the aura of the loss, the more vague, and the more heavily coated in the various languages of accounting. In contradistinction, memory, history, art, poetry, and folktales sometimes seek to testify to the aura of the non-compensated (or uncompensatable) loss, and sometimes even seek to invent it.

3.122   *In his famous essay "The Work of Art in the Age of Its Technological Reproducibility," Walter Benjamin describes the loss of the aura of the work of art when the means of reproducing it have eliminated the superiority and the uniqueness of the original, as well as the difference between the original and its copies.[4] The depreciation caused by this loss will never count as damage, for what was lost was, by definition, that which is inaccessible to an exchange system. The loss of the aura was supposed to have an aura of loss. But this aura of loss was soon covered by the huge expansion of the audience of art consumers and by the swift spread of commodification processes in the field of art. Looking at modern and contemporary works of art, Benjamin points to the lost aura, but in fact, as Ariella Azoulay writes, he describes the manner in which this loss was created and contributes a great deal to this process.[5] Therefore, despite all he sees in mass-produced art, Benjamin, for the contemporary reader, is like one who still testifies to the lost aura. Due in part to his influence, the aura itself has become a valuable commodity in the art market, and the loss has become a rich source of artistic creation, of the kind seeking to reproduce the loss itself and of the kind seeking to allow a new aura to emerge, using none other than the technical means of reproduction.*

3.130   Loss is an event in which the subject is extremely close to an unmediated encounter with a definite reality, but what was lost is always in doubt, whereas damage extricates what was lost into the relatively certain plane of truth claims, which are always prone to refutation and whose validity can be clarified through the conventional procedures of a given discourse — but at the price of ignoring the loss as an event. The statements of damage enlarge the distance between the reality of the loss and statements purporting to express it, though not because they are less precise but, on the contrary, because they may be more precise — that is, imprisoned within the rules of a single given discourse that distances or silences other possible ways of formulating the loss and molding it in discourse. In the words of Lyotard, one might say that the very act of speaking of damage rather than loss creates a *différend*, for it leaves a remainder of loss that is inexpressible in the language in which the damage is represented (3.003 and 3.104).

3.131 The debate about compensation between the party suffering damage and the party sued for damages is a controversy over how to
conclude the semiotic process begun when the loss occurred and
how to bridge this gap in the order of things, that is, how to
silence the *différend*. The party damaged and the party sued for
damages have different conceptions of the order of things, of the
price and the urgency of restoring this order. When restoring this
order — removing evidence of the loss — is an urgent matter for
the party sued, then the party suffering the damage benefits;
sometimes the damaged party is interested in leaving what was
lost without compensation so as to continue testifying to what
was lost, and to the loss as an event, and in such cases this party
won't rush to accept compensation. When the party being sued
has no particular interest in the disrupted order, the damaged
party will find it difficult to obtain the full compensation demanded. The treatment of civil lawsuits of those suffering damage
due to the actions of the Israeli army in the occupied territories
provides distinct examples of both kinds. In the period before the
second intifada, when the loss was a media event and an opportunity for embarrassing criticism of the Israeli government, such
treatment was swift, at least on the face of it; since the eruption of
a new series of clashes and terrorist attacks in October 2000, with
Palestinian losses becoming a routine that no longer causes excitement and the Israeli public and government no longer embarrassed by the disastrous consequences of Israel's violence, not
even by war crimes, treatment of such lawsuits has been diffuse
and has dragged out indefinitely.

3.140 If "damage" is a sign, then there is no possibility of stabilizing,
once and for all, the relation between what was lost, the signifier,
and the value of the depreciation, the signified. It is always possible to understand the meaning of the sign — that is, to determine
the damage — without reference to the addresser or, in other
words, to the event of loss, or to the addressee or, in other words,
to the sued party, the generator of the damage or the party responsible for its prevention. The move from the event of loss to
what was lost to depreciation doesn't necessarily have to pass
through the intention of the party generating the event, just as
the move from the event of signifying to the meaning of the sign
doesn't have to pass through the intention of the speaker. The
intention of the speaker or of the generator of the damage is an
additional signified to which some components of this relation
may bear witness, but not necessarily so.

3.141 As in every semiotic relation, the signified can at any given moment turn into a signifier.[6] A damage claim is a manner of representing loss, what was lost becomes the signified; every adjudication of damages signifies a loss. In legal discourse, loss is represented in order to sue for damages, and every civil lawsuit signifies a real or hypothesized loss; in moral discourse, loss is represented and signified (in order to justify it or deny its justification), and every justification of damage includes the representation of a loss that should be reinterpreted in relation to the improvement it allowed in a given order of things.

3.142 There is an ineradicable gap between the expression of what was lost (the signifier) and the depreciation (the signified) that this loss signifies. The damage is internally split, imprisoning within itself a signifier and a signified that are joined yet always separate, in a game of differences and traces, in the game of *différance*.[7] Like the sign, in keeping with semiotic concepts from Saussure through Derrida, or like goods, in keeping with Marx's quasi-semiotic analysis (in the first chapter of *Capital*[8]), the damage belongs at one and the same time to the phenomenological sphere in which the signifieds appear and to the conceptual sphere in which they receive their exchange values, and the issue in both cases is a sphere already permeated by relations of signification, that is, in which it is impossible to truly dissociate the phenomenal (or the experienced) from the conceptual, what was lost from the depreciation, or traces of what was lost from its value. "Damage" is an "objective" matter, a "thing" among things, part of what-is-there. Just like other things, it has a phenomenological side; it is a "phenomenon" which is not given to thought or expression outside a certain conventional grid of concepts that represents and evaluates it and which, at the same time, is inseparable from its phenomenology and from its subjective expression (of what was lost, of what was experienced) as someone's problem, which no evaluation can adequately express.

3.2 *Prevention*

3.200 A statement describing a loss as damage assumes, whether implicitly or explicitly, the existence of conditions in which it would have been possible to prevent the loss (3.023). A description of such conditions is an invitation of sorts to adjudications of damages. Just as it is possible to create loss by creating parties who have an interest in the disappearance (2.230), it is also possible to generate damaged parties by creating conditions in which the loss might be prevented or by creating an awareness of the existence of such conditions, or, in other words, by their representation (or by generating parties who have interests in the alternative conditions). Ecological discourse is a clear example of such a change of consciousness generating damaged parties who could not claim damage in its absence. Once the conditions for preventing the loss of some thing have been created, someone who has lost that thing can claim that the conditions which might have prevented the loss were denied him. The loss is represented as unnecessary.

3.201 The occurrence or prevention of an unnecessary loss requires sociohistorical conditions, and sociohistorical factors take part in its occurrence. In every case where conditions for preventing the loss can be pointed out, a denaturalization and a historicization of the loss take place (see 2.030–2.031). Damage claims assume a denaturalization or a historicization of the loss. An ox is declared dangerous, for instance, when "it is known that the ox was accustomed to gore" and is likely to cause damage; that ox is a part of nature that has undergone denaturalization. By declaring an ox likely to cause damage, one christens what is naturally damaging into a given social order, within which it receives a category of its own, and points out the need to take precautions against it. It is the duty of the ox's owner to protect the surroundings from the dangerous ox. If the owner fails at this, he is guilty of the damage. (But an ox is damaging even when it isn't dangerous, whereas a person is always dangerous.) [9]

3.202 Recent studies have led to the denaturalization of many diseases and malfunctions related to alcohol, smoking, and other types of substances, and have established the risks involved in the use of numerous instruments and materials that make up the daily urban environment in postindustrial societies. More and more injuries and harms are associated with identifiable, changeable factors; the losses they incur are manageable, and the damages they entail are preventable. The average citizen of any contemporary city is a risk-taking animal constantly shifting between failing to prevent damages to self and others and failing to take action (considered too risky) in order to prevent damages.[10] Knowledge of the material environment and its conceptualization in terms of risks have turned the experience of loss into an experience of preventable damage. Weber's "disenchantment of the world" has culminated in the "damage-ization" of loss. The genre of loss is tragedy; the genre of damage is the bureaucratic file. In postmodern, postindustrial societies, the tragic condition of human existence has become the object of investigation of commissions of inquiry. These are often appointed by the same authorities responsible for the production and distribution of the main bulk of damages within a society.

3.210 Is there a limit to the denaturalization of loss? There is, but the limit itself is not a natural given but rather a dividing line set through cultural means and redrawn again and again in the course of social struggles within various cultural fields. In contemporary culture, the naturalization of loss is the strategy of every damager; its denaturalization is the strategy of every conscious damaged party. The doctor in Haifa, Israel, will say that it is impossible to prevent the cumulative damage of muscular degeneration, that it is a natural phenomenon of aging, while the patient knows that in Houston, Texas, a drug has already been developed that will slow down this degeneration, and he doesn't understand why he is being prevented from obtaining it. For him, the doctor is part of a conspiracy of public medicine against him.

3.211 "The class that has gained self-consciousness" has become aware of and interested in what it lacks, which it identifies as something taken from it. In other words, it identifies the lack as loss and the loss as damage that would be preventable under other historical circumstances. But if capitalism is perceived as a necessary phase in the development of the proletariat as a conscious class, and the consciousness of the proletariat is perceived as a necessary condition for the liberation of the proletariat, then the conditions for prevention of the damage and the consciousness of the loss as preventable, as well as its interpretation as damage, come into being at one and the same time, inextricably intertwined.

3.212 In any case, strategies for representing loss actually allow or block suits for damages. They determine possibilities of transposing statements of loss from the realm of the natural or the purely accidental into the realm of the social and historical, and of shifting from an interest in the order of things to a struggle over social and political order. These strategies also determine the unfolding medium (the order of things) and affect the context (the conditions of prevention), thus determining the field of meaning that is the possible space for assessing the damage.

3.220 It is possible to identify and distinguish between types of natural or social surroundings in which the chances of incurring damage increase. Certain workplaces, for instance, are "accident-prone"; in other words, they spread damages among workers and among residents of the surrounding area. A high-risk environment — an army, for instance — is a dangerous environment, even between

wars. War is a social institution intended to harm, to spread loss
and damage, and almost no party that enters into war does not
suffer damage as a result. The same is true of poverty, illness,
or tyranny.

3.221 Ecological discourse en-tongues damage caused to the environment itself. Speakers in this discourse identify different types of
losses as their problem and try to persuade others that they are
everyone's problem. Many of these losses are formulated within a
general framework of the loss of a "natural" equilibrium that previously allowed the various systems of the biosphere to overcome
local damages through mechanisms of self-adjustment. Cumulative damage to the environment is a source of sundry damages
divided differentially among various populations. However, the
speakers in ecological discourse are afraid for the environment
not only because of the harm caused to human beings, to the
speakers themselves or to those they speak for; often the environment itself is perceived as one who suffers damage. The environment, conceived of in holistic terms as a system or organism,
becomes a subject of sorts; ecological discourse is the externalized consciousness of this subject, and the Greens strive to become its sensory and speech organs.

3.222 Poverty, sickness, and tyranny are all describable in ecological
terms, as environments that have lost some kind of "fundamental"
equilibrium and a "natural" capacity for self-regulation based on
feedback. As a result, the environment in question turns into a
harm-spreading one. This is precisely how Plato understood the
relation between the ideal political system, existing in exemplary
equilibrium, and any other political system, which unfailingly
causes some degree of imbalance — an imbalance that grows progressively as political systems move further from aristocracy
toward tyranny. In each political system, the fundamental imbalance is the source of a particular type of harm, corresponding to
the type of equilibrium that has been disrupted. This is how home-
opathy understands illness: an imbalanced organic environment
causing the body cumulative damages. In contrast to modern
Western medical treatment, which focuses on the damages and
their direct causes, homeopathic treatment treats the body as a
holistic environment, which it attempts to restore to the disrupted
initial equilibrium. The difference between Greek "political ecology" and modern ecology lies in their assignment of different
causes to the disruption of the "fundamental" equilibrium. In the
Republic, Plato ascribed it to a miscalculation of mating times in his
ideal city and, more generally, like some of his contemporaries, to

human hubris, to insatiable appetite and arrogance.[11] The moderns attribute the disruption of equilibrium to history in general and particularly to man's varying ways of intervening in nature.

3.223 The ecological description of the occurrence of damage is, as stated, a systemic, essentially synchronic account. The systemic structure defines those principles of the narrative that indicate necessary conditions for the occurrence and spread of the damage. This description contradicts a diachronic, historicist explanation, seeking to identify damage-creating factors at the moment of their historical appearance and to understand the institution, reproduction, and dissemination of these factors as a historical process that can be seen to form a characteristic structure only in hindsight, in light of the objective attained — despite or due to the factors in question. This structure is a diachronic one that does not exist at any given moment but rather determines the relation of a part to the whole only over time. In other words, the perception of the whole necessitates periodization and containment of the flow of time within an organizing structure. From the teleological point of view, the damages appear as necessary and fundamentally unavoidable prices of attaining the given goal — emancipation, liberty, liberalism, salvation, health or happiness, the flourishing of the nation or the race — the means sanctified, as it were, by the ends. Hegel can be easily identified here along with many of his disciples both on the right and on the left, Fascists, Marxists, and Leninists.

3.224 A third option for the denaturalization of damage is a genealogical description. From the outset, such a description views the historical appearance of the causes of damage as a matter of coincidence but sees and seeks to explain their institution, reproduction, and dissemination as the contingent crystallization of an order or structure and its maintenance over time.[12] An ecological description conscious of a given system's historicity will attempt to develop a genealogy of the disruption of balance. In such cases, we will be presented with two genealogies of opposing orientations: one of the creation and reproduction of the structured system, the other of the disruption and disintegration of the structured system.

3.230 In any case, speaking of a system in the context of the present discussion involves speaking of a structured regularity in the conditions and the means of production of damages of different types, of such a regularity in the differential distribution of specific damages among a given population, of a regularity in the ways in which damages are disseminated, and a regularity in the discernible rules and patterns of exchange relations between damage and compensation. This regularity also pertains to the ways in which the damage is "consumed": who can suffer damages of which kinds, who can demand compensation, who is capable of obtaining compensation.

3.231 When a volcano erupts, when an earthquake occurs, a movement of loss takes place (2.122–2.135), and it is accompanied by a movement of damage. At almost every site passed by the wave of loss, damages are caused, but the wave of damages is not identical with the movement of loss. It will tend to be less complex, with smaller intervals between the crests, traveling at lower frequencies and in more moderate curves. This is so because something — usually a great deal — is always lost or silenced, or suppressed, or dulled, in the translation of loss into damage. It is also so because the movement of damage depends on the production of goods and their distribution, as well as on the production of the loss and its distribution.

3.232 The differences between the movement of loss and the movement of damage can be typologically characterized, as can these two movements themselves. Perhaps there will be differences between types of disasters; there may be differences between a predicted natural disaster dealt with from the moment of its outbreak through state apparatuses designed to assess and administer risks and damages and an unexpected natural disaster that no social institution is waiting to monitor, as there may also be a difference between natural disaster and the planned dissemination of damage (in war, through acts of terrorism). In general, the more highly developed an economy is, the greater the difference in question will be; the more capable a regime is of intervening to a greater scope and depth in the life of the population it governs and administers, the greater the difference will be. At the opposite pole: in the state of nature — an idealized lack of regime with minimal, random, and totally informal exchange relations — the difference between the movement of loss and the movement of damage decreases until it almost cancels out. The geography and physics of the movement of damage should be subdisciplines within the framework of the geography and physics of loss, just as solid-state physics is a subdiscipline of physics. To the same extent, however, they should be subdisciplines of economic theory and political science.

3.233 The relation between the movement of loss and the structure of the system of production and dissemination of damages is similar to the relation between plots of love and betrayal in a relatively closed community and the structural patterns of kinship relations. But the relation between the physics of the movement of loss and the economy of the system of production and dissemination of damages is more like the relation between the anthropology and history of kinship relations and their explicit economy. The former should always take into account deviations that have not been formalized, tactics of delaying and eluding, singles and masturbators, while attempting to understand how the institutional patterns of kinship are supposed to deal with these. The latter refers only to that for which a price has already been determined, that is, only to what has already been instituted as a legitimate conjugal contract.

3.3 *Claim*

3.300 The relation between loss and damage is a matter of conceptualization and assessment. Damage judgments are based on certain and probable existential judgments (the loss as a fact; the probability of the conditions for possible prevention of the loss; the probability of the occurrence of a chain of secondary losses), on counterfactual judgments (what would be the case if the loss had not occurred), and on evaluative judgments (determining the value and equivalent of the lost thing).

3.301 Here, as always, statements determining existence and the probability of existence compete among themselves and engage in "struggles for survival," as it were, resulting in the chronic instability of objective description. Or vice versa: presuming to objectivity is a strategy to stabilize the system of representation of a given order of things in which someone has an interest. Someone's interest in some thing causes instability in its representation. Therefore, the ideal of a transparent language is always accompanied by the ideal of "a disinterested interest." The representatives of objectivity and the advocates of objective descriptions have a great deal of interest in this ideal, and therefore its representation suffers from serious problems of instability.

3.310 Insurance companies specialize in evaluating the depreciation involved in a loss, that is, in turning loss into assessable damage. They have, for this purpose, specially designed tables, various algorithms, and an entire discourse that links these together, validates them, and makes them objective. This discourse turns loss into something solid, tangible, possessed of immediate presence in a clearly defined field of phenomena, turns loss into an entity that can be classified, accumulated, transferred, exchanged. The interpretation of loss as damage changes from a hermeneutical act into a mathematical calculation. When loss is assessed, it is reified; its "subjective" margins are eradicated, and it is turned from an indefinite problem of the one who has suffered a loss into a definite object of institutionalized transaction. The loss is purged of everything that is not translatable into the terms of a relevant exchange system and its particular regime, usually the economic one. While there is no logical or historical necessity here, the economic discourse, and it alone, purports to translate every damage into its terms, thus becoming the imperialist discourse par excellence.[13]

3.311 Loss can be transposed into damage with the aid of rigid rules of calculation. A 30 percent degree of disability is an assessment of loss, a determination of damages and of their exchange rate in the insurance market and in the state welfare system. But for every disabled individual, these damages constitute a different loss, unique and singular, his own problem, which cannot be adequately expressed in economic terms. The evaluation of damages is a sign designating loss, but it is impossible to formulate rules that will turn the act of interpretation into an act of calculation allowing the replacement of loss with damage. Damage can only be exchanged for some other damage or for compensation. Speaking of irreparable damage involves moving back from damage to loss, reconstructing the aura of loss around the damage, and adding a hermeneutical dimension to the act of calculation. Assessment of the damage, the speech act that reifies loss and determines it as a quantifiable thing, is thus problematized and represented as limited.

3.312 However, the fundamental limitedness of evaluation is often perceived as an effect of the special nature of the thing that was lost, entirely independent of the social circumstances causing the loss, of the fact that prevention failed to occur, and of the social mechanism for evaluating the damage. Statements such as "beyond compensation" and "irreparable" frequently serve to block discussion of an evaluation of damages and of an assessment of compensation by implying "take it or leave it."

3.313 An assessment of damages is limited to more or less structured spheres of exchange relations. A loss whose damage cannot be assessed designates, beyond the metaphor, the limit of speech about damage and the threshold of exchange relations: death, extinction, despair ("not a trace will remain of..."), complete happiness or enormous sadness ("he was beside himself with..."), unlimited liberty ("he let go completely").

3.320 One who can suffer damage necessarily has some thing which can depreciate (3.001). The three axes of depreciation, according to which damages are assessed (3.021), are the viewpoint taken to identify the person suffering damage, to mold him as one with something to lose, and, since he has already lost it, to identify him as someone with a problem. The damaged party who expresses his damages and demands compensation has a problem that he can define; but the party assessing the damage (the insurance assessor, or the damaged party himself) attributes to the damaged party a problem that defines him (2.313–2.314).

3.321 Evaluations of damages posit the damaged party as having a problem, and posit the damage as an objective feature of the change in his condition. Recognizing damage as someone's problem is a means of subjectifying him; an assessment of the loss generated by the problem and its expression as damage are means of objectifying the damaged party. The two processes are bound together and intensify each other. On the one hand, claiming the identity of a damaged party and suing for compensation mean claiming recognition as one who has an interest in a particular order of things (bodily, financial, institutional) and whose body, property, and social position have become his problems. On the other hand, evaluations of the damage represent an objective description of the damaged party's condition, both implicitly and explicitly. They define him as having a definite interest and delineate his interest in the relevant order of things, as well as the change in his condition due to the loss; in other words, they delineate his problem (see 3.42).

3.322 As stated, objectification and subjectification — that is, positing the singular subject as an object of speech and gaze and constituting the individual as a subject — are two processes bound together that intensify each other. At least this is so in certain circumstances. The objectification of interested subjects — of their particular interests, and of them as interested — is a possible strategy for constituting them as subjects, and a possible strategy through which they constitute themselves as such. The constitution of subjectivity, the training and practice imparted to the individual until he is capable of taking a subject position, travels through the objectification of his body, his soul, his interests, his desires, and his entire world. Being damageable is but one aspect of these interacting equilibrium tubes; the more subject positions in various sociocultural fields an individual takes, the more factors there are that can cause him damage and the more losable things he possesses.

3.330 A nation, an environment, or a public company cannot identify itself as an interested party who has suffered damages; it needs representatives to identify it as such, to express the damage, and to claim compensation. The representative of the damaged party doesn't claim direct compensation for himself, only a fee: some percentage of the compensation, the symbolic capital acquired by one who is authorized to represent, the social status of "representative of." The representative will receive these dues by virtue of the act of representation, even if the party represented is granted no compensation. In such a case, the representation is metaphoric, in the literal sense of transferring (μετα-φαρειν): the representation transfers something from the represented party to the representing one — the authority to define him(self) as one who has a problem and to claim something from others due to it. In the metaphoric representation, the "personality" represented as one who has suffered damages is the content and effect, or a construct, of the act of representing. The representative's interest in the metaphoric representation is divided between the representing and the represented party according to the way in which dues are determined, according to the act of representation, or according to the claim's level of success.

3.331 But if the representative bears part of the damage himself, if he is part of what was damaged or if the damaged party represents itself, the representation is metonymic as well as metaphoric. What the representative of the damaged party receives will metonymically represent the compensation in its entirety. The represented personality is a borrowed extension of the representing personality, its projection, and it is constituted in the very act of representation, regardless of its contents or effects.[14] When representation is metonymic, the representative's interest is divided according to the way in which his connection to the represented party is determined or perceived.

3.332 In any case, claims for compensation situate someone or something as one who has a problem. The mentally disabled, the baby, no less than the rich customer or the commercial firm, are clients defined by their problems through the attorney representing them in a lawsuit. The damaged parties are the attorney's clients. The mentally disabled person, the baby, and the victim of disaster who has lost his memory together with his property all need someone to represent them from the outset. In such a case, the representative translates the loss into damage and turns the problem that someone might define as his own into a problem defining someone. He usually does so even when representation is not a necessary condition for the claim for compensation. In the first stage of the lawsuit, the rich customer himself is naturally capable of taking a subject position, and identifying a loss as his problem, while assessing the depreciation caused him and claiming compensation. However, from here on, the customer's problem is defined through the mediation of the means of representation that constitute legal discourse and, in the end, becomes what defines him (the customer) as an object of this discourse.

3.333 A damaged party must use the terms of a more or less well defined discourse and exchange system that enable the expression and the assessment of what he has lost; otherwise, he is simply loudly lamenting a loss. If he can take the subject position available to him in such a discourse and exchange system, what he can say or show is limited in advance by that position. When he takes such a position, he is representing himself not as possessed of this position but as having an interest in what he has lost. When the subject position is not available (or when the damaged party is incapable of taking it), the interest and the loss — but not the position in question — are ascribed to him through representatives.

3.334 In certain discourses and exchange systems, there are those who can claim damages only through representatives (the nation, the environment, a firm), those who can be represented but cannot claim damages, at least certain damages (for example, the Palestinian citizens of Israel whose lands were confiscated after the 1948 war), and those who can claim damages but cannot be represented (for example, German Jews after the *Nürnberg* Laws). None of these damaged parties is a subject in the full sense defined above (1.305–1.315). The damaged party is some one who (or some thing that) has something to lose, something that can depreciate, and who is now being posited as one who has incurred depreciation from among all the things he has to lose. This, however, still does not constitute that "ideal point of convergence of the one who speaks, the one who gazes at, and the one who touches/is touched by" (1.305). In the relevant field within which the damaged party seeks to express his damages, there is no subject position allowing him to situate "something, including his body, his sensations, his soul, or 'himself' (his identity), in speech-gaze-touch" (1.310), in relation to the damages he has incurred. His depreciation is ascribed to him by others.

3.340 On the one hand, "the subject is capable of identifying and expressing disappearance as someone's problem, and she can witness the loss" (2.420); on the other hand, "the subject might lose many of 'her' objects, but no object lost will in itself prevent her from taking the same subject position" (2.423). Therefore, the subjectivity ascribed to nations, football teams, or commercial firms is an illusory subjectivity, and nations, teams, or firms can never take subject positions in the sense defined above. "Persons" of this kind cannot witness loss other than via representatives who fabricate their testimony through various acts of representation. Neither are they immune to loss; on the contrary, what they have and may lose is what defines them, and if it is totally lost, they cease to exist. Their illusory subjectivity is based on the perception of them as ones who can lose, and on the blurring or repression of the fact that they can only claim damages through someone who represents them as parties suffering depreciation and as parties that can be damaged. Many plaintiffs claiming damages are not subjects. Because their illusory subjectivity is an effect of practices of representation, different practices of representation can multiply their number indefinitely, can deconstruct them, or simply send them to oblivion.

3.341 The difference between one who takes a subject position and one who has something to lose is the difference between the representing one and the one who is represented. The one who is damaged is always represented as having an interest in what was lost, even if he himself represents what he has lost. Representing himself, he posits himself, but he posits himself not as he who represents but as he who has lost some thing that he had, and that lost thing can never be the "ideal point of convergence of the one who speaks, the one who gazes at, and the one who touches/is touched by" (1.305). Of course, one can also lose a position from which speech-gaze-touch are made possible, but when this loss is represented, the ideal point at which speech-gaze-touch converge becomes a definite, measurable plane in some field of discourse. When the one who represents is said to have lost the ability to look and express, when his capacity to enunciate, to view, to touch is impeded, or when he has lost access to a subject position, he is already being posited as one who has something to lose (for instance, the subject position or part of it), and transformed from one who is speaking-gazing-touching into one who is being spoken of, gazed at, and touched, and this is so even if the damaged party is representing itself. In other words, the imaginary subjectivity of the damaged party is first constituted as an object.

3.4 *Compensation*

3.400 Assessing a loss as damage means claiming compensation. "Damage" and "compensation" are complementary terms, each of which is implied by the other, but in one case a claim or expectation (for compensation) is implied by the way things are (the damage), and in the other case the way things are (the damage) is implied by what-is-desired (compensation). Reference to compensation tacitly assumes that there has been damage; reference to damage tacitly assumes a claim for compensation and also implies that someone is expecting, or might have expected, such compensation. In more general terms, compensation is a sign that there was damage; damage is a sign for compensation (expected by someone).

3.401 Damage, as a fact, as some thing that exists, is situated between two types of possibilities: what could have been done to prevent it; what can be done to compensate for it (3.022). The first possibility is of that which is desired but will never be realized, a frustrated wish, a lost past; the second possibility is of that which is desired and has not yet been realized, an open future. Damage has no existence if it is not defined between these two types of the possible. The two types of possibilities delimit the concept of damage on either side like two asymptotes: the loss that could not, under any circumstances, be prevented, and the loss that cannot, in any way, be compensated, are not the objects of claims for compensation. The earthquake could not be prevented, but at least some of the damage it caused could apparently have been prevented. Bereaved families cannot be compensated for the loss of their loved ones, but they can be compensated for the accompanying damages related to the loss. Compensation posits the loss as damage. Assessing the loss as damage posits the inevitable as essentially preventable.

3.402 Nevertheless, insurance companies pay clients compensation for the damage caused by unpreventable earthquakes, for deaths that were already unpostponable. That is just the point: the client purchases from the insurance company the illusion of prevention and the possibility of exchange. The transaction is in fact a simple, commercial one. Life insurance is simply a kind of savings account that can be drawn from only on the condition that the saver dies; insurance for natural disasters is a kind of investment in the rehabilitation of a predictable loss. The contract between the insurance company and its client is a commitment to a conditional exchange, with an added calculated gamble on the part of both sides. Occurrence of the loss is the condition for activating the bargain. The client transfers his money to the insurance company and gambles on the possibility that the conditions in which he or his heirs will be paid double indemnity will be met; the insurance company receives the client's money and gambles on the possibility that these conditions will not be met. Most of the people insured, the solitary gamblers, lose their bets; their bets are too narrow: a specific type of loss befalling a specific person. Most of them gamble without assessing the chances that the loss will actually occur, or regardless of such an assessment. An insurance company usually wins the bet (or goes bankrupt), because it distributes its bet across a wide range of expected occurrences whose probability it calculates in advance. In any case, a claim for compensation from an insurance company is not necessarily a claim for damages. It is a claim to carry out a bargain whose conditions have been met (see also 3.434).

3.410 In determining how to compensate the damaged party, one must do more than determine the value of the damage, that is, assess the loss. It is also necessary to determine what context the damage was caused in, whether or not it was justified, who was responsible, who is responsible for compensation, and suchlike decisions essential to tort law. However, from the point of view of the damaged one, determining the damage is a claim for full compensation that will cancel out the damage.

3.411 Determining damage involves making a statement about what was there (what was lost) as what is there (loss assessed as damage), which is, in turn, represented as grounds for the demand for what should be there (compensation). The relation between damage and compensation is a manner of organizing time. The separation between past, present, and future is unequivocal: a loss occurring in the past causes a continuously present damage that produces secondary damages, and a future compensation that would in turn cover all or part of such secondary damages. A linear-time axis stretches from the past moment of loss to the future moment at which the claimed compensation is made, with the secondary damages gradually accruing along it. The intersections and the rate of motion along this time axis are suited to the exchange regime in terms of which the damage is assessed. The accrual, increase, and decrease of what is assessed are attributed to a uniform time axis controlling all exchangeable objects. In the ideal case of full compensation, when the cycle of exchange is complete, this time axis will be emptied of the particular damage that was granted compensation.

3.412 The temporality of damage is distinctly different from the temporality of loss. Loss is an opportunity to reorganize the temporality
of what-is-there and of he-who-has-an-interest-in-it, so that past
and future converge and are separated at one and the same time.
Represent-invent-ing what was lost means giving the past presence at present but also preserving in the past a grain of identity
from which the present is totally separate (2.101–2.103). While
the "intense presence of what (or who) was lost is the contracting
of the past into the present, and the extending of a present that
the interested subject fixes herself in" (2.112), "the presence of
the loss that becomes increasingly vague contracts the present
and extends the past" (2.113). In other words, when the loss is
forgotten, the time axis organized by this loss is not only emptied
of a certain object that formerly populated it; it is also totally
blurred to the point where it disappears itself. "The very act of
speaking of damage rather than loss creates a *différend*" (3.130)
due, as well, to the *différend* between the temporariness of the
loss and the temporariness of the damage.

3.42 Judgments of damage situate the damaged party as having an interest in an existing order of things and as having a claim to a
desired order of things. As stated (3.321–3.322), this is a dual
positing: recognition of the damaged party as a legal subject;
objectification of the damaged party as a subject. The frustration
often involved in compensation derives not only from the fact
that it is not complete (as, for instance, payment from an insurance company following a burglary when the victim is underin-
sured) but also from a sense that the damage doesn't do justice to
the loss, that it insufficiently approximates it, represses aspects of
it, leaves uncoded entire areas of disappearance that pose a problem for the subject. The regulative idea of successful assessment
of damages and of full compensation implies a complete objectification of the subject. In full compensation, the missing thing is
restored to its previous state. The damaged one receives full recognition as what he is, a legal subject and an owner of property or
its equivalents (a body, a position, and so on), but there is no thing
whose restoration can restore the subject as some one to his previous state. The regulative idea of full compensation is bound to
fail. This failure is a verification of the subject as a non-thing. The
subject complaining bitterly of the gap between compensation
(or damage) and loss verifies the impossibility of grounding what
he is on what he has and on what might have been the case, if it
weren't for the loss.

3.430 Judgments of damage not only situate the damaged party as having an interest and a claim; they also situate the person being sued as responsible for causing or preventing the damage or for providing compensation. If no one can be ascribed responsibility for causing the damage (the failure of its non-prevention, the act that didn't take place), or for compensating for the damage (the act that should properly take place), then the claim for compensation has no meaning.

3.431 In judgments of damage, at least four claims must be proved: that the damage was indeed caused; that the damage could have been prevented; that the fact that the damage was not prevented was unjustified; that there is someone responsible for causing the damage, or at least for compensating for damages of this type.[15] The party being sued will attempt to prove that no damage occurred; that the damage was unavoidable or could not have been reduced; that prevention of the damage was not his responsibility; that preventing the damage would have caused more serious damage and therefore the damage caused was justified and should not be compensated for; that there is no connection between responsibility for the damage and responsibility for compensating for the damage; and that the compensation is not his responsibility. In general, the party being sued attempts to sever his connection with the damage or with the compensation or both, or to sever the damage from the compensation; he tries to dismantle the semiotic tie between the two or, alternatively, to dissociate himself from this tie.

3.432 Justifying the damage through reference to more serious hypothetical damage that might have been caused if there hadn't been "a little" damage is an accepted way of dissociating the tie between damage and compensation. The justification shifts the discussion from one plane of exchange (in which there was a relation between the damage and the compensation) to another (in which there is a relation between "a little" damage and "serious" damage). It seems that every justification of damage can be expressed in terms of such a shift. The shift itself cannot be justified, except at the price of yet another shift, from the plane of the damage caused by the shift to the plane on which some other, more "serious" damage would have been caused. This infinite regress can only end with an unjustifiable decision to adhere to a certain exchange system (and the discourse within which the exchange relations are conducted), in terms of which the damage is described in relation to an assessment, "in the last analysis," of the entire economy of damages and the cost of their prevention.

3.433 One who is able and authorized to determine the discourse in which the damage will be described and in which compensation will be claimed in fact determines another ring in the aura of absolute loss — that loss which will never be compensated for — and draws its margins. Lyotard defines the state in which the damaged party and the party being sued agree on this discourse as a litigation or "arbitration" (*litige*) and the state in which such a discourse is forced on the damaged party as a "*différend*."[16] We have already encountered several configurations of *différend* that extend the reductive sense of Lyotard's definition (3.003, 3.130, 3.412).

3.434 In certain situations, someone is responsible for compensation without being responsible for the faulty act or injurious agent (the owner for the ox accustomed to gore, the parents for an obnoxious child, the state for the effects of drought). In certain social contexts, when certain political and economic arrangements hold, it suffices that there is someone to whom responsibility for compensation is ascribed for there to be grounds for a claim for compensation; there is no need to prove the responsibility of the sued party for causing the damage. Such are the arrangements allowing the compensation of people hurt by natural disasters, acts of terror, and so forth, regardless of the cause of the damage. Usually, such arrangements are intended to keep systems of exchange stable despite unstable conditions. Making compensation conditional on an ability to present a party directly responsible for causing the damage would exclude many damaged parties from the circles of exchange and destabilize the social systems of which they are part.

3.435 In some conditions, especially in the wake of disasters, wars, and economic crises, the state and other public authorities seek to restore the capacity of their damaged subjects to take part in a variety of exchange systems from which they have been excluded due to the severe damages they have suffered. The modern state — and this is one of its most important, quite recent, and quite neglected characteristics — has taken upon itself the responsibility of compensating its citizens for damages whose "authors" cannot be identified, located, or sued. Welfare systems, national agencies responsible for dealing with natural disasters, institutions such as compulsory car insurance, and the special assistance given to victims of terrorist attacks are all cases in point. Usually, such institutions are objects of political and social struggles; they pertain directly to the national or global economy of damages; and they are all deeply involved in the colonization of the lifeworld by state apparatuses and in the rapid advance of biopolitical mechanisms of power. The safety net the state grants its damaged citizens when they have no one to sue comes at a price: the ever-growing bureaucratization of daily life that makes citizens all the more administrable and governable.

3.440 When someone claims compensation for damage, he posits someone else as the party being sued, the debtor, thus making him someone who has an interest. The communication formula presented above (3.110) can now be reinscribed in terms of damage and compensation:

$$\text{damaged party (addresser)} \rightarrow \frac{\text{damage (signifier)}}{\text{compensation (signified)}} \rightarrow \frac{\text{the order of things (medium)}}{\text{possibilities of prevention (context)}} \rightarrow \text{sued party (addressee)}$$

3.441 Complete compensation for damage is, in principle, supposed to restore the condition of the damaged party to its former state and to cancel the damage. Complete compensation is commensurate with the damage. In principle, it is possible to provide complete compensation for every damage, because the damage is already coded in the terms of an exchange system, expressed in terms of what is reparable. Determining a damage caused to someone means determining what should be returned to him in order for his condition to be restored to its previous state and positing such restoration of the previous state as the object of the damage claim or at least as an expectation of the damaged party.

3.442 Usually, though, compensation is not a voluntary act in mutually accepted economic relations. The damaged party usually prefers not to suffer damages, and the sued party seeks to evade responsibility for causing the damage or for providing compensation. When compensation is received, it is usually lower in value than the full compensation that would cancel out the damage. This is because negotiation over compensation is costly, even if it does not involve expensive professional mediators. Also, the act of interpretation involves parties with different, sometimes conflicting, interests, usually at least four such parties: the damaged party; interested parties who stand to be damaged by the compensation; interested parties who stand to benefit by the compensation; parties who have an interest in the stability of the arrangements of compensation between damaged and damaging parties. Various interested parties have different perceptions of the compensation arrangements, and therefore the proper compensation is an object of struggle and extended negotiation.

3.443 The damaged party often loses such struggles. If the damaged party is also responsible for other damages and their compensation, he might finally gain from the gap between damage and compensation. This gap functions like the friction interfering with motion in a system of exchange relations. It can only be completely removed under ideal conditions, when negotiations take place between the damaged party and the compensating party with no mediators, under conditions of unimpaired communication where both sides attempt to reach an understanding and avoid manipulation, and which end swiftly, with both sides agreeing to the value of the damage and the size of the compensation that will cancel it.[17] This condition is analogous to the vacuum state in a physical system: a total absence of a mediating medium and of manipulating forces purporting to ensure the motion of the bodies with exchange values. In routine circumstances, such a vacuum cannot be created, and it is impossible to totally overcome the erosion caused by the mediating medium and the friction-generating forces.

3.444 Therefore, from the point of view of exchange relations, it is usually preferable to be in the position of the party responsible for compensation rather than that of the damaged party; it is better to cause damage than to suffer damage; and in general it is better to be prone to damaging than prone to suffering damage. ("Better" should be understood here merely in terms of the gains and losses measured in the relevant exchange systems.)

3.450 In every system of exchange relations, there are weaker partners, who are more susceptible to loss, and stronger partners, who are capable of tolerating damages more easily and possess various means (military, legal, economic, symbolic) whose regular and correct deployment is at risk of causing damage, not to speak of their deviant, faulty, or irresponsible deployment. Therefore, in a closed system of exchange relations in which loss is expressed as damage, the weak are not only more vulnerable to loss; they are also destined to become even weaker as a result of every such loss, while the relative power of the strong, who are prone to damaging, will only increase. In reality, of course, there are no closed systems of exchange, but some historical conditions approximate this state: a population living under occupation, for instance, or under totalitarian rule, and perhaps also a relatively isolated economy, preferably on a faraway island in a state of economic instability. The ongoing impoverishment of the weak (the subjects, the poor) and the growing power of the strong (the rulers, the

wealthiest capitalists) is the law in such systems. It doesn't necessarily occur as a result of meanness or evil intentions on the part
of those in power or those with wealth. It can result from the very
friction eroding the compensation of damages. In the circumstances of the global market at the end of the second millennium,
when capitalism has become the shared economic rationale of a
common, closed world market, the weakening of the weak and
the strengthening of the strong, but also the growing mutual dependence between them and the trickle of each into the other, are
geopolitical phenomena with a far-reaching historical significance
(see also 9.3).

3.451 The more unjust a system is, the more this friction is augmented
due to intentional acts performed by those in power. The more
just a system is, the more this friction will diminish due to intentional acts in the opposite direction. A just system is capable of
repairing itself and reducing erosion in the transition from damage to compensation. Because the erosion is a "natural" result of
the system's action, social justice will not be constituted without
"unnatural" intervention. No theory of social justice can be complete if it doesn't account for the perpetual need for repairing the
erosion and restoring what is lost in the exchange between damage and compensation.

3.452 Even if one considers only agreed-on damages, ignoring all the
disputes between damaged parties and sued parties, there is always, in every society, at every historical moment, more loss than
the damage can assess, and there are more damages than compensation. This is all the more so if one takes into account all the
damages being disputed within an accepted framework and all the
damages in a state of *différend*. There is always an eternally unexhausted remainder of damaged parties who have not yet been
compensated and of debtors who have not yet paid their debts.

3.5 *Translation*

3.50 As stated, damage belongs to the realm of facts. Like loss, it is the
object of statements of existence and probability and given to
truth games; in determining it, one can retreat to the usual tests
of fit used within a discourse, scientific, quasi-scientific, legal, and
so forth, for the examination of statements making truth claims.
In determining damage, one must, of course, do more than determine that there has been a loss. It must be ruled that the loss
caused someone depreciation in the terms of some exchange system (3.000). Very frequently, this determination is partial: for
instance, when it is determined that some one has suffered eco-

nomic damage due to the loss of property while ignoring the new opportunities that have opened up for him; or when it is determined that some one has received appropriate compensation for what he lost while ignoring the emotional damage involved. This partiality doesn't undermine the existential component of the damage claim. On the contrary, it validates this status as an existential statement that can be examined according to the conventional rules of a given discourse. The statement "Such and such an amount of damage has been caused here" is an existential sentence open to future refutation or reformulation that may change the assessment of the damage or the meaning of the statement determining it (compare 2.20 and note 14 there).

3.510 Damage is the object of assessments comparing what is there with what is not there, what was there and what could have been there (3.200). In any case, the comparison is between things and states, at least one of which no longer exists for the damaged party. In the case of car assessments, for instance, the comparison is between this particular car belonging to the damaged party after the accident and what it was before. The comparison is not made directly; it is mediated through the economic exchange value of the car in each condition. The car (or, more exactly, the parts of it that are no longer functional) is a signifier whose signified is a square in a table that is, in turn, a signifier whose signified is a sum of money (which in turn is a signifier, and so forth). However, the sum of money does not only act as an additional signifier; it also serves as an ultimate signified. This signified has priority over other signifieds not because it is "the final meaning" or because it is ascribed with an absolute, absent presence, but rather because of its almost infinite flexibility. Because the commodification of the lifeworld that characterizes the last phase of capitalism is so thorough, every thing can signify money, and money can signify (almost) any thing.

3.511 At the same time, it should be kept in mind that the relation between damage and compensation does not necessarily result from a capitalist economy, or from some other money-based economy (although such an economy of exchange gives this relation its own structure and patterns). Thus, for example, Sarah, who is infertile, perceives herself as causing damage to Abraham and therefore gives him her handmaid in order to compensate for this. When God compensates Job for all the damage he has caused him, he doubles his property but restores the same number of offspring he had before the devil's arrival. (To the offspring themselves, he restores nothing. True, Job asked for nothing and God is not a regular debtor, but the frame tale invites every reader to sue God in the name of Job and his sons.)

3.512 The table that establishes the car's value is a mechanism stabilizing the representation of damage. It acts like a translation machine. The activity of assessment is in principle unstable and hermeneutical, assisted by tables and assessors' indices, used like translation machines. And the same is true of the tables and indices of degrees of disability, of drought damages, natural disasters, or compensation (paid by the Israeli government) for the victims of terrorist acts. Professional assessment establishes the hermeneutics of loss on an elementary semiotics, with an infinity of signifiers on the one hand and a single, continuous, and clearly divisible signified on the other. Body parts, car parts, plots of land and fields, skills and abilities, future courses, investments and chances, each turns into the signifier of a sum of money or its equivalent. The index acts as a metaphor machine: it attaches to the organ, the piece, the bit, its universal economic metaphor, and allows the damaged party to somehow get through the hard times.

3.513 The translating machines are not automatons, and their action cannot be reduced to their inscribed algorithms. Parties with different interests will reach different results. Differently skilled people will obtain different levels of performance from them. When there is a dispute about an assessment of damages, the parties turn to the courts. The court neither installs the translating machines nor determines their translating programs. It acts as an institution of standards and measurements for translating machines and as a supervisor of the activity of those operating them.

3.514 The mechanisms for stabilizing the representation of damage form the basis for evaluating the compensation. Usually, when damages are assessed, the damage is but an additional signifier, and the compensation is the last signified in the chain. In the assessing business, the assessed damage is a signifier whose signified is immediately derived, in the very same table or index. At times, the damaged party knows only the sum of the compensation, from which he may surmise the damage. A damaged party who appeals the compensation determined for him reopens the chain of signification. In this semiotic and hermeneutical activity, the tables and algorithms are production machinery, but as in every semiotic activity their operation is allowed by the conventions determining their task and regulating their performance. Conventions and arrangements of this type are directly or indirectly based on law, regulated by the state, or retroactively authorized and sponsored by the state. Among the monopolies characteristic of the modern state (with regard to the use of violence, legislation, taxation, and so forth) is the monopoly of approval or disqualification of translation machines for the assessment of damages.

3.520 Economic discourse offers the most sophisticated and inclusive mechanisms of representation, mechanisms that, as stated (3.310), tend toward distinct imperialism: every thing is translatable into its exchange value, which can be expressed in (almost) any currency. However, exchange value is not the only stabilizing mechanism. In a society such as ours, there is at least one more kind of "stabilizing signifier" in assessing damages: the violation of rights. A sum of money serves to assess an object or an ability that was possessed, or could have been possessed, by some one; a violation of rights serves to assess kinds of things that some one can do in principle, using what he possesses, his hands, his mind, his language. The language of rights makes it possible to represent exposure to an entire realm of damages and to stabilize the representation of secondary damages.

3.521 A right that has been violated constitutes a principal type or category of damage. It designates a field of obstructed possibilities for action. It is almost impossible to assess all the damage caused by a violation of the right to free speech or of the right to freedom of movement or of the right to work for a living, because what is in question is not a chain of direct causal relations. At most, a comparison exists between the condition of a damaged party and the condition of someone similar whose rights have not been violated.

3.522 Generally, reference to the legal language of rights is a condition, and sometimes even a substitute, for reference to the exchange language of the market. Someone who is prevented from translating the damage caused him into the language of exchange can at least translate it into the language of rights. At times, he has to do so in order to claim compensation. In order to claim compensation from the state that has blown up his house, the terrorist's father has to prove that the state has unjustly violated his rights. When the state rejects his claim, it exposes him to an array of different damages due to the acts of another, committed without his knowledge and for which he was not responsible. Of course, the state has a well-ordered series of arguments justifying this injury, both the violation of the rights and the damage it entails. These are ad hoc and ad hominem arguments. They are disconnected from general principles according to which the state disseminates damage (through the mechanisms of punishment or suspension) and draw on unproved probabilities (that blowing up homes deters others from committing terrorist acts, that the revenge of innocent victims will not raise the level of violence even more, and so on). When these arguments are subjected to legal examination, they are hardly ever rejected by the Israeli court; on the contrary, by adopting them, the court provides a basis for inflicting additional injuries on people whose rights have been violated and for protecting the state from their claims for compensation.

3.523   A right is a mechanism that decreases prospective damages (by the state or by others) in a given realm, in advance, and enables claims for compensation when damages do occur. The denial, breach, or violation of rights creates an opening for approving damages distributed by the state and for blocking the access of damaged parties to positions from which they can claim compensation. A right is a mechanism that ensures damaged parties access to the position of plaintiff.

3.524   Different kinds of mechanisms for stabilizing the representation of damages have been adapted in different cultures at different times. The simplest mechanism (as regards the conception of representation) was "an eye for an eye." The damage is directly identified with the thing that has been lost; compensation is claimed in terms of the same lost thing. There is no substitution of loss with an equivalent, from the same order of things or from some other order. The exchange value of the damage is identical with its use value. In fact, the concept of damage is canceled: the loss signifies compensation that is claimed directly, without the mediation of damage as the meaning of the loss in some agreed-on currency system. However, the compensation that the lost thing signifies is that same thing itself as a thing of its kind. The claim for compensation conceives of the lost thing as a token, which it then turns into a type, while the expectation of compensation seeks to realize a type through a token.

3.530   Certain contracts, conventions, and economic and political arrangements dissociate responsibility for a failure or an omission from responsibility for compensation, recognizing in advance the responsibility of the authorities or the individual for compensation for damages not caused by them. Such social mechanisms render the translating machines more sophisticated and broaden the scope of their operation. He who is part of a system of exchange tacitly or explicitly understands that he may have to take the position of plaintiff or defendant in a damage claim, and he also recognizes the validity of the translating machines operating in the system in such cases. Some one who claims compensation and some one who is sued for compensation are, from the outset, partners in the translating game, whether willingly or not, and they enter into the scope of the machines' operation.

3.531 Every instance of a translating machine's operation makes someone a debtor. If "there is always an eternally unexhausted remainder of . . . debtors who have not yet paid their debts" (3.452), then this is a sign that the translating machines operate incessantly. They operate incessantly not only because new damages are created all the time and new compensations are being incessantly claimed, but also because the condition of previously damaged parties changes continuously, and because new possibilities occasionally open up for identifying the conditions of prevention and ascribing responsibility for compensation.

3.540 Translating machines operate on the basis of tacit or explicit assumptions about justice and injustice. Inappropriate compensation for damages is a case of injustice. Appropriate compensation for damages is a necessary condition for restoring justice. The discussion of compensating for a loss is at the basis of Aristotle's conception of restorative justice and of the entire tradition of political-legal thought ever since. In fact, already in Plato's work, the questioning of the idea of justice starts from the intuition that defines justice in terms of returning a borrowed object.[18] When the borrowed object is not returned to its owner and, from the latter's point of view, turns into a loss, an injustice occurs.

3.541 The definition of justice in terms of appropriate compensation for damages is an inversion of the justification of damage provided by a defendant in order to free himself from the obligation of compensation. This justification shifts the damage from one exchange system to another in order to avoid the price of restoring the balance of the first system; the definition of justice seeks balance within the same system and demands precisely that price. In the first case, the debtor attempts to replace the translating machine; in the second, he can only try to evade it. In any case, as long as he isn't freed from his debt, justice has not been restored.

3.542 The major theories of justice in the West, from Plato through Kant and up to Rawls, defined justice relative to a more or less institutionalized and definite discourse and exchange system, while assuming a known series of translating machines operating within these frameworks. However, the choice of discourse and exchange system could not be justified on the grounds of the concept of justice. The choice of system and translating machine determines what margin of loss will stay inexpressible, what margin of loss will be unassessable as damage, and what margin of damage will receive no compensation. By the same token, it distinguishes between owners of loss who can make claims for the damages caused by their loss and owners of loss for whom there is no assessment of loss, and between damaged parties who can sue for compensation and damaged parties who have no access to the translating machines (either because they are disenfranchised or because they lack the means).

3.543 The discourse in which loss is expressed, the exchange system in which damage is assessed, the translating machine that determines compensation, all draw the line between loss that is expressible and assessable as damage, due to which compensation can be claimed, and damage whose existence cannot be expressed, let alone proved. The institutional translating machines operate like black boxes. The function of the machine is to settle, postpone, or get rid of questions regarding what cannot be compensated for when lost, and all the more regarding losses that cannot be expressed. More generally, their function is to settle moral questions. The role of moral reflection is to reopen moral questions through dismantling translating machines. But who can afford to dismantle black boxes?

3.544 Lyotard: "A damage accompanied by the loss of the means to prove the damage is a wrong [*tort*]"; the victim of a wrong cannot prove that he has been damaged or that he has been wronged.[19]

PART TWO
What There Is

Second Curve

0.5 The line connecting disappearance, loss, and damage is a nonlinear curve. The further it progresses, the slower it climbs, and the phenomenological aspect is diluted. It becomes increasingly difficult to focus on the individual; institutional, cultural, and historical facets take up more and more space. This deceleration will be used to begin anew. Instead of moving along the curve to the next point, from damage to injustice, we will draw another curve, leaving another point of departure and reaching the same vicinity, if not the very same point. Instead of continuing along the line of disappearance-loss-damage, we will now draw the line of presence-excitation-suffering.

0.6 Suffering is greatly intensified excitation. Excitation is the intensification of presence. Presence is the way in which "being-there" exists for someone. That there is some thing there for some one, that there is some one who becomes aware of some thing that is there, is a simple relation, which it would be pointless to deconstruct, at least in the context of this discussion. The line will begin there: presence-excitation-suffering-injustice-wrong-Evil. These six concepts will, for the moment, be dissociated from their opposites: absence, indifference (apathy), pleasure, distributive justice, restorative justice, Good. A cumulative curve of sorts will be drawn through these six points.

0.70 Presence is a relation between some one and some thing. Excitation is the intensification of presence that occurs relative to the horizon of someone's expectations, which poses a problem for her. Suffering is intensified excitation that injures someone. Injustice is superfluous suffering, which may have been, or may still be, prevented or alleviated, but isn't. Wrong is suffering that is inexpressible (at least in a given dominant discourse) and/or whose existence cannot be proved. Injustice and wrong are cases

165

of suffering joined to an added something in one area, only to be declared cases of absence — lack of justice — in another area. Evil will be understood as the more or less orderly production and distribution of injustice or wrong.

0.71 Evil is an order of superfluous being and of a certain type of unexpressed being. Injustice and wrong intensify loss and suffering, each in its own focused, singular way. Evil is the ordered, systematic intensification of suffering and loss. It can be expressed as a growing repleteness of being-there that has gradually intensified, until the presence and the superfluity of the suffering, and the inability to express it, become increasingly complex and patterned, more and more ordered, to the point where they have taken up residence at the heart of the order of things (0.310). When suffering is joined by that something that makes it into injustice or wrong, it turns into something else, not twofold suffering, not suffering to the second degree, but injustice or wrong. The same applies to Evil: it is not worse injustice or wrong, but the ordered appearance of acts of injustice and wrongdoing.

0.720 On the face of it, there is a distinction here between an objective line (leading from disappearance to damage) and a subjective line (leading from presence to suffering). In both cases, though, the objective and the subjective are inextricably linked. The occurrence of loss is a way of constituting a subject, for it reveals that the lost object achieves its being as being-for-a-subject, and it reveals the subject as she who defines herself in relation to what she has, to what she might lose or has lost, and to what the thing she has lost was for her. A determination of damage is an opportunity to posit some one as a subject and a way of objectifying a subject who is measured in terms of her damages, some one whose losses can be evaluated. The same is true of suffering, which is apparently a subjective experience (like pleasure); suffering, it will soon emerge, is a way of turning the body into an object and also, at times, of presenting the soul as an object. Moreover, suffering is attributed to an objective cause (even if it resides "inside" the suffering subject) and has objective manifestations (perceived as interpersonal communication).

0.721 The first difference in this series is not between the subjective and the objective but between disappearance and presence. Presence is the opposite not of disappearance (the opposite of disappearance is appearance) but of absence. Neither is there any reproduction, here, of the difference between being and becoming, between permanence and flow, for what is present flows, if only to remain the same, to be what it is, whereas disappearance is not only a process and occurrence but a continuity-breaking leap from being to nothingness ("was once there and is no longer," "there was once a man and behold he is no more"). Accordingly, the difference between presence and disappearance is not an opposition, nor is it derived from an opposition. It is, rather, a more general, undifferentiated difference between two ways of being-there — more accurately, between two ways of temporalizing being.

0.73   In disappearance, a time gap is present because a certain being is absent; in presence, beings are present because a time gap is not. Furthermore, these moments are contained within each other. In disappearance, one is presented with traces, on whose presence attention is focused while other things are relegated to the background; in presence, the traces of what-is-already-gone and of what-has-not-yet-appeared disappear, or are at least relegated to the background. This disappearance, too, leaves traces, but they are shifted from foreground to background; there is no moment of pure presence. In disappearance, some one (she for whom what disappeared was what it was for her) concludes something about the absent being from the traces it (an absent being) has left in the present being; in presence, some one (for whom the presence is present) concludes the missing time from the traces that it (time) leaves in some beings through the disappearance and appearance of something else, something "secondary," making up part of the present being or of which this being is a part. The difference is the difference between image and background. In disappearance, the traces of what has disappeared are the image; in presence, the traces of what has disappeared and what has appeared (let alone the traces of the moment of [dis]appearance itself) are relegated to the background. They may blur and even disappear completely; the thing remains as is, exactly as it was. When the thing remains exactly as it was, in a world that remains exactly as it was, time stands still.

CHAPTER FOUR

Presence

4.0 *Wordless*

4.000 "Presence" is the simplest, most abstract term in the series. Being and nothingness are abstractions of presence and its negation, but they belong to another series. Hegel could have begun the science of logic with them, but not the phenomenology of the spirit. The fact that presence is described as a simple concept in the curve being drawn here does not mean that presence can be thought of as sameness without differences, without its opposite, absence, or without appearance and disappearance, consciousness and time. Presence cannot be taken for granted. It is not "objective," or given, but it always seems more certain, and sometimes also closer to the order of things. The things constituting "the order of things," or their characteristic signs, are present — or can be "summoned" to the surface and made present in the same space in which an order arranging things appears or is extricated. Presence is a way of being-there, a perpetuation of the being-there of some thing, a continual postponing of the transition of what is there back to nothingness, which conceals or suppresses the flow of time and already presupposes the temporalization of being by some one. I will call this someone a witness of presence, and, in short, a witness.

4.001 In perfect presence, both time and the witness for whom what is present is present disappears. This is the case with ideas in the thinking of Plato and Husserl; with the philosophical god according to Aristotle, Aquinas, and Maimonides; the substance according to Spinoza; and the thing-in-itself according to Kant. Perfect presence is a presence that has no need of witnesses, of someone for whom it is present. When the witness insists and attempts to witness the perfect presence, the latter annuls her subjectivity, integrates the witness into itself, erases the difference between them. Perfect presence is a substance in which the objective and the subjective moments converge, which is not for someone but

169

for itself, a complete, self-contained object whose perfection turns it into a perfect subject, as taught by Hegel. This perfect presence is situated (if it can be said to be situated at all) beyond time and language, and in fact beyond the possibility of thought and representation. Philosophy cannot think or express it without contradiction. If one is to identify the love of wisdom and the pursuit of truth with the desire for making the perfect being present, or for making present the contradiction embedded in the erotic drive to seek it,[1] then one must think the unthinkable and express the inexpressible.

4.002　But there is no need to identify the love of wisdom with the desire to make present the perfect being. Making present the perfect being is merely one possible attitude toward what-is-there, and it turns what-is-there into what-isn't-there for any witness other than that perfect being itself. The presence of what is there is always a presence for someone who is presented with this presence, someone who witnesses it (who is not necessarily an eyewitness).[2] Presence does not appear until the witness appears.

— But not just presence: nothing appears until the witness appears, for every appearance is a realization of the "for" relation; appearance, like disappearance, is always for someone.

— But neither does anything appear without something being already present. The appearance of some thing is always already a presence of some thing, even if it lasts for no more than an instant, even if what appears flashes by and something else appears and flashes by after it and there is no way of stabilizing the movement, arresting the duration. The duration itself comes into presence. When something appears for someone, there is always some thing that some one is presented with.

4.010　Presence is a relation, a relation between what-is-present and someone-who-is-presented with what-is-present. Therefore, presence, unlike existence, cannot be the predicate of an object without splitting the object itself or multiplying it into what is present and who is presented with it, or, that is, without attributing it to a witness.

4.011　Presence is never perfect, not even the presence of a perfect being. The fact that a present being is perfect will not turn its presence into a perfect presence, for presence is conditional on one-who-is-presented with it, even with regard to the presence of a perfect being, and in contrast to a perfect being the witness is always imperfect. Perfect presence can be only the presence of a perfect being to itself (if it has a self that can witness presence), and by definition such a presence is sealed to any witness who is not a perfect being in its own presence. Therefore, presence is an imperfect relation. And so the concealment of time in the presence of perfect being, too, is partial, always imperfect.

4.012 Since Nietzsche, various philosophers (Heidegger, Sartre, Lévinas, Derrida, Lyotard, and others) have spoken, each in his own way, of the irreparable absence of a complete, gap-free presence (God, Being, the signified), of the fact that what is there is riddled with cracks, differences, and gaps, that what is there is studded with traces of what is not there, what was there and is no longer, what is yet to come, or what has come but has yet to appear. In any case, the traces are present for brief or prolonged periods, while between the gaps some being persists, under the always-temporary auspices of which, and with relation to which, differences acquire their outline, their sense. Or vice versa: only under the auspices of those gaps and differences that are always already there/not there does the being that is "there" acquire the outline of its presence. This is what I would like to retain from the condition (which is not even a condition, because it cannot be *at present* as such) that Derrida describes, illustrates, and analyzes through his use of the term *différance*.[3]

4.020 The witness is present at some place where she is presented with (and at) what is present, what is present before her. Sometimes she is also presented with some thing of which she learns that it is this and not that.[4] She who is present is always present at some place where she is presented with something that is before (opposite) her.[5] She is thus presented (or may be presented) with the understanding that this or that is the way things are. Natural language is wiser (in this case, and in Hebrew more than in European languages) than the conceptual analysis that will now attempt to distinguish between the different presence relations. None of these relations on its own has an existence without the existence of the others, save the relation of being presented with knowledge, which may, but does not necessarily, accompany explicitly being presented with something. But even this relation is always there implicitly; it is only a matter of time and attention before some one presented with something present comes to know that there is something there, that this something is like this or that, and that she has now experienced it and come to know something about it.

4.021 When someone is presented with something at some place, someone else, real or imagined, is herself presented with her presence.

The spatial positing of the witness rules out the possibility of reducing she-who-is-present to the ideal point of a subject who never takes up space at any place. The witness is always there, at the place where she is presented with something.[6] Her presence there means that at any given moment she can be that thing with which the other witness is presented.[7]

4.022 *Heidegger rightly claims that being-there, merely existing among things and alongside them, among others and alongside them, precedes being presented with some thing or with some one from among all of these, some thing or some one with which one is presented when one posits it as present-before one, as an ob-ject.[8] Standing before some thing (or some one), positing it as what I am presented with, assumes some things (or some ones) that were already there, one of which was extricated and situated as a thing, as a single thing, as this and that thing, as such and such a thing, with which I am presented. Some of these things and ones will be things and ones that have occupied me, that I've been in contact with or even seen or heard, but without situating them as what or who is present for me, as what or whom I am presented with, and often without my ever being presented with knowledge of them, or without anyone's ever being presented with such knowledge. But what are all "these things," these and others, that have occupied me in one or another way without my being presented with them and without my positing them as present before me, all these things now re-presented in my writing and in your mind as you read my writing, through their verbal representations and their pictorial images, if they have never been presented, or present, to anyone? Either I can say nothing at all about them, save that there was something there beyond what I was presented with; or I can hypothesize that, generally, there were rocks, trees, cars, electrical appliances, children, adults, and suchlike things and ones there, of the kind that are usually present in such places and such conditions; or I can hypothesize more precisely that there was someone there, a specific person, who was holding this or that tool, wearing such and such, all based on the traces she left, which I am now presented with. In order to say something that makes sense about something or someone that was there, I need at least the presence of certain traces of what was there. True, as an ontological category, presence is not a beginning or a foundation, and it does not take precedence over other forms of the being of being-there (see 4.231). However, as a necessary category, it is always already there, when speaking, writing, and thinking begin, when some thing is said about something or someone (I'll return to this matter below: 4.100, 4.130, and note 19).*

4.030 Presence is always for someone who is presented with what is present. She who is presented with what is present is a witness who experiences presence. What is certain regarding presence is the experience of some thing and not the existence of the present thing in the world. In this sense, presence is always a virtual reality of sorts, a presence without the necessary existence of something in the world. In fact, presence as a form of being-there, a mode of existence of what is there, accompanies presence as an experience of being-there; in other words, the experience of presence is evidence of the existence of something, even if only of the experience itself (and certainly not of the I, as Descartes stated). Presence is the minimal level of some thing's being, not, however, in and of itself, but rather for someone. This is evident even in disappearance or appearance. In disappearance, the traces of the disappeared are present. In appearance, an environment is present in which what wasn't present before appears, and some thing that appears is present, the appearance of which "ruptures" the environment and damages the undisturbed experience of its presence.

4.031 Presence doesn't necessarily presuppose Cartesian relations between a bodiless thinking substance (which was later identified as the subject) and an extending substance (the object). What is present may be "inside" someone, not only "outside" her: a dream has presence, a fantasy has presence, as do pain and loss.[9] Each of these, when perceived as what it is — a dream, a fantasy, pain, loss, and so forth — is a way of presencing some thing possessed by some one and *for* that someone as something that can be hers alone.

4.032 Presence is an experience of the perpetuation of what is there for me. Hence presence is an experience joined by a determination of the existence of some thing. What that thing is, what I am presented with knowledge of when I'm presented with it, is a matter of language, discourse, point of view, and so forth. But the sensation that some thing is present, the sensation of the very being-there of some thing, here and now (the *il-y-a*, as Lévinas terms it, but in the light of day no less than in the dark of night), cannot be grounded on the expressions of presence or on its linguistic characterizations. The sensation, however, is not independent of these; it shifts along with them, and, like any other object, it requires a discourse expressing it in order to turn into some distinct thing.

4.033 A verbal description or a nonverbal representation of some thing may facilitate the thing's identification when it's "somewhere in the vicinity" and enhance the sense of its presence. But the opposite is equally true: a sensation of the presence of some thing with no verbal expression may motivate someone presented with it to find some way of expressing it, either in words or through other means of representation. There are moments, body touchings, sensations of views, the spread of a landscape, smells and memories of smells that will not find any means of expression and will slip by as a presence causing some affect. This affect is often etched in memory without words. This is especially true of the memories of smells (see 4.320). The fact that I use words in order to point out this presence, and even the fact that I attempt to express it in halting words that have no chance of producing an appropriate individuation of some thing ("that intoxicating sweetish smell"), cannot cancel out the fact that I have no fitting words to describe the presence and the excitation accompanying it, that language itself leaves me with a sensation of presence that overflows what it can express. Presence may remain without words to designate (or refer to) it, just as words' referents may remain without a presence that "completes" the act of referring.

4.040 When words replace an absent presence, the words, of course, have presence. Words, like all signifiers, take up space, differ from other signifiers in a space of differences, presuppose relations of figure and background, and bear the materiality of the medium within which they are borne. There is nothing remarkable about this. What is more difficult to understand is that these are precisely the characteristics of every presence: it takes up space, it differs from other presences in a space of differences, it presupposes a background on which it figures, and it bears the materiality of the medium within which it is borne. In other words, presence is an act of signification; what comes into presence is necessarily enmeshed in signifying relations, no matter how simple and elementary. Some one presented with a presence is put in the position of addressee; what-is-present is what signifies; the thing she comes to know when presented with what-is-present is the signified. What is there, this thing whose being-there is indicated by what-is-present, is posited as a referent, but at the same time it can also take the position of addresser: the one who (or the thing which) signifies, who/which sends the message.

4.041 However, if pain is present, too, or a memory, or a dream, what is the space of differences in which this presence occurs? What is the materiality of the signifier? Either we can get dragged into spatial metaphors of consciousness or the soul, as so many have done, from Plato through Kant up to Husserl, or we can reinterpret the reality of space and the materiality of the signifier.[10] The space in which signifying occurs precedes consciousness, precedes the distinction between consciousness and world and the distinction it entails between "inside" and "outside." More accurately, spatialization occurs along with signification itself; it is always already there when the act of reading signs takes place. Space is always already studded with differences that signify and signifiers that differ from each other; signification is always already spatialized. This spatialization precedes and enables the materiality of the signifier. Materiality is attributed to the signifier (see 4.100) on grounds of the sensation of its presence in a space of differences and identities, rather than the opposite.

4.042 And nevertheless, where is what was dreamed present? In the space of the dream; and later in the space of memory. And where is the space of memory? In the space of discourse or of the soul, or both. But are these questions more logical than the question: where is the space of phenomena? Or an intertextual space? Or the space of computerized communications networks? When this question is asked, space is represented as what takes a place within some other space, some thing that some one might be presented with; and what is present in a dream or in a memory loses its presence and even the traces of its presence and turns into the meaning or referent of a testimony. Different spaces are heteronomous with respect to each other. The homogeneity and the continuity of space are features of the space of physical phenomena, and this, too, only since the time of Bruno, Galileo, and Newton. We have no reason to assume that the space of physical phenomena contains all other spaces as discrete zones within it.

4.043 Understanding the semiotic aspect of every presence in this manner, and the spatial aspect of every signification, is the contribution of modern semiotics as well as post-structuralist theories of language and culture, first and foremost Derrida's deconstruction.[11] According to Derrida, language is spatialized, and everything there is, everything that appears or is present, is already en-tongued, in a way that entails a continuum between natural language and the "language" of things. I wish to distinguish between the general semiotic dimension of presence as such and the en-tonguing of what is present in this or that natural language. It will be a slippery distinction and require repeated, unsuccessful reformulation. But persistence is vital, not because something ought to be "rescued" from the imperialism of language — philosophical thinking has no obligation to rescue anything, just to describe what is there, to ask what might be there, and to contemplate what should properly (or ought to) be there — but because this imperialism betrays what is there.

4.050   Isn't "a sensation of presence that overflows what [language] can express" (4.033) a sensation of presence that has not been en-tongued? If so, doesn't this contradict the claim that "nothing exists for us as something that has not been en-tongued" (1.032)? No. It is impossible to say that something exists but has not been en-tongued without en-tonguing that something, at least as "some thing." It is possible to say that a sensation of presence that words cannot express is present for the witness, precisely because this sensation has been en-tongued — as it was in this sentence, for instance — but also as what was imprinted on your body as a quasi sentence when you heard a rustle or touched or smelled something. You distinguish the figure from the background, a signifier from a signified, before you've even made out exactly what the signifier is, and certainly before you've identified the signified (4.230). These sensations are already imprinted like statements with several vacant positions or instances: you are the addressee of a certain murmur, a scratch, something that shudders inside you, while the addresser, the referent, and the meaning of that murmur, scratch, or shudder are yet to be identified and interpreted. These sensations are statements, but not sentences in a natural language.[12]

4.051   When Derrida says that the text has no outside ("il n'y a pas de hors-texte"), he is saying something about the linguality of what is there, not about the unreality of what is not lingual.[13] In order to posit the text's boundaries and its outside, more statements are generated, and thus more text. The textuality of being is infinite because its finitude (any attempt to bring a text to an end, to declare its boundaries from the outside, to refer to its other — the world, the body, and so on) must be stated; that is, it is always already lingual. Gadamer says something quite similar about the linguality of being. Both continue Heidegger's concept of phenomenology that conflates the distinction between some thing's appearance and the Logos of this appearance, a gathering of what appears into speech. This should be understood not as a claim that everything that is-there is just words but as a claim that being has no "what," no characterization or expression that is not always already in language (and see 4.320).[14]

4.052   It is impossible to know, to express, to point at what is there without the mediation of language, but it is possible to know that something is there (without knowing what it is) without the mediation of words. Through feeling. That is the experience of presence. It is physical before it is verbal, while it is verbal, and after it has stopped being verbal. Words cannot encompass it; it cannot be grounded in words. But even when it is wordless, it is lingual (see 4.210–4.212).

4.1 Encountering[15]

4.100 What is sensed cannot be grounded in what is said, even if everything that is sensed is mediated through what is said and even if every sensation is en-tongued from the moment of its occurrence — and not every sensation is en-tongued from the moment of its occurrence.[16] Sometimes language precedes and guides a sensation, but sometimes it lags behind. At times, even presence lags behind sensation. Usually, sensation is an encounter with what is sensed that appears as present. Usually, a sensation signifies presence, but even this is not necessarily the case. For instance, at times one can feel discomfort in a sealed room due to the stale air or in the company of a nervous person whose conduct is disquieting. The discomfort steals up on one gradually, sporadically, and in an unfocused way; one can sense it for some time without its signifying the presence of what is discomforting. The encounter with what is present only occurs once the sensation has become stronger and focused. And then, when the sensation is focused and the encounter occurs, it is still possible to wonder for a while what precisely is present and causing one's discomfort. In such cases, en-tonguing is the slow process of raising into consciousness a sensation that splits the one-who-senses into a sensing subject and what-is-sensed, which becomes present, which turns into what-is-present as such and such (4.041). The non-en-tongued sensation can exist in such a consciousness only as a memory, a memory of something experienced without ever being present as what is being experienced and can no longer be experienced as such (for it has been en-tongued).

4.101 In cases where language lags behind sensation, what is sensed at the moment of encounter is not what is present, and what is present is not what has been en-tongued. When the encounter is reported, all this has already been en-tongued, of course. The gap between sensed and present has been erased, and what is present seems like what has already been gathered into the place allocated for it by the lingual signifier referring to it. Nevertheless, if language has indeed lagged behind sensation, en-tonguing occurred between the moment of encounter and the moment of reporting. Even if this process is very short, even if it can only be reported retrospectively (the report is its end), even if it only occurs on rare occasions, its very existence has a crucial meaning in understanding the relations between what is sensed and what is said. A memory of a wordless sensation will suffice to demonstrate the excess of what is sensed relative to what is present and the excess of what is present relative to what is said. Of course, this relation between sensation and presence and between the un-en-tongued excess of presence and the en-tongued presence results from reflection on experience, that is, from en-tonguing that gets increasingly entangled within itself like an old ball of yarn. But there is no reason not to try to capture in language the moment that has never been — and can never be — captured in language, to try to speak the unspoken, like trying to run a luminescent thread around the margins of a black hole.

4.102　A gaze encounters what is visible, listening encounters sound, an inner voice encounters an idea, a tongue encounters taste, a nose encounters smell, a cheek encounters tears, a body encounters another body, a body encounters itself, splits in two in pain, in thirst, in desire, hardens as an envelope out of which something seeks to erupt, or the body burdens something with its weight, or is compressed as flesh that something seeks to melt away so as to be swallowed into it. Every such encounter is the beginning of the experience of presence and the source of its incessant renewal, the secret of its duration. The experience isn't caused by the encounter; an experience of presence is an encounter that is incessantly renewed, like the world created by the Cartesian god. The experience goes on for as long as the encounter goes on, for the length of the meeting, until "the lines are cut," until disengagement occurs.[17]

4.110　What is present is not limited to the realm of sense data. A sentence uttered "in the mind," a poem reiterated by heart, a simile, fragments of a memory, an "inner voice," or a "stream of consciousness" all have presence of their own and their own ways of encountering whoever perceives and conceives them. And there is also the presence of hope, of longing, of desire, of anxiety. In Husserl's terms, it can be said that one can encounter not only the object of one's intention but also the intentionality itself, with which one is presented in a new act of consciousness that posits the previous act of consciousness as its object (see 5.000). Similarly, there is a presence of loss and suffering, of enjoyment and happiness, of horror and pleasure, sometimes even of pleasure at the presence of horror — as happens, for example, while watching a horror film or staring at the victims of a car crash.

4.111 Think of the tale Socrates tells in the *Republic*, in his discussion of desire, of "Leontius, the son of Agkaion, [who] was going up from the Piraeus under the outside of the North Wall, when he noticed corpses lying by the public executioner. He desired to look, but at the same time he was disgusted and made himself turn away; and for a while he struggled and covered his face. But finally, overpowered by the desire, he opened his eyes wide, ran toward the corpses and said: 'Look you damned wretches, take your fill of the fair sight.'"[18] Leontius encounters the dead bodies, which he spies from afar, then he encounters his desire to look at the bodies, then he encounters his aversion to this desire, and perhaps his weakness of will, too, and finally he encounters the horrific sight of the bodies at close quarters. The continuing presence of horror, of temptation, of a desire for expected pleasure at the sight, before the eyes have even encountered the bodies; and then the bodies present before the gaze until the desire is satiated.

4.112 How is what is present perceived when it is not perceived by the senses? Through consciousness. But consciousness is nothing but a name for a sense that is not perceived by the senses, that perceives what is perceived by the senses, including the traces of what was perceived that were left by the senses (memory) and including what is perceived as such and such a thing (a concept, an image). Consciousness is a non-sensual sense. "Is nothing but a name" hides a huge enigma, as old as philosophy itself. I'm not presuming to solve it, or even to discuss it. I will try to bypass it without damage, on the assumption that much of what is there can be described and understood without understanding the exact workings of that non-sensual sense that perceives and remembers what is there as such and such.

4.12 Presence goes on until the moment of disengagement. On the face of it, when disengagement occurs, something disappears, and something else appears. On the face of it, every severed contact is a new contact, a new presence — until death, or at least until one falls asleep, that is, for as long as some spark of consciousness is still awake. In fact, though, there are many states of being awake in the course of which no encounter is registered, or at least no encounter that leaves traces. For instance, when you play an instrument that requires simple and repetitious actions, the instrument is present-not-present, the gaze is suspended, attention is diverted, the mind is empty, and "you're not thinking anything."[19] The en-tonguing consciousness that suddenly pops up again (because it encounters something or is reminded of something, or just like that, for no particular reason) makes present the instrument and the series of mechanical actions performed on it. But even this may be exaggerated, for memory may remain empty; based on the consciousness of the act's mechanical continuity, both the presence of the instrument and the presence of the acting body are projected from the instrument and body currently present onto whoever is operating the instrument. Or, for instance, when one's face is pressed to the window of a moving car at night, the eyes are focused into the distance, into the thick darkness, and there is nothing. The self-consciousness that suddenly pops up will not discover anything that was present, the memory is empty, the screen of consciousness is empty, no movement was registered, and yet you know that you've been awake. Think of an open camera lens placed at the side of a road where cars are whizzing by: the moving cars inscribe stripes of light on the film; toward the edge, the stripe gradually dilutes, and there is a point at which it ends, or begins, a moment of encounter (or disengagement) between the light flowing from the headlights and the film; but beyond that point, too, in the area that remains completely black, the lens is open. Wakefulness is not identical with presence. One who is awake still needs to attain and take the position of the present witness. She needs to be alert. The difference between numb wakefulness and alertness is particularly prominent at moments of awakening, especially when waking up is difficult, or at moments of falling asleep, or in the course of a prolonged, enormous effort, like the end of a torturous boot-camp march. Lévinas, who writes of this with exceptional grace, also had in mind the effort of the workers in forced-labor camps.[20]

4.130 Appearance includes presence, the presence of something new that wasn't present before, but it also includes the traces of what was pushed aside when the new thing emerged and the presence of the novelty itself. It temporalizes being-there in a different way from presence, for presence blurs the present traces of something else that was there or of something that will predictably be there (or of the same thing that was or is present in some other way). Every appearance includes presence, and accordingly every appearance is an encounter, just as every encounter begins with an appearance. I encounter a pen lying on my desk, at my fingertips, that I hadn't noticed earlier; now it suddenly pops up before my eyes. I encounter her look; I suddenly perceive myself as someone who is looked at. I encounter an old poem; suddenly the familiar words appear and along with them a new stream of associations. Later the appearance ends, but encountering continues. I closely examine the decorated pen; her look touches me, caressing or wounding; the lines of the poem play out their rhythms. Later I'll pick up the pen, I'll turn my back to her, I'll put aside the book of poems; maybe I'll write a letter. All these presences will disappear. Others will replace and displace them without ever really taking their place, for place has an Aristotelian flavor in the experience of presence; it is defined by the object that occupies it — a presence in this case — and disappears when this object is gone.

4.131 What kind of encounter is it when an image floats into consciousness, when a phrase is suddenly thought as an idea, when a brilliant insight connects two objects of consciousness? An encounter is an occurrence split in two, the one encountering and the one encountered, the perceiver and the perceived. Every event is an occurrence that is split in two. When raindrops splash to earth, when a stray bullet hits a bird in flight, when rocks slide from a mountaintop and crash to the bottom of a ravine, and no one sees, and no one hears, and no one knows, the occurrence is one, undivided, a being-there without presence, for it has no one to be present(ed) to. All these encounters are enclosed within themselves, will never be known. Later the occurrence will become a meaning interpreted through its traces, traces that someone will be presented with during her mountain treks. "It has rained here," she will say, "the earth is wet." "This bird was shot down in flight; there are hunters around." "All the evidence indicates that these rocks just landed here in a landslide." These readings of signs will result from someone's encounter with the traces of something that happened there before — the occurrence. It's not the occurrence itself that's present but its traces. This is true of all the occurrences in my body and soul, if I have one, that are never split and whose traces alone I encounter: this headache, these palpitations, these memories, this contraction at the pit of my stomach.

4.132 When a consciousness, or maybe intentionality (in the phenomenological sense), or perhaps just a look, that is already equipped or not yet equipped with language cuts through the occurrence, an encounter is created, an event takes place, what is there multiplies into what is present and who is presented with what is present. The encounter is the event; presence is the trace of something that was there and the testimony to it. The occurrence is always something opaque, absent, already gone, or not yet come that is interpreted from what is present, that has no present without its being an object of speech.

4.133 An event is an experience of presence under an "objective" description, that is, an experience of presence described as an occurrence that happened to someone else. That someone else can be myself. The event is present in my memory, but what is present in my memory is the memory of the event, while the description of the event, including the experience of its presence, uses this memory along with other traces in order to describe "what was there." However, after I have described the event once, even to myself alone, the memory of the event and the memory of the event's description coalesce. It will never be possible to separate them again. Every attempt to separate them will require additional descriptions that will sink and settle, layer by layer, onto the first memory.[21] In other words, the first memory of the event has a very short life span, if any.

4.140 Loss is an event that can be remembered and described like any other. What holds for the first memory of every event holds equally for loss — and of course for the lost thing. But loss has a presence that does not depend on the memory of the event through which the disappearance occurred, and it exceeds the presence of the thing that was lost in the form of a lack. In the presence of loss, the presence of what is absent is accompanied by a memory of what is absent as something present and situated across that memory. The cutting character of this presence follows from the tension between the memory of what is absent and the presence of what is absent in memory, the tension between "was" and "is no more," and this is an event in its own right (2.113).

4.141 At times, nothing is left of the memory of the event, and only the presence of the loss remains. At times, the presence of the loss is erased, and what is left is just the memory of the events, of the disappearance and of the presence. At times the memory is reconstructed from the presence of the loss, and at times the presence of the loss is reconstructed from the memory of the event of loss. In any case, there is nothing "objective," and there is no "apodictic certainty" regarding what was lost that follows from the very presence of the loss (that is, regarding the identity of what was lost, but not regarding the mere fact that something was lost [2.213–2.214]). One reason for assessing the loss as damage is to stabilize a description of what was lost (3.301 and 3.512–3.514), or at least find a description of some equivalent. Frequently, an assessment of the loss takes into account only the event of loss and what was lost, not the continuing presence of the loss. When the authors of the Jewish Mishnah, in Tractate Baba Kamma, ruled that pain and shame were part of the reckoning of damage, they probably had in mind this presence as well.[22]

4.2 *The Experience of Presence*

4.200 The experience of encountering cannot be explained as a meeting between two bodies in space — someone encounters something — for the encounter as some one being presented with some thing includes the "internal" split of she who encounters and the "internal" space of her consciousness (or soul, or self), in which both the perceived things and the perceiving person hover. The experience of presence is a "wound" in being, for it posits some one who perceives in the face of some thing that is perceived,[23] without making it possible to ground the internal space of the presence in its external space (see 4.221).

4.201 The wound opened up by presence cannot be healed without relinquishing the position of the subject as some one, for it's impossible to think or sense or perceive without already thinking or sensing or perceiving this wound. This is the meaning of consciousness as nothingness in Sartre's terms. The wound can be healed for a moment or two, but always outside of time, in total abandonment or total surrender, in an ecstasy of love, carnal or spiritual-mystical love, or an ecstasy of action, and in any case in complete relinquishment of the subject position. However, if complete presence is not assumed as an ideal, if true love is not identified with achieving the full presence of the beloved who is there, there is no reason to sense this rupture as a wound and no point in trying to heal it. Death can be interpreted and understood, death can be held in awe and feared, death can be desired or tempting or enraging in many other ways.

4.210 The experience of presence is one way of temporalizing being-there. What is present is what persists over time. What is present is that in contrast to which the temporariness of what passes and perishes is measured. What is present differs from what is revealed and appears, in that within it the traces of what was there before it appeared gradually blur and fade. When some thing appears, its appearance bears traces of nothingness; it makes present what is no longer there and what is not yet there. When some thing disappears, its disappearance is sealed by something else, which is present as a trace of some thing that was and is no longer, a presence that makes the absent present. In this presence, nothingness persists and assumes the form of being-there, even if this presence is over in a flash.

4.211 What is present differs from what was there before its appearance through a difference of negation or absence. Determining what is present as present, its articulation in speech, its surrender to touch and gaze, assumes this emerging distinction from what isn't present by way of negation and absence. The sudden appearance of a teacher in class is one thing; the teacher's nagging presence, continuing until the sound of the bell, is another thing. At the moment of the teacher's appearance, the traces of the moment free from her presence in class are retained; they still possess a presence of their own. And the teacher's very presence is perceived against the background of the possibility — the wish or the apprehension — of her not being present in class. But in the middle of a particularly boring lesson, that possibility seems remote, possessing no traces in class. There is nothing in the teacher's continuing, tiresome, exhausting presence that indicates it. The teacher may be absent from class because she suddenly disappears, but disappearance itself, as a moment of transition from being to nothingness, is not a necessary part, or any part at all, of her presence. It's sufficient that a class with no teacher can be imagined.

4.212 The difference between what is present and what has appeared is different from the difference between what is present and what is absent (when the same thing is at issue). There is a difference between these two kinds of differences. Here is one way of expressing it: what has appeared and what is present are separated by a gap on a continuous time line; what is present and what is absent are separated by a gap on a discrete time line. When, for example, what is present causes the one presented with it happiness or pleasure, or when what is present is happiness or pleasure itself, the continuous temporalization is preferable. The one presented with the delighting presence wishes to intensify it, wishes to repeat the experience of its appearance over and over. Sometimes, when the pleasure has ended, she will longingly reconstruct the moment of its appearance. In contradistinction, when what is present causes the one presented with it sorrow, suffering, or damage, or when what is present is the sorrow, the suffering, or the damage itself, the discrete temporalization is preferable: the one presented with the troubling presence wishes to pass directly from presence to absence, to the moment of the presence's removal. The continuous process of disappearance merely postpones this moment. At times, when this passage is impossible, she will imagine the condition of absence so as to leap directly, though imaginatively, from presence to its negation.

4.220 The pictorial or auditory image, the fragments of speech retained in consciousness when a conversation has subsided, memories, thoughts, feelings, body, all "possess" presence. Someone has experienced their being-there and attributes it to herself. More accurately, she attributes it to herself in some way, without having to commit to this way as "hers," without the relation of possession explicitly positing some self that possesses this being-there and also without the self necessarily attaining a presence of its own (see 4.551). Her attributions may be mistaken, for presence has many possible and different modalities. There are presences that have spatiotemporal existence outside of someone's body (the teacher in class), others that have spatiotemporal existence inside her body (a toothache); there are presences regarding which body and soul cannot be dissociated (a visceral longing), and others that have no perceivable existence in any physical space (a murmur, conversation fragments, a dreamed image). In contrast, there is a presence of what is other than myself but mine, as an appropriated object, and there is a presence of what is mine but other than me, when my body appears to me like a foreign object, or like my son, my flesh and blood.

4.221 Attributing presence to a defined physical space-time is a famous source of error in judgments of existence. Philosophers dedicated much effort to determining these presences or some of them and finding the fit between them and things in the world. The presence of an image in consciousness is perceived as a re-presence, a re-presentation, of something present in the world. The philosophical error lay not in the attribution of certainty to the sensation of presence but in the attempt to turn this presence into a source of certain knowledge about the existence of what is present "outside," in the space of the nonself (Descartes, Locke, Berkeley); or in the attempt to create a typology of experiences of presence that would withstand all errors like the experience of presence itself (Husserl). The root of this error lies not only in the groundless projection from "inside" (consciousness) "outward" (onto the world) but also in the failure to understand that presence is always already spatialized, in the misconception that the distinction between inside and outside precedes presence, which is conditional on it (however, this distinction itself cannot be perceived without presence) (4.041). Presence is the encounter of some one who is always already split by it in a space of some kind into the one who encounters and what is encountered; before possessing any other meaning, and as a necessary condition for such meaning, this split is spatial; the interior of the person encountering and the exterior of what is encountered are just one possible sense of the split space.

4.230 At the time of the encounter, the subject cannot err as to the very experience of presence. Erring means being the addressee of a phrase expressing what is not present or not existent as what is present. It is only possible to err as to the issue of what is present, while the fact that something is present is above doubt, for even if there is "nothing there," the experience of presence itself is present. This doesn't entail that "I experience (and think about what I experience), therefore I am." It only entails that something is there. I encounter something (or experience the presence of something), therefore some thing is present.

4.231 The experience of presence is not "primary," "simple," or "unmediated" — all these are belated effects of a very particular philosophical idiom (see 5.013). However, it always implies a phrase of the type "there is something there," or "something is present there," which cannot be denied or removed, even if it isn't explicit. The experience of presence is prior to language at least in this sense: when being-there is attributed to some thing, and not just to words alone, this presupposes that the something in question, or at least what represents it, its traces, its remains and signs, was present for someone; someone witnessed it.

4.232 The experience of presence is the thing that "is given expression," not the expression that is given, not the statement, which may be in error. Like disappearance, the experience of presence is not a "simple" element preceding consciousness or language and underpinning it. It is reinterpreted in every reflection, and no reflection (linguistic or visual) can express it "in and of itself." What is present cannot be determined according to the experience of presence. But at the moment of encounter, presence is accompanied by certainty (and the moment of encounter is accompanied by the presence of certainty). Some thing is present. Every encounter is experienced as the presence of some thing, an experience of some thing present. There is no presence without an experience of presence, and there is no experience without the presence of some thing.

4.233 Critical reflection might deconstruct this certainty, whether by deconstructing the thingness of the very (some)thing that is present or through questioning its perpetual persistence as a presence. But no reflection will remove the experience of presence itself, the encounter as an occurrence split in two, without which the reflection would have no object, without which it would remain an empty intention.

4.3 *Being an Addressee*

4.300 When some thing is present, some one is in the presence of this presence. Presence implies some one who is present as an addressee of some thing present. Being an addressee of presence means filling the "for" role that allows something to be present. Someone wakes up in the morning and he is the addressee of an unmade bed, an aching back, and a bursting bladder, of daylight streaming too sharply through the shutter slats, of the toothbrush he picks up off the bathroom shelf in a mechanical motion, of a small boy who suddenly leaps at him with a playful shriek, because the child wakes up easily and the world has already been his stage for quite some time now. The waking man has not yet taken a subject position in the sense defined above (1.321 on), though he may take it at any moment: when he urges his son to end his game and get dressed and ready to leave for kindergarten. But meanwhile speech is difficult for him; his eyes are glazed, still half-shut; the presence of things is a matter of habit for him; no presence necessitates a deviation from his routine of near-automatic actions. The man who gets up in the morning this way is a prisoner of the order of things and of his daily agenda; he is activated by the things present in front of him more than he acts upon them.

4.301 The man who has just described the man getting up in the morning didn't take a subject position either. He was a prisoner of the magic of language, of the logic of writing, activated by thoughts that have already been typed into the computer. He would occasionally stare at the screen, momentarily absorbed in an ill-fitting word, replacing it with another, and would return to reading what was written, simultaneously concentrating and absent-minded, adding a comma here and there, correcting the text almost mechanically to meet stylistic conventions, not hearing the murmurs of the busy day filtering into his workroom, and all the while not feeling his body, or feeling it in an unfocused way that doesn't rise to the point of encountering some thing present. The text wasn't present before him either. Perhaps there was some vague idea from which he tried to extricate a coherent sentence, and maybe even that wasn't present. If he were asked, if he were requested to describe the experience of presence at the time of writing, he would en-tongue the traces of the sensations provided by his memory, but he would report all these presences in the past tense — as occurs in this just-written text, exactly. But from time to time, while writing the text and especially while rereading and re-editing it, when the man reads what's written from a certain distance, tries to pinpoint the rhythm, the serpentine description,

reconstructs traces of other texts here and there, his and others',
anticipates this or that reader — at these moments, the text is present; at these moments, his subject position as the future author
of this text is taken.

4.302 Suddenly a child bursts into the room and forces upon the writing
man a new presence and a lot of attention. The text's presence
drains off all at once, although the text remains present, but now
precisely as what cannot be encountered. The position of author
is abandoned, and the writing man is dragged against his will into
a parent position. Certain encounters force themselves upon one
and require the abandonment of one subject position and its replacement with another. When subject positions are exchanged,
one encounters new things.

4.303 Being presented with some thing that is present, being the addressee of presence, means temporalizing what is there thanks to
continuing presence and making time present thanks to the perpetual persistence of being-there, and in short identifying, even if
vaguely, the presence side by side, in the same space, of being and
nothingness, of some thing and what it is not, causing things to
persistently perpetuate their appearance, disconnected, for a flash
or forever, from the moment of their appearance and the moment
of their annihilation, belonging, wrapped in reality, for a flash or
forever, to the order of things of their kind (that a subject of
knowledge will later call "the order of things"). For such a presence, someone of the type of the awakening man will suffice, his
consciousness unfocused, his body aching, his motions prepro-
grammed. That which guides his actions — habit, daily routine,
roles that are taken for granted — still has no presence for him,
while the present things still don't — or already don't — guide his
actions. Action in an environment of things and the presence of
the environment of things are connected in a loose relation whose
character shifts from one context to another, in keeping with the
prevailing practices and the circumstances of each situation.

4.304 The experience of something's presence will not suffice in order
to take a subject position. And vice versa: one need not already be
a subject in order to be a witness. For someone to be a witness, it
is sufficient for her to be involved in an encounter through which
the occurrence is split in two. But in order to give testimony, she
usually needs to have already taken a subject position. Usually, and
not in principle, because witness can be borne coincidentally, in
an unstructured manner, and without the synthesis of gaze, expression, and touch taking place within a system of rules and related
sanctions and assuming the ideal meeting point between she who

speaks, gazes at, and touches (1.305). Not every addressee and not everyone bearing witness are subjects; but everyone who takes a subject position takes the position of addressee and takes the witness stand in the discourse that constituted her as a subject.

4.305   A subject is an addressee of presence in a more or less structured order of things and field of relations. The man who gets up in the morning and is presented with his son who has just awakened collects himself with a yawn and stretches, sweeps away the remnants of a dream, if there are any, makes an effort to focus attention on something, and slowly gains full wakefulness (4.12). This man is an addressee of presence who gradually takes the position of subject. The presence of which he is an addressee commands or invites him or signals to him or allows him to do something relatively well defined in a relatively delineated field of possible actions. The field is relatively delineated and the action is relatively well defined not in logical terms, of course, but in sociological terms. The social rationale of existence alongside, and with, others in a given context is what signals the possibilities, and this is what makes it possible to posit some one in the position of the addressee of a presence pregnant with such possibilities.

4.310   A presence devoid of anything save being a witness and some thing with which the witness is presented is a deprived phrase, a degenerate statement. She who is presented with and at the presence is an addressee, some thing's presence is the addresser; the meaning and the reference await "clearing," await the moment when the witness will herself take the position of addresser, will designate what is present, will name its name, will tell herself or others what it is that is present. Such a presence is a phrase in which the addresser, the referent, and the meaning contract and aspire to unite, for what is present eludes the position of the referent; the fact of its presence alone takes the addresser's position.[24] What is present is present as some thing that conveys something, but initially it just conveys that something is there, and only later that such and such a thing is there. In its initial, liminal moment, presence comes closest to the state of "there is" (*il y a, yeshno*).

4.311   In any case, when what is present "conveys" that some thing is there, it also "conveys" that what is there differs from what is present. Nothing is present precisely as it is "in and of itself," because what is there doesn't include the relation of "being for" the witness. The witness knows that what she is presented with is what is there, but not exactly. When her attention is diverted, she doesn't know even this; what is present contracts into what is accessible for touching, precisely the "Zuhandenheit" described by Heidegger. However, the minimal degree of attention to what is present returns and splits presence into what is present and what is really there. If attention is guided by interest, if what is present appears as a problem, then she who is present interprets what is there according to what is present. What is "really" or "precisely" there, that which provides an answer to the question "what is this?," is the meaning and referent of what is present: what the presence "wants to convey" is that such and such a thing (or occurrence, or process) is there; the being-there of this thing is presence's meaning; that same thing is what the presence refers to, is the referent of what is present. What is present is not just a signifier; what is "really" there is the signified. At the moment of presence, the signified includes both the meaning and the referent. Husserl, Sartre, and other phenomenologists understood this relation and the doubling up of presence in the witness's presence (consciousness, for them) created by this relation, but they failed to understand its fundamental linguality, and therefore remained stuck in what Heidegger and Derrida call "a metaphysics of presence."

4.312 In every event, some one (at least one) is posited as "an addressee of presence." Who posits her? Is what is present already "out there" as what is present, therefore serving to situate the person present in the position of addressee, or perhaps the person present situates herself in the position of addressee and is only then presented with what is present? When the point of departure is presence, the most complicated task is understanding what makes a subject position possible, because subjectivity is a transcendence of what is present. When the point of departure is the subject, the most complicated task is understanding what constructs presence as an event, for presence transcends (or at least indicates what transcends) the experience made possible by a subject position. Classical empiricists exemplify the first problem; Kant exemplifies the second. It is necessary to progress in both directions at one and the same time.

4.313 As long as the witness occupies the position of an addressee who is presented with some thing but does not know what that thing is precisely, what is present is what occupies the addresser's instance. The addressee may then identify what is present as such and such, as something whose whatness, or whose name at least, can be attached to some lead; at this moment, she is either taking the addresser's instance, telling — her self or others — what is there, or taking the addressee's position in another statement, in which some one tells her what's there.[25]

4.314 In whatever version, reflection arrives too late. When reflection arrives, someone is already in the addressee's position, being presented with what is already present. In reflection, everything is always "already." True, the reflective statement attempting to reconstruct the moment of presence can focus on the addressee's instance or on what is present or on what has occupied the addresser's instance. But if the reflective statement can return to anything, if it can replicate, look back at, or mirror anything, it falls back on an event of presence in which someone already takes the addressee's position, presented with some thing posited before her, and the reflective act must include her as well.

4.320 Presence is the embryonic lingual dimension of being. Or perhaps, more precisely, presence is the event in which what is there is christened into language, en-tongued. When what is there is present, it is lingual before someone even has the words to say what there is. It is lingual because of the relation between addresser and addressee that exists in presence and due to the split of presence into what is present, on the one hand, and what there is, on the other. The text has no outside (as Derrida has said), not because all there is are words and not because nature is written in a language that only God, or a mathematician, can understand, but because what is there is always perceived in relation to, and through, what is present. If something is there, then either it is present itself or its traces are present or it has no presence. If it is present itself, then it already posits someone in an addressee's position and conveys something to someone; if it has no presence, then it cannot be pointed at, shown, or experienced in any other way save being spoken or written of, that is, exist as the signified of some text; if only its traces are present, the traces (which are text themselves) signify what isn't present. In other words, what isn't present is the signified of traces of presence, and it either can in principle appear and come into presence itself (and therefore be part of a text, too) or cannot appear, in principle, and can therefore only be represented as the signified of some text.

4.321 When presence is the presence of a statement, the event becomes more complicated. Several levels can be distinguished in the presence of a statement, the moment of enunciation, which is an event of signification and meaning creation: the statement itself is present, even if briefly, as an event, as a collection of sounds or signs that appeared and "took up a place" in time and space. This presence may be accompanied by the presence of the statement's referent (or its traces) — though this is a possibility, not a necessary condition — or by the presence of its addresser (or its/her traces), or both. The latter differs from the former, for the referent may disappear without a trace, while in the case of a disappeared addresser the statement itself is its last trace. But this doesn't mean that the addresser is a source preceding the statement. As mentioned, when a statement is present, some one or some thing, present or intimated, real or hypothetical, is already posited in the addresser's instance. When a statement comes into presence, when the event of enunciation takes place, the addresser's position is placed alongside the statement's other position. A statement can be present without the presence of someone or something definite in the addresser's position; an addresser can't be present without being part of the presence of a statement. Of course, it's always possible to say of someone that she was the addresser of a past statement, but then the issue is someone who was the addresser of one statement who has been posited as the referent of another.

4.322   The statement's presence is the lingual event. The lingual event can exist without the presence of the referent (only a phenomenon can be a present referent), the addresser, or the addressee, and it always exists without the presence of the meaning, meaning being what is absent in principle from the lingual event. Naturally, other combinations are possible — for instance, a statement in which the addresser is also the witness of the referent. Although this is most often the case in everyday communication, the fit between talking about and showing is no light matter. A baby learns it gradually when it learns to understand the act of pointing, and later to point as well. Someone who trains to become a doctor, an engineer, a scientist, or an art critic learns it through a prolonged, more or less structured process of practicing gaze-guided communication and communicative guided gazing. A variety of social institutions (the laboratory, the clinic, the museum, certain television programs) train people to talk about what they see and look at or show what they are talking about.[26]

4.323   The addresser isn't necessarily a witness to the lingual event in which she's posited as an addresser. The addresser may speak about something absentmindedly, may concentrate on what she's talking about or on whom she's talking to and miss the presence of the lingual event itself. This is the usual situation. Usually, a statement is made present after the fact while suspending the presence of its referent or addresser and turning the statement itself into the referent of a new statement. But as mentioned, situations of double or even triple presence are possible, of the statement along with its referent and the statement's addressee or addresser. The simultaneous presence of the statement and its object is no different, in principle, from the simultaneous presence of body and sound, of written letters and a pen, and, more generally, of two material bodies. Right now, here, I'm writing you something on what is present here before me; at one and the same time I am presented with myself writing, with the thing on which I am writing, and with the act of writing itself. Were you to appear here suddenly, you would surely divert my attention. This double and triple presence demands high levels of attention and awareness. But if you appeared here suddenly, I might be capable of encountering you and my speech to you simultaneously. These are relatively rare events of communication. They engender linguistic phenomena such as irony, double entendre, and *ars poetica*.

4.324   In the process of reading, someone takes the position of addressee and reconstructs from the text the presences ensconced in the lingual event, all of them or some of them. In certain situations, this reconstruction is supposed to lead me back to one of the statement's "original" positions, to the thing under discussion, the person speaking, the person listening. This is how a police investigation is conducted, for instance. In another manner, paying attention to other aspects of the lingual event, this is how one learns to operate a piece of equipment using verbal instructions. In some situations, this reconstruction is, by definition, partial. This is the case when one tries to reconstruct the author's position from a corpus of literary texts. The reconstruction is partial because the author's position is preconceived and determines the relevant corpus.

4.325   As stated, what is never present in the lingual event is meaning, and therefore it will never be possible to reconstruct it completely. Generally, one who is called on to reconstruct meaning cannot adequately reconstruct the presence of the referent (and hence cannot be shown what "it" means) or that of the addresser (and hence cannot ask what she means). Meaning can be understood as a replacement for the presence of the addresser ("the speaker's intention") or of the referent, which can never appear as it is, in and of itself. The act of interpreting performed by every "professional commentary" in various types of interpretive discourse views meaning as a supplement to the missing presence, of the addresser or of the referent, and attempts to fill in what is missing through more and more signifiers that serve as meaning substitutes. Reconstructing meaning is either an open-ended, and hence infinite, project or a project abruptly interrupted due to external constraints. In truth, interpretation is an endless game that should never come to a halt.[27]

4.330 A lingual event is a particular case of representation. Someone is called on to be the witness of a presentation (of this computer screen, for example), which she is supposed to treat as a representation of something other than what is present (this screen, or this computer, for example). Acting as a representation, presence always makes absence present, too. What is represented may not be present at all, either at this given moment or ever (like the idea represented by the text on the screen), or it is not present to the same degree of immediacy as the representative (the computer with all its black boxes, and the surface of its screen), and in order for an addressee to be presented with it, to witness it, an act of interpretation, or deciphering, is required. Think about an exhibit, a play, a film, but also about a parade, a stage set, an interior and exterior design, and also about gestures of nonverbal communication, about dress codes and fashions, and so forth. Think as well of a scientist observing phenomena. Empirical scientific discourse (history, archaeology, and anthropology included), but also a discourse such as natural theology, multiplies what is present (everything that appears in the discourse's space of appearance) when it posits an observing subject in the face of phenomena that signify objects and processes.[28] Throughout the history of metaphysics, from Plato to Nietzsche, the phenomenon was presented as an entity whose reality had undergone devaluation; it is a presence perceived as less real than the absent thing it signifies. But clearly, not every presence is perceived as less real than the thing it signifies. Is pain, whose presence is so often undeniable, more certain than the presence of the cogito, less real than what (or who) has caused it (what or who, or at least the existence of which, is signified by the pain) or than she who suffers it?

4.331 When phenomena acquire a semiotic status, it is always possible to situate an implied addresser alongside — or behind — the hidden signified. If phenomena indicate an order, a regularity, or a logic controlling them (if they signify or represent it), perhaps that same order, that regularity, indicates a source that created them as they are (or constituted or situated them). If so, phenomena can be interpreted as a message from someone; they can be viewed as the presence of his traces, the testimony to his absent presence. A continuous line runs from archaeology, which interprets material forms as evidence of the intentions of human beings in the distant past, to natural theology, which interprets

natural phenomena as evidence of the very existence and attributes of God and also of his deeds in the world and the meaning
of his creation. In both cases, the addresser cannot testify himself,
that is, turn from a passive into an active witness. Every interpretation that attempts to explain the author's intention (and also to
provide an explanation in terms of this intention) is situated on
the selfsame continuum or at least is placed there after the author
dies. But even when the addresser is called on after the fact to testify to the event in which the witness was present as an addressee,
his testimony does not fall within the framework of the same
event; it is a separate event. It joins the memory of the event
without necessarily possessing a privileged status.

4.332 Sometimes I am posited as the addressee of a lingual event in
order to validate the presence to which the addresser testifies
(when she describes some thing for me, from memory or in "real
time," from a distance of time or space); sometimes just the
opposite occurs: I am posited as the addressee of an event in order
to validate the addresser as one who bears witness, to validate her
position as one who was present at the event. When the witness
takes a subject position, she is authorized to bear witness, but
additional witnesses are necessary in order to validate the presence to which she testifies ("at the mouth of two witnesses . . .
shall the matter be established," in law as in science). When the
witness isn't authorized to testify because she can't or isn't authorized to take the relevant subject position, she seeks witnesses
who will testify that she indeed saw, heard, didn't make it all up.
Sometimes no one is there, and she calls heaven and earth to witness, in vain.

4.333 "I swear in the name of God," says one to whose testimony God
alone can bear witness. This is how it sometimes is with regard to
what happened in her vicinity when she was alone; this is how it
always is with regard to what happens in her personal thoughts
and feelings. On such matters, she alone is authorized to testify;
she is the only person authorized to take the subject position.
Whether or not she is a subject authorized to testify, no one can
be present in her stead in what she is presented with: this pain
driving her insane, this longing, this desire, this anxiety, that
sweet memory. In such cases, what is present cannot be called on
to testify to the testimony or to the witness, and it is impossible
to rule out the possibility that false witness is being borne. Every
report of pain, suffering, and pleasure falls within this category.
On the one hand (that of the witness), absolute certainty of an
inescapable conviction, and on the other (that of her fellow

witness), a nagging, irremovable doubt (see 4.410, 4.422, 5.141, 6.024).

4.340 In certain events, presence is greatly reduced, and with it the scope of testimony. Someone is some one's or some thing's addressee, that's all. Something is simply there, something whose presence for the witness is its entire being-there, something that is present and that's all; sometimes this is also the whole beauty of it, or the whole pleasure of it, or the horrible pain of it all.

4.341 Think of the presence of a smell. Is it necessary to experience the smell (to encounter it) as some thing that represents some other thing? The smell may, but doesn't necessarily, evoke a series of associations, remind one of colors, places, people, be experienced as an excitation; and when it evokes associations, this doesn't mean that it represents or signifies these, that these colors or places are its referents or even its meaning. Think of the presence of pain or of some unremarkable object, an object that I know is there before I say its name, before it occurs to me how to use it. Aren't there presences in which the call of presence to the one who is present to interpret it (that is, to treat it as a representation) is blurred, repressed, or altogether erased? Think, for instance, of a piece of music when its listener "forgets herself," of a presence of sounds that is powerfully experienced; at such times, presence doesn't represent anything or anyone, at least not necessarily or immediately. Think of the presence of body to body in the course of the act of love. Courting is a game of signs, every presence is a sign for desired possibilities. Transition from courting to the act of making love is a (more or less) gradual erasure of the representing presences and an ingathering of those bodies encountering each other and interlacing into each other toward the moment that is entirely presence with no absence. I, who at such moments am more and more one with my body, do not stop being the addressee of your body, and if the presence of these bodies for each other carries some "implied message," it is none other than this: "Above all not to disengage now."

4.342 When suddenly, in the middle of the act of love, representing presences appear — the phone rings, a sleeping child cries out — the act of love is interfered with or suspended. The representation can ruin everything. But the play of representations and the suspension of erasing the representations may also intensify the bodies' presence for each other. Encountering the gaze of the beloved in the middle of the act of love restores the presences' semiotic dimension. They exist for someone else, too, they are something for someone, and this something is not what the presence is for me. Encountering a gaze is different from drowning in the eyes of one's beloved, which makes present this gaze of hers and is supposed to return the gaze to the body, to neutralize the source of the power that multiplies the presences. The other's gaze, says Sartre, "steals" away my situation; in the act of love, it forces me, first of all, to "return into a situation," that is, to return to a situation in which all presences, according to Sartre, have a semiotic dimension, because for me they are always organized as meanings.[29]

4.343 But there are also cases of the opposite: someone is longing, begging, for there to be another who will force her to return to a situation, even if he later steals it away, in which there is a bisecting gaze that multiplies presences and posits some relation between what is there and what isn't — yet there is no such other. This can be a state of terrible despair, paralyzing pain, depressing loneliness. The act of love in the non-representing presence of the other's body and an individual's despair at her loneliness in the absence of the gaze of an other promising stability in representation — each touches the borderline of the subject position at a different end, touches the limits of the very possibility of a subject position.

4.4 *Some Others*

4.40 The man who rises early (4.300) has not yet had time to remember who he is at all. Others "forget themselves" again and again in the course of the day, either more or less, either for better or for worse. In any case, a gap emerges between just being some one and being a subject. I'm referring to a real gap, not one that is totally given to the caprice of the one who would rather fake being just someone than be the specific someone she is supposed to be in this or that subject position. Someone can be absent-minded during a conversation at the office, during a lesson in class, beside a machine at the factory. This is the way she perceives her subject position for the moment. But at some moments, someone can simply evade, refrain from taking, any subject position at all; after work, for instance, before going home to husband and children, as she walks slowly along the tree-lined street, with an empty stomach and an aching head, her spirits are lifted by the play of light and shade along the street, and people sitting on a bench don't catch her attention (all these are presences without representation — there is hunger, there is a headache, there are pools of light and shade, someone is sitting on the bench; I, a subject of discourse, call them by name, but she, absentminded and tired, experiences them as some thing that is there) — until someone straightens her out.

4.410 When some one takes the position of addressee, she can stand alone in the face of what is present, even if it is the whole of Being. Usually, in the unremarkable presence of mundane things, being an addressee of presence means being coincidentally put in some position that anyone else could have taken. The greater the gap between the unremarkableness of the presence ("anyone else could have") and the singularity of the testimony ("but there's no other person who can"), the deeper the sense of loneliness. There is another kind of loneliness, too: when one who takes the addressee position experiences presence as if she alone were presented with what is present, she alone were there, she alone can be there, as if something were present for her alone. This is the loneliness of one who feels a sense of calling, of destiny, who feels she has a mission. But it may also be the loneliness of one who suffers, the sole addressee of an unbearable, incessant pain, of an enormous sorrow for an irreparable loss.

4.411 The loneliness of a mission, of a calling in the face of a revelation of some thing that is only present for someone — for the prophet, for the wise seer, for the blind man who gazes into the distance — is already within a field of discourse that situates the individual addressee in his illustrious loneliness in contrast to other addressees, his disciples or rivals, and in contrast to those who fail to see and cannot understand or fully know, and all these addressees already take subject positions in certain discourses and are accustomed to well-defined cultural practices. But one who suffers and remains an individual addressee of her suffering doesn't necessarily take a subject position, and her loneliness is not necessarily a form of distinction in a field of discourse or a product of cultural practices. Sometimes it cannot even become an object for others, in others' discourse.

4.412 Sometimes these two types of presence and loneliness seem to intersect: the Passion of the Savior, the suffering of the prophet. A description of this suffering is of course a familiar cultural topos attributed to a well-constituted subject position, but this does not rule out the possibility that Jesus was truly lonely in his suffering, and not just when he took the position of savior.

4.420 When someone takes a subject position, she is already placed, as stated, in "a more or less disciplined field of practices" that constructs her possibilities of speaking, gazing, and touching, and this, always, in cooperation, competition, and struggle with other subjects seeking to temporalize being and to make both being and time present, in their own way, in a manner that doesn't fully conform with her experience of presence (1.330). The subject position cannot be created *ex nihilo*, just like that. It is already there, in a more or less defined relation to a system of signs, instruments, observable objects, and others who take their own subject positions. One can take it or be situated in it or be cast into it, one can transgress it, redesign it (that is, reformulate the relations between it and other positions, texts, objects and so on), one can leap from it into another subject position, or one can evade it and be just no one in particular — but one cannot invent it on one's own without being already posited in some other subject position, already incorporated in a complicated web of relations spun around it.

4.421 In that "more or less disciplined field of practices," others are present as potential subjects, and other subjects are present as "potential usurpers of presence." When I acknowledge an other as a witness, I acknowledge her as a partner and a rival, one who potentially dictates and usurps presences.[30] An other as witness "provides" me with presences and also expropriates them from me. Alienation from an other may consist of a feeling that she will never be able to share my experience of presence, to be presented with what I am presented with. Sometimes it is the other way around, when I wish to hold exclusive access to a given presence and am afraid she might usurp what I am presented with. And, of course, I may switch position with the other, envy her exclusive access to a certain experience of presence, strive to get a share of, or mimic, that experience, to reinvent it for myself or even reinvent myself as capable of experiencing that same presence.

4.422 Existentialism, which strove to distinguish authenticity from an average, general everydayness, the singular from the common, created a clear difference and hierarchy between these two possibilities while of course preferring the first: the uniqueness of presence as what I alone am responsible for, the "for" that my consciousness inserts into being so that what is present is "for me" alone. However, the unique and the authentic are social and cultural constructs, no less than the unremarkable, average, general everydayness, and the latter may be a place of loneliness that only I alone can experience (4.333). In the presence of an other, who is always a supplier of presences and a potential usurper of presence, what counts is not the uniqueness of the event of encountering in which I alone am involved, but rather the difference, which may be removed momentarily but never once and for all, between what is present for me and what is present for an other. With regard to presence, all efforts at understanding, striving for agreement, for the mutual adjustment of points of view, including the unified education, taming, and discipline of individuals purported to take exactly the same subject positions, are doomed to fail. The difference will reappear. Being a witness of some thing in the presence of another witness means being presented with presence and testimony as unfailingly caught within a fabric of differences.

4.43 Only within such a fabric of differences can presence be determined as a fact. Or perhaps vice versa: determining presence as a fact means determining it within such a fabric of differences. Determining presence as a fact means signaling a possible bond and association between witnesses, and sometimes also the limits of this bond.

4.5 *Testimony*

4.500 Presence belongs to the sphere of facts. What establishes it there are statements of presence — which are distinct from presence as a statement. A fact is the meaning of an existential statement whose reference is a state of affairs; in this case, the state of affairs is presence as an event. The articulation of presence in discourse determines both the event and what is present as objects of speech, description, interpretation, and analysis, and also as part of a more general event or an environment in which presence occurs. As such, presence is an object of dispute and what is at stake in different kinds of "truth games" played in different fields of discourse.

4.501 Within modern scientific discourse, in its various forms, and within the many other types of discourse dependent on it, the things present are perceived as phenomena (4.330–4.331). Speaking about what is present as a phenomenon opens up a difference between the presence of an appearance, on the one hand, and what appears and is actually there, on the other: not everything that is there is present as a phenomenon; not everything that is present as a phenomenon is actually there. But what is present testifies in one or another way to what is actually there. Phenomena are semiotic presences, presences testifying to, signifying, indicating, disclosing what is actually there.

4.502 Every phenomenon is the presence of some appearance, and in every such presence there is a difference between appearance and reality. But not every presence is a phenomenon; not every presence is a sign of something different from it and more real than it.

4.503 What "is actually there," in truth, is supposed to be something that is present regardless of whether someone is presented with, and present at, its presence. The certainty of something's existence is manifested in the assumption that the same thing is present without its presence being accompanied by an experience of presence. The reliable witness who describes an event succeeds in creating an impression that what is in question is an occurrence, something that "was (actually) there" independent of the particular witness's presence or of the presences of witnesses in general. In giving reliable testimony, the witness becomes "transparent." Roland Barthes says there is a moment of such reliable testimony in every photograph.[31] Susan Sontag writes that this reliable testimony pertains only to the presence of the witness itself.[32] In an era of remote-controlled cameras, computerized simulations, and digital photography, it must be said that the sole reliable testimony pertains only to the presence of the picture-producing machine itself. The picture testifies to the photographic act; the act of photographing is situated in the object position, what is testified to. All the other things to which the photograph may testify are products of an interpretation that presupposes a photographic act embedded in well-defined practices, as well as in the discourse of which photography is a part.

4.504 In every case of testimony, testifying to a presence means testifying to the presence of the witness. The witness testifies to herself and to the presence of the thing she witnessed. A testimony to testimony (to being a witness, to the presence of the one testifying) must accompany every testimony to the presence of some thing. The photograph that testifies to the photographic act first and foremost testifies to itself as a photograph, and therefore to itself as capable of testifying. So it is with every signifier. But the witness presented with a photograph is not a signifier. In the first phase, she is an addresser of the photograph or of something that confronts her from within the photograph. In the second phase, she posits the photograph as a signifier that testifies to something else; at this point, she is the addressee relative to the photographer, to the editor who printed the photograph, or to whoever sent it to her; in the next phase, she occupies the position of addresser, points at the photograph, which becomes the referent, and interprets its meaning for someone else, explicates what the photograph testifies to. (Naturally, these phases can occur simultaneously.) The witness dubs the photograph; she gives testimony in its stead. She dubs the photograph until it turns into a reliable witness. When doing so, she gives testimony about the photograph, and in turn makes her interpretive intervention transparent. Every time someone turns from a witness to some thing who is presented with that thing, into a testifier to the presence of some thing and to some thing that is present, a process of "making transparent" takes place, relegating to oblivion the conditions of testimony that delimit and enable every testimony.

4.505 Is it possible to think of the moment of witnessing itself (the moment of some thing's presence) as a presence that does not depend on a witness? Is it possible to shortcut through the infinite regression of reflection (witnessing the act and event of witnessing) and arrive at a privileged moment of the pure presence of witnessing that becomes an anchor of certainty? This is what the Cartesian cogito and Husserl's transcendental ego should have been. But only a God who witnesses all occurrences, and who witnesses them all at once, all the time, can have his witnessing be a presence without a witness. A presence without a witness demands a witness without presence.

4.510 If an "encounter is the beginning of the experience of presence and the source of its incessant renewal" (4.102), this is because the encounter turns the one who encounters into a witness who is presented with what is present; it activates a cognitive mechanism that splits the occurrence in two (4.131). As she who is presented with what is present, the witness is simultaneously situated outside the occurrence (that she witnesses) and inside it (for it is within it that she encounters what is present). By virtue of the encounter, there is a material symbolic contiguity, a continuum of real objects, between the witness and the presence she encounters, even if what is present is just "an idea," a concept, or an image. There is no witness who isn't engaged, at least in the sense that she is involved in an encounter. And God included: transcendental as he may be relative to the world, he again and again encounters the horrifying sights, the cries of catastrophe, the elegies and the keening, the prayers. A God who is transcendental to such a point that he encounters nothing at all is not a witness either; enclosed within himself, he is totally foreign to, and alienated from, what occurs in the world. These are the wholly indifferent gods of Lucretius (who took no part in the act of creation either).[33] A transcendental god who is interested in the world and is presented with what occurs in it — regardless of whether he has merely conceded to contract himself in order to create the world, or of whether no human language can describe his attributes — cannot be completely disengaged from the world he is witnessing. Transcendence and testimony are a contradiction in terms.

Spinoza and Hegel avoided this problem by giving up transcendence, making their witnessing deity entirely immanent, identical with the totality of being. Lévinas moved in the opposite direction, separating the wholly transcendent from the moment of testimony, of being the addressee of a call whose source is always lacking.

4.511 The scientist's "objective" point of view is a manner of engagement. Since at least the seventeenth century, the scientist has been a witness seeking to encounter what is present in order to move — in the most reliable and direct way possible — from what is present to the thing revealed or appearing through this presence, and without encountering anything else that might dim the thing's appearance out of what is present. We have already distinguished (4.501–4.502) between what is present as a phenomenon, as the appearance (or disappearance) of something other than itself, and what appears, that something, not sufficiently defined yet, which leaves traces in the field of presence and which the scientist seeks to know as such and such. The scientist is a witness who seeks to reduce to the lowest possible degree her engagement in anything that does not pertain to the thing whose appearance she wishes to predict, describe, and explain, in order that she may be totally engaged in the encounter through which that thing will appear. In order to do this, she tries to control to the utmost the field of presence through which this thing she wishes to know will appear. This control reaches its climax with the institutionalization of the scientific experiment. Until the revolution caused by quantum theory, this ideal of presence consisted of the following idea: the scientist's engagement is responsible for the very appearance of the thing under defined conditions of experimentation and observation, but not for what appears. A series of appearances is extracted from nature, using more or less violent means of manipulation that never affect the nature of that which appears.

4.512 Experiments in quantum mechanics or opinion polls, on the one hand, and astronomical observations, on the other, are situated at the two ends of a continuum of conventional images of knowledge with regard to the nature of the witness's engagement with what appears: from clear responsibility both for its very appearance and for what it is that appears, to clear responsibility, at least on the face of it, only for its very appearance as such and such under defined conditions of observation. How can the interviewer totally erase the traces of his engagement from the responses of interviewees? How can an astronomer force a planet to be discovered? Or influence the nature of its presence through a telescope?

4.513 In contrast to this dichotomized image, many studies of the history of science teach us that the distance between the two poles is not as great as it would seem, and that the astronomer intervenes in the creation of the presence she observes whereas the pollster is not free to manipulate his data as he pleases. They demonstrate that the polarity between the disengaged astronomer and the intervening interviewer exists, if at all, only with relation to the ability to intervene in what appears (interviewees' opinions; the structure of the material composing a star) through manipulation of the presence (interviewees' verbal responses; blots on the screen of observatory equipment) through which something appears as such and such. With regard to the presence itself, the differences are less clear. The astronomer prepares herself for an encounter no less than the physicist and the sociologist and seeks to control it no less than they do. All seek equally to minimize their engagement with what does not pertain to the thing whose appearance they wish to watch, so as to be totally engaged in the encounter through which that thing will appear.

4.514 Even the standing by of a witness to a crime, an accident, or some other horrifying occurrence is a form of engagement. The bystander seeks to minimize the area of her encounter or to disengage herself completely. But she apparently derives some special pleasure or benefit from her presence as a bystander who does not disengage. The bystander is similar to the scientist who arrives at a laboratory that has been prepared in advance, where she will not have to make any effort, and where what interests her is not control of the conditions of the experiment, that is, the manner of encountering, but rather her ability to remain on the sidelines, in a witness's position, without having to change her manner of involvement in the encounter. It is worth noting here that the horrifying, like the beautiful or the delightful, has a presence of its own — as does pleasure, that is, pleasure in general and the pleasure of being a witness in particular. But the presence of this pleasure is already a presence that multiplies itself, as will be discussed separately (see 5.000 and 5.010).

4.515 Standing by is a form of presence, a way of taking the witness position, characterized by a special kind of encounter. It falls more or less in the middle of a continuum (or at the apex of a parabola) running from total disengagement from what appears to the witness's active intervention in the event she is witnessing. At each end — that is, either total disengagement or deep intervention — the witness encounters other things, and the presence of what is present fades away. When the witness disengages, she is free to become a witness to other things; when she intervenes, she may succumb to the action, reduce the area of her encountering, and swiftly forget everything she has witnessed. Severing contact with what is present, on the one hand, and immersing in intensive action, on the other, reduce the witness's areas of encounter.

4.520 The witness enlarges her area of encounter with what is present when she succumbs to the position of being-an-addressee. She attunes her reception, enhances her attention, sharpens her senses, and disengages from anything that is not already in her field of presence and from any action that may interfere with her concentration. She waits for what will come, closely following every change in what is present, every signal coming out of the field of presence. A child's fascinated observation of an ant drawing a tiny line in the sand; the tense attentiveness to nighttime murmurings of a soldier lying in ambush; Cézanne's turning himself into a continuously open camera lens in front of Mount Sainte-Victoire and observing it for many hours inactively;[34] the mystic's disciplined emptying of self of everything present; philosophical reflection (*teoria*, contemplation) in its classic sense — each of these is a kind of standing by. One who stands by and succumbs to presence turns herself into an eye, an ear, a smelling nose, a caressed body, an empty consciousness. Speech that bursts in suddenly, that makes present what is taken for granted, clogs the pores of attention and again reduces the area of encounter, frightens away what might have been at the threshold, what might have appeared, what might have come into presence.

4.521 Succumbing to an encounter with what is present is similar, in principle, for each of the above-mentioned types of bystanders. This similarity exists beyond the differences between the various senses focusing attention on the encounter, and beyond the differences between the different states of encounter. These are not where the fundamental differences between them lie, not even the ways of entering the position of "being-a-witness." The differences lie, rather, in the exit from this position. Upon entering it, the soldier who learns to listen to the nighttime murmurings, the artist who learns to watch the movements of color and of shades of light, and the monk who learns to surf on the waves of his thought engage in a somewhat common practice. In all these cases, the witnesses seek to return to the state of the fascinated child, who effortlessly "forgets the entire world," while honing and attuning their means of discernment more and more. At the exit point, however, there is nothing common to the soldier in attack, the artist returning to the canvas, and the monk descending from the mountain and entering the crowd. Each of them, in a different way, bursts the bubble of "succumbing to presence" in which he has been enveloped. The particular way in which one does this — in which one steals into or attacks other presences, whether daily and unremarkably or holily, but which anyone else could have witnessed — is what defines each type of standing by.

4.530   A bystander witness who has dismissed everything calling her to disengage or to intervene still faces two types of temptations in her encounter, originating in the presence itself: to disengage from the presence of something repulsive; to touch what is attractive, to draw near or approach it, to embrace it, to act upon it, to appropriate it, to hold out a hand to it, to save it. Temptation achieves its broadest sense here (one that includes a threat) — a seemingly sourceless call that nevertheless emanates from what is present, that exceeds the presence itself, that threatens the stability and the impunity of the witness's position as bystander. Though the call seemingly emanates from what is present, it has no source; it cannot be attributed to the "intention" of what is present or of one who has intensified its presence. In temptation, the tempter loses its status as some one, she or he who tempts, and contracts into the opacity of an object, of some thing; in order to tempt, the tempter needs to intensify its presence and blur its intentions, to be present as some thing whose presence overflows. "Seduction is a distracting presence, inviting and unattainable, that contains nothing but what is present . . . but nonetheless cannot be determined as that thing that has appeared and is present" (2.142),[35] for what is present includes the presence of excess beyond itself, to which it is indifferent.[36] "In seduction . . . the gap between signifier and signified is erased for the benefit of the play of signifiers or traces that suddenly acquire, within the signifying act itself, an unexpected reality, which takes over the entire field of presence" but threatens to destroy it from within (2.142). If the witness responds to temptation, if she is tempted, if she flees or pursues, she gives up her bystander's position and might lose the presence of the tempter together with the presence of temptation (see also 5.210 on).

4.531 Contrary to desire, in which some one oversteps the limits of self toward some thing, in temptation some thing oversteps its limits toward some one.[37] Temptation is the intensification of presence that exceeds itself, but in total disinterest. In other words, the tempting excess is not an aspiration of the exceeding presence to be something other than it is; it is an overflow of intensifying presence, the presence of a thing that seemingly seeks to become, or persists in becoming, more and more of what it is but with no authored intention. "Seeks" or "persists" is a projection of the one who is tempted; the tempter is indifferent to the overflow of its presence. This combination of overflow and indifference in what is present creates the attraction or revulsion of the one who is tempted. In contrast to the dynamic of desire, the replete presence of the tempter, not its absence, creates the characteristic dynamic of temptation.

4.532 But the excess in temptation exists only so long as the one presented with it remains a bystander. As long as the temptation persists, the subject projects her tendency to transcend herself onto it, on the one hand, and assumes an object-like attitude, on the other. The subject is not responsible for the presence exceeding its own limits, with which she is presented; she is only responsible for her response to this presence. When she is no longer that someone whom the tempting thing objectifies, when she stops surrendering to the temptation and seeks to act, so as to flee or pursue, to escape or attain, the tempter will revert to being an object receding into itself, and the tempted witness will revert to being one who longs, fears, or desires, exceeding the limits of her own self.

4.533 Flight due to overriding fear or revulsion, pouncing due to flooding desire, are common ways of leaving the bystander's position, of annihilating the temptation, of exterminating the tempter or conquering it, overcoming it by canceling the distance from it, or putting up a defense by increasing the distance from it, and in any case erasing the repleteness of presence overflowing what is present. When the witness confronts what is frightening or detestable and doesn't flee for her life, when she stands her ground facing what is desirable, the presence grows and becomes a temptation, but it grows and gushes out of what is tempting, with the indifference of boiling milk or of a flooding river, not emanating from within the one presented with it. Fear, revulsion, desire, and all the excitations arousing one to action may pour into the sense of temptation when the one presented with what arouses them collects herself into the position of bystander. And as demonstrated by the story of Leontius (4.111), even contradictory excitations can gather into temptation. (And by the way, the bodies that tempted Leontius to look at them are the embodiment of indifference in an object, the replete presence of death.)

4.540 When the presence oversteps the limits of self in temptation, the position of the bystander witness splits in two: the witness who is presented with what is present, the observer that is at most an addressee of sights, sounds, ideas; and the witness who is presented with what overflows from this presence itself, who becomes the addressee of a sourceless call. The temptation continues for as long as the witness remains a split addressee (or the addressee a split witness, either way) and refrains from abandoning any of her positions, turning from an addressee into an active agent, or from an addressee into an addresser, from a witness who is presented into one who gives testimony (see also 5.211).

4.541 Temptation is a call to act, to do a deed. The act — disengaging or intervening, fleeing or possessing — eliminates the temptation. Temptation contains a call to eliminate itself, to cause a change in what is tempting or in its environment, until it tempts no longer, at least not this witness. But this call is implied in the structure of the state of temptation, not in any content conveyed by what is tempting. The tempting presence calls the tempted one to do a deed, but what deed it is that should be done — this the tempter will never say. If the tempter says anything at all, if she expresses an intention or signifies a direction of action, she does so as some one who seeks or commands, who begs or suggests, but not as some thing that tempts. No meaning can follow from the temptation, only the force of attraction or revulsion, the force created with the overflow of presence beyond itself and existing only for as long as she who is attracted or repelled stays rooted to her place, in the position of the bystander witness, while there is no one to contain the overflowing presence.

4.542 Temptation creates a kind of categorical imperative — a call to action devoid of content whose form alone is known in advance, a call to action that is not conditional on anything beyond the tempting presence itself. The absoluteness of the tempting call is founded on presence as an end in itself, that is, on the total indifference of the presence to anything outside it. But this categorical imperative is an inversion of the Kantian one: instead of commanding respect for the end in itself — that is, respect for the overflowing indifferent presence — the command seeks to annihilate it. This inversion should be no surprise: Kant speaks of the repleteness of the subject's presence; I have been speaking (after Baudrillard) of the repleteness of the object's presence.

4.543 In this sense, the presence of the suffering of someone in distress is a perfect temptation. The presence of the suffering creates a temptation-command that derives not from the intention of the suffering one, or from her explicit cry for help, or from what she asks or demands (negotiations can be conducted regarding what she asks; it is a matter of discretion, always conditional on many other considerations), but from the distress itself. The distress has an overflowing presence that diverts the witness's attention. The overflow of presence may also be manifested in the words of the one in distress, but not necessarily so, or in the act of her cry for help, but not necessarily in its content. Distress itself has a tempting presence. Distress that is present before me is a temptation seeking to eliminate itself: to respond and help or to draw a curtain and disengage. The clearer the cry emanating from the distress, the more obvious the presence of the horror, the greater the temptation to depart from the bystander's position. Usually by drawing the curtain — it's easier. But there's no need to draw an actual curtain; annihilating the call will do, eliminating the tempting presence's excessive transcendence of its limits. The television can air the horrors of the whole world every evening without there being any temptation in the mediated presence of the horror. What is required is an evasion of the addressee position, annihilating it if possible; then one can remain in the viewer position, standing by all night, all one's life.

4.544 There are other possibilities, of course: it's possible to abandon the addressee position in order to act directly, so as to calm the call, to offer relief from the distress and the suffering in which it originated. It's possible to abandon the addressee position in order to bear witness and sometimes even to return and take the addressee position again, and then return and bear witness again, and so forth: a practice of testimony that is a way to move others to action and part of the act of offering help.

4.550 Temptation is a type of excitation. Someone for whom something is present perceives herself as a presence without anyone's being presented with her and positing her, for the encounter itself possesses presence that has intensified. Temptation intensifies presence and multiplies it; the tempted one is also present herself as the one enchanted by the temptation. A presence that has intensified to the point of doubling itself while positing the one presented with it as present to herself is an excitation.

4.551 In every presence, some one is presented with some thing but not necessarily present for some one. The fact that the witness is presented with some thing doesn't necessarily uncover her presence for some other, does not cause it to be experienced by someone. In order for the one being presented with some thing to become present for someone, someone else must experience her as some thing present. And so it is with regard to the other that someone else must bear witness to, and so forth: infinite regress, as it were. For everyone for whom something is present, there must be someone else who perceives her in her presence as some thing. In order for someone for whom something is present to perceive herself as present, to perceive the encounter as between two presences, to perceive the other who encounters — that is, herself — as someone who has presence, the presence of what-is-present-for-her needs to intensify and become an excitation.

CHAPTER FIVE

Excitation

5.0 *Intensifying Presence*

5.000 An excitation is the intensification of a presence that makes present the experience of the presence itself for one who is presented with some thing.[1] What is present can be perceived as present "inside" the witness or "outside" him, as "internal" or "external" to the witness, either possessed or not possessed by him, on the sole condition that the encounter constituting the event of presence be experienced as having a presence of its own.

5.001 An excitation is an event in which the presence of some thing acts upon one-who-is-present such that the encounter with that thing is shifted from background to foreground, becomes the image; the transfer of the event of encountering to the foreground takes place at the expense of the-thing-that-is-present, which is relegated to the background. The exciting thing has a "winning presence"; however, it's not the thing that wins over the one presented with it but rather its very presence, the encounter with it. "It is constitutive of emotion that it attributes to the object something that infinitely transcends it," Sartre writes in his *Sketch for a Theory of the Emotions*; this overflow of presence "evoke[s] the appearance of the same world," an imagined world, analogous to the world of dreams or insanity, with its special syntheses and its fixated relations.[2] What Sartre ignores, however, is that in this intensified world the event of encounter itself makes itself present, blurring the identity of the exciting element to the point where there is no knowing exactly what it is that excites — perhaps because for Sartre emotion differs from excitation. For emotion, what-is-present remains the focus of attention as a necessary addition to the affective intention, which takes on various shades of attraction or revulsion. For excitation, the presence of the encounter overshadows the presence of what is encountered — whether greatly or slightly — as well as the intentional character of the encounter itself.

5.002 Most theories of emotion perceive emotions as intentions toward an object arousing attraction or revulsion (and sometimes both) and classify the various shades of attraction to and revulsion at the object. Chapter 6 of *Leviathan* is a distinct example of such a taxonomy. In it, Hobbes collects all the emotions of attraction under the category "appetite" and all the emotions of revulsion under the category "aversion."[3] All the classical philosophical psychologists and moral philosophers from Spinoza through Mill follow suit, more or less. Someone with an appetite for something seeks to touch, to open up to, to swallow, to control, to appropriate, to know, to have; someone with an aversion seeks to distance himself from something or something from himself, to close himself to, to avoid encountering, to annihilate. Even Nietzsche preserves this perception in his distinction between two opposing orientations of the "basic will of the spirit."[4] Hegel developed a concept of desire that unifies these oppositions and is a fundamental template of all dialectical movement: emotion is a desire that has not been satisfied. When a desire is satisfied, the desired object is appropriated and destroyed at one and the same time; it becomes "mine" and is therefore preserved, loses its otherness and is therefore nullified. Emotion is the manner in which a subject has intentions toward an object arousing desire or revulsion, a "small beginning of Motion," as Hobbes put it, toward the object or away from it, and in fact there is no real difference among emotion, will, and act.[5] Emotion is the will to appropriate or annihilate; will is the beginning of the act of appropriation or annihilation. If, in the absence of an external obstacle, I nevertheless refrain from continuing the act, this is only because other, contradicting emotions exist, or because practical reason (*phronesis*, in its Aristotelian sense) controls desires and directs their realization.

5.003 The various traditions that share this perception of emotion — including psychoanalysis — ground emotion in desire and in fact perceive it as a movement toward the realization of desire and its elimination, and thus toward elimination of the desiring emotion. They ignore the presence of emotion between the moment desire is aroused and the point of its satisfaction. But with excitation, an intensification of presence, this presence is the heart of the matter; in excitation, the presence is winning. Kant could think of this presence only pertaining to the sublime, for awe and wonder at the sublime are characterized by a swift oscillation of movements of the soul between attraction and revulsion, which in turn neutralizes the possibility of viewing excitation as a desire to appropriate or annihilate the object or to cut off contact with it.[6]

5.004 Attraction or revulsion does not cease when the presence is winning — on the contrary. However, they are not real movements but rather images of movement, which is absent or insufficient at the time of encounter. Sartre, who still sees excitation as an act, is close to this conception of excitation when he describes it in his *Sketch for a Theory of the Emotions* as a magical act that changes consciousness but not the object. Excitation, according to Sartre, is "an [imagined] transformation of the world. When the paths before us become too difficult, or when we cannot see our way... all ways [to gain control of the object or to escape it] are barred and nevertheless we must act," and therefore they act upon consciousness.[7] When the one who is attracted or revulsed approaches or quickly draws away from the attractive or the revulsive, the emotion tends to fade — thus, the familiar tendency to suspend, for one more moment, a meeting with the desired object, or a total severing of connection with the repelling object, or its complete annihilation. It is precisely the lack of movement or its slowness relative to what is attractive or what is repulsive that provides an opportunity for the intensification of the exciting object's presence. In this sense, temptation or threat is a perfect excitation: its fundamental structure is based on a total freeze of movement and on succumbing to the huge tension created by such a freeze. But in desire (Hobbes's "appetite"), too, when the object attracts, the presence of its absence intensifies; and in revulsion, when the object repels, the excess and superfluity of its presence are intensified. Shifting the event of encounter to the foreground means making present the absence and the lack, or the excess and the superfluity, at the expense of the object attracting or repelling, and also at the expense of the attraction or revulsion itself. The excitation turns lack or superfluity into the forefront of what is there. When excitation intensifies even more, it no longer matters to the one who is excited what it is that is-there; what matters is that the object is immeasurably distant or crushing in its proximity.

5.005 Attraction to or revulsion at some thing can evolve into an excitation in which the absence or the superfluity of some thing intensifies. However, not every absence is a result of attraction, and not every superfluity is a result of revulsion; not every excitation is the intensification of an emotion seeking to appropriate an object or get rid of it; and not every excitation is a result of the intensified presence of lack or superfluity. Aesthetic excitation, what Kant calls "the pure disinterested satisfaction," does not seek to appropriate anything or to destroy anything; if it seeks anything at all, it seeks more and more of the selfsame intensified, unattainable presence through "mere contemplation."[8] And this is precisely what is sought by one experiencing temptation — as opposed to one who has already been tempted, who has lost patience and is now striving to appropriate or annihilate (4.542). The overflowing presence of the exciting thing doesn't need to generate a real movement of revulsion or attraction. We will later find that the same is true of care and compassion (5.341).

5.010 When presence intensifies and an encounter turns into what one is presented with, the witness encounters himself as well. After all, the witness is always involved in the encounter; he is always part of it — the encounter is something that "happens to him," something that "he undergoes." Now, when the presence intensifies, and makes present, the encounter itself, the encountering witness is made present as well. Excitation is an encounter in which the one-who-is-both-present-and-presented with some thing encounters himself, too, as someone-who-is-present.

5.011 Lévinas sees the repleteness of the presence of self as a primary structural characteristic of self. The self is an "entity replete with being." The relation between the I and its self is not the relation of a knowing or positing subject faced with a perceived or posited object but the relation of a "self-affected" entity present to itself in a tangible form of presence that precedes perception through seeing or intuiting, through the mind's or the body's eye. This sensation is one of satisfaction, enjoyment, joy in living, and, according to Lévinas, it takes precedence over all other excitations. Consequently, the subject's interest in himself precedes his interest in the entities around him; care of the self precedes interest in one's surroundings and in things; and the self's presence to itself experienced as joy in living precedes all caring, any positing intentionality of consciousness, every representation of objects other than the self.[9]

5.012 But how can we know which takes precedence, care of the self or care for an other? And why should joy in living be seen as a primary structure in the first place? Primary relative to what? The precedence, if there is any, is a precedence of abstraction, of generality — that is, of terms in language, not of an experience of existence. There is no fundamental difference in the scale of abstraction of self-care and care for an other, or of an intentionality positing an object and an experience of presence of self with no object posited "outside" the self. The presence of a self that involves self-care and the excitation of an I replete with itself is no more primary than the presence of an other (a mother for a baby, a beloved for a lover) or the presence of an object (water for the one who is thirsty, a fetish for a psychotic) that overflows the self and causes it excitation. Sometimes it's this way, sometimes it's that way, and sometimes someone moves through the world without having any excitation at all aroused in him.

5.013 *In general, it's necessary to get rid of the tendency to look for primary, "primordial" structures of experience; hierarchies of that type belong exclusively to the rationale of this or that descriptive language (4.231). This, however, does not entail a sweeping rejection of the phenomenological analysis of experience adopted by the poststructuralists. A phenomenology without an* archē *is a possible project: a phenomenology of linguistic phenomena, as part of the described experience and as an organizing principle of it; a phenomenology in which the described language itself is constantly visited by critical reflection that examines its rhetoric and historicizes its cultural horizons. Deconstruction can, of course, be exercised not only on the texts of Husserl, or other forms of analysis that presume to provide, once and for all and with exemplary certainty, the pure transcendental forms of intentionality, but also on any phenomenological analysis of experience, including Derrida's phenomenology of the sign in his early writings.*[10] *Deconstruction may no doubt be applied to this very text that I am writing now and its description of excitation, regardless of its awareness of the immanent linguality of experience and of its phenomenological analysis. Some are capable of performing the deconstructive act in the course of writing itself. Derrida is a master of this practice. Occasionally I try to indicate such a possibility, but it usually demands an effort of thought exceeding my abilities. If my words are of interest, let others come along and deconstruct them.*

5.020 This presence of one-who-is-present himself is not yet reflection, and it is important to emphasize this difference (pointed out by Sartre in *Sketch for a Theory of the Emotions*). Reflection is a statement in which the self is displaced from the position of addressee to the position of referent. In reflection, the self is posited as an object for gazing at, for expressing, and for touching by the one taking the addresser's instance and identifying himself as the object posited thus. But note that as one-who-posits, the addresser is already someone else, different from the posited self. (Sartre described this well in his analysis of the transition from "prereflective" to "reflective consciousness;"[11] Lyotard describes something similar in his analysis of the passage from a phrase positing some thing to a reflexive phrase positing the first phrase as its referent.[12]) In excitation, as in presence, one who encounters is an addressee and not an addresser. When one-who-is-present encounters himself, the self he encounters is not yet an object in its own right; it is an as-yet-undifferentiated part of the event of encountering. Sometimes, in an intensifying excitation, the encountering self gradually emerges from the image of the encounter; sometimes it is completely swallowed by it.

5.021 Self-reflection refers to a group of practices of other kinds that sometimes seek to make present the experience of presence. While all of them posit a "self," they differ greatly from each other according to the genre of writing, the type of discourse, and the cultural context in which they were written: Socratic "self-examination," confession in the style of Montaigne's *Essays*, psychoanalytic confession, phenomenological analysis of the transcendental I after Husserl, or a description of remembering in autobiographical writing à la Proust. In addition, these practices differ from each other in the role that the presencing of experience plays in the positing of self, in its description and analysis. Still another generalization can be proposed here: when reflection makes present an experience of presence, it distances it, and when it involves excitation, the latter doesn't necessarily follow from the repleteness of the presence of self. Nevertheless, in certain conditions, reflection can lead to such an excitation. This occurs frequently in the course of remembering. Someone relating an exciting experience is called upon to describe precisely what happened to him, and "reexperiences" what befell him, that is, experiences the memory as an overflowing presence and is unable to contain the excitation that floods him.

5.022 Excitation doesn't necessarily entail reflection either, but it may, in certain conditions, arouse it. An overflowing presence may cause an intensified presence of self possessed of a reflective moment, and may even cause such a presence of self to draw or entirely gather into an intensive experience of reflection, but the overflowing presence may equally cause a forgetting of self, a total erasure of the reflective moment vis-à-vis the winning presence of something else. I encounter an old photograph of myself in an album; the picture hurtles me in a flash into another place and time; I recall every detail of that distant event; staring into space, I'm swept away by the imaginative force of memory; people around me become invisible; I see through them, forget them, forget myself. Someone touches me, I hear a familiar voice, I reencounter myself, and all at once I am presented with the distance between me here and now and me as I was there and then. I think about who I was, who I am, who I will be no more. The excitation that has become reflection sucks the one-encountering who holds the position of addressee into the position of the referent while at the same time punting him from the position of addressee to that of addresser. But a movement in the opposite direction is possible, too. The same photograph that caused me to contemplate myself floods me with a sense of longing and loss. I feel the presence of time; I can almost touch it; I stare into space, forget myself, emptied of myself, left only with the sensation of loss and longing. The reflection that leads me to excitation turns my encounter with myself (and not my own self) into what is present.

5.023　What evolves from position to position here, from event to event, and from phrase to phrase or from statement to statement is not "the selfsame self." Assuming that it is the same self would amount to begging the question: that is, the question of the permanence of self as substance, as an object, and of its identity as some thing. These can only be generated by a reflective statement in which the self has already been posited as a referent that gathers into it the selves posited by previous statements; the reflective statement erases the differences between the different instances taken, each time, by each self, in every former statement or event.

5.024　Excitation and reflection are two ways of presencing an experience of presence, of turning an encounter with some thing present into the presence of an encounter. A third way of making present an experience of presence is an other's look or speech. The other's gaze or voice, but also other traces of his presence, immediately posits the experience of presence as an object with which I am presented. The other's presence causes the presence I've experienced to appear within a statement in which I perceive myself to be the referent (in which I sometimes, though not necessarily, perceive myself to be the addressee as well). Sartre and Lacan showed, in different ways, how encountering the look of another multiplies my experience of presence, for by its very presence the look causes me to internalize another's point of view and at one and the same time to place myself in the position he allots me, both as an addressee of presence (mine) and as an addresser who posits what is present (me). Like reflection, the gaze or speech of another leads sometimes, but not necessarily, to an intensification of presence, to excitation. Excitation is based on the intensification and concentration of presence: on repleteness and excess. Reflection and another's intervention are based on the multiplication of presence: a split and a rift, in case the I is assumed as an integrated substance; multiplicity, in case this image of self is relinquished.

5.025 Sometimes another's presence is an overflowing one, capable of making present the experience of presence and thus causing excitation. The gaze of the other, but also his hidden face, the presence of the look interpreted as recognition that is granted to me by the other who recognizes my presence as a witness, but also a denial of recognition, whether intentional or because he just happens to ignore me, each of these possibilities may cause me excitation (see 5.301), though not necessarily and not always. And of course, there is also the excitation caused by the other's absence, his temporary or final disappearance. (What-was-lost and the loss as an event are objects of excitation no less than what appears suddenly and appearance as an event.)

5.030 Here is a concise description of excitation:

> I received a letter (from Sarah)
> stars went red in their courses, the heart
> shed a tear. Like a flower in the wilderness like a flower
> in the wilderness like a flower in the wilderness.[13]

The direct presence of the letter and the implied and interpreted presence of its writer are experienced as an event of metamorphic force. The experience of presence changes the perceived world ("stars went red in their courses") and intensifies the presence of the experiencing I, described through metonymy (the heart) and two metaphors, one of which is grounded in the other (shedding tears "like a flower in the wilderness"). Together and all at once the tropes afford the experiencing I a dimension of depth (the weeping heart) and breadth (the wilderness). But the I experiencing itself is not posited as an object — of contemplation, description, or excitation. It establishes itself from the outset in the speaking position, at the addresser's instance. The reader may view this as the I to which the poem refers. But such misunderstanding occurs only when he has hastened to shift it (the I) from the addresser's position to that of the referent, in keeping with his conventional reading habits. This poem is an inscription of the presence of an overflowing presence. The I is merely a trace of the first encounter, the event in which it (the I) encountered the letter (Sarah's traces), preserved in the presence that followed it.

5.031 A poem is a means of expression that may not only describe the intensification of presence but also arouse emotion, intensify presence itself. In a poem, in fine literature, in works of art in general, there are many examples of the intensification of presence, or at least that is how many readers and viewers are accustomed to experiencing their presence. Heidegger, in "The Origin of the Work of Art," and Gadamer after him, in *Truth and Method*, seek to determine the capacity for "collecting presence," for concentrating and intensifying it as the distinctive feature of high-quality artistic representation. "The picture [by van Gogh] that shows the peasant shoes, the poem ["Roman Fountain" by C.F. Meyer] that says the Roman fountain, do not simply make manifest what these isolated beings as such are...; rather, they make unconcealment as such happen in regard to beings as a whole. The more simply and essentially the shoes are engrossed in their essence, the more directly and engagingly do all beings attain a greater degree of being [*alles Seiende seiender*] along with them."[14]

5.032 Which presence is intensified in a work of art? There is no point in offering a general answer to this question; it depends on the cultural context, on the conditions of exhibiting or receiving, on the training of the listener, the viewer, the reader, on his preferences, on his condition and his mood, and so forth. After all, presence is an encounter, and it depends on the listener, the reader, or the viewer, no less than the artistic object. In any case, at issue here is not the presence of what is represented (the speaker, the addressee of the letter in the poem by Avraham Ben Yitzhak), for what is represented is absent; at issue, rather, is the presence of what represents (the continuum of sounds, the language of the poem, the picture on the canvas, the series of images in the projector, the three-dimensional object that cuts through space). More rarely, what is intensified is the presence of the act of representation itself, the presence of the lingual act (or the visual, theatrical, or musical act), which sometimes is and sometimes isn't present as a representative of something other than itself.

5.033 The artistic medium with the most highly developed capacity for intensifying presence is music. Who isn't moved by some kind of music? One need not be a skilled listener in order to be moved by music. And in every culture there are people skilled in producing and receiving moving music. This seems to be universally true. Dance may be second in line after music, but the cultural differences are greater in this case, as are the skills demanded of the viewer. I can't say much about these matters. But I can report on the excitation caused me by listening to a particular kind of music or by watching a particular kind of dance. What is basic about this experience, in the present context, is the force with which the presence of an encounter with sound or with body movements is intensified, to the point that sometimes, at the peak of excitation, it actually suppresses the very sound of the sound or the sight of the body movements.

5.040   If what-is-present can be suppressed (or caused to fade into the background) by excitation, this is all the more true of what-is-represented by what-is-present. The signifier's status as a work of art derives from its possessing an intensified presence that makes present what is present (sound, movement, image) at the expense of what is represented (or signified, or symbolized), an intensified presence causing the viewer, listener, or reader to slow down on his way toward what is represented, to pause over the representative and wonder at it, sometimes to the point of erasing the very relation of representation. The intensified presence of the representative suspends the relation between what is present and what is absent, the referential function of the work, its status as an act of representation, while emphasizing its status as a presence in its own right. The work is presented — and this depends completely on the conditions of its display — as if it aspires to attain an uninterrupted presence. Attempts to achieve abstraction in various phases of modern painting, poetry, experiential theater, or cinema are examples of experiments in ridding the work of art of its referential dimension. Because every work of art of this kind is present in some more or less structured field of other works of art, because it refers to other works, intimates them, communicates with them, and because it is offered to the consumer within a structured cultural field, mediated by interpreters and critics who dub it and restore its suspended meaning through discourse of various kinds, this attempt is doomed to fail from the outset or is at most transient, capable of existing only on the occasion of a viewer's first encounter with a new form of artistic expression.

5.041   Of course, at issue here is modern art or a particular conception of it; the conception demonstrated by Marcel Duchamp by means of a single pissoir, forcing its thematization and problematization upon the world of visual art for the whole twentieth century. At issue here is a presence that is intensified as a result of collaboration between the cultural institution that declares the signifier a work of art to be paused over and the consumers of art who have been trained to pause over what has been sanctified as a work of art. Intensification of the signifier's presence that turns a signifier or an object into a work of art requires specific historical and cultural conditions in which subjects who are trained to become consumers of art learn to pause over the work of art and meditate on it through the mediation of the experts authorized to en-tongue it.[15]

5.042 The enchanting presence of the work that wins over the viewer's gaze, holding it in fascination, is permeated from the outset by a rift between what-is-present and what-is-there, which is not exhausted by what-is-present. "The minimal degree of attention to what is present returns and splits presence into what is present and what is really there" (4.311), and the artistic work, at least the "enchanting" one, with its "winning presence," not only demands attention but takes it. The enchanting work, even if it doesn't send the viewer beyond itself, beyond what it "represents," invites him to interpret it, even when this occurs in the most restricted sense: that is, understanding which thing enchants him. This thing, that which enchants, is there but isn't exhausted in what-is-present. A work of art declares this about itself: there is more in me than meets the eye, more than reaches the ear. But when interpretation becomes the main issue, when "which thing it is that enchants me" is more important or more urgent than the enchantment or, to generalize, when what-is-there precisely is more important than that it is there, the excitation dulls.

5.043 In contemporary Western culture, the art world provides trained subjects with designated sites where the presence of objects (images included) is systematically intensified. The trained sub-jects become capable of excitation in the presence of objects christened as art. But not every work of art succeeds in intensify-ing presence, not to speak of enchanting, in the same way or in every situation. And other cultural mechanisms produce some-what similar experiences: tourist sites, for example, with regard to landscape, and religious ritual with regard to sacred objects. One can always experience the intensification of everyday objects on one's own, with or without the mediation of the advertising industry of our consumerist societies, in one's private fantasies or perverted imagination. Fetishism may be described as the ten-dency to be enchanted by the intensified presence of objects while disregarding their use value, thus creating a vast gap between their use value for the fetishist and their exchange value.

5.044 And yet an object does not have to become a fetish to have an in-tensified presence for someone. Everyday, unremarkable objects may happen to excite someone in particular — and him alone — in very specific circumstances, and only then. Circumstances of recollection or recalling, for instance. Like Proust's famous madeleine or an old picture that one encounters in an album. Like the blue flowers my mother used to form into tiny dancers when we were walking along that stone wall on our way to kindergarten, when I saw them again, many years later, cascading out of the cool wall in the same Jerusalem alleyway. The difference between unremarkable presence and intensified presence, excitation, cannot be ascribed to the character of the object one encounters or the character of the one encountering it. It lies in the circumstances of the encounter alone. A museum creates the circumstances for an exciting encounter with artworks, but many viewers remain indifferent. A particular poem that used to excite may now seem inane, or vice versa; you reread it after separating from someone, or after having read things others wrote about it, and suddenly your heart misses a beat.

5.050   An unremarkable presence, too, can leave a tail end of excitation; a highly intensified excitation also leaves margins, a faded background of unremarkable presences inside the situation. There are two discernible poles here, two extreme moments of experience that exist, if at all, in mystical transcendence, in the outlet of insane happiness, in searing pain: on the one hand, total self-emptying by the present witness and the situation's repleteness with the excessive presence of everything other than him; on the other hand, a witness replete and obsessed with himself who heaps the situation with his presence to himself and empties it of any other presence. These two poles converge and touch, as stated above (4.343), at the perimeter of the subject position.

5.051   But in principle this difference is similar to the difference between disappearance and loss. In presence, as in disappearance, what happens happens for someone, without someone being presented with what is happening experiencing what is happening — present, disappearing, occurring — as his problem, that is, without the presence of a subject who posits himself as someone to whom some thing is happening. In excitation and loss, someone appears for whom what is happening — already present, now being lost, going to occur any moment — makes him present to himself as having an interest and posits him as one who is present, or at least posits this experience of presence as his problem.

5.052   What has popped up here is some one that "in its very Being, that Being is an issue for it" (the outmoded existentialist tone of these last paragraphs cannot be denied, even if what is under discussion is an experience of presence rather than the-one-present). It is worth remembering, though, that none of this applies to "man" in general (or to *Dasein*, or to consciousness). It applies, rather, to some one who takes a subject position in specific, more or less defined historical conditions. Someone can abstain from taking any subject position at all, he can take a break from his existence as this or that type of subject (see 1.344 and 4.300), and he can also take a subject position without necessarily turning himself into his own object of care.

5.053　A subject who posits an excitation taking place "inside himself" as the object of a reflective statement identifies the presence of some thing as his problem but is actually preoccupied with the objectification of his own self. Something of "his" is determined as some thing, and he is presented with it, from here on, in a new experience of presence. Like loss, excitation "could be an axis in the constitution of self-identity from that same subject position and throughout a transformation of this identity" (2.423). But this analogy is misleading. Loss can only be a focus of identity and identification for some one who is already a subject; where there is loss, there is already a subject. In contrast, excitation can be a focus of identity and identification for one who is not taking a subject position. Sometimes creating loss requires subjects who have an interest in the disappearance, subjects who see the disappearance as their problem (2.013). Sometimes taking a subject position requires an excitation that will turn someone into an interested party, one who faces a problem. The problem of the one experiencing the loss is not enough to make the loss exciting. That requires something whose form is determined by the subject position but whose occurrence per se doesn't depend on this position alone; it requires an intensification of presence. And in contrast, an occurrence of excitation is merely an invitation to take a subject position, insufficient in itself for someone to have already taken a subject position. This requires something preceding and independent of the excitation: a field of relations between some of those presented more or less together with what there is, what appears and disappears.

5.054　The move that posits excitation as the object of a reflective statement reaches its systematic climax in Husserl's "phenomenological reduction": the thinking I seeks to posit as an object not his own private excitation but rather that same excitation as a specific realization of excitations of its kind, and the excitation of its kind as a specific realization of excitations in general, and the excitation in general as a specific realization of the structure of the intentionality of consciousness in general. In a correct phenomenological analysis, every event of excitation can lead to the transcendental structure of subjectivity. In order to extricate the form of the intentionality of an experiencing consciousness, presence must be intensified, or an intensification of presence must be imagined (and expressed in language and failed in the attempt due to all the fallacies plaguing phenomenology through its blindness to the lingual nature of experience), turning the experience of an intensifying presence into an object of fresh reflection. The intensified presence is just a means; it is dimmed instantly in the process of reflection. As contemplation of it runs on, an increasingly abstract idea of presence replaces the intensified presence. Philosophical hubris seeks to hold on to the particular presence and the private experience in order to constitute the universal structure of subjectivity of all creatures endowed with consciousness from here to eternity.

5.055 Excitation, even when it breaks step with every semiotic order (see 5.212), is not primary in any sense. Therefore, the phenomenological project (as well as the existential one dependent on it) is doomed to fail from the outset. It's impossible to anchor anything in excitation; what is identifiable in it, over and over, is simply the continuing (and sometimes intensifying) distance between language and experience in particular and between representing words and present things in general. But perhaps Husserl is merely taking a mundane phenomenon to great extremes — someone grasps an excitation, uses it in order to constitute a subject position for himself. As stated above (1.400), a subject position is always realized vis-à-vis a problem facing someone who takes the subject position. Someone who can't, or doesn't wish to, take a subject position in the face of problems that "reality" poses him invents excitation as his problem, as an anchor of his subjectivity, and displays it in the presence of others: an emotional type, in its many forms, a neurotic type, a sentimental type, screams of enthusiasm from a pack of young girls, cries of admiration when a vista suddenly comes into view.

5.1 *Expression*

5.100 The encounter that creates the excitation isn't between one-who-is-present-as-a-tabula-rasa and some-thing-present that inscribes a "pure" mark on this slate. The one-who-is-present reaches the encounter equipped with conventions for the expression and interpretation of excitations, with paradigmatic gestures, representations, and explications of excitations, or, more precisely, with a tangled web of remainders of all these. His ability to be present, to focus on an intensifying presence, to experience presence itself, depends on the means of expression at his disposal, on the various types of discourse open to him, on the positions he is capable of taking in each of them. But it does not follow from this dependence that the excitation can be reduced to the discourse expressing it.

5.101 "It is only in normal cases that the use of words is clearly pre-scribed.... The more abnormal the case, the more doubtful it becomes what we are to say," says Wittgenstein.[16] For him, pain, fear, and happiness are normal instances with characteristic ex-pressions. The ordinary nature of their appearance allows their expression through normal language games: pain, for example, is replaced by a common expression, which is supposed to arouse the common reaction of offering help or expressing empathy, sympathy, and suchlike. However, an excitation is perceived at the moment of its occurrence as unusual, even if an occurrence of precisely this type is remembered from the past, and one who encounters the exciting presence usually needs to improvise. Even one who improvises is usually understood, for improvising is play with the materials of common language games and impro-visation itself is a familiar language game. In any case, whether one is dealing with a "normal" feeling or with excitation as an "abnormal" eruption, the expression belongs to conventional lan-guage games or to improvisation among language games and not to the exciting encounter, for someone can feel excitation to the depths of his soul without expressing it at all.

5.102 There's a stressed relationship between excitation and expression. "Excitation" denotes the encounter itself here, regardless of the expression of the excitation, of the "authenticity" or force of this expression; "expression" denotes everything pertaining to the relations of signification within which the excitation is the signi-fied. Expression cuts through presence, multiplies it, depletes one-half of it, suspends and delays its other half. Expression relates what is present to what is absent in a way that shows the former to be lacking, dependent, existent by virtue of its relation to some thing other than itself, and time and again intimates an order controlling what-is-present without its being present itself. The excitation intensifies presence and broadens it while simulta-neously preserving the unity of presence beyond the split that tears it apart from within and spreads it across distinct things. Excitation blurs differences between things that were formerly distinct, makes present what is absent, but it also weakens the link to what has no presence here and now.

5.103 Excitation is an experience of intensified presence that seeks expression for itself. This expression is culturally structured and has a degree of "freedom of expression" that varies from one context to another. At least up to a point, even cries of pain or roars of joy sound different when they come from speakers of different languages, from men and women, from adults and children, or from people of different classes who speak the same language, and the same goes for nonverbal gestures. People learn to express excitations from infancy as part of their acquisition of language, culture, and a particular *habitus*. Certain types of discourse specialize in expressions of excitation, which they structure in more or less systematic forms: the discourse of rhetoric, poetics, ethics, or psychology. And tables of emotion serve the orator, the tragedian, the moralist, the psychologist. The emotions expressed in this or that discourse are the objects of that discourse, posited or constituted like any other object, in more or less defined conditions of speech, gaze, and manipulation. One never knows precisely which excitation they generate in the addressee; all one can know is whether the addressee has learned to express his emotions properly, that is, whether he knows the proper use of the means of expression at his disposal, whether he in fact takes the position that discourse allocates him, and whether he speaks and acts within the framework authorized for him by discourse. Excitation, like every experience, is formed within discourse and has no meaning outside it.

5.110   Nevertheless, despite the impossibility of identifying an excitation without the mediation of expression and despite the vanity of the attempt to express "the excitation itself," there is no justification for reducing excitation to its expressions, verbal or nonverbal, either in part or in their entirety. The impossibility of reducing excitation to expression is a facet of the general principle according to which what is sensed or experienced is not reducible to what is spoken (another facet of this general principle is the irreducibility of what is seen to what is spoken [4.100]). Clearly, both "the experienced intensification of presence as an excitation" and the difference between "excitation" and "expression" are products of discourse. Clearly, too, the gap between excitation and expression cannot be erased by means of another expression; it can only be signified (or "captured") by means of another expression. This gap may even become a well-structured strategy within a discourse assuming "emotional life" to be something that is partially hidden somewhere, at some depth, and always partially expressed, while expressions of dissatisfaction at this gap (themselves falling into familiar patterns) are manners of distinction within discourse. Even this fact doesn't turn excitation into the exclusive product of expression. Excitation has a repleteness of presence that no expression can fully exhaust; only the impossibility of exhausting it can be expressed.

5.111 Admittedly, many excitations are direct products of forms of expression that describe or articulate emotions; it's vital to reject the phenomenological attempt to anchor certain knowledge in the primacy of privileged experiences; it should be determined that no discourse can reach a primary experience preceding differentiations within a space of signs permeated by *différance*, which are conditions for the possibility of relations between expressions. Despite all this, it does not follow that the limits of excitation are the limits of discourse; it certainly does not follow that there is, out there somewhere, some "authentic" or "faithful" or "precise" discourse of emotions capable of erasing, or replacing, or representing the experienced intensification of presence and taking its place. Can you imagine a discourse that relinquishes the difference between what is experienced and what is spoken? Only if you can imagine creatures whose language is their entire soul, or mental life, or consciousness. But indeed the impossibility of such imagining, testifying here to the excess of excitation relative to expression, is an outcome of discourse, too, as well as a testimony to its limitation.

5.112 "Pure" excitation, disconnected from expression, may perhaps exist for a short time, in a state of ecstasy, at the climax of an act of love, in insane pain, in paralyzing depression. But even the most terrible presence of pain can find some respite when it is expressed in discourse. It is not exaggerated (though not fully precise) to draw an analogy between the opposition of excitation versus expression and Nietzsche's opposition: Dionysian versus Apollonian. As well understood by Nietzsche, in the absence of the Dionysian, the Apollonian would freeze to death in the pure, distinctly differing forms uncontaminated by any hybridity; in the absence of the Apollonian, the Dionysian is consumed in the fire of desire for, or crumbles in self-negation under the burden of, a terrible truth. Thus, "having looked boldly right into the terrible destructiveness of so-called world history," gaining "an insight into the horrible truth," and having been vanquished by limitless loathing toward absurd existence, one finds solace in art, which "approaches as a saving sorceress, expert at healing."[17]

5.113 An expression of excitation in discourse without the intervention of an overflowing excitation represented through this expression may exist for a very long time; such an order of discourse is the ideal of every bureaucracy. But even the most rigid bureaucracy needs a shot of charisma from time to time. The charismatic personality arouses excitation in its very presence; the traces it leaves here and there suffice to create an excited anticipation for presence, in which the mere possibility of a meeting with the charismatic figure floods the one anticipating with images (re-presentations) of the anticipated presence.

5.114 The secret of the unique presence of power lies in the game of reciprocal relations between excitation and expression, between the intensification of presence and its suspension. Power cannot be present in action all the time. Power cannot suspend the presence of its action forever.[18] Suspension and existence, which is always limited by the boundaries and order of the discourse, are what ensure the proper functioning of a system of exchange in a given area (the power of conventional arms, of capital and merchandise). The difference is not between the presence of the power's representation and the presence of the thing (power) "itself." The signs of power are the presence of power in action as well; the action of power has a signifying effect, too. The difference is between an intensified presence that doesn't cease signifying and a suspended presence in which the suspension itself doesn't cease acting. A military parade, columns of tanks rolling by with a deafening roar, a chest covered with medals — the signs of power excite, intensify the presence of power, and the excitation itself may signify yet more power.

5.120 Like a scratchy mirror image of power, like the mold of its bas-relief, suffering, too, appears and is enmeshed in the same game of reciprocal relations between excitation and expression. The permanently excited presence of suffering is an insufferable presence — from time to time suffering, too, must sidestep into expression. Yet a permanent expression of suffering in any discourse, never accompanied by an outburst of intensified presence, is not credible, is suspect, and, as in a bad play, lacks any effect. It would seem to be disconnected from the thing it is supposed to express. Here, too, the difference is not between the presence of the representation (of the suffering) and the presence of the thing (suffering) "itself." The signs of suffering, too, are a presence of suffering "in action," that is, in the act of suffering, of bearing and "absorbing" it;[19] the presence of the very state of suffering has a signifying effect as well. The difference is between an intensified presence that doesn't cease to signify and a suspended presence in which the suspension itself doesn't cease to act, that is, to annoy, depress, torture.

228

5.121 Power acts through the threat of causing suffering and through in fact causing suffering, which is simply an intensification of excitation (5.51), and also through the threat of additional suffering signified by the excitation itself. The representation of power and the suspension of its operation and the signification of suffering and the suspension of its appearance are interconnected. Suffering and power meet inverted in the reciprocal game between excitation and expression: power in action (or violent power, force) is the moment at which suspension is eliminated and power shifts from potential to action; suffering is the moment at which excitation, which cannot be suspended or from which one cannot suspend oneself, becomes insufferable. In both cases, when suspension is eliminated, other powers might erupt at any time, or other suffering might befall one at any time, and there is a threat that stays suspended. For one who suffers, for one to whom power is applied, there is always something else to wait for — and something to lose. But activating power represents as well — more power not yet activated — and activating suffering represents more suffering not yet caused.

5.122 Power, like violence, has an exciting presence that may prevent or directly cause more activation of power (or the activation of more power). There is always an excess of violence "in the air," whether or not it is contained and whether or not it is actually taking place: present-absent violence that may deter or torture (both those generating it and those bearing it), may cause to rise up or annihilate. At the point where violence and suffering meet, there is an intensified encounter in which the reciprocal game between excitation and expression, suspension and realization, spins and accelerates. The end of the game may be a collapse of the entire system of signification and suspension — self-devouring violence, annihilating suffering — but there may also be suffering that toughens and is not yet intimated through any external expression, or power that has been internalized and as yet leaves no traces, until they again erupt. The master may annihilate his slave — whom will he exert his power on now? The slave may fall to his knees under the burden, but may also be strengthened in his work, may bear his pain in silence and secretly plan the moment of rebellion. Power needs suffering and a consciousness of suffering in order to act without consuming itself. Suffering needs power in order to take place without annihilating the one suffering.[20]

5.130 In excitation, an experience of presence becomes someone's interest or problem, a repleteness of presence flowing out of the-thing-present to one-who-is-presented with the thing (1.43). A subject is one capable of translating his problem from the realm of experience into the realm of some discourse in which it can be expressed. The instinctive reaction to pain can clarify this matter, for it lies at the edge of the relation between the one experiencing and his experience. In instinctive reaction to pain, the reaction may not be experienced at all and certainly isn't experienced as a reaction, except in hindsight. One who is in pain and reacts remains in the realm of excitation both before and after the reaction. The pain may be brief, may be removed immediately through the reaction, may be swiftly forgotten. But when the excitation continues, the one presented with the intensifying presence will probably seek a subject position in order to respond, to interpret the excitation to himself, to interpret himself as one who is experiencing an intensifying presence, to express himself, to act so as to end the excitation or to retake control of it.

5.131　The intensification of a presence can neither create nor damage a subject position. A subject position taken in excitation is pre-prepared, even when it is taken or abandoned as a result of the excitation. The subject position opens and limits a field of possibilities in which the excited one can intensify presence and respond to the intensification of presence (express the excitation, suppress it, call or focus attention to or on it, use the excitation as a source of motivation or a reason for action, and so forth). An excitation can intensify someone's own presence for himself but cannot intensify subjectivity, for subjectivity, by definition, is not present; it is an ideal pole and an enabling condition of some one's being present. Excitation is a relation between one who is present and the state of presence, between one who is experiencing presence and the experience of presence; subjectivity is a feature of a position held in a field of relations between those experiencing presences and those responding to them.

5.132　Therefore, excitation cannot help one-who-is-presented with some thing take a subject position that will authorize him to describe what-is-present, to represent it, to use it, or to act upon it; at most, excitation can justify one who struggles in taking a certain subject position or freeing himself, for a moment or forever, from a certain subject position. Taking a subject position means being able to control excitations, to balance the intensification of presences through a correct distribution of attention among other presences in the situation, to disallow the intensification of any presence to the point of totally conquering the witness.

5.140 There is a stressed relationship between the excitative and the subjective, which is similar, in principle, to the relationship between excitation and expression. The subject belongs to the order of discourse that allows expression; excitation threatens that order along with everything belonging to it. This is why a victim's testimony is always suspect, because he is still subject to the winning presence of pain, suffering, humiliation. This is also an excuse for disqualifying the legal testimony of women in a culture that associates them with over-excitation. The testimony of a woman who has been raped — victimized by a man whose subjectivity is not customarily questioned — is all the more suspect, as is the testimony of the black victim of a white person's assault, and in general the testimony of a member of a vulnerable and subjected group, a subaltern, ruled over as an other. One way of addressing this state of affairs is translating the excitation into discourse from an authorized subject position; another way is clearing a space for the excited victim within the order of discourse, with particular attention to his limitation (that is, from the point of view of the hegemonic discourse), or, in other words, broadening the boundaries of the discourse so as to include the expressions of excitation and acknowledge them as faithful testimonies.

5.141 From the perspective of one seeking to posit someone in a subject position, to recognize him as the subject he wishes to be, to respond to him, there is not much point in trying to distinguish between a simulation of excitation and a "real" excitation. The issue is recognizing the one present as a reliable subject, as one authorized to represent excitation, and not approving or denying his excitation (see 4.333 and 6.024). Excitation can erupt into the order of discourse where expressions take place but cannot determine it. The excitation itself does not really matter. The witness's testimony cannot be disqualified on the grounds that there was no excitation; testimony about excitation can only be disqualified on the grounds of a suspicion about the witness himself: his sincerity, the legitimacy of his subject position, his authority to take such a subject position that always presupposes the institutionalized conditions of expressing excitation (not believing an actor who weeps onstage but believing him when he weeps in the street, for instance, or vice versa). Excitation is always for a witness, for myself as witness, shut and sealed for another, because the only way to distinguish between reality and a simulation of reality is through the mediation of an understandable expression in a more or less structured discourse, from a given subject position, and with the aid of other subjects. In the course of excitation, the witness can ask himself, "Was it only a dream? Was it I?," but only in relation to things, never in relation to the experience.[21]

5.142 Once the excitation has died down, it's impossible to reconstruct the intensification of the presence, and it's impossible to distinguish between the presence of the traces of the first excitation and the traces of the memory of the first excitation, or the traces of the memory of all the excitations that occurred when the presence of these traces intensified (this holds equally for every event [see 4.032]). It is only possible to fabricate a representation of the first excitation within a given discourse. But the constraints on the order of discourse and expression do not constitute constraints on the world. The limits of my language are not the limits of my world — Wittgenstein could not be more wrong about this — and I am presented with this fact every time I try to describe an experience or reconstruct an experience from someone else's description. Something stays inexpressible, and that very something is part of my world. It is not the same something relative to or within every expression; in every lingual act or other act of representation, the background changes, the margins change, what is left out changes. Something is always left out, and even if I speak until eternity, and even if I speak poetry, language will not catch up with the experience. Language, the language of poetry above all, continuously creates new experiences of presence, and how could it catch up with the old one, now fading away in memory?

5.143 What a blunder it was to grant language such power, to attribute to it the capacity to exhaust the experience of presence. It is not just Being — understood as what is there but hidden, concealed, what has not yet been brought to the point of presence in someone's presence — that language cannot exhaust; it cannot even exhaust presence. There is no mystery here. Like the attributes of God in Spinoza, so the attributes of consciousness: the experience of what is seen, heard, smelled, tasted, spoken, sensed through external touch, sensed through internal touch, dreamed, all that is sensed without touch — every such experience is translatable from one order of consciousness to another, but never reducible; one sensual medium cannot be grounded in the other. There are, of course, "translation softwares," and — as in every translation — something is lost in the process, something else is added, but there are no "compatible" attributes of consciousness. Language, of course, is the most sophisticated of all translating tools, possessed of the broadest presumptions, and in comparison a shelf in a perfume shop is a very poor translation tool indeed, but this nevertheless does not make language compatible with experience or render superfluous the repertoire of perfumes and nameless scents.

5.150 If it were possible to make excitation present to myself and to others, to present it alongside its representations in the space of interpersonal communication, as a product is presented in the commodities market, to return to it in the space of memory, as one returns to a book in the library, we would surely tend to speak of it less. The expression and interpretation of excitations are what is at stake in different types of "truth games" — in poetry, literature, a variety of psychotherapeutic discourses, medical discourses, phenomenological analysis — and they are at stake in different ways, in different cultures and historical epochs, combined in different ways with additional factors that form the encounter with what excites: the education of the subject capable of excitation; the patterns of movement, observation, and contact in the space in which encounters occur; the presence of others assigned this or that role in the excitation or from whom the excitation is supposed to be hidden; the manner of their inclusion in the exciting experience, in its expression or its interpretation; and so forth (5.231–5.232). There are different kinds of experts on various types of excitations, equipped with different typologies. Especially prominent in modern culture are the experts on the "authentic" expression of "deep" excitation, but both "authenticity" and "depth" are products of a very specific discourse. Regimes of discourse that operate under the rationale of "authentic expression" tend to represent excitation as some thing that no expression can truly grasp, and this is precisely why the discourse in question is obliged to seek the appropriate expression from here to eternity. These practices of representation give form to the encounter with what excites (5.111), but no excitation can be derived from them. People feel "deeply shocked" in the face of an abused child, for these are the words at their disposal, but it is hard to gauge their possible reaction to the very same child had they other words at their disposal.

5.151 Obviously, it is impossible to express the inexpressible; at most it can be intimated — but what precisely can be intimated? A discourse conducted under a regime of authenticity needs the inexpressible. Without it, the representation of excitation would simply be judged as true or false. And for exactly the same reason, such a discourse can never stabilize the representations alternating within it, for it will never have a criterion for distinguishing between the authentic and the inauthentic, because it can never compare the authentic expression with the inexpressible. As a result, evaluations in terms of authenticity tend to turn into acts of censorship. Instead of a necessarily hopeless search for authenticity, it might be possible to clear a space in language for those margins of excitation that are inexpressible: to clear a space — not necessarily so that some day they will be expressed (and the margins pushed to some other site), but so that testimony to the impossibility of expressing something completely will exist now.[22]

5.152 The same logic that foils the presumption to authenticity holds for every attempt to express what is inexpressible in other areas — the sublime, for instance. From the witness's point of view, the sublime is an excitation without an object. From the interpreter's point of view, the sublime is the complement of excitation. Every attempt to express it is doomed to failure due to the same force and motivation that drive the witness who attempts to find an expression for an inexpressible excitation. There is a point in preserving an unoccupied space in language for the excitation exceeding any expression; but it is unclear if there are similar reasons for clearing a space for the sublime. Isn't it possible to phrase the sublime in terms of an excitation that has no object? In other words, perhaps the sublime is no more than the preeminence of excitation relative to its visual and verbal representation.

5.153 "Nature is thus sublime in those of its appearances the intuition of which brings with them the idea of its infinity. Now, the latter cannot happen except through the inadequacy of even the greatest effort of our imagination in the estimation of the magnitude of an object."[23] If "infinity" is replaced with "inexhaustibility," "effort of our imagination" with "expressive ability," and "estimation" with "excitation in the face of some thing," the result is the conclusion of the previous paragraph. It seems to me that this is a possible way of understanding a central matter in Lyotard's proposal for reading Kant's *Critique of the Power of Judgment* and the link the former creates between the concept of the *différend* and that of the sublime.[24]

5.154 Understanding excitation as always exceeding what is expressible doesn't necessarily mean placing it in the "depths" of man's soul, but ever since the soul has had such depths, there has been a tendency to place it there. That said, if excitation is spoken of in terms of the intensification of a presence flowing out of the thing-present towards one-presented-with-the-thing, then the vertical trope may be replaced with a horizontal one. This will not make it possible to represent the excitation itself or to find the idiom that expresses it faithfully, but it will allow us to discard the illusion of authentic expression. From here on, representation of an intensified presence will depend on the ability of the representing medium to intensify presence through the expressions at its disposal. Representation will turn into an act of displacement in which the repleteness of presence (which, as the reader may recall, has flowed out of the present-thing to the-one-presented-with-the-thing) is transferred to the representing medium and flows back from it to the one presented with what represents. Naturally, this is not the "same" repleteness of presence, and it is even difficult to speak of isomorphism here, for there is no primary form to compare it with.

5.155 A more reasonable metaphor is the wave image (2.130). The language (or painting, photograph, and so forth) that represents excitation seeks to create a wave in which a replete presence will flow from one-who-is-present to an addressee who isn't present. The discourse that interprets excitation seeks to freeze the wave and extricate another wave from it — that is, the one that passed from the present-thing to the one-presented-with-the-thing — and even more than that it is interested in reconstructing the conditions (the personality structure and history, the structure of the experience and of the situation) that allowed the occurrence of this wave.

5.2 *Heterotopia*

5.200 An excitation is the result of a repleteness of presence at a certain point in the situation space experienced at the expense of the situation's other components, which move to the background. To produce an excitation, one must cause some presence in a situation to over-replenish. To dim an excitation, one must return from the experience of encounter to what-is-present; this, for instance, is the demand that one be "to the point" about something, that is, focus on "the thing itself" and not on the accompanying outcomes of the experience of its presence. In more general terms, in order to dim an excitation, one must cause the presence to re-disperse across broader areas of the situation. This is what happens in every attempt to "turn attention away from something" (in contrast to turning attention to something, which enhances some thing's presence). How easy it is to divert a hurting child's attention by making faces, showing him a shiny object, or giving him some candy. How hard it is to divert the attention of one absorbed in himself, for whom excitation is a means to make himself present, who needs this presence of self and refuses to disperse presence, even very slightly, across other elements of the situation. He isn't prepared (or is simply unable) to make space for others, to allow others to make themselves present, or to make anyone other than him present, and he demands all the attention for himself.

5.201 The larger the space of the relevant situation across which the presence disperses, the weaker the force of the presence of every element within it and the smaller the ability of some thing to command attention. Broadening the space of attention is a means toward dimming excitations, depleting the intensity of the witness's presence to himself, a technique for emptying self.

5.210 In temptation, excitation is created by a concentration of presence in a restricted area of the situation space. Something that is present wins me over in its presence ("she has a winning presence"), causes me to feel myself present in the face of it — not merely present-to-myself but present-to-myself as subject to the grace of some-thing's-presence. In every temptation, there is a threat to the border between the one present and the tempting thing present before him. However, in contrast to desire, temptation threatens not the thing desired, which the desirer wishes to swallow or otherwise integrate into himself, but the desirer, who submits to an addiction to the presence of what is tempting (4.532).

5.211 A presence may be tempting, winning, precisely because what is present testifies to itself as being a mere hint of what is concealed within, because it is full of the promise of something still buried within it, something whose appearance, whose emergence into the world, whose surrender to touch, will intensify its presence sevenfold, bestowing enjoyment and other pleasurable excitations. Therefore, temptation is a dangerous matter. The tempter may be dangerous if "his heart belies his lips," if the tempting presence conceals another repulsive, destructive presence. But there is a difference here between a tempting object (food, a piece of jewelry) and a tempting body. The tempting body's position, its movements and gestures, the alluring look, are dangerous not necessarily because another disastrous presence is hidden behind them but because this presence could disappear at any moment, when the body, the look, suddenly turn from what, for me, is a source of brimming presence into someone who draws presence to himself, who seeks to be presented with himself, who turns me into some thing that is present for him, too, or even into some one who is present. Temptation disperses when the other suddenly recognizes me as one who is presented with him, as one who is now supposed to respond. Temptation is the suspension of reaction (4.530).

5.212 Temptation (like pain) is intensified presence per se. In temptation itself, there is intensification not of lack but of presence. This distinguishes what is tempting from what is desired in its various forms. In desire, presence includes an anticipation of some expected but absent thing. In longing, presence includes a memory of the presence of some thing that was lost. In mourning, presence includes missing the presence of some thing that will never again be present. In all these cases, the excitation is a result of the intensified presence of the representation of what is no longer present, what is not yet present, or what will never be present. In temptation, the semiotic dimension embedded in principle in what-is-tempting is absorbed, as it were, into the surface of what-is-present. The string of pearls at her throat can signify social status, the sweater thrown haphazard over her shoulders can signify a character trait, the book she is holding may give some evidence of her taste, of her education level. All these, however, will only be reconstructed later, in the process of recalling, then joining the image that will engender desire and longing for the sweet moment of temptation. At the moment of temptation itself, all the signs refer to each other and not to anything beyond the moment of presence itself. What is tempting is simply present, there, demanding, winning attention, erasing all signifieds.

5.220 As mentioned above, temptation is a type of "concentration of [the] presence" of some thing in a situation, and there are surely other types as well. It may be possible to compile a typology of "techniques for concentrating presence." The best-tested technique is causing pain. Strong pain is an example of a swift flow of presence, which may extend from making self present to a forgetting of self (5.022). Certain words give form to pain that is already there, and other words invite pain that would not have been caused without them, but pain has presence before it has words. In other techniques of concentrating presence, language plays a more active role — for instance, in frightening, in threatening, in making present the loss of some thing or some one dear. Refinement and gentleness will be measured, on the one hand, in the capacity for differentiation and subtle distinction as to what is present, and in a high excitation threshold, and, on the other, in an ability to surrender to the excitation caused by certain distinct presences. Accordingly, rudeness will be characterized by an indiscriminate excited reaction, which is indifferent to differences in what is present, on the one hand, and by an inability to surrender to distinct presences, on the other.

5.221 The contrast between refinement and gentleness and rudeness in excitation intersects with another contrast, between apathy and ecstasy, or indifference and addiction. Apathy is a failure to respond to what is present; no thing present in the situation has an overflowing presence, the one who is presented is devoid of excitation. Ecstasy is a total response to the winning presence of something, to the repleteness of its presence, until the experience of presence empties the one presented with it of anything other than the presence of the addictive thing. Ecstatic addiction can be reached through increasingly refined sensibility and increasingly brutish rudeness to the same extent; apathetic indifference can be crawled into equally through controlling a delicate or a rude response. Being emptied of any excitation and overflowing with excitation are opposite poles between which the whole of emotional life is organized.[25]

5.222 Language plays a crucial role in refining sensibility to distinct differences in the space of presences, but here, too, this role is not exclusive. The professional wine taster, the professional scent smeller, hang distinctions on language like a coat on a hanger. They can seemingly take them off the hanger whenever they wish. In fact, when they try, the hanger gets caught in the coat. For the newcomer, words such as "bittersweet," "fruity," "velvety," and "full-bodied" are capable of designating the different tastes of wine only if the winemaker accompanies them with a case full of bottles. But language is a necessary and cardinal means, even if not the only one, for developing and nurturing others' sensibility, including their sensibility to taste and smell. With regard to certain excitations, language may well shrink into a hanger, but that hanger will always remain the property of some public dressing room.

5.230 Can the presence of some thing intensify in the same way for two witnesses? Two witnesses trying to coordinate between them an experience of some thing must put aside, at least for a while, every excitation. Excitation in the face of some thing tends to foil attempts to unify and regularize the perception of what-is-present. In relatively rare cases, when the presence of some thing is intensified in a similar way for two or more witnesses, grounds for solidarity are created. This is one of the important effects (and perhaps also one of the important functions) of ritual. Ritual institutionalizes excitations — joy as well as sorrow, but more sorrow than joy — through creating a system of coordinates that allow the division and distribution, the coordination and tuning, of excitation among many witnesses presented with the intensified presence of some thing. Ritual creates a new balance of excitations within a given community: it dims the excitation of those involved with the thing (the exciting thing: birth, death, love) by granting it rigid and regular patterns of expression; and it enhances the excitation of those less involved with that same thing and more involved with the possessor of the thing, making them partners (compare 5.150).

5.231 An assured way of creating solidarity is creating conditions in which the presence of some thing will be intensified in the same way for different witnesses. Shared excitation is a basis for solidarity. When excitation is experienced separately, it singularizes, splits, and eats away at the sense of partnership. One important difference between television viewers and theater audiences (but also, though less distinctly, between audiences of street theater and those seated in a fancy theater hall) is the link between the intensification of presence and solidarity. The conditions of creating excitation on television allow every viewer to be presented with the intensification of presence on his own, to experience it independently of other viewers. Television dismantles solidarity. The conditions of creating excitation in theater, and mainly in the ancient theater or today at rock concerts, for instance, intensify presence under similar conditions for many different viewers, and indeed employ the presence of the other viewers whose excitation is displayed as a means of intensifying presence for every one of the viewers. This is part of how theater functions as a rite.

5.232 The conditions of viewing a film are usually similar to those of viewing television, but there are some exceptions, attempts to create theatrical-ritualistic viewing conditions — *The Rocky Horror Picture Show*, for instance. In contrast, the experience of excitation in the face of a work of visual art in a museum or gallery is completely private. A basis for solidarity will only be created here, as is the case with reading texts, in a limited circle of people with similar taste. Some special conditions of speech are intended to create more of a mass excitation in the presence of texts — rituals, dramatizations, readings, public storytellings. More intricate rituals also create common conditions of viewing and contact. They are responsible for the fact that participants in an exciting event will "hit" the exciting encounter in the same way, more or less, and will temporalize the exciting event in a more or less coordinated manner.

5.233 Such conditions for generating excitational solidarity create heterotopic spaces with a space-time of their own, suspended from everyday space-time, where things take place as usual. The theater hall, the laboratory of modern science, and the museum are spaces of this type, as are cruise ships, holiday resorts, birthday parties, and boot camps.[26]

5.234 Actually, excitation is a primary core of a heterotopic space, a sort of skein of heterotopia. The exciting event is a moment of suspension from the ordinary progress of things. Sartre understood this well in *Sketch for a Theory of the Emotions*: "In excitation, it is the body which, directed by the consciousness, changes its relationship with the world so that the world should change its qualities. If emotion is play-acting, the play is one that we believe in."[27] While excitation tends to produce heterotopic spaces, the latter tends to create excitation, for example, in rituals, during the viewing of a work of art, in certain television programs that aim to bring someone to excitation and to excite the audience through this excitation, or in candid-camera films.[28] But it may also be a condition for the endurance of excitation. One who wishes to preserve his excitation for himself, like one who has just received a love letter or a notice that he has been fired, seeks out a corner, a pause, and a moment of isolation. Certain cultural practices allow swift organizing for the creation of such a heterotopia so as to enable one who has been hurt by an encounter to be alone with his excitations. Other cultural practices organize equally swiftly so as to return the excited person to the usual routine, get him back in line, back into the order of things. The community creates a liminal status for the mourner and a heterotopic space in which his excitations can continue to exist, but only with the mediation of others and in their presence. The patterns of conduct in this heterotopia are completely beyond the mourner's control.

5.240 Excitation tends to produce heterotopias because, when it takes place — in pleasure as in pain, in pleasurable pain as in painful pleasure, and across the entire spectrum of excitation, from revulsion and abhorrence through longing and desire — the organization of the situation is damaged, along with the equilibrium of the presences within it, the equilibrium between the presence of things for the one who is present, the making present of the event of presence, and the presence of the witness to himself. If the encounter with some thing is "the beginning of the experience of presence and the source of its incessant renewal, the secret of its duration ... [and] an experience of presence is an encounter that is incessantly renewed, ... [that] goes on for as long as the encounter goes on," between the one perceiving and the something perceived (4.102), then excitation is an encounter with wounded victims. When there are victims in an encounter, the exciting event develops within a space-time that is distanced from the common, general social space-time by a gap and by incompatibility. The intensification of presence and its overflowing into the event of encounter itself reorganize the temporality of the event: what is incessant now, what continues indefinitely, is not the thing encountered but the encounter itself.

5.241 Presence is a way of temporalizing being. In presence without excitation (more precisely, in presence where excitation is dimmed or strongly suppressed or has not yet arrived), the passage of time, the continuum, is perceived relative to the perpetuation of that thing which is present; since its presence endures, since (and as long as) time does not leave traces on this presence, it appears to be freezing time. It is a fixed point relative to which time differentiates space and changes can be perceived. In intensified presence, the being of the one present also becomes part of what is temporalized. The one present is suspended from the usual, unnoticed progress of time. Sometimes "time stands still," sometimes it "flashes by in an instant," and in any case when something "is upon us," the unified continuum of the time of things cracks while the excitation seems to occur in a temporal continuum of its own. From the point of view of the excited person in question, the time of things is suspended, or lags behind the exciting time, or anticipates it. It's not that the excitation as a thing hastens and arrives or procrastinates relative to something else that emerges or disappears earlier or later than it does, for the excitation is an event drawn out along a split temporality: the exciting presence, overflowing its boundaries, acquires a time of its own (gradually or all at once, depending on the type of excitation), which is not coordinated with the measured time in which the rest of things present at the event continue to take place. In excitation, a split occurs between the temporalization of the being of everything being-there and the temporalization of experience of the one presented with what is there. This split is responsible for the fact that in excitation, time itself acquires a degree of presence, too.

5.242 At times — depending on the type of excitation — space, too, acquires a degree of presence for itself. Suddenly a distance springs up between me and my body and between this body and other things around it. Sharp pain, insane desire, or exquisite pleasure suspends the body or one of its organs from the space of things and organizes everything around it, relative to it, at an infinite distance or an unbearable proximity.

5.243 To an onlooker — that is, to one who is already (or still) not excited — no difference can ever be discerned between the two time lines and the two timetables, or the two spaces superimposed on each other. But this is just because from the alienated point of view of the other, someone else's excitation is a phenomenon or a thing with presence just like all the other things in the situation — until the excitation infects the onlooker, too.

5.244 *In excitation, time and space stop being "transcendental forms of intuition" (Kant) and turn into modalities of being (Heidegger, Sartre). Reflecting on excitation, one sees that the time of things and the space of things as transcendental forms of intuition were only made possible by the suspension of excitation, any excitation. Kant's analysis in the chapter on transcendental aesthetics depends on the inhibition of the presences and their measured distribution across the space of the experienced situation. This is attained at the price of canceling the witness's lived presence to himself, of rendering him abstract and universalized, of distancing him to a focal point beyond the boundaries of experience (that thinking I who "must . . . accompany all my representations").*[29]

5.3 *For an Other*

5.300 When the overflowing of a presence intensifies, this may make the witness present to himself in a way not yet distinct from the presence of the encounter (5.010 and 5.020). In Hegel's terms, but explicitly inverting his intention, one might say that excitation is the beginning of the process through which the witness ("consciousness") turns from "being in itself" into "being for itself" through the mediation of the other (the object, what is present); however, this happens not because "consciousness seeks to appropriate its object" or to overcome the difference that separates it from its object, but rather because the object (what is present) wins it over, enchants, excites. And also opposing Hegel: the reflective moment in which the self is posited as a distinct object of presence is not the necessary end of this process. When presence is intensified still more (5.022), this may cause the witness to forget himself, again turning him from being-for-himself into being-for-another (what-is-present).

5.301 At the first, exciting moment, the witness is presented with his state of being present; at the second, reflective moment, the one-who-is-present is extricated from the experience of presence and becomes a self-present object, an object present to itself; in the third moment, the one present loses his distinctness for himself and is reabsorbed into the exciting encounter, but in the process his presence intensifies for others.[30] In the last two cases, the one who is excited becomes an object, making itself present, in the first instance for itself, in the second for others. A kind of hyperbola forms along the witness's axis of presence to himself: at one end is the experience of presence whose addressee has not yet been posited as an object (or whose object has not yet been identified as a subject); at the other end is the experience of presence in which the boundary blurs between one-who-is-present and some thing that is present; along the curve in the middle lie experiences of presence in which the addressee of the excitation is present to himself as one-who-is-present. In any case, when the person in question does not restrain his excitement, others, too, are presented with it. The overflowing presence wins (or threatens to win) them over, too.

5.310 Someone else who is present in a situation along with me can dissipate excitations, multiply presence, restore the tempter's semiotic dimension (5.212), but can also intensify some one's, or some thing's, presence. Think of some thing that surfaces, or some thing that is revealed as something else, as unbearable, as desirable, just because someone else is looking at it. In his very presence, his gaze, his speech, an other competes with me for the distribution or the dissemination of the force of presence throughout the situation. Just as he can dim presence, he can intensify it, too. But is there a special effect of the intensified presence of the other himself? Are there excitations that belong exclusively to the presence of the other, that characterize it?

5.311 Being tempting, for example, or being desired isn't necessarily characteristic of the presence of someone with a vested interest. What is tempting, what is desired, can be some thing, not necessarily some one. Intensified presence can bring about caring for an object, no less than a human being. But is it possible to love an object as one loves a person? And an animal? As long as one is "in love," the presence of the beloved is an intensified presence. What causes that? Falling in love is an intensification of the presence of an other who becomes a beloved. Being present together, alongside each other, for a long time erodes the ability of spouses to intensify one another's presence, and the presence of each vis-à-vis the other. Thus the importance of parting, suspending, separating, in every love relationship.

5.32 The presence of someone else may intensify, cause excitation, when he acknowledges you as someone, makes you present as one-who-is-presented, and almost always when eyes meet. But it can also intensify when this acknowledgment is denied, when someone ignores you, for instance. The excitation accompanies the moment of the recognition's appearance, or the moment of its disappearance (denial), while only very rarely (at "moments of grace") is it accompanied by reciprocal relations in which recognition is assumed to go without saying. This touches on Hegel's famous discussion of the transition from consciousness to self-consciousness.[31] Hegel sees recognition by the other as a condition for the development of self-consciousness, but the master's lack of recognition is also a necessary element in the emergence of the slave's self-consciousness. A need for an other's recognition, rudely denied, ruthlessly, indifferently, inattentively withheld, may intensify his presence again and again, just as the presence of his absence may intensify the experience of presence itself, the encounter with the other at the expense of the other encountered. Denied recognition may form grounds for a project of organizing the subjectivity of the one in need of recognition, who posits himself through this excitation and is possibly conscious of himself as one in need of recognition.

5.330 The presence of someone else can intensify when you recognize him as one undergoing excitation, as one presented with some thing whose presence is intensified. There is no need for you to be presented with the thing that excites him in order for you to experience its intensified presence; sometimes his excitation intensifies its presence for you, and sometimes his excitation excites you. This is what happens when tears are contagious, when laughter is contagious (see 5.420). Certain typologies of excitations designate a special place for excitations that are triggered by someone else's excitation. Excitations of this kind are familiar from watching fragments of erotic films; you know the dissipation of the excitation (this type of excitation; sometimes there are others) when the film turns into pornography and the sex becomes mechanical. The mechanism of identification and catharsis in Greek tragedy operates on the basis of exciting excitations. Excitations of this type are brought about certain descriptions of suffering intended to enlist the empathy of readers, listeners, or viewers — certain descriptions, because other descriptions seek to enlist empathy without making present the specific excitation of the sufferer, and some descriptions seek to enlist empathy without creating any excitation for the addressees.

5.331 In one spectrum of excitations, the witness is afforded enjoyment by the excitation of an other, affording the other nothing but pain, either physical or emotional — from gloating through sadism. And a different spectrum of excitations has an inverted structure: an other's enjoyment intensifies his presence and causes me sorrow, repugnance, jealousy. My excitation is not directly caused by his, but is always mediated through the intensified presence of the excited other. This intensified presence is, of course, not ensured by the presence of the other's excitation. The witness can always note the other's excitation — his sorrow, his joy, his depression, his pain, his anger — like one more piece of furniture; for such a witness, the other can make present his excitations just as he makes present components of his identity on an income tax form.

5.332   Compassion is an excitation caused by the intensification of the suffering or distress of an other as one who takes a subject position due to the very fact of his suffering, by virtue of his "capacity to suffer," his suffering faculty, that is, by virtue of his biological features, his very belonging to the human race, and even by virtue of his simply being a living creature.

5.333   Everyone can feel compassion, everyone can be an object of compassion. "Meditating on the first and simplest operations of the human soul," says Rousseau, "I believe I perceive in it two principles anterior to reason, of which one interests us ardently in our well-being and our self-preservation, and the other inspires in us natural repugnance to see any sensitive being perish or suffer, principally our own fellow men."[32] Rousseau calls the second principle compassion or commiseration or pity (*pitié*), without offering any clear distinction between the terms, and sees it as "a virtue all the more universal and useful to man ... and so natural that even beasts sometimes give perceptible signs of it," a disposition that becomes "more energetic as the observing animal identifies himself more intimately with the suffering animal."[33] In the human species, compassion is compared and opposed to the impulse of self-preservation (amour de soi) and its degeneration into self-love (amour propre) and all its aberrations. According to Rousseau, requests for help as well as compassion are common to man and animal, belong to a natural, primary level of communication and moral sensibility (see 6.022). However, the animal's response to a cry emitted by a sufferer cannot count as truly moral. Only a human response can count as moral, for only man is able to refuse the commanding "gentle voice of nature."[34] What is a refusal to the commanding voice of nature in this context? Ignoring the distress of a suffering other. Indifference or cruelty (see 6.554 and 7.105). Morality will appear the moment cruelty appears; language will appear (at the selfsame moment) upon the appearance of the gap between the first phrase (request) and the second (compliance).

5.334 One who feels compassion ascribes to the one he feels it for a subject position, even if only a very depleted one, such as one could ascribe to an infant or an animal (1.211 and 1.340). One who feels compassion already ascribes to the one suffering an ability to identify the disappearance or the pain as his problem, as well as a certain range of possibilities of expressing what was lost or what hurts him, possibilities of looking at and touching him, and possibilities of acting: he ascribes to him the identity constituted as an ideal focal point synthesizing these possibilities of touch, look, and expression. He also ascribes to him an insufferable gap (it is this, "the insufferable," that causes the suffering) between what he is and what he seeks to be or not to be. Sometimes this gap is perceived from the position of the subject who feels compassion as the difficulty of making suffering present independently, of expressing it and dealing with it independently, without the mediation of a witness. The subject for whom compassion is felt makes present his suffering through the mediation of the witness, who becomes responsible for the presence of the other's suffering in the world (as he might be responsible for a loss befalling him [see 2.030 and from 6.533 on]).

5.340 Patronization and paternalism, which are usually associated with compassion, mean not annulling the subjectivity of one who is suffering but rather acknowledging it and taking responsibility for it. In compassion, acknowledgment of the other as a subject is unidirectional; even if acknowledgment from the other for whom I feel compassion causes me contentment and even excites me, I don't need it in order to feel compassion toward him (otherwise how would one explain compassion toward an infant or an animal?). I acknowledge the other as suffering, as desperate for help, as seeking to be other than what he is, whose very presence as one suffering exceeds what he is — I acknowledge him as non-thing, as some one. The intensified presence of his suffering or his intensified presence as one suffering flows over to me and makes me present to myself as one who recognizes some one who is suffering. I don't need recognition from the suffering other in order to take the position of the compassionate subject. But I do need recognition from others who may, like me, (have) take(n) the same position.

5.341 Forgoing acknowledgment from the other is part of the disinterested interest that one who feels compassion shows toward one who is suffering. Compassion may, of course, be accompanied or driven by other interests — various side benefits may be drawn from an interest in one who suffers — but it itself is "disinterested," no less than aesthetic contemplation. Compassion is an excitation that may be completely devoid of attraction or revulsion in relation to the exciting object — as it is, for Kant, in relation to the beautiful object; more likely, perhaps, as regarding the sublime in Kant, it includes a swift oscillation between revulsion (at the horror of the tortured body, the aching soul) and attraction (to what is desperately in need of help in the sufferer).

5.342 "An imprisoned man ... sees outside a wild beast tearing a child from his mother's breast, breaking his weak limbs in its murderous teeth, and ripping apart with its claws the palpitating entrails of this child. What horrible agitation must be felt when witnessing this event which holds no personal interest! What anguish must he suffer at this sight, unable to bring help to the fainting mother or to the dying child."[35] Rousseau borrows this episode from Mandeville, author of *The Fable of the Bees*,[36] and he sees it as testimony to the fact that he, too, the most radical theorist of egoism and self-interest known until his time, was "forced to recognize man as a compassionate and sensitive being" and even to depart from his "cold and subtle style" in order to paint that "pathetic image."[37] The excitation overflows its rim: for the sufferer in desperate need of help, for the witness observing him in emotional turmoil, and for the viewer of the picture from a distant time that is mediated by descriptive text and then through re-quoted quotation. The witness's compassion and the excitement of the reader viewing the image of the excited witness through his mind's eye follow not from the care of the witness and the reader for themselves but from a sense of disinterested empathy for a tormented other, combined with an inability to offer the other help (or an abstention from any intention of doing so).

5.343 The sensations of excess, superfluity, absence, and lack present in compassion are a reflection of the presence of what is excessive or lacking for the sufferer. Compassion is an excitation in which the one feeling compassion seeks neither to appropriate for himself nor to disconnect himself from the intensified presence; he seeks to end it for the suffering other, or at least to reduce its repleteness. And as long as it is impossible to offer help, the one feeling compassion is continuously swung to and fro between the desire to help and helplessness. This continuous motion is what excites him, what causes him to feel that his "heart goes out." What excites one whose heart goes out radiates from the presence of the repleteness or lack torturing the sufferer, on the one hand, and from his own helplessness in the face of the insufferable excitation, on the other (see 6.522). Sometimes helplessness alone is enough to give the suffering of an other a winning, or perhaps in this case overpowering, presence. Ensconced in this helplessness — that is, in the heart that goes out — is a demand to rush to the aid of one who is suffering, to dim the repleteness of the presence tormenting him. How this demand is ensconced, how it goes out with the heart, and how it bursts out of that and injures the one who feels compassion — all differ from one excitation to another, from one context to another. In certain institutionalized contexts, the one who feels compassion is also the one who acts immediately: a mother and her son, a lover and his beloved, a Florence Nightingale. In other contexts, it doesn't even occur to the compassionate one that he is called upon to help, and he will not know this until someone shows him the way to the position of addressee — that is, until someone unfolds the demand ensconced in compassion (5.350). But the content of the demand, the deed to be done, is not interpreted by the excitation. Compassion is very similar to temptation, for it is a preparation, as it were, for "a call to action devoid of content whose form alone is known in advance" (4.542).

5.344   In compassion, the excited one surrenders to the other even if he takes no action on his behalf; this is the essence of "being-for-the-other." Moreover, if he acts to alleviate the other's distress, his immersion in action dims the excitation (5.004). Therefore, compassion should sometimes be denounced if it slows down assistance, if the one who feels compassion enjoys the feeling of compassion itself, as well as his status as one who feels it, and so tends to linger on it. But this is not to say that it should be disqualified completely, as Spinoza and Nietzsche are understood to claim. When the subject is thought of as a position in a field of relations, not as the response of an entity seeking to preserve itself (Spinoza) or to intensify and overcome (Nietzsche), there is no fundamental problem with an excitation in which the self succumbs to its being for another, as happens with compassion.

5.345   Certain types of excited caring are similar to compassion. For instance, one might care for an other, yet in his excitement he seeks not to eliminate the cause of care or to appropriate the object of care but to preserve that object for himself. A dear one, but also a valuable object, a memento, or a work of art, may arouse excited care of this type. Characteristic of preservation-minded care is the objection to or the impossibility of translating the object that arouses care into the terms of a system of exchange. But this is not enough; the care must be disinterested as well. Some cultural institutions specialize in nurturing objects that arouse such disinterested care: museums, nature preserves, archaeological sites, and so forth. Nurturing disinterested care for the preservation of select objects (selected, of course, by the institutions in question) is the work of the preserving institutions. The preserving institution acquires symbolic capital, and through the mediation of this capital acquires other types of capital, by producing and distributing one type of excitation: disinterested care for the preservation of irreplaceable objects.

5.350 Temptation and compassion have a similar structure (as do the above-mentioned forms of disinterested care): both of them assume a kind of standing by, a disinterested interest, at least on the face of it, a restraint from appropriating the object of care or from severing connection with it; both of them call on the excited one to go beyond himself, to intervene, in an unconditional, content-less call that is ensconced within the excitation (compassion) or present on its surface, causing it to split (temptation). The one being tempted and the compassionate one are ready to follow their object of care, to give themselves to it, regardless of its response — sometimes a lack of response, an indifference, or a total helplessness on the part of the object of care excites them the most. In both, the antithesis of the excitation is not a negative excitation of rejection (as in sorrow and happiness, pain and enjoyment, repugnance and desire) but rather indifference, a mere absence of excitation. Perhaps it is against the background of this similarity that one should understand Christianity's insistence on a strict antithesis between the two. Succumbing to temptation was perceived as the source of evil, dedicating oneself to an other, in fact self-sacrifice, as the source of good. And vice versa: demonstrated indifference to temptation and the power to overcome it were perceived as an ultimate test of piety and righteousness; demonstrated indifference to the suffering of another was perceived as an insignia of evil, a kind of cruelty.

5.351 Nietzsche, who detested Christian morality in general and the compassion it praises in particular, continues to think of himself as trapped at the heart of the same structure and even develops it in a "unity of contradictions" of sorts: the ultimate temptation is compassion. That is the "last temptation" of Zarathustra, the ultimate test of self-restraint. Self-restraint is self-cruelty, indifference to the suffering self, and it is a key to all emotional and cultural sensibility, to all restraint and maturing. In self-cruelty, both temptation and compassion are denied, and indifference is shown for oneself as for another. One who is cruel to himself restrains his tendency to reject intensifying suffering, and through this his will to power and his power to will grow as well. The entire history of culture can be told as a dialectical development of cruelty and compassion, self-cruelty and gentleness.[38]

5.4 *The Masses and the Market*

5.400 When one who is hurt in an exciting encounter doesn't restrain his excitement, others are presented with it, too. The excitement has a winning presence that threatens to win them over, too (5.301). Frequently, someone's excitation is itself exciting. The closer the excited other is, the more likely it is that his excitation will generate excitation among those around him; or vice versa, an excitation that excites is a (not necessarily conclusive) sign of proximity — between friends, spouses, parents and children, siblings, and so on. And in turn vice versa: an excitation that doesn't excite can testify to alienation, to marred relations, to the disintegration of the family unit, to the end of a love affair, to a calculated relationship in which the other is merely a means.

5.401 One of the classical sociological distinctions between a community and a society (after Tönnies) or between mechanical solidarity and organic solidarity (after Durkheim) can be translated into terms of exciting excitations and unexciting excitations. A society where there is what Durkheim calls "organic solidarity" has developed mechanisms for neutralizing the spread of excitation among its members. Groups that nurture the spread of excitation among their members retain the "primordial" traits of a "community." However, it isn't true that "alienated" societies are without any spread of excitation or that communal societies practice no neutralization of excitation. At issue are two totally different patterns of controlling the spread of excitation. In "alienated" societies, the spread of excitation is channeled through economic and political systems of exchange. In communal societies, the neutralization and spread of excitation are channeled through highly developed codes of ritual and ceremonial conduct. Modernization, according to these distinctions and in this context, improves and enhances the cultural and social mechanisms that reify and commodify excitations.

5.410 In any case, excitation spreads through a dense social and cultural medium; a society does not leave it to the inclinations and whims of individuals. The movement of excitation can be imagined as a wave, like the movement of loss (2.130), a movement that is a transition not from unremarkable presence to intensified presence (and vice versa) but from the intensification of one presence to that of another, a movement of intensification and dissipation from addressee to addressee. At every frozen moment of this movement, someone else is excited, the one excited at the beginning of the movement is not the one excited at its end, but the excitation itself may move "like a low-pressure area, like the eye of a storm" (2.130). However, unlike the movement of loss, which may spread over large expanses and last for a long time and does not require direct physical proximity between the ones losing, excitation usually moves through a limited environment, and its movement requires physical proximity or sophisticated means of mediation. The relation between the movement of loss and the movement of excitation is similar to that between macrocosm and microcosm, between physics and microphysics, between geography and topography.

5.411 This is not just an analogy; causal relations connect loss and excitation, as well as their movements. A movement of loss leaves in its wake traces of excitation, "pits of longing, of sorrow, and of mourning" (2.130). In this case, a movement of excitation will be the wake of the movement of loss whose dynamic will dictate it (2.132): concentric or eccentric circles in the case of disaster, a spiral course in the case of an excitation resulting from bankruptcy, and so forth. However, in such cases the wave of excitation doesn't spread independently; it spreads only through the mediation of the wave of loss on which it rides or is carried.

5.412 A movement of excitation can, in turn, create a loss, too (although the relation is not symmetrical); it can do so by creating a party interested in what was lost or by creating the thing that will soon be lost, the excitation itself. The microphysics of excitation and its topography are not even fledgling sciences yet, but study of the movement of excitation is nevertheless more highly developed than study of the movement of loss; there are beginnings of it in social psychology and mainly in studies of mass behavior.

5.420 It's possible to imagine the movement of an excitation, such as that from the first audience ever viewing *Romeo and Juliet* to the audience viewing it today; generations of viewers, readers, and interpreters are the medium within which this movement occurs (compare 2.131) — but this example almost stretches the metaphor to its limits. The movement of an excitation is an actual movement. Excitation is contagious — like contagious laughter in a group, like desire arousing desire, like the applause of an enthusiastic audience, like the arousal of a crowd by a charismatic orator or by a display of power. When a couple takes pleasure in lovemaking, the contagious excitation is an inseparable part of the act of love. The couple's relative isolation is a condition (though most likely a culturally dependent one) for the occurrence of the pendulous movement of pleasurable excitation. A sense of others' presence instantly freezes this movement. But when a voyeur looks on undiscovered, or the sex act is put on display in a porn show, the presence of the sexual excitation spreads waves of excitation through the audience of voyeurs. A contagious excitation in pendulum movement between two individuals — laughter, anger, anxiety, nervousness, desire, pleasure, and so forth — is the exception; in most cases, the movement of contagious excitation is a mass phenomenon.

5.421　Elias Canetti began researching the movement of excitation through masses in his book *Crowds and Power*.[39] Canetti distinguishes five types of masses according to the type of excitation bounding about within the mass: a "baiting crowd" (the desire to kill or to view killing), a "flight crowd" (threat), a "prohibition crowd" (rebellion, resistance), a "reversal crowd" (aspirations of liberation from oppression, revenge), and a "feast crowd" (lust, pleasure). Canetti ascribes the movement of the mass (such as pursuit or flight) to the type of contagious excitation in question. The contagious excitation serves as a glue creating the mass as "a single body." Therefore, one who does not participate in an excitation, doesn't pass on the movement, is seen as a spoilsport. The obstructed excitation may naturally change, but the results of its obstruction are the same: movement is stopped. Canetti, however, doesn't offer a separate account of the movement of contagious excitation itself, nor does he refer to the possibility that the cohesion of a mass, as well as operating within a mass, itself acts to intensify the movement of excitations.

5.422　The density of the mass — in a demonstration, in a theater, during a rock concert or a group tour — creates conditions for the excitation to spread and generates the physical proximity and intimacy of those who share a single "fate" (that is, a situation), all of which helps to create the medium through which the movement passes. Of course, the movement of excitation may also spread via more complex mediating mechanisms, through various communication media but also through a "display of presence" in the public sphere.[40] Think of President Sadat's visit to Jerusalem, of the night the Berlin Wall was torn down, of the night Yitzhak Rabin was assassinated. Certain media events, like a crucial sports event or a thrilling political event, distribute excitation swiftly, all at once, through an entire population. Think of the radio broadcast from Lake Success on the night of November 29, 1947, when the UN made the decision to partition Palestine, or of the television broadcast of the ceremony in which the Israeli-Palestinian Declaration of Principles was signed on the White House lawn in 1993. Does the excitement sweeping through a TV-incited audience make it a mass? Probably not. The excitement scatters into innumerable homes, makes waves in front of the television screen, and dissipates, dies down quickly and separately in every house. But on the night of the UN resolution in November 1947, there was no television in Palestine, and people listened to the radio broadcast in large crowds, at home, and in many public spaces. Their excitement gushed out; crowds of people soon made it to the streets; the excitement created the mass.

5.423   Often, after an exciting event, the next morning's newspapers attempt to preserve it. Sometimes it is translated into spontaneous displays of presence, but these, too, soon fade away. Unlike loss, whose scope of movement is enormous and whose duration is almost unlimited, the movement of excitation (at least its independent movement) is spasmodic, short-lived, and limited in scope.

5.424   But on the night Yitzhak Rabin was assassinated, November 4, 1995, a movement of excitation emerged that continued for quite a while. The patterns of mourning that sprang up at the square that night were filmed on television and reproduced the next day, and filmed again and again reproduced, until the whole country was full of candles and melancholic songs. Later many wondered where all this had disappeared to in the days that followed, and how it could disappear so fast that by June 1996 a new right-wing government had come into power. They didn't understand that this was simply a movement of excitation, not necessarily a movement of loss, that movements of excitation are always spasmodic, even when a "beloved leader" is murdered, and all the more so when the victim is a leader who becomes beloved only after he is murdered. Neither did they understand that the television breathed life into the movement of excitation, in an artificial respiration of sorts, and that the movement stopped the moment the respirator was disconnected.

5.430   In contagious excitations in a mass, or in a pendulum movement between two individuals, the spreading excitation more or less retains its form; what spreads is an excitation of the same type: laughter, fear, veneration. But obviously, an excitation of one kind can trigger excitations of other kinds: pain may arouse compassion, but also anger or revulsion, for instance, and sometimes all three at once; happiness may arouse sorrow or hatred; pleasure may arouse desire or hatred or both together; and so forth. Usually such movements of excitation are of limited scope and duration and depend on a cultural repertoire of excitations and responses to excitations, and on the character traits of the one presented with the excitation of another. (However, "character" will in turn be defined, among other things, through patterns of excitation and response to excitation, and culture is characterized, among other things, by its repertoire of excitations and responses to excitations.) Certain social situations and cultural mechanisms form such movements of excitation: the ritual ceremony through which an excited individual or individuals infect an entire audience with their excitation; open gloating at others' misfortune that seeks to arouse sorrow, shame, or humiliation; philanthropic propaganda that disseminates images of suffering in order to arouse compassion. The latter is very close to the direct distribution of excitations through images — in advertising, in the media, in politics, and in many other venues of culture. However, at issue in this case is no longer the physics of the movement of excitation but the economics of excitations: production, exchange, distribution, and consumption of excitations packaged and communicated with the high sophistication of product designers and marketing executives.

5.431   Clearly, the production of excitations is not limited to the direct distribution of packaged products in various representational technologies (virtual reality, porn films, horror films, rousing speeches, and any form of rhetoric). Some excitations are produced as perishable merchandise (love songs, horror films); some are supposed to generate an entire wave of excitation (through a love letter, an inciting sermon); some are intended to activate every individual separately and to exhaust themselves in the private sphere (in music, in advertising); some are designed to activate a group in an enclosed social space (in a ritual ceremony); and some are distributed in an open public space to an undefined population of addressees and consumers (at a parade or procession, through election propaganda). Modern society has various means for intensifying presences — for instance, through psychotherapy (in which the presences of loss, or of the mother's or father's figure, and so on are intensified) or at "workshops" for "rediscovering" religion, for developing a consciousness of self, or some other form of "spirituality." There are workshops for contagious excitations (group therapy and support groups for patients and for members of two declared "identity" groups that are in conflict), and there are religious sects or cults that train their members to stifle certain excitations and intensify others.

5.44　The economics and politics of excitations are matters of major importance for every religion, for every form of psychotherapy, for every military drill, and in general for the training of individuals as individuals or as a group sharing a particularly demanding task. The orator at public assemblies is supposed to be a master at arousing and channeling excitations; the poet is a master at arousing them while changing their forms and objects. The job of controlling excitations, forming and nurturing them, was, in ancient and medieval times, mostly a matter for unique individuals, elevated persons, and was conducted in a closed economy of excitations in religious orders, in convents, in academies, in the prince's family. In modern times, however, the economics and politics of excitations turned into a matter concerning entire populations and were conducted in a closed economy within closed institutions — schools, factories, and the barracks of people's armies — and then in an open economy, in full view, in the public sphere, in the media, through skilled salespeople and sophisticated distributive mechanisms. Parts of this story are told by Foucault in his series of studies, from the history of insanity through the history of sexuality. With regard to the formation and control of excitations, these studies are simply an implementation of Nietzsche's program in the genealogy of morals. But Foucault doesn't deal with the last phase of the history of excitation, that is, with the commodification of excitation and its distribution in the modern public sphere and across virtual postmodern spaces.

5.5　*Surfeit*

5.500　Some excitations are such that the witness learns over time to desire them or seek more of them. These excitations cause enjoyment and pleasure. The child shrieking on the huge waterslide, on the roller coaster, or in the fun house at the fairgrounds derives enjoyment from fear and, perhaps more precisely, from the way in which fear intensifies the presence of the world around him. The masochist derives enjoyment from pain or, more precisely, from the way in which pain intensifies the presence of his body or the presence of another's pain-inflicting body. Some excitations are such that the witness asks for their cessation immediately, or in time. These are tormenting excitations that cause pain, sorrow, fear, revulsion. Here, too, pleasure and pain, enjoyment and fear, may be intermixed.

5.501 Every excitation, even the most pleasurable, of which the witness requests more and more reaches a point of surfeit in the end — whether because the desirer has fulfilled his desire, or the novel and unexpected have become boring,[41] or because the pain accompanying the pleasure has become insufferable. An excitation reaching its point of surfeit, becoming overmuch, becomes insufferable, becomes that which one seeks to suffer no longer. There is some impermanent threshold, not known in advance, beyond which the excitation becomes an encounter with casualties who seek to cut off contact with it.

5.51 The body and consciousness of a finite creature cannot continue an incessant excitation perpetually. Only God can love (himself, of course) forever; only God can hurt (the hurt of man, who else?) forever. The flesh-and-blood finite witness needs a rest, must sleep, has to leave every presence for some time, to remove all presences for some time. Besides, more and more presences are always coming, demanding attentiveness, seeking to gain attention for themselves, too. When the intensified presence is insufferable, but at the moment cannot be left, when one prays for the excitation to stop and nevertheless cannot be rid of it, the excitation becomes suffering. Suffering is an encounter with casualties in which one refrains or is prevented from disengaging.

Chapter Six

Suffering

6.0 *Disengaging*

6.000 Suffering is caused in an encounter with casualties in which one refrains or is refrained from disengaging. Suffering is an excitation whose intensified presence is excessive and becomes unbearable, but the one who is present is refrained or refrains from removing it. Suffering is the duration of the encounter with the unbearable; the unbearable is precisely what one bears when suffering, what one suffers from.

6.001 The reverse of suffering is pleasure: an excitation whose presence is amplified to the point that the one who is present wishes, "May it never end."[1] Pleasure is an encounter that makes the one involved in it hold on to it, refuse to let go. This articulation of the reverse relation between suffering and pleasure seems to repeat the classical opposition between excitation that causes revulsion and excitation that arouses attraction.[2] This opposition is subjected to the logic of desire ruling the thought of philosophers from Plato to Sartre: the intentionality of a lacking subject wishing to negate itself and fill the lack either by attaining the desired object or by disengaging from the repulsive object. The articulation suggested here tries to avoid this logic: it presupposes not a lack in the subject but an excess in the object, it does not identify pleasure with a desire that wishes to annul itself by attaining the desired object, and it identifies suffering not as a result of the presence of a repulsive object that raises the desire to disengage from it but as a result of the inability to disengage from an excitation that overflows its limits.

6.002 Suffering is an increase of a presence to the power of three: something is present; some one experiences this presence (as sorrow, anger, pain, fear, and so on) and herself as experiencing it; the experience of the presence itself, the excitation, is present as what one wishes to remove but cannot or may not, or not now anyway. Sometimes it is impossible, in principle, to remove the tormenting excitation, because what was lost will never return or because what is hurting is beyond the control of the one hurt; sometimes one cannot remove it easily, the way one opens a window, or changes the channel on television, but only through something that is lacking at present (money, a rare medicine, a distant lover); sometimes one chooses not to remove the tormenting excitation in order to prevent a loss that will bring damage or a pain that is much more intense to the one who suffers or to an other; sometimes one chooses not to remove the tormenting excitation because the same encounter also brings pleasure. Sometimes it is impossible to remove the tormenting excitation because someone is systematically preventing its removal, as in torture. One paradigm of torture, which is the prototype of causing suffering (6.403), is sleep deprivation, when the fundamental need to remove oneself from any presence is denied: the suffering occurs because one forces some one to be awake — that is, to be present — because she is prevented from removing herself from the situation, prevented from getting out.

6.003 Lévinas writes poignantly on this matter:

> I am going to lay stress on the pain lightly called physical, for in it engagement in existence is without any equivocation ... physical suffering in all its degrees entails the impossibility of detaching oneself from the instance of existence. It is the very irremissibility of being. The content of suffering merges with the impossibility of detaching oneself from suffering.... In suffering there is an absence of all refuge. It is the fact of being directly exposed to being. It is made up of the impossibility of fleeing or retreating. The whole acuity of suffering lies in this impossibility of retreat.... In this sense suffering is the impossibility of nothingness.[3]

Lévinas says these things about physical pain, which he distinguishes from mental anguish or moral pain (*la douleur morale*), and then immediately moves on to talk about suffering (*souffrance*). He is inaccurate about two things: physical pain does not necessarily cause suffering; suffering does not necessarily include physical pain, and even physical sensations that may accompany suffering caused by loss or humiliation are not necessarily sensations of pain. But if one ignores the way Lévinas narrows down the definition of suffering to physical pain, one can use his words as they are.

6.004 No excitation in itself is suffering. Even excitations of pain or fear, great sorrow or terrible anger, are not necessarily cases of suffering. Not all continuous pain necessarily causes suffering.[4] As was said, the masochist enjoys pain; the trained warrior or the man lying on a bed of nails can ignore it. But for the masochist, as well as for the warrior and the circus performer, there is a threshold beyond which the intensifying pain will cause suffering. Beyond this threshold, in performance as in war, suffering begins — even if the pain is still tolerable, even if one refrains from removing it only to keep up her part. The body pleads to end the encounter, to disengage; some one, who is posited as an addressee of this call, ignores it, being cruel to herself or to others, and the pain carries on. In any occurrence of suffering, some one is posited as the addressee of a call to disengage, and the encounter goes on. In self-cruelty (from abstinence through developing stamina and willpower to the self-mutilation of the hysterical), the suffering doubles the-one-who-suffers before it causes her to wither. It simultaneously posits her as the addressee and as the addresser of the demand to disengage. Maybe for that reason Nietzsche describes a scale of "cruelty against oneself" as a sublimating instrument in the development of self-consciousness.[5]

6.010 The excitation can become excessive either because it continues for too long or because it goes "too deep" and becomes too intense all of a sudden. In any case, at the moment it is crossed, the threshold of the tolerable is suddenly illuminated. A deafening noise can cause suffering at the moment of the encounter itself; the barely audible sound of a dripping tap becomes excessive gradually, very slowly, until the nuisance becomes torture and the one who hears it cannot take it anymore. One drop, one too many, has made it excessive. Suffering begins when a sharp sense of "too much" comes upon the one who is overcome by the feeling — "I have had enough" — when something inside some one cries out, "No more, stop it!" The presence of what is exciting turns into a presence of a surplus that cannot be disposed of.

6.011 This presence can go on for a very long time. There is no necessary connection between the pace at which the excitation builds up and its duration until it becomes too much, or between the duration of the excitation and its pace after it becomes torture. In general, one can distinguish a decentralized, prolonged suffering from a concentrated, intense, short suffering.[6] The deafening noise that caused suffering immediately could go on and on, meddle with other sounds that try to overcome it, and not let go. In situations of extreme mental tension, the dripping tap that gradually becomes excessive could drive the one who hears it insane; she will scream in order to silence it, will fight to the death anything that stands in the way of her attempt to get rid of the stupefying, stultifying dripping.

6.020 If the excited one did not express her excitation before, she will tend to do so at the moment it becomes excessive — in bodily gestures, in facial expressions, in a held or rushed breath — and such an expression is anticipated even if the suffering is not physical. To suppress spontaneous or instinctive expressions of suffering at such a moment, and in different ways at all the moments of suffering that will follow, one must practice self-discipline, restraint, and self-control. When these are lacking or insufficient, the moment of excess is also the moment in which the suffering becomes present for others who can decipher its traces in the sufferer's body and behavior. But not always is there some one there, and if she is there, she is not always capable of or interested in noticing; sometimes her attention must be demanded. There is a difference between involuntarily expressing suffering and deliberately entering a communicative situation. The utterance that expresses suffering could remain unanswered in both cases, but in deliberately entering a communicative situation, the-one-who-suffers takes on rules of expression that are not derived from the suffering itself.

6.021 And so suffering is an encounter with casualties in which it is impossible, or one is unwilling, to disengage, to cross the threshold again, this time in the other direction, to a place where one can contain the excitation or dispel it altogether. When one comes across the exciting presence and cannot disengage, one reports the casualties, cries for help, requests to be evacuated. Suffering positions the sufferer, if she is still capable of it, as an addresser in a communicative situation, real or imaginary, with an addressee, real or imaginary. "Mayday, Mayday." "My God, my God, why hast thou forsaken me?" "Mommy!" "Doctor, it hurts. Here." "Where are you, my boy, why won't you come home, my boy, come home, come home already." "O Jesus." "O brother, where art thou?"

6.022 "Man's first language, the most universal, the most energetic and the only language he needed before it was necessary to persuade assembled men, is the cry of nature ... this cry was elicited only by a kind of instinct, in pressing circumstances, to be for help in great dangers, or for relief in violent ills" — the words of Jean-Jacques Rousseau.[7] For Rousseau, the cry of suffering is a primary, germinal communicative situation, a pre-social language that "was not of much use in the ordinary course of life, where more moderate sentiments prevail."[8] The massive excitation that is unbearable throws man into a communicative situation. For Rousseau, that means that the individual, who can survive in the state of nature as a solitary creature most of the time, needs his other, but can also respond to him. The primal linguistic relation is also the primal social relation. For us, that means that the individual is thrust into a communicative situation that is structured socially and linguistically, a situation whose structure and repertoire are always already there.

6.023 As was said, the communicative situation is not necessarily a speech situation. In any presencing of suffering for others (as distinguished from its presence for the sufferer), through speech, a cry, a body posture, or the image of a posture, some one presences or represents an amplified presence (of excess or lack) that becomes too much, whose excess or lack have become intolerable, and some one is positioned as an addressee who is called — at least implicitly, at least in principle — to enable the sufferer to disengage. This "call" is not necessarily related to any explicit utterance of the sufferer or the one who represents her. It comes from the presence of suffering as an encounter that has turned excessive and that can, in principle, be disengaged from. The sufferer suffers because she cannot disengage, or because she chose not to disengage in order to prevent more suffering (for her or for others). But to acknowledge her as the one who suffers means to acknowledge her as the one who is yearning, begging, craving, aching to disengage. Suffering turns the sufferer into a living communicative act, whether or not she cries for help. The sufferer who chooses restraint hides her pain, stifles her tears, and deadens the utterances of suffering that her body produces.

6.024 Of course, the opposite situation is also possible: some one is not "really" suffering, yet her body produces utterances of suffering. The one who cries for help does not need to "really" suffer in order to posit herself as a living communicative act. Suffering can be displayed, just like any other excitation, and the addressee has no way to determine in advance which is real suffering and which is its simulation. An attestation of suffering cannot be disqualified by going back to the expressed experience; one can only doubt the witness or the institutionalized conditions of expression of her suffering (compare 4.333 and 5.141). A common and convenient way of avoiding answering the call of the sufferer is to interpret her utterances of suffering as pretense and to present her as an impostor. One pretends to know that the other pretends to suffer.

6.025 To pretend: to pre-tend, to disconnect the immediacy of the internal tendency from the external articulation of it.[9] To impersonate: to disconnect the persona from the inside. To accuse someone of pretending: to assume a rift between the internal and the external, and, prior to that, to assume that there is an inside, that the inside can articulate, sometimes through and sometimes despite the outside, what really is "in there." How can you know that the sufferer really suffers in there? How can you know that the external persona is really transmitting messages from inside?

6.030 The presencing of suffering for others is the presencing of the craving to disengage, before and beyond any other attitude toward the encounter and its causes. This craving is always an event in which the sufferer is posited — finds herself posited — in a communicative situation in which she begs someone, an implicit or explicit addressee, she or her others, to disengage. The presencing of this craving that is encapsulated in the presencing of the suffering is an explicit positioning of an addressee.

6.031 In order to be the addressee of an utterance of suffering, one need not be at the presence of that craving itself; its representation is enough, that is, the presence of what represents the sufferer. For the witness, there is no difference between an "immediate" presentation and a "mediated" representation of suffering. The sufferer's suffering is always merely an excitation that can be represented, identified with, interpreted and understood, imagined more or less tangibly, but never presenced "in itself," that is, as it is for an other. One can never appropriate an other's suffering (or her other excitations), not even in the way one appropriates an object in a gaze. In this sense, suffering (like other excitations) is different from an idea, from meaning, and even from intention, which are also always already representations for an other — that is, they are present in a mediated way and yet can be appropriated. But suffering, which is an excessive, relentless excitation, is also different from other excitations (for example, sadness, boredom, and gaiety) that can be experienced as amplified presences without having to be doubled as representations for an other. Suffering, or at least continuous, escalating suffering, compels the sufferer, after crossing a certain threshold, to present her suffering for others. Beyond that threshold, which varies from individual to individual and from culture to culture, the sufferer enters, whether she likes it or not, into a transmitting position. Appropriately, this threshold can be called "the transmission threshold."

6.040 When suffering goes past the transmission threshold, some one, real or imaginary, is positioned as the addressee; or rather, an addressee position opens up, which can be occupied from then on. In order for the addressee position to be occupied, all the conditions for the existence of communication must be fulfilled: open lines, clear codes, some one who listens. When the line is open, the code is clear, and there is some one who listens; the listener is an addressee of a cry for help.

6.041 It is reasonable to assume that the primary code is biological: humans can identify animals that suffer according to their postures and cries; animals can identify other animals.[10] In effect, the code is culturally shaped. In any case, there is no point looking for the universal common denominator — the biological infrastructure — of all cultural codes, even if it could be identified and agreed upon, because suffering is not necessarily physical and because evolutionary primordiality is not a moral category; what is communicated in a more primordial code is no more important, decisive, or terrible than what is communicated through more developed codes.

6.042 In the speaker position, all the rules of the communicative situation, of discourse and genre, apply to the-one-who-suffers. But the utterances that announce the suffering (6.021) only announce the existence of the situation of suffering, announce the speaker as the one who suffers, that is, as some one engaged in an encounter from which one does not disengage. Sometimes, but not necessarily, the utterances indicate or explicitly point to the cause of suffering as only the one who suffers grasps it. To call a rescue team, one need not describe the experience of amplified presence; one needs only to report the casualties, to communicate that it is impossible to disengage. When suffering is horrible, the sufferer (or the one who identifies with her) will usually prefer to show the suffering rather than describe it. In acute cases, even the linguistic description will strive to show — that is, to presence — the suffering in full force and immediacy.

6.043 Even such a transmission can be a simulation of suffering. Whenever it is possible to transmit, communicate, or signify, it is also possible to lie. ("Semiotics," says Eco, "is in principle the discipline studying everything which can be used in order to lie."[11]) Some one reports casualties when there are none; some one asks for a rescue squad when there is no terrorist attack. As with any transmission, the addressee has to determine the credibility of the transmission according to hints given in the context. But the simulative effect decreases the further you are from the addresser position and the nearer you are to the addressee position. There might not be a sufferer, but there is no doubt that someone has been placed in the addressee position, because there was a cry for help, or its simulation. This is commonly the case with a civil servant — for example, a soldier or a policeman — who has become an addressee of a cry for help that displays a suffering that might never have been, certainly not *hic et nunc*, but is produced because of another suffering, whose expression is impossible or forbidden in the present communicative situation. Even when the addressee suspects a simulation of suffering, she must take into account the possibility that it is a genuine attempt to communicate. Yet if the addressee completely overlooks the possibility that it is a simulation, a deceit, she might find herself cooperating with extortion.

6.044 Here are two seemingly contradictory claims about the structural conditions of suffering: (1) There is an inverse relationship between the efficacy and efficiency of the communication channels (the credibility of transmission, the density of the network, accessibility, transparency of the message, and so on), on the one hand, and an increase in the suffering and the price it exacts from the suffering individual and her environment, on the other. (2) Developed, efficient, and functional communication channels will increase the suffering that is expressed, will increase the willingness to express suffering, will reduce the will and ability to deny suffering, and in general will open new possibilities of experiencing suffering. There is no reason to assume that suffering is not an excitation that becomes more refined as its means of expression and representation become more sophisticated, just like any other excitation. This is not a paradox, but a combination of two processes or cultural conditions that coexist and even feed off each other. In any case, it is always preferable to have an increase in suffering that is a result of the refinement of its means of expression in a developed communicative network than an increase in suffering that is a result of a block or a collapse of a communicative network. The difference is visible. In the first case, the new conditions of communication produce a more refined sensibility to suffering both in the sufferer and in the addressee, and they enable both the call and its response. In the other case, the addresser and the addressee disengage, and the call remains hanging in midair, which becomes a suffocating, dense atmosphere.

6.045 Utterances of suffering have no primary epistemic status; they are no more certain than other utterances. Their object has no primary ontological status. Even if suffering is an excess of presence, it is not the only presence that could make the situation excessive. Nonetheless, utterances of suffering have a singular pragmatic status. They are descriptive utterances that make the witness an addressee of a prescription, at least in the sense that a call for disengagement is a command for action.

6.050 One should clearly distinguish between the presencing of suffering in the communicative situation, directly or through a representation, and giving the suffering meaning — a matter that the literature of suffering deals with extensively. These are two very different speech acts. The one who cries for help has no time to give meaning; she is interested in relief, not interpretation. The one who interprets her or someone else's suffering defers rescue, or speaks retrospectively, sometimes posthumously, about the suffering of the convalescing or the dead. The one who answers the cry for help must give a causal, immediate interpretation, has to answer questions such as "Where is the point of contact?" "From what should the sufferer be disengaged in order to alleviate her suffering?" In this case, suffering is an effect of an estimated cause; its appearance is always grasped as a metonym whose deciphering is fragmentary, because its semiotic web is abandoned the instant one knows how to act. For some one who wishes to endow suffering with meaning, some one who engages in a hermeneutics of suffering, suffering can be seen as a symptom of an individual or a group, as an attestation of the sufferer's past, or as an ominous sign announcing her end, and anyway as a sign — metonym or metaphor — in a context in which the horizon of hermeneutic activity is open to infinity. Suffering can be seen as a metaphor of someone else's suffering — God's, for example — or as a metonym of the anguished homeland, and then it becomes a means for focusing and displacing attention. In any case, the hermeneutics of suffering is of no interest to the one who is posited as an addressee by the cry for help, at least not here, not now. If she is interested in it, if this hermeneutics becomes her problem, it is because she has already detached herself from the position of the addressee of the prescriptive cry for help.

6.051 The causal interpretation of the expression of suffering is a necessary condition for alleviating or preventing suffering — one has to know something about the causes of some one's suffering in order to know how to help her — whereas the hermeneutics of suffering can only function in the justification of suffering or its damning, in justifying the verdict or in demanding justice. These are two alternative exchange systems. In the causal interpretation of suffering (which is somewhat similar to estimating damage [see 6.330]), a certain type of suffering is offered a certain type of relief; what is supposed to replace the expression of suffering is the reply to suffering, the act of relieving it. In the hermeneutics of suffering, the expression of suffering is only a symptom or an indexical sign of the state of the general exchange system extending over a time and space that go far beyond the space-time of the event of suffering itself. In this system, each event of suffering is supposed to balance the sins of the past, of the sufferer or of others, or to stand as a future credit for the sufferer (or of others who are worthy of her suffering). In cases of theodicy-like justification, the expressions of suffering are taken to testify to the internal balance of the system; in cases where suffering seems unjustifiable, this lack of reason for suffering is taken to prove the weakening of the system, its breakdown, "breaking of the vessels," an "eclipse," and other such exaggerations.

6.052 I admit that this description is based on a prejudice against the religious interpretation of suffering and takes the distinction between a reason and a cause for granted. It is possible that from the perspective of the religious interpreter and the sufferer responding to the offered interpretation, the meaning of suffering is, precisely, its cause. It is possible that from their perspective, the religious sermon is a true response, because it offers the sufferer relief, even if only because she now understands, but also a relief that will be achieved as a result of devoting herself to religious discourse and because of the internal turning point, the remorse, the penitence, and the good behavior that might follow. Whoever insists on entering such a debate will eventually need empirical arguments. These may not convince the believer whose dogmas are irrefutable, but the traditional theological questions will remain open, as ever: the chronic problem of a certain imprecision in divine providence (the righteous who suffers) and the question of the creation and existence of Evil in a world created by an omnipotent, benevolent God.

6.053 Both in the causal explanation and in the hermeneutics of suffering, the present suffering attests to what is missing: putative causes of suffering or conditions of its relief in the first case, the meaning of suffering in the second case. But in the first case, what is absent is present elsewhere, in another time, and could return and reappear at any moment for the-one-who-suffers, or for the witness of her suffering. In the second case, in the hermeneutics of suffering, what is absent will always remain absent, by definition, from the space where suffering appears. The meaning of suffering — its place in the exchange system that goes far beyond the time and place of the suffering event — will never appear in the same space in which some one witnesses the suffering of another. The hermeneutics of suffering is a form of transformation from presence (which is always excessive in suffering) to absence, and from the real space of the appearance of suffering in the world (which is a semiotic space in which signified and signifiers serve intermittently) to the imaginary space in which meanings "appear" (which is a space of signified without signifiers). This is where the picture of reality begins to flip over, exchanging a figure for background, positive for negative. The hermeneutics of suffering is the camera obscura of the sufferers, the birthplace of ideology. Any critique of ideology has to position itself, at least once, at least for a while, in the other direction, in the passage from the hermeneutics of suffering to a causal reading of suffering.

6.054 Even the most successful hermeneutics of suffering cannot completely eradicate its pointlessness for the one who suffers. Suffering, says Lévinas, always appears in its "interiority" as suffering in vain, "*pour rien*."[12] When I try to give it meaning, I cannot assume that that meaning cancels the suffering other's experience of "for nothing." "Suffering...as meaningful in me, useless in the other."[13] It is true that in many cases, the meaning given to suffering can relieve, encourage, even uplift the spirit of the one who is proud of her resilience and her ability to suffer for a worthy cause, to the point where she begins to like her suffering. But this does not annul the "for nothing" feeling as immanent to what Lévinas calls the "interiority" of the suffering, the principal form of the experience of suffering. Even the just administration of suffering (or rational management, which Lévinas discusses in the same context[14]) cannot achieve this. Suffering needs interpretations and sermons precisely because it is experienced as unfounded. The hermeneutics of suffering supposes the experience of suffering as unfounded, and that is precisely the outrageous dimension in the experience of suffering it tries to eradicate.

6.1 *Touching Words*

6.100 I "own" my suffering, at least until I "lose control," "can take it no more," until I am controlled by my suffering. My suffering can control me more than an other can. An other frightens me, threatens me with suffering, or causes me suffering, but does not really control me, because I can always refuse him, even if at a terrible price. When suffering controls me, it truly controls me, because it expropriates my self and takes over me, seizes my ability to decide when to keep silent and when to scream, until it expropriates my ability to act at all. Suffering paralyzes me. That is why an other who threatens me with suffering or causes me suffering — even if only through the anxiety that the threat arouses in me — best controls me.

6.101 As long as I own my suffering, I can decide whether to scream or keep quiet, whether to turn the suffering into a cause for action or for paralysis, whether to work through the suffering as a "corrective experience" or repress and silence it, whether to do things with it or let it do things to me. More than anything, I decide when to "broadcast" the suffering to others and to what extent, how much, in what means of communication and under what conditions, who the addressee will be and what the context will be, what form this suffering will have — a complaint, a shout, a sob, a plea — and what the contents of the communication will be, if it will be possible to separate form from content in the phrase of suffering, and what the cost will be. I am responsible (to the extent that I am responsible for my expressions, my body language, the language I use, my obsessions) for entering my suffering into a circulation of communication and exchange, or for removing it from circulation. And this is precisely what I cannot do with the suffering of the other. I can ignore her, I can respond to her, I can pretend that I am responding and actually continue ignoring her, but if she decides to broadcast, I cannot completely eliminate the communicative element in her suffering. To censor, to repress, to remove, to prevent access to communication channels, to communicate in a way that neutralizes the cry — all these are responses in the face of the suffering of the other, in my ring of communication, but each response can only be made once I have already been the addressee of this suffering.

6.110 The description of the suffering "in itself," a description that tries to "express" the suffering, to pass on the experience to someone else who can supposedly imagine it and imagine herself in the place of the sufferer, this description requires time, concentration, an ability to distance oneself from the suffering, to disengage momentarily, an ability to focus on images and expressions that are supposed to represent it, to measure, time and again, the mold of representation against what is represented. The sufferer who is capable of doing that might sink into the presence of the representation, be taken over by it, in a way that dims, a little or a lot, the unbearable excitation she wishes to express. Sometimes this process takes place until the excessive excitation dies out, and the expression of suffering assuages the suffering. But even if the unbearable excitation does not die out, the process of representation inseparably combines the representing expressions with the continuing experience of suffering until it is no longer possible to talk about the "original" experience of suffering.

6.111 In any case, "original" is a momentary and specific matter, one that does not yet have an explicit representation, that exists "for itself" only until the explicit representation appears, and is afterward placed there like an absentee, to whom the expression points again and again without being able to grasp or attain it. The continuous presence of the suffering does not necessarily cease or lessen due to the hazing of the suffering in its representations; it merely becomes an inseparable part of the act of representation itself. And vice versa, the act of representation becomes an inseparable part of that presence.

6.112 Between the presence of the suffering and the language that describes it (or other means of representation) stretches a gap that separates the excitation from the expression (5.102–5.120). In certain cases, this gap, and the unbearable presence of an unceasing excitation, could lead the sufferer to seek new, special means of expression; sometimes it brings her to infinitely speak her suffering, so that the "touching words" will touch, will find consolation. This speech, which constantly reinvents new representations of suffering and changes the way in which the unbearable excitation is perceived, constantly moves away from the traces of the presence of the suffering in the past, the traces of the encounter from which it emerged, if it emerged from it at all, and never catches up with the presence of the suffering in the present. Nonetheless, it could refine the spectrum of sensibilities of the sufferer and of the one who witnesses her suffering and is willing to listen.

6.120 But all these things do not apply to speech as a cry for help, to a notification of an encounter with casualties and no possibility of disengaging. They only apply to what can be called "mimetic representation" of suffering, which in real time, when everything is so urgent, has almost no place. In real time, the one who suffers wants to disengage from the encounter, and it does not matter in what sense and in what way this encounter unbearably excites her. An expression of suffering that posits the witness as an addressee of a call for help is supposed not to "imitate" or "mirror" the suffering, but to urgently presence only the "unbearable" or the "intolerable" in it; everything else is less pressing. Suffering may demand a private language that will express it with absolute precision, that will recognize its singularity and the exclusive relationship of the one who suffers to her suffering, but when there are casualties, the need to call for help becomes greater. The sufferer who asks to be rescued must be understood. For that purpose, culture has prepared several familiar communication channels and a few lexicons. The physician has such a lexicon, quite impoverished within the context of modern Western medicine, because it sees in suffering first of all, and sometimes also all in all, only an unreliable symptom. Clinical psychology has a richer lexicon, which also gives the sufferer a new language and new kinds of excitations. And there is a lexicon of distress that is displayed in the public sphere by photojournalists and television crews, a lexicon of demonstrations, sound bites, body language, and images of horror.

6.121   A mirroring representation of the suffering becomes more vital the more distant or unperceivable its presence is. It is unnecessary, or it can be rejected, when the suffering can be presenced as soon as it is caused, at the moment when the sufferer wants to disengage. In other words, the message can be extremely coded when the nets of communication are open, the information flows freely, and the addressee is listening fully. But when the nets are obstructed, the information fragmentary, and the addressee distracted, the suffering has to be presenced in a way that will capture his attention again and make him *identify* the condition of the sufferer as that horrible condition: an encounter with a presence that is excessive, in which there are casualties and no possibility of disengaging. First of all, to identify (who, where, in what condition); the matter of identification (with) will be discussed later. The patient lying on the dentist's chair announces her suffering with a short cry, an instinctive recoiling. The dentist drilling into the tooth immediately understands and stops. Later, perhaps, if necessary, the patient may try to describe her pain to the dentist, or the dentist might ask the patient to give him such a description. The lover tormented by longing for her loved one who has gone away needs first of all to rehabilitate her communication network. Only later can she poetize in order to describe to her lover the suffering she experienced at the separation. Her words will try to touch the lover's soul, because now nothing other than words can touch. Those stranded in a war-stricken city (I am thinking of

Mostar or Sarajevo in Bosnia), or homeless people in the streets of a busy metropolis (I am thinking of Tel Aviv), require, first of all, access to the communication network. Then they need the necessary information to operate the network, to code their message, and, finally, they require a listener. In order to reach her, her communication network, and her code, they have to presence their suffering through representations that mirror this suffering and not just announce its existence. Such a message presupposes healthy communication, open access to the broadcasting position, and a listener keen to identify messages of suffering.

6.122 It is not always possible to report casualties or call for help. Sometimes the radio is damaged, sometimes the radioman is wounded, sometimes the entire network is silent — perhaps the broadcasting station is damaged, perhaps someone switched off the radio on the other side and "the communications are down." One must reach cover, return fire, or hide and wait for a cease-fire or for death. Or give up and surrender — to one's enemy, to one's suffering.

6.130 The one who suffers could cope with her suffering in action, in a speech act, or in another form of response. But she may also devote herself to it, and this devotion could be a kind of action. Sometimes she collapses into the abyss of her suffering and never rises again. Sometimes she adorns herself in preparation for it, yields to it in a celebratory manner, holds on to it in order to be constructed by it, in order to construct from it the privileged sufferer with its special rights, the suffering subject.

6.131 Suffering gives the suffering subject her identity, her being for others. But the one who suffers wants much more from the suffering than simply her identity; she wants attention, sympathy, material profit, and all this with the mediation of the compassion that she arouses in the witness of her suffering. "Compassion is an excitation caused by the intensification of the suffering or distress of an other as one who takes a subject position due to the very fact of his suffering"(5.332). This is precisely what the sufferer tries to achieve through displaying and representing her suffering. And she can do this with or without giving the compassionate one recognition in return for his ruth, his sympathy, or even his noble charity. In the same way that the compassionate one does not need recognition from the sufferer, the sufferer does not need to recognize the compassionate one in order to call him to help her by displaying her suffering.

6.132 The pitied subject position has unique characteristics, which change historically and culturally, but it is hard to imagine a culture lacking institutionalized ways to display suffering together with the helplessness and the inability of the sufferer to cope independently with her suffering, or even to express it and gain others' attention. In a culture such as ours, the suffering subject that arouses compassion is typically depicted as some one who is almost incapable of talking and almost unable to touch, a subject that has nothing left but a gaze, and even that gaze is turned not toward the world, to perceive it, sort it, and control it, but toward the one who posits her, to express infinite suffering and woe. This subject has a mute body, limp and lame, and only a pair of eyes or a screaming mouth, like transmitters of distress signals. Like the open mouth of the woman on the bridge in Munch's painting *The Scream*, or the look shot out of the eyes of the tortured in Goya's paintings, or the look in the eyes of the hungry African child who decorates so many humanitarian appeals.

6.140 These characteristics of the pitied subject are rooted deep in the Christian tradition and ethic, and they are transformed in the age of mass media, electronic media, and the turning of human rights into a new civil religion. In fact, the pitied subject is perhaps all that is left from the universality of the subject after the critique of philosophers such as Nietzsche, Heidegger, Althusser, Foucault, and Derrida. The pitied subject's suffering is recognized, when it is recognized, without regard for his religion, race, gender, nationality, or class. He is pitied "by virtue of his 'capacity to suffer,' his suffering faculty, that is, by virtue of his biological features, his very belonging to the human race, and even by virtue of his simply being a living creature" (5.332). What happens to the witness until she recognizes this suffering, and how she responds to it once she recognizes it, are matters determined by historical, social, cultural, and personal variables. But at the moment of recognition — that is, during the encounter that produces the presence of the suffering for the witness as an excitation of compassion — the sufferer is recognized as "one of our own," part of the same species of those born to suffer. The recognition that compassion is overflowing or failing to appear within the compassionate one because she witnesses the suffering of a Jew or a Gentile, an extremely wealthy or a very poor person, a black or a white person, a man or a woman, is a retroactive recognition that is not part of the excitation itself. A compassionate witness might all of a sudden realize that she is pitying the "wrong" subject, and may become remorseful or ferocious toward the sufferer for causing her such a conflict between what she was supposed to feel and what she actually felt.

6.141 Displayed or represented suffering could release the one who suffers, at least for a while, from the limitations and disadvantages that her social place imposes on her, because recognizing her as a sufferer forces others to relate to her identity through her suffering and not the other way around — to treat her suffering through her identity, which is more common. Usually, these are fleeting moments during a particularly acute distress. Often they appear during a disaster, mainly when there is a temporary and unusual affinity between "brothers in fate." The oath of Hippocrates is an ancient attempt to institutionalize this moment in the medical practice. But although these are fragile, fleeting moments, their mere possibility is enough to move sufferers to devote themselves to their suffering and presence it in the appropriate social situations; they hope to gain something in this way from the recognition, attention, or help that they are deprived of because they belong to an inferior group. In certain situations, in certain cultural contexts, suffering could be a mechanism of social mobility. But of course one has to already have certain cultural resources in order to extract this profit from one's suffering.

6.15 Devoting oneself to suffering is a less radical, or more defeated, form of cruelty against oneself (6.004). Here, too, suffering is joined by a delay of response, sometimes to the point of obtaining pleasure from the mere desire to disengage and end the encounter. But even if someone suspends the disengagement, holds on to the unbearable excitation in order to purge herself, purify herself in agony, she does not eradicate the suffering. On the contrary, she affirms it, turns it into something in her psychological or social economy, in order to exchange it for something else, to use it in an exchange relationship, or to turn it into an instrument in her self-construction, the construction of her personality.

6.2 *Duration*

6.200 Suffering occurs when it is forbidden or impossible to "disengage from an encounter with casualties," and so the temporality of suffering as an unceasing duration is part of the essence of its presence. "The content of suffering merges with the impossibility of detaching oneself from suffering," says Lévinas (6.003), and this impossibility is always a question of time. If "in excitation, time itself acquires a degree of presence" (5.241), then in suffering this temporalization is intensified and presenced: the being of the-one-who-suffers is experienced as time, a time of continuous suffering, an expectation for the moment it will cease.

6.201 As in any excitation (5.240 on), but with increasing intensity, suffering as temporalization expels the sufferer from time's ordinary imperceptible progress and bifurcates the flow of time. Sometimes time grinds to a halt, the excitation that causes the suffering goes on for eternity, and the suffering continues on a different time span. The-one-who-suffers measures time by the increase and pace of pain, by whether the end of the workday is near or distant, by various traces on her body that indicate the duration of contact and the expected end of the painful encounter. Sometimes time solidifies, becoming as present as the suffering itself, like an empty stomach, a throat burning with thirst, or a tooth screaming with pain.

6.202 Simone Weil says: "Suffering is nothing, apart from the relationship between the past and the future, but what is more real for man than this relationship? It is reality itself.... We cannot think that it simply *is*. That is unendurable."[15] But this is precisely the thing one suffers from in a disaster, the "simply is," a presence that chains the-one-who-suffers to her present, a present that powerfully magnetizes both past and future to itself, the remembrance of things past, the hope for what will be, and the anxiety; a present that magnetizes the relationship to the past and the future to itself until they are sometimes completely compressed into it. Then, in opposition to what Weil says, disaster is precisely the nothing that remains of this relationship to the past and the future. But not every event of suffering is a disaster.

6.203 In the course of suffering, temporalization has specific characterizations as the synthesis of a past, present, and future — a past that is presenced through its traces, a present that never is, and a future that is preceded by its omens. The distance from the past greatly diminishes. A clear line separates the past that precedes the suffering from the suffered past. The past that came before the suffering is first of all — sometimes exclusively — present through negation: a long time ago, before this terrible affair began, it wasn't like this. The suffered past is drawn into the continuous moment of the present, the distance between the presence of traces of suffering in memory and the presence of suffering itself is blurred or erased. The entire duration of suffering folds into the present moment of suffering; every moment of the present carries with it the entire duration of suffering. There is a clear line drawn also in the future, separating the future that belongs to the suffering and the future that is preceded only by negation: the moment when the suffering will cease or diminish. The present is nothing but the duration of suffering, the intolerable excessive presence in the space of presences, the space between the sufferer and her body, her body and the presences of the things that cause suffering, or the things that stand in front of her in complete indifference. The intolerable presence continues incessantly. It folds the suffered future within it, as additional distress and anxiety that are almost indistinguishable from the painful excitation itself.

6.204　The ability to dissipate suffering is related to the ability to deconstruct this temporality and sometimes based on it. The one who offers the sufferer help will attempt to retell his past and state what awaits him in the future, to link him back to the past that preceded the suffering and to the future that will come after the suffering ends, and to indicate places and events that transcend the space taken over by the suffering and the possibilities that the suffering hasn't yet temporalized. How difficult it is to do this for a sick woman, addicted to her disease, or for a depressed man, drowning in his despair. How terrible it is to do it for someone who is brought toward his end by horrendous suffering.

6.210　Intensified suffering is a duration that defines experience in its totality, as long as it lasts, including the short-lived cessation of suffering, the moments in which the suffering calms down or is temporarily forgotten. But at the same time, any one of the moments of suffering as duration is also a focused center that organizes the situation, wounds it, saturates it, and doubles the presences in it, dictating the relationship of the sufferer to things, to others, to herself. These two moments exist also with regard to the space of the encounter: on the one hand, a focused center that is located in the tormented body or the anguished mind and organizes the situation around itself, the space of things; on the other hand, the immediate surroundings of suffering as an enclosed space, the space that the sufferer can (or "can afford to") move within ("in such a terrible situation"), the shortening range of the hand, of the objects of interest, the narrowing horizon of memory, of anticipation, as one's entire lifeworld is taken over by the winning presence of suffering. Suffering is an extreme excitation that generates a heterotopic space-time (5.233 on) whose unique structure is highly resilient.

6.211　The heterotopic space-time of suffering, as the organizational center for the experience of the encounter and the form in which it folds into the totality of the experienced event, is transformed completely when suffering is represented by some one who witnessed it. Some one takes on a responsibility for the memory of the suffering, hers and mainly that of others, because she tries to turn this suffering — that is, to turn its representation — into something of value in some exchange economy, emotional or cultural, private or social. In such a case, she will displace the unique duration of suffering from private experience to the communicative channels of the remembering culture. She will try to reconstruct, in discourse, in the imaginary, a continuum between the suffered past and the remembering present, to erase the distance between the presence of the traces of suffering in the memory and the presence of suffering itself, without suffering itself having any presence. The temporal continuum will replace the presence of the past suffering. Then she will unfold this furrow and present time as a continuous duration. Or rather, her images will move from the folding of the past into the present, to the spreading of the continuous duration from the present to the past, and back from the past to the present. Christians do it in relation to Jesus. Zionists do it in relation to the Jewish victims of the Holocaust and the Jewish casualties in the Arab-Israeli conflict. Palestinians do it in relation to the Palestinian victims of the conflict. This displacement appropriates private suffering durations by giving them a context and a meaning within historical time, but it represses or denies the untranslatable moment of private suffering, its opaqueness, and its exclusive temporalization. The cultural representation of private suffering as part of a common suffering, which is the fate of a whole group, destroys the private heterotopia of the sufferer, even if it represents the entire culture as a heterotopia of suffering, as "another planet."[16]

6.212 Is it possible to remember suffering, in particular the suffering of others, without fabricating a common temporal continuum and a homogeneous space? The truth is that it is possible to really remember suffering only if one renounces this attempt to fabricate; the continuum between the one who remembers and the suffering preserved in memory and presenced out of it is a form of forgetting, because it erases the unbridgeable difference between the temporality of the suffering and the temporality of those who remember (and this is a clear case of a *différend*). The suffering that gathers the past into the present of the-one-who-suffers cuts her off from common time, even if it is the common time of those who suffer in similar circumstances. Common time is always time and memory offered by a culture to the suffering individual in order to invest his suffering in it, diminish his suffering, and eventually forget it. A responsibility for the memory of suffering that does not deny the untranslatable moment of private suffering will relinquish in advance a unitary and unified historical time into which suffered time is gathered. Such a memory of suffering will deconstruct any historical metanarrative, even that of the subaltern.

6.220 When suffering is the result of anxiety about a future event, the folding of the future into the present is emphasized, whereas the future that will come after is blocked. When suffering is the result of a loss and the presence of an absence becomes excessive, the folding of the past into the present is emphasized, whereas the severance from the past that was before the loss is present and presenced time and again as a testimony to the loss, a mirror that reflects an empty hole. It is not the memory of who or what was lost that causes suffering, but the way it is presenced. The image of the lost person or his traces can be present as a source of consolation, in which case the image is emphasized while the lack of the signified and the signified lack become implicit. When the inverse is the case, when the image of the lost person or his traces are present as a source of suffering, the image blurs in the background and the lack is emphasized.

6.221 Devoting oneself to suffering is folding the suffering I into the temporalization of suffering, gathering its memories and expectations into the past and the future that fold into a continuous moment of suffering. The distance between the sufferer as such and such a person — who has wishes, hopes, memories, and a body that are not experienced as part of the suffering itself — and her suffering diminishes, if not completely disappears. Such a contraction of the sufferer is the cause of loss (of appetite, friends, assets, or possibilities). Some of these cases of loss could cause more suffering, and the increase of this suffering could accelerate the movement of loss. Suffering and loss ignite and feed on each other in a vicious circle. If the sufferer or someone else cannot break into this circle by external intervention, it could become a vortex that will lead the sufferer to her destruction.

6.222 A struggle against suffering is an attempt to posit, time and again, an object of ambition, hope, or memory that is not subjected to the temporality of suffering, that is not caught in its duration, that stands within it like an island in the current that one can hold on to during the flood, that one can hope for as a safe haven. The battle with suffering is an attempt to preserve the autonomy of a temporality that is not the temporality of suffering. And a denial of suffering (in this sense, suffering is like other excitations) is an attempt to cancel the autonomy that a temporality that is not part of objective time demands.

6.230 In battling suffering, the-one-who-suffers strains to disengage from the encounter event. In the denial of suffering, the sufferer behaves within the encounter event as if she has already disengaged. But it is difficult to determine the difference between "as if" and "actually" disengaged, between simulated relief and real relief. In an injury, for example, the body can sometimes disengage, as when a person stops feeling an injured limb. Sartre describes in *Sketch for a Theory of the Emotions* a denial of emotion as a magical act that influences consciousness, and in extreme cases could cancel it altogether, like the case of a person who faints before a "ferocious beast."[17] If an encounter is what happens to the witness in the event of presence, then the fainting person has disengaged, left the witness position, ceased to suffer. If the encounter is what happens to the body, disengaging could prove fatal — the fainting person could be devoured by a beast, murdered by an enemy, or run over by a speeding vehicle. But the dazzling fear disappears, and it is unclear in what sense we can attribute suffering to one who is frightened at this stage, at least as long as she hasn't been devoured or run over. An event of suffering (and excitation in general) in which there is no suffering (or excitement) is like an unthought thought, an unfelt emotion, a sight unseen. That is why the denial of suffering (by the sufferer) may be a form of diminishing suffering, and sometimes it is the most efficient way available to the sufferer. (But when the witness denies suffering, she usually causes its increase.)

6.231 The denial of suffering is efficient only with regard to a certain object perceived as the cause of suffering or to a certain range of behavior within which suffering is caused. Often denial turns out to be a displacement of suffering to another area: a projection of the source of suffering onto new objects or the attribution of suffering to a different behavioral environment (but there is no reason to assume that denial is always tied to displacement). In psychoanalysis, denied suffering is reconstructed, based on the assumption that it should be reexperienced in one way or another in order to remove a distortion in the emotional economy, a distortion created by the denial. It is not the "same" suffering that is reconstructed, of course, but a new suffering that is re-created in the therapeutic interaction when the excitation-producing presence is replaced with memories and images of such a presence. The experience of an encounter from which it is impossible to disengage is created in relation to these images, and it is created through the mediation of an other who makes these images appear and (allegedly?) prevents their removal.

6.232 Denial severs the duration of suffering, or the continuum of its presence for others. Speaking of suffering in terms of denial shifts attention from a diachronic level to a synchronic level. Denial presumes a system in which what is denied continues to exist. Denial of suffering — at least in psychoanalytic terms — removes the presence of suffering but takes its toll through the disturbances it creates in cognition, function, and behavior that might cause further suffering. But not necessarily. Sometimes the suffering involved in reconstructing the denied suffering is larger than the suffering involved in the denial itself. The unconscious is that part of the psychic system that enables the continued presence of what no longer has presence for the sufferer, in order to enable its continuing flow in the exchange cycle of the psychic economy. In this way, the unconscious increases the volume of possible suffering. In order to decrease suffering, one can try to presence the denied, but one can also simply forget it (assuming that "simple," sheer forgetfulness, that is, forgetfulness that is not a displacement, is possible). In both cases, the volume of the unconscious is decreased.

6.240 Torture and therapy, an increase of suffering and a decrease of suffering, are questions of time. When the conditions responsible for the unbearable excitation continue for a while, time itself seems to be the cause of suffering. Any nuisance could become torture if it goes on for long enough (the dripping tap). On the other hand, it is possible to feel a very sharp pain without that causing suffering, that is, without its becoming excessive, if one responds quickly and disengages, or efficiently removes the source of pain, like a burn that is immediately chilled. The sufferer takes part in principle in the speed of reaction. The reaction can be particularly swift. An instinct is the top limit of a quick physical response; denial, hysterical blindness, immediate distraction, are the top limit of a response that involves mental processes. The response can be deferred either by a hostile environment or by the sufferer. When Jacob heard about the death of his son Joseph, "all his daughters and all his sons rose up to comfort him; but he refused to be comforted; and he said, For I will go down into the grave unto my son mourning."[18] The mourner creates time and again the image of the person she has lost, the lover represents to herself time and again the memory of the lover who deserted her, so as to return to and remember the irreparable loss.

6.241 Suffering that is quickly removed is almost incapable of participating in any exchange system. In order to be solidified as a valuable object in an exchange system, suffering must exist for a certain duration (that cannot be predetermined), so that when it appears, one can point to it, and when it is absent, one can point to its absence. When suffering is removed quickly, the sufferer can demand compensation for damage, no more. That is, prolonging the duration of suffering, deferring the response, has value for the mental and social economy of the sufferer, but also for those who are supposed to compensate for suffering or might be demanded to make reparation for it. Only suffering that has gone on for long enough can be presenced and displayed in a way that will enable one to assess it, that is, that will enable it to be integrated into some exchange system. The one who may be asked to compensate someone for her suffering has an interest in removing the presence of suffering for others, whether by quick response (and disengagement from an encounter involving the sufferer) or by disregard and denial. Every time suffering occurs, a whole system of opposing interests comes into action, whether wanting to calm it, let it be forgotten, or continue and presence it, to the point of taking pleasure in and gaining benefits from its display.

6.3 *Use Value and Exchange Value*

6.300 Suffering puts into action different exchange systems, which are sometimes competing, sometimes coherent and feeding off each other, and sometimes contradicting each other. These exchange relations exist on at least two levels. On one level, suffering creates need: everything that is needed to assuage it and to compensate for the damage it causes. On another level, suffering creates symbolic capital or (and sometimes also) symbolic bankruptcy: everything that the sufferer demands or "deserves" because of her suffering and everything that she has been deprived of because of that suffering, or because of the feelings it arouses in others (identification, compassion, disgust, contempt, guilt, arrogance, shame, political solidarity, and so on).

6.301 The needs created by the suffering are not just the result of what causes suffering; they are a complex outcome of the sufferer's socioeconomic state. The needs of the sick homeless woman are different from those of the house owner in whose doorstep she is crouching in her rags and who has the same disease. The needs of an agonized lover whose beloved has forsaken him are different from the needs of the lover (from a similar social background) whose lover deserted her. And the same applies to the symbolic losses and gains that accompany the presencing of suffering, although here the dependence on the socioeconomic situation is even greater. The needs generated by suffering are determined by biological factors, not just social and cultural factors, whereas the symbolic capital that suffering accumulates or loses is completely determined by the social situation of the sufferer.

6.302 The one who witnesses someone's suffering will enter an economic, social, or political relation of exchange, either to get rid of the suffering or to get rid of the suffering other, to remove him from one's sight and from one's mind. When a resident of a metropolis who can afford to buy an apartment bumps into a homeless person lying, half-drunk and half-asleep, at her doorstep, she may enter both systems at once: she will toss some change to the homeless person, perhaps give him an old coat, and then demand that her janitor keep the front stairs clean of any nuisance and that her representatives on the city council get homeless people out of her neighborhood once and for all.

6.310 Certain environmental conditions delay, in principle, the attempt to disengage in response to the suffering of some one, and other conditions accelerate it. The mere existence of these conditions is not necessarily a moral issue. Sometimes an environment is produced in which the response to suffering is deliberately slow — in training for various needs, for example. Sometimes an environment is produced in which the response to suffering is deliberately accelerated because the expected amount of suffering is particularly large and the quick response enables the system that produces the suffering to function efficiently — for example, army paramedics, airborne doctors, and similar means for getting help quickly to those who are sent to kill and be killed, smashed, crushed, and dispersed, limb after limb, on the battlefield.

6.311 A delay in the response that relieves suffering and the prolonging of suffering worsen the condition of the one who suffers. But the worsening in one order of things could turn out to be an improvement in a different order of things. "What is hard in training is easy in the battle," says a well-known slogan that justifies suffering in army bases; the condition of the soldier who suffers during training is worse in the order of things of the daily military routine, but it is better in the order of things that will be dictated by war. The patient suffers terribly during his treatment, but his life has been saved. The lover suffers when his beloved says good-bye, but he has great happiness awaiting him when she comes back. The girl suffers when her lover leaves her, but when she gets over him, she will say, along with those who want what is best for her, "Good riddance to that troublemaker." The father who has lost his son refuses to be consoled, although he knows that if it were not for his son and his brave friends, the city would have fallen into the hands of the enemy and all its residents would have been killed.

6.312 "The condition of one who suffers damage is always worse than it was before the damage" (3.011); that is not the case with the situation of the one who suffers. The sufferer could eventually improve her condition and therefore would be willing to further delay disengaging from the exciting, agonizing encounter. In the meantime, she suffers. Her condition is bad as long as the suffering continues. "He that goeth forth and weepeth, bearing continuous suffering."[19]

6.313 Suffering may cause damage, and damage may cause suffering. Suffering has an experiential aspect that an evaluation in terms of depreciation and gain erases. Even when the evaluation of damage includes sorrow and shame, even when it includes the suffering caused by the loss, the translation into terms of damage and compensation is supposed not to "express" the experience but to posit an indexical, although indistinct, sign for it within a system of exchange relations. The sign is indexical because the evaluation is tied to the suffering; it is indistinct because the same evaluation could be tied to different kinds of suffering (see 6.330 on). On the other hand, suffering has an economic aspect that is erased by the experiential representation of suffering: the things she needs in order to ease her suffering; the things she loses as a result of her suffering; the things she can get hold of by presencing and displaying her suffering; or the things she receives on account of that suffering. The hero is a type whose entire existence is based on an exchange market of the same kind: suffering for fame, women, sometimes wealth.

6.314 Suffering generates pressing needs that require an urgent response. The sufferer is a consumer of what may alleviate her suffering and is willing to pay an extraordinarily high price for an ordinary product or a tremendous price for what has no price. Her suffering is an event of overpricing. And there are other ways in which suffering could be a coefficient that multiplies damage, which might, in itself, increase the suffering. Suffering could impoverish the sufferer not only because of the urgent needs it creates but also because it decreases her symbolic capital when she is treated with contempt or disgust on account of what the suffering does to her. This impoverishment simply adds to the other kinds of loss and damage that the suffering causes and joins other causes for suffering to increase its presence and widen the zone of the encounter. In impoverishment, damage and suffering move together, held to each other in the spiral movement of loss (2.134 and 6.221); if there is no one or nothing to stop them, the movement will continue from loss to perdition. The insolvent is the reverse image of the hero, who makes a career out of suffering.

6.320 Sometimes suffering forces some one into exchange relations, and sometimes some one introduces suffering into an exchange market. The two should be clearly differentiated.

A. Suffering forces some one into exchange relations when it creates need and generates damage. The sufferer or those who want to help her (or both) now have new needs they must satisfy, and therefore they must change, by little or by large, their earning (or production), exchange, and consumption patterns. When new needs arise without a change in the earning, consumption, or exchange patterns, the suffering continues and is magnified. The more the suffering grows, the more the sufferer encloses herself in her excited heterotopia, and so grows the burden that her suffering places on the emotional economy of those around her and on the social, economic, and political exchange market open to her and to them. In continuing and growing suffering, there is a demand for the reorganization of entire social systems. The larger the number of individuals who are suffering in a certain social environment, the more the demand for reorganization increases. For that purpose, the sufferers need not suffer in the same way or from the same things. It is enough for them to be tied to the same social systems and to the same economic and political exchange markets.

B. Some one introduces suffering into an exchange market when she attributes an exchange value to the suffering itself. To receive an exchange value, the suffering has to be displayed or represented so that someone else is willing to give something in return for its production, reproduction, display, or removal. In certain political and cultural situations, television and newspapers are willing to pay a handsome sum for the permission and opportunity to photograph suffering. In certain social or familial situations, someone is willing to pay a great deal for the removal of the nuisance caused by the continuous presence of suffering at her doorstep or inside her house.

6.321 The presencing of suffering and its commodification are not necessarily situations in which an individual deals in his own suffering. Some one could display the suffering of an intimate other in order to gain financial or social profit both for the sufferer and for his environment. Parents often use their children's suffering in front of welfare officers or television cameras, hoping thus to reach the authorities. Sometimes this is a function of demonstrators' tents, people striking in front of a government building, the homeless, the unemployed, the underprivileged, and other deprived people who appear every morning in front of a government building. A group could deal in individuals' suffering within it for the same purpose. When individuals' suffering is removed from their possession, it is instrumentalized and politicized. Needless to say, in these cases there is a strong incentive to preserve the suffering and even magnify it, at least temporarily, at least as long as the communicative situation continues. Palestinians and Israelis alike have become experts in exploiting suffering for political purposes.

6.322 The use of suffering has its own history. The people of Israel groaning under the whips of the Egyptians displayed their suffering to God in order to convince him to help them in their plight: "And the children of Israel sighed by reason of the bondage, and they cried, and their cry came up unto God by reason of the bondage. And God heard their groaning."[20] The praying Jew says before the blowing of the shofar in Rosh Hashanah verses from Psalms and Lamentations: "I called upon the Lord in distress. Thou hast heard my voice; hide not thine ear at my breathing, at my cry."[21] And in the prayer for Yom Kippur (Day of Atonement), he describes in detail the torment and agony of exile and reminds the Lord of the suffering of the ten martyrs in the time of the Roman Empire:

> These martyrs I well remember, and my soul is melting with sorrow. Evil men have devoured us and eagerly consumed us. In the days of the tyrant there was no reprieve for the ten who were put to death by the Roman government.... Thereupon the tyrant ordered them to cast lots, and the lot fell on Rabban Simeon, whose head was stricken off with a sword.... Rabbi Ishmael was flayed, suffering with great fortitude; he wept only when his executioners reached the place of tefillin.... Thus were slain men of spotless conduct and profound learning.... They lacerated [the] body [of Rabbi Akiba] with combs of irons. Full of devotion, Rabbi Akiba recited his prayers with a peaceful smile on his face while undergoing extreme torture.[22]

Every religion has texts and ceremonies in which the address to God is accompanied by a display of suffering, sometimes to call for his help, but sometimes also to vouch for the addresser, like the praying man on Yom Kippur who acknowledges his sins and cleanses himself in his anguish. And in general, the cultural practice that displays suffering is not always intended to recruit help for the sufferer. Sometimes it is supposed to declare the power and affirm the authority of the one who causes suffering as a display of his power. Sometimes it is supposed to be part of the punishment of the one who was caught in the act and serve as a moral, advocating good behavior for those not yet caught. In any case, the politics of suffering is always, first and foremost, the politics of the representation of suffering.

6.330 The most widespread institutionalized way to introduce suffering into an exchange system is by representing it in terms of damage and a demand for compensation. Suffering involves claiming compensation by its very nature, but also because and to the extent to which it has caused loss — of time, health, quality of life, material resources, and so on. For suffering to be the basis for a compensation claim, it has to have everything that was said with respect to a compensation claim for damage: that there were conditions under which it could have been prevented (3.200 and 3.401); that the one who could have prevented the suffering knew about it or about the possibility of its occurrence and could also have stopped, or at least given a warning about, it (3.112). As with damage, it is possible to generate a ground for a compensation claim by creating conditions in which suffering can be prevented or by creating an awareness of the existence of such conditions, that is, by representing them (3.200). But the analogy is incomplete: when new prevention conditions become apparent, some one may appear as a subject of damage who has a reason to demand compensation. Damage can be ascribed retrospectively. But it is impossible to suffer in retrospect, and suffering does not intensify just because it transpires that it was preventable (although additional suffering could be caused; think, for example, of parents who find out that their son, who allegedly died a hero's death in the battlefield, actually died in an accident as a result of his officers' negligence).

6.331 There is another analogy between an appraisal of loss and an appraisal of suffering. Experts appraise suffering, translate suffering into damage. The appraisal of suffering is a very inaccurate business, because of the chronic instability of the "objective" description of suffering, and even of the "subjective" description, from the sufferer's point of view (which changes in different moments, out of a different involvement in the act of remembering, and out of a different evaluation of "what she got out of it").

Suffering does not have an agreed-on grid in the discourse that describes it and has no clear institutionalized affinity with a given exchange system. The experiential aspect of suffering, its being an intensified expression of a painful and relentless excitation, the conventional link between suffering and its expressions in other languages and means of representation, and the fundamental gap between excitation and expression (5.102–5.120) — all these do not permit the institutionalization of a grid that will enable an ordered commodification of suffering. But anywhere damage is appraised, it is possible, in principle, to agree on a codification of types of suffering (according to the type of loss, the rate of the "basic" damage, and so on) and to try to quantify them. In defined exchange conditions within an exchange market, the appraisal of suffering is no different, in principle, from the appraisal of loss.

6.332 To identify some one as suffering and assess the damage caused to her means to recognize her as an interested party in a certain order of things (bodily, economic, institutional). That is, whoever has a body, property, or an institutional position so that her body, property, and position are her problems. On the other hand, the judgments of suffering present, implicitly and explicitly, an objective description of the sufferer's condition; they define her as an interested party and define her interest in the order of things as relevant and the change in her situation as a result of her suffering. The regulative idea of a successful appraisal of suffering and full compensation posits the sufferer as a complete object, some one who became some thing that has a replacement, and it is bound to fail exactly like the regulative idea of damage appraisal (3.42).

6.333 An evaluation of suffering leaves a lot more unrepresented suffering than the evaluation of loss leaves from the loss, because it is about excitation, an excess of presence overflowing its bounds beyond the expression it could find in a certain discourse. What the damage has left from the unrepresented loss can now be interpreted in terms of suffering: the continuous presence of what was lost and will not be returned, the unreturnable, the unbearable excitation overflowing from this presence, the impossibility of disengaging, of forgetting what cannot be returned even in the face of what has been returned after all, even after the compensation. And besides that, the compensation for suffering, presenting suffering as a necessary evil to achieve something vital, or to prevent a more terrible suffering, all these do not cancel the suffering, do not muffle the presence of the pain, and do not assuage the powerful longing. A perfect, simple exchange relation is possible, in certain cases or at least in its ideal form, between damage and compensation, whereas the relation between suffering and compensation — always, even in its ideal form — seems more like the relation between the seen and the said.

6.334   There are no direct semiotic relations between suffering and damage. Suffering does not signify damage, and damage does not signify suffering (as opposed to the partial semiotic relations between damage and loss [see 3.100 on]). The phrase that expresses damage may relate to the loss caused by the suffering or caused as a result of the suffering (loss of consciousness or of memory, for example). In every case where the relation between damage and suffering is mediated by a determination of loss, it is a relation of deduction between phrases, not between things in the world. But suffering can be evaluated directly in terms of proper compensation. The Mishnah proposes a procedure of appraisal for evaluating suffering in the case of bodily harm: to the damage, time spent recuperating, and the expense of healing, it adds two other excitations that cause suffering: pain (literally: sorrow) and degradation (or shame relating to the humiliation of being harmed). It suggests a precise way of assessing the exchange value of sorrow: "Pain? If someone burned him with a spit, or with a nail, even on his fingernail, a place where it produces no wound, we assess how much a person in his situation would be willing to accept to undergo such pain."[23] But there is no similar way of assessing the exchange value of shame, except for the statement that the appraisal has to take into account the differences in the social status between the one who shames and the one who is shamed. In this case, too, the evaluation does not presuppose and does not enable semiotic relations. As was said earlier, many different kinds of suffering might be coded in the same compensation; different compensations may serve as an index of different kinds of suffering.

6.340   The fact that suffering has been placed in an exchange system, has an exchange value, and that the one who suffers is supposed to gain something from it (utility or pleasure) does not change the "use value" of the suffering, the suffering as what is suffered. In this sense, suffering differs from loss even more than it differs from damage. Loss should cause harm for it to worsen someone's situation (3.000 on). I wish I would lose some of my appetite, a little weight, a few debts. In everything related to the worsening of the situation, the analogy is not between the pair loss/damage and the pair suffering/damage but between loss/harm and excitation/unbearable excitation (or an intensified encounter/an encounter from which one wishes to disengage). An excitation must reach saturation, cross the threshold of the unbearable, to be considered the cause of the worsening of the sufferer's situation. Damage has been described as a sign in which the signifier is loss and the signified is depreciation. Accordingly, it is possible to describe suffering as a sign in which the signifier is an intensified presence (some kind of excitation) and the signified is the threshold of the unbearable excitation that has suddenly been lit when the excitation becomes excessive. Instead of the substrate of a given order of things in which the loss is expressed as a deficit, one has to posit a substrate of a given emotional world (or an order of presence) in which the excitation expresses the limits of the tolerable. Instead of the context of a possible prevention of loss, one should posit as a context the conditions for disengaging from an encounter with casualties (compare this to 3.110 and 3.440). And this in the following way:

Communication: addresser → signifier/signified → medium/context → addressee

Damage: the event of loss	→	$\dfrac{\text{what was lost}}{\text{depreciation}}$	→	$\dfrac{\text{the order of things}}{\text{possible prevention}}$	→	assessor of the damage
Suffering: encounter	→	$\dfrac{\text{excitation}}{\substack{\text{threshold of}\\\text{the bearable}}}$	→	$\dfrac{\text{emotional world}}{\substack{\text{conditions for}\\\text{disengaging}}}$	→	someone who suffers

6.341 The one who suffers, like the one who is damaged, is the addressee of the event. The moment the addressee becomes an addresser and posits someone else as an addressee of the suffering or of her damage (in a claim for compensation or a cry for help) the signifying relations are reorganized. The sign "suffering" becomes a signified for an other who witnesses the suffering, an addressee of a call. The previous signified, the threshold of the tolerable, can only be interpreted by the witness through presencing the tormenting excitation (a bodily fit, a cry of pain, a letter, a photograph). But from the witness's point of view, the threshold that has been crossed is already part of the suffering as signified, which the presenced excitation points to as a signifier. For the witness, presenced suffering signifies an experienced suffering like loss signifies depreciation and losings. In this sense, for the witness the suffering of an other always marks a worsening in his condition.

6.342 This evil belongs simultaneously to the suffering's space of appearance, the space in which gestures and phrases that express suffering appear, and to the conceptual space in which the suffering receives its exchange value (as a pressing need, as a demand for compensation). In both of these spaces, the separation between the phenomenal and the conceptual cannot really be maintained, the separation between the expressions that signify the tormenting excitation and the excitation experienced as a crossing of the threshold of the tolerable (which is also the threshold of a need or demand for compensation), between the traces of the excitation and its price. "Suffering" is an "objective" matter, a "thing" among other things, a part of what is. "Just like other things, it has a phenomenological side; it is a 'phenomenon' which is not given to thought or expression outside a certain conventional grid of concepts that represents and evaluates it and which, at the same time, is inseparable from its phenomenology and from its subjective expression (of what was lost, of what was experienced) as someone's problem, which no evaluation can adequately express" (3.142).

6.350 In the equation in which the loss estimated as depreciation is the signifier, the compensation is the signified; suitable compensation will cancel the damage completely. In an equation in which the experienced suffering is the signifier, disengagement is the signified; a successful disengagement will cancel the suffering, or at least will bring to an end the effect of its most persistent cause (even if it does not cancel all its traumatic traces, which might themselves be a cause of further suffering). An expression of loss in terms of damage introduces what was lost and the loss as an event into one of the exchange systems accessible to the one who was damaged. An expression of excitation in terms of suffering puts the excitation into a different kind of exchange system: on the one hand, a cry for help; on the other hand, a response in the form of a disengagement from an exciting encounter. In both cases, the response was supposed to cancel the source of the call: full compensation cancels the damage; successful disengagement cancels the suffering. But with two important differences:

I. Compensation closes an exchange circuit, whereas disengagement opens a new exchange circuit (the price of disengagement and the debt of the one who suffers to the one who responded to his call).

II. Compensation could cancel the damage with no residue, whereas disengagement cancels the suffering only from the moment of disengagement (and only the suffering caused in the encounter itself); nothing can cancel the past suffering.

6.351 When compensation erases damage, the loss remains, from the damaged person's perspective, as a signified without a signifier — the silenced, the denied, the expelled. Or, from the perspective of the exchange system, as a signifier without a signified — the meaningless, the residual, waste. The worsening of the situation is displaced from the presence of the thing that was lost to the loss of the ability to presence loss. But compensation cannot erase suffering. As long as the suffering is experienced, one can insist on presencing it, giving it expression in different exchange relations. Suffering is an evil that can be inserted as a harassing, aggravating sign into any system of interpersonal relations.

6.352 A condition of justice is an appropriate compensation for damage on the basis of an agreed-on process for appraising loss. Inappropriate compensation is injustice (3.540–3.542). In ideal conditions, an appropriate compensation equals the damage; its exchange value erases the value of the damage (and by and by turns it into an event in the economic genre [2.003 and see also 6.551]). If the damage is not minimized, although it is possible to do so, one can still justify it through appropriate compensation, that is, in terms of a larger utility or pleasure. In contrast, no compensation can erase suffering, and it is hard to agree on an appraisal of suffering. The translation machines activated whenever damage takes place (3.512 on) are not reliable when suffering occurs. Suffering can be measured, if at all, in small communities within which there is complete agreement over the representation and evaluation of pain and shame, sorrow and humiliation, that is, in conditions of unusual identification between the ones who suffer or are about to suffer. When suffering is at stake, compensation is a necessary but insufficient condition for justice. In the context of suffering, the main interest is prevention and alleviation. Justice has to do first and foremost with the conditions for preventing and diminishing suffering. Distributive justice is a just distribution of unavoidable suffering and of the conditions that enable a decrease in the number of unbearable encounters and the quickest disengagement possible when they do happen. A justification of suffering, as different from the hermeneutics of suffering, has to include an analysis of the social modes of production of unbearable encounters and of the conditions for disengaging. With the concepts developed so far, it is (still) impossible to talk about a justification of suffering.

6.4 *The Exit Toll*

6.400 Suffering always appears as the gap between the unbearable (the excitation) and the impossible (the action needed in order to make it bearable). It is located in the gap between the rejection response in the face of an unbearable excitation and the lack of ability or will to disengage, to remove the intense presence that causes the excitation.

6.401 Suffering is a gap between a presence that has increased excessively and the powerlessness that undercuts the attempt to disengage. Sometimes, when suffering increases, the powerlessness itself is made present, sensed by the sufferer. This sense of powerlessness, in turn, tends to become a source of more suffering and raise feelings of loathing, rage, hatred, which can also be a source of suffering, both for the one who cannot disengage and for those around her. The sufferer's powerlessness is also a rich source for the witness's compassion; it produces compassion as an excitation that holds within it a cry for help (5.343). But when the witness is presented with her own powerlessness in the face of suffering, she might become alienated from and indifferent to that suffering (see 6.522). All this is true only for suffering that is not chosen.

6.402 Sometimes one chooses to suffer: it is possible to disengage, but one does not do so — for some thing, for some one — because the price of disengagement is high, because one enjoys suffering or the joy of overcoming it. Suffering that is chosen is based on a gap between a presence that has become unbearably excessive and a determined will to overcome it and not disengage. Sometimes, especially in a context of a seemingly free choice, when suffering increases, the willpower that makes it possible to overcome and not disengage is presenced, and it can be a source of happiness, self-love, pride, confidence, arrogance. This narcissistic feature of suffering from choice will interest me less in the context of the present discussion. Sometimes, when the choice itself is perceived as forced, the increase of suffering presences the coercion even more, and with it the powerlessness that might, as was said, become an additional source of suffering (see 6.404 and 6.410).

6.403 The Catherine wheel is the paradigmatic example of a mechanism that creates the gap between the intolerable excitation and the deed needed to stop it. This mechanism perfects the gap. But cruelty need not be so premeditated, organized, and extreme. In the more common type of suffering, the gap between intolerable excitation and powerlessness in the face of it is the by-product of a relationship in which no one had the intention of being cruel to anyone. The gap is produced incidentally, "naturally," on the military training course, within a marriage, under investigation, or in the examination room. More generally, it is produced in any institution that specializes in organizing events from which free exit is denied, or where the exit toll is extremely high, so that many prefer suffering to leaving. This gap can be produced by natural disaster (a landslide, for example, when you lie there, crushed, waiting for the rescue team), disease, and injury. Disease, poverty, the family, a tyrannical regime, and secure institutions (a convent, army barracks, school, hospital, mental institution, nursing home, prison, and such) are all environments in which suffering is produced through mechanisms that prevent free exit from situations in which an intolerable excitation occurs, or exact a high exit toll.

6.404 The dilemma that forces a choice between suffering and the terrible price one pays for disengaging is a common structure of closed environments that produce suffering. Usually, one can leave: a prison is not a Catherine wheel and can sometimes be broken out of; a military camp is not a prison, and one can almost always defect; marriage is not an army camp, and one can always leave home for good. But it is almost impossible to escape the dilemma, the need to choose between suffering and suffering, or between suffering and damage or loss. As was said (6.402), the coerced presence of a dead-end dilemma could increase and become intolerable in itself. In the background of the moment of choice, there often lies the fundamental structure of suffering as a gap between an intolerable presence and an unbearable exit toll.

6.405 Terrible suffering can cause the one who suffers to grasp "life" itself, life as the totality of all experiences or as the totality of all the excitations "life" brings, as an institution that prevents free exit. When she insists on leaving, we talk about suicide. The one who commits suicide wishes to disengage once and for all. She also wishes to cancel herself as someone interested in her own loss, in all her possible losses; she loses herself so that she will not lose anything anymore, so that she will never suffer any loss again. The suicide attempt is a response to the inability to bear a loss that has become intolerable. The one who commits suicide, who cannot replace the loss and knows no better way to cancel or muffle the interest in what was lost, annihilates all her losses by annihilating the interested person inside her. But sometimes suicide is an attempt to force loss onto others in order to break down their wall of indifference. The one who commits suicide wishes to make herself — all that she has or had, and all that she was, is, and could have been — into the loss of others, who might now finally take an interest in her.

6.410 In an environment in which one is not free to leave, during an encounter with casualties, when it is difficult to disengage, mechanisms that duplicate suffering are developed. The sufferer who cannot disengage becomes a source of suffering himself. Think of an unemployed man and his relationship with his wife; a battered wife and her relationship with her children; an abused child and his relationship with his friends; a grieving mother and her relationship with herself, with her husband; the endless demands of a sick man; the vengeance of the humiliated, the betrayed. As a rule, if there is a single cause of suffering that generates more suffering than any other, it is earlier suffering. This is not only because of the spiral movement of impoverishment of suffering that causes damage and loss, which produce more and more suffering (6.314). The suffering that the sufferer produces and spreads around her seems to function as a mechanism of discharge and compensation within her psychic economy. The sufferer becomes a suffering-amplifying system. The suffering input activates an entire set of images, excitations, desires, and needs in the suffering "unit"; these then activate violent reactions — anger, hurt, depression (the output) — which turn the presence of the sufferer into a source of intolerable excitations for those who come into contact with her, and each one of these is a suffering-amplifying system in itself, and so on. As a result, the closed system becomes a powerful amplifier of suffering. The family, particularly where one member permanently suffers from something (frustration, depression, mental disability, chronic disease, drug addiction, and such), can serve as a paradigmatic example of this situation. And there are other examples: a detention camp, a village under curfew, traveling in a bolted train car crammed with people. Under such conditions, self-discipline and self-control are essential to muffling the suffering a little; they disconnect a few wires in the amplifying system.

6.411 Sometimes the overbearing presence of the suffering caused to an other is enough to distract the one who suffers, create a simulation of disengagement, and bring temporary relief to the sufferer, who is being cruel to others. More often, the sufferer devotes her attention to the overbearing presence of disappointment, anger, hatred, or vengeance, which distracts her from an unbearable excitation, usually only in order to create another. The short break in suffering and the torture of the next unbearable excitation increase the sense of defeat of the sufferer, who wanted to find relief in others, and now join the sense of disappointment she has from all those around her who cannot help her, and add to her sense of powerlessness. And so the failure to find relief from suffering only duplicates the suffering, and reproduces the sufferer's cruelty to those around her in a vicious circle, until someone from outside interrupts this circular motion, or until this motion itself finishes off the one trapped within it.

6.412 This circular motion, coping with suffering through displacement and projection of excitation, is a distinct example of the magical power Sartre attributes to excitation — the attempt to intervene in the exciting situation not through disengagement or removing the unbearable excitation but through a change in the excited consciousness (5.004).[24] But this example also points to the limitations of Sartre's analysis, which are, typically of his early phenomenological writing, the limits of an observation of an individual consciousness reducing the entire world to a series of meanings in its noematic space. The "magical action" that allegedly changes consciousness rather than the world turns out to be an action in the world that increases the unbearable excitation of the one who devotes herself to it and spreads various kinds of suffering around it. The "magical" coping with the excitation is a typical example of the dynamics of the movement of suffering in social situations and institutions that extract an excessive exit toll — this time the price the others, who witness the suffering, have to pay.

6.413 These displacement and projection mechanisms must be more complex, and their description requires psychological presuppositions that are not relevant here. Such suppositions will provide various explanations for the movement of suffering that the sufferer spreads around her, perhaps even different descriptions. But different and embedded in psychological theories as they might be, they are descriptions and explanations of the movement of suffering, a portion of its physics and geography. They will enhance our understanding of the movement of suffering, its spreading and increase in closed systems, but will not dispute, I suppose, the general assumption that relatively closed systems, which extract a high price for leaving, amplify and duplicate suffering, are responsible for its accelerating movement and amplified presence.

6.414 Here is, for example, the simple description Simone Weil gives for a double movement of suffering, inward and outward:

> Human mechanics. Whoever suffers tries to communicate his suffering (either by ill-treating someone or calling forth their pity) in order to reduce it, and he does really reduce it in this way. In the case of a man in the uttermost depths, whom no one pities, who is without power to ill-treat anyone (if he has no child or being who loves him), the suffering remains within and poisons him.[25]

The lonely man, "whom no one pities, who is without power to ill-treat anyone," is an enclosed cell of suffering that has no origin and no end and is incessantly multiplied.

6.420 Earlier suffering might produce more suffering than any other cause, but this earlier suffering, too, has conditions that accelerate its production. The contingent causes of suffering are always intertwined with more or less structured social conditions. A negative social environment might create more opportunities for the contingent causes of suffering to act, accelerate their action, and slow down, complicate, and raise the cost of responding to suffering. The production and distribution of suffering can be described as by-products of social structures and processes: the suffering that goes with unemployment and poverty as a by-product of stability and wealth in an economic system; famine in some areas as a by-product of a destabilized ecosystem, joined to the corrupt administrators in charge of relief work; the horrors of war as a by-product of power struggles between political forces; and so on. But the production and distribution of suffering (and of loss, of course) can also be described as unique characteristics, sui generis, of defined social systems: war, military occupation, or prison, for example, or the family, or the transportation system that "specializes" in the production and distribution of loss, damage, and suffering that result from road accidents.

6.421 Historical research into every one of these social situations and settings could reconstruct the structural conditions responsible, among other things, for changes in the mode of production of suffering and in the patterns of its movement, in its distribution, and in the attempts to assuage or erase it. Does the Western bourgeois family produce more or less suffering than the traditional Arab family (assuming that these categories have relatively clear value and meaning)? What is the effect of changes in the structure of the Western family in the second half of the twentieth century (women in the workforce, single-parent families, the transfer of more and more tasks to external forces that are paid for their services, and so on)? How do reforms in mental hospitals or in prisons affect the production and distribution of suffering within them?

6.422 One can now attempt to evaluate an entire social order according to the means of production and distribution of suffering it permits, encourages, or deliberately causes. This is a highly complex task, but it can be imagined, at least under certain conditions, sort of controlled-experiment conditions that regulate some of the variables. Twentieth-century totalitarian regimes supplied one set of such conditions. Hannah Arendt was one of the first to discover that. Her research on totalitarianism can be seen as an attempt to understand the totalitarian regime as a huge system that creates suffering out of its internal logic, independently of the evil intentions or the cruel character of those working within it.[26] Arendt called the systematic, bureaucratic, faceless production of suffering "the banality of Evil."[27] Continuous situations of occupation, like the Israeli occupation of the Palestinian territories, provide other controlled conditions. And maybe one can examine in a similar vein a feudal kingdom in the Middle Ages, or the Athenian polis in its day. In the last case, it is important to remember that around 100,000 slaves were taken into the laboratory, about ten times the number of free citizens in Athens (see 6.541–6.544).

6.430   Systems that regularly produce suffering tend to naturalize it, to represent it as a result of bad luck, an uncontrollable and unpredictable coincidence, which is moreover impossible to prevent: "fate," "God's hand," "natural disaster." A critical discourse will try to redescribe the suffering, its production, spreading, and distribution, in order to denaturalize the socially produced suffering (or the suffering that is not prevented or alleviated). (See 7.042 and 8.340 on.) Such a discourse will try to reconstruct the historicality of suffering, the unique sociology of the institutions that produce, distribute, and legitimate it. In order to do this, one need not concentrate on the phenomenology of suffering or its typology. It is enough to identify the social conditions that prevent or make it very difficult to disengage from various forms of encounter (physical pain, hunger, yearning, boredom, humiliation). The conditions that prevent disengagement — the law, a brick wall, false consciousness, fear, guilt — are enslaving conditions. Increasing the ability to disengage is liberation.

6.431   Liberating the sufferer from conditions that attach her to the source of her suffering is not an end but a means — a means to assuage the suffering and attain the ability to choose between different kinds of suffering. For liberation to be an end in itself, one must posit the liberated thing as an autonomous and fundamental value. What is liberated? People, men and women, or a people, a nation. That is, one posits humanism or nationalism as a value worth fighting for. But the man we are supposed to liberate, let alone the people, is not flesh and blood but an idea. Only an idea can be a value in itself and the source of other values. For us, liberation is a means — not a value stemming from the absolute value of what is being liberated — that serves a goal: better conditions that allow for faster disengagement from an unbearable encounter, at a lower price. Interpreted in this way, liberation is a matter of degree, not a case of all or nothing. It is supposed to ease the suffering of the sufferer, be it man, beast, or God, and allow him to choose to suffer as he wishes — to disengage from one place only to encounter an unbearable presence in another.

6.432 The sufferer benefits from freedom of choice, but one need not sanctify the freedom of will or declare it an absolute value. The choice itself is a means, not always successful, to assuage suffering or to use it properly, to produce an exchange value out of it, because it allows the sufferer to choose what causes her less suffering or a suffering that causes her less loss or brings her more profit. Sometimes the sufferer knows what causes her more or less suffering, how to decrease her suffering, and how to benefit from it. Sometimes she is wrong. The prevention of such mistakes is often used as an excuse to justify conditions that prevent disengaging from a tormenting encounter. Sometimes this is a perfectly sensible justification, like in the case of a young child forbidden to leave the house even if she suffers from boredom or nightmares when she is left alone, or the case of a toddler who is not allowed to let go of her mother's hand when they cross the road. Sometimes this claim seems reasonable but unlikely, as in the case of a mental patient whose condition is bad, who the doctors say might suffer outside the mental institution, left to the mercy of passersby, more than inside it, subjected to the experts' treatment. In many other cases, those justifying the continuation of the conditions of subjection gain something from them; in addition, they use the ignorance of the subjected in relation to their suffering and welfare, and even cultivate it, only so they can continue to justify those conditions. But this does not imply that the freedom to disengage is the sole concern of the sufferer or that it belongs to him as an inalienable right. This freedom is always also the business of all those who might encounter the one who demands conditions in which she can quickly disengage in case of a previous intolerable encounter.

6.433 Nonetheless, one must acknowledge that denying this freedom might in itself be the cause of suffering (out of frustration, hurt, or rage), even without the unbearable encounter, in relation to which it is supposed to limit the possibilities of disengaging, taking place. This is so because the freedom to enter and exit different relationships is perceived as a consecrated or supreme value in our culture, and the one who is denied it experiences the denial as an irreparable loss. Different kinds of "liberation discourse" —

sexual liberation in psychotherapeutic discourse, national liberation in nationalist discourse, women's liberation in feminist discourse — tend to en-tongue some hidden essence that must be
liberated and give it the power to evaluate, measure different values according to their affiliation with it.[28] The thing now is not to
cancel the yearning for liberation and return to a satisfied consciousness, happy with the state of subjection. The thing is to distinguish liberation as a struggle to increase the ability to disengage
— of more people, for longer, in variable conditions, in more areas
of the social space — from liberation as a striving for the realization
of some hidden essence, or for reclaiming rights that were with-
drawn, even though they are qualities of that essence, immanently
belonging to it, "inalienable."[29]

6.44　Over all, one must remember that sometimes it is appropriate to
assuage the sufferer's suffering and sometimes it is not. Sometimes it is right to let the sufferer choose her suffering, and sometimes it is not. When exactly? We still lack the apparatus needed
for the deliberation this kind of decision requires.

6.5　*Having No Expression, Getting No Return*

6.500　Some social conditions defer a response to suffering (6.310), and
some accelerate a social denial of suffering. In social denial of suffering, the presence of suffering is removed for witnesses of the
suffering, not for the sufferer, and the chance to claim, let alone
get, help or compensation decreases.

6.501　The psychic unconscious is "that part of the psychic system that
enables the continued presence of what no longer has presence
for the sufferer, in order to enable its continuing flow in the exchange cycle of the psychic economy" (6.232). In reverse analogy,
the social unconscious is that part of the social system that allows
the un-presence, the ongoing concealment, (or prevents the presence) of the suffering of individuals and groups in the "public consciousness" — that is, prevents its visibility in the public space and
its expression in various discourses in the public sphere; this concealment occurs despite the continued presence of the suffering
for the sufferer and her immediate environment, and in general it
occurs in a way that enables the removal of the unexpressed suffering from the exchange cycles of the social economy. The psychic unconscious "increases the volume of possible suffering" for
an individual (6.232). The social unconscious increases the volume of possible suffering for individuals within society. To reduce
mental suffering, "one can try to presence the denied" (6.232);

the denied must be presenced in order to reduce the overall suffering in a society. To reduce psychic suffering, one can simply forget it, whereas on a social level complete oblivion only increases suffering and perpetuates it.

6.502 A more precise definition of the social unconscious will also include damages that have no presence for others, a loss that remains unexpressed. The social unconscious is defined by suffering and loss that have no presence in the public sphere. Of course, this does not mean the un-presence of suffering and loss for all the others. The sufferer's neighbors, relatives, and friends continue to witness her suffering and loss; they might try their best to help, to give her the attention she "deserves," to get rid of her suffering or of her. At stake, rather, is the impossibility of representing suffering and loss in a way that enables them to have an exchange value in one of the more general exchange systems within society (see 6.543 on). In other words, in the social unconscious, displayed or represented suffering will not activate general exchange relations that reduce or remove suffering. The sufferer is left alone, attempting to relieve her suffering with her last strength or burdening a small social group — family, neighbors, or a few friends. That group may be an entire social minority whose members lack adequate representation in the public sphere.

6.510 The social unconscious, together with "collective consciousness" or "social mentality," is not a psychic entity that lacks a spatial presence. It is not an abstract entity, a concept or a motive that resides in the minds of people in general and researchers and scholars in particular, somewhere beyond the world of appearances, in the depths of social reality, behind its curtains of ideology, or within its hidden, denied desire. The social unconscious exists in time and space. It exists in time and space in the sense that suffering exists, within suffering individuals, in places of unbearable encounters. It is not a unified and homogeneous entity but is unequally distributed among groups and classes in a given population. It is always defined in relation to the suffering that is present in the public sphere, that is represented and exhibited in the various means of representation, and in relation to the social environment that is perceived as relevant to assuaging suffering and caring for sufferers. The size of this unconscious can change according to changes in the production and distribution of suffering and in its representation, but also according to changes in what is perceived as the public sphere and in the social environment relevant to caring for sufferers.

6.511 Social change with relation to suffering can also be described as a change in the ways of re-presencing unacknowledged suffering. The agents of change will try to uncover the mechanisms of denial in society and to flood the social consciousness — that is, the various kinds of public discourse — with representations of denied suffering. They can do that in several ways, only a few of which are anchored in familiar practices of ideology critique or a therapeutic-like exposure of the repressed. Among other things, one can help the sufferer represent suffering that has not been presenced earlier for others; one can locate existing representations of suffering that the public discourse ignores, that is, existing cries for help that are sounded off into blocked communication networks and help them get "airtime"; and one can lay out again the communication networks and re-mark the broadcast range, that is, retrace the borders of the social environment relevant to the cries for help. Certain types of critical discourse match this characteristic, but what they do — with other strategies of representation and discourse, and usually more effectively — the journalist, the poet, the television cameraman, the film director, the political orator, the graffiti artist, the pamphlet writer, the demonstrator, and sometimes the terrorist also do.

6.520 There are several ways to change the broadcast range, first and foremost by changing the real approach conditions — for example, when the army allows journalists to come in and out of a city under siege, or when a passage to a disaster area has been cleared. A change that is no less real could be caused by a change in the accessibility to a represented situation (as a result of changes in the approach conditions or independent of them). This happened, for example, when feminist critics began to change the reading practices of legal texts and historical documents. In a different context, this also happened when someone in the Israeli press realized, sometime in the late 1980s, that it was possible to interview Palestinians about the situation in the occupied territories, even when the Israeli government defined them as terrorists.

6.521 A change in the perception of relevance itself could also bring about a change in the broadcast range. Here are two examples that present different interpretations of "relevance." When the Ethiopian immigrants who came to Israel were declared Jewish, many members of the Jewish public in Israel were moved by their complaints, and their suffering raised compassion and empathy; the broadcast range expanded in this case because the borders of the community within which someone's suffering got attention expanded. In the 1980s, when more and more Israelis understood that Palestinians in the refugee camps were suffering as a result of Israeli policy, they felt that this suffering was relevant to every Israeli and became more attentive to it; the broadcast range expanded because the borders of responsibility changed. In the first case, a change of identity created a change of responsibility; in the second case, a change in the conception of responsibility brought a change in attention, and possibility in self-identity. In principle, the relevant social environment is the one within which one can reduce someone's suffering, as well as cause or increase it. But the relationship between causing the suffering and reducing it is not necessarily symmetrical (like act and omission, for example [see 7.422]).

6.522 In the age of electronic mass communication, anyone can be present in direct representations of suffering of people from all over the world; the once-forsaken multitudes of sufferers now stand a chance of having their suffering represented all around the world. But the amazing improvement in access to means of communication, which can reach suffering almost anywhere and at any time and broadcast it all the time, is disproportional to the means of intervention of governments and other public bodies that could, in principle, intervene. The gap between the accessibility to suffering that various producers of images and representations have and the accessibility of the average viewer, who finds himself staring at the TV screen faced with a deluge of images of suffering, is larger still. No wonder, therefore, that this viewer tends to withdraw from the addressee position, stops hearing the cries for help, watches suffering as a spectacle. When the representation of suffering includes a representation of the distance and the accessibility of the sufferer, when this distance is very large and the accessibility is very low, the witness can acknowledge the suffering without occupying the position of the addressee of the utterance. When a love scene is represented on the screen, I am not invited to kiss; when a war is represented on the screen, I am not invited to enlist; when the permanent, endless political jabber is represented, I am not invited to participate in decision making; when footage of bombed cities, hunger-stricken villages, plagued refugee camps is shown, I am not invited to offer help.[30]

6.530 When a very distant or very foreign suffering is presenced — in particular that of those who are long dead, or never existed and are just a figment of the imagination in a play or a story — the witness is the addressee not of a cry for help from the sufferer but of the suffering spectacle in its totality. The communicative situation, original (if it ever was) or fictitious, is represented from the "outside" and not activated from the "inside." The addresser who cried for help refers the situation to someone else, who now represents the suffering of the dead or of the fictitious protagonist, in order to convey a message, teach a lesson, create a meaning that is no longer relevant to the one who suffered. This message could be irrelevant not only to the original communicative situation, if there was such a situation, but also to the one represented while representing the suffering. This is so for the representation of suffering in the history of painting (Hogarth or Goya, for example) or literature (the descriptions of poverty given by Hugo or Dickens) or Greek tragedy. Think about the entire tradition of pietà paintings, how much suffering is presenced in them, and how minute is their function as a cry for help.

6.531 Unless the viewer is of the Christian faith and is still capable of being moved by the suffering of Jesus. For her, the pietà may be a direct cry for help, for she is capable of taking the addressee's position when Jesus is represented as suffering. It is true that it is not Jesus whom she must redeem, but herself, but this makes little difference, because suffering, and also redemption, are completely universalized through the mediation of the image of Jesus. Here is God's suffering come down to walk among us, here is the suffering that God has suffered for man, here is the suffering that represents all the suffering that has ever been and is yet to come, here are the anguish and agony that all the suffering in the world cannot redeem, the suffering that is the substitute of all suffering and its end. The Christian believer is called to insert her suffering into a cosmic exchange relation: she will respond to the voice rising from Jesus's suffering and will turn to him, will believe in him; in exchange, she gets a promise of compensation for her suffering, which will come when Jesus returns.

6.532 The religious sermon rehabilitates the position of the addressee in the face of the suffering of Jesus, a position that has been greatly eroded in an era of heresy and antireligious contempt. It develops an economy of suffering that is then duplicated in other relationships, with or without religious faith: faced with the suffering of someone distant and foreign, the witness becomes a direct addressee who is supposed to act; the act demanded of her has no direct reward in this world, but her payment is promised in a more general exchange relation, the one of the hereafter. This pattern repeats itself in those strands of Marxism, nationalism, and other modern movements and theories that contain motifs of salvation and world reform. The individual becomes the addressee of all the suffering in this world or of all the suffering of his people. The promised reward for the sacrifices she is forced or called to make in order to reform the world is guaranteed in the new world that will come after the revolution. This pattern becomes almost impossible in a culture like ours. In culture that has turned incredulous toward any utopia, it is hard to promise a future reward to the one who responds and comes to the help of those who suffer; this culture is inundated with a pornography of suffering from all around the globe coming through the media, a suffering met with almost total powerlessness. In this culture, it is very hard to sustain the position of the addressee who is called for help and is asked to sacrifice without a promise, with no guaranteed return for his gift.

6.533　This is the context in which new mediators of suffering appear in our culture. In the past, their role was filled by the religious preacher, the ideologist, the social critic, the writer, or the artist. Today it is filled by reporters and photographers and in particular social activists, local Israeli groups like B'Tselem, Physicians for Human Rights, and the Anti-torture Committee and global groups like Amnesty International and Doctors Without Borders.[31] These mediators do not settle for turning the suffering of others into a set of images, marketed for mass consumption. They work to restore addressee positions that have been destroyed, create new ones, and connect the distributed images to new positions, in which anyone or almost anyone can be situated, or at least those with standing in certain areas.

6.534　Sometimes, to create this addressee position, the mediator, photographer, journalist, and reporter must give up the position of addressee (in this sense, their position is different from that of the doctor at the disaster area). The mediator must be transparent, invisible, the inevitable human attachment dangling behind the eye of a camera, from the ear of a tape recorder. To enable others to be witnesses of suffering, she must become, in the presence of the suffering itself, a witness of an occurrence worth reporting, a current affair, an event of informative, political, or aesthetic value. The fact that instead of pulling the camera string she could have pulled the trigger, that instead of activating the tape recorder she could have activated contacts and money in order to help, is usually eliminated from the report. But testimonies that mediate the presence of suffering — that is, everything that tries to say about the suffering "this was there, this is still there," and the photograph perhaps more than all — also leave traces of the one who was there or at least traces of the fact that there was someone there, that there was a possibility of offering help. This kind of testimony, and not just the direct testimony of the presence of suffering, is necessary in order to restore the addressee position of the cry for help.[32]

6.535 Sometimes the reward the mediators promise the one who responds to the call still relies on old promises of world reform and payment in the hereafter, but this has no chance — it never had any chance — without the existence of local reparation mechanisms in terms of prestige and social symbolic capital. And yet side by side with the cultivation of such mechanisms, and in an increasingly convincing way, a new reward appears: the removal of suffering itself. In a postmodern culture, the new mediators of suffering wish to inject suffering into the bourgeois sitting room as a nuisance that must be removed, and they want to convince the addressee that to remove the suffering, one must do more than press the button on the remote control — one should and can act. But beyond all that, they wish to teach him, through everything the exchange relations put at their disposal, to do deeds that entail a total renunciation of reward, because the deed that must be done cannot be rewarded within any exchange relation, not the existing ones and not the one promised for the future.

6.540 A representation of suffering, direct or mediated, is accompanied by a cry for help — explicit, implicit, or erased: someone asks to be rescued, asks to be helped (or asks for help for someone else, on behalf of whom she is speaking) to disengage. Representation of damage may also be accompanied by an implicit or explicit demand: someone has lost so-and-so, this and that, and she is entitled to such and such compensation (3.400 on). But for the one who was damaged, it is not enough to display her damage; she has to prove she really deserves something. The sufferer, on the other hand, has nothing to prove; there are reasons and motivations to offer her help, even if she deserves nothing. Even if the response to suffering is always part of an exchange relation (and it is not always so), the presencing of suffering includes a call to ignore the rules of the exchange system, to transcend them, to give something without getting something in return.

6.541 Sometimes the thing given to the-one-who-suffers has no reward in one exchange system but does have value in another. In other words, the response to suffering entails a conversion of capital between different exchange systems. Conversion is an exchange relation in which capital is transferred from one field of action to another, and its value, which was previously stated in the terms of one field, is now translated to another: money buys respect, respect buys authority, knowledge buys admiration, and so on. Often a capital conversion is required to buy a cure from suffering, because the conditions of disengagement from the exciting encounter cannot be obtained through ordinary exchange relations. It is impossible to convince the court to change its verdict, but it is possible to bribe the warden; it is impossible to change a political decision that causes suffering, but it is possible to join the injured ones in a demonstration of solidarity and share with them even a little of their suffering; it is impossible to buy a cure for the disease, but it is possible to give the sick person love, care, and dedicated attention. More generally, conversion is an exchange in which a value cannot be stabilized within an accepted system. M is homeless; she suffers. S gives her shelter in return for gratitude, perhaps also for other services. But there is no exchange, because the shelter, which has a certain value in the market, was offered for free and without condition, the gratitude and the meaning were offered voluntarily, and in any case they have no exchange value. S is sad. M tells him a story about his sadness, gives his sadness meaning. She receives affection and love in return, perhaps a meaning to her relationship with S.

6.542 Some channels of conversion are always blocked: situations in which one cannot give love, work magic, activate authority, or give meaning. Perhaps someone on the other side is unwilling to accept; perhaps there is an obstacle on the other side — law, a policeman, a heart of stone. Such blocks can be coincidental, and they could be a deliberate result of social actions. But more often they are an unintentional but systematic and non-coincidental consequence of social power relations. Giving meaning is the simplest, most general, and usually the least effective conversion under conditions of suffering. What does the one who gives meaning (to suffering, to loss, to a life thus wasted, to the world's cruelty) give? A little time and the effort of listening. What does the one who accepts the meaning get? Almost nothing, nearly everything, depending on the circumstances, the depth of her despair, her ability to enter the circulation of meanings, to enter the place where giving takes place. Exterminating the ability to give meaning is the worst, most radical, and most general impediment to the possibility of conversion in the face of suffering, but not because it is the factor that has the greatest capacity to cause suffering; quite the contrary. It is the most fragile factor, the most "airy" one, virtually weightless, that can cope with suffering. When one reaches this ether where the movement of meaning takes place, out of which meaning is "given," one hits rock bottom.

6.543 It is possible to characterize social situations, social order, and political regimes in terms of the exchange relations they institutionalize and the conversion channels they enable or block. Michael Walzer defined tyranny as a regime in which the individuals in power can convert their power into capital from any other social sphere without having to enter the exchange relations accepted within each sphere.[33] So, for example, the feudal prince who realizes his *droit du seigneur* easily revokes the separation between the political sphere and the private sphere and converts political power into sexual pleasure. Liberal democracy is characterized by high partitions between different spheres of action, which greatly reduce the conversion possibilities: one cannot legally buy a trial or a public position; one cannot translate knowledge or respect into political prerogative; and so on. But when it comes to suffering, the situation is reversed: the more conversion channels are open, the easier it is to reach the sufferer and help her. For the feudal prince, to whom most conversion channels are open, the channels concerning the reduction of suffering are also open, whereas for the feudal subjects most of these channels are blocked. In other ways and in another measure, this is also true of the relationship between those in high posts in a democratic state and most of the other citizens. The rights of conversion are a common basis for discrimination between social groups. In some societies, discriminating prerogatives prevent individuals in a certain group or class from freely converting their capital in order to cure suffering; in other societies, channels of conversion are accessible only to members of certain groups.

6.544 The ability to reduce or increase the possibilities of conversion is a structural quality of social institutions and of control mechanisms. The liberal regime, for example, blocks many conversion channels in order to maintain the relative autonomy of the different spheres within it but is supposed to ensure its citizens a more or less equal access to exchange relations in the different spheres. This is an example of an equilibrium between exchange and conversion that in an ideal situation at least is supposed to enable every citizen to utilize social resources to relieve her or someone else's suffering. On the other hand, when the social space is closed off, in the ghetto or under a curfew, the possibilities of exchange are blocked, and there are more and more attempts to find conversion channels, which the authorities block as well. One can deduce from this two ways in which a regime can increase suffering in a society. A regime can exclude an entire society or groups within it from institutionalized exchange relations and still allow conversion in various channels, but it can also block the conversion channels to which they turn in their despair. Curfew under occupation is an extreme example of exchange blocking, but even here there are gradations. Here are two examples of conversion blocking: instilling a market economy into a tribal society, and enforcing a "rational" bureaucratic rule under conditions of colonization.

6.545 The amplification of suffering reaches an apex when both the exchange systems and the conversion channels are blocked. Who can help the prisoner in his cell, the tortured on the Catherine wheel, the starved in the work camp? The Gulag and other concentration camps are modern instruments that create an environment that produces suffering. Such an environment has almost no resources that enable one to place suffering in an exchange relation, and the channels that enable the conversion of suffering are systematically destroyed.

6.550 Every conversion has a certain measure of gratuitous giving. That is not because some hallowed aura surrounds the conversion, but because without an institutionalized exchange system it is impossible to ensure the equality between what is given and what is accepted in return. When the exchange relation breaks open and the regulated exchange cycle decreases, the part of gratuitous giving grows. When someone comes to the help of an other who is suffering, converts capital between various spheres of social action, and at the end gives what was acquired (shelter, therapy, the right to exit) to the sufferer, she further increases the dimension of gratuitous giving in the mutual relationship. She had given up her time and her honor, for example, to get someone dear an improvement in his detention conditions. He will be grateful to her and, if he can, will pay her back in some way. But the gap between gratitude, even if it is accompanied by financial compensation, and the lost honor may be irreparable. In any case, until the gratitude and compensation arrive, if they ever do, the giving remains gratuitous. It is gratuitous because it is not conditioned upon what will be returned by the sufferer. The one who pities does not require acknowledgment from the pitied (5.340). Often the one who helps the sufferer does not expect any reward.

6.551 The rule of the economic genre, says Lyotard, is that someone's (x) cession of something (a) to someone else (y) must cancel y's cession of something else (b) to x. The exchange is the combination of the first phrase "x cedes a to y" with the second phrase "y cedes b to x," which cancels the debt between the sides.[34] In a conversion, x cedes a to y, y cedes b to x, but the combination of the two cessions does not cancel either one of them; each retains an aura of what is irreplaceable, what was gratuitously given. In a conversion, someone always remains in debt. In a conversion intended to help someone who suffers, x cedes a to y but gives b, which was given to her in exchange from y, to z, the sufferer. The graver the suffering, the more prolonged it is, and the worse it makes the situation of the sufferer, the smaller the chances that the last cession will be canceled, or rather, the bigger the gratuitous share in this cession. The rule of the philanthropic genre is that someone's cession of something to someone else who suffers is not supposed to be canceled within that relationship. But usually the philanthropic person gives gratuitously in one sphere in order to be rewarded in another (honor, recognition, appreciation, fame, "influence"). Philanthropic giving exceeds any exchange cycle if the final cession is not supposed to be canceled in any other system. Such is the case, for example, with anonymous charity. But even an anonymous charity that was given "for God's sake," "not to be rewarded," could be interpreted as a giving whose reward is promised in heaven. The Kantian categorical imperative or ethical responsibility according to Lévinas entails a cession that is not conditioned on the chances of its cancellation in any exchange relation, not on earth or in heaven, not here and now and not come Judgment Day.

6.552   One can describe solidarity as familiar practices of and readiness for gratuitous conversion meant to relieve some one who suffers. This solidarity is structured and produced within particular social frameworks and eroded in others; it is socially and culturally cultivated in relation to individual members of certain groups, affiliated with the one who cedes gratuitously, and is perceived as impossible or unwanted in relation to others. This applies to the family, the platoon, and the paupers in one's neighborhood. The nucleus of social solidarity lies in relatively small communities in which individuals are willing to infract the existing exchange relations time and again in order to relieve some one's suffering. Under certain conditions, this willingness is transported to a more general social space, such as the extended family or a tribe. The more general the object, the more abstract it becomes, but it is still the suffering of people, flesh and blood — until one reaches a totally abstract object, the nation, the homeland, whose suffering is always imaginary. But the affiliation of the tight nucleus of solidarity with its abstract object is not unequivocal. Sometimes the suffering of a homeland contradicts the suffering of a mother or a lover (as in Sartre's famous moral dilemma). Sometimes the nuclei of social solidarity are precisely what threaten to destroy it from the inside. The regime, which has an interest in displacing the solidarity onto the most general and abstract object, will always seek ways to cancel this threat, whether by eroding the solidarity in the small nuclei or by injecting images in which devotion for the abstract and the general is perceived as a widening of the devotion for the concrete loved ones. That is why every soldier in the front must know that he is directly protecting his parents and children in the rear.

6.553 These infractions of the exchange-relations logic and the demonstrated readiness to make them are themselves part of a mutual-exchange relationship — helping you today is a sure investment for the future, for the day I will need your help; this promise is the reward of gratuitous giving. But even these mutual-exchange relations are broken through; in the readiness to help the-one-who-suffers one finds that the reward, its timing and value, is uncertain. The stronger this uncertainty, the larger the weight of the gratuitous and unconditional giving, the sacrifice. And sacrifice for the other, to the death, is the height of being for an other. For Hegel, Being for an other is the height of objectification. Here we are dealing with the height of transcendence, but it is not the height of subjectivization, because it always also transcends the position of the subject. It is the height of self-overcoming, but it is not a height of self-realization, because there is no "potential" self prior to the overcoming of the self beyond itself that can or cannot be realized. This is the excess of expenditure (see 8.5).

6.554 Sacrifice to the death is one end of a continuum whose other end is self-preservation at all costs. But this is a continuum of being for an other, and therefore self-preservation has a unique meaning: absolute indifference to suffering that cannot be responded to in any exchange relation. Between sacrifice and indifference lies the "community of suffering." A community of suffering is distinguished by its threshold for suffering, by its distinctions and classifications of different kinds of sufferers, by the way in which its exchange mechanisms and conversion channels are organized, and by the way in which it encourages, rewards, or blocks the expenditure entailed by sacrifice for the suffering other. A community of suffering is the correlating opposite of the social unconscious, a kind of island of social recognition in the face of social nonrecognition and misrecognition (*méconnaissance*).

The presence of suffering beyond the threshold of a certain community of suffering will not activate any of its exchange relations (6.300). In the most extreme case of indifference, the presence of suffering that is beyond its sensitivity threshold will have no expression in any discourse.[35]

6.555 When it is impossible to express suffering so as to make others find relief for it, suffering becomes a case of wrong (*tort*). The one who bears such suffering is a victim. The passage from suffering to wrong is similar to the passage from damage to wrong (wrong being the case of a damage that cannot be established [3.544]). The victim of a wrong cannot prove that she suffers or that she has been wronged.

Aside

To this point, the present text has progressed along two parallel axes, two separate curves: from disappearance to wrong, from presence to wrong. From here on, the two curves converge. Before proceeding along the single ensuing line, I would like to pause briefly over this "proceeding," in particular over the character of the text's transition from one concept to the next, and in general over its use of concepts.

Excitation is no more fundamental than presence and is not derived from the latter; certain presences can be learned of only through excitation, through the intensification of another presence. Suffering is no less primary than excitation and is not derived from it; suffering may moderate excitations or annihilate them. "Being-there" is no more primary than dreams or suffering, nothingness no more "primordial" than bereavement. The differences are ones of abstraction, of dissemination, of exchange value within defined conceptual systems. When I move from disappearance to loss or from presence to excitation, I move from the abstract to the concrete, and from the more common to the rarer. But when I continue from loss to damage or from excitation to suffering, the picture gets more complicated. Points of view and discursive regimes begin to branch off.

A mountain climber knows if the base camp where he has left some of his gear and rescue equipment was properly chosen only after reaching the top, or relying on the experience of others who have already mapped out the area and discerned its conditions under changing weather patterns. In my own journey, presence and disappearance are two base camps situated at the foot of the mountain, on either side. The apex is the concept of Evil; the view from the top is a new field of morality.

While climbing to the top, I will send out skilled messengers — native metaphors and local terms — so as to bring back missing equipment from the valley and send down injured climbers. The goal is to reach the summit, not necessarily to conquer it, in order to look out *from there at as large an area as possible, which I intend not to control but to return to and roam through. Doubtless, this is not the only way to do so. Anyone who knows another route is welcome to go his way. It may very well be that other routes will lead in the end to nearby summits. It may well be that from other summits another, more awesome vista can be viewed, that visibility conditions are better there, that access is more convenient, that the view on the way is more breathtaking. The journey should be tested in these terms. In order to do so, one needs to be a skilled climber and to climb in the company of other skilled climbers. Those who stay down in the valley need at least the skill of deciphering aerial photography. But it should be kept in mind that no photograph will be taken from a bird's-eye view here. Feet are constantly committed to the ground, breathing comes hard, there is always need of something to catch hold of so as not to stumble. None of the things caught hold of will be the base of the mountain. One can only catch hold of stakes one carries on one's back and of rock nodules encountered along the way. There is no way to prevent stumbles, downward slides are to be expected at every turn, especially at the height of the slope, and the risk of a total crash should be taken very seriously.*

Still, this is not Neurath's raft. The supply of stakes is not limited to what one can bring from home or carry in a knapsack, and anything found along the way can serve as a handhold. Even if we were at sea, there would be not one but several rafts, and they would have different designs. But we aren't at sea. In the territories of thought, as at sea, the horizon is always out of reach, and holding a steady course won't bring you back to the point of departure. The always flowing rivers do not reach the same sea. Sometimes the earth grows swiftly under the climbers' feet; sometimes it contracts. Every journey begins from a house, even if it ends in the Himalayas. Some people climb mountains near their childhood homes; others were born near the summits.

What I write is as faithful as possible to what I feel, know, am familiar with (although with some texts, the more you write them, the more you feel, know, for the text works incessantly and there are more things to feel and know — such is the present text for me). In any case, I am examining not just "what" I feel or know but also the boundaries of what I can imagine someone really feeling, understanding, or knowing — about presence, loss, excitation, and so forth. A boundary is one of the meanings of abstraction. I abstract and recombine. When your sensibility is offended by what I write — that is, not when you don't understand what I mean but when you do and can no longer follow me, when you feel I'm speaking of someone else, not of you — you can draw my boundary line from the outside and go on roaming without me. For instance, if you think — because you know from your own experience or from that of others whose reports you trust — that some excitations are caused by the draining away of presence rather than by its intensification (and it's impossible to describe such draining away in terms of the intensification of another presence); or if you can conceive of a kind of damage that doesn't involve loss. Through the process of abstraction, I mean to reach the boundary of what I can imagine as real, but I know my mind is quite limited. Wherever you choose to depart from the course I've taken, I will try to follow you so as to broaden my mind, on the condition, of course, that you have come to terms with it at some previous point on the journey. The route you choose will interest me in this context as long as you go on searching for the same destination: that is, if you go on trying to figure out how bad things appear in the world, if you go on trying to extricate the concept of Evil from what is there — the experience, the sense of it, the things and the others around you, the deeds, the tools of construction and the tools of destruction, the social, economic, and political relations, the institutions and rules regulating them, the language, the cultural activity and its products; that is, if you forgo from the outset the assumption that Evil is the opposite of some "positive" value and do not succumb to deriving Evil from good, or justice, or liberty, or authenticity, or some other value that is always present as an absolute value, exceeding the phenomenal realm and therefore forever absent.

On the way to this destination, I cross innumerable paths that others have traveled — most of them on the way to other destinations. Only a few interest me enough to make me want to outline here the boundaries of their thinking. It is very likely that this will be the relation between you and me as well. You happened upon me in your wanderings toward other places. You try to broaden your mind without fathoming the boundaries of mine. You join me for a stretch, then leave. You take something from me and make some use of it, perhaps, and then discard it. Later you may come back for something else. Or maybe not. The things you take from me, even when these weren't taken from someone else, are naturally not mine but my text's. When you take them "from me," I am already no more than a creature of this text. And that is precisely what you are, too, at least at this or that stage of your encounter with this text, at this or that stage of your taking.

Nevertheless I, who simultaneously create and am created by this text, roam along the way to some destination that gradually emerges through the act of writing. The act of writing, in turn, is simultaneously a wandering along the way toward and an invitation to set out. This text invites the reader to join it along the way to the summit I have called Evil. This sort of invitation is a common matter in text-reader relations. Less common, perhaps, is this text's invitation to the reader to leave it at any moment so as to go there his own way. Of course, this "there" will be rewritten by every reader who writes, though at the point of divergence it is still possible to speak with appropriate reservations of "that place there" aimed at by the roaming. If you continue on your way to that place, you may find in time that my route, too, the one you left at this or that stage along the way, is of interest to you, whether it broadens your mind or merely serves you for discovering the limitations of mine. The common destination and a few meeting points along the way (understanding presence as an encounter, for instance, or understanding loss as a disappearance that becomes someone's problem) define a common ground. That will do. There's no need to determine the boundaries of this area in advance. There's no need to declare the rules of the partnership in advance. But the form of the partnership should be introduced: agreement on statements describing what is there. There is no reason to forgo from the outset the universal claim implied by descriptive statements, which is the form this partnership assumes. It should just be kept in mind that this claim isn't to be taken too seriously. It should be noted that the universal claim is no more than a form of partnership, and as such is a product of language games and particular discursive frameworks, the rules of which we never understand completely, for understanding itself activates new rules, and so on and so on. It should be kept in mind that even if we don't know exactly how at the moment, these descriptions are conditional and limited, like all those before them, and thus cannot provide solid ground for anything important — and who says important things need solid ground anyway?

More important than the universal claim of the descriptive statement, however, is the move toward abstraction, the striving toward the limit — usually one and the same. Abstraction is the limit or boundary of what is thinkable. This claim itself is no more than a description of one of the laws constituting the game — at least the game I think I am taking part in, the one I think you are taking part in, too, if you are still reading me. (The invitation to take part in the game appeared in this text in many forms, explicit and implicit, long before the appearance of the invitation to progress toward "that place there," and the two should be distinguished from each other.) What counts in my attempts to talk about the concepts with which I work is not the universality of their application but the preciseness of their abstraction relative to my experience and relative to what I know, what I am capable of thinking, about your experience and that of others. In this matter, I am still "a lover of these processes of division and bringing together," and I wish to remain faithful to those "two principles . . . that of perceiving and bringing together in one idea the scattered particu-

lars, that one may make clear by definition the particular which he wishes to explain... [and] that of dividing things again by classes, where the natural joints are, and not trying to break any part, after the manner of a bad carver," as Plato says in Phaedrus.[1]

Of course, the generalizations and intersections indicate not the current things or their eternal forms but only the boundaries of what I can imagine as real. The question is whether you can imagine as real something that has been left out or something else that can still be abstracted. The question is whether I wound your sensibilities when I exceed the limits or whether I burden them with foreign elements, bringing in the superfluous from without. But in order to ask yourself this question, you need to be prepared to roam beside me for a time, that is, inside and along with my text. My text seeks to teach your sensibilities a few new words. It seeks as well to teach your words a few new sensibilities. You need to be prepared to entrust yourself to it for a time before you start asking questions. That is the process of socialization into any cult: you cannot ask before you understand something; silence is golden for starting out along the path. Science and philosophy are no different in principle. Socratic investigation is an invitation to take a journey; it is not the journey itself. When the real journey begins, Socrates's partners fall silent, or at most nod their heads, yes, yes, yes. The difference between the philosophical journey (and, hopefully, the scientific investigation) and the dogmatic rigidity that some of Plato's dialogues gradually take on lies in a readiness to stop the journey from time to time and take an outside look at it, to take an "outside" view of the territory, the destination, the point of departure, the bridges and tunnels at difficult passes, the forestlands and swamps, the deserts and populated cities. The point is to take a look from the outside — that is, from someone else's territory (as stated, there are no bird's-eye photographs, or is it perhaps that birds, too, have a limited territory and point of view?) or from the roaming of a nomad who suspends himself from the logic of the given time and place, a foreign user of a space not his, who has no idea what role has been assigned him by others, what others expect of him. Philosophizing of the most limited type, which is most of what is taught in universities, makes do with an outside view without taking the trouble to check or declare within whose territory exactly the point of view is placed. Philosophizing of a slightly less limited type, also commonly taught, makes do with an inside view. The virtuoso philosopher knows how to amaze with both types of games, without completely separating them, without disconnecting them entirely. This virtuosity is the birthplace of philosophical irony.

When I write "excitation is . . ." or "damage is . . . ," I don't intend to provide a dictionary definition, to epitomize common usage taken from daily language (Whose, precisely? On exactly which days?), from one or another structured discourse, or to establish a corrective norm against such usage. More than intending anything, I act upon something. I construct a concept as a tool for thought, and in the process I conduct some trial runs, simultaneously thinking it through and thinking through it. After constructing it, I tune it as one tunes a musical instrument. If there is some important sense of the term "intent" here, it is similar to the one used in ancient discussions of prayer, which requires an intent of the soul like the tuning of an instrument. Later I play it a little, my concept, maybe a bit more than needed in order to make it produce a typical sound. And then, gradually, I change it through additions, enlarge its sound box, add strings, broaden its keyboard, to the point where you can speak of a new instrument. But the first instrument in my series was also created from other instruments. There are highly complex instruments that produce very simple products (a "subject," for instance) and very simple instruments that produce relatively complex products (a "loss," for instance). And in every case, no tool can be made without a tool. Attributing primary status to the abstract concept is like trying to base an orchestra on the tambourine.

A concept can be thought of as a musical instrument, but also as a working tool. Both metaphors should be used with reservations (I can't remember where I borrowed the first from; the second was taken from Nietzsche's toolbox, and from that of Deleuze). In speaking of a musical performance, one emphasizes the game element, the clear delineation between the game/performance and all other areas of activity, and the suspension of all other activities for purposes of the game. In speaking of philosophizing as a musical performance, one must not forget that the notes were not written in advance, even if a few motifs and musical phrases and more than a few instruments are already waiting in the hall for anyone who begins philosophizing. The contract signed with the impresario rules out any possibility of ever securing an empty hall. In speaking of philosophizing as work, one wishes to emphasize the link between philosophical thinking and society's other production lines while pointing out that products of this cottage industry possess commercial value in other cultural exchange systems. In speaking of concepts as work tools, one must not forget that to onlookers, the philosopher often seems like an unemployed loafer or an inventor of tools whose purpose and manner of operation no one knows, like Jacques Carelman, who invented unfindable tools that, when found, are inoperable and that, when operated, lead to no good.[2]

I wish to operate these two metaphors alongside each other, each embedded like a spear in the ribs of the other. Work tools are supposed to remind any who might wish to forget it that philosophizing is a serious game, that there are defined social conditions which allow it to take place, that it generates products which do not end once the curtain falls. Musical instruments remind any who might wish to suppress it that philosophizing is an immensely pleasurable diversion, that not just anyone can pick up an instrument and operate it, that the work in question is conducted in the presence of an audience, that applause, too, has value, that something does, after all, end when the curtain falls.

And there is more work to be done yet and just a short time to play. Back to the journey.

As stated, until now this text has proceeded along two parallel axes, two curves. In both cases, the principle of progress was similar: development of a concept to its very limit, closely following the concept along winding paths, to the moment when something was added that caused a new concept to appear: a principle of accumulation. On one curve, loss is disappearance with the addition of an interested party; damage is loss that causes depreciation assessable in a given order of things; injustice is superfluous damage that could have been, or can still be, prevented; wrong is damage accompanied by a loss of the means to prove the damage. Analogously, on the other curve, presence is the manner of the existence of being-there for someone; excitation is an intensification of presence; suffering is a kind of excitation so greatly intensified as to become unbearable; injustice is superfluous suffering that could have been, or can still be, prevented; wrong is silenced suffering, suffering that has no expression, which can therefore not be prevented or reduced. The two curves converged at the concepts of injustice and wrong. The area of their convergence is foggy. Injustice and wrong are suffering or damage at turning points on the cumulative curves: when something is added to them, something from one area is subtracted from them. Their excess (a superfluous damage, a superfluous or overburdening suffering) is also their lack on another plane of existence, the plane of discourse (what is superfluous is unjustifiable; what is silenced is inexpressible), and at the same time this lack can be described as an addition in a defined area of moral discourse, in the region of what ought and what ought not to be done, what is proper and not proper.

What is superfluous or silenced is unjustifiable in principle, what is unjustifiable is not proper, and what is not proper should be eliminated. What is not proper gives birth to the proper, by definition, but *itself is born of what is there. There is no unbridgeable gap, no chasm, between the proper and what is there. All that lies between them is the intensification of something and the depletion of something else. What is proper is not detached from what is there and does not hover above it like a ghost. It grows out of it, appears from its complexity, like a life appearing out of the complexity of inorganic matter, like a consciousness appearing out of the complexity of organic matter. The Evil that will appear later out of the many wrongs will be a result of the complexity of being. When something is added to suffering or damage, turning it into wrong, it is a case not of twofold suffering or damage squared but of suffering or damage becoming something else. So it is with Evil: not a terrible wrong, but a terrible order of wrongs.*

It should be kept in mind that there is no full symmetry here. On the one hand, damage cannot overburden or exceed anything; there is no upper limit to exchange value; such an excess of being does not transfer it from one order of things to another. Conversely, loss overburdens not because of the depreciation it causes but because of the suffering. On the other hand, though, some of the unpreventable suffering — or at least the suffering perceived as such — is overburdening, and when it is given expression, there are those who respond, but it can nonetheless not be alleviated, or at least this is how it is perceived. Horrible as this suffering may be, nothing in its intensification transposes it or the one presented with it to the plane of what is or is not proper; its presence does not generate a moral claim. Or it generates a moral claim, but posits in the position of addressee the one who could have prevented and alleviated it only because he is omnipotent. This suffering, lying beyond what can be changed by humans, which — for just this reason — can be termed metaphysical, belongs to the moral realm only if God can be placed within this realm as a defendant. And perhaps God is no more than the one taking the position of addressee in a statement of suffering for which no human addressee has been found — in other words, God as a bulge appearing somewhere along the accumulation curve, long after what is proper has appeared from within what is there, when the suffering accumulates continuously and the human addressees gradually disappear.

However, we know that the historical process was in fact just the opposite. We know that God vacated the sphere of morality at just the time when men and women began taking addressee positions, responding to complaints about suffering and damage that might have been prevented, and history itself became the field of moral action (it is irrelevant which was the cause and which the effect here, and it is likely that both were both). This historical knowledge does not blemish the accumulation curve: the ontological-phenomenological description of the moral being of what is there has only been possible from the moment history has been perceived as the realm of moral action and the historicity of being as one of its main interests, but this does not turn such a description into a historical description.

PART THREE
The Superfluous

Third Curve

0.800 Damage and suffering are kinds of evils. Evils are part of what-is-there. They are the particular part of what is there that may have a moral existence. The centrality of the concept of Evil justifies a digression here. Although this text has reached the concept of wrong in its progression along both curves, and although the concept of Evil is in fact already implicit in two of the previous chapters ("Damage" and "Suffering"), the next chapter begins with it. The first steps will be based mainly on things stated already in these earlier chapters. The text returns to roam swiftly through two regions it has already crossed, collects and classifies the old findings, discovers a few new ones, and goes on from there.

0.801 The two curves now converge into one with the concepts of injustice and wrong, and I will continue to trace this curve as it moves from injustice and wrong to Evil. However, before converging completely, the curves already verged on each other at the points where the similar semiotic structures of damage and suffering emerged (3.110 and 6.340) and where damage and suffering emerged as "things," as part of what-is-there, what is at hand, with their own space of appearance and conceptual grid (3.142 and 6.340). Starting at those points of convergence, I was able to begin a move combining the two concepts into a single new concept whose use I have so far evaded — evils. Evils are things, events, or occurrences in the course of which someone's condition deteriorates. Damage and suffering are evils. Evils are signs whose signifiers are events in the realm of experience (loss or excitation) and whose signifieds are values or measures in terms of which the experienced duration is interpreted (depreciation or a move across the threshold of what is sufferable).

0.81 Evils serve to connect the two curves and to allow continued accumulation along a single curve. They allow both the two curves' convergence and the transition from wrong and injustice to Evil. The concept of evils has a relative advantage: it distinctly belongs at one and the same time to the realm of moral discussion and to the phenomenology of experience, to the physics of the movement of loss or excitation, to the geography of damage or suffering. Evils are both a link in the order of things and a link in the proper moral order. This, though, is an imprecise formulation. In fact, the concept of evils eliminates the radical difference between what is there and what is (morally) proper, or, to use the common idiom, between is and ought. If a single intuition guides this text throughout, it is that there is no radical difference between what is there and what is (morally) proper, that human reality, as what is always already there, contains the possibility of morality as organic matter contains the possibility of life and life contains the possibility of consciousness. This intuition hangs on the concept of evils like a picture on a nail. Evils are simply those bad things that happen to human beings and make their lives difficult. Evils are among those things that human beings cause other human beings, produce for them and distribute among them. For the one who consumes them — the one who is hurt — evils are always superfluous; for the one who produces and distributes them, evils are always preventable; there is always another way.

0.900 Morality appears in this area between the possible and the superfluous. The fact that it is always possible to do evil in other ways — that evils can be reduced or intensified through social action, management, control, and resistance — makes what is proper (the reduction of evils) possible; the fact that evils are always superfluous for the party suffering them makes part of what is possible (the reduction of evils) proper. To understand which part precisely, which evils should properly be reduced, we need to understand superfluity not just as an aspect of the subjective experience of suffering and loss but also as a category of objective reality.

0.901 On either side of the coin, of the possible or of the proper, the issue is what there is and what could be: on the one hand, the possibilities of managing the production and distribution of evils differently are an inseparable part of the existing order of reality; on the other hand, the superfluity of evils for the one who is hurt and the demand to remove them are an inseparable part of the experience of evils. In general, the moral realm includes the deliberation, the types of discourse, and the social practices, rituals, and customs that mediate between what is superfluous and what is possible in the production, distribution, and prevention of evils. Or differently put: every social practice is situated in the realm of morality if it includes a problematization of the link between what is possible and what is superfluous regarding the evils involved in it.

0.91 Evil is part of what-is-there, much of what-is-there is steeped in Evil, but Evil in and of itself is not the end of the world. The lives of numerous people — behind barbed wire, in occupied territories, in the depths of mines and at the heights of scaffoldings, in dreary offices, in terrible homes — are controlled by the systematic production of superfluous evils, and these people nevertheless laugh and love, create and invent, feel joy and take pleasure, between the lines, in the intervals, behind the guards' backs. In the gaps between the islands of Evil's order, they steal moments of grace, learn to take pleasure in torment, develop entire and rich cultures of perseverance, survival, ignoring, transcendence, and simply mundane routine alongside the horror. We are not yet at the apex of the cumulative curve.

0.92 The intensification of Evil can be traced in terms of the length of time over which evils are suffered, of the geographic space throughout which they are distributed, of the depth of their penetration into various areas of living, of the force of their rule over the matrix of the lifeworld of individuals and groups, of how systematically they are distributed, of the chances of escaping the system that produces and distributes them. There is mundane Evil, with which one lives daily and from which an entire culture arises; there are disasters and tragedies in which some die and others are crushed; there are catastrophes in which masses die and entire lifeworlds are shattered and whole civilizations are turned into ruins. And among catastrophes, too, some are more terrible than others. In these times, one catastrophe has become a symbol and a name for absolute Evil. The general name is the "Shoah," the Holocaust; the particular name is "Auschwitz."

0.93 The thinking presented here on the subject of Evil will seek to understand catastrophe as one of the more sophisticated forms of Evil in these times and will seek to reread the concept of Evil through the catastrophes characteristic of these times (while in the process scrutinizing the meaning of the delineation and identification involved in thinking about "these times"). This thinking, however, will make an effort not to presuppose a scale of Evil whose climax is Auschwitz, placed there in its full horror like some negative pole to which every discussion of Evil in these times must inevitably, teleologically lead. The thinking on Evil presented here makes an effort to think without presupposing any meaning for the signifier "Auschwitz," partly in order to rethink the catastrophic event named "Auschwitz," but mainly in order to think that Evil which, even if less horrendous than Auschwitz, is much more urgent to think due to its being still foreseeable, Evil that can still be prevented. The most horrifying catastrophes may perhaps be not those that have already taken place but those that are yet to occur. The fact that they are not inevitable turns the thinking that seeks to understand them and to ward off their occurrence into the most urgent thinking at hand, both morally and existentially.

0.940 Among the catastrophes yet to occur, the most terrible may be those hastening the end of the world. The catastrophes that have already occurred allow a displacement of the thought of the end of the world from the realm of religious messianism and eschatological mythology onto the history of the present. They also allow thought about several tangible forms of this end: the true end of the world, in the worst case, or the end of the human world, or the end of the world for entire civilizations. This is the not-inevitable pole that every discussion of Evil in these times should address. This is also the climax and the culmination of the cumulative curve that the present discussion wishes to draw and the point where it will end.

0.941 In the last part of this discussion, which covers half of the book, the pace of the journey will change. The movements will be slower and broader; I will pause more often over the classical philosophers, and later over some historians; at times, the discussion will exceed its measured dimensions and run on beyond its usual format. Despite this, the discussion will go on conforming to its pattern of progression along the cumulative curve: from evils to injustice and to wrong; from injustice and wrong to Evil; from Evil to the catastrophes of our times; from catastrophes that have already occurred to those yet to happen, first and foremost those threatening to bring the end of the world.

CHAPTER SEVEN

Evils

7.0 *Prevention, Assistance, and Compensation*

7.000 An unbearable excitation or a loss causing depreciation worsens the condition of someone who has been hurt by it. The occurrence in which a worsening in someone's condition takes place is an evil.

7.001 I know of two major types of occurrences (that may be intertwined) that worsen someone's condition: when he incurs loss or damage (in terms of certain exchange relations) that has no compensation; and when someone or something causes him suffering. Two types of evils. There are, of course, occurrences that worsen someone's condition because they increase the danger that he will be harmed without directly causing damage; in this case, the evil comes from the future damage and from the indirect loss caused as a result of the need to protect himself from the expected damage. This is a type of evil of the first kind, a type of damage, even if it is indirect or futural. And there are different types of offenses — pain, humiliation, disappointment, and so on — that do not cause suffering, because their excitation is not intensified, not yet or no longer. These offenses can be seen as a small-scale model or fetal stage of an evil of the second type. If they do not become suffering or do not constitute loss, they are transient, or at least secondary in importance and urgency.

7.002 Unpleasant emotions, "negative" excitations such as sorrow, disappointment, and insult, and everything that injures without causing suffering can spoil someone's mood, pester and plague, without becoming unbearable. These are encounters from which one does not wish to disengage. Sometimes some pleasure is to be gained from them. In any case, it is difficult to attribute to them a substantial worsening of someone's condition. And the same holds for a loss that does not cause suffering but also does not cause depreciation, because there is no exchange system that can express the loss it causes. Loss makes someone's situation worse only if it causes depreciation or suffering (or both, of course). In

other cases, the hazy margins of what was lost and has no substitute can be present as those encounters from which one does
not want to disengage, as a longing, a yearning, or a sadness.
Sometimes they can be mixed with a "sense of sweetness," arouse
nostalgic reminiscing. The encounter of loss can cause whoever
experiences it to withdraw, or to come out of himself, to distract
his attention from something, or to refine his emotions about
what was lost or about an entire plane of presence in which the
absence is presenced. But in all of these cases, it is difficult to
attribute to the sensations that accompany the loss a worsening in
the condition of the party interested in what was lost.

7.003 Are there other kinds of evils? I cannot imagine any. Or more precisely, I suppose that any other imaginable kind of evil could fall
into the category of hurting someone, the clearest form of which
is suffering, or the category of hurting something that belongs to
someone (or what could have been his), thus causing loss and
damage. Suffering may be followed by loss, and loss may be followed by suffering. Other harming effects of suffering and loss
can be reduced to the latter. Here are two examples:

Humiliation: the person who is humiliated is hurt, feels terrible
frustration, suffocation, powerlessness, wastefulness. He feels like
a useless, redundant object in the world of the humiliating person
but has no way out of this world and no way of changing his position and status in it. When these excitations increase, they cause
suffering. They are structured in a suffering-creating framework
from the start—an encounter (with the humiliating person and
with the feeling of humiliation itself, with frustration and helpless
rage, and with intensified and intensifying excitation) from which
it is impossible to disengage. The suffering involved in humiliation could lead to action—from defiance of the humiliating person to a full-blown mutiny—and such action could, in its turn,
cause loss and damage and increase the suffering. This does not
mean that we can reduce humiliation to the suffering and damage
it causes. It only means that humiliation is an evil, measured by
the suffering and damage it involves.

Restriction on the freedom of movement: this kind of restriction is tied to a loss of the possibility to act, which causes
losses (damage), hurt, frustration, an unbearable sense of suffocation (suffering), and the increase of population density in the
restricted area, which causes, in turn, more damage and suffering,
and so on. Such restrictions also create new possibilities that
could improve the condition of the one who was hurt: the lengthy
stay at one place could lead to social ties, give merchants and

craftsmen new possibilities, and so on. Restrictions on the freedom of movement constitute an evil only insofar as they entail loss and suffering.

7.004 Could you imagine other types of social action, such as restrictions on the freedom of movement, that are evil? If you say "the denial of rights," for example, I would reply that a right belongs to one or several defined exchange systems and the loss of this right is a depreciation in terms of these systems. The denial of rights represents "exposure to an entire realm of damages" (3.520). "A right that has been violated constitutes a principal type or category of damage. It designates a field of obstructed possibilities for action" (3.521), the kind of damage that could be caused as a result of that and obstructing access to the plaintiff position, which prevents compensation and perpetuates the loss (3.523). And what about a lack into which one is born that cannot be described in terms of loss, because this person never had anything to lose? This kind of lack, I admit, is an evil only insofar as it causes damage or suffering. There is nothing wrong with a lack that does not cause either damage or suffering. In order to represent lack as evil, we attribute to the one who was born into it possibilities whose fulfillment is blocked. Various humanist philosophies, including Marxism, treat these possibilities as a potential that is part of human essence and whose fulfillment (which belongs to man no less essentially) has been denied. The various realizations of this essence constitute a closed exchange system: when there is shortage, the fulfillment of a certain potential is at the expense of other realizations. But in a utopian society, which will overcome the lack and distribute what it has fairly, the exchange relations will only take place as a time economy: "In communist society ... society regulates the general production and thus makes it possible for me to do one thing today and another tomorrow, to hunt in the morning, fish in the afternoon, rear cattle in the evening, criticize after dinner, just as I have in mind, without ever becoming hunter, fisherman, herdsman or critic."[1] The shortage that prevents the individual from fulfilling his human essence appears thus, like the right, as a principal category of damage.

7.005 And what about a loss that worsens a person's condition but cannot be prevented in principle (memory loss as a result of aging, for example, or weight loss as a result of a malignant disease)? This loss is, by definition, not damage, because the possibility of prevention is a necessary condition for the existence of damage (3.030). Is such a loss, which is not damage, not an evil? It is an evil only if it causes suffering and only with respect to the suffering it causes. Let us suppose that the memory loss is unpreventable and does not directly cause any suffering. It only decreases the possibility of enjoyment, intellectual activity, and socializing of the one afflicted by it. These losses do not count as losses, because they could not have been prevented. But they indirectly cause preventable losses (preventable through correct treatment, assistance for the person affected by the condition, and so on) and unpreventable suffering. Because of these two (loss and suffering), this is still an evil. If there were no secondary suffering or damage, there would have been nothing wrong in the loss; the loss would not be an evil. There are countless things a person loses every day that cannot be thought of as evils, precisely because they do not involve any suffering or any damage.

7.010 Obviously, the same kind of occurrence could cause both damage and suffering, but in different ways, in different circumstances, and for different people. Compare, for example, the suffering and damage involved in the same chronic disease for an insured and an uninsured patient. Or think about the loss of a dog: a child loses his beloved dog, which he rescued from the street — how great is the sorrow and how small the deficit. And compare that to a blind person who loses his recently acquired guide dog; it is very likely that the sorrow over the lost dog is insignificant compared to the sorrow over the loss of money, because the dog was so expensive.

7.011 The way in which an evil is experienced is inseparable from the evil as an occurrence, something that happens in the world, and the difference between harming someone and harming something that someone has is an ontological difference, not just a matter for a subjective perception of the occurrence. This is an ontological difference — in which the demarcating line is not determined a priori but always expressed ex post facto — between a space in which damage and loss appear and the space in which suffering appears; between the conceptual web into which the expressions of loss and damage are weaved and the conceptual web into which the expressions of suffering are weaved. The same goes for the exchange relations and possibilities of conversion open for each of these. You can harm someone by harming his body, his property, his honor, and his hopes and dreams as long as the injury arouses an excessive excitation. The limits of excessive excitation are the limits of the injured, suffering self. The limits of damage are the limits of what one has that is alienable, the limit of the exchangeable components of one's self (including one's body) — an unbearable excitation against a growing deficit, an economy of intensified excitation against an exchange economy, without forgetting that an excitation has an exchange value and that both the act of exchange and the value exchanged have exciting effects.

7.012 Perhaps this is just another version of the radical difference between subject (harming someone) and object (harming something someone has). But instead of returning to these metaphysical concepts, we will note that this is a translation of the metaphysical distinction into two kinds of economies, which give this difference an earthly, concrete, and contingent sense that is historically and culturally embedded. In other words, what will excite excessively, and how one isolates something, gives it an exchange value, and attributes ownership to it, are matters that distinctly depend on economic, cultural, and historical contexts. They do not belong either to human nature or to the immanent nature of man's exchange relations.

7.013 Damage is an estimate of losses that depends not only on the perception of loss of the one who is harmed. Suffering is an experience of excitation that does not depend on the real damage caused to the sufferer. The concept of damage guarantees that it will be possible to also speak about evils that befall happy, insentient, or insensitive people. The concept of suffering enables us also to speak about evils that befall those who lack nothing. Now we can, at the cost of a certain repetition, bring together the results of the two parallel movements of damage and of suffering.

7.014 "The condition of one who suffers damage is always worse than it was before the damage" (3.011); "that is not the case with the situation of the one who suffers. The sufferer could eventually improve her condition and therefore would be willing to further delay disengaging from the exciting, agonizing encounter. In the meantime, she suffers. Her condition is bad as long as the suffering continues" (6.312). "In this sense, suffering differs from loss even more than it differs from damage" (6.340). A loss has to cause deprivation in order to be considered damage (2.531), but suffering does not; suffering is an evil by its mere occurrence. In this sense, it is analogous to damage: loss relates to losings as excitation relates to the threshold of the tolerable; an excitation must cross this threshold (as loss must change the balance of loss and gain) in order to be considered an evil.

7.020 The gesture or the verbal expression that conveys excitation bears dubious witness to the place of the threshold of the tolerable, the moment of its crossing, or the fact that it has already been crossed. But there is no other testimony. What was lost, and in fact its representation in a word, a photograph, a sentimental description, bear dubious witness to the deprivation caused by the loss. There are other testimonies, but they are all tied to a displacement of the representation from one discourse to another, and to attempts to stabilize the representation and increase the reliability of the signification with the help of an accepted translation mechanism (3.512). Either way, evils appear as a complex sign in which a previous signification event — of suffering (3.102) or of an unbearable excitation (6.340) — functions as a signifier, and the worsening — in terms of depreciation or of crossing the threshold of the tolerable — is the signified. The surplus of the signifier belongs essentially to the semiotic form of Evil (3.110). Between the expressions of the excitation, or the representation of what was lost (the signifier), and the losings signified by the loss, or the crossing of the threshold exposed by the excitation, there is an indelible difference (3.142).

7.021 Like any sign, an evil belongs simultaneously to the space of appearance of loss or of tormenting excitation, the phenomenal space within which the signifiers appear, and to the conceptual texture in which they receive their measure and exchange value (as a pressing need, as a demand for compensation). In both spaces, the separation between the phenomenal and the conceptual, between things and words, between the experienced and the said, cannot really be sustained, but neither can the former be reduced to the latter. An evil is an objective matter in relation to excitation and suffering, just as it is in relation to damage and loss. It is unthinkable and inexpressible outside a certain discourse, within which damage or suffering is represented and appraised. Nonetheless, it is inseparable also from the phenomenology of loss and excitation and from their subjective expression (what was lost, the intolerable excitation) and their inexpressible residue as someone's problems that no appraisal can adequately express (3.142 and 6.342).

7.030 Damage always relates to a certain exchange system within which what was lost finds expression and an exchange value (3.011), whereas suffering is what transcends exchange relations and exists independently of any exchange system. But suffering, too, is often placed in exchange cycles, by being represented in terms of damage and a claim for compensation. Suffering is a matter for a compensation claim by its mere existence, but also because and

if it causes loss — of time, health, quality of life, material resources, and so on (6.330).

7.031 There are experts for estimating suffering, translating suffering
into damage, as there are experts for translating loss into damage.
But because of the chronic instability of the "objective" description of suffering, the appraisal of suffering is extremely imprecise.
Suffering has no agreed-on discursive grid that describes it, and it
has no clear affinity with any exchange system (6.331). The experiential aspect of suffering, its conventional expression patterns,
and the fundamental gap between the excitation and the expression (5.102–5.120) prevent the institutionalization of an agreed-
on grid that will enable an ordered and orderly commerce of
suffering. But anywhere damage is appraised, it is possible, in
principle, to agree on a codification of types of suffering (according to the type of loss, the rate of the "basic" damage, and so
on) and to try to quantify them. "In defined exchange conditions
within an exchange market, the appraisal of suffering is no different, in principle, from the appraisal of loss" (6.331).

7.032 Hence, in certain exchange conditions, evils of both kinds are the
object of compensation claims and have an exchange value that is
placed on the scales in the struggle between different partners of
these exchange relations. But the mere attribution of an exchange
value to loss or suffering creates a *différend*. That is because the
exchange value leaves a residue of loss, an unbearable excitation
that has no expression in the idiom in which the damage and compensation are represented (3.130 and 6.112). Full compensation
erases all damage because the damage is already coded in terms of
what is compensatable in a given exchange regime (3.42), whereas
something always remains uncompensated in loss and suffering,
even when compensation is given rapidly, generously. It is impossible to give full compensation for loss, only for its exchange value.
It is impossible to erase suffering or even ease it with compensation by anything other than disengagement from the exciting
encounter and a return to the other side of the threshold of the tolerable. When compensation erases damage, the loss remains, from
the perspective of the damaged one, as a signified without a signifier — the silenced, the denied, the expelled. Or, from the perspective of the exchange system, as a signifier without a signified — the
meaningless, the residual, the surplus. The evil is displaced from
the presence of the thing that was lost to the loss of the ability to
presence loss. But this is not the case with suffering. When compensation erases the damage that caused the suffering, and even the
damage caused by the suffering, and there still is an experienced

suffering, it is always possible to continue to presence what has no compensation and insert the evil itself "as a harassing, aggravating sign into any system of interpersonal relations" (6.351).

7.033 Often an expression of loss or of a tormenting excitation introduces what was lost and the loss or excitation as an event into one of the exchange systems available to the harmed one or the sufferer: damage on the one hand and compensation on the other; a call for help on one side and a response to the call (in the form of helping one to disengage from an exciting encounter) on the other. In both cases, the response is supposed to cancel the source of the call: adequate compensation will annul the damage; a successful disengagement will cancel the suffering (it is possible, in principle, to annul every suffering by disengaging from an encounter with casualties, even if the price is total disengagement). When the matter is damage, the compensation closes an exchange circle and could, at least in principle, annul the damage with no remainder. However, when the matter is suffering, disengagement cannot annul the suffering that has already been experienced, only any future suffering, and it opens an exchange system in which the sufferer becomes a debtor (6.350). In general, evils that come from damage have a different status and function from the evils whose source is a tormenting excitation, but in both cases evils are an inseparable part of the exchange market. Evils are an object of social manipulation, negotiation, and bargaining; they are produced, distributed, and consumed.

7.040 Evils take place between two types of possibilities: what could have been done to avoid their production or their distribution; what could have been done to ease the suffering or harm of the one who was injured by them or to annul the injury itself through compensation or disengagement (compare 3.401). One possibility is a desired state that will not be realized, a missed opportunity, a lost possibility buried in the past; the other possibility is a desired state that has not yet been realized, an open future.

7.041 Damage has no existence if it is not defined between these two types of possibilities. Like two asymptotes, these two types of possibilities limit the concept of damage on both sides: an unpreventable loss and an uncompensatable loss are not subject to a compensation claim (3.401), whereas suffering is indifferent to the possibility there was to prevent it or to the existing possibility to annul it. Either way, it is present and demands a response; when total disengagement is impossible, it calls for alleviation, even if only temporary.

7.042 But what could have been done and was not done is a recipe for what can be done so that evils of this kind will not recur. Exposing what was possible in the past and pointing to what is possible in the future are not disconnected from each other. The lost past of the one who has already been harmed is the open future of others who may get hurt. The denaturalization of evils (3.201–3.210, 6.430, 8.340, 8.342) has a crucial part in representing the possibilities of prevention, which in turn has a crucial part in the preventive action itself. In other words, the social ideology that represents the differential distribution of evils as natural, as God's will or the hand of fate, and as necessary and unpreventable, and the radical social critique that reconstructs the condition for the production and distribution of evils and exposes their contingency (see 8.341) are among the factors that determine the modes and relations of producing and distributing evils. Ideology and critique are partners in the reproduction of these patterns and the struggle for their transformation. Even under the most stable social conditions, the reproduction of evils is never a complete reproduction, due to fluctuations in the representation of evils, their naturalization, and their denaturalization. How much change is allowed, and how long can reproduction be maintained? That depends on the historical conditions and the social forces at play.

7.043 One characteristic of modernity is the belief that a correct representation of evils will contribute to the desired change in their modes and relations of production and distribution. Of course, that is not how things are phrased, but this is the significance of the belief that has been directing the ideology of the Enlightenment since Voltaire, the Marxist critique of political economy and the post-Marxist ideology critique, the scientistic conception of social change from Saint-Simon or Comte to Popper, the different technologies of intervention in the life of the individual in various disciplines of the humanities, and the "correctional" institutions (from the school to the madhouse), within which and in relation to which the sciences of man have developed.

7.044 All these philosophies and ideologies of progress shared the belief that social evils have one common source, the root of evil, that can be identified from a distance, without the representing person himself being involved in the production and distribution of evils, and that it is enough to identify this root and eradicate it to bring progress and improve the human condition. The ideologists of the Enlightenment attributed evil to ignorance and superstition. The Marxists attributed evil to capital, private property, and the oppression and exploitation tied to them — they are all moments in the present historical shape of the class struggle. Correctional institutions assumed that the root of evil lies in perversion, distortion, or a disease of the individual's soul or personality. Thinkers such as Popper and other ideologists of social technology assume that the root of evil lies in irrationality, which they identify with dogmatism, ignorance, closed-mindedness, and an unwillingness to test beliefs. Modern evil has almost always been perceived as a disease for which a cure can and must be invented, a pathology of a malfunctioning system, within which one disease or disorder was usually posited as the root of all evils and all other disruptions were represented as its symptoms.[2] But we no longer believe that evils have a common source, and we do not believe that it is possible to represent evils without involvement in their production and distribution. This is not to say that the question of the source of evil is futile, but one has to ask it time and again, every time in relation to a specific sociohistorical context, and the question itself is no more primary or fundamental than the question "What form does evil take?" or "What is its intensity?" It is not pointless to try to give evil an idiom, to en-tongue evil — perhaps there is nothing more worthwhile — but one must also acknowledge that every act of expression is entangled in power relations and every representation is also an erasure, and that as such they can always also generate evil. I will return to these two principles later.

7.050 Suffering could be the basis for a compensation claim if everything that was said about a compensation claim for damage applies here as well: the existence of prevention conditions, knowledge of these conditions, and the ability to prevent or at least warn of expected suffering (6.330). But there is a non-reducible difference between the one who is demanded to give compensation for suffering, like in a common case of damage, and the one who is demanded to respond to suffering. With damage (whether it is an estimated loss or an estimate of suffering that causes loss), the addressee could evade the demand. He has several ways to do so (3.431): he could try to prove that there was no damage (refutation of existence); that the damage could not have been prevented or minimized (refutation of possibility); that the prevention of damage was not his responsibility, or that the responsibility for the damage has no affinity with the responsibility for compensation and that although he is responsible for the damage, he is not responsible for compensation (denial of responsibility); that preventing the damage would have caused more severe damage and therefore the damage that was caused is justified and does not entitle anyone to compensation (justification). The one who demands compensation for damage has to block — with arguments — all these evasions. In principle, a compensation claim is always an invitation for negotiation; it is the first step in a discussion whose end we cannot know in advance. In suffering, the situation is completely different. If the addressee tries to prove that there is no suffering (refutation of existence), or that it was impossible to prevent it (refutation of possibility), or that causing the suffering or its prevention is not his responsibility (denial of responsibility), he simply does not understand the suffering phrase addressed to him. He is like a soldier who responds with applause to the command "forward march," or someone who in response to the command or request "shut the door" explains why the door has been left open.[3] Unlike the damage phrase, the suffering phrase is not an invitation for negotiation but a call for action. The addressee who chooses to open negotiations is indifferent to the call of the sufferer; he responds to someone else. There is a *différend* between his language game and the sufferer's language game.

7.051   In only one case is there a similarity between a rejection of a compensation claim and a rejection of a suffering phrase: when the rejection is explained with the worry that the desired intervention may cause suffering and damage that are more grave than those it is supposed to prevent. We cannot say about someone who tries to justify suffering in this way that he did not understand the call or did not respond to it appropriately. His response is not necessarily indifferent to suffering. It may show overconsideration, an understanding of the causes of suffering or its end, just as much as it could be a cover for evading responsibility. But it could be an evasion of responsibility precisely because it is a relevant response, as opposed to the responses discussed earlier. The one who responds by justifying the suffering in terms of a more serious suffering or damage is leaping from one language game (in which he is asked to respond with action) to another (in which he explains to the sufferer why she should suffer), but this leap itself does not cancel the interest in the suffering of the one calling for help and is sometimes justified by this interest.

7.052   The proper compensation for damage is a complex matter related to every one of these factual or statistical claims. The parley about proving damage and responsibility for compensation is usually disputed by several interested parties in addition to the claimant and the defendant, such as other interested parties for whom the compensation will be damage or a party interested in the stability of compensation agreements between damaged and damagers (3.451). In general, the defendant will try to sever his relation to the damage or to the compensation, whereas the claimant will try to ground these kinds of relations. When it is a case of suffering, the one who is demanded of is demanded to act urgently, to help the sufferer to disengage. The proper action in the face of someone's suffering is allegedly a less complicated matter. When one faces suffering, there is no point in dealing with prevention conditions, responsibility for the damage, or compensation. What matters is whether the one called upon to respond can hurry to the rescue of the one who suffers and help him disengage. One should also consider whether such a response might cause further suffering, to the sufferer or to others, now or in the future. The proper compensation for damage and suffering demands a mapping of prevention conditions, responsibility domains, and the predicted consequences of canceling the damage. The proper response to suffering must consider the price of responding from at least three perspectives: the perspective of the sufferer; the perspective of whoever might be harmed or suffer as a result of responding to the suffering of an other (and this includes the one who offers help); and the perspective of the one interested in stability or in a reform of the arrangements for offering someone help.

7.053 Usually, the question of prevention (as a missed possibility) relates only to the compensation claim. The situation in which those confronted with suffering insist on discussing the missed opportunities to prevent this suffering has a tedious dimension and a distractive function like that of the hermeneutics of suffering (6.050–6.053). To discuss missed opportunities right now means to postpone the help; to offer help means to postpone dealing with the prevention conditions. The revolutionary thinks he knows what the missed opportunities are and how one can act to fulfill them; he would be willing to ignore the suffering of a concrete other facing him in order to ease the suffering of many others, who are more or less abstract. He has to teach himself and those around him to overcome pity, to repress ruth. From his point of view, the benevolent one who hurries to help only affirms the existing order and reproduces the conditions for the production of evils of the kind he is now facing and with which he is trying to deal locally, on a small scale. From the revolutionary's point of view, this is the difference between aspirin and a root canal. But from the point of view of the one crying for help, this could be the difference between life and death, or between concrete and immediate alleviation of suffering and future redemption, which is always delayed. The revolutionary ignores the urgency of the call for help; he is cynical about what is and naive about the relation between the proper and the possible. The benevolent one ignores the social order that produces evils and distributes them; he is naive about what is and cynical about the relation between the proper and the possible. The revolutionary type and the benevolent person are two ideal poles: naïveté versus cynicism, procrastination versus urgency, false belief with regard to the inevitable appearance of a different future versus false belief in an inevitable selfsame present that will never change. Every plan for social action that is not inherently torn between these two poles ends up collapsing into utopian terror or becomes the faithful servant of the existing order.

7.054 The right balance between these two poles must be found anew time and again, out of some kind of participation in the social systems that produce and distribute evils, without being able to completely stand aside (both ideology and radical critique take part, as was said, in shaping the modes and relations of the production and distribution of evils [see 7.042]). The urgent need for action in the face of suffering does not cancel the responsibility to prevent further suffering and the need to consider whether the urgent action hastens or thwarts the creation of further suffering. Understanding the possibilities of different production patterns and new distributions of evils, and the new field of action that such an understanding signifies, do not rescue the critic from the position of the direct addressee of the call for help, and they are not enough to silence or cancel the demand for help.

7.1 The Unbearable

7.100 Evils can only be justified by appealing to more grave hypothetical evils that could have been caused if the prevention or disengagement actions had taken place (3.432). The justification displaces the discussion from one order of exchange, in which the one harmed tries to create a link between damage or suffering and compensation, to another order of exchange, in which the defendant tries to create a link between evils that occurred and evils that might have occurred. Such a displacement is justifiable only at the price of another displacement, and this infinite regress stops arbitrarily at the order of exchange in which the definite and defining damage and suffering are described, the ones that are used as an estimate of the final or total loss (3.432).

7.101 The "ought" appears as a measured line stretching between the real and the possible: between the evil that in fact occurred and the evil that may have been prevented. The "ought," the guiding line of moral action, relates here to the preventive action: evils that should (and anyway could) have been prevented. What kind of evils can be prevented? Those whose prevention would not have increased the grand total of evils in a given system and would not have distorted their distribution within it. Or, simply, one ought to prevent unnecessary evils. Also, one ought to compensate the one harmed by these evils.

7.102 To justify evil means to attribute it to a certain exchange system within which its superfluity is canceled. A superfluous evil is one that by definition cannot be justified. With respect to an evil, to justify is to turn the evil into something useful for someone, something that takes place in order to achieve or avoid something. This achievement or avoidance relates to damage or suffering, utility or pleasure, in short, to other evils and goods. This utilitarian conception of justification does not sit comfortably with an essentialist conception of rights or values as the basis for moral justification. According to this form of essentialism, an evil that is not superfluous but is nevertheless unjustified is possible, because it harms someone's right or some common sacred value that has been taken out of the exchange cycle and that the exchange economy posits or is supposed to serve. By the same logic, a superfluous evil that is justified is also possible, because it stems from or guarantees someone's right, or it is entailed by the need to safeguard a sacred value. But there is no reason not to perceive a right or a value as a kind of privileged good, and introduce it into its own exchange economy, to measure it by what one is willing to invest in order to guarantee rights or values and by what one expects to receive or prevent with these guaranteed rights or sacred values. Rights guarantee access to the claimant position in different exchange systems (3.523) and so function as an efficient control mechanism guarding against an uncontrolled distribution of damage, or turning a particular group into the permanent victim of a certain kind of damage. The denial of rights is, as was said, a principal category of damages (3.521).

7.103 Some evils can be justified — under certain conditions, always under certain conditions — and within the system that justifies them, they are not superfluous. Some superfluous evils cannot be justified but can "somehow" be tolerated "for now." In this case, the temporariness is not necessarily a promise for a near annulment of the superfluous evil but a sign, which could be stable and exist for a long time, of the general price that the existing order

charges for its very existence. In other words, an unjustified evil
that could somehow be tolerated, even if only in fact, let alone in
theory, is a sign of the high price that the attempt to point to the
superfluous nature of that evil could have. Some superfluous evils,
of course, must never be tolerated. And next to all these are evils
that have not been en-tongued or could not be expressed as superfluous or as justified. Justified evils could be horrendous; superfluous evils could be transient and insignificant from the point of view
of the one who suffers or has been damaged by them; evils that a
discourse does not allow to be expressed could be of either sort —
when they find expression, they could turn out to be superfluous
or justified, horrible or tolerable. In other words, all these distinctions, as important as they might be, cannot offer a scale of evils.

7.104　A superfluous evil that must not be tolerated is an *injustice*. An
unexpressed evil or an evil whose expression has no addressee is a
wrong.[4] The meaning of a wrong (*tort*) here differs from that in
damage law, and the concept must be narrower. The difference
between injustice and wrong is one of knowledge and recognition, or their lack. The discourse that justifies some of the evils
and declares others superfluous can recognize injustice but not a
wrong, because this notion stems precisely from its inability to
recognize the evil as such (see also 7.220). If the wrong results
from the impossibility of expressing an evil, the evil generated by
the wrong is all the more inexpressible, hence one cannot even
say it is superfluous. Only by transgressing the limits of a certain
discourse and transforming its rules, or switching to a different
language game, can one en-tongue the inexpressible evil. At this
point, one should distinguish between a first-order evil, the one
that did not find expression, and a second-order evil, the one tied
to the prevention of expression. Recognizing the wrong enables
one to represent the first-order evil as not unpreventable, and
hence one can represent the second-order evil as preventable.
From this moment on, the second-order evil is superfluous: perhaps one can justify the evil that was not expressed earlier, but
not the evil that is caused when there is no possibility of expressing that same evil. The recognition of a wrong is the sign of the
superfluous nature of the evil tied to it.

7.105　Evils appear between two thresholds of moral sensibility. On the
one hand, there is the low threshold, beyond which are evils that
leave the witness indifferent — the threshold of indifference. The
witness remains indifferent because these evils have no expression
in a discourse in which they may appear as superfluous or as justified, or because he has no interest in this discourse. On the other

hand, there is the high threshold, beyond which are evils that arouse intolerance and revolt, the unbearable evils — the threshold of insurgency. "Insurgency" is a precise term, because it enables us to speak simultaneously about excitation ("he felt a surge of anger toward that thing") and about violent action ("the Palestinian insurgency, the intifada, broke out because of a violent clash that was one too many") and to present the line stretching between these two ends.

7.110 The concept of the "community of suffering" (6.554) should now be broadened to the "community of evils," but it will be easier to simply talk about a "moral community." Members of this community are blind and deaf to certain kinds of evils and learn to revolt against other kinds. They learn to identify the latter evils as superfluous and to think of some as particularly intolerable and revolting. A moral community is defined by its thresholds of moral sensibility. This sensibility — its character, range, and stability — is a factual matter. It varies between cultures and eras, like many other sensibility thresholds.

7.111 The passage from the amoral domain of evils, as facts about the occurrence of damage and suffering, to the moral domain, in which evils appear as wrongs and injustices, does not take a leap of faith over an unbridgeable gap. No Rubicon is crossed in the passage from an "is" to an "ought." The ought appears under a description of what is that is mediated by the moral sensibility of a discursive community. This sensibility is related, on the one hand, to the ability to identify and recognize evils and, on the other hand, to the ability to express and represent the evils in different (and competing) exchange systems and to come to recognize their superfluity. This is not an extraordinary capacity. Someone will always claim that a certain evil is superfluous, and immediately the addressees of this claim will be liable for a moral account of the proper distribution of evils.

7.112 An unbearable evil is a superfluous evil that must not be tolerated. Of course one usually does tolerate it, but the point here is the sense of revolt. A refusal to acquiesce characterizes the crossing of the moral-sensibility threshold, not necessarily the actions taken afterward.

7.113 For the one who suffers, "the unbearable is precisely what one bears when suffering" (6.000). For the witness who revolts in the face of suffering — that is, in the face of the unbearable — the unbearable is what is absolutely impossible to tolerate. But in fact the impossibility of tolerating the unbearable is a common char-

acteristic of the sufferer and of the witness of his suffering. This is
the essence of the presence of suffering: that it cannot be tolerated, that even the one who "can take it" cannot silence the appeal
for relief that his body and soul call for. Suffering turns the sufferer into a witness of an appeal for respite, of the cry "enough."
This is also the essence of the unbearable evil for the witness who
does not suffer: an appeal for respite that rises out of a presence
that cannot be tolerated. The sufferer cannot acquiesce in an
excessive excitation; the one who revolts cannot acquiesce in an
excessive evil. In the first case, the excess is a measure of individual experience; in the second case, the excess is a measure of sensibility about another's experience. The wounded sensibility in
the face of an unbearable evil could be a private excitation, but
first and foremost it is a judgment whose sources and addressees
belong to an entire community. The experience of suffering could
contain a similar judgment, out of revolt or passing blame, but
first and foremost it is an experience whose exclusive addressee is
the individual. Such oppositions are possible because there is a
common denominator here: the unbearable, what cannot be put
up with, a presence that is a statement calling for respite and positing someone as an addressee who must disengage.

7.114 It does not matter to the witness whether the unbearable evil is
suffering or damage, or even whether the unbearable damage (for
the witness) does not cause any suffering to the damaged (this
situation is in itself quite rare). An unbearable damage is a superfluous damage that must not be tolerated. Of course, the presence of such damage is usually mediated in a much more complex
way than the presence of a superfluous suffering. The witness recognizes such damage only if he has access to the discourse that can
express not only the damage but also the complete system of its
production and distribution and the conditions of its prevention
or reduction. A similar caveat applies also, in varying degrees, to
superfluous suffering that cannot be perceived as such without
knowing something about its prevention conditions. In any case,
the refusal to acquiesce and the revolt in the face of unbearable
evils, even if originally they were an animal-instinct type of
response, are the results of a sensibility that is socially acquired
and refined and determined by countless cultural variables.

7.115 The low threshold of moral sensibility, the threshold of blindness
to certain kinds of evils (or victims from a certain social group), is
anchored in different kinds of discourse — moral, legal, political,
therapeutic, theological, literary, and so on — but can only be perceived outside of them, from a point of view that turns discourse

itself into a subject and uncovers its regularity. In this sense, the threshold of sensibility is similar to the threshold of the visible or the expressible (1.303 and 1.330). The high threshold of moral sensibility, the threshold of the unbearable, could have a more or less explicit expression in some of these discourses. This expression often takes the shape of a moral statement that has a general validity claim and, in any case, a pretension to transcend the limitations of the concrete historical and cultural situation.

7.120 This sensibility is common, as was said earlier, to an entire community. In relation to unbearable evils, the moral community acts as "a kind of island of social recognition" (6.554). When one is within its domain, when one turns to the sensibility that characterizes its members, it is enough to point to this evil in order to place someone in the addressee position, the addressee who is called upon to help, prevent, or compensate. This sensibility appears when it is offended, that is, when it confronts unbearable evils. On the one hand, the appearance of moral sensibility is not conditioned on its possible thematization within a moral or critical discourse, and here, too, the gap between the excitation and the expression remains intact. When offended, moral sensibility becomes an excitation. It occurs after one has taken the position of the addressee of an event — the occurrence of an unbearable evil. This excitation is neither a necessary outcome of nor a necessary condition for a moral speech act, but it is an invitation to take up a position in a moral discourse in particular and in the moral sphere in general in order to perform some proper speech acts. On the other hand, members of a moral community develop a similar sensibility threshold for damage and for suffering, beyond which it is impossible to recognize evils, and if they can be recognized, there is no agreement about their superfluity, about the need to prevent or minimize them, or about the need to compensate for them. One's relation to evils beyond this threshold is indifference. This indifference marks the bounds of the moral sphere in that society or community (see 7.310). To place someone in the addressee position in relation to these evils, one must do more than point to the evil: he will not see it; if he does see it, he will not know what to call it; if he does know what to call it, he will immediately also know how to justify it, with ready-made clichés, if the need to justify arises at all. And he will never be alone there; this indifference is always also a form of association with others. In order to place someone in the addressee position with respect to these evils, one must challenge not only the addressee's moral-sensibility threshold but also his mode of belonging to his community.

7.121 The stability of the moral-sensibility threshold changes historically and culturally, and yet it always appears as what transcends concrete historical conditions and particular social interests (or at least some of them). Obviously, more traditional societies have stricter thresholds; in hyper-developed late-twentieth-century societies, one can find many fragmented thresholds of disintegrated moral communities that intermingle, merge, and split at a high rate.[5] In such societies, the moral-sensibility threshold is more flexible but also more lax, that is, less efficient. I propose to measure efficiency here by a community's ability to come together in order to act or activate its institutions for the benefit of those who have been exposed to superfluous evils, evils that cannot possibly be justified (within the common moral discourse). That "cannot possibly be justified" means that one can imagine other situations, different from the ones here and now, in which the same evils occur and nonetheless also find them equally unbearable. That "cannot possibly be justified" means also that someone's mere attempt to justify is perceived as an abomination. The unjustified becomes unjustifiable, what is in principle incapable of being justified, ever, and the unjustifiable turns into what one should never justify.

7.122 In any case, the thresholds are always anchored in the interests of dominant groups and in the power of the forces battling them. The biblical text describing how God hardens the heart of Pharaoh also hardens the heart of its readers, so they can later celebrate with no pangs of conscience the ten plagues God brought upon the Egyptians. Their hearts were so hardened that in a later period, interpreters endowed with a different moral sensibility saw a need to ask "why the creatures of my hands are drowning in the sea and you sing praise."[6] During the Spanish conquest of South America, several theologians led a campaign in the name of universal values, such as "human form," against a new sensibility threshold that erased the evils that were showered on the Indians by the Spaniards and decreased the ability to answer their cries. Those theologians — Bartolomé de las Casas is the most famous among them — lost, because the new interests operating against them were several times stronger than the tradition in whose name they spoke.[7] And in our time, in almost all the struggles of minority groups, or "the subaltern others" — blacks, women, homosexuals, ethnic minorities, and so on — one of the main things at stake is the new threshold of the "hegemonic" moral

345

community or of the ruling class, which will not leave its members indifferent (the low threshold) and will not let them put up with (the high threshold) the evils suffered by members of the subordinate groups (see 7.132). But perhaps this is most prominently expressed in the struggles of Green groups and animal-rights groups to make us sensitive to the suffering of the environment and of animals.

7.123 Every challenge to the moral-sensibility threshold is made from within another moral community, imaginary or real, in which that threshold is drawn anew, in a different place (see also 7.130). Every moral judgment necessitates presupposing such a threshold, and there is no procedure for an argument that can *a priori* guarantee a preference for one threshold over another, let alone its stability and absoluteness for a substantial period of time. Sensibility to evils is a matter of negotiation, of an acquired ability to listen, of an interest in being exposed to what is different in order to distance or contain it, of the power of redescribing suffering and damage, and of the readiness to identify with others and to identify others' interests as one's own. No argument could predict where such an array of social interests and cultural practices could lead.

7.124 When a moral-sensibility threshold is questioned, the challenger tries to break the threshold of an other's moral indifference, because beyond this there are suffering others to whom he cannot remain indifferent. One community's threshold of moral indifference, which is the limit of its moral sphere, is thus posited as a subject of moral interest at the heart of another community's moral sphere. This means that where it is possible to challenge the threshold of moral indifference, it is impossible to speak of a homogeneous and coherent moral sphere. The moral sphere is heterogeneous and fragmented, if it is a sphere at all. Perhaps in the same society or under the same political regime, there are several moral spheres, partially overlapping or completely foreign to one another. A key question in political thought would be a political regime's level of tolerance toward different moral spheres, its ability and willingness to force a unified moral sphere on all those under its rule.

7.125 The mere existence of heterogeneous moral spheres in the same political space undermines any attempt to base the political regime's legitimacy on a social contract, hypothetical or historical. If the contract presupposes one moral sphere and its sensibility threshold, it cannot compel those whose moral sensibility is shaped and expressed within the bounds of another moral sphere.

In order to force everyone subordinated to political power to obey the same rules, a common moral sphere and a universal sensibility threshold should be presupposed. There is no such sphere, and every attempt to imagine and portray such a threshold is always limited by a given moral perspective. When moral sensibilities clash, each side can only try to introduce its thresholds of blindness and revolt into the other side's moral sphere. Liberals do this when they preach human rights, and racists or nationalists do it when they spread xenophobia and demonize the other whose exclusion is the basis for their collective identity.

7.130 From the premise that the sensibility threshold has a central role in delineating the domain of superfluous evils (that cannot be justified, that must be prevented or reduced), it is possible, at least at first glance, to draw two opposed conclusions. On the one hand, it is impossible to force someone to obey rules and regulations that, in order to be justified, presuppose a radically different sensibility threshold from the one that delineates his own moral sensibility.[8] Members of different moral communities live in isolated islands of moral discourse, and there is no way to bridge them. This bridging is prevented not because a common language is lacking but because a common measure for evaluating unjustified superfluous evils is lacking. On the other hand, awareness of the historicality and temporariness of the sensibility threshold requires a willingness to examine it time and again, to respond to the challenge other moral communities place in front of it. This also means that the freedom to reexamine the moral-sensibility threshold is a necessary (and insufficient) condition for justifying political authority.

7.131 The response to the challenge of other moral communities is possible because the lack of a common measure does not entail a lack of a common language. This response is necessary because the threshold of moral sensibility has no justification. It is morally unjustifiable because it is a condition for every such justification. Like Foucault's *episteme*, it is the "historical *a priori*" of moral discourse, a contingent, cumulative result of hermeneutic traditions, rituals, and discursive and institutional practices in the domain of using and legitimating power, jurisdiction, punishment, family matters, private affairs, faith, and knowledge.[9] Out of this historical *a priori* in the moral domain, and with the influence of the broad spectrum of different and conflicting interests that it allows, serves, and cultivates, a more or less clear delineation of the "impossible to imagine" emerges, around which spreads a twilight zone, painted in gray. As opposed to the *episteme*, the thresholds of moral sensibility can be brought up and presented as a central problem of this discourse again and again. The two thresholds are not accessible in the same way; there is a difference: usually the unbearable is easier to thematize and problematize than the threshold of indifference. But the possibility of problematizing exists, in principle, in both cases. This possibility exists first of all because, as opposed to the diachronic perception of the *episteme* in Foucault's *Order of Things*, there is no situation (certainly not in contemporary culture) in which at a given period one discourse dominates the entire cultural space.[10] Different discursive regimes exist next to one another (and not just one after the other), their borders exposed to mutual penetrations, and there is no need for a transcendental or ahistorical leverage point from which to move a discourse. It is enough to have a few dissident practices with insights or in a language supplied by a competing discourse.

7.132　The widespread contemporary debate about "the other" — the subjected other, the persecuted, subsumed, silenced, marginalized other — is to a large extent a problematization of moral-sensibility thresholds in different communities that constitute their self-identity in relation to this other. (And perhaps they are rediscovering — or discovering for the first time — their selves by problematizing the threshold of their moral sensibility.) Feminist, postcolonial, and queer discourses are familiar participants in this debate, but a similar moral thematic can also be found in socialist or nationalist discourses. This moral thematic would usually be formulated in universal terms; it aimed to include the excluded other within the community from which he was expelled, or to constitute a community of his own for him, or else to transform his community into a universal human community. But the moral point of departure of all these kinds of discourses and political and critical endeavors is similar: the outrage of putting up with a continuous offending of a subjected other. The body of this other, his property, his honor, the fruit of his toil, his liberty and his rights, his desire, and even his life (or a combination of several or all of these) are beyond the high threshold — transgressing them does not count as an unbearable superfluous evil. Sometimes they are also beyond the low threshold — transgressing them is not perceived as an evil at all. Otherness is expressed in a distinct, explicit manner according to the fundamental difference that is opened up between two kinds of evils that are identical in every other respect: the unbearable evil when they hurt "us"; the same

348

evils that are tolerated by us (if we even perceive them) when they hurt "them." The evils may appear similar, the differences between them do not differentiate them — until the victim's identity is found out and the difference that makes the difference appears: is he "one of us" or "one of them"?

7.133 The difference between the liberal position and a more radical one — Marxist, feminist, or postcolonial — can be redescribed in terms of the problematization of moral-sensibility thresholds.[11] The liberal makes do with a formal universalization of both the victim and the evils; differences between victims (according to race, sex, religion, nationality, and so on) do not change the degree of superfluity or bearableness of the evils they have suffered. Some of the more radical critics take this position for granted and try to extend it in different directions. But some demand a change in the moral-sensibility threshold so that certain injuries to subjected others are considered unbearable while the same injuries to members of the dominant groups are tolerable under certain conditions. The justification could be affirmative action toward the subjected other or a militant struggle against the one who subjects that other. In both cases, such bending of the high moral-sensibility threshold is dubious, because it replicates patterns of domination over the other, his exclusion and silencing, even though it reverses their direction. There are, of course, historical and cultural differences in the conditions under which the discussion of the sensibility threshold takes place. The attempt to change this threshold under conditions of violent struggle for liberation from a repressive regime does not resemble a peaceful debate in the relative calm of civil society in a developed Western country. But one should also remember that regardless of its dependence on specific historical and cultural conditions (7.115), the revolt threshold appears in the horizon of moral action as precisely what transcends changing historical conditions and the interests of this or that group, and it cannot be subordinated to the immediate needs of the struggle, justified as it may be.

7.134 In principle, the liberal is a universalist who does not distinguish between one victim and another, and no victim leaves him indifferent, but there are many kinds of evils he is too blind to see. In other words, universalization in the liberal position is limited by the kinds of evils taken into account. But in practice, it is also limited by the kinds of others-as-victims taken into account, because the liberal usually sees universalization in terms of citizenship in the state, whose existence and governance he takes for granted. That is why naturalization is so often at stake in contemporary critiques of liberalism. With respect to the type of evils, the liberal usually excludes from the list of relevant evils damage that results from the type of participation in the market economy, which he also accepts as a given. That is why impoverishment stands at the center of his disagreement with the socialist or the new Marxist. And evils that result from the objectification and commodification of a woman's body and her sexuality are at the center of his debate with the radical feminist.

7.135 But that is not the end of the debate, or the end of the differences and similarities. Liberalism, Marxism, and certain feminist theories, in particular early feminism, all partake in the attempt to develop a universal sensibility to an abstract other, whereas contemporary feminism and postcolonialism (and this is a postmodern dimension in both of these critiques) tend to develop local sensibility to specific others. The liberal discourse developed a special sensibility to evils that could be formulated as an infringement of universal rights; the Marxist discourse developed a special sensibility to evils that could be attributed to a difference in the access to and control of the means of production. In the feminist and the postcolonial discourse, there is a special sensibility to evils that can be attributed to two kinds of differences: differences in access to the means of representation in culture and in access to the means of care of the body and the enhancement of ways of using it. These are evils that the liberal and the Marxist discourse have left beyond the low moral-sensibility threshold.

7.140 Is it possible to claim progress in the cultivation of moral sensibility, with regard to others and with regard to the range of evils in the domain of the unbearable? In a quick glance over modern history, it seems that the answer is yes, at least in the West — but only with respect to the types of others. With respect to the types of evils, matters are much more complicated and much less clear. In both cases, one should not conflate progress in the cultivation of sensibility with progress in the decrease of evils. It is very likely that the cultivation of sensibility is a direct or indirect result of a massive growth that took place in modern times in the breadth, range, frequency, magnitude, and diversity of evils that are socially produced and distributed. Has there been such a terrifying growth? I suppose so, but an appropriately qualified answer would rely on empirical research that will combine insights from future disciplines — the economy, physics and geography of loss, damage and suffering. Only later would it be possible to identify precisely the affinity between historical changes in the patterns of production and distribution of evils and changes in the various thresholds of moral sensibility.

7.141 Of certain notorious evils it is usually said that any civilized man or woman would "reject them with revulsion" and no civilized man or woman could imagine any argument that would justify them, that would make them tolerable. This is how the horrors of Nazism — first and foremost the extermination of the Jews — and with a lesser consensus the other genocides and mass murders of the twentieth century (from the Ottoman Empire to the Gulag, from Cambodia to Rwanda) are usually represented in most Western countries. But it is worth remembering that civilized men and women found ways of justifying every one of these gruesome bundles of evils, not to mention ways of participating in their production and distribution, and that civilized men and women justify or excuse them in retrospect. Genocide could turn, in these cases, into a regrettable killing during a war (like the attempts to absolve the Turks of the blame of exterminating a million Armenians), and political cleansing could become a necessary action taken by a regime against those who oppose it (by the occasional defenders of Stalinist regimes and of South American, Southeast Asian, and African dictatorships). But even though this clean language might weaken the impression of horror, the problem is not in the factual description but in the extraordinary moral flexibility of the potential addressees of these descriptions of horror. The problem is that the moral-sensibility threshold is a very thin barrier against the spread of unbearable evils, because the regimes that excel in producing such evils, and their threatened subjects, also excel in changing their moral-sensibility threshold.

7.142 Often the situation is roughly like this: on one end, there is a group, usually not very large (the hard core), of determined people for whom mass killings and the systematic production of evils are the only way. They perceive the evils that they produce and distribute as necessary or unavoidable in order to bring about some good or to prevent worse evils, which could allegedly occur, to them or to others, if they do not behave cruelly enough to those around them. At the other end, there is a group, usually small and depleted, of determined people who refuse to put up with the unbearable evils and actively oppose the regime, and therefore suffer themselves from the evils that the regime produces, sometimes especially for people like them. Many join the first group in order to gain some benefits and to prevent the evils that standing aside, not to mention actual opposition, could bring about. The moral threshold of those people is flexible enough for

351

them to put up with what was, not too long ago, "unimaginable" and perhaps even justify it. Few people join the other group, and their mere joining makes their moral threshold more rigid — in the other direction, of course. In between live the majority of the members of that society, collaborating — in a more or less regular way, to a greater or a lesser degree — with the various apparatuses that produce and distribute evils, denying these evils as well as their own cooperation in their production, and repressing their memories. Those with a more flexible moral threshold will be willing to expose themselves to the "facts" about the horrors and act out of an awareness, at least a partial one, of the role that they themselves play in their production. Those with a more rigid moral-sensibility threshold will deny and repress.

7.143   Despite every regime's distinct power advantage, and despite the fact that the moral-sensibility threshold is a slack barrier, a weak defense against the increase of the horrors, the struggle over these thresholds, over their precise location and the means of their expression, is not superfluous. It is not superfluous because drawing these lines and the design of their surroundings — the representation of evils as bearable and unbearable — are channels of normalization, naturalization, and legitimation of the regime, of every regime and of regimes of evil among them. Even the worst regime of terror needs a clean language to speak about the evils it produces, and collaborators whose consciences are clear. On the other hand, those who struggle against the regime try to presence evils that had no expression, to present them as unbearable, and to redraw the line that delineates the unbearable so that it will include evils that at this stage are still tolerable.

7.150   As was said previously (7.120), when one's moral sensibility is offended, one is called to take up a position in the moral discourse. Whoever takes up such a position professes that the unbearable evil is a superfluous evil. How do we determine what a superfluous evil is? How do we determine what proper compensation is? With an agreed-on exchange system, within a discourse in which the various compensation claims are supposed to be formulated. And how are these to be determined in the absence of an agreed-on exchange system? With a discourse that is supposed to bridge the competing exchange systems (but not between the different compensation claims; for example, an exchange of commodities that have an economic value and rights that have a social and political value). But every discourse is in itself a mechanism for the exchange of validity claims, and there is no metalanguage

352

that would bridge, once and for all, these competing discursive systems. More precisely, all metalinguistic claims are local; the bridging work is infinite.[12]

7.151 The discourse in which evils will be described and the exchange system in which evils will be appraised and compensation will be claimed determine, in fact, the difference between arbitration and *différend* (3.433); they also determine when justice is the background and injustice the figure, or when justice is the figure and injustice the background.

7.2 *Justice and Injustice*

7.200 The main theories of justice in the West defined the term in relation to a discourse and an exchange system in which the appropriate prevention, relief, and compensation are set (3.542). The one who justifies evils (because he is involved in them and is demanded to make reparation for them, or because he benefits from them) tries to displace the damage from one system of exchange to another, so as not to pay the price of restoring the balance in the first system. The definition of justice, on the other hand, seeks a balanced distribution of evils within the same system and demands precisely this price (3.541).

7.201 Failing to prevent an unnecessary evil and giving inadequate compensation for an evil are injustices. Preventing or reducing unnecessary evils is a necessary condition for restoring justice (3.540). Distributive justice is the just dispersion of the evils that are not preventable and of the conditions that enable one to lessen the amount of evils and to respond to them appropriately when they occur (6.352). In a just society, one needs to imagine a metasystem that looks over and bridges several exchange systems, that is, a metasystem that determines the exchange values between them, not just within them. This is supposed to be the task of moral discourse, within which a theory of justice is constructed, but in fact the only system that comes close to the status of a metasystem is the economy, which pretends to offer an absolute exchange value for all exchange systems. This absolute is, of course, relativity par excellence: the monetary value.

7.202 Within such a system, injustice is the figure, and justice is the background; injustice is a deviant violation, and justice is the default option of the system; injustice is exposed and sticks out but always attests to its negation, justice, which is nothing but the correct functioning of a balanced system. When the system works seamlessly, with no screeching and scraping, no distortions, in a balanced way, its action is silent and unnoticeable — it is taken for granted as natural. Natural justice is nothing but an image of the immaculate functioning of the most sophisticated cultural system — so immaculate that the figure of justice appears as external and foreign to that system, independent of its concrete historical and political conditions, until it can be given a general and atemporal status. As was said, within that system, justice is a background, not a figure. If the system really functioned immaculately, if it had no injustices in it, justice would be invisible, like a background from which all the figurative lines were erased. Paradoxically, in an exchange system that functions immaculately, justice needs injustices in order to be noticed at all.

7.210 Here is a familiar philosophical move that has been repeated in many versions: (*a*) expressing discontent as a result of apparent and obvious cases of injustice in the near or distant environment of the philosopher; (*b*) observing the figure of abstract justice through the appearances of concrete injustice, as the negation of these appearances and as a condition of their prevention; (*c*) constructing a "just" polis, community, society, or regime, which is hypothetical, utopian, and abstracted from concrete historical reality (it is a social form that embodies a balanced and immaculate metasystem that regulates exchange relations in different walks of life). Sometimes this move was accompanied by an analysis of the psychological and social structures that cause the tremendous gap between a reality full of injustice and the ideal of a just society; sometimes the concrete social conditions that are supposed to ensure the realization of the ideal were discussed as well. But only very rarely did philosophical thought linger on injustice itself in an attempt to understand it independently of justice, or at least without hurriedly redefining it as the negation of justice. Concrete evils were almost always perceived as signifiers whose absent signified was justice. Political and ethical thought almost always rushed from the signifier to the signified, without taking an interest in the order of the signifiers themselves. Justice was almost always an absent signified. It was seen as a "negated value" that served to retroactively interpret the appearances that got into the phenomenal space of ethical discourse: evils and injustices that were visible, demonstrable, and expressible within the discourse that defined justice, that is, those evils that were within the limits of the visible and the sayable of ethical discourse.

7.211 Marx and Engels made crucial contributions to a social analysis that focuses directly and from the start on evils: Engels in his remarkable report on the state of the working class in England in the mid-nineteenth century;[13] Marx in his *Economic and Philosophic Manuscripts* and in *Capital*, particularly in Chapter 10, "The Working Day."[14] Marx's and Engels's contributions to the discussion of evils are little noticed, because these texts were drawn into the Marxist tradition and ideology and their interpretation was too often required to take a stand for or against Marxism as a political and ideological movement. Moreover, Marx and Engels, as well as most of the secondary literature on them, declined in advance an affiliation with any tradition within ethical discourse in the West.[15] Their rage against the exploitation of the proletariat and its disgraceful subjugation, and moreover the early Marxist critique of the alienation and dehumanization of the worker, entered various fields of ethical discourse in the form of demands for equality, freedom, and humanization of work conditions but almost never as the most comprehensive account to date of the "ordinary" production and distribution of evils. Foucault's genealogical research on the madhouse, the prison, and the history of sexuality can also be read as an attempt to give a systematic account of the production and distribution of evils, which is external to the established ethical discourse and is not committed to the prism of a preestablished idea of justice.

7.220 *Ever since the Sophists' debate about the relativity of justice, philosophers have known that there is more than one exchange system and more than one discourse offering definitions of justice. Even those who think that there is such a thing as natural justice, or at least that — in modern terms — the universal claim to one theory of justice can be sustained, cannot justify their choice of a discourse and exchange system in which justice is defined on the basis of the concept of justice itself. Rawls, for example, constructs a model of rational deliberation before he defines the concept of justice; Habermas chooses the ideal communicative situation and its rationality (that is, the one he attributes to it) — these two examples should suffice, the two most prominent ones in the discussion of justice in the second half of the twentieth century.[16] The choice of system and its translation mechanism determine the margins of loss and suffering that will remain inexpressible, that is, the margins of loss and suffering it will be impossible to assess as damage and the margins of damage that will have no compensation (3.542). In Rawls's theory of justice, it is impossible to express what cannot be articulated and quantified in universal terms that are used to describe advantage and disadvantage in the situation of individuals with no particular identity. In the Habermasian discourse-ethics, it is impossible to express what cannot be translated into utterances articulated as validity claims. Even if the retreat to a "primary" discourse that determines what is just can be justified (Habermas does this through a quasi-transcendental analysis of communicative action; Rawls by constructing a model of rational choice), this does not cancel the damages incurred by this move. And these damages can only be justified on the basis of the argument that causes them.*

7.221 The discourse in which an evil is expressed, the exchange system in which damage is assessed, the translation machine determining compensation, all of these draw the line between an evil that can be expressed, its damage assessed, and compensation demanded for it, on the one hand, and an evil whose existence cannot be proved, on the other (3.543). The institutionalized translation machine that functions within an accepted exchange system is a black box that confines moral questions about what cannot be articulated or compensated behind the curtain dropped by a single, just system. The ability to demand reparation, like the ability to express suffering or to find someone who will listen to your cry for help, precedes the injustice and defers it; being adequately compensated for damage or answering the cry for help erases the injustice before it even takes place and retains the interaction between the prosecutor and the accused in the amoral space between the arbitrariness of the case (bumping into a rabid dog, for example) and the logic of the exchange system (receiving full compensation for damage, pain, cost of cure, lost time, and degradation).[17]

7.230 Even if partners in social interactions agree on the discourse and exchange system for the debate about the prevention of evils that have not taken place and about compensation for the ones that have already happened, and even if this agreement exemplifies or comes near the Habermasian ideal communication, some evils will not find expression within that exchange system. There will be evils whose prevention cannot be discussed, evils whose affliction cannot be reduced, and evils that cannot be compensated for. More generally, in relation to every accepted exchange system and discourse, evils will remain whose existence cannot be proved. Such evils constitute a situation of a wrong, and the one who suffers from them is a victim.[18] A wrong is culture's "state of nature," the prevailing situation before an agreement on the exchange system is reached, between agreements and after them, and especially during the agreements, with regard to everything that has been erased as a result of the agreement itself. Now the tables have turned: the wrong is the background, and the figure of justice, its idea, occasionally shines out of a prevailing exchange system and discourse.

7.231 In other words, a wrong is caused when the one called upon to acknowledge an evil, to give compensation or help, fails — or refuses — to read the body of the victim, his property, or his mind as a text, cannot recognize the presence of loss or tormenting excitation as a signifier, and cannot attribute a specific signified (or exchange value) to the loss or suffering. These semiotic relations are perceived in a totally different way by the three actors involved in the situation: from the perspective of the victim, the signifiers of evil are irreplaceable in his own idiom but remain without a signified in the addressee's idiom; from the perspective of the addressee, these signifiers are invisible, have been ignored or erased so as not to interfere with the ordinary process of communication; and from the perspective of the critical witness (the reporter, the investigator from the human-rights organization, or the philosopher), only traces of these signifiers exist, for they have been systematically erased by the *différend* between the victim and the addressee of his call. In other words, for the victim, a surplus of signifiers; for the judiciary system, a due process of deciphering and interpretation; for the witness, erased signs (*signes sous rature*) of distress or of a situation in which one side forces on the other his form of *différance*, which erases the signs of his distress and prevents his access to regulated exchange systems of what can be given meaning and what can be commodified.[19]

7.232 Often even the one who was harmed cannot acknowledge the evil that has befallen him. Discourse conditions limit him, a lack of consciousness or cognitive maturity prevents him from noticing the appearance or disappearance of evils that make him miserable, let alone from recognizing the conditions of their production and distribution, and he cannot see these as his problem. What does a pagan peasant know about the losses he accumulates for Judgment Day as a result of the sins of his ignorance? What does a woman in a traditional patriarchal society know about the oppression and exploitation she is under as long as she knows no other gender relations? What does an illiterate junkie know about the accumulating harm to his body? What does a coal miner know about shortening his life expectancy? Someone will tell them. At a certain moment, others will appear, others who play a patronizing, missionary role, who will try to alter the consciousness of certain types of victims who are structurally and systematically damaged by the production and distribution patterns of evils in society. They should know something the victims don't know — about Judgment Day, about patriarchal hegemony and the oppression of women, about abnormal metabolism and brain damage, about the accumulation of carbon in the lungs. Paradoxically, those who know are now responsible for the appearance of wrongs, for the creation of *différend* (that is, appearance and *différend* for the victims). Through the ones who know, the victims will learn to identify the evils that befall them as their own problems and will encounter others who are unable or unwilling to enable them to prove the existence of these evils and demand prevention and compensation.

7.233 The wrongs were present, of course, even before the change in the victims' consciousness — for the one who identifies evils and who understands the one unable to express them. After the consciousness transformation, wrongs appear in the field of vision and in the discourse of the one damaged by them, simply because he learns to take part in his "patron's" discourse, in which the wrongs first appeared. Wrong is an objective matter, like evil, damage, and suffering, and that is precisely why it depends on discourse, on the conditions of speech and observation.

7.234 Under conditions of domination and oppression, the one who rules cannot or will not see the evils that befall the one who is ruled. The one who is ruled cannot prove the existence of the evils that damaged him in a way that will turn the ruler into an addressee of a cry for help or a plea for prevention and compensation. Sometimes a third party can describe the *différend* between the ruler and the ruled so that the limits of the ruler's discourse and the evils that befall the ruled are both perceived. The one who can perceive the limits of the ruler's discourse has already taken part in it. It makes no difference, for the appearance of a wrong (perhaps only for that), whether the one who occupies the third-party position is a ruling subject who transgressed the ruling discourse to the extent that he can recognize evils that befall the ruled and identify with their suffering, or whether he is a ruled subject who has been socialized into the ruling discourse, can perceive its blindness, and can transgress it from within. That is why Gayatri Spivak's rhetorical question "Can the subaltern speak?" should be met with the trivial response: "Yes, if she learns to speak the language of the rulers but has not given in to it completely."[20]

7.235 When a wrong takes place, someone bears the evils the other refuses to acknowledge, and someone denies the existence of evils the other suffers from, which the denier himself helps produce and distribute. The victim demanding the removal of the wrong, not just the removal of the evil, creates a subject position for himself that feeds off the discourse of the one who caused the wrong and struggles with its constraints. The one who acknowl-

358

edges his part in creating injustice and wrong (because the evils have been expressed and are now perceived as superfluous, or as waiting to be justified) designs for himself a subject position that feeds off the discourse of the victims and struggles with its constraints. This is the hybrid situation in which some post-colonial and feminist discourses find themselves. The hybrid situation continues as long as those who speak the ruling discourse acknowledge that they are the addressees of a demand directed at them from the outside, from subalterns, calling upon them to take responsibility for the evils that are inexpressible in their own discourse, and as long as the subalterns struggle for recognition of the evils that have befallen them. The hybrid situation will be canceled if the ruler once again completely ignores the evils he produces for the ruled, or if the ruled fight for the removal of these evils without requiring the recognition of the ruling discourse. In these two cases, one can predict extreme situations of violence. This violence will not only seek justice and vengeance (the demand of the ruled) or the restoration of order (the demand of the rulers); it will also seek to destroy the possibility of hybrid situations in which the complexity of the relationships between ruler and ruled is exposed as well as the difficulty of stabilizing a binary relationship between them, a relationship based on a series of simple dichotomies.[21]

7.240 In order to be precise, we should rephrase the conditions for the impossibility of proving evil. Sometimes it is impossible to prove because the evil, as an object of discourse, transcends the limits of the visible and the expressible: wrong is the consequence of the discourse limits. Sometimes one cannot prove it because the evil is perceived as impossible to prevent or compensate for; there is no one to whom one may appeal to demand compensation, and all that remains is irreparable loss: wrong is the result of the way the limits of exchange relations are set. And sometimes — this is a private case with a certain importance — when the damage can in principle be proved and compensation can be claimed from someone, a person refuses to acknowledge the evil out of coldheartedness, malice, or blindness, and it is recognition from him in particular that the one who was harmed demands. Think of a woman whose damage (caused by her husband) has been acknowledged by a court, and the court is willing to punish her husband and force him to pay compensation; but she demands recognition from her husband, the one who was her man, and will not rest until she receives it from him. In this case, the one who was harmed demands that the other not only (perhaps not at all) return the evil to an exchange cycle, where it is expressed and annulled as damage; she demands recognition of the occurrence of evil itself, of the loss and suffering, and/or recognition of his responsibility for causing the evil. When this recognition is denied or deprived, it becomes an irreparable loss and has no expression, because it can only exist within the intimate and relatively closed relationship between the partners and their private language game. This situation is also familiar in other intimate relationships (parents and children, siblings, soul mates) but can actually take place wherever two sides of a confrontation are close partners (former or future ones) in a mutual relationship that the conflict breaks up or prevents.

7.241 Sometimes recognition itself enables evil to be returned to the exchange cycle, even if that evil is irreparable loss or suffering: someone recognizes his responsibility for causing evil to another; he apologizes; in return for recognition, the one who was harmed forgives, absolves. The exchange cycle is closed; the two can be partners again; the oppressing memory no longer blocks or undoes the net of relations woven between them.[22] Punishment might stop the evil, but it can never cancel the wrong; forgiveness might. When someone refuses to acknowledge responsibility for causing an evil, it stays outside the exchange cycle, and the injustice remains. But the same thing happens when someone refuses to accept recognition and is unwilling to forgive. She seeks to keep the exchange cycle open and the other in debt and maintains for herself a victim position.

7.242 When, in the early 1950s, the Israeli government, and with it the Jewish public in Israel, accepted "payments" from Germany for the slaughtering of the European Jews, they showed a double readiness to introduce the evils caused by the Nazi regime into exchange cycles between two nations and two states. In that, they cleared the path for future cooperation between Germans and Jews. The readiness was doubled because part of the evils were introduced into the exchange cycle as damage and suffering that could be compensated for and because those who claimed to represent the Jewish people accepted the payments as a symbol of the German people's and the "new" German state's recognition of their responsibility for the Nazi crimes. In order to keep the exchange cycle open — what kind of exchange cycle could contain the infinite evils of Nazism that were already expressed and recognized then? — the Israeli officials and intellectuals who supported the "payment agreement" distinguished between forgiving the Nazi criminals and recognizing the citizens of "the new Germany." Forgiveness was declared impossible, and this impossibility has since been constantly reaffirmed through a nonstop stream of clichés. Recognition was considered a clever and justified political and economic act. A certain division of labor among Jewish intellectuals and political leaders with regard to the West German Republic ensured a relatively happy coexistence of the unforgivable and the forgettable, the incalculable crimes and the calculation of growing profit out of the new relationship. This coexistence was established in the presence of surviving victims and while many Nazi criminals walked freely, sometimes not even in disguise, in that new Germany, some of them even vigorously participating in constructing the new relationship.

7.243 Hannah Arendt identified the non-forgivable with the non-punishable and saw in both a mark of "radical evil": "Men are unable to forgive what they cannot punish and … are unable to punish what has turned out to be unforgivable. This is the true hallmark of those offenses which, since Kant, we call 'radical evil' and about whose nature so little is known, even to us who have been exposed to one of their rare outbursts on the public scene. All we know is that we can neither punish nor forgive such offenses and that they therefore transcend the real of human affairs and the potentialities of human power, both of which they radically destroy wherever they make their appearance."[23]

7.244 Eruptions of radical Evil into the public arena are no longer rare (perhaps they never were). We know about them — Arendt knew as well — a few things other than that they transcend the possibility of punishment and forgiveness, and it is obvious that "the true hallmark" that characterizes them is not enough. At this stage, I wish to adopt only Arendt's notion of the unforgivable and the unpunishable as two ends of a continuum of forms of denying forgiveness. Denial of forgiveness and punishment occur much more frequently than an eruption of radical Evil. When such a denial occurs, it means that some evils remain outside any exchange cycles. Evils could remain outside the exchange cycles because they cannot be proved (in the broad sense described in 7.240) and so there is no one to punish and it is impossible to forgive, or because there isn't anyone to forgive or anything to forgive for. And vice versa: these evils could remain outside the exchange cycle because there is a refusal to forgive (even if there is someone to forgive) and one does not wish to punish (because there is no point), or one refuses to consider punishment a reason to forgive. In any case, someone always remains in debt, and someone else remains "without recognition"; a debt is present somewhere, an account is yet to be settled.

7.250 Between the positive and the negative, between justice as figure and justice as background, there is one more possibility: conversion. The response to evils that cannot be estimated, prevented, or repaired within an exchange system forces a conversion of capital between different exchange systems (6.541). Conversion is an exchange relation between the regulated systems and outside them. The more the evil that afflicts someone is amplified, the more difficult it is for him to enter the regulated exchange relations and the greater his need for more conversion channels; the more conversion channels are open, the easier it is to reach and help the one who is harmed (6.542). A just society sustains an equilibrium between exchange and conversion, and each of its members has, at least in principle, an equal opportunity to navigate between the different exchange systems and to use social resources to ease his or someone else's suffering. Both exchange and conversion relate to evils, not just to goods, and a concept of justice that aims to regulate the access to exchange systems and conversion channels, as well as the balance between them, has to take into account the patterns of production and distribution of evils.[24]

7.251 Under such a system of justice, it is possible to distinguish between justice as it relates to patterns within a system and justice as it relates to patterns between systems. In a situation of injustice, superfluous evils are caused because of an infraction of the exchange rules within a system, or an infraction of the balance between systems. In such an infraction, citizens or subjects are pushed out of exchange systems into conversion channels, but the conversion itself is forbidden. Or vice versa: they are pushed from conversion channels into exchange systems, which for them are still inaccessible (6.543).

7.252 Since it is usually easy to identify the exchange rules within one system, it is easy to identify injustice as the breaking of rules. It is much harder to determine the right balance of exchange and conversion between different systems, especially if one wants to avoid the reifying descriptions of society as a closed metasystem offered by the hegemonic discourse. Moreover, since the separation between the systems and their autonomy is usually also — and sometimes only — an image every system seeks for itself, and is therefore part of the stakes in its internal struggles, it is more urgent to expose injustice related to the access to conversion channels and to the balancing mechanisms between conversion and exchange. But what is more urgent is also more difficult and jeopardizes the existing order, and perhaps that's why it is usually overlooked. Most talk about justice remains on the first level, of the allegedly separate exchange systems, and even when such a debate is highly sophisticated, as in Michael Walzer's *Spheres of Justice*, it unknowingly contributes to the reifying description of the exchange systems.[25]

7.253 A concept of justice that takes into account both the exchange systems and the conversion channels between them has a clear advantage over a concept of justice prescribed by one of the exchange systems. But such a concept presupposes a metasystem, a totality of exchange relations and paths of conversion ("society" in contemporary theories of justice), and the description of such a metasystem is conditioned and limited by and competes with other descriptions, and in this sense is no different, in principle, from the description of any other exchange system. Such a description can serve as arbitrator, bridge, or intermediary between competing exchange systems only insofar as they presuppose the same metasystem that the description relates to. But competing exchange systems and discursive fields will produce competing descriptions of society as a metasystem that will always exclude some evils which cannot be expressed, proved, prevented, or canceled.

7.254 Conversion enables one to answer the call of those harmed by evils, a call resonating outside the regulated exchange systems, and this without its containing any expectation for return payments and balance (6.550). Open conversion channels are a condition for a just society, but justice only requires keeping the channels open, not using them. In every conversion, something is given with nothing in return; someone remains indebted (6.551–6.553). Using the conversion channels means giving while getting nothing in return, that is, transcending what is deemed appropriate by the criteria of justice, which are always determined in relation to a closed exchange system and a predefined discourse in which evils are assessed. Gratuitous giving is a form of sacrifice. Sacrifice transcends justice, since justice is determined by the delicate balance between the given and the taken, the existing and the possible, which determines which evils are superfluous, and always stands in relation to given exchange systems (7.101 and 7.200).

7.255 Sacrifice is a response to a call. Someone suffers, someone is hurt, someone is the victim of unexpressed suffering or loss or of uncompensated damage. The mills of justice are closed off to the one who was harmed, or they churn too slowly, and his call receives no reply, his loss remains irreplaceable, his suffering does not cease, his damage is not canceled. At a certain stage, the presence of the loss, or the tormenting excitation, exceeds what the harmed one can contain. He suffers; he cannot or does not want to hide his suffering. His suffering is present as an utterance; even if nothing has been said yet, his suffering is a cry for help. One can show him the way to the common exchange channels, take him to the social-benefits office, to the emergency room, lend him some money. One can drive her to the women's shelter, lend her a blanket, listen to her story for a few hours in order to pass it on, through this or that communication channel, in the hope that the cry will reach the person who is supposed to treat cases like hers. Even these simple actions are an infraction of regulated exchange relations, because they take place on the way to the exchange system, not within it. The infraction becomes an "irreparable" sacrifice when the shelter is in your home, when the neighbor plays the role of the social-benefits officer, when the friend is the bank teller and gives up in advance both the interest and the capital. This sacrifice results from the sense of urgency that rises from the cry for help. If not now, when?

7.3 *Indifference*

7.300 Sacrifice may, but does not have to, be part of mutual exchange relations (between the one who responds to the call and the one who is harmed), which it transcends, but there are always other economies in which it may be included. The one who responds to the call could get a decent return for what was allegedly done gratuitously. This could be money, honor, social prestige, contacts or social relations created as a result of the intervention, the thrill that the one who helps enjoys, self-recognition, self-esteem, and, more generally, a way to construct her self-identity. And yet this kind of return is usually not guaranteed; even when the response has a predetermined value (the set payment for a newspaper article or a firefighter's shift), the response to the call is a form of giving that the financial payment is not supposed to and cannot compensate for. An everyday response to the call of one who is harmed (as opposed to the responses demanded of one in dramatic or heroic situations) could also transcend the exchange relations, the calculated utility and loss, the self-interested deliberation of the closed economy of the self. There is a measure there, whether large or small, visible or hidden, but almost never removable, of care for the other who has been harmed, and this care is tied to a certain measure — which is not always measurable — of excess (8.425 on).[26]

7.301 Allegedly, all these actions are more than fair; they are beyond moral duty, based on generosity and a voluntary spirit, on the devotion to gratuitous giving, on the power to spend and expend, to act contrary to the laws of self-preservation and the tendency for self-love, on the willingness to place care for the other before care of the self. Allegedly, virtuous individuals perform these actions, which cannot be forced on the entire public as a duty but can at most be posited as a model and praised after the fact (or condemned, as in the case of Spinoza and Nietzsche). But in truth, all these actions and their qualities are very close to the limit of the moral domain itself (in the specific sense given to this limit and to this domain here). Avoiding them means ignoring the distress of a suffering other. A vast space stretches between total sacrifice and a brief, indecisive attempt to mediate between the one who suffers and the one who can help the sufferer within proper exchange relations, but already in this mediation there is sacrifice, and in its omission there is indifference to the other's suffering. Indifference to this suffering is the limit of the moral (see also 8.405 on).

7.302 This echoes the position of Hume, who regarded indifference as the opposite of moral sentiment: "Extinguish all the warm feelings and prepossessions in favour of virtue, and all disgust or aversion to vice: render men totally indifferent towards these distinctions; and morality is no longer a practical study, nor has any tendency to regulate our lives and actions."[27] Overcoming this indifference — that is, the existence of a moral sentiment — is the condition of moral judgment. But both the sentiment and the judgment, according to Hume, are responses to actions and qualities of others rather than to their condition. On this matter, I am closer to the position of Hume's friend and intellectual interlocutor Adam Smith, who opens his *Theory of Moral Sentiments* thus: "How selfish soever a man may be supposed, there are evidently some principles in his nature, which interest him in the fortune of others, and render their happiness necessary to him, though he derives nothing from it, except the pleasure of seeing it. Of this kind is pity or compassion, the emotion which we feel for the misery of others, when we either see it, or are made to conceive it in a very lively manner."[28] Nonetheless, my articulation is both more narrow and more far-reaching. It is more narrow because it deals only with the misery of the other, not with his happiness (see 8.1) or with his actions or qualities; it is more far-reaching because non-indifference will be presented here as the condition not only of moral judgment but also of the existence of the moral as a field of interest and a form of intentionality.

7.310 Indifference to suffering, and more generally to the presence of evils someone else suffers from, constitutes the limit of the moral, just as indifference to a mistake determines the limits of the epistemic (in the broadest sense, any activity seeking knowledge). The epistemic domain begins where and when the truth claim is posited as a problem for someone who takes an addressee position, and the latter is not indifferent toward a possible mistake. The moral begins where and when the presence of evils becomes a problem for the witness of evils that harm someone else; that is, when and where indifference to the suffering of the other stops.[29]

7.311 The "moral" — I must discuss here what should come later — is the domain of the struggle over the distinction between proper and improper, just as science is the domain of the struggle over the distinction between truth and falsity. The improper is not the immoral but precisely what the moral enables one to identify. The opposite of the moral is the amoral, the domain of indifference to the suffering of an other.

7.312 Within the huge space of the epistemic, the domain of "truth games," as Foucault calls it, one can distinguish a changing threshold of "the scientific" — changing historically and culturally and in relation to various topics. This is a differentiating line dividing those areas that contain a systematic, relatively autonomous, structured, and regulated striving to separate truth from falsehood, and to produce true statements, from a broad and non-delineated area — from the viewpoint of science — in which the separation between truth and falsehood exists (again, from the viewpoint of science) arbitrarily, using ad hoc rules and with no agreed-on authority (see also 8.514 on). But this is also the undefined area in which the rules of scientific discourse itself stand the test driven by a will to truth. The distinction between the epistemic and the scientific has no cultural equivalent in the moral domain. Or more precisely, in modernity — and this is one sign of modernity in the West — when the autonomy of modern science was institutionalized and its inner structure was formed — and that of law, economics, or art in parallel — the agreed-on institutions, rules, and authorization procedures of the moral domain dissolved. The moral domain (in the modern West) has no specialization, no authorization mechanisms, and no set rules accepted by an institutionalized discourse community for distinguishing the proper from the improper.[30] When the legal system was established as a relatively autonomous cultural system — one that had the pretension to systematically distinguish the proper from the improper, by set rules and on the basis of accepted procedures of authorization and decision making and relatively free from "alien interests" — it was removed, more or less systematically, from the moral domain. The traditional concept of right (*Recht, droit, mishpat*) designates, in biblical discourse as well as for German idealism, the inseparable meshing of law and morality, but the determining issue of modern law is legality, not morality. The separation of legality and morality (which was already accounted for philosophically by Kant and Hegel[31]) keeps the legal distinction between proper and improper within the limit of the law alone and lets the judge use moral deliberation only when he has to fill lacunae in the law.[32] When the judge enters the moral domain to interpret the law, he might try to convert the cultural capital given by his legal position into the capital of a moral expert, but this is an impersonation, because the moral domain has no experts (since there are no accepted authorization procedures). The judge is an authorized interpreter of the law, not of morality, of morality by the law but not of the law by morality. When we wish to understand the morality of law and of the judiciary process, legality itself stands on trial. (These matters will be discussed again in 8.423, 8.424, 8.443.)

7.313 A false statement (a mistake, a lie) falls within the scientific ("within truth," Foucault would say) just as much as a true statement. The limit of the epistemic is not the mistake but indifference to a claim that might be mistaken when it appears as dubious, or indifference to doubts. The limit of the economic is not the inefficient or loss-causing action, but indifference to the expected profit or loss. The same goes for the moral: the limit of the moral is not cruelty but indifference to evils that befall someone else. Deriving pleasure or benefit from evils that befall others is a position within the moral just as much as devoted assistance to the one who is harmed is. Separating the true from the false is determined within the scientific discourse; it is the project of that discourse. And so for the moral discourse: separating the proper response to evils that befall others from an improper response is determined within the moral discourse. A moral theory can, of course, proclaim that indifference to the suffering of the other is a form of cruelty, but it can only condemn cruelty because it has already distinguished between a proper and an improper response to the suffering of the other and only on the basis of this distinction.

7.314 The demarcation principle suggested here is allegedly based on the interests of the interested subject, a compassionate (or cruel) subject interested in the misery of others. But in fact the demarcation is based neither on the interested subject nor on the object of interest. The demarcation is positioned in the moment something appears or disappears as an object of interest, which is also the moment someone appears as an interested party. The demarcation principle lies in the invisible line between subject and object, in the moment the distinction between an interested subject and an interesting object appears. This moment precedes and conditions both the subject and the object. To be an object is to already be within the subject's field of interest — a scientific, moral, or aesthetic subject, and so on. To be a subject is to already take up a position of someone interested in the objects belonging to a field defined by a certain type of interest, such as the scientific field or the moral field. Here, too, the determining factor is not the phenomenology of the subject but the logic of the field of relations within which the subject positions are placed. The interest in superfluous evils defines the moral domain. There is no superfluous evil that has no victim. That is why the moral interest is an interest in the other as a victim, potentially or actually, this other or that one, as the one who is harmed or might be harmed by superfluous evils (see 7.331).[33]

7.315 Cruelty, cynical exploitation, and sacrifice — these are all possible positions in relation to suffering and loss caused to an other. In cruelty, one continues to hurt the victim in order to derive pleasure or benefit from the mere fact of his torment; in cynical exploitation, one avoids damaging the victim directly but continues to take an interest in the evils that befall him only in order to benefit from them; in sacrifice, one goes to any length to relieve the victim's suffering. In order to determine the moral dimension of all these responses, we must go beyond the simple formulation presented here, because once concrete others are posited in place of the abstract other, it turns out that a selfish or sadistic interest in someone's suffering could be part of a caring interest in someone else's suffering and the attempt to offer her help. And vice versa: one can derive both pleasure and benefit from sacrifice for the other (7.300). But there are also borderline cases, the ideal types — pure cruelty (see 7.524), pure cynical exploitation, and pure sacrifice. All these responses are within the moral domain because they are within the range of interest in the other as victim, although only the latter response is a proper moral response.

7.320 In sacrifice, one walks that extra mile to relieve the suffering of the victim. The extra mile beyond what? Beyond what convention, custom, state law, or moral law dictates, or beyond what is deduced from one's personal interest. In any case, sacrifice is an infraction of a normative system that dictates actions of cession under certain conditions and sets their exchange values. The sacrificer willingly leaves one exchange system and gives something, big or small, with nothing in return. Cruelty, too, breaks the rules of normal exchange systems, but in another way: the victim is the one who "gives" with nothing in return; what he "gives" is taken from him by force, with violence or under threat, within an exchange system he is forced into, without the possibility of disengaging. The cruel one, who invests force, violence, and sometimes also time and money to derive from the victim what is supposed to satisfy his desires or needs, gives nothing in return; the more excessive the cruelty, the more the victim is subjected and becomes raw material or an instrument serving the cruel one in gaining pleasure or benefit.

7.321 The one who sacrifices with nothing in return might gain his subjectivity by devoting himself to the other to the point of becoming an instrument in the other's service; but subjectivity does not necessarily emerge. The devoted one might forget himself in the act of sacrifice and completely renounce his selfhood; he will be seen as an instrument only from the perspective of others who accept the terms of a certain exchange system (see 8.425–8.435). The cruel one affirms his subjectivity by subjecting the other, making the other an instrument in his own service. In both cases, the subject position of the one responding to the other's distress is determined in relation to the victim and while transgressing "normal" exchange systems, that is, ones in which both the victim and the one facing him take up certain positions and can enter negotiation. Between these two extremes, the third response, cynical exploitation, leaves everything as it is: someone caused the victim suffering and made him needy; this neediness opens a new system of exchange relations (6.300); the one who enters this system to satisfy the needy one has an interest in continuing the suffering and increasing the victim's dependence on his help. This does not make the cynical one directly involved in causing suffering, just as the help he can offer does not release the victim from his position as a victim. The exploiter takes up a ready subject position within existing exchange cycles. These can serve to decrease the evils that befall the victim but also to preserve or increase them. The cynical exploiter chooses the second option without changing any rules of action or discourse and without switching to another exchange relation. The moral situation does not change him; it does not even affect him — affections do not count here. The exploitation of opportunities is the name of the game in any exchange system in which gain and loss are at stake. Right action in the moral situation obliges us to suspend this game.

7.322   Three types of improper responses follow: taking an interest in the victim in order to gain profit or pleasure from his suffering, even wishing to increase his suffering for that purpose (the negative pole within the moral domain); taking an interest in the victim without disaffirming the superfluous evils that befall him (the limit of the moral domain); ignoring the situation of the other as victim and therefore not disaffirming the superfluous evils that befall him (outside the moral domain). From a moral perspective, it is improper to be outside the moral domain — that is, to be indifferent to the other's suffering — and therefore these three cases are improper responses, which can be placed on a continuum from interest to disregard. Let us first take a look at the two ends of this continuum. On one side, an improper response comes from the type of interest in the victim; the victim is an object of meanness, malevolence, destructive desires, sadism. I would like to call the improper moral response close to this pole wickedness. On the other side, an improper response comes from disregarding the victim: an obtuseness of moral sensibility, insensitivity, not knowing, and not understanding. But this disregard comes also from the general limitations of the discourse and the exchange system and power relations that produce and nurture it. The improper response close to the disregard pole I would like to call moral blindness. Wickedness is a type of interest in the victim, a matter of taking a stand, realizing the subject position, and a way to express desire and have pleasure; moral blindness is related first and foremost to power relations, the discourse structure, and the conditions of exchange, to taking the subject position in a given field (although it could also express a particular response and a personal obtuseness of moral sensibility). The principal difference is that in acts of wickedness, one must assume an explicit intention of the interested subject, whereas in acts of moral blindness, the objective conditions in the subject's field of action are enough, and there is no need to assume any conscious intention. Moral blindness is a result of a limited field of vision rather than a necessary fault in the "soul" or "personality" of the subject. Wickedness can be expressed through disregard, of course, but then it is disregard as a form of interest, which entails a conscious effort to dispel the object one must ignore. Blindness cannot lead to wickedness, because it means zero interest.

7.323 Between wickedness and moral blindness there is an improper response that entails both interest and disregard: the one interested in the victim is well aware of his situation and vulnerability and is interested in them so he can better exploit the victim's weakness for his own benefit. He might also help the victim, but only out of self-interest and only within the limits of what will benefit himself, immediately or in the future. This response, which we already defined as moral cynicism, actually describes a familiar utilitarian position. The utilitarian hopes that the person interested in an other's suffering will avoid exploiting the victim's weakness, because he assumes that considerations of mutuality are an efficient barrier against exploitation. The interested party understands that he might someday be in the victim position and at the mercy of others, and he does not want to be exposed to the threat that others will do unto him what he is tempted to do to the victim now. But the symmetrical situation between the cynical one and the victim that is presupposed by this argument is hypothetical or a mere fantasy; considerations of mutuality have no realistic basis because of the differential power relations that characterize any society. Because of these differential power relations, there is also no reason to assume that the exploitation of the subjected, especially when they are identified with a rejected and "inferior" group, will not eventually increase the "general good" or the overall utility. Either the utilitarian is assuming nonutilitarian limitations to the cynical one's interest in the victim, or he has no good reason to subdue exploitation.

7.324 The humanist formulation of Kant's categorical imperative — "that the person never be used as a means except when he is at the same time an end" — is directed primarily at the cynical response to misery in any of its forms.[34] But the two other types of responses have margins, whose width is unknown, in which the categorical imperative turns out to be irrelevant. It is especially hard to see how the Kantian imperative, in both its humanistic and its formal formulations, is useful in the case of moral blindness. In the humanistic version of the imperative, disregarding the other's agony includes also disregarding the other as a possible means for promoting the disinterested one's aims. In the more rigid formal version, disregarding the other cancels in advance the appearance of a possible content to which the universalization principle can be applied as an empty formal principle. The case of wickedness is less clear-cut, but it is at least questionable whether the Kantian imperative forbids wickedness if, for example, the wicked one's interest in his victim can be described as an aesthetic interest. Aesthetic wicked interest can appear as a disinterested interest in which the vision of horror becomes an end in itself and not a means for attaining the pleasure of the wicked, which only accompanies his aesthetic interest as an unintended by-product.[35] Even in the case of sadistic interest, in which the witness derives pleasure from the sight of the tormented other, it is difficult to talk about the interest of the wicked one, for whom cruelty is its own end. In the extreme case, the torturer does not wish to derive anything from the torture other than the torture itself. The torment of one is the pleasure of the other. The two are inseparably intertwined, part of the same event, which has no aim beyond merely taking place (just like, mutatis mutandis, an aesthetic delight or sexual pleasure).

7.325 It can be said, of course, that improving the moral sensibility and distancing the blindness threshold should be guiding principles of the rational will. But this is the exact moment at which the real source of the moral imperative appears. The general imperative to distance the blindness threshold is not a self-legislated law, created by the subject when he posits himself simultaneously as the source and author of the law and as its faithful subject. This imperative is also not an *a priori*, sourceless demand for empty generalization, whose content is bound to the circumstances. This imperative is an *a posteriori* generalization, given by induction, out of ungrounded demands and obligations, whose source must be rediscovered each and every time, and they are always external to the subject. The subject is never the author of those demands and is never free to move away from them. The generalization through induction uncovers a mutual dimension in them: the call to respond to the suffering of a concrete other, to overcome the indifference to the call whose source he (the other) is.

7.330 Within the tradition of moral discourse dealing with moral character, most of the interest is devoted to virtues, and only a small portion of it to vices. It is worthwhile to mention three exceptions: Aristotle, who devoted the seventh chapter of his *Nicomachean Ethics* to vices; Michel de Montaigne, whose *Essays* includes numerous discussions of various vices; and Judith Shklar, a contemporary philosopher influenced by Montaigne and a renovator of the interest in vices.[36] But these, too, only noted improper interest in the victim (wickedness), not moral blindness. The response stemming from zero interest in the victim received very little attention, and this, too, almost exclusively in the context of the "idle bystander," whose inclusion in this context is doubtful. Standing idly by might appear as curiosity without intervention, which is a type of aesthetic interest in the victim and therefore falls distinctly within the moral domain as defined here. And it might appear as an omission of intervention, despite the primary revolt in the face of the superfluous and unbearable evils endured by the victim, and so, too, fall within the moral domain. Casual disregard for the victim on the part of the one who has not even become a bystander is a topic that, for the most part, has remained beyond the scope of moral discourse, constituting one of its unjustified limits. This kind of disregard for the victim plays a crucial role in the regular social production of evils.

7.331 From the point of view of the harmed one, the determining factor is what decreases the evils that befall him and what increases their accumulation. Some wicked deeds improve his situation (whether because they were done to others or because of the ordinary, ever-renewed gap between intention and consequence), and some allegedly proper deeds try to reduce unbearable evils (his or someone else's) but turn out to be harmful to his condition. Actions and practices outside the moral domain, in the undefined sphere of action that lacks any interest in the victim's hardship, have both kinds of consequences, of course. But the interest of the one who was harmed in the evils that befall him (in contrast to those that befall others) is not a moral interest by definition. The victim focuses on his own agony, not on that of others. Distress is posited as the object of moral interest only from the perspective of an other taking an interest in the harmed one as victim, or from the perspective of the victim himself when he considers actions that are intended to prevent the distress or that come from its continuation according to the measure in which they might damage others. From this new perspective, every action that affects the accumulation or reduction of evils befalling someone is "within the moral domain" or has a moral "dimension" or "meaning." The amoral domain becomes part of the moral domain insofar as the actions taking place within it are relevant to the situation of an other (whom someone perceives) as a victim.

7.332 It is very likely that the moral interest in the amoral domain is more urgent, broader, and more complex than the interest in the actions, practices, institutions, and qualities within the moral domain, that is, those that have an explicit affiliation with the other as a victim. This is so simply because it is very likely that more superfluous evils are caused by action in the amoral domain, and because these evils are graver, more threatening, and accumulate faster than those produced within the moral domain. It is more urgent to take an interest in these evils, since indifference to them is the result not just of obtuseness but of blindness and ignorance, which are caused, among other things, by the discursive conditions that prevent such evils from being expressed. But this is precisely what makes a moral interest in amoral domains so much harder to have. Therefore, it is not surprising that moral discourse has mostly neglected this field. Questions of virtue or the just society are a lot more accessible. Moreover, every theory of justice standardizes and mechanizes the moral interest, in an attempt to dispel the distress accompanying it. Here is a mechanism for the abolition of unnecessary evils, here is the formula for operating the mechanism, here are the technicians who will operate it, here are the quality-control inspectors who will supervise them. The bourgeoisie can sleep in peace. The work of the pious — the work of justice — is done by others.

7.333   An evil that is impossible to express or prove cannot exist in the dominant, common discourse, within which the harmed one is supposed to express the damage or suffering he incurred, and therefore the addressee of the compensation claim or of the cry of distress remains indifferent. If "the moral" means not being indifferent to the distress of an other — that is, making the presence of evils that injure an other the problem of the one who becomes aware of them — then such an addressee is simply outside the range of moral interest. Someone who has no interest in epistemological questions does not stop being wrong because of that; someone who is not interested in his investments does not stop losing because of that; someone who is blind to the presence of evils does not stop being involved in the production of injustice and wrong because of that. A lack of interest in epistemological questions (or the inability to grasp the problematics of different knowledge claims) nurtures mistakes. A lack of interest in interest rates nurtures economic losses. A lack of interest in the existence of evils (or the inability to grasp them when they are pointed out) nurtures injustice and, in particular, wrongs, since a wrong is an inexpressible or non-provable evil (3.544 and 6.555). As was said, this indifference is not necessarily a mental position, coldheartedness, or wickedness; it demarcates the limits of listening, which is the other side of the limits of the expressible. Indifference to evils that harm others is the flip side of the wrong, which is "an evil accompanied by a loss of means to prove the evil."[37]

7.334 If a wrong is the other side of the limit of the expressible, then when a wrong takes place, it is impossible to turn suffering or loss into the problem of a third person, who is present as a witness. The evil remains the problem only of the one who was harmed. A wrong takes place in relation to others who are in a position to adjudicate the existence of (superfluous) evil and fail to do so, thus remaining indifferent, unwilling or unable to make that evil their problem. But indifference may also come first, and then be followed by a failure to adjudicate the existence of superfluous evil. For the victim, the result is the same. The misery of a sick child in a refugee camp placed under curfew or a blockade is the immediate problem of his parents and a few relatives; later it might become the problem of neighbors and friends, welfare officers, or a local leader; but when the family reaches the army checkpoint with the child, in hopes of making it to a hospital on the other side of the blockade, a few bored soldiers are standing there. The soldiers follow orders. For one moment, they might take an interest in what's happening in the car, they even ask their officer for instructions, maybe they can act benevolently in this case. But an annoyed sergeant on duty tells them that their officer is gone, that no one may come or leave, that they should take down the details of the car that violated the curfew, and that in general they should stop bothering him at such a late hour. From here on, the soldiers' problem is the car that broke the curfew and not the awful condition of the child. The sick child and his parents have no way to express the incurred suffering and damage; they have no one to go to in order to demand compensation or relief. This is one of the more familiar images of a wrong for many Israelis and Palestinians, albeit from opposite sides of the checkpoint.

7.335 This is also one of the most distinct and characteristic pictures: the presence of evil on one side; the indifference of the other called on for assistance; the inability of the sufferer to break the barrier raised by a system that operates through clear and well-known rules and regulations that erase the particular evil by articulating the injury in the euphemistic terms of the ruling system, spreading the responsibility, and displacing it from the one who faces that evil to the rules and orders he is following. Every bureaucracy produces such wrongs on a daily basis; every bureaucracy contains a kernel of occupation. (And perhaps also: a state of occupation, at least a modern one, always tends to rapidly evolve into a bureaucratic system.)

7.340 Indifference is a rarefaction of presence whose apex is apathy (which means literally a lack of passion and affection, having no excitation and first and foremost no suffering), to the point of total erasure of what is present for the one who is (or might have been) present. What is present is not a problem for the one who is present, or rather, for the one who is not present (for the sufferer), the one who is present (or involved) in something else and does not see the evil, even though it is standing in front of him. A problem is a "disturbance in the order of things that demands attention, treatment, action, speech.... [It] can be caused by the disappearance of some thing or by the appearance of some thing, immediately manifested as lack or excess in the presence of some thing" (1.400). In lack or loss, the absence is present, and its presence saturates the one who is present. Therefore, even in a case of loss, evil is an excess of presence, whereas a wrong is an encounter between the excess of presence and the rarefaction of presence: an excess of presence for the one who was harmed; a rarefaction of presence for the one who remains indifferent, the one who takes the addressee position in a discourse where evil remains unexpressed, with no one to address it, with no response. Wrong is always a case of irresponse-ability.

7.341 The presence of an evil withers for the witness when the discourse within which the victim seeks expression or the exchange system within which he seeks compensation or relief cannot contain the evil that damaged him. As was said, this happens not because of coldheartedness or wickedness but because of the structure of discourse and exchange relations (7.322). A new aspect of the movement of accumulation and overflowing that characterized the transformation from presence to excitation and from excitation to suffering is uncovered here. Excitation is an overflowing presence, suffering is a spillover of excitation, and out of this accumulation of excitation, as it crosses some reception threshold that is hard to reconstruct, the experience of the one who bears the overflowing excitation is transformed (5.501). But despite the intensity of the change, an excitation does not cease being a presence; it is more present than presence. And suffering does not cease being an excitation; it is more exciting than an excitation. On the other hand, a wrong is an evil whose harm overflows the exchange relations and the bounds of discourse that are supposed to enable its presence, an evil that the discourse or exchange system cannot contain — and therefore they tend to erase it completely. From the witness's point of view, when an evil is turned into a wrong, it is erased with it, whereas for the victim the wrong joins the evil and is carried on it as another evil that has no expression, that causes another wrong, and so on. And so, in an infinitely rapid cycle, grows an irreparable Evil.

7.342   The wrong is multiplied like an image reflected in a closed hall whose walls are all mirrors. The infinite is gathered in this run back and forth between the enclosed walls, the walls enclosing an evil that has found no expression. The same social order — structured fields of action and discourse — that produces the evil determines that its victim will have no access to the subject position from which it would be possible to express and address that evil. Any attempt to demand the prevention of that evil, its reduction, or the compensation due for it will be delivered like a cry into empty space and will remain unanswered. Under these conditions, the representation of evil — the cry, the complaint, the demand — is doomed to dart around the tormented soul's mirrored hall. No wonder that many victims of wrongs seek to leave the enclosed hall — in madness, political struggle, or a combination of both. Michael Kohlhaas could be the perfect example of — in fact the model for — such a combination, a crazed struggle to invent the field in which an addressee of the wrong's suppressed call will be found, as well as a response to the compensation claim, where the wrong will find rest from its infinite spiraling. And the end of this struggle is, as we know, devastation, both for the victim and for the victim's victims.[38]

7.343   The intensification of evils as a result of the appearance of a wrong in the victim's field of vision is also why the condition of victims who acquire a new consciousness (2.322) might worsen, temporarily or permanently. As a result of consciousness-raising, victims learn to identify the evils that befall them and also the discursive rules that have prevented them from recognizing these evils so far, and still keep them from claiming prevention and compensation (7.232–7.235). From now on, the victim knows that he is being robbed not only of his time, labor, body, and honor, but also of the right to claim compensation and change his condition. The "liberating" moment might instill paralysis, and the "aroused" consciousness may lead to despair. This is the source of the paradoxical responsibility of the "redeemer" (in the figure of the therapist, the feminist activist, or the nationalist leader) for the (temporary) amplification of the suffering of the oppressed one, who should be liberated. Any social action or political struggle that has a moral intention should take into account these possibilities, too. Under certain conditions, some victims might be left in the blissful dark. But who is entitled to decide whether to disseminate the knowledge or prevent access to it? And which doubt is bigger, the doubt whether knowing is cursed or the doubt whether patronizing corrupts? These doubts cannot be resolved in advance and cannot be gotten rid of without delving into both the details and the general context of the moral situation. And even when one interprets the situation well, the doubt remains hanging, sin lieth at the door.

7.350　The wrong is multiplied here because it has no way out. In principle, a wrong is a type of suffering, because it, too, is an encounter with no possibility of disengagement — unless the victim is willing to give up his demand for compensation, expression, or recognition. This paradoxically makes the harmed one responsible for his condition as victim: if he stops asking for expression and reparation for what has no expression or reparation, he will cease being a victim. If he did not demand, he would not be a victim.[39] Such a cession is a way to cancel the hybrid situation (described earlier) in the relationship between those who speak the dominant discourse and the subaltern victims of that discourse (7.234–7.235), since the victims not only cede proving the wrong (while they continue to face the evils independently of the dominant discourse) but also cede expressing the evil itself. Total cession reduces the possibility of violence; it is in the direct interest of the one causing the wrong or making a living from the evils that are silenced time and again.

7.351　Nonetheless, one cannot ignore that under certain conditions — when change is hopeless and insistence on the demand takes too heavy a toll — such a cession might also be in the victim's interest. Paradoxically, the victim's interest in ceding the demand and preserving the binary relationship grows in direct relation to the deterioration of his condition. And vice versa: the interest of the speakers of the dominant discourse in forcing the victim to cede his demand, in making him pay a dearer price for the ability to express his complaint, grows in a direct relation to the amplification of the evils for which they might be prosecuted. This is the logic that nurtures, especially in situations of extreme oppression, submissive behavior in the victims and cruelty in the oppressors. The victim's passivity and the oppressor's cruelty are constantly feeding each other.

7.352　But ceding the victim position is not only a strategy of victims under extreme conditions of oppression. In everyday situations, other conditions are possible in which the victim has an interest in ceding his complaint. This is a crossroads at which familiar mental and social pathologies meet. On one side is the inconsolable mourner, devoted to his mourning: the one who reproduces, over and over, the image of loss and the unaddressed complaint, the one who runs his entire life in the infinite gap between the image of loss and the unaddressed complaint. On the other side are various social agents trying to convince the victim to stop asking for expression or compensation for what is beyond any expression or compensation, agents of forgetting and denial, the manufacturers and distributors of soul erasures. And in between, different kinds of religious discourse (or semireligious, or mystical, and in general a metaphysical solace discourse) offer such victims alternative linguistic channels that can, after all, express the inexpressible pain, as well as an imaginary tribunal in which some or all of the damages will be compensated for and what was lost will be restored. And alongside those, more modern and "enlightened," are the various "therapeutic" agents taking part in education, normalization, and social control. These agents give the victims alternative genres in which they can find an expression for their suffering and loss, find compensation in the mere possibility of expression until the exhaustive expression that will liquidate the damage, leaving no inexpressible residue, is found.[40]

7.353 The obsessive mourner might need the help of a consoling discourse, religious or therapeutic, and consider it suitable. But this need does not blur the affirmative role of the therapeutic or religious discourse: to reaffirm that the evils were justified or not preventable, or that there is no one in the world from whom one can claim compensation. Once again these agents deny the possibility of giving another expression to the evils that were actually caused, a different mapping of their distribution, a different account of the possibilities of preventing them. Once again the possibility that someone is responsible, if not for the prevention of the evil, then at least for giving compensation, is denied.[41]

7.354 Religious and therapeutic discourses are similar in that they both try to slow down the rate of the accumulation of evils, to increase the angle of the centrifugal spinning motion that began with the appearance of the wrong, to drain evils in several separate channels that are allegedly disconnected in order to prevent the possibility of accumulation. Both types of discourse promise that the evils not recognized now will be recognized elsewhere, at another time. They disconnect the evils from the social context of their production and possible prevention and dispatch them to heaven's gate or gather them within the soul of the tormented individual; they discover positive sides to them, new possibilities, and a new arena for modeling the self and for the struggle for its position in the world. And every time, they lift a small partition over the arena where the encounter between the presence-congesting evil (for the harmed one) and the presence-diluting indifference of the addressee is supposed to take place. If the spinning of evils is like an electric current made up of the gaps between the "positive charge" of the excessive presence and the "negative charge" of the addressee's indifference, then the consoling discourse is a capacitor for the accumulation of charges and the reduction of tension, and eventually a lightning conductor.

7.355 A moral subject guided by justice — the one who asks for recognition of the evils and demands an expansion of the domain of the concept of justice in order to prevent, redistribute, and compensate for evils — can only exist in a field in which the same tension between the two levels of presence prevails, the amplified presence of the evil for the victim and the diluted presence of the victim for the one blind to his distress. The subject in the position of therapist, psychological or religious, thrives on dissipating the tension in this field — channeling the excessive presence and its dilution into the mental economy of the individual or into the cosmic economy within which the individual faces his creator (or both). If we judge by the relation to wrongs, and solely by them, the subject position in moral discourse and the subject positions in therapeutic and religious discourses are mutually exclusive. But if we take into account the relation to the evils themselves, the matter is more complicated. Different kinds of therapeutic or consoling discourses, and the practices attached to them, help the one who was harmed to disengage and open new exchange relations to him in which he can find compensation, even if a poor one. In this, the relation between therapy and solace, on the one hand, and the "pure" moral interest in justice and injustice, on the other, is similar to the relation between an act of compassion and a revolutionary practice (7.053). And here as well we can say that "every plan for social action that is not inherently torn between these two poles ends up collapsing into utopian terror or becomes the faithful servant of the existing order" (7.053).

7.4 *Responsibility*

7.400 The wrong splits the construction of subjectivity. "A subject position is always actualized vis-à-vis a problem encountered by the one who holds it.... A problem is a necessary correlate of a subject position" (1.400 and 1.402); "the one who has a problem already occupies a subject position, and her dealing with the problem is an important part of her shaping as a subject" (2.310). In the case of a wrong, the same object, a certain evil, is a problem for the victim who cannot express it or prove its existence and is the limit of problematization for the indifferent addressee. On the one hand, the victim who considers the inexpressible evil (or the irreparable loss, or the incessant suffering) his problem takes and shapes a subject position that depends on the occurrence and persistence of a wrong. On the other hand, the indifferent addressee reduces his listening range and as a result reduces the range of his subjectivity. His preoccupation with the evil that befalls someone else has, at most, the form of removing a nuisance. With regard to the evil in question, his subjectivity is reduced to fulfilling a function. He gives up the possibility of transcendence, which belongs to the very structure of subjectivity (1.314).

7.401 For the one who remains indifferent, who refuses to turn another's problem into his problem, the subjectivity of the victim of a wrong is as unrecognized as the evil that turns her into a victim. Her cries for help, her complaints and demands, her horror stories, and her pleas for justice are all just noises to be silenced, a nuisance or obstacle to be removed. Sometimes, to justify his indifference, his silence, his deafness, or his blindness, he will endow with subjectivity the system in whose name he is acting and whose rules he is following and try to hide in its shadow. But this justification means that the indifference has already become a problem, that the blindness, deafness, and silence are not "natural" or self-evident, that they are chosen from among other options, and that their existence requires a certain effort.

7.410 The split construction of subjectivity in the case of a wrong, its intensification in the victim and its reduction in the indifferent witness, is a reversal of the situation of temptation. In temptation, the object is characterized by indifference (4.531). The witness is filled with excitation; he is enslaved to his subjectivity and arrested within the bounds of his subject position by an other that is completely drained of subjectivity (but could at any moment take up a subject position again). The witness's position is internally split, because he is an addressee simultaneously arrested by a seductive presence and forcefully drawn elsewhere by a call for action (4.541). "Temptation creates a kind of categorical imperative.... The absoluteness of the tempting call is founded on presence as an end in itself, that is, on the total indifference of the presence to anything outside it" (4.542). That is why the presence of the suffering of one in distress is a perfect example of temptation (4.543), in which the other becomes an object but his presence is excessive and forcefully draws the witness's attention.

7.411 This temptation was also familiar to the Nazis, who regarded the SS men as heroes who could control their desire. The problem, writes Hannah Arendt, "was how to overcome not so much their conscience as the animal pity by which all normal men are affected in the presence of physical suffering. The trick used by Himmler ... consisted in turning these instincts around, as it were, in directing them toward the self. So that instead of saying: What horrible things I did to people!, the murderers would be able to say: What horrible things I had to watch in the pursuance of my duties, how heavily the task weighed upon my shoulders!"[42] The image of the immoral subject is structured like the reverse portrait of the Kantian moral subject. Both are torn between duty and "inclination," obliged to overcome their desire, guided by the law — the moral imperative or the Führer's command — to which they owe unconditional obedience, because the law is an end in itself and obedience to the law cannot be reduced to any other motive that will turn it into a means. The immoral subject does not respond with indifference to the terrible suffering he causes. On the contrary, the presence of the other in his suffering causes him deep shock. But he is as strong as a lion, and he overcomes the shock. He overcomes it with the strength of his psychological economy and self-discipline, which is also what enables the man of pure duty to overcome his inclinations. In the face of inclination, as in the face of surging emotion, the moral — or immoral — position is a constant test of the moral subject's selfhood, its habitat, its place of greatness.

7.412 The proper moral alternative to the immoral position is not unconditional obedience to a categorical imperative beyond time and place, but a response to the call of a concrete other, here and now (although not necessarily a response to the call of transcendental otherness, or of the transcendence of otherness, which allegedly transpires in a trace, through — but also hidden beyond — the concrete other, flesh and blood, a voice and a cry, and, beyond everything else, a face and a gaze). If one decides not to respond to the call, this is neither because one overcomes temptation nor because one strives to preserve temptation and devote oneself to it, but because concern for the other overflows from the here and now to the future awaiting the other, or because the concrete other is one of many, and one should calculate the response according to its foreseen influence on the future of that particular other and so the many others. The proper way to cope with temptation in the face of an other's suffering is to try to multiply it, hypothetically and in practice, by many other presences of suffering, in the relevant context of the social, spatial, and temporal environment of the evils within which the distress of the sufferer is placed (see also 7.500 on). The proper moral position is split not between inclination and the categorical imperative but between the seductive presence of concrete suffering and a whole cognitive apparatus of calculation, evaluation, interpretation, and prediction of the social production — that is, the one susceptible to change and manipulation — of evils in the relevant context. What is the relevant context? This is part of what needs to be determined every time within the framework of that epistemic activity. [43] The moral subject is a subject of knowledge guided by excitation and of an excitation guided by knowledge. His interest in the victim is always simultaneously affective and epistemic.

7.413 Moral blindness contracts the subject position in both the epistemic and the affective domain. The ability to empty the presence of the other's distress of everything that makes it increase and overflow (but not by freezing the desiring movement or overcoming it, in an attempt to preserve the exciting moment) is a perfect example of indifference, a dying of both the epistemic and the affective interest. By the same logic, by the same economy of presences, in the case of a wrong the witness's indifference is a constitutive factor of the sufferer's subjectivity. In his indifference, the witness creates a space that the victim can then occupy so he can shape his identity as the one harmed by the lack of recognition of what is harming him.

7.414 These things should be emphasized against a common complaint or battle cry about turning the subaltern other from subject to object. The therapeutic response to the other's suffering holds more danger of objectification than does ignoring the suffering; the oppressor's cruel indifference endangers the oppressed's subjectivity less than the righteous devotion of those who display their solidarity with his struggle. This does not mean that for the good of the other one should stop expressing solidarity with or be cruelly indifferent to him. It only means that different patterns of behavior, moral and immoral, have a changing, nonhomogeneous role that is not completely predictable in the constitution of subjectivity, in fixing someone in a subject position, and in an increase or decrease of the range of subject positions available to him. Before they subdue one's personality, wrongs develop it (in the same way that alienation and lack of recognition on the side of the master are constitutive for the development of the slave's self-consciousness in that famous section of Hegel's *Phenomenology of Spirit*).

7.415 Accordingly, the splitting of subjectivity in a wrong and its narrowing in the indifferent witness are a mirror image of the doubling of subjectivity in sacrifice (or in cruelty). The one who responds to the cry of distress turns an other's problem into his own problem, and that same problem becomes an axis of his self-shaping. The one who responds to the call and transgresses, even if only for a moment, even if only by a little, the institutionalized exchange relations transcends his role anyhow. Instead of projecting subjectivity onto the system in whose name he is acting, he takes on a responsibility that he borrows from the system in the place of which he is acting. But in both cases, subjectivity is displaced, responsibility is passed on, and the subject position is transformed with respect to its defining field or system of relations.

7.420 Whether the result of a wrong or a sacrifice, subjectivity is shaped as a flexible set of relations between a witness and the presence of an evil, and these relations are spread out in the space between the subject position and its defining exchange system or field of action. The subject never bears sole responsibility for the moral meaning of his response to an evil that harms an other, neither in the case of indifference nor in the case of response and sacrifice (he has sole responsibility only in extreme cases of wickedness, when he volunteers to harm the victim well beyond the harm that his subject position obliges him to inflict). This is so not only and not necessarily because he does not bear responsibility for causing the evil, but because the discourse rather than its authors, its speaking subjects, determines the limits of what is expressible, and because the exchange system and its mechanisms — not the subject who intervenes or remains indifferent — determine where exchange stops and conversion begins. The moral subject intervenes or ignores according to what can be done with the evil he is witnessing (what can be said about it; what can be done to prevent, cancel, or reduce it; what its value is in terms of compensation; and how it can be compensated for). The field of these possibilities is a feature of the discourse and of the particular exchange systems within which a subject position is taken up; the one who acts from this or another subject position does not determine the discursive rules or the features of other exchange systems, and he cannot be seen as responsible for their limitations, even if sometimes he can affect them — slightly or considerably, but almost always very slightly. A subject position is a post in this field, which has maneuvering possibilities and different strategies, each with its own toll, as well as "'lines of flight,' fissures, and ruptures through which one can escape, at varying degrees of risk, into other spaces of action, stealing into other subject positions, reshaping the boundaries of the expressible, visible, and touchable" (1.330), of the exchangeable and the convertible.

7.421 A discourse, a field of action, and an exchange system (at this level of discussion, the differences between them are insignificant, and so from now on I will simply call them "the field") are not subjects to whom actions, decisions, or choices can be attributed; but neither are they objects in the full sense of the word, because they cannot be attributed a defined identity, fixed, clear borders, a finite and rigid structure. This field is a cumulative result, renewing and reproducing itself, of the actions of all the subjects that take up positions within it; it is intersubjectivity itself. Its articulation — as a structure, as an order, as a set of relations — is nothing but a freezing of regularities, probabilities, and semi-patterns into a structural description that erases spatial and temporal gaps (that is why every description participates in the reproduction or breaching of regularities in the field). While the action of the one who takes up a subject position is not a result of a single arbitrary decision, an absurd leap, neither is it a "necessary" result of inclinations and response patterns that are part of his "natural essence," "personality," or "psychic structure." Every concrete action taken from a certain subject position is the result of a choice of one possibility in a structured field of positions, relations, and possible actions, and this choice in its turn participates in structuring this field, in reproducing or breaching regularities within it.

7.422 One should therefore distinguish between responsibility for causing evil and responsibility for a wrong. The wrong is located not in the nature of the evil, the circumstances that caused it, or the motives of the one who caused it but in the inability to translate it into the terms of an accepted exchange system. Usually, an evil is the result of many causes — social, ecological, psychological, and biological — and of the complex relationships between them. Sometimes it is possible to attribute it to the action of a single agent, not necessarily a subject, who under certain conditions, intentionally or unknowingly, acted in a way that harmed someone. But responsibility for causing an evil, if it can justifiably be attributed to a single agent, does not entail responsibility for causing the wrong associated with that evil. In fact, the cause of the wrong and the cause of the evil should be separated completely. A wrong is caused by whoever or whatever prevents the victim from expressing, proving, or preventing an evil. More precisely, a wrong is caused as a result of an encounter, which could be completely accidental, between a particular evil and the conditions that limit the possibility of a response in the face of such an evil.[44] This possibility is a result of the limits of the visible, the expressible, the preventable, the exchangeable, and the convertible within and between defined discursive fields and exchange systems.

7.423 As was said earlier, the limits of discursive fields and exchange systems are a cumulative result, renewing and reproducing itself, of the actions of all subjects in the field, a result that regularizes structures and sets of relationships. Speakers and actors obey the regularities thus created without choosing them or necessarily being aware of them. This means that like some evils, a wrong could be caused without its being possible to place responsibility for it on any partner in the field of action.

7.430 If a wrong is the state of nature, a kind of background against which certain figures of justice float (7.230), it occurs without any necessary relation to a specific agent acting from a subject position, but it must exist in relation to the subject positions that activate the field within which the evil in question is denied recognition, expression, and compensation and becomes impossible to prevent. A wrong acts on the subject that causes it like a solution, dissolving its subjectivity into functions and relations that make up his position in the field, whereas its effect on the victim is that of a superglue, riveting the harmed one to a subject position that no one recognizes. Responsibility for causing a wrong is therefore based on the ability to isolate from the components of the subject position what contributes to blindness to the evils that befall others, on the one hand, and what contributes to the production of these evils and their distribution, on the other. This ability always depends on the place of the subject position in the complex set of relations that determine the authority to act from this position and the possibilities for action that open up from it. But to determine this, one needs to be outside that subject position.

7.431 Responsibility for causing a wrong derives from the "extent and form of cooperation with an existing system that causes wrong."[45] The extent and form change depending on the subject positions and on how these positions are perceived by different individuals. But no subject can know clearly and distinctly, from the subject position he takes up, the extent and form of his cooperation; reflection is never that clear-sighted. It is possible to estimate a

subject position's extent of cooperation with systems that produce and distribute evils only to the extent that one is outside it
(and them). Therefore, when we attribute moral responsibility to
someone, we should not fix him in a subject position; and when
we attribute a subject position to someone, the moral responsibility we can attribute to him is very limited.

7.432 Obviously, a teacher has a responsibility for the evils his pupils
suffer from, and cannot express, in class; the judge, for the defen-
dants she sends to prison; the journalist, for the strikers whose
struggle he is supposed to report on; the policeman, for the woman whose complaint he does not know how to formulate; and so
on. In all these cases, responsibility is linked to fulfilling one's
role, expectations, doing what must be done under these conditions, and so forth — that is, it requires a correct, sensible, and balanced activation of a certain subject position. The teacher must
be receptive to his pupils; the judge cannot act preferentially in
the trial and must take into account all the facts, use her best
judgment; the journalist must be precise in his report and listen
to the strikers' discourse, not iron it immediately into the language of objective facts of a capitalist economy; the policeman
must listen politely, search for a solution within the means at his
disposal, sometimes even transcend the narrow definition of his
role, go beyond acting by the book. But acting impeccably, in any
of these subject positions, is nothing but taking responsibility for
the concrete act within the limits that the subject position allows;
it is not taking responsibility for assuming the subject position
itself, for the extent of its involvement in the field's general
action, of for what lies outside this field's limits of expression,
exchange, and conversion. In order to listen to what is beyond
these limits, one already needs to transcend them. In order to
take into account what does not enter the exchange relations or
conversion channels, one already has to transform their structure.
In short, in order to take responsibility for assuming a subject position, one must hover between this subject position and another
position. Real moral responsibility can be attributed only to the
one who hovers, and can be demanded only of him.

7.433 From this stems an argument of principle about a new domain of
moral thought and theoretical practice: applied ethics. A new subject position appears in this area, taken up by experts at solving
moral dilemmas that arise during a routine activity in defined
fields of action: the military, medicine, education, business,
media, and so on. The expert operates under clear and relatively
strict "conditions of invitation": he acts under the auspices of the

hosting institution (hospital, school, business firm, government office, and so on), the moral dilemmas he is required to deal with are expressed in the common discourse of a defined area, and the position from which he is supposed to answer questions is defined by the field of action in that area. If the expert were to try to redescribe the dilemma or the situation that creates it in terms foreign to the hosting institution and the conditions of discourse and action within which it functions, he would not be listened to; if he adopts the common discourse and sticks to the position the hosting institution provides him with, he limits in advance his ability to reflect. The expert has to adapt his reflective "hovering ability" to the conditions of the system he is called upon to serve. The constraints — political, economic, and institutional — that he operates under tend to make the expert at moral dilemmas make do with the responsibility given to him by the position he has been invited into. His questioning of the institution and the practices that cause the dilemmas he is called upon to solve is limited in advance. For example, he may not be free to question the exclusion of alternative medicine when serving as a consultant of a conservative hospital, and he cannot question the government's military policy and the justice of war (*jus ad bellum*) when advising army officers about justice in war (*jus in bello*). In other words, he will find it hard to hover between different subject positions. Under these conditions, it would be difficult to attribute real moral responsibility to him, let alone expect him to make a valid moral judgment.

7.440   It is possible to speak of the one who hovers as the one who takes up another subject position, for example, the teacher as a citizen, the judge as a mother, the journalist as a friend. In such a case, we are (merely?) exchanging the attribution of responsibility for a concrete act within one subject position with the attribution of responsibility for a concrete act within another subject position. Changing subject positions, and looking at one position from the vantage point of another, especially if the latter belongs to a different field, is a way to hover. But it is also possible to suspend entering the subject position, to leave it vacant and wait for a while, or forever, without necessarily taking up any other position. One can wait outside, attentively, and try to listen to what will not have a voice on the inside.

7.441   Who hovers? Someone who wishes to hear or say something that has not yet been heard or said, or show something that has not yet been shown. The one who hovers has not yet taken, or no longer takes, a subject position. To say who he is exactly, to tell his story, to attach some public biography to him, to attribute motives and interests to him — every such action will miss the moment of hovering, which is a transgression of such positioning. The transgression is always from certain positions that can be pointed to, but where exactly is the one who hovers located? It is impossible to ever know precisely. It seems that someone's position is subject to a law of indeterminate positioning similar to Heisenberg's principle of indeterminacy: it is impossible to determine the location and the movement of a single unit at the same time. When the position is located, the movement (the hovering) is indeterminable; when the hovering is described in some detail, the location is indeterminable. So how can hovering be described? Retroactively, and only according to and in relation to the differences between two stable subject positions, the one that precedes and the one that follows the act of hovering.

7.442 But this is an exaggerated, somewhat romantic description of the suspension involved in entering the subject position. This suspension, which I call hovering, could be the result of a big disruption, a traumatic event, or a disaster, but also of a very happy and surprising coincidence, an unexpected fortune or misfortune, a stinging failure or success, a sudden or prolonged disease, a terrible disappointment, an uprooting, the death of someone close, or a bankruptcy. And then it is really difficult to position the subject, in particular if the one harmed by the big disruption is not cooperating, is avoiding displaying his position. But usually, even those harmed by the worst troubles rush to occupy ready subject positions, even if unknowingly and helplessly (a terrible catastrophe destroys even these positions, and that is obviously one of its characteristics). More often, hovering and suspension are the privilege of people who have time on their hands, for whom nothing is too urgent. Usually a disruption is not enough; one also needs a certain skillfulness, the strength to enclose oneself, the power of restraint, the capacity to look and listen. Some subject positions, in art and poetry, in religious or philosophical discourse, prepare the one who takes them up for such restraint and listening.[46] But in such cases, restraint is a pattern of action that a subject position in a certain cultural field enables and encourages, whereas the suspension itself is virtual. That is because the philosopher or the poet or the artist never really took up the position of the judge or the policeman or the political leader whose field limits he is trying to break in the act of hovering, which is nothing but a metaphor used for talking about reflection.

7.450 Reflective activity uncovers the moral responsibility of the one who takes up a subject position in a certain field in the face of evils that stand at his doorstep and push him into an addressee position. One can exaggerate, like Plato, and say that only complete knowledge, the knowledge of the uppermost object of knowledge — the Form of the Good — could predetermine which subject positions should be taken up (and who exactly should occupy them) and how one should act from within them. But in the lack of such philosophical knowledge, we have to make do with a restrained, skeptical reflection, released as much as possible from the weight of subject positions in defined fields of action and discourse; to make do with it and the wrongs it retroactively uncovers. The monk, the philosopher, the poet, the artist, could uncover from the outside a responsibility for causing wrongs that is attributed to a certain subject position and call upon the one in that position to stand up to his duties, in the hope that the message will not be lost in transmission. One can also try to give fresh recruits basic training in skeptical reflection as part of the accreditation process for taking up a subject position in various fields of action. Imagine a judge, a teacher, a journalist, a scientist, or a political leader who learns to hover, who practices hovering as part of his training.

7.451 There is a belief here, which is not entirely founded, in the power of one component of what is perceived as "enlightenment" — that is, critical, skeptical reflection — to make the world a better place. This is a worthy and noble belief perhaps, because it may give hope (mainly to those who practice reflection anyway), but it is useless, and not only because it is unsubstantiated (this alone does not disqualify it) but because hovering has many ancient traditions, none of which has ever become popular. The paralyzing dimension of skeptical reflection threatens any institutionalized system, in which dysfunction is always perceived as sabotage. In this matter, nothing has changed since Socrates. Skeptical reflection bites like a mosquito or, at most, injects its stinging venom like a bee and dies as soon as the venom begins to take effect.[47] And that is all. There is something pathetic, one must admit, in this heroic effort to spend so much time, intellectual expertise, and sublime abstractions on mosquitizing.

7.452 As if this were not enough, one should add that dealing with reflection and with its function in uncovering responsibility for the wrong has little effect. Perhaps I have been following, unreflectively and uncritically, one of the prejudices of moral discourse: to see the array of evils that are socially produced and distributed only through the perspective of improper deeds, because they are morally reprehensible, that is, deeds that can be attributed to an agent responsible for the improper deed and its harmful consequences. But one must distinguish between responsibility for improper deeds (wrongs and injustice) and responsibility for causing evils in general and superfluous evils in particular (7.422). If the moral is defined by non-indifference to evils that befall someone else, then the central, urgent matter is the decrease in the overall sum of superfluous evils and not just correcting wrongs.

7.453 Because so much of moral discourse is organized around the concepts of justice and injustice, and the concept of rights that accompanies them, even the most urgent dealing with the most horrible evils that are denied by no one is mediated today in Western societies by a rhetoric of justice and injustice within the framework of the human-rights discourse. These rights are universal and are non-appropriable under any conditions. When rights are defined in this way, transgressing them is a morally improper action by definition. In order to defend victims of these and other kinds of state terrorism, exploitation by the capitalist market, and the oppression and humiliation produced by both, we incessantly widen the realm of reference of the concept of right and include in it the evil that befalls the victim in a particular case: tortured detainees have a right to a fair investigation; the starved have a right to bread; the unemployed have a right to work; chronic patients have a right to die in dignity; women have a right to abort their fetuses, and fetuses have a right to be born; the systematically murdered have a right to live, and animals, too, have a right to live (and the rights are no longer "human," but the rights of the living, or of the sentient, or of nature itself). That is how organizations for human rights, animal-rights groups, and many relief organizations function. The evils are expressed and affirmed; they are acknowledged, and an attempt is made to reduce them; the cry for help is responded to with different levels of urgency — depending on the context — but almost always at the price of reifying evils in terms of a violation of rights. Evils become violated or denied rights that must be rectified; the right precedes the evil and is the condition of the possibility of talking about it, making it visible, and showing it to others. Looked at from the perspective of rights and their denial, evils tend to conceal the sui generis institutionalized mechanisms of their production and distribution. The denial of rights is presented as an infringement on a normal routine: the arrest and investigation are morally authorized, only torture is declared improper; a curfew of a city under occupation is acceptable, only the shooting of those who violate it is noted; the relationship between employer and employee in a capitalist regime gets moral authorization, only unemployment is declared improper, and it, too, is normalized; and so on.

7.454 The discourse of rights normalizes and legitimates existing systems for the production and distribution of evils at the price of a clear distinction between the proper and the improper within those systems. Its advantage is that it allows one to isolate what seems, from a certain point of view, the most urgent moral matter and give it a relatively efficient treatment. Its main weakness is that it tends to legitimate, and perhaps also nurture and enrich, the system that creates the conditions for the appearance of such urgent cases, sometimes even produces them directly, and, within that, increases both moral blindness and the narrowing of the horizons of the moral discourse.

7.5 *Urgency*

7.500 Urgency is a moral category, because time has a constitutive role in causing suffering. "Suffering is the duration of the encounter with the unbearable" (6.000). It occurs "when it is forbidden or impossible to 'disengage from an encounter with casualties'"; its temporality is "an unceasing duration" (6.200). "Torture and therapy, an increase of suffering and a decrease of suffering, are questions of time. When the conditions responsible for the unbearable excitation continue for a while, time itself seems to be the cause of suffering" (6.240). The continuation of suffering is central to its intensification; a rapid response to suffering could be central to its assuagement. In general, the presence of evils requires quick action.

7.501 Deferral and suspension accumulate an evil on top of an evil. And yet suspension is not indifference to suffering but restraint that is already within the moral domain. It presupposes non-indifference, a readiness that has to be overcome, restrained, at least for a while. Immediate response is not necessarily a proper deed. Compassion could override deliberation and damage the moral judgment, that is, the ability to take into account the conditions of prevention and the conditions of the discourse of the one who was hurt, the chances of his rescue, and the price that coming to his aid will exact from him, from his surroundings, and from the one who has come to his aid (see 7.412). Justice attempts to remove the temptation posited by compassion.

7.510 Restraint and moderation are also moral categories. That is because time is needed and normal activity must be suspended in order to listen to the evils that cannot be expressed in the common discourse and in order to determine the relevant subject position's "extent and form of cooperation with an existing system that causes wrongs" (7.431). A proper action requires "temperance," but not necessarily for the reasons presented by Plato and Aristotle. Temperance is a condition of the possibility of reflection, and reflection is the condition of appropriate moral judgment, which is always supposed to take into account the possibility that the existing conception of justice leaves some evils unexpressed (and therefore causes wrong) and that the response to these evils is more urgent than the response to the explicit evils expressed by the common discourse. In general, the assumed presence of wrongs demands suspension and listening, temporary disregard for what seems most urgent (7.432).

7.511 An immediate response carries the danger of disregarding the one whose suffering is invisible, whose befallen evil has no expression. Immediate response could add a wrong to a wrong. But the price of suspension is certain. Suspension takes a toll, in damage and in suffering, which grows with every passing moment without a response to the call for help. The suspension of judgment is a form of torture. And the sufferer does not care that judgment is rightly suspended and that justice tortures justly. And when judgment tortures and justice afflicts, it sometimes seems that they develop an indifference to the suffering accumulating in the one awaiting decision. This indifference is necessary for the normal functioning of the systems that institutionalize deliberation over the suspension of judgment in the face of unbearable evils and the ways to administer it. But such indifference, or at least the deliberate disregard for an other's suffering, despite the surge of seemingly superfluous evils and the surge of excitation in the witness who cannot put up with them, is necessary, especially for anyone who wishes to examine critically the distribution of evils itself and the discourse in which a just distribution is determined. Either way, whether one wishes to find out the proper response to an evil according to the existing conception of justice, or whether one demands the justification of the conception itself, whether one revolts against an injustice, or whether one revolts against a wrong, once again moral sensibility fights the temptation posited by compassion (5.342 and 5.350). The one who pities and wishes to respond to the call must overcome the barriers placed by the "cruelty against oneself" of the proper.

7.512 This is, first of all, cruelty against oneself, which is a condition of due process that ends in justice. But in every instance of such cruelty, the one whose call is not responded to is also harmed. The concept of justice oscillates between the demand to decide immediately and respond to the call and the demand to suspend judgment and defer the response. To act justly means to act immediately; to act justly means to take everything into account — an endless reflection and infinite suspension of the decision. For Derrida, who formulates this dilemma as one of three aporias of justice, this is a paradox with no solution.[48] All that is left to do is to locate the traces of this paradox in every judgment and leave traces of it in every decision, leave an opening for correction in the next step, refrain from giving any decision the status of closure. Ultimately, the paradox of moral judgment is the paradox of any determination of meaning. The worst thing of all is the closure of the borders of the discursive game; that is why one must join any force that keeps the borders open, until the next possibility appears, with an ungrounded hope for correction and healing (but resignation and despair are also ungrounded, and just as much so).

7.513 Derrida is right about the aporias of justice, which for him actually means (in this context at least) what I have designated "the proper" or "the right thing to do," where the distinction between improper and proper is the basic, most general moral distinction. In other words, these are aporias of moral judgment in general. But one should bear in mind that it is only since Kant that the question of judgment dominates moral philosophy. This was not always the case — biblical literature was concerned mainly with the upbringing and education of the pious; the Greeks were concerned with virtues; the philosophers of the Scottish Enlightenment with sentiments; and the English utilitarians with the greatest happiness or utility. And this also should not be the case. If indifference to an other's suffering is a limiting and enabling condition for morality, then not judgment but effective care should be the utmost concern of the moral philosopher.

7.520 Is it possible that indifference to the suffering of an other — which defines the moral domain negatively, from the outside — is a necessary condition for a just decision and a moral judgment? Is it possible that an imperative that seems to stand at the heart of the moral domain and to organize it from within — to care for others in distress — is based on practices on whose negation the domain itself is differentiated and founded?

How *could* something originate in its antithesis? Truth in error, for example? Or will to truth in will to deception? Or the unselfish act in self-interest? Or the pure radiant gaze of the sage in covetousness? Such origination is impossible.... This mode of judgment constitutes the typical prejudice by which metaphysicians of all ages can be recognized.... The fundamental faith of the metaphysicians is *the faith in antithetical values.*[49]

Truth is produced from a lie (that has been established by the will to truth); beauty appears out of ugliness (which demands for itself the exact same wondering attention); justice grows where cruelty is channeled in precise conduits and becomes a systematic disregard of certain evils that befall others, so that it will be possible to create a balance between other evils. The one who no longer believes in the metaphysical status of opposing values, the one who does not rule out in advance the possibility that something will be created from its opposite, from the accumulation of the thing opposed to it, or from its purification and refinement, will not find it hard to understand that cruelty, both the kind directed against the witness and the kind directed against a suffering other, is a condition of the possibility of justice and that a disregard for the suffering of a certain other is the condition of care for and devotion to a different other. This is also a possible, even if unorthodox, interpretation of the saying from Ecclesiastes: "And moreover I saw under the sun the place of judgment, that wickedness was there; and the place of righteousness, that iniquity was there."[50]

7.521 Nietzsche called the research that reconstructs the creation of something out of its opposite "genealogy" and posited it beyond good and evil. Genealogy is a kind of critique, which in itself does not necessarily lead outside the moral domain; it only forces us to suspect the motives of every moral discourse, the interests it serves, and the life-forms it cultivates, and, mainly, such a critique reconstructs the traces of the life-forms on whose ruins this discourse grows. Nietzsche was not only a genealogist but also a metaphysician (or at least it is often tempting to read him as such). Against the prejudice of the metaphysicians and their oppositions he posited his own opposition, between what promotes life and what arrests it, between two types of a will to power and two types of a will to truth, and in this sense, at least, he also remained a metaphysician. Nietzsche tried to turn Western values on their head, and in fact to completely deconstruct them, in order to find a place beyond good and evil from where it is possible to measure anew the value of all values. The new value according to which all other values should be measured is their responsiveness to life, their pointless flow, their limitless diversity, their devotion to bounty, to generosity, to excess, to risk taking, and to putting to the test, all of which developed in the most sophisticated forms that life grew from within it, and above all their response to the way in which these forms of life promote or arrest self-overcoming. Self-overcoming entails cruelty, in particular self-cruelty, an indifferent expenditure of power and an excessive indifference to suffering, the suffering of the one who overcomes himself and others. Indifference to suffering is a condition of self-overcoming, but in order to reach it, one must overcome one's self — as was said earlier, pity is the last temptation of Zarathustra (5.351). This indifference to the other's suffering, and not the declaration of a place beyond good and evil, is what positions the Nietzschean text outside the moral domain — but of course only at the place where such indifference actually prevails. Usually Nietzsche takes a strong interest in suffering, its presence, tempting us to pity the cruelty that produces it. Because of this matter, the thought that wishes to sail beyond good and evil almost always remains within the moral.

7.522 When Nietzsche exits the moral domain, he does so in the name of the hierarchy of the final opposition of values that he sanctifies in order to deconstruct through it all other oppositions: the hierarchical opposition of abundance and parsimony, plurality and uniformity, motion and rest, passive and active forces, a will to power and a will to nothing. The transcendence of the moral domain in Nietzsche can only be achieved at the price of reintroducing the same dualistic metaphysics that Nietzsche overcame in and through his genealogical critique. Rejecting dualistic metaphysics together with Nietzsche, we may remain faithful to genealogical critique without abandoning the moral, whose necessary and insufficient condition is overcoming indifference to the suffering of an other.

7.523 Overcoming this indifference could entail self-overcoming and could imply a change in the consciousness and discursive practices of others; the two are not mutually exclusive. Despite Foucault and the ancient Greeks he describes in his late work on the history of sexuality,[51] the care of the self (*souci de soi*) and the concern for it are not moral matters in themselves, according to our definition of the moral domain (8.511 on). The care of the self is a moral matter only from the moment it is prescribed by a concern for the suffering of an other (7.331), whereas the concern for the other is the constitutive rule of the moral discourse (7.301 and

7.313). It is important to clarify that the care itself is not founded on any prior value or on the negation of any opposed and inferior value. It is its own end in the strong sense that theology attributed to God and Kant attributed to the categorical imperative. It is, at the same time, unconditional and unjustified. Every attempt to condition it on something else — personal utility, an abstract general interest, ties of belonging to one group or another — throws the argument and the arguer out of the moral domain. Every attempt to justify it on the basis of something prior to it is an attempt to deduce the constitutive principle of the moral domain itself from one of the values that this domain makes possible (the good, justice, equality, liberty, and so on), or to subject it to another domain (of utility, domination, or knowledge) that is foreign to it in principle.[52]

7.524 Richard Rorty says something in a similar vein, following Judith Shklar, who in turn appeals to Michel de Montaigne: "Cruelty comes first" (in the ranking of vices).[53] An uncompromising opposition to cruelty is the mark of any liberal position (and, implicitly, of every moral politics), thinks Rorty. The cruelty that Shklar and Rorty discuss is the causing of suffering for its own sake, which is the clearest example of superfluous evil, unbearable, not just unjustifiable but beyond the possibility of justification. One should revolt against anyone who does not revolt against such cruelty. But this unconditional rejection of cruelty has no prior basis, it cannot be deduced from any previous rule, and, in short, it itself does not have justification. Against unjustified cruelty, pointless cruelty that has no end but is an end in itself (7.324), stands care for its own sake, just as unjustified. In both cases, we are talking about the limits of justification, that is, the conditions of moral justification itself.

7.530 Victims of cruelty are an extreme case (even if not the most extreme) of others we should care for. There are many more. The care for others gets its concrete expression in the space between urgency and deference. Urgency is always related to a concrete other, near or far, who is in dire need of help. The reflective deferral opens the way for an other that has not yet appeared, that is not yet known, or for evils that have not yet been expressed. Deferral, as we said, obliges us to ignore, even for a while, the evils that befall concrete others; it cultivates toughness that could become cruelty. Contemplation requires time and space, and there is almost no major thinker who did not take much of it for himself at the expense of others in his immediate environment;

lesser thinkers, too, are competent at being cruel to those around them. But even the urgent response compels toughness toward the ones whose suffering is silenced for the time being, or forever (because the unbearable evils of others are perceived as more urgent), or toward the ones who have to suffer in order to decrease the evils that befall others. Every struggle, armed or unarmed, is based precisely on this logic. The urgent response — offering to help or to restore the just order of the distribution of evils — compels a redistribution of evils even for the one who has no affinity with the suffering other and no interest in his troubles, let alone the one who benefits from the evils that the other is harmed by. The deferral in order to reexamine the order of evils, aiming ultimately at a more just distribution of evils, participates in the existing distribution and reaffirms it in silence. In both directions, the moral deed forces us to readopt a "cultured," "cultivated" kind of indifference to the suffering of others, indifference mediated by reflection, which is nothing but a kind of restraint. But one should remember that moderate deliberation could always turn out to be an excuse for moral indifference, and expressions of restraint may be nothing more than pietism toward the victim whose treatment is deferred for now. Beyond the veil of justifications, there could always hide that unmediated indifference, whose overcoming defines, from the start, the action as moral.

7.531 One can never know. There is no one who will search deep into our hearts; there is no place from which we can judge moral judgment without encountering the same obstacles of self-deception, pietism, and hypocrisy that hide indifference behind a veil of moderate deliberation. That is why moral judgment is always dubious. This is the source of the rejected victim's frustration and rage; it is also the source of his hope: maybe he can still break through the veil of justifications and shock the one indifferent to his suffering. This is also one of the clearest arenas of critical discourse: to uncover the moral indifference — and not just the interestedness — at the basis of a reasoning guided by arguments that justify a resource distribution within which we ignore the call of certain victims and respond to that of others.

7.532 On both sides of the calculated restraint lie slippery slopes: on the one hand, the baseness of the mediated, self-conscious indifference that entails not only restraint but falling out of the moral domain; on the other hand, the growth of pleasure out of the inevitable refinement of excitation in the face of the suffering of others, a pleasure that culminates in the torment of an other as an end in itself, cruelty for its own sake as the apex of the negative pole within the moral domain, "the improper in and of itself."

7.533　There were always those who climbed these slopes. The climb has been fragmentary in a historical time and space and also in the moral space: from unconscious indifference to a recognition of the evils that befall others and from recognition to revolt; and a parallel climb from taking pleasure in the suffering of others to revulsion at such suffering and revolting against it (see 8.042). Everyone who has tied morality and knowledge or consciousness together, from Plato to Marx and from Marx to the radical feminist and postcolonial thinkers, has contributed something to the climb on one side of the slope. And whoever has tied morality to sentience and sensibility, from Aristotle to Adam Smith and from Hume to the humanist reformers of education, punishment, and the treatment of various others, has contributed something to the climb on the other side of the slope. The various critics of the Enlightenment pointed to the ways in which this type produces its models of cruelty. In this context, one may be reminded of Nietzsche's words on the three stages of religious cruelty and his firm determination that high culture in its entirety "is based on the spiritualization and intensification of *cruelty*."[54] Also called to mind is the amazing opening section of Foucault's book *Discipline and Punish*, the scene of the execution of Damiens the regicide, which is juxtaposed with a series of regulations that governed the lives of inmates in a juvenile correctional institution. Foucault thus posits against each other two types of relations to the suffering of an other.[55]

7.534　To prevent any misunderstanding, I should like to emphasize that we are talking not about a general historical process but about cultural and psychological changes, which are partial and local. We are talking not about historical progress toward a more moral culture but about changes in the position and function of the moral domain within culture. The fragmented climb takes place within the moral domain and does not determine the main thing: the rhythm, power, and range of the production of evils in a society and their distribution and dissemination. At most, it mirrors these factors or takes part in them. It is likely that most evils are caused by actions that take place in the indefinable space outside the domain demarcated by moral discourse. It is also difficult to know in advance what part of the totality of unbearable evils is caused by morally improper actions. And in any case, sliding down the slope, to amoral indifference or to cruelty for its own sake, is not a real factor in the moral deterioration of a society, but at most a result or a symptom of such a process. The moral deterioration of a society means first and foremost an increase in the amount, power, and range of unbearable evils caused within it. There is no reason to assume that such deterioration comes from the state of moral discourse or even from the moral virtues of the members of society. The real conditions of such deterioration should be at the top of the agenda of a moral discourse.

7.540 The most urgent thing within moral reasoning, the thing for which we must pause (and thereby deconstruct the radical opposition between urgency and deferral), the thing for which we must defer the ready response to unbearable evils and attune ourselves to what has not yet been said, to silenced and repressed voices, but also to what has been endlessly repeated and is therefore no longer heard, this thing is the understanding of the "moral condition" of a society. This means understanding the conditions and the modes of production and distribution of superfluous, unbearable evils in society and the institutionalization of certain, always circumscribed, limiting channels and patterns of expression of these evils, the injustice and the wrong.

7.541 It is important to emphasize that some superfluous evils are not wrongs: they are both those produced by a wrong and given expression at a later stage, on the one hand, and those that do not take place in an affinity with others who are aware of the evil and remain indifferent, on the other. This last type of evil occurs even though it is preventable (which is why it is superfluous) and even though some attempt has been made to prevent it (which is why it is not a wrong). In a hospital, for example, patients might suffer because of a deficient organization of the medical care or because of the general way the hospital's bureaucracy treats individual patients. The same may happen in a school or in a city stricken by an earthquake. These cases of suffering could take place even though they are expressed and responded to with the sincere care of those in charge of cure, education, or relief, and nonetheless they are superfluous. It is not right to treat them as wrongs. It is also not right to exclude them from the list of superfluous evils.

7.55 The totality of conditions, modes, and actions involved in the production and distribution of superfluous evils in society is "the order of evils" or the "general evil." But the order of evils is always only a hypothetical projection of a certain discourse, whereas the "generality" of the general evil is only a name: a family name, which is ultimately a proper name, the proper name of that family. And if we want to talk about this totality in a language familiar to all the moral theories in the West, from Isaiah and Socrates to our times, the family name is Evil.

CHAPTER EIGHT

Evil

8.0 *The Order of Evils*

8.000 What, precisely, is the relation between evils and Evil? Are we
already on the path opened up by Heidegger when he questioned
the ontological difference between beings and Being? Aren't we
obliged to ask, at this stage, what the evilness is that inheres or
subsists in evils, all the while warning ourselves not to think of
Evil as a substance, or as the form or essence common to all evils,
or as the totality comprising them all and at the same time independent of them, exceeding their sum? In fact, we have already
answered this question. We can save ourselves the long Heideggerian detour and postpone to a later stage, for another book, a
possible reconstruction of the entire history of moral philosophy
from the point of view of relations between evils and Evil, and of
the "forgetfulness" of the question of evils (not Evil – the analogy
is not perfect, which makes it all the more fruitful). Our answer
has been that an evil becomes Evil when it is superfluous. We
should thus say a few words about this superfluity's mode of being.

8.001 As a first approximation, we may think about Evil as the superfluity common to all superfluous evils in a society. For the sake of
brevity, though not entirely innocently, let's call it "the common
Evil." "The common Evil" does not indicate the universality of
Evil (conceived as an abstract idea); what it designates, rather, is
the concrete ensemble or assemblage of all the superfluous, insufferable evils that a certain collective of people share. To have a
share in the common Evil does not necessarily mean to share the
burden of the same evils with others; it may also mean to have a
share in the production and distribution of any or some of those
assembled evils. Those assembled evils: all those evils that are
there now, at this moment, at the moment the term is uttered,
whether or not they are given specific expression, whether or not
they will – at some future time – meet with rescue, compensation, or benefits. Such an ensemble is not – and cannot be – the

real object of any discourse (the referent of an existential statement), not even if we were to collect all the various kinds of discourse used for speaking (of) evil. Seeking expression for this
commonality means seeking the discourse or the metadiscourse
into which all the various kinds of discourse speaking evil will be
translated, the discourse that will en-tongue all the wrongs that
appear wherever evils are denied expression. Such a discourse is
impossible in principle, and accordingly the ensemble of evils is
inexpressible, except as an abstract idea. And yet every single evil
is a finite state of a finite being, and there is a finite number of
beings subject to evils, and a finite number of evils that could have
been, but were not, prevented at the price of lesser evils, due to
which it is possible to speak of the sum of evils at any given
moment. This sum is like a family whose members are scattered
throughout the world and for whose simultaneous census there
are not enough census takers, registration logs, police staff, or
databases, and who — even if there were sufficient resources —
would be known to different speakers by different names, ruling
out the possibility of ever reaching a single agreed-on list of
names. But it is nevertheless possible to speak of all the family
members in one breath, under their shared family name — the
common Evil.

8.002 The common Evil is neither universal nor really common, or at
least not common to all in the same way. The commonality of Evil
is the commonality of a sum, an agglomeration of things of the
same kind: superfluous evils, in which I, too, have a share. Superfluity is their common essence, but it is an essence of a special
kind. Superfluity is not a predicate of Evil in the same way that
worth is a predicate of damage, or a strong, searing sensation is a
predicate of insufferable pain. Superfluity is the way in which an
evil is suffered, experienced, and assigned expression or compensation, the way it addresses a call, invites response, opens up a gap
in someone's existence. Superfluity is the manner of the Evil's situatedness and embodiment in a concrete field of social relations,
its way of being-there as a being placed within an individual, an
injured victim, but only by virtue of the individual's placement
within an immeasurably complex system of relations reaching far
beyond him, and as a concrete realization of this relation. An evil
cannot be superfluous or un-superfluous in the way that a line
can be straight or curved or a book can be interesting or boring.
When an evil is superfluous, it is superfluous in the way that a
roof leaks, that milk boils over, that a riverbank is flooded, that a
hole opens up suddenly in the ground, that a wooden pole gives

and snaps. More precisely, a superfluous evil is the boiling over of the milk, the flooding of the riverbank, the caving in of the earth that opens up the hole, the splintering of the wood — an occurrence situated within a concrete object, but only due to the placement of the latter within a complex assemblage of power relations, the intersection of which, at some particular point, is excessive. This peculiar essence that superfluous evils have in common ensures that they have no shared source, no single "root" (see 7.044), for all the boilings over taking place right now, for all the floodings now upon us or upon others, or for all the superfluous evils. And the superfluity of Evil is not an exclusively material event, such as the boiling over of milk and the flooding of a bank, which themselves are not actually physical events devoid of meaning, for their appearance depends on creatures, human and others, who experience and specify the essence of this boiling over and flooding, according to the way they've encountered them. At the same time, there is, at every moment, a finite number of boilings over, of floodings, of superfluous evils (for there is a finite number of individuals, human beings and other creatures, who can be hurt, at least on the face of the earth).

8.003   When speaking of "the common Evil," we obviously allude to "the common Good." Like the common Good, the common Evil must be ascribed to some social commonality or collective — the polis, the people, the state, mankind. At issue is not a random collection of superfluous evils but superfluous evils that always appear within a particular form of social association and that arise from the peculiar characteristics of the partnership of which it consists. If this were not the specific form of the social partnership, perhaps the evils would not have occurred; calling them superfluous obviously means that some other form of social partnership could have prevented them. Therefore, every superfluous evil participates in the common Evil, which is the Evil characteristic of a particular social commonality at a given historical moment. Moreover, the term "the common Evil" seeks to denote a form of social partnership responsible for the production and distribution of superfluous evils while at the same time denoting the possibility of an imagined, alternative social partnership whose negative pole of convergence is its partnership in superfluous evils.

8.004   Admittedly, "the common Good," like "the common Evil," is inadvertently reminiscent of overbearing philosophical creatures such as "the general will" and opens up paths to a perception of the general Evil (or Good) and of the commonality whose Evil it is, as a substance or essence, existing "above and beyond" the sum of its partial manifestations. There is a tendency to speak of this essence, due to habit or unshakable faith, as if it logically or historically (or both) preceded any concrete ensemble of superfluous evils, defined in space and time. There is no substance here, though, but a combination, a transient form, its relative stability notwithstanding, of patterns of association and communication, and a weave of power relations spread across a more or less defined space of social, political, economic, and cultural relations, beyond which they also often extend. It is not an association entered into voluntarily, as one enters into a business partnership or joins a group tour, and in most cases it is not a social partnership that can be dissolved whenever one wishes. It holds even between people with nothing in common — neither property, family, language, history, nor a homeland — but for whom what they share or have situated between them determines their existence together, alongside each other, in the face of or against each other. They share particular ways of being together — language, patterns of association and communication, power relations, property relations, ways of distributing labor — now, for the moment, or over time. These are the forms in which and through which they discover themselves and the manner of their belonging to each other, their interdependence, their mutual foreignness, their reciprocal imitation and distinguishing of self.

8.005   Contemporary philosophers such as Hannah Arendt, Michel Foucault, and Jean-Luc Nancy all emphasized the weblike, incessantly weaving and unraveling character of "being-with," of existence together, alongside, opposite, and the fact that every *a priori*, permanent, established structure and every general essence or substantive being attributed to this web are merely acts of representation, attempts to contain its infinite complexity in some figure or gestalt, none of which can be dissociated from the attempt to control or rule the web.[1] This should also be true for the common Evil. Therefore, I resist the temptation of this notion and prefer another name for the family of superfluous evils — the order of evils. It should be kept in mind, however, that there is no real order here either, at least not if one understands order as some regularity existing apart from the complex that is ordered by it. What there is is an inconclusive collection of temporary regularities, constantly reproducing and changing, according to the cooperation and resistance of all those whose actions and conduct these regularities order or are supposed to order.

8.010 All Western schools of thought recognized superfluous evils by their first (phenomenal, experiential) name, but almost all of them erred in identifying the family (the root, the origin[s]). When the thinkers of ancient times spoke of "Evil," they thought of hubris, the transgression of nature-given boundaries, or of sin, the transgression of divine law; the moderns thought of the arbitrariness of will or of the excess of self-love or of the destructive drive and the death wish. The superfluity of evil was attributed to some thing that was missing: to ignorance, and particularly not knowing how to distinguish good from evil; to a lack of temperance, of piety, of respect for the law, of stable government, of emotional equilibrium, of order. Most such thinkers failed to understand, or did not accept, that there is nothing beyond the superfluity of evil, nothing, in other words, that belongs to the same family, other than the order of the evils' production and distribution. But, as stated, that order, too, if there is one, exists not beyond the ensemble of superfluous evils, only within the ensemble itself.

8.011 Of chief interest here is not the ensemble of evils but the regularity within it. The ensemble complex is essentially unremarkable, random, and meaningless. Regularity is a pattern of not-inevitable repetition. Regularity is a changeable order, an order dependent on repetition, a repetition dependent on the cooperation of the one repeating, on the response of what is repeated. The possibility of changing the order, its contingency, is its meaning. This is true even when the order appears as natural, primordial, necessary, and unchangeable. The meaning of the regularity will then be precisely its zero possibility of changing, its necessity.

8.012 Because repetition is at issue, the reference is not to random, surprising, seemingly inscrutable, and groundless outbursts of natural forces or wicked forces causing evil. Such outbursts cannot be predicted (prediction presupposes repetition), and it is therefore doubtful that they can be prevented; if they are unpreventable, then they cannot be counted among the sum of superfluous evils (those that should properly be prevented [7.101]). It is possible, of course, to speak of general safety measures in order to prevent unexpected outbursts that are, nevertheless, expected, based on experience. The surprise element then remains the precise time, place, and character of the bad things supposedly destined to occur surprisingly. But this assumes some degree of regularity in the surprise itself, and confidence in some degree of regularity in the preventive measures. Many evils occur as a result of the failure of these assumptions and the breakdown of those preventive measures taken in accordance with them. Such a failure can come as a complete surprise, and then we're no longer dealing with an evil that was preventable (in given conditions of knowledge and social and technological preparation); or there can be some degree of regularity in the failure, too, and then we're again dealing with a superfluous evil. Insurance companies specialize in such regression and are supposed to insure against it, but they often fail, and their failure to assign the regression a quantitatively calculable expression may in turn possess some degree of regularity as well — the regularity of the conditions of economic, medical, or technological discourse that always "leaves out" evils of this type.

8.013 If repetition were not avoidable, we would be faced with a predetermined order, preceding the practices generating and determining evils and making them inevitable or necessary. That which is necessary cannot be superfluous. In the moral domain, superfluity, not contingency, is the opposite of necessity. What is contingent might never have existed (it is not inevitable), but nothing prevents its existence; what is superfluous is that which is contingent that should never have existed. Clearly, if some thing is perceived as necessary to the very existence or the manner of existence of something else, this is limited necessity; it is contingent on the necessity of the contingent thing and on the validity of the contingency statement. (For instance, this war is necessary if and only if this war is truly a necessary condition for securing national independence in the present circumstances, and if national independence is indeed a necessity; a free-market economy is necessary if and only if a free economy is truly a necessary condition for a flourishing economy and a flourishing economy is a necessity.) Unconditional necessity exists only when the necessary thing is truly necessary for the existence of something necessary. Necessary to what? Why and to what are national independence and a flourishing economy necessary? To the existence of some other necessary thing. Either one leads to another and this is infinite regression, or the only way to think of unconditional necessity — that is, of absolute necessity — is to think simultaneously of all there is, of necessity as the totality of Being, of the totality of Being as what is necessary. At the tail of every attempt to justify, there lurks the deceptive demon of totality.

8.014 Spinoza's dismissal of the reality of Evil, like that of Leibniz and other rationalists, is based on the totality of necessity and on the necessity of the total. Everything is necessary, nothing is superfluous, and therefore Evil is not part of being. However, only God can think simultaneously of all there is; only he can know that everything is truly necessary and that nothing is superfluous throughout the whole of reality.[2] But either there is no God or we don't know what he knows, which amounts to the same thing: from our point of view, there will always be superfluous things, and some of them at least will be governed by certain regularities, of production, distribution, and exchange. Recognizing this superfluity and understanding the regularities that govern it are the objectives of a theory of morals — in diametric opposition to Spinoza's *Ethics*.[3] For Spinoza, understanding the totality of necessity and the necessity of the total is both the objective of an ethics and the internal logic driving it. Lévinas has already undermined this logic, also shared by Leibniz and Hegel, and established an ethics that is an almost-symmetrical alternative to it — in fact, his entire philosophical project can be viewed as an attempt to do just that.[4] Lévinas seeks to break out of Spinoza's total necessity through a recognition (that lacks any positive cognition) of the transcendence of Being whose traces are encountered within the heart of Being. Lévinas disrupts Spinoza's necessity of the totality through the presence, within being, of the traces of the transcendence of "the other" that being cannot contain and that language cannot endow with closure and which, therefore, is infinite. Otherness, transcendence, infinity — this is Lévinas's way of talking about God in "Greek," that is, in the language of philosophers. Whereas Spinoza equates the totality of Being with God, Lévinas identifies it with Being's complete exteriority. For us, however, neither the totality of Being nor its complete exteriority is an option. We are stuck with an always-partial grasp of Being and always-limited moments of its transcendence. God does not dictate or ground or condition our morality; he does not even give it its direction. We insist on staying within the boundaries of Being, of the finite, the actual, and the possible, within the limits of what is there and what might be there. In order to break through the Spinozistic totality, we need merely insist on the superfluity of — and in — being. This is how our *Ethics* could begin, with a definition of superfluous beings (evils) instead of a definition of the totality of Being (God). Superfluous evils are part of what is there. Our experience of Evil is an experience of their excessive being and of the being of excessiveness. The suffering other and her suffering are also part of what is there, even if I don't know how to perceive them through the conceptual and linguistic means at my disposal. The experience of the other's otherness necessitates thinking not about an otherness that is "otherwise than being" but about other ways of being-there and being-with, about other, perhaps unknown modes of being. And the experience of Evil does not lead beyond being but, conversely, rivets us to being all the more forcefully, unbearably.

8.015 Unbearably, but also with the understanding that things could have been otherwise and the longing for that other possibility. This transcendence from the actual to the possible is also part of being, and more concretely of what actually is. Transcendence is unfailingly finite, from one form of existence to another, from one system of relations to another, from a certain regularity of superfluous evils to another. Lévinas might view the other possibility as exactly what is beyond being, or at least as what might lead us there or prepare us for it, or open us to it, or perhaps, and more precisely, he might argue that another possibility cannot be really different without presupposing and being open to that ultimate transcendence of an infinite other. I wish to insist that the other possibility is completely down-to-earth, sometimes trivial, sometimes heroic, sometimes self-evident, sometimes clarified only after a long journey of the critical mind. The other possibility is that of sabotaging the serialization of the production of this particular "line" of superfluous evils, of interrupting the repetition, stopping the machine that reproduces Evil. Moral theory should teach how to cut the fine cords of the serial repetition that Evil is made of. It should also teach that only some, if any, are ever cut, and always at the risk that new ones may appear in their place, that is, without waiting for a Messiah and without hoping for salvation.

8.020 Serial repetition is not a substantive trait of the social association, whatever its form, but rather the pattern of a relatively limited network of relations, carried from moment to moment in time, re-created through innumerable free decisions, like the world that is incessantly re-created (by a single decision each time, though) by a Cartesian God. The pattern reproduces itself in time, for at every given moment it seems to the individuals embodying and actualizing it that this is precisely what is proper, or that "there is no other way," or that the price of any other action is greater than they could bear. Digressions, forgettings, small deviations, and minute differences between one act and another, between different points in the series, differences that accumulate and that could produce a decisive difference that would make the difference, all these are immediately corrected by the network's mechanisms of representation, to the best of their capacities. To the best of their capacities: at times, the gradual accumulation of negligible differences nevertheless generates change, whose appearance can be sudden even if it has grown out of a series of differences that, if perceived at all, seemed negligible at every given moment. The "leap" or the "break" always occurs only from that moment when change is represented, and sometimes exclusively in the realm of representations. In the meantime, between one leap and another, the representational mechanisms, through their regular operation, blot out deviation and the very possibility of deviating and supervise the distribution of images of the commonly practiced pattern as "necessary" or "normal" and normative, or in time even taken for granted. The representational mechanisms in fact succumb to the same logic guiding the serial repetition, for there is no fundamental difference between acts of representation processing texts and images and other acts processing other materials. However, what is possible and what isn't, how, precisely, the field of possibilities is laid out, and what prices the various possibilities will exact –all this is not naturally or even socially given; it isn't given at all, but rather it is what is produced in the act of social reproduction itself. As a consequence, resisting Evil is always a struggle over the limits of the possible.

8.021 Every serial repetition is enmeshed in another regularity, and in fact in very many regularities. The personal computer I'm currently using to write with is a precise repetition of a series of computers of its kind. These computers were produced in several industrial plants that repeat the same actions of exchange and coordination over and over. In each plant, many patterns of more or less serial activity exist concurrently, some whose regularity is very dense and immediately discernible — the labor of the Thai women who assemble the chips, for instance — and some whose regularity is loose and more difficult to see: managerial meetings, contacts between the shift supervisor and the assembly-line workers. (Here is a measure of freedom: the more dense the regularity, the smaller the amount of freedom.) Each assembly-line worker comes back to her workplace every morning after having performed several roles at home — mother, wife, neighbor, and so on — all of which have some degree of regularity of actions in general and of acts of association and communication in particular, of a particular pattern, more or less defined, of authorized deviations from this regularity, and also of a particular regularity in the sanctions imposed on any deviations from the pattern of authorized deviations, and so on. All these patterns of regularity are interwoven and intertwined, more or less coordinated in a specific social

space-time, by social agents who are engaged in more or less violent conflicts with some other agents that succumb to other patterns in other social space-time, practicing a particular regularity
of correction and change in cases of maladaptation, conflict, violent clashes, and so on.

8.022 Because all the regularities are limited in space and time and
because their reproduction is not inevitable, there is no limit to
the changes in the overall order made of the sum of these regularities, of their intertwining and mutual disruption. However, the
same logic we identified above for the family of superfluous evils
applies here, too. It is impossible to count all these regularities
simultaneously, not to speak of counting the order of their intertwining (and clearly the representation of regularity is part of the
production of the regularity, and there can thus never be a full
description of the entire complex), but it is nevertheless possible
to assume that at any given moment there is a finite condition of
social regularities that can be assigned a (family) name: the Social
Order. And maybe simply "the Social." In other words, society is
not a substance but a web of relations, of associations and communications, without beginning or end, without a source or a
basis, finite yet without an end, limited yet boundless (save the
source, the end, the basis, or the boundaries imagined and illus-
trated in various acts of representation, which are in turn boundless). This web, both limited and open to infinity, ensnares
innumerable (because uncountable) intertwined regularities that
are incessantly changing and time and again erasing the changes
they undergo, all the while reproducing the image of their permanence and order.[5]

8.023 Some regularities are inscribed on the bodies of people who
hardly know a thing about them, while other people know how to
read them and sometimes even turn a single regularity of this
kind into an identifying personal mark (her fleeting, almost invisible smile when she's embarrassed; his averted look, cutting off
eye contact when he loses patience). There are regularities that
people can recite time and again to demonstrate that they know,
that they are able, that they are allowed (the procedures and
explicit rules of games of every kind). There are regularities that
people know and deny, deny and know (the regularity of cases of
love at first sight among members of the same sociocultural class;
the regularity of cases of suicide among soldiers). The discourse
that gives expression to such regularities is critical and violent. It
forces knowledge, disallows denial; it compels people to admit to
what they wished to deny and pressures them not to take part in

it or, conversely, pushes them to deepen their denial. And there are regularities (though this is a very partial list) that are known to no one and cannot even be denied until they are given expression (for instance, the regularity of the appearance of cancerous growths among workers exposed to a substance not yet identified as carcinogenic; the regularity of violent outbursts among people with a particular hormonal problem; the regularity of military training accidents characterized by specific command features). The discourse that gives expression to such regularities is less violent (and perhaps less critical, too). It allows people to see the general pattern that they are part of or destined to; it allows people to try not to participate, which of course creates a new arena of struggle and denial.

8.024 One regularity is intertwined with another, sometimes this way, sometimes that. A visible regularity often testifies to a hidden one. To understand what sustains a given regularity, you visit another: from the regularity of miscarriages among a particular group of women to the regularity of their economic or family conditions, from the regularity of armed violence in a particular population to the regularity of power relations between various groups within it. Sometimes the passage is difficult: from the regularity of power relations between a teacher and his students to the regularity of power relations in the family, in the educational system, or in the complex system of relations spread among family, market, law, and an entire network of "care" institutions. In any case, the passage is never finite or complete. Only the regularity of mathematical games has a relatively simple formula, but even a complicated formula will not suffice, for the act of representation itself involves the reproduction and fragmentation of regularities, and the final decision on, and full understanding of, regularities are only possible within the complete order, the order of the totality, which is inaccessible even if it is there. Knowledge of the order is always partial; the complete order is just the family name of the complex of regularities, always but a name — God, Spirit, infrastructure, Being, a peg to hang all else on — and in fact nothing, no content, no form.

8.025 If knowledge is always partial, always of partial regularities, limited in time and space, then at issue here are complex contents and forms. We know a lot about various regularities in the production and distribution of superfluous evils: the economy of hunger in Africa; the outbreak of an epidemic; the sudden outburst of evils in the course of an act of terror and their more or less regular distribution over the unremarkable days of a routine state struggle against terrorists; the broad scope, the power, and the prolonged persistence of the movements of loss, damage, and suffering in times of war; crime, unemployment, and the destruction of the social fabric in the poverty-stricken inner cities of the world's megalopolises; disintegration within the family; the exemplary order of industrialized death in the Nazi camps and the less impressive, but no less distinct or effective, orders of annihilation on the Siberian steppe, or in the jungles of Southeast Asia and central Africa. A partial list. The physics, the geography, and the economics of loss and suffering are sciences that will one day appear (if science itself is not lost), but today we are already all too familiar with the regularities that they shall eventually study. Even if these sciences become highly sophisticated, they will never provide a final knowledge of a necessary order, only partial knowledges of regularities that are not inevitable. And there is no need to wait for such final knowledge. Even the partial knowledges at hand provide a basis for a very broad agreement on the kinds of regularities that should properly and urgently be disrupted due to the superfluous evils whose production they enable. The possibility of erring due to partial or doubtful knowledge is dwarfed by the certainty of the massive presence of Evil in certain parts of the world and in certain areas of the social sphere.

8.030   Every regularity is composed of discrete elements: actions, relations, products. A regularity of relations is always more difficult to discern than a regularity of the material products for whose production and appearance the relations are responsible. Marx knew that to understand the regularity of economic relations, he had to begin by understanding the discrete product, the commodity.[6] Soon enough he discovered that the discrete product itself led a double life: a unique, "sensual" life expressed in its use value; and a nonunique, "non-sensual" life expressed in the exchange value. Marx argued that the regularity of the appearance of commodities, what we may call the phenomenology of their production, exchange, consumption, and accumulation, could only be understood through deciphering the logic controlling the regularity of the exchange value of commodities (as the theorists of classic political economy already understood), and he proposed to understand the regularity of exchange values through the regularity in relations of production. The passage from a material and local regularity to seemingly more and more abstract, general, and "fundamental" regularities did not eliminate the phenomenological regularity of the appearance of commodities, that "a-sensual sensuality," as Marx called the commodity, because of its double life and the inversion of this duality in the consciousness of the naive bourgeoisie. I propose to think in a similar way about the regularity of the appearance of evils.

8.031 In the "naive bourgeois" consciousness, rich people have more commodities and more opportunities to enjoy them because they are rich, and the poor have fewer because they are poor. In the same way, people have more "troubles," that is, evils, and more opportunities to suffer from them because they are unfortunate, that is, rich in troubles, and the fortunate have fewer troubles because they are fortunate, that is, poor in troubles. But if we are to understand the regularity and accumulation of commodities/evils, we can't stay at the level of the "naive bourgeois" consciousness. It's necessary to identify the discrete product, the commodity/ evil, and to understand its double life, its sensual, experienced, "useful" facet from the "consumer's" point of view and its general exchange value: what a consumer is prepared to give in exchange for obtaining a good/preventing an evil. The exchange relations should be understood according to the regularity of the relations of production: who controls the resources producing the commodities/evils; what profits can the owners of the means of production gain from producing the commodities/evils; in what ways are they capable of organizing the production and accumulating the profits. And just as the capital owners are not generators but one type of product, among others, of the capitalist system, no less than the laborers they exploit, the owners of the capital employed for the production of evils are not the generators of any system for the creation of evils; their very participation in the production of evils, as well as their manner of participation, results from the system. However, the system is one of regularities; no participation is unavoidable.

8.032 The discussion up to this point (and especially in Chapters Three, Six, and Seven) can now be interpreted as an attempt to reify evils. Needless to say, this reification is a necessary stage in the attempt to deconstruct the reification pertaining to the production of goods and the reproduction of the social order in which this production has been naturalized. Reifying evils was a crucial step toward identifying the singular unit constituting the economy of Evil. Capitalist economy endows the commodity with the aura of a fetish, identifying it as a distinct unit, "preparing" it for the analysis of political economy. But this fetishization is a unique trait of capitalist economy without parallel in the moral realm. At the point where naive bourgeois consciousness knows how to identify the commodity as taken for granted, the naive moral consciousness only knows how to identify "evil states" — war, plague, unemployment — but not necessarily how to isolate the different units produced by the different kinds of Evil labor.[7]

8.033 However, the problem isn't just the naive consciousness of Evil but also the very complex social character of the production of superfluous evils. A distinctive expression of the difficulty in identifying a singular product of the system producing evils, and of the consequent difficulty in understanding the regularity with which the system operates, can be found in the catastrophes typical of the "postmodern condition" — a nuclear accident, an environmental disaster, mass terrorism, AIDS. The catastrophe is, as it were, a very large-scale experiment that all watch like sleepwalkers. In a catastrophe, not only the boundary lines between the different spheres of social action are blurred, but also the very capacity to distinguish between separate objects. The same object (the immune system, the stock market, a religious cult, or a nuclear reactor gone berserk), the same series of related occurrences (a nuclear leak, a hijacking, a bomb blast), the same event — the disaster is a target for the simultaneous yet different treatment of experts from all the social spheres.[8] And every individual expert operates in keeping with the logic driving the system she comes from; she has difficulty understanding the constraints of the other systems and their experts' modes of action. She finds it difficult to communicate with them, needs mediators, catastrophe experts. But catastrophe and expertise are diametrically opposed. There can be no experts on catastrophe. Catastrophe is the moment when the hyper-sophisticated coordination and interaction among spheres of actions become a mess of collapsing systems, a postmodern tower of Babylon. Catastrophe entangles almost all systems; the space for any action failing to conform to the logic of one of the social systems disappears; there is no grounding for even one foot placed so as to stay outside the systemic regime, although, and perhaps because, this regime is collapsing, imploding.[9]

8.034 But a catastrophic event may also be described as a culmination of the chronic problems of the "normal" state of affairs spread throughout the entire social space. The chronic problems of postmodern society — transport, pollution, particularly violent neighborhoods — are similar in character. They are handled simultaneously by experts from different systems, with uncoordinated tools and without the capacity of any one system to offer a synthetic point of view for addressing the problem. The same is true of dis-

tinctly civic issues such as preserving green lungs in densely populated areas (a matter handled by experts in the fields of urban
planning, transportation, real estate, recreation, and so on, representing science and technology, the market, local and central
government). Attempts by the various authorities to alleviate the
distress, to treat the "ailment," seem more and more like pissing
into the wind. No one really knows the "cause of the ailment";
getting to the "root of the problem" is an election slogan; and
holistic social medicine is a utopian vision that can no longer be
entertained. And all this is not because of the false consciousness
or blindness of a particular class or group to the suffering of
another, but because in the postmodern social space the problem
or the ailment usually has no "roots." "Postmodern" evils spread
through the social space like the "rhizome" described by Deleuze
and Guattari.[10] They are an immanent part of the operation of the
combined systems, not a sad deviation or a localized malfunction
causing disaster. "Systemic malfunction" is the permanent state of
the intricate web of social systems and a condition for their correct operation. Such, for instance, are traffic accidents, seemingly
"built in" to the structure of modern life, a phenomenon we are
doomed to accept along with cars and freeways in a package deal,
or "the drug problem," or "white-collar crime," and the varied
spectrum of "corruption scandals." Perhaps similar terms can also
be aptly applied to diseases such as cancer and AIDS,[11] not to
speak of enclosed institutions such as prisons, hospitals, and other
kinds of institutionalized "shelters,"[12] and all the more so of an
enclosed territory under occupation.[13]

8.035 The "investigative commission" is a political institution typical of
"systemic malfunction." It is none other than the belated, and all
too predictable, flip side of disaster. Its role is to quarantine the
malfunction now burst into public consciousness in the "deviant"
slot, thus providing a clean bill of health for the system in which
the real deviation is the correct operation that upholds its formal-
istic image. In those rare cases where attempts are made to implement the conclusions of an "investigative commission," when a
governing system actually tries to deal with the evils it distributes,
the result is often the transfer of suffering to other regions, a
redistribution of damages, and a continued inflation of the system,
creating more and more jobs for caretakers of various kinds in the
new mechanisms along with myriad opportunities to produce
new evils and to accelerate the distribution of existing ones. So it
is that every time the system's institutions confront disturbances
of the peace or disruptions of the order, as they do repeatedly,

they change the "open-fire regulations" applying to the instruments at their disposal. This is the onerous logic of the modern welfare state, linked through a clear continuum with the regime of occupation: through control mechanisms and the capacity for their rationalization (à la Weber), through good intentions and the competence to rationalize these (à la Freud).[14]

8.040 The globalization of Evil goes hand in hand with other globalization processes in all the spheres of human activity: the economy (especially through the transfer and exchange of money, commodities, and labor), the media, governance, the sciences, warfare, terrorism, tourism, sport, civil society (consisting of anything from humanitarianism to antiglobalization movements). Like capital, poverty, unemployment, epidemics, environmental pollution, terrorism, and drugs all know no borders. Each of these evils has its characteristic economy; each is embedded in other economies of horror, in just plain troubles, and in all kinds of goods, whose production is enabled by the production of evils and their specific modes of distribution. One regularity is intertwined with another; a visible regularity testifies to a hidden one.

8.041 The globalization of Evil has engendered new areas of knowledge and new mechanisms designed to care for injured and injury-prone populations. New bodies of knowledge and forms of discourse about the outbreak of epidemics, environmental pollution, drug use, burns, or toxic effects are integrated into the new care mechanisms operated by the state and by national and international civic authorities. In parallel, either in response to the globalization of Evil or as an integral part of other processes of globalization, organizations continuously founded worldwide, since the end of the nineteenth century, offer voluntary aid to the victims of various areas of horror. Some of these care mechanisms and most of these organizations, however rare and powerless they may be, are a distinct (though not exclusive) site of morality in these times — "site of morality" in the same sense that a museum is a site of art, a courthouse a site of law, a church a site of holiness, and a library or laboratory a site of knowledge. The logic guiding at least some of the activity of such morality sites derives from care for an other in distress. This care cannot be grounded in motives or values preceding the other's distress or in benefits that may be gained from it, even when such motives, values, and potential benefits are indeed combined with the care. This remainder of disinterested care for an other in distress is always at risk of being swallowed up by the structured "steering systems"[15] — the state, the market, or the media — and at risk of being manipulated by the powers at work within them, which exploit humanitarian action as a medium for manifesting their own interests. (In this aspect, too, the place of the moral is similar to the place of knowledge or of arts in modern Western society.) Under what conditions can moral action maintain its autonomy, and how does it combine with, or contradict, the logic of the action of other social systems? A discussion of these questions exceeds the limits of the present work.[16]

8.042 Since Kant at least, progress is perceived as, among other things, asymptotic progression in the realm of removing superfluous evils from the life of "humankind."[17] Is the world indeed progressing (at least since Kant's time)? A legitimate question. There are more than enough areas in which evils can be quantified: victims of war, of ethnic clashes, and of acts of terror; victims of natural disasters, of epidemics and famines, of urban violence, of poverty, of unemployment; changes in life expectancy and infant-mortality rates; and so on. Although no one datum will teach us anything much, ignoring the accessible data is tantamount to "unlearning." The huge growth in world population needs to be taken into consideration, of course, as does the connection between the growing capacity for expressing, documenting, and quantifying evils and the changes in their distribution, the dense entanglement of parameters for every single datum. It should also be kept in mind — this reservation is crucial and puts any kind of quantification into perspective — that not all evils are superfluous and that moral progress is relevant only to the latter. But the question's increasingly tangled complexity is not sufficient reason for dismissing it.

8.043 When the physics, the economy, and the geography of loss and suffering appear as independent areas of knowledge, it will be possible to start answering this question in an orderly manner. The answer should supposedly be "scientific" in any case, that is, experimental, hypothetical, and refutable (which obviously includes the ungrounded answers that we can already provide today). Meanwhile, be that as it may, it is worth posing the question clearly, keeping it on the agenda. Under no circumstances should we make do with the deep sigh over the state of the world emitted by the painter at the beginning of Shakespeare's *Timon of Athens*, whose tune Derrida admits repeatedly into one of his works. "It [the world] wears, sir, as it grows," says Shakespeare's painter. Echoing these words, Derrida adds, half-interpreting, half-completing them, "the world is going badly, the picture is bleak, one could say almost black."[18] "Le monde va mal," the state of the world is indeed very bad, but what point is there in such a statement if Shakespeare and Derrida can make it in such a similar way, can repeat and quote each other as if the four hundred years between them, the whole of modernity, simply didn't exist? Instead, it is worthwhile asking again, along with Kant, "Is the human race (as a whole) continually improving?"[19] We should properly begin asking how much evil, where, how, and why. In other words, one should study the regularities involved in the production of superfluous evils and their distribution, as well as their geographic and historical patterns of change, just as rainfall or the production of merchandise is studied.

8.050 Such a question, such sciences, such an arithmetic of Evil, needs to start out by standing Leibniz's theodicy on its head, by turning it upside down in at least three senses: thinking of the worst possible rather than the best possible world; replacing a principle of faith requiring proof with a hypothesis requiring repeated refutation; replacing the static state of the world guaranteed from time immemorial and forever with a historic process possibly leading to total catastrophe. The hypothesis to be refuted: that we are embroiled in a process of escalation toward the worst of all possible worlds or toward the worst possibilities for our world.[20] In other words, not only can the world be involved in moral regression, but the worst is yet to come.

8.051 This inversion will guard another axis central to the logic of Leibniz's argument. As we know, Leibniz thought that we live — and have always lived and will always live — in the best of all possible worlds. He saw Evil as situated in the particulars, in the partiality of the understanding of particulars torn from their place within the whole, and on this matter he had no argument with Spinoza. Good is perceived through thinking of the world in its totality and relative to all other possibilities, each as an independent ensemble and all together as the ensemble of all that is possible. At the same time, Leibniz's sanctification of what exists paradoxically allows him to be precise where others cut corners. Who can know the depths of the despair hidden behind his rationalist optimism? The truth is that only when you try to think our world as an ensemble — an ensemble of the regularities of social relations and the patterns of action responsible for the production and distribution of superfluous evils — do you begin to grasp how horrendous Evil is. Leibniz did not deny the factual dimension of Evil. Evils are not erased in Leibniz; they remain real beings vital to the achievement of good. In the best of all possible worlds, the fewest possible evils allow the greatest possible good. Accordingly, in the worst possible world, the smallest measure of good requires the greatest amount of evils. In other words, possible worlds may be compared in terms of the amount of evils required in each in order to produce the same amount of good. Evils that are necessary in a worse world become superfluous in a better one. In other words, in a bad world, or at least one that is comparatively worse, the amount of good achieved may perhaps be the same as in a better world, but it is achieved through evils that are superfluous in a better world.

8.052 Perhaps Leibniz was guided by deep despair, and perhaps, although he witnessed the destruction and horror caused by the Thirty Years War, he knew and saw only a fragment of the Evil of which man is capable. We, however, who have heard, read, and seen more, know that if this is indeed the best world that God could have created, then he merits the pity of the human beings he created (and perhaps this was his sole reason for creating them? Food for theological amusement). Either God is not truly good or he is not truly omnipotent, and in any case it's time to oust him from the game and free thinking about Evil from its tendency — due to him — to sanctify what exists. Without a God who, of necessity, chose the best of all possible worlds, it's necessary to talk about this world, the only one we have, and we can consider all the imaginable possibilities for this world to be other than it is. If the existing world is not an enclosed system that must be sanctified, then there is no need to move from one world to another, that is, from one possible total system to another; suffice it to repair the existing world. Repairing the world means erasing superfluous evils. The more superfluous evils accumulate in our world, the more it seems like the worst of all possible worlds. The more superfluous evils are erased from our world, the more it will seem like the best of all possible worlds.

8.053 There is no God to ensure growing proximity to the best of all worlds, and there is no devil who decrees a growing proximity to the worst of them. In fact, there are insufficient grounds for assuming that anyone ensures the repair of the world in advance, and insufficient grounds for assuming that anyone prevents such a process of repair in advance. But if repair occurs, or to the extent that it does occur, it is guided by the same demand that led Leibniz: to banish unnecessary, superfluous evil so as to ensure the goodness of the world. Banishing superfluous evil is man's, that is our, moral mission. Ours, if we are not prepared to acquiesce in or concede the Evil, if we are "inside morality," if we seek to do the job that God was too shortsighted to finish, or incapable of finishing, by the seventh day, or if we wish to repair what human beings made a mess of after God left them to their own devices. Because we live, forever and ever, on the seventh day, the day God rested from all his work which he had made.

8.1 *Good (or the Finitude of God)*

8.100   We know nothing about Good. More precisely, we know nothing about it in general, and we know nothing about it that allows its grounding in other concepts. We have no idea what Good is in and of itself. We have no concept of Good; Good is not a concept. Good is not in goods, even if a minimum of goods is a necessary condition for the possibility of happiness. We know there are miserable people "who have everything." There is no point in the various goods that a person can strive for and achieve — in all the forms of capital and reward, in spirit, in material form, in treatment — if they bring no enjoyment or fail to ensure the future possibility of enjoyment. (Or if they fail to reduce suffering and loss, but I've said enough of that.) Better put, the point of goods or their end is the enjoyment they make possible and the evils they help to prevent. At times, enjoyment is equated with pleasure and pleasure with happiness. We should first briefly outline a distinction between enjoyment and pleasure, and then dedicate a few more words (in passing) to happiness.

8.101   Enjoyment will be understood here as the opposite of pain, and pleasure as the opposite of suffering. The difference is a matter of intensification, turning a quantitative difference into a qualitative one. The opposition between pain and enjoyment consists in the difference between a disagreeable excitation, which I can bear, and an agreeable one, which I can do without. In suffering and pleasure, the excitation is intensified, and the opposition turns into one between "enough, I can't take it anymore" and "more, more, let it never end" (6.001). I believe that happiness is a form of enjoyment, not of pleasure, one agreeable excitation among many. I will try to characterize it. I think, for instance, of the excitation that floods me at specific moments in the presence of my children. Unlike the excitation that floods me when I meet my beloved after many days apart, excitation in the presence of my children is free from desire, free from any wish to achieve something, and neither is it the enjoyment accompanying an already-satisfied desire. It is the enjoyment that floods me when I'm presented with the expressions of a small child's love, with his smile, with his innocent joy, his complete enjoyment. I want more of this excitation, but this "more" is not the opposite of the excruciating "enough" in an excitation causing suffering; neither is it similar to the pleasurable "more" in the process of realizing desire. It is not demanding as they are, and when it ceases, it will not arouse sudden distress (the opposite of the relief when a tormenting excitation stops), nor will it arouse the frustration of an as-yet-unsatisfied desire.[21] This excitation doesn't make me aspire to exceed the boundaries of myself — so as to become an other, to turn into an other, or to merge with an other — or to appropriate the other, making her part of myself. It is an excitation that doesn't gather me into myself either, doesn't make me present to myself like someone in a state of autarky (according to the ancient ideal of being a free man), for clearly I need the enriching presence of my children in order to feel such excitement. Perhaps it is an ideal, transient state of complete equilibrium in my being with others: neither rejecting nor being rejected; neither swallowing nor being swallowed; neither striving toward nor being threatened by; neither evading the other nor wishing the other would disappear, leave me alone for a while or forever; neither standing guard in fear of her unwanted actions nor conspiring to get or hide something from her. The feeling of happiness in this case involves the very presence of the other, the very fact of my being in the other's presence, which makes present being in another's presence as a pleasurable encounter that one wants more of, without seeking to change a single thing in the encounter itself. The sense of self-sufficiency, the sense that I am sufficient for myself, which may fill me at some such moments, is not essential to the happiness. Each can exist without the other. At the same time, the sense of "together being sufficient for ourselves," myself and the others in whose presence I feel happy at the moment, is essential for happiness.

8.102 In excitation, "the presence of the encounter overshadows the presence of what is encountered — whether greatly or slightly — as well as the intentional character of the encounter itself" (5.001). In a happy excitation, the overshadowing encounter is with being in another's presence that causes me happiness. When I encounter my son's radiant smile, my daughter's free-flowing joy, I forget what I meant to ask of them, what I wanted to tell them; I experience myself experiencing their presence without asking anything more in particular. I encounter the very fact of my being in the presence of my children, and all I ask is that this encounter go on. The feeling of happiness that floods a child whose beloved dog or

423

cat has been lost when the pet suddenly returns can be thought of in a similar way. Or the feeling of happiness that floods me when I encounter myself in a landscape, when I am presented with an "outside," be it nature or a city, not just as something other than myself but as an environment in which I am situated, as a "world" that is my world, a world where I belong, and belong as what I am and what I may be without my being ever ceasing to be of this world. In happiness, I encounter this encounter as devoid of demands, not belonging to those paths of desires and wishes seeking satisfaction, of needs seeking fulfillment, of threats seeking preventive measures. If I know a sense of happiness when I am alone, with myself, this is not because I am full of myself but rather because I have reached that equilibrium of being-in-a-world that is my world. The feeling of happiness involves the very presence of the world around me, making me present to myself as one who has been lucky enough to have such a world and making present to me my being-in-a-world of this kind as "a pleasurable encounter that one wants more of, without seeking to change a single thing in the encounter itself" (8.101). I experience myself abandoning my self to the "outside," to my surroundings, opening up to these, because they open up to me, reveal themselves to me without disclosing any dark secrets or uncovering suspicious traces, without tempting or threatening, without soliciting or frightening, in that presence of "being-in" to itself seeking nothing for itself, other than continuing to be such, in peace and tranquillity or in the exhilaration of some action.

8.103 If this is the case, then happiness is not the self-affirmation of a self sufficient for itself, distancing itself from the other in an arrogant in-dependence. Neither is happiness the self-affirmation of the self that appropriates or merges with the other. Happiness is the very presence of self in the presence of another, the presence of being-with-another (and this other can be a person, an animal, an environment, a view, a work of art) that makes itself present as sufficient in itself without demanding anything either from the excited self or from the other whose presence is a condition for this happiness or its direct cause. Happiness is the antithesis of worry, not of suffering (see 8.114).[22] Happiness is not a continuous state or an emotional characteristic following from the removal of worry, but rather an excitation that contradicts it.[23] Because different excitations can coexist, beating in the same breast, struggling with each other within a single consciousness and body, someone can sometimes even be simultaneously happy and burdened with worries (contrary to Epicurus's view).[24]

8.104 More generally, perhaps happiness is an excitation following from the intensification of feelings of joy or gladness and peacefulness in the company of others, an excitation excited by the sense of sufficiency. However, it is not a self-sufficiency but a sufficiency of being-with-others or of being-in-an-environment and, even more generally, of the fact that I find sufficient my being myself alongside, or in the presence of, or around what I'm not; I find sufficient my "becoming-present-with-in-the-presence-of," in which "becoming-present" doesn't turn into "being-faced-with" or "being opposite," and the presence (of the other and of myself alongside the other) does not become a confrontation. Affirmative self-sufficiency belongs not to my self but to being-among-and-with-others or to being-in-the-world. Maybe this is what was understood by those who saw *vita contemplativa*, a life of contemplation, as the height of happiness. Maybe this was the belief of the Stoics, who equated happiness with wise resignation to the order of things. Perhaps this was what Spinoza, for instance, was thinking when he equated happiness with the "amor Dei intellectualis," namely, the thought of infinity from within finitude, accompanied by man's complete acquiescence in his place in the world and the world as his place.[25] Maybe that was what Socrates, Plato, and Aristotle were thinking when they equated philosophical dialogue with a kind of company (even if it takes place as "the conversation of the soul with itself," in Plato's words) that is present and experienced as sufficient for itself, not belonging to the daily course of desires and threats, a company achieved when all its members wisely direct the erotic arrow — or the will to power, the anxiety, and the lust — toward a common object of knowledge. There is no competition regarding this common object and shared objective. No one can achieve them by herself, and no one can keep them to herself, for the object of knowledge is a product of discourse and exists only within discourse, and the discourse (the Logos), according to its images in Plato or Aristotle, is none other than dialogue, a kind of company, a presence together of the participants who desire the very thing that all can share, seeking nothing but each other's company for the sake of that thing, until, out of the shared progress toward that thing, the amusement with it and with its images, the company is sufficient for itself.

— This ideal of a life of contemplation collapses in the face of Socratic irony, or in the face of the erotic view of knowing in Plato, in the face of the Nietzschean critique of the will to truth or Foucault's construal of discourse, and no wonder that even in ancient times there was a prevalent tendency to equate a contemplative life with the loneliness of the thinker rather than the company and comradeship of partners in philosophical discourse.

— True, but there is a lovely image and ideal of happiness here. And its structure conforms to a model similar to the figure of happiness I presented above. Because what is in question is a phenomenology of excitations that testify to themselves and not a disclosure of the truth about what "really" excites, there is no reason not to believe one who testifies that contemplation excites him in such a way.

8.105 It seems to me that I'm characterizing a kind of excitation that suits what other people, both close and distant, experience, but I have no reason to assume that others should not feel happiness or describe happiness as excitations of other kinds, and might even equate it with what they lack, which is not an excitation at all. Aristotle, too, to whom it is customary to attribute the equation of happiness with a life of contemplation, understood that happiness as perceived by "the wise" has no advantage over its perception by "the many." He places the various opinions on a single plane:

> Verbally there is very general agreement: for both the general run of men and people of superior refinement say that it is happiness, and identify living well and doing well with being happy; but with regard to what happiness is they differ, and the many do not give the same account as the wise. For the former think it is some plain and obvious thing, like pleasure, wealth, or honour; they differ, however, from one another — and often even the same man identifies it with different things, with health, when he is ill, with wealth when he is poor.[26]

I wish to join "the many" while proposing that they make precise distinctions: for instance, refraining from identifying every enjoyment as happiness and also the satisfaction of desire as happiness. But they can insist; they can always construct another "grid" and describe their own happy excitations within it. Possibly, I don't experience the same excitations they do, or don't experience them in the same way. When my beloved and I are excited together, I can't say whether her excitation is like mine; even if we prod our excitations all night long, we will still never know. So how can I claim as much of other, more distant people? How can I dare to claim as much of people from other cultures, far from mine in space or time? And why would I want to claim this at all? In any case, if happiness is a kind of excitation, one among many, and if these are its characteristics, it cannot be said that a definite kind of goods is capable of creating happiness, not to speak of construing happiness as the end aspired to through the obtainment of goods of any kind (8.101). Many goods create excitations, provide enjoyment and prevent suffering of other, various kinds. It is not clear whether happiness supersedes all of these or why it is purported to be the end of all other excitations. More precisely, in order for the happiness understood in this way to be the end of all other excitations, it has to receive its value from something else, placed at the top of the scale of values in another order of the real: self-sufficiency, for instance, or freedom, or knowing. But we do not have sufficient grounds to assume such a scale of values, and we definitely have no grounds for assuming its general validity. Thus, happiness is left an excitation among excitations. And it obviously cannot be equated with Good.

8.110 Instead of equating happiness with a kind of excitation and committing, in the process, to a unified typology of the expression and classification of excitations, we could define happiness in a more abstract, general, and less obligating way as the intensification of enjoyment, a kind of "full enjoyment," or a state in which one can partake of full enjoyment unimpeded. I assume that "unimpeded" is a more general and less obligating way to speak of removing the threat of dependence, on the one hand, and removing the compulsion of need or of desire, on the other. "Unimpeded" is a general, weakened form of "self-sufficiency," or "peacefulness," or "tranquillity." Even in the framework of this type of general discussion, I wish to insist on the difference between enjoyment and desire — a difference in concept, even if not always in experience as different people live it. Every desired object is desired in order to reduce suffering and/or increase enjoyment. But not every satisfaction of desire increases enjoyment, and not every enjoyment brings happiness. Sometimes people seek to satisfy a desire simply in order to remove the annoying want causing it; sometimes they seek the enjoyment of the satisfaction itself. Desire and enjoyment can be obtained at the price of torment. Many people make do with enhancing satisfied desires (or with reducing tormenting desires). Sometimes they also seek to reduce the tormenting excitations involved in the satisfaction of desire, but sometimes they seek to enhance these (for instance, when satisfying a desire causes greater enjoyment the worse the torment becomes, and the desirer is strong enough to withstand this torment, even though it also generates the contradictory desire to be rid of the torture). Relatively few people seek to enhance their enjoyments when this involves torment.

Even fewer seek happiness in its abstract sense or, in other words, attempt to organize their lives to create the conditions allowing them the largest possible amount of, and the most complete, enjoyments, unimpeded. Sometimes they equate happiness with a single, very intensive, continuing enjoyment. Sometimes they wish to subject the wild economy of enjoyments and desires to the single enjoyment they identify as happiness, to subjugate all other enjoyments to this one while totally denying them. Philosophers in particular have shown such a tendency. Suffice it to mention Plato, the Stoics, Spinoza.

8.111 This economy of desires, enjoyments, states of happiness, of want, of torment, is not enclosed and insular; it is not guided by hierarchical principles of attaching value or by set rules of exchange. This evening I long for love, and tomorrow morning I will be happy to again be absorbed in my writing. Or vice versa. I know what it is to satisfy a desire without enjoyment of any kind, and what it is to enjoy without any accompanying desire, either prior to or after the enjoyment. I enjoy massages enormously, but almost never feel any real desire to make an appointment with a masseuse. I know how to enjoy good food even when I'm not hungry. Enjoyments of the same kind bore me when presented to me too frequently, but I know that others can succumb to the selfsame enjoyment time and again. I know there are desires (not just satisfactions of desires) that people are prepared to pay for, in which it wouldn't occur to me to invest a cent, and there are enjoyments that other people hold in very high regard which leave me completely indifferent. I also know there are desires and enjoyments that are seen by many as inferior, prohibited, and even immoral — a view that may intensify the desire and enhance the enjoyment — which I, for my part, either desire or am indifferent to, yet prepared to satisfy, and able to enjoy in complete indifference to their value for others. I have no interest (and of course no desire) in subjecting the many-branched economy of possible desires to a single controlling law and in setting a uniform scale for measuring the values of enjoyments. Even if I had such an interest (or desire), this economy could not be unified. A uniform scale of values of enjoyment, or at least a procedure for evaluating enjoyments and desires, necessitates a single moral language and the erasure of the *différend* between different genres of enjoyment discourse.[27] The philosopher, who was supposed to stand "witness to the *différend*," cannot build on its erasure. Moreover, the teachings of Plato's *Symposium*, too, should be kept in mind (Plato perhaps provides the paradigm of such an erasure, of which all future erasures will present but pale repetitions): the huge amount of denial and sublimation invested in that erasure. Admittedly, it was from this work that philosophy itself sprang: the love of wisdom, the love of Good, the love of beauty, the rational love of God, the love of destiny. An eroticization of the concept, devoting oneself to Eros as a concept, making love to reason, all this might have been no sin if it weren't for all the forbidden touches and all the touched forbiddings it engendered. But one born in sin need not go on sinning. The eroticism of the concept is not the end of philosophizing; neither is it a condition of philosophizing, not to speak of being a substitute for other kinds of erotic relations. At most, for those thus blessed, it is a small side benefit.

8.112 Therefore, I have no interest in a general procedure allowing the evaluation of objects of desire and enjoyment as a basis for the development of an instrumental morality necessitating the reification of enjoyment and tending toward erasure of the positive presence of suffering by turning it into enjoyment or its negation. In fact, it should be questioned whether desire and enjoyment are moral categories at all, and if they are, how they have turned into these, and whether today's permissive culture allows the re-separation of desire from morality. However, these are questions for a genealogy of morality, of desire and enjoyment, which I cannot address here.[28]

8.113 If desire and enjoyment are not moral categories, it follows that happiness, too, when perceived as complete enjoyment or as a state that enables unimpeded complete enjoyments, is not a moral category. Not even when I seek the happiness of another, save when that other in her state of severe distress is longing for a moment of happiness. When the other is in distress, regardless of what has caused it — lack of happiness, lack of water, lack of love, a toothache, boredom, humiliation, hurt, or loss — I am always called upon to help. I can help the other longing for happiness by causing her a little happiness, or by enabling her to cheer herself up, or by teaching her to suffer less in the life she is forced to live, which allows so little happiness and so little chance of attaining more happiness. Does the lack of happiness make a difference in terms of morality? That is, is happiness a thing whose lack creates a specific evil? And conversely, does a longing for happiness generate specific evils? I don't think there are any grounds — phenomenological or conceptual — for a general affirmative answer.

8.114 As stated above, happiness, as an excitation situated in the realm of the enjoyable, is not the opposite of suffering. Suffering is the converse of pleasure, not of enjoyment (which is the converse of pain) or of happiness (which is the converse of worry [8.103]), and pleasure is not identical with happiness. If happiness is perceived as a kind of excitation, pleasure cannot be identical with it, for it is defined as the enjoyable intensification of excitation in general, of any excitation (6.001); if happiness is viewed as "full enjoyment" or a state allowing one to "partake of full enjoyment unimpeded" (8.110), then pleasure cannot be identical with happiness, for it can occur in terrible tension, in the face of various kinds of interference. Moreover, when happiness ends, it is not necessarily followed by suffering, and when suffering ends, it is not necessarily followed by happiness. The unbearable superfluity of suffering (at least from the sufferer's point of view) has no analogue in enjoyment, the lack of which can be borne easily. Even the deprivation created by tormenting desire is one not of enjoyment but of the satisfaction of what is lacking, whose tormenting presence can be spoken of in terms of superfluous suffering more usefully than in terms of a lack of enjoyment. True, suffering is perceived as an overburdening excitation, an encounter in which one seeks to cut off contact (6.000), and enjoyment can be said — inversely, as it were — to continue for as long as the enjoyable excitation occurs in good measure. But suffering can be grounded in the "overmuch," in repleteness, in superfluity, for suffering is caused by the excessive burden, regardless of what it is that overburdens, whereas enjoyment cannot be grounded in the good measure, for there can be enjoyment in excessive measure (of food, for example), and the good measure requires knowing the good measure of what (and not every beneficial thing administered in good measure — medications, for instance, dietetic foods, or physical exercise — causes enjoyment).

8.115 This can also be formulated in a picturesque form as follows: enjoyment, pleasure, and happiness, and the Good whose components the former are purported to be, are as elusive as foam on the waves; suffering and loss, and the Evil whose components these are, are forever stuck like some hump in the state of affairs. It's easier to grasp them, as one grasps a protuberance, in order to pull the description of the state of affairs from what is to what ought to be, in order to describe the state of affairs under a moral imperative. Evil appears regularly, the regularity of its appearance is its way of being, and it is not easy to escape it when it is present or made present (or represented), even when it concerns very distant others. In contrast, happiness is elusive and random. Therefore, I tend to miss it time and again, even when it is my own happiness, and all the more so when it is the happiness of others. I hardly know how to recognize it when it appears among others close to me, and I know even less about how to cause it to appear. I have, on several occasions, attempted to bring my loved ones happiness and failed, because I did not achieve the right measure, right time or place. The happiness of more distant others interests me less, and I invest no effort in it; the happiness of even more distant others interests me not at all — "it's none of my business." There is no call in this happiness, no imperative, not when it is absent and definitely not when it is present. And as for my own happiness, if I seek to surrender to it, to take care of myself, invest efforts in myself, submerge myself in self-love, so as to become happy — that is not a moral matter (except by way of negation, for this self-love may prevent me from hearing or seeing others who need my help, or it may impede my acting on their call).

8.120   This fundamental difference between Evil and happiness, and the Good it is purported to stand for, and the difference in the possible use one can make of these concepts as moral categories are implied as far back as Socrates, when he claims, in Plato's early dialogues, that it is better to bear evil than to do evil. According to the legend told by Plato, Socrates knew how to identify Evil with relative ease and could therefore avoid it with relative ease. While Socrates attributed this ease to a demon that warned him against doing evil every time he might have been tempted, not one Athenian citizen entertained any doubt that the things forbidden to Socrates by the demon were evil deeds. On the other hand, Socrates in the early dialogues doesn't know what Good is, and therefore Good cannot serve him as a moral guide. He says nothing positive about Good in the early dialogues. Notably, though, when Socrates seeks to avoid doing evil, he is caring for himself, his soul, his virtues, his existence as a "good and beautiful" citizen of the polis. It is not care for the other that guides him but rather care for himself. In this sense, Socratic care of the self, which stresses the avoidance of doing evil, amounts to one version of an ethics founded on "care of the self" and on making the self exemplary.[29]

8.121   Happiness was a central category of ethics in ancient philosophy, and the proper regime of enjoyments was a focal point in the problematization of ethical discourse. Plato, and all the critics of hedonism who followed him, saw the regime of enjoyment or pleasure[30] as an insufficient basis for creating an example of a virtuous life, no matter how refined and civilized the enjoyments or pleasures subject to this regime. Enjoyments need a law, a tyrant even, or they may impose their own tyranny through the desires they arouse. For Plato, this tyrant is the Form of the Good.[31] Christianity, which absorbed Neoplatonic elements, construed this tyrant as religious law, epitomized in the ideal of celibacy. Later, the link between happiness and Good gradually weakened, until its complete disappearance in modern times. Modern Western ideologies presume to administer and regulate enjoyment and pleasure, but not happiness, socially. When justice or freedom replaces Good in modern times as the supreme moral category, the social law of enjoyment is supposed to ensure the universality of the right — and sometimes the universality of the opportunity — to obtain enjoyments and of protection, either common or particular, from the injury caused by unbridled attempts to obtain enjoyments. Even the utilitarians, who grounded Good in the maximization of utility and enjoyment while ensuring a maximum amount of enjoyment to the maximum number of people, could not promise anyone happiness other than the sum of all enjoyments and pleasures.

8.122 Good is not happiness, although happiness can be boundless Good. As is well known, happiness is fleeting. A moment after it is gone, I may understand that the very thing that made me so happy hastens my ruin: the woman who is happy tonight in the arms of the man who will torment her for the rest of her life; a happy evening in the company of friends who will betray me tomorrow or simply divert my attention away from what is most important for me; a whole world "opening up" to me only to eventually enslave me; a happy appointment to a coveted position that will turn me into a lackey of the power and authority I hold. These clichés are well known (but sometimes truth is clichéd). And nevertheless, wasn't happiness, at the moment of happiness, a realization of Good, or at least its locus? Of course not; in all these examples, it was the locus of imminent disaster. And the excitation itself, is there no point in identifying it with Good? No. Happiness is enough, a sufficiently elusive concept; Good adds nothing to it. Of course "it's good to be happy," but this Good depends on an active unknowing attitude toward whatever engenders the happiness. People who seek a moment of happiness with all their hearts are prepared to deny and forget a great deal, to look away, to protect their happiness with the force of their cheering ignorance. An understanding of the impending ruin creeps into the happy moment itself and destroys it from within. And there is no need to know every future thing that the happy moment will bring; a consciousness of the moment's finitude is enough. To be

happy, one must forget, or at least pretend to forget, how close the
end of happiness is. This is a mirror image of the view put forth by
Solon, who was so painfully aware of this finitude that he sought to
delay evaluation of a person's happiness until the day of his death.
The price that Solon, Plato, and Aristotle were prepared, gladly, to
pay was the dissociation of happiness from enjoyments and other
agreeable excitations and a distinction between what a person
knows about her happiness and what others know about it. If happiness is equated with a person's good condition as perceived and
evaluated from the allegedly general or objective point of view of
an other, purporting to encompass her entire life, no wonder the
ancients found it so hard to distinguish between happiness and
Good, and to this end needed to enlist new arguments and even to
distance Good beyond the limit of human reality, or beyond being
altogether. But if happiness is a kind of excitation, the excited one
is its only witness; the others can only be partners in this act of
witnessing indirectly, and their testimony doesn't count. It is possible, then, to try to restore Good to the realm of human experience as a general moral category without grounding it in the
calculus of enjoyments. And yet I don't know precisely what this
Good is beyond enjoyment and utility, though I know that many
have tried to speak of it. If my point of departure is excitation,
then I can account for happiness as a general category of a type of
private experience but not for the common Good as a moral category. From a moral point of view, an account of happiness neither
adds nor subtracts; meanwhile, lacking a reasonable and acceptable account of the common Good, we are all the more pressed to
look for a reasonable account of the common Evil. But I'm anticipating later parts of this discussion.

8.123   If happiness is transient and its finitude seeps into the consciousness of one-who-is-happy to the point of deflating the excitation,
then a certain degree of unknowing is vital to happiness. If happiness is nevertheless equated with Good or seen as one of its components, then a certain unknowing is a condition for Good. Is it
possible that Good is grounded in unknowing, that a happy ignorance is among its components? Plato saw the Form of the Good as
the supreme object of knowing and what grants thinking the very
possibility of its existence, by granting entities their intelligible
being.[32] But Plato never said what Good was. Is it possible that at
the end of the long journey we will find that the desired object of
knowledge was to know unknowing as a condition of happiness?
Perhaps this is not so different from what mystics have thought,
both in the East and in the West: unknowing of entities as what

they are, and of time as that which changes entities, which creates and annihilates, renews and ages, intensifies and corrupts; voiding the self of all knowledge of the emergent and ending entities in order to succumb to eternal Being, but devoid of any particular object. However, at issue here once again is happiness alone, the happiness of the individual whose journey of self-voiding achieves success. Good doesn't become a concept this way, although one might say a few things about the means of attaining it, which would again be no different from the attainment of happiness.

8.124 Good can be thought of as an idea in the Kantian sense — a concept unintelligible to the senses and denoting a totality that cannot be realized in experience. Ideas can be thought but not known, Kant believed, and it can therefore be said that the idea of Good is foreign to knowledge and a certain degree of ignorance might, in principle, be one of the components of the historical processes reducing the gap between reality and idea. After all, didn't Kant (who anticipated Hegel on this matter, as on many others) think of human shortsightedness, including the stupidity of war and its calamities, as a necessary moment in the process of progress, which is progress toward supreme Good?[33] Happiness in Kant's moral theory is meticulously separated from moral law, but so is Good. The unconditional duty to obey the law as a general form of moral judgment is neither good nor happy, but simply what ought to be done, the right or the proper thing to do. The good-will involved in this judgment is nothing but the will to do one's duty. The Good itself is the (happy?) union of doing one's duty (what ought to be done, the right or proper thing) and attaining the happiness of which one is worthy.[34] One who obeys the law, making it the supreme guide of her actions, one who orients herself toward the law as to an end in itself — that is, acts out of honor for the law and transcends any consideration of self-love when it contradicts the law — both acts properly and properly deserves happiness. Where does that notion of being worthy or deserving happiness come from in Kant? From the remnants of the theodicy left by his critical philosophy, things that cannot be known but whose possibility may be rationally believed and whose realization may be hoped for. And where did hope come from? From the longing for happiness. This longing is a demand for harmony in human existence, a quasi-aesthetic demand for the removal of the superfluous and the unjustified (the wicked who are happy and the righteous who are miserable), and for a just distribution of happiness. In Kant's view, this is a necessary completion of the categorical imperative — being interested in, and working toward, bettering the world.[35] In any case, when one who properly deserves happiness indeed finds it, Good is realized. The "supreme" Good is the situation in which such a happy coincidence becomes history's regular course. Hence the Kantian Good is not totally foreign to happiness; it contains it as a necessary but insufficient component. One who is happy achieves Good only if she acts morally and if she properly deserves her happiness. One who acts morally and properly deserves happiness attains Good only if she really reaches happiness.

8.125 Kant's supreme Good is an idea of harmony between happiness and the moral desert of happiness. Lesser good is what advances this harmony, which is the best of all possible worlds. Even in the best of all possible worlds, Evil will not be eliminated, according to Kant, for radical Evil will remain, the Evil inherent in the root of human nature (see below). Will Evil recede? On the one hand, Kant speaks of progress in the realm of moral conduct, until "the human being always behaves in accordance with moral laws," and, on the other, he discusses a balance between reward and punishment such that "[we see that] the wanton criminal would rather not die until he has suffered the well-deserved punishment for his misdeeds."[36] This is not sufficient, for Evil is not necessarily a result of immoral conduct, and the prevention of Evil is not necessarily a result of moral conduct, and in addition the torment of the criminal who "gets what he deserves" only adds suffering upon suffering. But it should be kept in mind that for Kant, Good is the opposite of wickedness, a characterization of the subjective rule guiding action, or, in other words, a characterization of intention and not of results; so a reduction of this wickedness is ensured when a person conducts himself in keeping with moral laws. In a bettered world, there will be fewer wicked people, more people will be properly deserving of happiness, and fewer people will suffer the superfluous evils caused by people who have acted improperly, putting considerations of self-love above moral law. Kant doesn't explain exactly how such a world will be attained, but he claims that some historical indications point to the possibility of approaching it — the moral aspiration of humanity revealed through the French Revolution, for instance, or the achievement of a lasting and sustainable peace among nations on the horizon of political action.[37] Viewing the French Revolution as a sign of progress requires overlooking the horrors it generated (see 8.312),[38] and admiring the general progress in realizing freedom requires overlooking the fact that this progress also opens up new possibilities for causing evil. We can continue this train of thought by talking about the superfluity of the evils caused by wars, "the greatest evils which oppress civilized nations,"[39] or alternately of "the grave of universal despotism," which is even more "incurably evil" than war (8.311).[40] But whether we demand a just distribution of happiness or the reduction of superfluous evils, the concept of Good itself will again turn out to be superfluous. Kant would have been more faithful to the critical spirit if, rather than speaking of the imperative to approach the supreme Good, he had spoken of the obligation to reduce the common evil.

8.130 If we take into account the need to better the world, we must also consider the following: even an action motivated by the best of intentions and performed out of complete respect for moral law, an act guided by careful and serious considerations of all the possible consequences, even such an act can do evil. Even an actor who possesses all the virtues listed by Socrates as traits of the good and beautiful man — temperance, courage, piety (or righteousness), and wisdom — is only the beginning of a chain of actions and reactions, the end of which is unknown. The human act is infinite in principle, Arendt says in this context; it generates a new beginning, but it cannot control what this beginning will in turn generate.[41] "A deed's end lies in the thinking that precedes it,"[42] but the deed has no end, its outcome is infinite, due to the finitude of thinking, due to the limited human ability to calculate the expected outcome. The gap between intention and consequences calls for and is immediately filled by new deeds. This gap is incalculable. What makes its calculation impossible, foolish, and hopeless is the existence of others who are free, whose every action is also a new beginning, a new chain of actions and reactions. Human freedom involves an immanent unknowing that undercuts the possibility of knowing whether the thing aspired to is truly good, what its side effects will be, which effects will follow from the act intended to attain Good.

8.131 This logic obviously applies as well to an action directed toward reducing Evil. But abstaining from action is itself a kind of action, a form of conduct one chooses from among several alternatives. As in every case of choice, the advantage of every alternative should be considered relative to other alternatives. And even if someone proves that inaction is always preferable, this entails multiple acts (persuasion, study, contemplation, setting an example) to distribute an ethic of inaction. Whether Good or the reduction of Evil is taken to be the end of moral action, there is no certain knowledge guiding this action, only presumptions and conjectures that a practical reason (*phronesis*) carefully considers. In both cases, one acts according to what, in the given circumstances, seems to be proper — the act ensuring the maximum Good or the maximum reduction of Evil. But the two possibilities are asymmetrical. The expected results of the action are equally shrouded in mist, but not the point of departure. In the first case, the decision to act involves a hypothetical image of the state of Good; in the second, it involves a concrete knowledge about Evil present in the real world in which the action is taken.[43]

8.132 Presence alone is not evidence, at most it is a temptation to know (4.530–4.531), and the presence of Evil, unlike the presence of suffering or loss, needs to be interpreted based on the traces of the regularity with which superfluous evils are created. The victim's call is never enough. Nevertheless, the difference stays intact. If Good is the source of the imperative to act, it is not what is good for me and you at this moment, that which will cause us enjoyment or prevent us from suffering, and it cannot be grounded in or reduced to something other than itself — Evil, happiness, suffering, or pleasure. The Good that prescribes the proper act is what is good in general, Good in and of itself, or perhaps the concept or the Form of the Good. But Good in and of itself cannot be interpreted from its traces in the world, because the Good itself is always absent, its presence leaves no traces, there is only Evil that testifies to Good as what is always still not or already not there. Good has imagined figures that may be represented by certain situations and states of affairs in the world, by allegories and metaphors indicating its absence and substituting for it. Our visual culture is replete with such figures: a child's happy smile, the peacefulness of a rural home, a man and a woman embracing, the grateful look of a miserable person whose call of suffering has been answered. Our textual culture is less familiar with them — the moment one tries to en-tongue Good, the idyll begins to crumble. Evil, on the other hand, needs no metaphors; there are myriad metonyms for it (later I'll mention a few of them by name [9.000 on]).

8.133 From this point, there's a possibility of swiftly reaching Plato's conclusion: Good is situated beyond Being. There is no need to continue along Plato's path, to determine as he does that Good exceeds Being in its awesome grandeur and power, granting Being its very existence and intelligibility.[44] Maybe it's enough, as proposed by Lévinas, to extricate from this key text of Plato's his main insight: the view of Good as a stubborn resistance to the closure of Being in thought, to the folding of being-there into a consciousness of being-there, to the understanding of Being as a totality becoming clear to itself through the Concept (Spinoza, Hegel), or hidden, forgotten behind concepts (Heidegger), but always enclosed, contained within itself as one, containing within itself all its contradictions, all its negations, everything it is not, and even nothingness itself. Resisting this conception of Being, Lévinas wishes to identify Good with breaking the apparently closed economy of the ego and the transcendence of the I toward that complete otherness that lies beyond being yet bursts into it, leaving there its traces in the face of concrete others, calling upon the I to open itself to what exceeds the being that encloses it.[45] This possibility cannot be dismissed just because of its religious pathos. There's no way to simply banish the thought demanding the right to speak in the name of a radical alterity that will never be revealed and whose traces are nevertheless everywhere. One cannot ignore the magical power of the other's face, the magician in another's face that always reflects something beyond the visible, testifying to this absent presence of otherness[46] — testifying to its being beyond human essence ("au-delà de l'essence"), which the face symbolizes, and to its not being some thing that is there like any other ("autrement qu'être").[47]

8.134 But why equate transcendence with Good in the first place? That is possible only if the totalization of Being is equated with Evil and if the dialectic between the same and the other is overcome by a thought capable of thinking the other without naming it, without positing it as an object of thought and without ascribing to it any form of being. If the totality of Being is indeed Evil — that is, if it is possible to transcend this Being without that transcendence immediately becoming another mode of being, and if the other to which transcendence aspires can indeed be desired by the I transcending itself without assuming any reciprocal relation of the other to this I — then Lévinas's equation is valid, and ethics should indeed be preoccupied with the Good, that is, with transcendence. But these assumptions, on which Lévinas bases both his ethics and his critique of metaphysics, are dubious. One may and should reject them without falling back on the metaphysics rejected by Lévinas. It is not Being as such, either its (imagined) totality or its (impossible) closure, that should be equated with Evil, but only the superfluity in Being. It is true that some superfluous evils may be ascribed to the attempt to imagine the closure of Being and to action taken on the basis of this closure, but this is no reason to associate Evil with closure itself, which in any case remains an imaginary construct of thought. The transcendence of being is a mode of being of the I, a basic feature — an existential (*existenzial*) structure, Heidegger would have called it[48] — of its relation to others, both concrete (one's neighbor, one's mother) and imaginary (God, demon), both particularized (this landscape, this work of art) and generalized (the state, the nation). As Derrida has convincingly shown, radical alterity is not merely an empty signified that has no relation to the language in which it is signified and about which nothing can be said, but a discursive figure as well, and as such it is forever entangled with a series of signifiers, differences, and negations, through which it is constituted as what it is (not).[49]

8.135 Lévinas is careful to equate Good not with what is beyond being — for nothing can be said about that, not even that it is beyond being — but with the transcendence of being itself. But the pathos of the first lines of his book *Totality and Infinity* leaves no room for doubt: human reality is a war in which everything human is embroiled — politics, economy, culture. Peace is the total negation of the historical form of the human world, not of this or that state within it; peace is a messianic state of being beyond history. Messianism is an unprecedented outburst of total otherness into being. Ethics is preoccupied with this otherness and is therefore an eschatology.[50] Even if this is the case (or precisely because this is the case), all we can do in the meantime, until the Messiah comes, is leave Good to the Messiah and go on talking about the Evil in this world, about the concrete individuals, others, but never complete or pure others, who suffer from it in defined and changeable political circumstances, and about the very down-to-earth possibilities for creating change.

8.140 By positing evils as the first object of a moral interest and as morality's utmost concern, we have actually proposed a theory of morals that is neither an "eschatology" nor an "optics,"[51] but rather a special branch of ontology, of an ontology that has long given up the dream of an enclosure of Being (or of history, or of the text) and thinks the possible as a modality of being and thinks what is there in light of what could have been and could still be there. A theory of morals that has gone through the ontological turn has no interest in Good. Good neither adds nor subtracts in moral matter. We have no interest in Good, whether it is understood as happiness or as what gives happiness its value and weight, just as it gives value to any other entity that is-there, that isn't there, or that should properly be there. Not the Good that isn't there, but the superfluous loss and suffering, present in their excess, is the imperative. Not the absent Good, not even the absence of Good, but the presence of superfluous evils. Not what is lacking or even the lack itself, but the superfluity of the tormenting lack, the lack that can be fulfilled and removed. Not the generosity or the fairness, but the humiliation and the injury that can be avoided and removed. Not the virtue but the unnecessary brutalization whose results should be stopped. People who have undergone horrible suffering or irreplaceable loss may never again know how to be happy. Memories will haunt them, mistrust toward every person may sabotage every relation they seek to create, torment of mind and body will continue to plague them. The imperative to stand beside them concerns not their future happiness but their present torture.

8.141 This, however, is not a claim for prioritizing present over future and past in principle. The people whose lives are saved and whose torment is prevented by correct planning on the part of health services, flight controllers, administrators supervising travel in dangerous areas — in short, by anyone responsible for reducing risks in various circumstances — will not be happy due to their protection from an epidemic, a plane crash, an earthquake, or falling off a precipice. Most probably, their lives will continue as usual, mainly passing in mundane daily existence; they will be preoccupied with the worries or pleasures of the trip that might have ended in a disaster of which they know nothing. All this has no necessary connection with Good or happiness. The steps taken to prevent their suffering and loss were guided by the capacity to predict these, by the capacity to prevent them, and by the imperative to prevent superfluous suffering and loss.

8.142 It's possible, of course, to define Good as the prevention of superfluous suffering and loss. But such a statement would neither add nor subtract, only provide some work for an unemployed concept. The reduction of superfluous evils is the definition of what is right, or proper, in short what ought to be done. How does "Good" add to "what ought to be done" in the statement "Good is what ought to be done"? Does it change what should be done? Should one act differently now that one knows it is good to do what ought to be done? Was not the ought enough?

8.143 When the predicate "good" is added to the descriptive statement "this is what ought to be done" (a description of a prescription), one gets a statement of appreciation: "it is good to do what is to be done." An appreciation implies, among other things, a point of view: there is someone in whose eyes it is good to do what is to be done. The addressee of the prescription may need that point of view; she may be too weak to overcome her hesitation and pay the price for doing what ought to be done. Although the predicate initially refers to an act (the act that ought to be done), its slide from act to person is too often quick and unnoticed. Good people always do what ought to be done; lesser people do that less often; weak and wicked people constantly fail or refuse to do what ought to be done. Goodness is a way to psychologize morality and put an end to moral questioning.

8.144 The need for an external eye that accompanies the doer of good deeds cannot be denied. Some need their mother, others their best friends; some need a "big other," and for many this other is still God. In fact God is the ultimate other in whose eyes acts (and consequently persons) appear and are measured as good or bad. He is omniscient, and hence knows the outcome of every action and therefore cannot err about what ought to be done. But everyone would readily agree that it is good to do what ought to be done, for this statement is a kind of tautology. In this case, even God is redundant.

8.150 Either there is or there isn't a God. If there is a God, it is necessary to explain why a world that could have been less evil is so replete with superfluous evils. All answers that ascribe Evil to human limitations should be sent back to their authors with the demand for an answer to why an omnipotent and boundlessly good God created human beings (and animals) so limited, why human limitation must be expressed through such a variety of horrendous forms of suffering, and why human beings need such suffering to understand that Evil is merely an "absence" (which animals won't even understand for all the suffering in the world). After dismissing answers of this type and insisting on the reality of the presence of Evil, we are left with only three possible answers: either God isn't omnipotent, or there are limits to his goodness, or both. Perhaps God created the world in a moment of weakness, in a spirit of wickedness; or perhaps he was exhausted by previous attempts at creation and could do no better. Maybe now he is exhausted, too, or not good enough to repair his work. Holding on to a transcendental God, the creator and leader of the world, entails separating the transcendental from the absolute or, conversely, making do with the enormous, in fact infinite, gap between human finitude and divine finitude. It is possible, if one insists, to grant God virtual infinitude. It is even possible to restore all his potency or all his goodness. But it is impossible to restore both. In other words, the unavoidable choice is among a wicked God, an exhausted God, or a dead God. And the responsibility for making this choice is ours.

8.151 Let's examine the possible answers briefly, one by one.

A. God isn't omnipotent. If he could have, he would have created a better world. Because he didn't create such a world, he is apparently not omnipotent. If indeed his potency is limited, this is not his fault. Accordingly, God should be exempted from feelings of guilt and pangs of conscience for failing to prevent such a terrible world when the possibility of a less terrible world exists. We would be better off were God to try to repair the reparable parts of what he ruined rather than suffer for what is irreversible. The last time God repented his deeds, he piled evil upon evil and caused a horrible disaster that spread from one end of the earth to the other, a disaster of which the rainbow, intended to make us forget it, reminds us every time it appears as a sign of the renewed covenant God made with man.[52] And what is this covenant if not an eternal sign of God's tormenting remorse?

B. God's goodness is limited. He could have but didn't wish to. If so, we're better off with his suffering in silence rather than sharing with us his pangs of conscience for the evil that he caused us when he created our world the way it is. He can, and maybe does, have other worlds, and perhaps he's playing among them, switching them with each other without our knowing. Maybe right now he's watching over some other world altogether. We, in any case, neither have nor can have any other world. Let the good God leave us to ourselves to make do somehow with what there is. If he's so inconsiderate as to wish to be the victim of the horror that he himself created, we would be better off trying to rid ourselves of him, along with all his emissaries and spokesmen.

C. God is not omnipotent, and there are limits to his goodness. Every line in the Book of Job testifies to this. Were he omnipotent, he would have had no need to enter into negotiations with the devil. He could have restored to Job everything he robbed from him. Although Job fathered new sons and daughters, God did not restore his dead. If I were Job, I would not be comforted by this lesser evil. Were God boundlessly good, he would not have been so arrogant toward the poor man in his speech from the tempest. He would not have robbed him of the only thing Job asked for after all the horrors he went through, the ability to give meaning to his misfortune. A better God would have helped Job find such meaning and would perhaps have uttered a word of remorse. If God has some calculus of good and evil that we'll never understand, it is irrelevant to happiness and suffering in this world; it is outside the realm of moral discussion, beyond Good and Evil. If it is outside morality, would God and his spokesmen and interpreters, adherents and messengers, doubles and substitutes, all kindly leave the premises and free moral discussion both from the absence of his presence and from the nagging burden of theirs.

8.152 Some theodicies limit God's omnipotence, but not one of them limits his unbounded goodness. The reason for this, Francis Wolff explains, is that any damage to God's unbounded good would pull the rug out from under the moral address directed to him.[53] What point will there be in seeking his salvation in troubled times? This logic is doubtful, for in principle there is no difference between the two limitations on God's absoluteness. What point is there in seeking the salvation of a God whose capacity to save is limited? Perhaps he can't provide salvation for the case in question; perhaps he's busy with something more important at the moment and is unable to take the time it would require (only an omnipotent God can take the time required for everything all at once). However, the point in seeking mercy is that you never know. Maybe God will nevertheless be able, and be good enough, to provide salvation here and now, for myself and my dear ones. There would seem to be a point in seeking God's mercy only if he is not omnipotent and not boundlessly good, for otherwise he would do whatever is needed regardless, and if it wasn't good he did me, then I must have deserved it. Setting limits to God's boundless good and omnipotence makes space for the religious attitude rather than eliminates it. But there's only a slight distance between this position and the views of Adeimantus and Glaucon presented early in book 2 of Plato's Republic, according to which prayer and ritual serve to "varnish" rather than truly worship God.

8.153 If a benevolent God has been a bit negligent in creating the world, or continues to fail at its administration, it is not difficult to imagine the force of his pangs of conscience, his great remorse, and his unbearable burden of guilt. Perhaps God is so severely tormented by the world he created that he needs our pity. Perhaps his distress is so great as to obligate us to respond to his call for help. Perhaps his call for help even contains a call for sacrifice — not to the sacrifice of a sacrificial lamb. A sacrificial lamb can be commanded; a sacrifice cannot. Just as love cannot be commanded. A religious stance will seek to develop an identification with God to alleviate his sorrow somewhat, the sorrow of the world. The feelings of guilt that should initially have been ascribed to God are internalized, while the wish and intention to alleviate some of the suffering are externalized, projected onto him. God is the absolute other who calls for help and becomes the supreme object of moral intentionality. Meanwhile, human beings stay in deep shit.

Believers can try to en-tongue God's evil, the suffering he undergoes, to place it alongside the suffering of the rest of the world,
and all concerned can judge for themselves. One thing is clear: if
God's pained conscience alone is at issue, then this is negligible
vis-à-vis superfluous human suffering, just as the pained conscience of the rapist is negligible vis-à-vis the pain of his victim.
Let the representatives of religion cease troubling us with God's
pangs of conscience, which they have internalized as theirs.

8.154 These are all different ways of expressing God's finitude. The difference between these various ways of declaring his finitude and
the famous declaration of his death amounts, mainly, to the following: man's liberation from the pangs of conscience properly
deserved by God. Even Nietzsche's mad messenger continues to
suffer for his responsibility for the death of God. ("*We have killed
him* — you and I! We are his murderers. But how did we do this?
How were we able to drink up the sea?"[54]) Man's own painful
conscience due to what he has caused and could have prevented is
quite enough. Man might just be able to better concentrate on
these were he liberated from God's painful conscience, which, in
principle, concerns all the Evil that humans could not prevent.
God's finitude does not mean that man, or anything else, can take
the place that human culture has assigned to God, and of course
still assigns him in the view of billions of believers the world over.
His finitude means that humans are on their own to face the Evil
for which they are responsible, to face the Evil that they can prevent or reduce.

8.155 "Are on their own," if one continues longing for an absent God.
Such theological or cosmic loneliness has no relevance to the
presence of Evil. Outside the shadow cast by this void, humans
remain with-each-other, alongside-each-other, against-each-
other. They incessantly do each other evil, in ways that are becoming more and more sophisticated, more and more refined,
more and more effective. They multiply with amazing speed, and
Evil multiplies with them. It is imperative to try to understand
what prevents them from reducing evil in the world somewhat
and what causes them to multiply it so greatly. (And the answers
should not be sought in the realm of psychology, for the soul is a
product of the same society that produces Evil and of the same
culture that approves it, rather than the opposite.)

8.2 *Necessity*

8.200 Many philosophers thought of Evil from the point of view of God
and were therefore preoccupied with the superfluity of Evil. If

they hadn't assumed an omnipotent, boundlessly good, and generous God, perhaps Evil would not have seemed superfluous, or perhaps its superfluity would have posed no problem. But because they did assume the omnipotence and boundless good of God, they needed other solutions. If, for instance, there were a fit between sin and punishment, then superfluous evil would disappear. The monotheistic religions developed imagined economies of sin and punishment ensuring this wondrous balance, establishing celestial courts for this express purpose, and extending generously the time at the disposal of the true judge, the king of kings. Various philosophers attempted to provide this celestial harmony with rational defenses, ignoring what they could have learned long ago from Plato — that it takes an unbelievable myth to persuade people to believe this "tale," or perhaps to make believe it. "Marketing" an unconvincing tale (an article of faith: there is harmony, there is no superfluous evil) with the aid of a convincing one (a myth) — this is precisely what Plato attempts to achieve in the myth of Er that concludes the *Republic*, the dialogue "on Justice," that is, about the disruption and restoration of balance.[55]

8.201 "Real" Evil is whatever is left after the justified payment, after the system has been restored to equilibrium. Accordingly, Evil is an excess in the system of reward and punishment. Where does it come from? In rationalist thinking, justifying this excess means making it necessary and eliminating it as excess. What remains excessive remains unintelligible, and Evil is none other than the Unintelligible, that which cannot be understood or justified. The scandalous nature of Evil has been perceived since ancient times in terms of the lack of fit between suffering ("physical Evil") and the deed that caused the suffering ("moral Evil"). Every theodicy included an effort to assign superfluous evils a meaning that would erase the scandal. Giving meaning means placing Evil within a system of justification that re-creates the disrupted equilibrium, and does so without changing the facticity of evils; it changes only their "surplus value."

8.210 As for the distinction between physical Evil and moral Evil, it could be said that the victim experiences the physical, suffered Evil and the sinner experiences moral, caused Evil. A balanced system in which superfluous evils are eliminated achieves equilibrium not only between sin and punishment but also between the active and the passive, between production (sin) and consumption (suffering). Evils move around the world like marbles across a perforated game board — in due time, with enough patience,

445

and when the board is completely level, all the marbles will eventually roll back to their respective holes. Until then there will always be homeless marbles and marble-less holes, or as yet unpunished sinners and as yet innocent, un-sinning victims. From the point of view of the latter, suffering is superfluous. They are impatient. If they wait long enough, they will find that every marble reaches its hole. But even if they eventually understand their suffering according to their placement in the common order, no theodicy can compensate them for the suffering of not understanding, for the time that passed before they understood and resigned themselves. Which theodicy has taken this suffering into consideration?

8.211 Evil remained unintelligible for so many philosophers because they were thinking of God, through God, and in his place, from his point of view, and also because the world of God, or the world as God, was for them — by definition — rational, intelligible, and ordered. Even when God himself or the idea that replaced him — Good, Totality, Being — was declared unintelligible, not to be understood here, now, by us, there remained a radical difference between this unintelligibility and the unintelligibility of Evil. God, or Good, or Totality, is not intelligible to us; each testifies to our limited capacities and limited minds. But in and of itself, each is a self-elucidating necessity, the total and all-encompassing transparency of the logic of reality. Grasping this transparency was both philosophy's promise and the object of its desire, the beloved of philosophical Eros. Evil, on the other hand, was that stubborn thing, that black hole, that would stay unintelligible even after this complete clarification, if it left intact any reality at all. The superfluous remainder of Evil was illogic, disorder, a surplus remainder that was a scandal of superfluity: the remaining evils and the Evil of this very remaining. An Evil multiplied and denied, by virtue of its very existence, by a logic that resists it.

8.212 This is the case in Plato, for instance, at least according to one possible reading. Good, it will be remembered, is the supreme Form, and it exceeds all being (*epikena tes ousias*) and grants things their existence and intelligibility.[56] But Good grants neither existence nor intelligibility to the absence of understanding itself, to the gap between the intelligibility of the thing and its unintelligible, pointless existence. Think of the gap between what the participants in the dialogue (*Republic*) imagine about Good, through the fables of the sun, the cave, and the divided line, and what they are unable to understand because of their limited grasp — what Good itself is.[57] This gap has to do with finitude and limitation, with the body, with distracting desires, with phenomena in general — with everything whose existence is lacking from the point of view of the intelligible, everything that longs for an idea so as to be granted intelligibility, in order that its very existence may be explained. This gap arises, however, not from the corporeal or the phenomenal per se but from the meeting between the corporeal-phenomenal and the ideal, between what it is that requires explanation and what it is that grants meaning. The idea can explain only what is ideal within the phenomenal; it cannot explain the phenomenality of the phenomenal, that which is missing from it, the lack of regularity and of permanence, the transient, that which is in flux. It explains only the imprints left by the permanent and the eternal within the phenomenal.[58]

8.213 Augustine, who formulated explicitly what Plato left between the lines concerning this matter, identified the gap in question as Evil, for it is Evil that separates what exists in reality and whatever this was supposed to be according to its concept; and Thomas Aquinas followed suit.[59] Augustine called this gap absence (as opposed to simple negation) and declared its nonexistence. The gap between the finite being and its concept, which is the beginning and the end of all Platonic philosophy, is declared that which is not.

8.220 An absence, however, is hard to get rid of. If the gap were eliminated, if what appears were identical with its concept, then things would appear as they really were, would testify to their being what they were and no more. What is there would be perceived instantaneously as what actually is — nothing in excess, nothing missing. But then there would be nothing more to think. Not even this thought itself (more precisely, the thought would become a motionless reflection of ideas, and its erotic dimension, which is also its dimension of action, would be totally annulled). Thought itself, as an aspiration and an activity, is evidence of the gap, of the presence of absence. And if Evil exists within this absence, thought itself should be a witness to its existence, if it is not one already.

8.221 That which mere words can make extinct can be resurrected by the stroke of a pen. This "absence" is part of what is there. Evil is a transgression of the intelligible within Being itself; it is what remains unintelligible after reason has articulated intelligible being and endowed it with meaning. This Evil exists, is experienced and suffered as the insufferable itself. Its presence is a demand for intelligibility, which in Plato, Augustine, and throughout a long rationalist tradition (perhaps ending only with Kant) is equated with an aspiration for Good. The demand for intelligibility that activates thought is an imperative, within what exists itself, to transcend what exists and to change it — even if all it changes is the existence of she who is thinking or the mode in which thought exists. But what is sought by the thought that equates the Good with what is intelligible? Such a thought seeks to reduce the gap between Being in its being as what is there and the Good it reflects. It seeks to overcome the gap in order, somehow, to dwell within the eternal, the perfect, the absolute, all of which are somehow identified with the Good. There and only there, at long last, will we be rid of the unintelligible dangling from existence from beginning to end like an excess appendage. It is there that existence, any existence, will meet its true meaning, its raison d'être. To the extent that philosophical thought has been seeking to grasp the totality of Being, it has always been willing to explain away for this purpose the finitude of the finite and the singularity of its limitations. Philosophy has been prepared to relinquish corporeality, sensuality, desire, along with all earthly things, and finally life itself (philosophy is preparation for death, says Socrates, the first of a long line of self-annihilating philosophers [see 8.511]).

8.222 All this violent nullifying of self is invested in order to overcome finitude, the origin of the absence that is Evil. And nothing guarantees, nothing has ever guaranteed, that this violence will stop at the threshold of the philosophizing individual prepared to annihilate himself. As it turns out, the idea of Good (or God, Totality, and so on) clutches in hand an evil-generating power. But those philosophers who were held in thrall by the magic of this power denied this evil, just as they denied the factual (positive) being-there of unintelligible Evil. From Plato through Hegel, everyone who assumed the possibility of a complete illumination of reality in the clear light of reason was complicit in this denial. They failed to understand where the superfluous being came from and did not study its essence, because they placed it from the outset at that infinite distance between the finite and the infinite, or the imperfect and the perfect, a distance that itself remained inscrutable, unthought, and not accounted for.

8.230 Evil is the transcendence of being itself from being. It is the excess or superfluity of what is there that divests what exists of its sense, of the very possibility of understanding it, as well as that of accepting and affirming it. But finitude is not Evil, nor is the limitation of the witness presented with Evil; Evil is what is outrageous about this finitude, its scandalousness. In philosophies of totality, this scandal is a result of the meeting of the finite, the imperfect, and the infinite or the absolute and wholly perfect. The annihilation of the self in philosophers burning with desire for an understanding of the absolute and for the perfection of understanding is not an acceptance of finitude but rather a denial of the scandal, making thought or the entire life of contemplation an arena in which the scandal is simultaneously displayed and denied.

8.231   This is the case in Spinoza, for instance. Evil, which is perceived from the point of view of the totality that is causa sui, disappears, for within this totality all is both necessary and justified, nothing is superfluous. The individual who understands this necessity in full — that is, in its totality — and who views himself and all evils befalling him from the point of view of the necessity of the whole, has no reason to lament or feel sorrow. For him, from now on, good and evil will be affections of attraction to and revulsion at what is useful for, or harmful to, his subsistence and persistence as a distinct entity. Evils are the result of an individual's aberrant attitude to an object that lessens his strength and causes him to aspire to (or generate) that which will harm him.[60] The suffering involved in his revulsion will of course remain; only its superfluity will disappear. It will reappear only when the individual, at a weak moment, is tempted to compare the world as it is with the world as it seemingly should have been. But speaking of what should have been the case, in opposition to what is, means rejecting the totality of what is as it exists, and this is an idle attempt, for totality is necessary. Evil disappears in Spinoza within a system that is inclusive and balanced, justified and necessary. And Spinoza's entire philosophy comprises nothing but the traces of a desire for a totality in which Evil disappears.[61] This desire, which is obviously contingent on the absence of the total presence of the totality, is an active yet denied presencing of this absence, an articulation of the scandalous meeting of finite and infinite.

8.232   Even Nietzsche, to the extent that he was still a philosopher of totality, was complicit in this simultaneous denial and display of that which is denied. A display of what is denied (and a trace of denial) is mainly located in a few formulations of his idea of eternal return. A display of the denial (and a trace of what is denied) can be found in a few of Nietzsche's nonchalant remarks about death,[62] and, most strikingly, in his very presumption to place his new thinking on the finitude of man and on a world without a God "beyond Good and Evil." The fact that determining values is represented as a belligerent interpretive activity, embroiled in incessant struggle, and that both giving meaning and determining values are reduced to the will to power makes no difference here, for Evil is not located beyond being and in opposition to it, but is a scandal of unjustified superfluity boiling over at the heart of being. The death of God leaves a world orphaned of supreme Good but not of Evil, which now becomes identical with being itself, with being in its totality, for being without justification, meaning, or end is now superfluity in and of itself. When Nietzsche seeks to celebrate cruelty, to turn prodigality into the test of strength and generosity, and to laugh in the face of this abundant superfluity, he actually seeks to accept it, to blunt and blur its edge, to approve it in its totality, just like Spinoza the wise, with a single difference that means little from our point of view: *amor fati*, the (intellectual) love of fate, instead of *amor Dei*, the (intellectual) love of God.[63] When all is equally superfluous, nothing is truly superfluous. But Nietzsche's genealogy, restoring every judgment of values to the forms of life and historical accidents from which it stemmed, cannot eliminate the being of Evil as a superfluity of suffering and horror unnecessary even for the emergence of a new man destined to overcome that which is human in man. And neither can it think this being when it situates itself "beyond" it, as it were. Thus, "real" Evil, "truly" superfluous Evil, again remains as before — denied and unthought. The only thing changed is the pattern of reason's violence.

8.240 Spinoza and Nietzsche, who are prepared to approve everything there is and being (or becoming) in its totality, must either deny (Spinoza) or resist (Nietzsche) the presence of negation in reality so as to eliminate the negation of the world manifested in the call of the sufferer. For them, the sufferer's negation appears to be an inferior or external or false and meaningless attitude of this sufferer to his condition; it is no more than a particular, limited case of the existence of a being that fails to understand the meaning of its own limited existence. However, the sufferer's negation is not an external attitude to suffering, but rather its mode of existence, an essential facet of it. Suffering means being an entity that seeks to break off contact, to be, within the experience of suffering itself, a relation to an excess of being and to a lack in being: the "enough," the "being enough," itself, the self as "being enough" to the verge of "enough of being." Determining that the negation of suffering is external to the sufferer, evaluating it as inferior, or judging it to be a matter of false consciousness means deconstructing suffering or negating its very existence and forcibly attaching it like a hump of illusions to the aching body of the sufferer. But the sufferer exists in the course of her suffering inside — and as the negating relation to — this suffering that is overmuch.

8.241 There is a fundamental difference between a sufferer who cries out "Why do I deserve this? Why me of all people?" and one who cries out "Enough, enough of this torment, this suffering is superfluous, it could have been prevented, it can be stopped right now." The call of sufferers thought of by Stoic philosophers, as well as Spinoza and Nietzsche, is of the first kind. They seek justification for the particular in the framework of a pointless totality, or they seek a change in the distribution of suffering within an insular economy of suffering in which the negation of suffering appears as an act performed in vain. The call of the contemporary sufferer is of the second kind. Beyond a search for meaning or in total disregard for it, her speech act contains a demand: stop tormenting me, us. This demand is based on the knowledge that the economy of suffering is not insular, that it is possible to create an excess of superfluous suffering, and that it is also possible to avoid this. The sufferer who makes this demand is seeking not a justification for the particular in the framework of a pointless totality but rather a preference for one possible system for producing and distributing suffering to another possible system. In other words, if the suffering is preventable and has not been prevented, then its superfluous presence is a result — whether direct or indirect — of a choice of some kind. This is the moment when Evil is associated with freedom.

8.3 *Freedom*

8.300 Descartes associated Evil with freedom, but he did so in an onto-theological context, not a political one. Descartes thought of Evil as possessing the positivity of some thing that is there when it shouldn't be, rather than the negativity of absence. He saw Evil not as "subsisting" (*moindre-être*) but as an actually existing contradiction of what should have been and is not. The problem is that this contradiction, this positivity, needs a reason, and God cannot be that reason. Descartes locates the reason in human finitude, in the proneness to sin and error of this creature who is free to sin or err, just as he is free to avoid this.[64] The Cartesian God (unlike the God of Leibniz) is capable in principle of choosing sin and error, but his perfect wisdom and goodness disallow the realization of this possibility. Man, like his God, is free, but limited in his wisdom and goodness, and therefore prone to choosing evil. The question why God created a world whose creatures' finitude involves Evil, and whose choosing evil is inevitable, remains unsolved (compare

8.151). The main point is the absence of a solution, rather than Descartes's extended theological deliberations. Descartes leaves Evil in the very bosom of human freedom without erasing it later in the course of another theodicy. The freedom that has come to house Evil is the same freedom that was willing to doubt everything and negate the reality of whatever seems to exist. It is the same freedom that encountered the unremovable facticity of the doubting I, that is, of its own self.

8.301 The facticity of Evil in Descartes belongs to the facticity of freedom as the epitome of self. Evil is freedom in its finitude. Every mistaken or sinful choice produces a superfluous evil that didn't have to be; it ought not to have existed itself, and indeed it could have not existed. But even if this bad choice were prevented, some other choice would have occurred that might have been as bad as, or even worse than, the first — this is necessitated by human finitude. A person can avoid doing bad at least part of the time by learning wisdom, avoiding error, nurturing his piety, and avoiding sin. Evil, according to Descartes, finally remains a matter whose necessity is general and common, while its prevention is private, in the realm between the individual and his God. The longing for the elimination of Evil remains a longing of the finite for the infinite, for the Lord of creation.

8.302 What was implicit in Descartes acquires central status in Rousseau and Kant: Evil is immanently and explicitly tied to the structure of human freedom or to the structure of humanness as freedom. Like many of the Enlightenment philosophers, Rousseau and Kant identify Evil not with a sinful or erroneous choice but with "self-love." Rousseau interprets self-love as an exaggeration in care of the self and as perception of the self not in accordance with its "natural" needs but in comparison to and competition with others.[65] Kant interprets self-love as the prioritization of happiness over law, meaning the choice of a particularity that is not expressible as a general law.[66] "Radical Evil" is Kant's term for the placement of the particularity of the acting self where a general law should have been placed as the action-guiding compass. Instead of subjecting the particularity of will to the general form of the good will, which is a rational will, Kant's wicked man makes this form conditional on the law of self-love or, in other words, turns a specific, momentary particularity into an ad hoc substitute for the general form of determining his will.[67] Kant, like Rousseau before him and Schelling or Hegel after him, equates the moment of Evil's appearance with an adherence to the particular and a rejection of the universal.[68] This adherence is a permanent tendency of human nature, "an innate disposition" toward transgression and wicked acts.[69] Rousseau's innovation, given systematic expression by Kant, is to equate the tendency to prioritize self, or exaggerate self-cultivation and self-care, with the facticity of freedom, the differentiating difference (*differentia specifica*) of human selfhood. This tendency preestablishes the fundamental dichotomy that will cut across freedom's field of possibilities: at every moment of its appearance, at every moment of a new beginning, free will must decide between the general law and personal whims of vanity and self-love, between overcoming and succumbing to the temptation to do evil. And given that, according to Kant, this disposition to succumb to self and ignore the general law pertains to the facticity of freedom, freedom can be no less mysterious, for which reason Kant disqualified any presumption to exhaustive knowledge about matters concerning the origins or the nature of freedom, matters lying outside the boundaries of critical knowledge.[70] Accordingly, for Kant, Evil, or at least its source, the origins of its being — that is, its ontological status — remained "inexplicable to us," inscrutable. Thus "radical Evil" is an epistemic substitute of sorts, an "incomprehensibility," for an ontological absence, "limitations of our nature," that cannot be assumed as a reason in the kingdom of freedom.[71]

8.303 But this talk of the inborn drive of man to adhere to the particular — that is, to evil — testifies in the Kantian text to a denied desire to understand it. What is this "innate disposition" that it is possible not to obey and that it is impossible to obey without freely deciding to do so if not a hybrid concept, a half-breed creature bridging the gap between two unbridgeable realms of reality? "Radical Evil" in fact proposes a translation between two types of discourse, between which a *différend* has been declared: on the one hand, the mechanistic discourse of laws of nature, whose objects are knowable in principle for anyone who practices this discourse; on the other hand, the moral discourse of freedom whose objects may only be thought or imagined, and represented indirectly. This inborn disposition is not a necessity but a tendency that can be overcome, a phenomenal regularity not governed by laws, from which, as Hume already recognized, it is impossible to derive knowledge. Freedom cannot be spoken of as a phenomenal regularity, but a phenomenal regularity can be spoken of as a manifestation of freedom, as evidence of its disposition to do evil (on the condition that no one presumes to derive knowledge from this regularity, that is, to derive a set of mechanical rules controlling the regularity of the way nature is governed by its own laws). Every time moral law is realized — that is, every time reason legislates the maxims that dictate the will — and the good will, that which is determined by reason, guides action, the regularity testifying to freedom's disposition to do evil is disrupted. The hope, which cannot be eliminated in Kant (for his critical philosophy guarantees the logical possibility of its realization), for a non-accidental, historical, complete actualization of moral law is the hope for a consistent contradiction of freedom's disposition to cause evil.[72]

8.304 The disposition itself cannot be totally uprooted. Evil must remain a possible object of free will; otherwise the good will would not be a free will. In the end, there is nothing radical about Kant's radical Evil, save the recognition of the tendency toward the particular at the root ("radix") of human existence. And the fitting term for this disposition is in fact not "Evil" (*Bosheit*) but "wickedness" (*Bösartigkeit*).[73] When this disposition is formulated explicitly as the will to deny the universal and to make this denial general — that is, to anchor it in the law of reason and turn reason itself into "evil reason" — Kant speaks of a "subject" that "would be made a diabolical being" and says that man cannot become one.[74] In fact, this "diabolism" is but a manifestation of radical wickedness in the form of a general rule of the will, the rule demanding systematic resistance to the moral imperative. In principle, this resistance is no more than the sanctification and intensification of the tendency toward self-love and a denial of the possibility of erring in the interpretation of moral law while imagining and devoutly believing an aspect of self-love to be the command of conscience and a general rule of reason.[75] What didn't occur to the innocent man from Königsberg was the sanctification of hatred for another. Wickedness — whether diabolical or radical — is located in freedom's denial of the generality of the nonself (and not of the other in general, or of just any other).

8.310 Kant understands that this wickedness may lead, in certain social conditions, to cruelty and suffering that are completely pointless, to human destruction as an end in itself.[76] But in his main discussion of wickedness, these are mentioned in passing as examples of the radical nature of wickedness, not of the wickedness of the roots. In other words, they cannot teach us expressly about Evil's specific mode of being. For Kant, the being of evil, its facticity, and even its various historical and cultural manifestations belong in anthropological theory, not in moral theory itself. From a moral point of view, there are three decisive elements: the presence of

evil as a permanent and unremovable temptation (the temptation
— and not just the capacity — to do evil constructs freedom, belongs to the structure of its existence); the form of Evil as form-
less particularity, that is, as an aberration of the possibility of
generalization and a disruption of the general form of moral law,
which is the inevitable underside of freedom; and the possibility
of repairing Evil — Evil as a temptation that can be overcome,
freedom as the freedom to break free from Evil. Longing for the
elimination of Evil is not a matter between man and his God but
rather a matter of human history and culture. This is where Kant's
modernity appears, and the difference between him and Descartes
is crucial. Incessant progress from Evil to Good is logically possible,[77] culture provides tools for man's moral formation,[78] and
history provides signs that the progress is indeed taking place
(8.125 and 8.312).

8.311 Kant understands the freedom to do evil and the Evil embedded
in freedom with no connection to the evils that befall human
beings due to the state of society and the character of the cultures
in which they live. While he recognizes the social and historical
source of the most terrible evils, he links them not to the facticity
of freedom but to the specific historical state of the external
political and cultural form in which freedom can be realized as
rational freedom. The most terrible evils are those caused by war
and, even more, by the orderly, incessant preparation for war.
These evils, however, are presented as a necessary condition for
progress:

> We have to admit that the greatest evils which oppress civilized
> nations are the result of war — not so much of actual wars in the past
> or present as of the unremitting, indeed ever-increasing preparation
> for war in the future. All the resources of the state, and all the fruits
> of its culture which might be used to enhance that culture even fur-
> ther, are devoted to this purpose. Freedom suffers greatly in numer-
> ous areas, and that state's maternal care for its individual members is
> replaced by demands of implacable harshness (even if this harshness
> is justified by fear of external threat). But if the constant fear of war
> did not compel even heads of state to show this respect for humanity,
> would we still encounter the same culture, or that close association
> of social classes within the commonwealth which promotes the well-
> being of all? Would we still encounter the same population, or even
> that degree of freedom which is still present in spite of highly restric-
> tive laws? We need only look at China, whose position may expose it
> to occasional unforeseen incursions but not to attack by a powerful

enemy, and we shall find that, for this very reason, it has been stripped of every vestige of freedom. — So long as human culture remains in its present stage, war is therefore an indispensable means of advancing it further.[79]

In other words, even though people may seem to suffer from the terror of preparations for war, these evils are not superfluous.[80]

8.312 In any case, whether it is Evil at the root of human existence or a flow of evils lubricating the wheels of human progress, Evil is not a scandal to Kant. He depicts the "long melancholy litany of charges against humankind," expressing despair or outrage at Evil, as the result of a one-sided perception of the human condition that fails to acknowledge that evils are vital to progress.[81] Even the horrendous terror that accompanied the French Revolution pales against the backdrop of the new hope it arouses. The fundamental importance of the French Revolution doesn't lie in the enormous deeds and crimes performed in the course of it, or even in the overturning of entire social structures. The Revolution "may be so filled with misery and atrocities that no right-thinking man would ever decide to make the same experiment again at such a price." But this is not the main issue. The fundamental importance of the Revolution lay in "a sympathy which borders almost on enthusiasm" that it excited in the onlookers, despite the danger involved. The sympathy they revealed toward the Revolution is the main point, for this testifies to the morality of the onlookers, the ensemble of actual onlookers and the onlookers as representatives of the whole of humanity. That sympathy "cannot therefore have been caused by anything other than a moral disposition within the human race."[82] This is "the sign of history," a testimony to the existence of a moral power acting in history and allowing the belief that progress from wicked to good is not only possible in principle but also taking place in actuality.[83]

8.313 Kant's acceptance of, or resignation to, the Evil caused by war and revolutionary terror differs from the denial of Evil in Spinoza's *Ethics* and from the *Aufhebung* of Evil in Hegel's dialectical logic, which perhaps is precisely why it is even more outrageous. Kant knows not only that wickedness is an inborn disposition but also that evils have a structured and intelligible social source, such as war, which "creates more evil men than it takes away."[84] In addition, he knows that the world is reparable, but he believes that this repair is taking place "behind people's backs" while foiling their intentions and causing various disasters. Unlike Hegel, he doesn't presume to know the course of this reparation; he's prepared to make do with identifying signs of it in historical reality. And these are steeped in acts of unsurpassed cruelty. He registers the cruelty and, alongside it, the necessity of moral progress itself, as a matter of fact. Of course, this fact can never justify any act of cruelty, not as an end in itself and not as a means to a noble aim; moral law contradicts both the first and the second kind of justification. But this fact cancels out the superfluity of Evil and makes suspect and doubtful, if not downright superfluous, the act of intervention intended to remove it, the political deed seeking to reach the social root of evils. In addition, this fact represents the historical moral imperative — work in this world to bring nearer the supreme Good, that is, to realize morality in history — as a righteous yet relatively uninformative formulation.[85] On the one hand, this act is superfluous because evils are necessary for progress — note, for instance, how the civilizing process has been brought to a halt in China. On the other hand, the act is superfluous because, based on all the evidence, "the crooked tree" grows upward regardless, in ways beyond our comprehension.[86] Progress toward the "final end" seems sure, and there's no knowing which acts of wickedness or horror may help hasten it. The signs of progress and the cunning of nature that give catastrophe positive meaning make redundant the need to think of the Evil occurring at present. Evil is thought of relative to the roots of its being and its mysterious beginnings only in order to ensure the inevitable element it contains and also to ensure that it is not totally irreparable.

8.314 The Kantian concept of freedom has far-reaching implications in the political sphere, and yet despite the immanent link between Evil and freedom these stop short at the threshold of thinking about Evil, which remains external to any political context. Perhaps this is because radical Evil is located at an impossible juncture between nature and freedom, at the heart of the *différend* that, for Kant, separates the discourse on what can be known from the discourse on what should properly be done, due to which it is almost impossible to say anything about the superfluous evils that "radical Evil" generates. Evil contradicts this distinction in its very being as being-there, because it is a superfluous being that appears as a demand to take action, to do something. More precisely, Evil is an occurrence in which superfluity appears, gains presence, and something that appears fails to cross the threshold of justification and emerges as superfluous, emerges in all its superfluity, while this appearance of superfluity and this superfluity of what appears address their witness with an ungrounded demand: to remove the superfluous. The form of this demand is similar to the transcendental claim of the moral law in Kant. But a thought whose point of departure is the divide between what is knowable and what ought to be done will most likely be blind to that "tumor" of superfluous being that is simultaneously both knowable (like other phenomena) and unconditionally commanding (like moral law).

8.320 The first modern philosopher who systematically thinks through the line between Evil and freedom in a political context is Hobbes. Actually, Hobbes is very close to Spinoza's logic of totality, but he limits his concept of totality to the human-political context and confines it to the realm of power relations through his concept of the sovereign. Sovereignty is total in Hobbes, and its totality is necessary for its very existence. Partial sovereignty or its partial or temporary surrender deconstructs the concept of sovereignty from within. Everything the sovereign commands is necessary, because this is his sovereign wish and because the sovereign reaffirms his sovereignty with every act of will, even when he allows his subjects to do as they will in certain areas. The sovereign who chooses to limit himself is sovereign to reappropriate for himself at every moment the domain from which he has chosen to absent himself. Hobbes's sovereign is a pantheistic god of the political sphere: the sovereign is the totality of the political, just as Spinoza's God is the totality of reality. As long as sovereignty exists, there can be no real gap between the law (what the sovereign commands and what the subject is commanded to sacrifice as a result of the sovereign's wish) and morality (the subject's condition as it ought to be). In the final analysis, in the realm of the sovereign's rule there is no gap between is and ought.[87] Hobbes, however, recognized an anarchic moment of transition from one sovereign to another, which is a return to the moment of constituting sovereignty itself, the transition from the state of nature to the civic state.[88] At this moment, the totality is ruptured; and at precisely this moment, Evil bursts into the world —a return to the state of nature in which "every man is Enemy to every man":

> In such condition, there is no place for industry; because the fruits thereof is uncertain: and consequently no Culture of the Earth; no Navigation, nor use of the commodities that may be imported by Sea; no commodious Building; no Instruments of moving, and removing such things as require much force; no Knowledge of the face of the Earth; no account of Time; no Arts; no Letters; no Society; and

which is worst of all, continuall feare, and danger of violent death; And the life of man, solitary, poore, nasty, brutish, and short.[89]

In this state, everyone can claim ownership of everything, and no one has a right to anything; every case of the use of force is equally justified, and necessity turns into utter arbitrariness. This state itself, rather than any specific action in it, is what becomes unjustifiable, superfluity realized to the fullest. At this moment, not only is everything equally superfluous, but superfluity is all there is. In her struggle for survival, the wretched, deathly fearful individual loses everything human and is cast about with no sovereign to protect her and no way of escaping the excess of being: the excess of power that can place every individual as superfluous at any moment; the excessive presence of the fear of death in the face of this immanent superfluity; the excessive presence of the other, whoever she may be, the ever-threatening other, who can never be trusted. The state of nature is radical Evil, according to Hobbes. The political state is its active negation, a constantly renewed decision on political principles and a power structure capable of defending one from it. Longing for the elimination of Evil is the individual's longing for the guardianship of an all-encompassing and perfect but earthly sovereign.

8.321 For Hobbes, radical Evil is not simply the state of nature but the natural state of freedom, and not simply of unbridled freedom but of freedom in the plural, the freedom of many who are equally powerful, without law or hierarchy.[90] Evil is a multiplicity of freedoms left alone with freedom itself, without any law or limitation other than that imposed or forced by another freedom. Evil is freedom that is fear-stricken by the multiplicity of freedoms around it, freedom that lashes out in the deathly fear that overcomes it in the face of the terrifying excess of freedom. In the state of nature, violence feeds itself to the point of destruction; this is the logic of freedom as illogic. But the negation of the state of nature is a manifestation of freedom, too — the transfer of all rights to the sovereign is consented to freely, in obedience to the laws of reason.[91] Consent is what ends the cycle of violence; that is the logic of rational freedom. Freedom is both a source of evil and the possibility for its elimination. Whether sovereignty is the elimination of freedom or its paramount manifestation, freedom's subjection to reason and to the principle of sovereignty that reason entails follows from a completely personal and private experience — the terror of death[92] and an utterly egotistic opposition to Evil. The reason that constitutes sovereignty is the general reason of the individual I, the common law of the particular. Both the superfluity of Evil and the possibility of eliminating it are totally subject to the point of view of the individual I, an I that longs and desires, that fears, that senses deathly fear of death, that grasps the logic of its state and is prepared to succumb to the total otherness of the sovereign in order to be rid of the fear of radical Evil. Philosophers who thought through the concept of sovereignty after Hobbes — Locke, Rousseau, Kant, Hegel — were left with the task of removing the alienation between individual and sovereign and reducing the moment of arbitrariness in the rule of the latter, that is, of turning sovereignty into an explicit result of the individual's self-constitution and allowing the individual to recognize herself in the sovereign otherness to which she succumbs.

8.322 When this conceptual scheme was brought to fruition with Hegel, freedom, originally a condition for both the possibility of Evil and its elimination, had turned into the unfolding story of this historical development of the appearance of Evil and its actual sublation. The arbitrary totality of the Hobbesian sovereign appears in Rousseau as the totality of the general will that imposes freedom on every individual, whereas in Hegel it becomes the totality transformed from potential to actuality through the necessary process of the realization of freedom.[93] The carefully argued, but imagined, leap that Hobbes proposed, from the state of nature to the regime of sovereignty, and from the logic of the violence of freedom in the plural to a singular rational freedom, was given metahistorical grounding by Hegel, who claimed to ensure the necessity of its realization. The external conditions for the rational realization of freedom (as viewed by Kant [see 8.311]) were integrated into freedom itself and became conditions of its self-actualization and a necessary moment of it. A two-faced immanent necessity covered the entire process: rational freedom giving birth to itself and realizing itself in the structures and institutions of human society; the development of this freedom's self-consciousness as a consciousness of total necessity or of the totality of necessity.

8.323 Within this totality, Evil is, again, not superfluous. On the contrary, it is a manifestation of a particular kind of lack. Evil is a result of partiality and abstractness, a flaw in the totality of the principle of sovereignty or in the absoluteness of its rationalization. Therefore, in principle, every state in which the ruling power is lacking, including the state of nature itself, is perceived as worse than the existence of a sovereign rule. Any disruption of the principle of sovereignty is seen as an outbreak of Evil. Thus, in

Hobbes, Kant, Rousseau, and Hegel, disobedience is seen as an uncontainable threat, and obedience a sacred principle, even when the regime is clearly the main producer of evils. Rousseau makes an exception for states of occupation and slavery,[94] for it is impossible to claim that sovereignty exists in such conditions if sovereignty is none other than the active manifestation of the general will.[95] Kant speaks of an enlightened ruler in an epoch of enlightenment and forbids any form of active resistance to the regime other than addressing the sources of its legitimacy.[96] But from the moment the process of constituting the sovereign is equated with rationalizing the political, disobedience and, more generally, any resistance to order can be nothing but manifestations of particularity, irrationality, and partiality that are finally identified with Evil.

8.324 In Hegel, Evil appears when a particular freedom fails to recognize its general law, when a capricious conscience recognizes the form of moral law without knowing its contents, when the abstract moral law has not yet achieved realization in the culture and institutions of a concrete moral community. "Conscience, as formal subjectivity, consists simply in the possibility of turning at any moment to evil; for both morality and evil have their common root in that self-certainty [of the content-less conscience], which has being for itself and knows and resolves for itself" due to the contingent connection between knowledge of what ought to be done and the nature of the actual decision.[97] An evil person turns her good intention, or her desire, and in any case the particular and arbitrary manifestations of her will, into a general law instead of molding them out of her recognition of the general law and without trying to "supersede" (aufheben) the inalienable arbitrariness of the will through the mediation of the general law. An evil person says, "I am ... beyond this law and can do this or that as I please. It is not the thing [Sache] which is excellent, it is I who am excellent and master of both law and thing; I merely play with them as with my own caprice.... In this shape the subjectivity is ... empty of all ethical content in the way of rights, duties, and laws, and is accordingly evil (evil, in fact, of an inherently wholly universal kind)."[98] Hegel could have spoken similarly of the classical tyrant, but he chose to speak of the person of good conscience, possessed of a capricious soul, full of good intentions but lacking understanding, failing to grasp the necessity of general laws. Finally, Hegel's person of good conscience cares for himself. His interest in moral law is limited; his main interest lies in his appearance as a moral personality. Thus, Evil appears out of the mere interest in the particular and its prioritization over the general law.

8.325 "The origin of evil in general lies in the mystery — i.e., the speculative aspect — of freedom," Hegel adds in this context.[99] But the mystery of freedom will disappear in the process of reality's self-clarification and emergence into lucidity; it will persist only for those who have not yet understood. Once again, Evil is no more than a type of ignorance. In order for Evil to be superseded, the individual must succumb to the only sovereignty possible, the sovereignty of the totality of Being turned into an Idea, of a substance becoming a subject and a freedom revealed to itself as a necessity. Reality as a whole takes on sovereignty, and freedom is revealed to itself as a necessity, when consciousness and freedom arrive together at the end of their historical journey (and at the end of history); as "absolute spirit" appears onstage, the totality becomes conscious of itself, and the concept is fully actualized. And whatever this absolute spirit may be, it is obviously also that wonderful realm in which the difference between good and bad is lost: "If Evil is the same as Goodness, the Evil is just not Evil, nor Goodness Good: on the contrary, both are suspended moments — Evil in general is self-centered being-for-self, and Goodness is what is simple and without self."[100]

8.330 "Universal despotism" is "incurably evil," more terrible than war itself, Kant says. There is a "monstrous" dimension to the complete annihilation of freedom under a reign of tyranny; its "disintegration" drags in its wake "virtue, taste and science" and, in short, the destruction of humanity as a civilization.[101] The picture is very similar to the one Hobbes paints when describing the state of nature as the complete annihilation of any ruling power (8.320–8.321). A mirror effect emerges here: freedom without rule and rule without freedom are perceived in almost the same terms, as complete Evil, the limits of humanity. The complete absence of hierarchy among a mass of free individuals and the complete lack of freedom in the one-dimensional hierarchy of a single individual give rise to the same monstrous terror, which is the true ruler in the frontier zones of humankind.[102] Evil can be a result of an excess of freedom or an excess of rule, but in exactly the same way: an arbitrary and capricious realization of freedom, by masses or by an individual, in total absence of general laws and of a rule to enforce them.

8.331 The political problem of freedom is viewed in both classical and modern philosophical thinking as a total imbalance in the distribution of freedom between the two poles of a regime, between the ruler and the ruled. Evil appears when too much freedom, perceived as a distributable resource, is compressed into one of the poles in the polarized relations of government: an excess of freedom for the ruler or an excess of freedom for the subjects. A disruption of balance can be viewed thus because the relations of government are seen from the outset as binary. Injustice in political thought, both classical and modern, is perceived as a distribution of resources that disrupts this or that principle of equality (arithmetic or geometric equality in Aristotle's terms[103]) projected onto social relations. Evil that is linked to terror is viewed in the mainstream of political thought as a complete aberration of the distribution of freedom in a field governed by this or that principle of hierarchical polarity. The political task is not to equalize the freedom to act at every point in the field — that would be a return to the state of nature — but to provide protection against excessive freedom at the dominated pole — that is, freedom spread out among subjects — and to ensure a safe space protected from excessive freedom accumulated at the ruling pole. Both the political problem and the political task are thought of in terms of justice, balance, equality, and freedom. The presence of Evil is situated somewhere on the horizon of this discussion, but the concept of Evil is almost completely pushed aside. Evil is present but remains unthought. It is used to think with but almost never thought through. More specifically, in the main traditions of Western political thought, Evil is not a category for thinking through the allocation of freedom, but, conversely, freedom is a category for thinking through the appearance of Evil. Evil appears in its full horror in the extreme states of the accumulation and realization of freedom.

8.332 Eliminating political Evil thus requires educating and restraining the ruling freedom and at the same time forming and regimenting the subjected freedom according to principles that will ensure balance in the allocation of liberties. In schematic terms, a double move could be described here whose contents undergo a thorough change in the transition from ancient to modern times but whose dual structure is kept intact: on the one hand, formation of the ruling freedom; on the other, the elimination, internalization, or administration and government of the freedom of those who are governed. Classical political philosophy was mainly interested in the formation of the ruling freedom, the freedom of every citizen of the polis as well as that of the tyrant and the oligarch. The formation of the ruling freedom was conceived as the best way of controlling the freedom of the ruled, the many or the mob. Hence the importance of education for political theory. Modern political theory was mainly interested in the controlled expression and containment of the freedom of the ruled and subjected it to the general laws of morality and the state. The proper administration and "normalization" of the freedom of the governed were conceived as the best ways to ensure proper government and control the accumulation of freedom at the sovereign's end. Interpreted in these terms, Machiavelli's *Prince* is situated at the precise turning point between classical and modern political theory.

8.333 Plato proposed the classical paradigm of the elimination of political Evil in his utopian guardian state, with the philosopher-king as an example of virtue and as a flesh-and-blood realization of the knowledge of Good. Marx proposed the modern paradigm, with the elimination of state and the full realization of the rule of commonality and the commonality of rule in Communist society. Commonality now appears not only as that form in light of which, and through the mediation of which, freedom is actualized; commonality is also the form and the end of the process of liberation itself, that is, the process of realizing freedom. At the end of the road, the Marxist will meet with a humanity that has become sovereign and with a sovereignty that is now shared by humanity as a whole. These are none other than the realization and humanization of Hegel's totality, and Marx's interpreters had sound grounds for claiming their equal "necessity." Nevertheless, sovereign humanity is a future task, a future to be achieved, yet to be realized. In other words, unlike Hegel, who "superseded" political Evil, or Kant, who took note of it and was even willing to aestheticize it (emphasizing the audience's role in the drama of history over that of active participants in it [8.312]), both Plato and Marx, despite the many differences between them, allow the present to be measured relative to the Evil present in it.

8.334 Despite the many differences. Plato classified and analyzed five types of governments, based on those he was familiar with in the ancient world, and proposed a measured but noncontinuous line connecting the best regime, the guardian state, and the worst regime, tyranny. Tell me what regime you live in and I'll tell you how bad off you are, how far from the Good. In Marx, the badness of conditions and the distance from the Good (interpreted as a triumph over alienation, as liberation and equality) can be measured according to placement in the historical process. Tell me how close the revolution is and I'll tell you how terrible the state of affairs is.[104] But the connecting line isn't straight. The evils produced by capitalism are necessary for creating the conditions for a revolution. The proletariat must have nothing more to lose save its chains; that is, every loss and all the suffering of the proletariat can be interpreted as hastening the revolution. From Kant through Hegel and up to and including Marx, evils were assigned a significant role in the historical process, on the way to progress. But Marx is the first to say that evils are excessive, that it is time to move from the distant observation point into the field of real action, that such a move from interpretation to action is not just a moral imperative (as in Kant) but also a necessary condition for the reduction of Evil. It is now, only now, that Evil appears as truly superfluous and in the truth of its superfluity, whether or not it is directly connected to the resplendent journey of freedom. Was it the logic of Hegelian dialectics that formed this move, or was it the call arising from the suffering and loss of Europe's downtrodden in the course of the Industrial Revolution? Both readings of Marx's early writings are possible and do not exclude each other. Real action in history complies with the moral imperative, but in its own right it — like the elimination of Evil it will finally bring — has a place, predetermined or justified in hindsight, in the process of the realization of freedom.

8.340 Philosophers and theologians, from Augustine through Maimonides to Leibowitz, grant man free will and the knowledge of good and evil and a capacity for choosing between them, thus clearing God of responsibility for the presence of Evil in the world. Free will serves as a kind of clutch that disengages the divine cogwheels moving a world of total Good from the human actions generating a world steeped in evils. But even if God is perceived as finite and limited, this clutch must be kept in place so that human beings can be assigned responsibility for the reduction and prevention of Evil. In the absence of God, the clutch partitions the determinist mechanism of nature, or the hand of a random but inscrutable and uncontrolled fate, and the morality of the actual world. Machiavelli was perhaps the first to express this consciousness on the eve of the modern era, in a famous passage from *The Prince*:

> Nevertheless, so as not to eliminate human freedom, I am disposed to hold that fortune is the arbiter of half our actions, but that it lets us control roughly the other half. I compare fortune to one of those dangerous rivers that, when they become enraged, flood the plains, destroy trees and buildings, move earth from one place and deposit it in another. Everyone flees before it, everyone gives way to its thrust,

without being able to halt it in any way. But this does not mean that, when the river is not in flood, men are unable to take precautions, by means of dykes and dams, so that when it rises next time, it will either not overflow its banks or, if it does, its force will not be so uncontrolled or damaging.[105]

Even if Machiavelli is dealing here not with moral matters but with issues of government and the management of state, he is clearly dealing with the reduction of evils: this reduction is possible, there are evils that people can prevent, and the matter is given to their discretion and their free decision. This necessitates the assumption that not all is in the hands of heaven, "cruel" nature, or "blind" fate. Notably, Machiavelli mentions all three in this single passage, attaching no importance to the onto-theological differences between them. And indeed, from a human point of view, it makes no difference what the factor is that cannot be controlled or whose conduct cannot be predicted — God, nature, or fate. The only question is whether something can be changed in the progression of things predetermined independently of human action. The condition for the possibility of such a change is the existence of an element of human action that is not part of "the progression of things predetermined." This is the role of freedom in most moral theories that seek to ascribe to the individual moral responsibility and see the possibility of ascribing moral responsibility as a condition for the possibility of moral judgment. I, too, am obliged to assume this minimum. The fact that in the theory of morals presented here, the appeal of a concrete other takes the place of a universal law or a categorical imperative makes no difference regarding freedom. There is no condition of being-an-addressee without the possibility of being-free-to-respond. The freedom of human action must be assumed, at least as a measure of indeterminacy. Now the "clutch" of freedom separates the serial repetition of the practices generating evils (8.020), a repetition viewed as necessary or taken for granted, from the possibility that the action in question may differ and discontinue the regularity of the production of evils.

8.341 The difference between the various postulates of freedom lies in the metaphysical commitments they entail. In Machiavelli, freedom appears all at once as a working assumption and a given fact, needing no contemplation or examination. In Augustine or Leibniz, human free will appears as a deus ex machina so as to save God from the fruits of his creation and make possible both sins and salvation. It doesn't conform to the orders of the cosmos (for it contradicts both the determinist and the teleological views of

466

nature) or to the radical difference required between God and man (for it creates a dangerous continuum between God and man — the capacity to choose, and thus to generate something new, to begin something afresh). In Kant, the postulate of freedom necessitates a factual, nonempirical knowledge that is not of the order of experience and that nevertheless seeps through the boundaries set by the critique of reason. The Kantian postulate creates a dangerous combination of things and phenomena, causing several anomalies that Kant goes to great lengths to dispel, not always successfully. I hope that for the purposes of the theory of morals I am presenting here, there is no need to assume any more than I already have: a space of social relations comprising regularities of relations and practices; these in turn are constructed of not-inevitable repetitions of unitary actions and gestures taken and made by individuals (8.011). The freedom to act otherwise is perceived here from the outset as part of what-is-there, and not due to any uniqueness unjustly granted to man but rather due to the contingent character of social reality, perhaps of any reality.

8.342 Yemima Ben-Menahem proposes distinguishing two sets of oppositions, between which philosophical thinking has often slid indiscriminately: causality versus chance (lacking cause), on the one hand; necessity versus contingency, on the other.[106] A necessary occurrence results from a variety of different causal chains and will take place in any event because it is "relatively insensitive both to initial conditions and to potentially disruptive intervening events." Such independence of initial conditions may follow from the existence of some sufficiently powerful "essential feature" or "primary cause," such that its very existence in and of itself necessitates the occurrence and its outcome. A body that has started to move in a medium of any given density (that is, not in a vacuum) will come to a halt in the end, of necessity. What has been born will die in the end, of necessity. In contrast, a contingent occurrence depends on the initial conditions and demonstrates "a high sensitivity to initial conditions and intervening factors" (which can be described as reorganizations of the initial conditions), so that many small changes in the conditions of occurrence may prevent it or change its results. Once launched, a missile will take its predicted course, and once born, a creature will die, on this particular day only if all the relevant conditions for this launching, this death, are met.

Causal occurrences may be non-necessary, that is, contingent; logically, nothing prevents necessary occurrences that are independent of initial conditions from being causeless; a contingent

occurrence can be either causal or random, and a random occurrence can be either necessary or contingent. It is not the degree
of randomness (absence of reason) that determines contingency
but rather the degree of dependence on the initial conditions and
the sensitivity to interventions (or "interferences," or changes in
the initial conditions). Thus, for example, the development of
cancerous cells or an addiction to drugs is an apparently contingent, and not necessary, causal process, whereas the precise placement of a subatomic particle may be random but may also be
independent of the initial conditions of its disintegration and
therefore necessary. The study of chaos in recent years and earlier
probability studies sought to understand occurrences in physics,
meteorology, geology, evolution, and sociology as contingent
occurrences whose overall patterns may be described and explained in causal terms, even though their effects cannot be predetermined. It is impossible to determine the effect not because
the process is causeless or because its cause is unknown, but because its occurrence is contingent on the existence and continuity
of a large number of initial conditions, of which it cannot be
determined in advance that they will hold and persist.

The opposition between what is necessary and what is contingent, according to this view, is not dichotomized; there is a
continuum between the two absolute poles of being more or
less necessary/contingent, and it is possible to speak of levels of
necessity and contingency.[107] Death is apparently a necessary
occurrence that befalls every living creature and cannot be prevented; but this particular death in a traffic accident last week
might have been prevented, for many interventions and changes,
even minute ones, in the initial conditions (the state of the drivers
involved, the road conditions, the state of the vehicles in question) might have warded it off. Death due to malignant disease is
inevitable (necessary), but massive clinical intervention may be
able to postpone it for some time. At certain historic moments, it
is possible to say that a conflict between two parties has reached a
"point of no return," that clashes are unavoidable and only enormous changes, whose occurrence is unlikely, may ward off what
seems necessary; but highly aware people know that even in such
a situation, they need not be hurt, for the predictable distribution
of evils is contingent and sufficient changes can still be generated in the initial conditions in order to reduce unnecessary evils.
The main advantage of the distinction between the random and
the contingent is that it circumvents the classic formulation of the
question of free will and obviates the need to decide it. Free will

is simply irrelevant, at least in the context that interests us here — the possibility of preventing superfluous evils. On the one hand, even free will won't change the expected outcome of processes that are, "by nature," necessary, that is, characterized by a high level of necessity; on the other hand, given contingent processes, even an action that is determined, in principle, in a causal manner (which we don't often know how to reconstruct) may cause a difference and prevent what should properly be prevented. This determination allows a reformulation of earlier statements: attributing contingency to a loss-generating occurrence is a necessary condition for the description of loss as damage (3.200) and for the presentation of suffering as superfluous suffering (6.430). Finally, the view attributing contingency to historical occurrences and ridding them of "the hand of fate," nature, or "God's will" and his will plays a vital role in preventing preventable evils (7.042).

8.343 Furthermore, freedom should not be placed "inside" the individual, perceived as a subject, or be viewed as a feature immanent to the individual. There is no need to attribute to the individual the status of the primary "source" of freedom and no reason to see freedom as what defines the individual in her singularity. The role of "clutch" assigned by philosophers since Augustine to the individual's free will, in order to separate the necessity of a world order — whether rational, good, or meaningless — from the human deeds to which good or bad can be ascribed, is one that I wish to assign to a contingent system, without subject, end, or reason, the processes of which have an inner logic but are devoid of necessity. This is a system whose inner logic (that sensitivity to initial conditions and occasional interferences) always leaves an empty (or vacant or free) space for play, change, resistance, and prevention of improper results.

8.344 What is left for the individual? The nagging question persists. The question of free will is not easily circumvented, and the concept is still difficult to get rid of, even after Nietzsche deconstructed the concept of a will possessed of freedom and even if the concept of contingency proposed here obviates the need to ascribe freedom to the will.[108] The following idea can be tried out: the individual is left with the ability to discern the vacant space and to respond or not to the possibility that it offers her for acting differently. Freedom is conditional on the ability to identify, to make present, to imagine, to represent the contingency of a social occurrence, and to use this image as a temptation for new action. The capacities required for this — both cognitive and affective — are most probably both inborn in the individual as a creature of its kind and nurtured culturally. But these capacities are a condition for freedom, not freedom itself. Freedom itself appears the moment someone responds to the temptation and fills the vacant space with new action, or overcomes the temptation and goes on adhering to the routine of expected actions, which she continues performing in keeping with the familiar regularity. In the face of the vacant space, the individual's decision to respond to or ignore temptation, to deviate from the regularity or reenact it, may be determined by causal chains whose beginnings are unknowable, but not by the contingent occurrence in which she intervenes. Freedom is not eliminated by the existence of a causal explanation for the decision, for it is not located within it or within the individual "enacting" it. Freedom is a relation that holds between the individual and the vacant space in a contingent system. Freedom is embodied in the unpredictable manner in which the individual fills in or avoids filling in this space, the manner in which she takes up the space and utilizes it to do a deed, only to go back and re-create it at another site in the system, or the manner in which she performs the same act over and over so as to avoid being forced to encounter this space. Freedom is embodied in the individual's attitude toward the place allotted to her by the prevalent social regularity and toward the space opened up to her by the contingency of this regularity. Freedom is realized in the way the individual fills in a space.

Perhaps this can also be put as follows: freedom is the fact that what bears the individual's body between one move of the social game and the next is not inscribed in the game itself or in the body itself (for the rules of the game are never fully inscribed in the body). The contingency of the social game means that the next move of every participant cannot be derived either from the rules of the game or from the characteristics of the individual. And nevertheless the next move arrives. When it does, it is possible to reconstruct all the reasons and causes that generated precisely this move, but this reconstruction will never lead to a place from which it is possible to derive the next move in advance, even if we have full knowledge of all the factors involved in the game: body, consciousness, what is at stake, how the others are perceived, and so forth.

8.345 — But isn't it the case that granting the individual the freedom to resist (to resist repetition, sequentiality, the reproduction of the patterns of action producing superfluous evils) returns freedom to her as an immanent attribute?

— I don't see the individual as the source of this freedom, and I don't see the freedom as an attribute of the individual. The individual takes the freedom to act differently from the social game she is taking part in, and she always leaves it "in the middle," as what is situated between her and others participating in the game with her. Thus, for instance, language grants the individual speaker the freedom to choose words and forms of expression, while her inborn linguistic competence — whatever it is — is but a tool through which she can take this freedom for herself momentarily, so as to formulate the unexpected in an unexpected way, and in the process rewrite the space of possibilities and redraw the figure of freedom for other speakers in the discourse. And what is true of language is true of all the other social games taking place in and through it. The individual is a body bearing varied and complex types of competences that allow participation in social games. Nothing in the body dictates either the rules of the game or the moves made in it, that is, the response to the use others make of the freedom lying "in the middle." Social games — all of them, by definition, by virtue of being games — leave space for improvisation, for resistance, for rule breaking, for disrupting the repetition, for a representation that affects the order. What leaves no such space is neither a game nor social. And nevertheless, the moment of resistance — isn't it a moment of freedom?

— Yes, but it is exactly like the moment of repetition or of cooperation, if these take place in the face of the possibility of acting otherwise. The active presence of the possibility to act otherwise — that is, the consciousness of the contingency of the social game in which one is involved — is a crucial matter. Freedom appears and exists only when the other possibility appears as a temptation. It may be that most people, most of the time, do not notice this temptation and act without any consideration of the empty space in the social game, or of the contingency of the processes in which they are involved, and therefore without causing freedom to appear. It may be that for most people, most of the time, existence lacks the reflection and sensitivity that allow one to identify the vacant space, and that they accordingly respond unthinkingly to the systemic logic of the social game and to what is generally expected of them. I think, for instance, of that famous waiter to whom Sartre ascribed freedom, regardless of whether he throws a plate in the face of an irritating customer or goes on serving him faithfully despite repeated humiliations. I mean to say that this waiter takes his freedom — either to go on or to stop playing his role as a waiter — only occasionally in the course of the evening, the week, or his entire career. This happens only when the waiter is tempted — or overcomes the temptation — to scream at his boss, to slap a customer, or just to sleep another hour and arrive late for work. Our social life is full of cultural, ideological, and legal mechanisms that attempt to cause "the other possibility" to be forgotten and erase the temptation in it, and it is equally over-flowing with temptations that simulate these "other" possibilities, whose realization merely reproduces existing regularities and blurs the traces of their real contingency.

— And it can still be claimed against you that the freedom vested in the individual is what allows the contingency of human reality and consequently the social game, rather than the opposite.

— If this were the case, it would be necessary to view games as unique to man, and that is not true — animals play, too — or to grant freedom to animals, at least those who play.[109] And indeed, it seems completely reasonable to me to attribute to some kinds of animals the ability to identify "the other possibility," as well as the capacity to be tempted by it, to prefer or forgo it. If animals are granted the freedom to play and to embody freedom, then we must recognize freedom in nonhuman nature. If there is freedom in nonhuman nature, why limit it to animals? Why not identify freedom in nonhuman nature whenever a game takes place be-tween elements and parameters whose interaction doesn't dictate effects in advance, doesn't generate predictable results, because the causal process in question demonstrates a high level of sensitivity to every change in the conditions of its occurrence, that is, to contingent systems? In other words, the idea of a continuum be-tween what is necessary and what is contingent can be further developed and presented as a continuum between varying levels of consciousness of contingency and its representation in a rele-vant scene of action. This continuum will cross the animal king-dom, but also the human world, as I wished to demonstrate with the aid of that weary Parisian waiter.

8.350 On the one hand, a distinction is drawn between contingency and randomness (indeterminacy); on the other, the view of freedom as an independent source of power vested in an individual, which is capable of acting on all her psychophysical systems and by which she is not acted on, is abandoned. The combination of these two allows a reduction in the metaphysical commitment implied by the theory of morals proposed here. Sufficient for the purposes of the present conceptual economy is an irreducible degree of con-tingency "lying" between individuals in all their encounters and interactions. What is saved is manifested not only in terms of metaphysical assumptions but also in the possibility of moving without delay from metaphysical discussion to social theory. Contingency is located in all social games and in all forms of government, though not to an equal degree in each. For social and political theory, one should distinguish between social games in particular and social conditions in general according to the level and shifting patterns of contingency allowed in each. For moral philosophy, one needs to explain the conditions for irreducible contingency in the production and distribution of evils. The underlying assumption is that in all the regularities involved in the production and distribution of evils, there is a degree of contingency sufficient to allow the individual to resist. One who resists is not creating her resistance out of thin air; she takes it from the existing repertoire of possible responses in the game, or at least creates it by creating a difference relative to one or more element of the repertoire. Even when she invents a totally new gesture of resistance, she usually composes it from some other existing repertoire of speech and action. Sometimes she does so by borrowing elements from the repertoires of other games. Therefore, the most important parameter of a political regime from the point of view of freedom is the ability to maneuver between one social setting and another, one game and another, and the price of each of the moves. All this will suffice for re-ascribing to human beings the responsibility for reducing and preventing superfluous evils.

8.351 It is helpful in this context to enlist Claude Lefort's formulation: "In democracy the locus of power is an empty place."[110] This empty place creates a space open to political and social interactions and associations, making it possible to maneuver between different social games without paying too high a price for the transition from one game to another. This space and this maneuvering capacity progressively contract the lower the level of the regime's democracy, and the price of transitions rises for the entire population of subjects, while a small group of overprivileged people enjoys a high degree of low-priced maneuverability. This group gradually takes over the empty space of power. In a totalitarian regime, the vacant space is packed to capacity with innumerable threatening representatives of the ruling power, and no free space remains. The entire social space is open to a very small group free to maneuver at a very low price among the social spheres and the games taking place in each; all others are riveted to permanent places in the social space and can participate in a small and set number of social games, with very little maneuvering capacity within each game and very high prices exacted for every attempt to move from one game to another. Of course, both totalitarianism and democracy have additional characteristics, but these will suffice for the purposes of our discussion. A totalitarian regime creates structural conditions in which it is impossible to disengage from encounters with casualties, or to cut off harmful contacts even when the intensified encounters produce unbearable suffering and damage, and in which it is much more difficult to respond to calls for help. A democratic regime creates structural conditions that facilitate both cutting off contact and responding to calls. This, in a nutshell, is the difference between them from the point of view of the production of Evil, and one can formulate it without knowing another thing about the specific mechanisms of oppression in a totalitarian regime or the mechanisms of welfare and the protection of fundamental human rights in a democratic regime.

8.352 Based on the same logic, a decisive difference can be formulated between the Evil produced through economic domination and the Evil produced through political domination. The Evil produced in the economic sphere concerns the capital at the disposal of individuals in various systems of exchange, that is, the means allowing maneuvers among games, as well as cutting off contacts and responses to calls for help. Poverty and exploitation tend to wear down the possibilities of conversion but do not block its channels (7.250–7.255). Moreover, practices of resistance that may have an exorbitant economic cost may prove profitable in terms of the cumulative capital in other spheres — political authority, social prestige, cultural reputation, and so on. When Evil is produced through political domination, damage is caused to both the means and the channels of exchange. The resultant loss and suffering spread instantly throughout most, if not all, of the social spheres in which the individual is involved. The more powerful the mechanisms of social oppression and the deeper its colonization of the lifeworld, the greater the speed and scope of the spread of loss and suffering and the greater their impact on all the webs of association and communication in which the individual takes part. This is one manifestation of the elimination of the social and the political in a totalitarian regime.

8.353 Political freedom is a necessary and insufficient condition for the reduction of Evil. Its absence is a sufficient but unnecessary condition for the production of Evil. In democratic regimes, there are oppressive state mechanisms designed to protect political freedom, but these are insufficient, for there is an ever-present need to protect the dominated from an excess of freedom obtained through the accumulation of economic capital, the abuse of political authority, and the benefits of group affiliation and symbolic capital. In totalitarian regimes, there are oppressive state mechanisms designed to protect the system from the irreducible ontological freedom that is always, in every state of affairs, excessive from the regime's point of view. But these are insufficient, and there is an ever-present need for mobilizing this freedom into the regime's mass projects — war, occupation, transfer, reeducation and restructuring of the society, and so forth — through which continued support for the regime and the reproduction of its oppressive policies are enlisted. A political theory of morals has to take into account these two sides of the coin of freedom: the excess of freedom and the need to take measures to contain it; the excessive chaining and management of freedom and the need to find enough cracks in the system, enough lines of flight, to allow its proper expression. In both cases, the starting point must be ontological freedom, and that means that one has to presuppose the existence of heterogeneous social games.

8.354 The only thing we should assume regarding ontological freedom is the non-inevitability of the regularity of human action and the existence of vacant space for a new move in any social game (8.011–8.013). Freedom in itself, that mysterious nonentity in the depth of human nature or at the juncture of body and mind, is not necessarily beyond the scope of our critical knowledge, as Kant argued, but it is beyond the scope of our interest, as what should be of interest in the domain of moral theory. Certain actions may be necessary, and some of their harmful effects might be inevitable as well; in such a case, evils are not superfluous, and the talk about Evil is lamentation devoid of moral significance. However, to the extent that human action leaves a space free of necessity, it determines the evils as not inevitable and makes the discussion of Evil the most urgent matter in moral affairs. The different historical ways of forming political freedom, the different social ways of allocating it, of compressing it and distributing it across the various fields of social domination, the different ways in which it is invested or imprinted in those who learn to imagine themselves to be its generating source, its "subjects," all these need to be rethought from the point of view of the superfluous evils that these ways and forms produce and allow.

8.355 Evil is the underside of impersonal freedom, with no source in any subject and no location in any self. Its place, if it has one, is precisely in the space between one individual and another, between one act and another, between one representation of regularity and another. And perhaps, if you wish, its place is in the space between one moment and another. But one must understand that no subject bears this space within him, or in any way gives birth to it, and that, conversely, the subject can be imagined as that self-identity encompassing within it difference and otherness only to the extent that this space is erased and only at the site of its erasure, in the various acts of representation out of which that sticky, indiscrete metaphysical mud of the self appears. Freedom is the space that may not be erased, this permanent spacing, and Evil is the excessive, superfluous being that appears out of this spacing and whose presence is institutionalized when such a particular spacing repeats itself in a set pattern, in a series of practices.[III]

8.4 *The Limit of Waste*

8.400 On the origins of Evil: human beings are finite and limited creatures who produce superfluous evils both intentionally and inadvertently. As finite creatures, human beings lack the imagined perfect benevolence and omnipotence of God. They can prevent and reduce some superfluous evils but don't wish to, because they are not good enough; they wish to prevent and reduce some superfluous evils but cannot, because they lack the wisdom and strength to do so. Therefore, Evil does not lessen in the world. And even as they seek other things — comfort, welfare, riches, political power, knowledge, fame, and fortune — and continuously improve the means of attaining them, they also improve the means of producing and distributing evils and the social order capable of maintaining ever more sophisticated regularities of the production of evils, which in fact cannot exist without them. Therefore, Evil multiplies in the world. But for precisely that reason, because they produce so many evils through such sophisticated means, humans can reduce at least some of this malaise and misery, at least some of the time. They can do so either by abstaining from inadvertent Evil or by abstaining from intentional Evil, but most of all by knowing how to identify the regularity of the production and distribution of evils and taking action to disrupt it. Because they can, possibly they must. It is not the duty that entails the ability, as Kant thought, but the ability that entails the possibility of duty (see 8.404).

8.401 Perhaps there is an evolutionary ladder here: small animals sometimes kill smaller or weaker animals that cross their paths; large animals hunt for prey; the ancient human-animal that improved the means of hunting learned to lay traps as well, to prepare snares, and began to direct these means against other, competing human-animals, too. Gradually, people separated killing from the other tasks of existence and survival and turned it into a means that could be employed for other, less urgent ends; under the protection of this means and under the threat it created, other instruments of torture and destruction evolved, and existing means initially designed for other uses took on new roles in the realm of producing evils. "The rise of man" is patently also the growing sophistication of the means of causing evil and of their integration, like that of agriculture or commerce, into the distribution of labor and the social order as the latter became increasingly complex. But even if it's possible to reconstruct such an evolutionary course, this doesn't justify the saying "man's heart is evil from his youth." If there is an original sin here, it is that of God, who created man so far from perfection. Evil came into the world not because man's heart is evil from his youth but because he is an imperfect creature who incessantly completes himself, a limited creature given no limits, an unbridled creature creating, inventing, changing and being changed, improving and being improved, commanding physical and social powers to cause evil that are forever immeasurably greater than the wisdom, the courage, and the mental strength he commands to bridle the production of Evil.

8.402   Man is not born evil, and the reduction of Evil does not necessitate the reprogramming of childhood. There is no need to labor over the correction of individuals' souls, to await a straightening — somehow — of the crooked trunk and hope the boy will shake off badness and mature to good deeds. On the contrary, the organized correction of young souls is anchored, at least since the eighteenth century, in disciplinary procedures that have themselves become centers for the orderly production of superfluous evils. Today, we know a lot about the ways in which these evils are manufactured and distributed. We know very little about educational institutions that have ever succeeded — perhaps ever since the establishment of educational institutions — in bringing up an entire generation of people who participate less than others in the production of superfluous evils. Education is not an instrument for the reduction of Evil but a set of apparatuses that take part in its reproduction. It is one of those distinct areas in which the orderly production of superfluous evils calls out for civil resistance — resistance, struggle for reform in the educational system, not in order to reform the young person but in order to protect her.

8.403   To be precise, the power to do evil and the power to reduce evil (and the capacity to create, and even the capacity to invent, evil) belong not to "man," or to any man in particular, but to societies of human beings. It is not "at the disposal" of any man or woman, it is not inscribed on the genes of any particular individual, it is not in anyone's possession, whether an individual or a public, and it cannot be inscribed on anyone, although at times it is seemingly easy to identify those in whose bodies and souls it has settled. It is created and exists only in human coexistence, in competition, in the distinguishing differences between individuals, in the struggles waged everywhere for every kind of limited resource, and it is always implanted in the webs of association and communication within which individuals are born and from which they are constituted. Just like freedom, Evil subsists between individuals, not "inside" any one of them. What is "inside" the individual — wickedness, malice, cruelty, vengefulness, sadism — doesn't necessarily concern the regularity of the production of superfluous evils. The wicked man can take part in resistance to Evil no less than the innocent and pure-hearted can take part in the production of superfluous evils.[112] Evil is a superfluous being that appears out of a certain regularity in the organization of freedom as that "spacing" between singulars — individuals, positions, acts, images, signs, gestures (8.354). Freedom is taken within the social game from the empty space that always exists between one step and the next, between one individual and another, between one act and another, so as to re-space, so as to do a deed. Just as Evil is situated within the social game that regularizes the production of superfluous evils, the moral act is that spacing which will discontinue this regularity.

8.404   Because in principle this can be done, there can be a duty to do it. Whence comes this duty? The duty arises from the call of the other in distress. The concrete other is the probable but not necessary source of the call; the call can be real or hypothetical, conjectured or imagined, and as such ascribed to someone suffering here and now or to someone in danger of suffering at some future time. The duty arrives from an other who is or who may be in distress. It comes from there but isn't logically derived from there, not from there and not from any other place either — the call is not the source of the duty. The duty has no source. The duty doesn't follow from the call; it is its displacement from one language game into another. In the first language game, the other — real or imagined — is the speaker who posits me as an addressee of a description (of suffering, or disaster, or pending danger that has befallen or may befall someone else) embodying or implying a call for help, or as an addressee of a plea for help containing or implying a description. The call posits me directly as an addressee of a plea and indirectly as an addressee of a description (or vice versa), but what counts at this stage is the description. This description will become part of a moral discourse if it opens up the question of the superfluity of the evil — is it or was it preventable and at what price? The plea, the entreaty, the call, too, will become part of the moral discourse but only through such a description. A description of distress in terms of preventable superfluous evils is an enhancement and extension of the call of distress in terms allowing a moral justification for the action: failure to act, the malfunction, the abstinence from preventing the evil, or the act intended to prevent it. The justification itself can be given only in terms of greater or lesser evils that may presumably be caused as a result of the act or the failure to act. But the justification does not entail a duty; it assumes one. Neither does the call entail an obligation; sometimes it seeks to express or activate one. The duty is situated in the very transposition of the moral description onto the second language game in which I simultaneously posit the other as a referent of a prescription and myself, along with others, as the addressee of this prescription. In this language game, I stand concurrently in the position of addressee and in the position of addresser. From the description I extract a prescription instructing "This superfluous evil must be prevented," and I see myself as the addressee of this prescription, along with others, in the event that they, too, could stand in my stead in the speaker's position and extract the same prescription. And vice versa, someone else may be the addresser who extracts the prescription from the description, while I see myself as the addressee of this prescription because I myself could be its speaker.

8.405 The duty itself, and the obligation it creates, are merely a translation of the call of the other in distress into the language of a principal guiding action. The two language games are separate; in Lyotard's terms, you might say that a gaping *différend* lies in between. But the two language games belong to moral discourse. Moral discourse is characterized by the presence of these two language games, alongside each other, so that they cannot be separated without departing from moral discourse, without being "outside morality." These are two separate language games, divided by a usually unbridgeable gap, and sourceless duty commands a move from one to the other. The duty is not the prescription itself but something else, a kind of supplement or addendum, accompanying the prescription. This addendum is at one and the same time that by virtue of which the leap from game to game is occurring and that which is dragged along in the passage from game to game, from description to prescription: non-indifference in the face of the superfluity of the evil (see 7.310–7.315). The duty is the principle of the leap from the describing to the prescribing language game. More precisely, it is the principle that determines the impossibility of disconnecting the two. This principle is a necessary, transcendental condition for the possibility of moral discourse that constitutes the boundary of the moral: the moral begins where indifference in the face of an evil befalling another ends; indifference to an evil befalling others is the end of moral discourse. And also its threshold: once it is crossed, you have entered morality. This principle cannot be justified without being assumed. It constitutes moral discourse the way a checkmate constitutes chess: it's impossible to play chess when you're indifferent to the fate of your king; this indifference means the end of the game. Defending the king is the basis of the game. An other in distress is the king of moral discourse. There is no other king, and there is no law preceding the king. The king in chess comes into the world along with the law constituting the game. Duty comes into the world along with one in distress.[113]

8.410   As stated, duty assumes ability, but the ability allowing the occurrence of duty as a passage from a descriptive to a prescriptive statement is limited. In fact, it is not an ability in the sense of a potential ready for realization, vested in an instrument awaiting use. Such an ability is not vested in the individual as the potential for motion and transportability is vested in a car and is implemented when the car's engine is ignited, or as the potential for measuring time is vested in an old watch, to be activated if only someone would wind its springs. The ability in question is probable and contingent, a chance of changing what is non-inevitable — like the fast dribbling of a player that can lead the ball into the hoop, or a chess player's successful move that can decide the game, and, even more, like a strike at an industrial plant that can begin a wave of strikes that eventually paralyze the economy and foil government policy, or like a petition that can move people into the streets and ignite civil resistance to war. Some actions have a likelihood, somewhat greater than zero, of generating a break in the regularity of the production of evils in a particular area, within a particular range, in a certain sphere of life. That's all. And because the chance is there, one should try.

8.411 Until the right conditions are created, resistance remains weaker than the mechanism reproducing the regularity. In contrast to what many Marxists have thought, there's no knowing when the suitable conditions will arise or what signifies their ripening. Instead of looking for signs of the coming revolution, and waiting for the Messiah, we should search for cracks in the reproductive machine, those that exist there now, that always exist — because continuity is a false image of assorted reproductive machines — and drive stakes into these cracks.

8.412 Am I faced with a crack or a trap? Will the match light a flame or die out before it singes the page? There's no knowing. Ever. The act is always performed in conditions of uncertainty. Worse still, there's no knowing that the act will not generate more superfluous evils than those it set out to reduce or eliminate. There's almost no doubt it will generate some evils that will be superfluous from a given point of view. Children feel abandoned, feel the pain of separation from the woman who has joined some struggle and is now investing her all in it; the strike may bring many families to near-starvation, might end in the closing of the plant, as the owners threaten; the demonstrators demand moderation of the cruelty inflicted on terrorist groups and less oppression of the population among which they are hiding, but these steps may enhance the terrorists' appetite and engender yet more terror, as the state experts on terror predict. And of course there are even more extreme situations when the rebels endanger an entire population. There's no knowing, but it's always possible and obligatory to guess, to hypothesize, to assess the probabilities, both through detached deliberation and through trial and error. Even one who opposes change and is not prepared to try can only hypothesize in conditions of uncertainty; she may be in control of more information sources and more means of representation, but she isn't necessarily in command of a more practical wisdom that allows her to know that the proposed change will worsen the situation. She only knows what has been tried in the past, which in any case confirms the repetition, which is also the repetition of approving or putting up with what exists. One who seeks to reduce Evil must disrupt the regularities that produce it. She must attempt the new.

8.413 Evils can only be reduced through a social struggle. A struggle is social even when it destroys the social fabric, in revolution, in rebellion, in total war; but the more destructive the struggle, the less definite its connection to the reduction of superfluous evils, the more distinct its contribution to the production of new superfluous evils, and the vaguer and more dubious its moral horizon. The social is always existence in strife and struggle (but not necessarily in a struggle for survival): the "being-with" is always also "being-opposite"; the "being-alongside" is always also "being-against."

8.414 Needless to say, real struggles for social change are not conducted as exclusively moral struggles. Every party has interests — real, imagined, and perhaps also virtual — in the preservation of what exists here and now and in different directions of change. From an extra-moral point of view, it is possible to describe what moral duty demands as one interest among many, in agreement with some and contradictory to others. The moral interest demands changes in the order of evils that will reduce the general Evil. Those extra-moral interests that are in agreement with the moral interest will appear in the social struggle as carriers of the moral (or of the Good; there is no difference at this point); those extra-moral interests that contradict the moral interest will appear as carriers of Evil. But make no mistake: the former are not necessarily guided by an aspiration to make things better, and the latter are not necessarily guided by an aspiration to make things worse. The motives involved in a social struggle — for the maintenance of a social order, for its partial transformation, or for its total overthrow — should be distinguished from the moral significance of each. Kant, Hegel, and Marx recognized the gap between the morality of motives and the moral significance of the results, but believed it could be overcome in the end. The first saw war as nature's cunning bringing about man's moral improvement in its aftermath; the second spoke of the actualization of Good through evil as one facet of the cunning of reason in history; the third spoke about the revolutionary power vested in the oppression of the proletariat, and his disciples translated this in a vulgar form to statements along the lines of "the worse it gets, the better it will finally be." The possibility that bad will or a bad state of affairs will finally lead to the reduction of Evil was interpreted as a law of human nature or of human history. However, there is no law here, only a possibility following from the distinction between the nature of the interests motivating the social struggle and the moral significance of the struggle. Kant, Hegel, and Marx were right to claim (each in his own way) that the moral interest alone cannot generate a moral change and also to look for its historical partners, but they were wrong (each in his own way) both in assuming that such partners would necessarily exist and in believing that their path was destined to succeed.

8.420 The moral interest demands changes in the order of the evils that will reduce the general Evil. The horizon of the moral interest's intention should always be the general Evil, that Evil thought through to the limits of moral sensibility, rather than the one befalling a particular sector and experienced as common within that sector — a family, clan, community, people, nation, class, or any other group — and emphasized in a more or less calculated dismissal of evils befalling others. The (more or less) calculated dismissal of evils befalling others is the inner negation of the moral, the negative pole within morality itself, the equivalent of a lie, or the conscious acceptance of error in the cognitive domain, of a consciously illegal act in the judicial sphere. The moral interest, "naturally" directed first of all to those nearby (though the precise range and character of "naturally" change from one culture to another), cannot be guided by the dismissal of those who are distant. On the one hand, it must always be open to criticism that reveals the limits of moral sensibility and seeks to broaden it. On the other, it must be open to criticism that reveals the amoral interests working to narrow the relevant range of the moral interest and seeks to curb them.

8.421 On the one hand, the interest in reducing the general Evil is a moral interest only up to a point, as long as it remains abstract and doesn't refer to particular others, those who have a larger share of the general Evil than others. In contrast, the particular care I apply to my family members, members of my people, noble as it may be, is also, in and of itself, only a moral interest up to a point. It is moral by virtue of containing care for an other; it is limited by the fact that the extra-moral interests I have in the social group to which I belong, to which I am close, or in which I am invested emotionally or economically restrict this care for an other. These are extra-moral interests to the extent that they concern me, my identity, my way of life, what I hold dear, what I am close to, the meaning I can give this life.[114]

8.422 When I care for my family or my close friends, I am serving two kinds of interests, and I often confuse them. In especially extreme conditions of danger, suffering, and want, such as those created in battle, in time of disaster, or in concentration camps under totalitarian regimes (see 9.1), a conflict of interest appears between the self and the other that leaves no space for doubt: Evil separates the self from the other and destroys social partnership; care for the other that survives in extreme conditions follows from a moral interest and contradicts other interests of self-love, and the very will to survive. Under more relaxed conditions, it is easier to err and to mislead, but the further one gets from the "circle" immediately around the self, the easier it is to locate the difference. Here is one example: agents of national culture tend to forget and obscure this difference when they assist the members of their people in remembering a common national past and preserving a gradually disappearing heritage. Those with cultural capital who seek to develop and teach their tradition and culture to others have a distinct personal interest in this tradition and its transmission (after all, this is the capital they deal in) and a doubtful moral interest in the others to whom they wish to teach the tradition (for these cultural agents labor to create the need for this tradition among the public, along with a sense of identification with it and a fear of losing it). So even if they cater to the interests of others, these cultural agents too often cater to interests that they themselves have created in others out of their own self-interest. At times, a similar phenomenon can be discerned within the close family circle: it is sometimes easy to identify the parent's distinct personal interest in passing on to her children what she knows how to give, thus affirming herself, gaining her identity and authority, and more difficult to identify the child's interest in accepting what the parent demands that he take. And yet I don't intend to deny the possibility of a partnership evolving between people such that it becomes pointless or even impossible to distinguish between care of the self and care for the other, or between an extra-moral interest and a moral interest, and I will return later to this form of partnership (8.443 and 9.303–9.304). I only wish to be careful about the ways in which an interest is represented as moral. The bourgeoisie, said Marx, represents its particular interest as a universal interest. This is the entire critique of ideology in a nutshell. What is true of the relations between the bourgeoisie and society at large is true of every group, from the family through the nation, as regards the relation between the dominant elements, who have the means of representation, and the group for which they purport to care. When such a partnership forms, it usually concerns the political rather than the moral or, at best, the morality of the political. This is the rare moment, utopian or imagined, in which the common Evil can be spoken of as the platform unifying a human association, endowing a diversified and fractured community with its moral common ground.[115] But contrary to the common good, which is merely an idealization both of Good and of the association, a utopia of another world, when one speaks of the common Evil, the utopian element concerns the nature of the association alone, not the Evil, and the utopia is of this world.

8.423 The matrix of problems involved in identifying an interest as moral and in representing interests as moral is irrelevant to the guiding principle of the moral interest — care for an other, which involves a willingness to harm personal interests to the point of self-sacrifice. Within the moral realm, care for an other suspends other interests and overrides them, and it makes no difference whether by "other" I mean my dear ones, or my people, or my distant relatives, or whether I mean the distress of the convert, the stranger, the widow, and the fatherless who are in thy land within thy gates, or of those among whom we dwell. Care for the other overrides other interests when these are articulated within a moral discourse and as long as they remain within the moral. This always pertains to the possibility that I will be required to sacrifice my particular interests, not for the sake of the common, general interest, but for the sake of the particular interests of concrete others.

8.424 I'm not referring to an absolute imperative situated opposite other hypothetical imperatives in the vein of Kant. The moral imperative is always conditional on a general discretion that determines whether the conditions exist, in a given state of limited and fragmentary knowledge and considerable uncertainty, for doing this or some other deed in order to reduce superfluous evils, in order to answer the call of someone in distress. But this is a variation of sorts on another Kantian principle, that fundamental difference and that unbridgeable gap between considerations of moral duty and considerations of pleasure, enjoyment, and utility. The moral interest makes its demands in an open field of action in which there are — together and always in total confusion — considerations of all kinds: political, economic, aesthetic, and so on; excitations accompanying these interests and other excitations not guided by identified interests. This field can be represented from a point of view that is emotional, economic, political, aesthetic, and so forth, and each time a different value will be assigned to the various interests operating within the field and to the various demands — of emotion and of logic, to the extent that these are distinguishable — within it. Therefore, a political or aesthetic or religious game can always exist within the economic or the ideological game, and so forth, and vice versa. But these representations and these games have a common denominator only if they are organized from a third, independent point of view. Thus, for instance, the political representation can assign its own values to economic and aesthetic interests and create their common denominator; but this common denominator will disappear from an aesthetic or economic point of view, which will also erase the superiority assumed by the political representation. All this is no more than a clumsy formulation of one facet of the idea of *différend*.

8.425 Moral deliberation, that branch of practical reason oriented toward the other, is none other than the rational calculation of wasteful prodigality.[116] Moral deliberation does not consider, or account for, personal interests, for when it is activated, these interests have no focus of selfhood to attach to. Moral deliberation is self-forgetting, a form of submergence in an other, succumbing without limit, an absurd investment, a sacrifice, and a waste. This waste can bring forth great happiness, or suffering and pain, pleasure or loss. But be they happiness or suffering, the excitations accompanying the waste or the moral sacrifice and the benefits it provides are not what makes them morally proper or obligatory. A philanthropist can build a reputation out of the waste, and a masochist can take pleasure in the suffering she willingly takes upon himself. From a moral point of view, these motives and these profits neither add nor subtract. What determines the proper moral act is only the propriety of the response to an other in distress. Because moral interest is unfailingly directed toward the other, moral deliberation deals not with the motives of the self in addressing the other but only with the question whether the effort is proper, whether it is made to the right degree, whether it is guided by a reasonable judgment of the expected results for the other toward whom the action is directed and still others whom this action neglects or may indirectly involve or inadvertently affect. People can respond to the call of the other due to the pleasure this affords them or despite the terrible pain it causes them. Moral deliberation may turn a certain pleasure or a certain profit into the bearer or the conductor of a moral action and attempt to reduce the pain or the loss involved in responding to the call. But nothing can change the fact that the proper act demands expenditures, which are beyond the account of profit, pleasure, and pain.

8.430 The self is the limit of the prodigal waste involved moral concern. The self is not an internal essence but rather a boundary line that one concern draws for another. The self is first of all a limit of self-sacrifice, which is conceived and expressed as such only after a limit to one's expenditure has been set. Setting the limit allows a self to recognize spending as its own and giving as self-sacrifice. This limit precedes the constitution of self as an object of reflection and as a hypothetical focal point that seemingly unifies all the acts of self-consciousness. Selfhood is posited, affirms itself, grants itself identity and meaning, through the way in which the limit to sacrifice is drawn and according to the matter of interest on which it was drawn. Every other form of self-care, self-nurturing and self-development, self-positioning and self-interpretation, in the various social fields, through the various media of culture, assumes this divide, reaffirms it, and manifests it according to the rules of the given social game and cultural discourse.

8.431 Until selfhood appears, concern for the other is not perceived as sacrifice. From the moment of its appearance, and even if the practical, real interest in the other continues, succumbing to an other seems to be self-sacrifice. Selfhood delineates the realm of prodigal expenditure for the sake of an other; it determines the economy — of goods, emotions, ideas — from which what is detracted is detracted and in which what is invested is invested, and it declares prodigal expenditure to be sheer waste. In extreme conditions of danger, suffering, and want, when conflicts of interest between care of the self and care for the other unravel the social fabric (8.422), sacrifice is the only way to retain its remnants.

8.432 Until selfhood appears, sacrifice for someone is not perceived as concern for an other. When selfhood appears, concern for an other can be instrumental — the other as an instrument for the satisfaction of my needs — or a form of sacrifice. The dichotomized relation between self and other appears along with a clear boundary line between the self's calculated and insular economy of exchange and the waste that deviates from this for the sake of someone else. And this relation appears only when such a boundary line is in place.[117] But selfhood — like otherness — does not always or necessarily appear. The web of social ties within which every individual is placed is not created through the connection of individuals where every one is a self unto herself and an other to everyone else; more or less loose associations, more or less solid social formations, are not constituted through a dialectical negation or a miraculous overcoming of this imaginary and seemingly most fundamental difference between self and others. Webs of social ties precede self and other and enable their appearance, their placement opposite each other, the polarity, the contrast, and the negation, as well as the interaction, the sharing, and the partnership. Through these webs, things and talk, objects and messages, sensations and excitations, enjoyment and suffering, property and loss, are constantly passed from hand to hand, from ear to ear, from body to body. The individual is connected to others by various ties, knitted and unraveled,[118] before she is separated from them in an act that determines giving as waste and before she situates her selfhood as a limit of waste and the limit of waste as a foundation for her selfhood. Selfhood is not an essence waiting for an announcement of the waste that harms it or of the sacrifice that glorifies it; it appears out of this announcement and along with it. Understanding giving as waste within the web of social relations is a way of positing selfhood; drawing a boundary line for waste is a way of shaping the self. One who understands giving as waste and situates herself as a limit for this giving separates herself from the web within which the giving and the exchange relations take place so as to don the image of her selfhood, and in the process to situate other concrete individuals as her others.

8.433 A transition from exchange to waste and from calculated transactions to giving for free, to devotion and sacrifice, is always possible. The polarization between self and other can be established, stabilized, and protected through cultural, social, economic, and political practices and institutions, but it is just as possible to eliminate, transform, or reformulate it. Affirming the self through the negation of an other is possible but not necessary, and it is just as possible as tying one individual to another, an association of body with body and soul with soul that is beyond one and beyond the other, that is outside the selfhood of the first and beyond the alterity of the other. Such is the transition from desire to love (over and over again), or from economic investment to secret almsgiving, or from the authoritative speech of an author to a free-flowing conversation rewoven into some tradition.

8.434 In one direction, from waste to exchange, individuals disconnect — for most of the time perhaps, but even in a culture like ours not for all time — from their web of "uneconomic" association in order to take a place in the exchange economies (of emotions, messages, or objects) offered by the various institutions of society and culture, from the family through the psychologist's clinic, from the hairdresser and the postman through the discourse of art and communities of taste. In the other direction, from exchange to waste, individuals disconnect from this or that economy of exchange — disconnect for a moment, or an hour, but usually, in a culture such as ours, not for much longer — and dedicate themselves to someone else, who is already not wholly an other, and open up to what she is conveying, listen to her, give her some thing, and connect with her "with no strings attached." In other words, they do this without taking account of the calculus of the enclosed exchange systems. But here, too, this happens outside of society and culture, always inside and in relation to various traditions that establish exemplary figures and images of social ties, love, empathy, solidarity, compassion, and sacrifice unto death. And also, frequently, too frequently, this happens inside traditions that establish images of the social self — clan, class, or nation — under whose auspices, and there alone, is such an association, such a sacrifice, made possible. But it should be kept in mind that when the social self appears, it is merely because the boundary line of waste has been pushed aside momentarily, diverted and redrawn elsewhere, inscribed forcefully and unambiguously as that threatening borderline between us, "we" and all those like us, and them, the others, those different and separate from us. In other words, there is no moral sacrifice that is not a sacrifice for the sake of concrete individuals; when sacrifice is demanded for the sake of the homeland, the nation, the land, and any other value concealing a collective subject behind it, we have ceased talking morals.[119]

8.435 As Hegel demonstrated, and as is argued by psychoanalytic and anthropological discourse (Lacan and Mead, for instance), self-hood appears in a complex process of gradual individuation, out of the submergence of what will become a self in what will become an other. The self loses itself in the other only to rediscover itself in the mirror with which the other faces it, and negates the other only to discover its dependence on the other it negates and on the very act of negation. But why attribute to this individuation, and to the complex of dialectical relations between self and other, a single source, a single time, a single end, a single valid "resolution" or "result"? Moreover, why limit it to what happens to the slave discovering his selfhood through the consciousness of mastery reflected from his master, or to the master discovering his dependence on the slave, or to the baby separating from its mother? Why limit submergence in the other to need for the other or dependence on him, to desire for him and enjoyment attained or sought from him? Why see all the appearances of the individuation of self as manifestations of a single common essence, whose two extreme configurations are signified by narcissism and ecstatic surrender to the other, two forms of self-annulment? Submergence in the other and individuation from him can take on many faces, can occur at many points throughout life, can be more or less dramatic, can be refreshingly novel or tedious and repetitious, and all this without their sharing a common source or a unifying basis. Submergence in an other can express various types of interests and be anchored in different kinds of associations, engendering different types of individuation. Playing a ball game, I can submerge myself in the other's face, in his physical gestures, in order to prepare for his pitch, his transmission. In a conversation, I can submerge myself in the other's face and await a new message, a word I wish to hear, or a certain gesture that would tell me more than is said. A man can submerge himself in his beloved, during an act of love, or a dance, in the wonderful tension of untouching-touch, and from afar, while writing a letter or a story. While giving, I can be totally submerged in the trouble of another. When contact with the other (or others; there can always be someone else there) is especially intense, especially dramatic and stormy, and I disconnect from the other and reaffirm my selfhood, I sometimes feel that I left the encounter a different person. Clearly, disconnection from the other, from the others, from my being-alongside-and-opposite others, can always occur as a negligible matter of diverted attention. The self will not appear in every case of diverted attention. But when the self appears, it is almost impossible not to divert my attention from the other, from the otherness in the other. The self appears as a focus magnetizing a field of "personal" interests and magnetizing the other into that field, spreading her within it, dismantling, interpreting, and analyzing her, in order to extract from her something that belongs to her enclosed economy.[120]

8.440   When "human" made its debut in the eighteenth century, Foucault claims, it first appeared as a boundary line. Before it became the essence of man as a creature of his kind — that is, before "Man" came into being — "humanness" functioned in attempts made by members of a rising middle class to tame the sovereign's excessive, arbitrary power and to set limits to his supreme authority to punish.[121] "Humanness" was also a sort of code for calculations and a rule-deciding principle, allowing one to assess in advance, to predict and plan wisely, the steps of the sovereign, to include him, too, within the rational economy of civic interactions and negotiations, in making contacts and contracts. All subjects are endowed with a certain ineradicable value, which they shared equally, and which set recognizable limits on the sovereign's authority to hurt or harm them. I wish to identify a similar but inverted logic in the moment of the appearance of a selfhood that affirms itself as a limit to self-sacrifice — the self as a limit to what can be relinquished, to what can be eradicated from the self. A similar logic: only after selfhood/humanness has appeared is it possible to identify what occurs on the other side of the boundary line as waste/ arbitrariness and to demand a rational calculation of investment/ exercise of power. Inverted logic: the appearance of selfhood, magnetizing the other into the field of the self's interests, is the moment when the moral interest is suspended, the moment when care for the other ceases or is relegated to the background. The appearance of humanness, magnetizing the sovereign to the political field of a civil society, is the moment when the political birth of moral interest is made possible — the institutionalization of a moral interest (as care for the other) as political matter.

8.441 By analogy, but only by analogy, one could speak in the same vein about the self-affirmation of a group as possessing identity and clear boundary lines. Thus, for instance, the modern state that absorbs immigration formulates its selfhood (usually in terms of national identity) as the limit of its generosity in absorbing additional immigrants. But until such selfhood or "national identity" appears, along with the entire nationalist discourse that accompanies it and along with the mechanisms of state that nurture and enforce it, a willingness to absorb immigration is not considered generosity. With respect to the state, it is almost always retrospective generosity that is cited, and this in the past tense: relatively open borders are represented as generosity in order to put an end to generosity. An end is put to it in the name of the threatened national identity, in the name of the joint interests of all those whose identity this is purported to be, and on the basis of the principle of their national sovereignty. Modern sovereignty is a projection of selfhood that has intensified beyond measure. When interpreted in terms of subjectivity, this intensified selfhood engenders the destructive power of the nation, the race, or the class and the leader that embodies them. Such an intensified selfhood threatens to eradicate the unique selfhood of the individual, for it binds the truth of the individual to his part in the collective subject. In those fortunate places where sovereignty is interpreted as an intensified projection of formal and vacant selfhood, the selfhood of rights, borne by the individual as a unitary atom, an alienation appears that undoes the threads of social association and destroys the bases of solidarity constituting it. This abstract selfhood is always willing to abandon the individual to himself, for it binds his truth to the vacant form of his selfhood.[122]

8.442 If it were possible to restore humanness to being no more than a limit — a general law applying to the arbitrariness of the sovereign's exercise of power — and if it were possible to think selfhood as an inevitable limit to sacrifice for the sake of an other, would it not then be possible to totally overturn the conceptual constellation of sovereignty-citizenship-selfhood lying at the base of most forms of "the political" in the West and in some of its chronic problems? Sovereignty would then appear as a projection of that inevitable limit of common waste, appearing on the social screen inescapably, in sporadic flashes, with no unity or essence of its own. Such sovereignty would draw its legitimacy from the sacrifice it allows, that is, from the principle of its *tzimtzum*, its self-reduction.[123] Social solidarity would not be forcibly imposed on behalf of a collective subject and would not be cast into its smothering lap, but would be able to grow in that vacant space where actions of care for others can take place. The formal principles of citizenship would be preserved, but they would be free from any assumption of humanness as an essence, serving only as a limitation on the sovereign authority's exercise of power. These principles would not be exploited to ensure social cohesiveness or justify abandoning the other to his troubles and misery.

8.443 The generality of the law enables the formation and representation of the moral interest in the other as a political matter but does not determine it as such. Political interests in the moral must also always be expressed in terms of laws, borders, rights, rules of negotiating, exchange, and allocation, norms of action, procedures, and measures. This is so because establishing care for another as a political problem (its political problematization) must be carried out according to what is common and general, what pertains to the public interest, to the things common to the collective, the *res publica*. The common requires a certain generality of rules and a certain, at least temporary, consent to rules and to rules for setting the rules — that is of course a point of incessant struggle, which aims at the authority to establish rules and at the rules to be established, and in which access to the ruling power and the welfare of the ruled collective are both at stake. In contrast, moral interest in the political always bears a seal of the singular, of the exception to the rule and the authority to make exceptions, what cannot be made to answer to a rule and cannot be measured, a seal of sacrifice and waste (see 8.515).[124] This is so not because moral interest is indifferent to what is dictated by law or owed by right, nor because it refrains from struggling over the law, the right, or the rule governing the allocation of what is owed to one or to many. On the contrary. This is so partly because moral interest is always an interest in the singularity of suffering that cannot be expressed and irreparable loss that cannot be assessed. This is so partly because moral interest makes these demands on behalf of others, above and beyond personal considerations, oblivious from the very outset, from the moment of its clear differentiation from other interests, to the care of the self, save its thought of waste without measure, save its virtue of doing the right thing.

8.444 A certain degree of waste — of time, money, and other resources — occurs on a miniature scale in almost every demonstration, every act of organizing for a civil struggle. A certain degree of sacrifice (a degree that cannot be measured) occurs every time someone takes it upon herself to bring the distress of the other into the common space, to bring to light in the public sphere her complicity, and that of others, in the regularity of the production and distribution of the superfluous evils befalling others, to place these superfluous evils on the public agenda. Not just waste and sacrifice, of course. There are almost always various benefits, too, and above all the benefit born of partnership, of the knitting of new ties, of the strength imparted by the solidarity of those given to; the benefits gained from participation in the social sphere that is formed by the moral act and the space created within it for new associations.[125] But there's always the chance and the risk of a sacrifice going too far, beyond what can be returned or even measured. In the twentieth century, Mahatma Gandhi and Martin Luther King Jr., for instance, exemplified a moral interest in the political that involved not only a willingness to take risks but a sacrifice unto death. However, one need not be a hero, a saint, or a martyr like Gandhi or King to be driven by moral interest and to take the risks it involves.

8.445 Clearly, in cases where the political is totally nonexistent, under occupation or under a tyrannical or totalitarian regime, risk and a willingness to sacrifice are conditions for the struggle and not accompanying moments of it. Many additional factors combine here, some pertaining to the shared values for which the struggle is waged, which are not necessarily moral values (national dignity, personal and national freedom, and so on), and some pertaining to ethical — but not moral — questions: how should individuals properly live and die under this bad regime? [126]

8.450 Nietzsche: self-restraint, self-discipline, and cruelty to self, which lead the self beyond itself and realize its potential to overcome itself and aggrandize its will to power, are all the refined climax of a will to the power of a "strong spirit," of a noble, virtuous man who has ventured beyond good and evil. There is a sense in which Nietzsche was right: abundance and generous spending do characterize noble men and women, strong spirits, who are also willing to take risks in experiencing what is new and exposing themselves to the strange and foreign. But Nietzsche was wrong: these extraordinary traits should be attributed to ordinary people who do the right thing—beyond good perhaps (and its many images), but not beyond Evil. The right thing to do, what ought to be done, emerges only in the presence of, and due to, Evil.

8.451   Morality is the sphere where the self transcends itself, the sphere of elation. The self will always appear outside the moral, through self-affirmation or self-positioning, or due to self-care, nurturing, forming, and invention, and always at the expense of care for others.[127] This is a zero-sum game, but only in terms of intentions or, more precisely, in terms of the exchange relations between possible justifications, and only if self and other are isolated from the dense web of being-with-together-alongside-against many individuals ("intention," it should be remembered, always assumes an isolated individual vis-à-vis the world and vis-à-vis others). When the results, which have no existence outside this web, are taken into account, the whole structure may be overturned: care for another may injure him, and submergence in self may annihilate it; self-care may aid a particular other while injuring others still; care for a particular other may glorify the self and harm yet others or do them good. As far as possible, moral deliberations must take into account the moral advantages of self-care (that is, their advantages for others) and the moral risk of neglecting it, as well as the disadvantages of care (and excessive care) for the other and the desirable and undesirable side effects of both kinds of care.

8.452   Given all this, it may be that self-sacrifice is not an efficient instrument in the struggle to reduce Evil. This sacrifice pertains only to the aspect of waste in moral considerations, not to "rational calculation" (8.425). Rational calculation is a cold calculation. It is impressed by the pathos of sacrifice in accordance with its usefulness to those for whom it was intended, according to its effective range, always determined in keeping with the subject position from which the sacrifice is performed (from 7.430 on). Should the enthusiastic youth join the underground or care for his ailing mother? Sartre presents a famous form of a moral dilemma. The Sartrean youth's free consciousness, devoid of grounds or ends, could do with a little less pathos and a bit more consideration for the purpose of carefully examining which of the two actions will prove more successful in an attempt to reduce Evil. If the young man stands only a very slim chance of being significantly useful in underground operations—of doing more than distribute leaflets, for instance—or if the underground operations endanger the civil population more than they trouble the regime, the youth had better stay home. Instead of making an arbitrary choice between absolute values that cannot be justified, he should choose, based to the best of his abilities on relevant reasons, the most useful waste of his energies. Underground activity itself is an example of a waste of energies, resources, and lives, which should properly be as rational and efficient as possible. A member of the underground seeks to identify the Achilles' heel through which to harm the regime — to strike at the ruling mechanism using minimum means to achieve maximum results. But what is true of the power relations between a wicked regime and the underground fighting is true of every site at which a mechanism producing superfluous evils can be identified, and at which from an almost powerless stance an attempt can be made to disrupt the normal progress of this mechanism as far as possible.

8.453 Because regularity in the production of superfluous evils does not conform to some inevitable law, there is unfailingly such an Achilles' heel in every mechanism producing evil. Hitting it doesn't necessarily require a head-on collision, either open or clandestine. The more sophisticated, but also much rarer, rational calculation does not exaggerate the importance of the pathos of resistance, of its heroic image. At times, it is wiser to employ the internal logic of the mechanisms producing superfluous evils against themselves, rather than directly resist these mechanisms and step up their operations. It may be more useful to employ viral action, disrupting the systems by activating their own means rather than trying to halt them head-on.

8.454 Frequently, it turns out that reforming the mechanism of evils and reducing the evils it produces are interests of both the reformers and others for whom these reforms were not intended. In such cases, there is no point in sacrifices and no need for a willingness to make them. Instead, one needs to persuade all concerned that the reduction of evils being caused to others is in their own interests, too. Such cases are very frequent, and therefore negotiations are usually preferable to any other form of action, especially since other forms may cause many more superfluous evils than attempts at persuasion. However, it is important to see dialogue as a strategy of struggle and to clarify that its choice is a result of the given conditions of the sociopolitical struggle. Reformers usually try to represent their proposed reform as a common interest, a "common good." Such a happy coincidence is an exception to the rule, and perhaps merely an idealization of an exception to the rule, a false representation of both the rule and exceptions to it, but many theories of morality and state have set it as their point of departure. In most cases, what takes place is a struggle between conflicting interests or between what the social partners perceive as conflicting interests, and it makes no practical difference which. Some suffer from superfluous evils, and some profit from them. Some profit from the evils' mode of production but are prepared to give it up out of moral considerations. Such individuals are willing to make some degree of sacrifice. And others are unwilling to do so and seek to go on profiting from the troubles. In this case, there is no point in addressing the common interest or in presenting an imagined interest of this type, which social experience will, sooner or later, contradict anyhow. In this case, continuing the moral struggle means a clash, civil or otherwise, which may harm all concerned.

8.455 In other words, even the rational calculation of waste may lead at any moment to a point requiring a choice between retreat — abandoning the case and the others, shutting oneself up in the economy of self — and sacrifice in continued dedication to an other. There's no getting rid of the willingness to sacrifice, or of the inherent tension between dedication to another within the realm of the moral and self-affirmation as the limit of the moral. Even the coldest calculation can turn out to be wrong; even the most careful act of resistance can turn out to be dangerous. In every public confrontation, a violent thug may suddenly appear; the most tolerant regime may suddenly go berserk; a policeman who is willing to open fire may pop up at any demonstration. Is this the moment necessitating retreat? And what happens in situations where the willingness to sacrifice life is a necessary strategy in the power struggle? Is it truly proper to die for others? In order to begin thinking about this question (and I can trace only the beginning of a thought here), we need to think about death. More precisely, about dying and killing.

8.5 *Unto Death*

8.500 My interest in my own death is not a moral interest. When Camus speaks of the absurdity of choosing existence, of the groundless "nevertheless" with which a man seeking and failing to find some sense to life cleaves to his existence, he affirms this statement, among other things.[128] The only moral element in the act of suicide concerns the loss and suffering it may cause others. The moral interest in my death (or in its prevention) belongs to others. Apart from my concern for those who may feel my death as a loss, my own death interests me in a totally amoral way, in the most self-interested way possible, for I am interested in the possibility of continuing to exist as an interested party, in the very possibility of being interested at all.

8.501 I may think that my death is a moral matter only if I give up the continuum between myself and the man I will be when I die. I may care for the man who will die in my body, or in what others would recognize as the same body that bore "me" in the past, that is, at present.[129] My body is closer to me than to any other person, and nevertheless it is not identical with me. But by distancing my death and attributing it to the other man I will be when I die, I miss death as an immanent possibility constantly accompanying me at any moment of the present. My death, imminent at any moment, is an immanent possibility of my existence as a finite entity conscious of the fact of its nearing death while having no knowledge about the manner of death's arrival. The man who is going to die at any moment is the writing, thinking man who is trying to locate the limits of his interest in himself, beyond which the other appears and the possibility of moral interest in others opens up. This man cannot care for his own death as he cares for the death of an other.

8.502 Even if we ignore the immeasurable proximity to death for a moment, it is difficult to bear the thought that some other man will someday die in my stead. Even if it were possible to assume such a disconnection, such a rift in identity, it would still be impossible to limit it exclusively to what concerns my imminent death. When the price of this disconnection emerges in other areas — for instance, in my relations with my children, with my beloved, in my ability to represent the man I was and the things I did in various, changing economic, political, and social contexts — then I will no doubt give it up in what concerns my death, too.

8.503 It doesn't follow from this that I must attribute to myself an identity and a unity that are not mine. Selfhood is not a substance but rather an agglomeration of areas of self-interest, which do not necessarily have a common basis, a unifying principle, or a coherent structure, but which include various fragments of continuities, repeatedly reimagined in keeping with the way that others, and I myself, represent me. Contrary to what Heidegger thought, even the selfhood constituted through my interest in my personal death, out of care for a finitude that has become conscious of itself, cannot provide a more primordial or more comprehensive structure, encompassing and giving measure to all other domains and aspects of self-interest. My interest in my children, in my free time, in my desires and enjoyments, in my professional career or my injured pride, does not necessarily succumb to the logic of the authenticity seemingly stemming from the singularity of death or from its intimate proximity that has reached self-consciousness. This is so even if this self-consciousness, from the moment it appears, accompanies all my other concerns and "bends" them along its lines. In other words, even if a consciousness of my finitude accompanies all the other manners and modes of my being in the world, it will not provide a unified basis constituting a unified self.

8.504　At the same time — and this is the decisive matter in the present context — in order for there to exist a relation of otherhood between myself and the one who dies while bearing my name and inhabiting my body, consciousness of death as self-consciousness, as the most distinct form of self-consciousness, must be erased. When I care for myself with regard to my imminent death and act to postpone the end (diet, medical tests, avoiding unnecessary risks), I may sometimes forget that it is I myself in question. But in order for me to ascribe to these cares a moral sense, in order for me to see them as a matter of moral interest, I must truly cause myself to forget the singularity of death that has reached self-consciousness. This happens on occasion, but it is easier for reflection to correct the mistakes that stem from this erasure than those mistakes that stem from the cementing and sanctification of the line connecting myself in the present and the other who will die under my name.

8.510　Well, then, is willingness to sacrifice unto death the right action? Right in what sense? Relative to life as it should properly be lived. Properly for whom? For me.

8.511　In this form, the question is not from the sphere of morality, although the whole history of ethics echoes through it. The history of ethics, not of morality (8.514). An ethics deals with the life that is good or proper for me, the life that it is right for me, and sometimes also for others like me, to live. At the end of the day, an ethics is an aesthetics of the existence of the self, as Foucault has shown so clearly in his later studies on the history of sexuality,[130] a quasi-aesthetic ideal of self-design that the individual acquires, but also forms and improves on, in the course of his education while forming himself in accordance with it.[131] Dealing with the good life also entails an engagement with the good (or beautiful) death, the proper way for a lover of wisdom to go to his death. As is well known, Plato states on Socrates's behalf that this is the whole point of philosophy, that philosophy in its entirety is but a preparation for death.[132] Many philosophers — first and foremost Spinoza — have repeated this, either self-righteously or candidly, meanwhile implicitly or explicitly establishing ethics as a "primary philosophy," or at least as what motivates philosophy and therefore precedes it. For Spinoza, ethics is the primary philosophy, the ultimate expression of the rational love of God, of metaphysical interest in the totality of reality, but all for the sake of knowing what is good, knowing good and evil, which for Spinoza finally meant what is good or evil for the body itself, the correct understanding of excitation and desire.[133] Since the self is perceived as finite and its finitude is perceived as a lack, as an evil to be overcome, care of the self becomes a wish to overcome the finite and cling to the infinite, because "love towards a thing eternal and infinite feeds the mind wholly with joy, and is itself unmingled with any sadness."[134] Overcoming finitude means being liberated from the limitations of the self, from the self as limited and finite, and it therefore culminates in death.[135] On the way to death, while dealing with the finite, the infinite, and the relation between them, philosophical discourse gets stuck in the dead end of self, even if it attempts in vain to overcome it.[136] This may explain why theories of morals (unlike ethics) tended to become anecdotal collections of proper rules of conduct rather than a real object of philosophical inquiry. The establishment of interest in another as a philosophical problem and its location at the heart of moral study did not occur in philosophical discourse until Kant, did not become its main issue until Marx, and was not thematized as moral concern for the other until Lévinas.[137]

8.512   Others, too, can learn from the philosopher's study of the good life and the appropriate death: those who view the philosopher, his life and death, as exemplary and worthy of emulating. Obviously, the appropriate death concerns every man. But this is so merely in passing. The main interest in ethical discourse is in the philosopher's good life and appropriate death. Had he truly been interested in his close friends rather than the truth and his soul's intimate relation with it, Socrates would have heeded their pleas, fled prison, and granted them a few more years of that rare combination of wisdom and eros that made him so dearly loved. However, contrary to common knowledge, Socrates was taking care of himself. Even when he tried to move others to care for their own souls and ask questions that would lead them to the essence of the good life, he was initially caring for himself, not for them.[138] He needed skilled interlocutors, quick-witted and razor sharp, opposite whom he would be able to examine his hypotheses about virtues, Good, and knowledge. Therefore, it was more important to him (or to Plato) to teach them the rules of the philosophical game than to tell them what Good is.[139] Aristophanes, Xenophon, and Plato, each in his own way, report additional anecdotes conveying Socrates's enormous concern for his own self. Official histories of philosophy relate this concern to the famous command "know thyself," as if self-knowledge were less egocentric than self-love. In addition, they emphasize that this interest in the self is none other than a transcendence beyond the self, toward the Logos, the Ideas, the Good, or God, while obscuring that what takes place is a dialectical process at the end of which the knower returns to himself, even if he loses himself completely in the object of his knowledge. Lessening the distance between the soul and the ideas it longs to know doesn't do a thing to lessen the distance between the soul of the philosopher and the soul of his friend, even if they travel the same route together. On the contrary, a life of contemplation forms a man who is capable of making do with himself and has no more need of friends (although the presence of these may always be beneficial).[140] I have dwelled somewhat on this matter because its importance extends far beyond Socratic ethics. Clearly, this is the canonical model for philosophical activity as a kind of care of the self, that is, as an activity outside the moral.

8.513 Anticipating later parts of this discussion, I wish to mention here that some of the familiar dilemmas pertaining to the conduct of the Jews under the Nazi regime — first and foremost the question of rebelling or "going like sheep to the slaughter" — can be interpreted as ethical, not moral, questions. True, many of those deliberating on these questions have perceived them as moral; yet the dilemmas originated not in care for an other but in care for something else, something that finally returns the deliberator to self, to the individual or the nation. The aesthetics was an aesthetics of death, but at issue in most cases was the manner in which individuals, those who were able, chose to design their own deaths, in view of the exemplary acts established by others and in order to set an example for others (see 8.521 on).

8.514 In contradistinction to ethical discourse, moral discourse deals, or should properly deal, not with "our" good life but with the bad lives of others, and not with the appropriate death of the one who philosophizes but with the ugly, horrifying, and senseless deaths of others. If this interest helps me or us, too, inadvertently, if it contributes to my or our good life, all the better. But moral considerations cannot be based on this, and it cannot be seen as the point of moral study. It cannot even be said to be right for me to live a moral life. All that can be said is that it is right to live a moral life, that is, to conduct a life guided by attentiveness to others and by a willingness to act to alleviate their distress. But this rightness is nothing more than another formulation of what is morally proper, and is equally general. It does not pertain to me personally or especially. Moreover, in order to say this, one must already be "within the moral" or, in other words, must already conform with the regime of moral discourse, which establishes care for the other as a limit and a constituting rule (from 7.311).

8.515 It is thus possible to conceive of care of the self and care for an other as two separate branches of the "theory of measures."[141] I propose to call the first branch "ethics" and the second "theory of morals." The semantic gap between "theory of measures" and "ethics," as well as that between the biblical and contemporary meanings of the Hebrew *musari* (moral), alongside the phonetic and graphemic associations of the Hebrew term, allow a redefinition (in a manner that might seem somewhat technical) of the three terms: "theory of measures," "ethics," and "theory of morals."

A theory of measures will denote here an interest in anything for which a measure is sought, in order to determine its correct or good measure, because in principle it lacks a measurable measure. Clearly, we are talking not about a measure of length or breadth, or riches, or motion, or any other quantity, but about something whose measure is immeasurable: authority and obedience, love and friendship, courtesy and custom, education and punishment, life and death. For something whose measure is measured, its measure is external and coincidental. Among those whose measure cannot be measured, two kinds can be discerned: (*a*) that whose measure is an internal restriction, a restraint of a self legislating to itself, which is its quality or its very essence, so that deviating from the measure is a possibility essential to it, posing a risk of transgression, destruction, elimination, or negation of the possessor of the measure; (*b*) that which has no measure and for which any attempt to draw a boundary line so as to signify its measure amounts to an arbitrary, external restriction that misses the point and voids the essence.[142]

Ethics is a branch of the theory of measures that deals with the archetype of those with measures of the first kind, the self. Ethics carries with it the Greek *ethos*, the prevalent custom, the habitual, the homely, the rules of etiquette and correct conduct, that which belongs to the way of life usual to myself and others in the same vicinity, that which is formed within this *habitus*, and therefore, also, that which pertains to my inclinations, my character. In the end, ethics encompasses everything that concerns good measure in the sphere of the lives of myself and those like me, including self-restriction, restraint, self-discipline, self-control, and the formation of self. In most of the ancients, the good measure of the self that lacks a measurable measure is an aesthetic one. In most of the moderns, the only way to determine a measure for self is to strip it of all its singularity and present it as subject to a general law, whether that which it legislates for itself (as a rational, autonomous being) or that which is enacted for it by the state and its judiciary or is regulated for it by social disciplinary institutions or mechanisms of normalization. The state judiciary, the rules and regulations of disciplinary institutions, the unwritten norms of social life, all these hedge in and set measures to the individual as a member of a group, in relation to a universal law essentially foreign to the immeasurable singularity within him. The individual's good measure or her virtue is but the measure of her conformity to the collective. A few moderns, such as Nietzsche, Heidegger, and Foucault, who criticized this view of common, ordinary, or normal and normalizing measures, tried to take an example from the ancients and restore the aesthetic measure. The other possibility didn't occur to them: acceptance of the infinite character of the immeasurable measure and, rather than an attempt at its restriction either aesthetically or through self-legislation, a redirection of it from self toward the other.

A theory of morals is the other branch of the theory of measures, the one dealing with the attempt to determine, despite all this, a measure for the immeasurable relation to another. If the theory of measures deals with everything that has no measure and ethics deals with the good measures of self, then the theory of morals deals with immeasurable giving and giving oneself to the other, that is, with transmission of whatever is transmitted for the sake of the other and with spending, devotion, and submission at the expense of the giving self.[143] Transmission is different from tradition, even if the former takes part in the latter and allows it.[144] Tradition pertains to everything transmitted, to the different processes of cultural transmission, and to transmission as an anonymous act without a distinct source and destination. Transmission, conversely, has a definite destination even when it has no source. Transmission is focused on this or that concrete other. The messenger transmits a message or a package or some other object, and leaves. The point is that the message, or that which was transmitted, reaches its destination. It's always important to know to whom precisely the object, the message, was transmitted. The sender may remain anonymous, the messenger be swiftly forgotten; she is supposed to transfer what is transmitted to its destination, to the one receiving, and no more. The messenger transmits, or transfers, but not in order to receive something in return. Transmission is transfer, not exchange. Transmission is just one leg of an exchange relation, and it is the only leg with which a theory of morals deals. Transmission can be imagined as an interrupted exchange, an action lacking its counterpart, not reciprocated. But this lack appears as such only if the transmission is examined from the point of view of exchange, if an attempt is made to reintegrate it into this or that system of exchange. The transmission lacking an immeasurable measure is located outside of exchange relations; it is parallel to them, and it establishes an alternative to exchange relations.

8.516* Relation to an other belongs to the second kind of things, the group of things with no measurable measure, things that cannot be fit with a measure and for which boundary lines are arbitrary restrictions that void their essence (which is to lack an immanent measure). It is necessary to distinguish here between the immeasurable and the infinite. Time and space, for instance, are infinite but measurable; the attempt to measure them is essential to the very interest in them as physical objects. Love is immeasurable but finite; the attempt to measure love kills it, while the anxiety related to the anticipation of its end is part of its essence. Lévinas equates the other, the otherness that subsists in any particular other, with the infinite (what is not finite and what the finite self is not), and infinity with immeasurability. The other is that which lacks any common measure with the self. Anything pertaining to the relation to the other becomes immeasurable as a result of these equations. I would like to distinguish myself from this position as clearly as possible: only the relation to the other is immeasurable in moral affairs, not the other herself, and it is immeasurable not because the other is infinite, or because there is no common measure between self and other, but because there are no predetermined limits for what it is proper for the other to ask from the self and for what the self ought to give to the other. These limits cannot be predetermined, because they are forever drawn and redrawn in and through the act of giving itself and because the very distinction of self and other proceeds from them and depends on them. The otherness of the other follows from the impossibility of restricting the relation to the other according to the predetermined measures that the self carries within itself. When

---

* The text exceeds its measure here, and I exceed the measure I set for myself in the present book and allow myself a measure of further elaboration on this matter.

restrictions are set, the other can be brought — as an other — into the economy of the self. Her otherness is implied in the often-repressed but never completely erased traces of the arbitrary nature of the restrictions.

8.517 No measure is common to the self and the general law. The law is a rule applying to every individual of its kind, and the common measure of all the individuals of their kind is a general law, but the self, as an object of care and interest, is contained in the individual's relation to herself in a way that cannot be grounded on the measure common to her and all others of her kind. Therefore, the individual's relation to the law can be seen as a kind of relation to the other, and the demand to "respect" the law in the Kantian theory of morals can be seen as a formulation of the appropriate measure of relation to the law in the absence of a common one. The categorical imperative, the "fundamental law of pure practical reason," says: "So act that the maxim of your will could always hold at the same time as a principle in a giving of universal law."[145] The "fundamental law" is a general law that makes the test of generality a criterion for the moral validity of the guiding principle of personal will. Kant terms it "the moral law" (*Sittengesetz*).[146]

8.518 The "maxim" or guiding rule of the will in Kant is none other than a linguistic, formal embodiment of self, from the time that self commits to the terms of the moral discourse demanding the formulation of rules for even the most ephemeral of whims.[147] With the appearance of the general law and the ungrounded demand for this "dependency under the name of obligation" between it and the personal will, otherness appears as an explicit moment of opposition. In Kant, the opposition between self and other in the moral context is manifested as the relation between the finite and the infinite: "the utmost that finite practical reason can effect" and which the finite will guided by it can seek is to "only approximate without end" to this "model" of "holy will."[148] A holy will unfailingly conforms to moral law; "the relation of such a will to this law is *dependence* under the name of *obligation*, which signifies a *necessitation* ... to an action which is called *duty*."[149] There is no limit to drawing ever nearer to the model of a pure moral will, that sacred will, for the personal will and the general law are incommensurable. Despite his criticism of Kant's view of infinity, Lévinas, writing in another context, still proves useful here: "The idea of infinity ... the idea of the perfect is not an idea but desire; it is the welcoming of the Other, the commencement of a moral consciousness, which calls in question my freedom."[150] The infinite moment in Kant's theory of morals is not separate from the total otherness of moral law. But does this desire to draw nearer to the idea of perfection follow from care of the self seeking perfection and seeking for itself a will as similar as possible to the pure moral will, or does it follow from an interest in the other, in the general law determining that pure will? Kant gives an unequivocal answer: only respect for the law can be a legitimate motive in moral considerations.[151] This should be added to Kant's direct and explicit opposition between the "law of morality" and self-love or care of the self. Where the latter appears, the validity of the former ends. Therefore, Kant's conception of morality can be seen as a special case of care for another (and hence of a theory of morals rather than an ethics), where respect for the moral law is the constituting rule of the moral sphere and indifference to this law is where morality ends.

8.520   Giving and transmission do not depend on reward. Giving is not a belated reward and doesn't beget a belated reward. Therefore, sacrifice unto death, which is a total giving of oneself for the sake of another, is the epitome of moral waste: the gift of life has no reward. The gift of life puts an end to the giver and to the giving. There is no more exchange, and there will be no reward, ever. This is the moment at which morality is differentiated from religion, including the "civic religion" of the state. Religion commands sacrifice to a nonmaterial, abstract, and absent other and usually promises rewards. Religion also allows certain others, under certain conditions, to transmit the property and souls of others and to sacrifice them for the sake of that abstract other.[152] Morality unfailingly refers to tangible transmission of the self and from the self to always tangible, present, or presentable others. This transmission, and the sacrifice it entails, are something one takes upon oneself but can never command of others. One can never make the leap from is to ought for another, the move from a description of superfluous evils to the obligation to reduce these. The moral leap, like the leap of faith, is a singular matter, and a matter for the singular individual.

8.521   One who purports to derive rules of sacrifice is speaking within another discourse, ideological, religious, or political but not moral. Or, at the very least, she has ceased obeying the rules of moral discourse that this discussion seeks to reconstruct here. In her discourse, there must be absolute values necessitating the sacrifice. The reference here is to "Values," to that which assigns value and determines something's worth, not to something that is valued, whose worth we seek to measure. Only a Value can determine what someone's life is worth. The reference here is to absolute values, for only an absolute value can command an absolute surrender, an absolute loss, and the elimination of the interested party. There is no return from sacrifice unto death. It is the very edge and end of all networks of exchange between self and other. The demand for sacrifice can be carefully qualified, as is the demand for sanctification of the Name in Jewish Halacha. Or it can be extremely sweeping, as is the modern state's demand that masses of its "sons," forcibly conscripted into its army, be ever ready to lay down their lives for the homeland, or as is the leader's demand of his people that for the sake of his honor, their honor, or the common national honor, they refuse to lay down their arms until either victory or death.[153] However, this demand is always made in the name of values through which one's personal death, the most absolute thing possible, becomes relative, and through which the superfluous deaths of many others become justified. Nevertheless, giving oneself over to an abstract entity endowed with absolute values seems to be a relatively common phenomenon, certainly more popular than moral sacrifice. Perhaps this is so because, given human finitude, only an absolute value can give value to the absoluteness of the individual's end.

8.522 But nothing can eliminate the absoluteness of my personal death. My own death unfailingly causes me indignation. I cannot resign myself to it at any time. I shudder at the thought of a possible moment when I might have to be killed for something — in order to save my son, for instance — and I don't know whether I'll have the strength to do it. But I know that some people are resigned to death and some people hope for it; I know that some people have given their lives for things great and small and that many others say they are willing to do so; and I know that some people commit suicide. This relation, of the individual to her own death, is anchored in various cultural codes and shifting life circumstances, but I'm not convinced that these do anything to advance its examination from a moral point of view. Assuming that the individual's interest in her death is not moral, no command or measure can be derived regarding the limit of sacrifice for an other out of the utter indignation of an individual refusing to die or out of the utter submission of the individual willing to take his life in his hands. There is a moment at which the individual draws a limit to her sacrifice, positions her selfhood as the boundary line of submission for the sake of others, at the price of departing the moral realm or retreating within it. This moment cannot be set *a priori* on the basis of values, laws, duties, or other rules from within the moral itself. There's no knowing it in advance or deriving it from any grounds. The individual who has given her life or risked giving her life for others can be presented as exemplary, can be glorified as a saint or a hero, but no rule obliging others is derivable from her conduct.

8.523 — Yet people have to have absolute ideals and values to believe in, in order to be willing to risk their lives.

— Some need them and some don't. The need is an acquired cultural one. People must be taught to get rid of this need. They must be taught that the only thing capable of justifying the sacrifice of a life is a real other in extreme distress, not an abstract value of any kind.[154]

— That's too easy. Many studies show that in extreme situations, people who are devout believers in absolute values are better able to retain their humanity, their dignity, and their capacity for considering others than unbelievers are.[155]

— Perhaps, but just as many studies indicate a clear correlation between a belief in absolute values and the appearance and persistence of extreme situations. It would seem that the damage done by absolute values overrides their usefulness. It is impossible to answer the question of how absolute values aid and damage moral life through an analysis of the concept of a value. An empirical study of the institutions and the situations in which such values function is required. We are already committed to measuring absolute values according to the amount of damage and usefulness they contain. Could we possibly now go back and teach them as absolute?

8.524 In the moral discourse presented here, there are no absolute values. Actually, there are no values in it at all. It is a value-free discourse. Therefore, sacrifice unto death cannot be derived from it. In fact, death cannot be derived from it at all, neither the license nor the duty to give one's life, neither the duty nor the license to take life from others (with the exception of the license to kill in self-defense, and this, too, only by way of negation [see 8.545]). But within such a value-free discourse, which does not provide justification for either the license or the duty to kill, or for the prohibition of being killed, will it be possible to justify a prohibition of killing?

8.530 In order to prohibit killing, one must know what is bad about the death of others. In other words, what is bad for others in their deaths? The dead other is beyond good and evil. A dead man or woman is the single human thing that is beyond good and evil. A dead woman is already a thing and is still human, for those who remember her alive and also for those who see the dead woman, or speak of her, or care for her. But although the dead woman retains some humanity, nothing can worsen her situation, for she can no longer be a bearer of situations, an interested party capable of excitations. She can no longer encounter a thing; nothing will hurt her. If her corpse is mutilated, this will at most hurt her "dignity," the dignity of the dead. The cultural codes pertaining to the dignity of the dead require preserving the remnants of her humanity and establishing them as a limit for those caring for the dead body so as to remove it or to use whatever can still be used of it. But it is impossible to speak of the dead woman herself in terms of suffering and loss, either inevitable or superfluous. Death is the source and site of immeasurable suffering and loss not for the dead woman but for those around her, who are not the ones in question here. What is in question is an attempt to clarify what evil death causes the dead woman. As it turns out, there is no such evil.

8.531 Are we capable of grounding the first, most ancient, and most general moral command — "thou shalt not kill" — without relying on divine authority, without sanctifying life (whose? in whose name? by what right?), and moreover without sidestepping to the suffering and loss of the kith and kin, near and distant, who are hit by this death? The command includes nameless and kinless people, too, and it includes those who are not conscious of their impending death, whether due to shortsightedness or limitations, or due to disinformation or to being murdered in their sleep or being killed instantaneously without having even a nanosecond to contemplate death, like those tens of thousands who evaporated all at once the moment those mushrooms opened in Hiroshima and Nagasaki. Is it possible to ground the command "thou shalt not kill" without invoking the fear, the loss, and the suffering of those who are going to die? For killing does not always involve these evils, and if its prohibition claims to be universal and un-equivocal, it should include those who die before experiencing any evil.

8.532 First of all, it should be recognized that in all cultures, at all times, this command has been broken, is broken, and will go on being broken, explicitly, in a manner perceived as legitimate, in the devout belief that its breach is proper. The biblical text that introduces the prohibition of murder combines it immediately with license to kill. In the same breath, the biblical verse prohibits murder and allows "legal" killing: "Whoso sheddeth man's blood, by man shall his blood be shed: for in the image of God made he man."[156] In the text that includes the canonical commandment "thou shalt not kill," exactly twenty-four verses separate the absolute commandment and the formulations eroding its absoluteness.[157] It is permissible to kill a killer; it is permissible and, indeed, an obligation to rise and kill one who is coming to kill you. It is permissible to kill the enemy in war. It is sometimes permissible to kill the sinner and the tempter to sin, to issue a fatwa against the desecrater of the holy name. It is permissible if not obligatory to kill witches. It is a duty to kill Amalek. It is permissible to kill traitors and spies in times of war or when war is pending (that is, always). It is sometimes permissible to kill dangerous criminals, rapists, murderers, and robbers. It is sometimes permissible to kill (out of mercy) one whose suffering is horrendous and who has no chance of living. It is sometimes permissible — though only in very difficult circumstances — to kill one who becomes a terrible burden upon her friends and relatives. In any case, the state kills according to law, the Church kills according to the principles of faith, medicine kills out of mercy, and science kills for the sake of truth. Besides which, most of us eat animals that others kill for us.

8.533 In all these cases, an entire mechanism of explanations and justifications is enlisted to annul the superfluity of the death in question and present it as an irreproachable necessity. Superfluous death is a moral scandal. The justifications for killing — formulated by all the cultural agents that assemble to justify killing — seek to eliminate the scandal but not necessarily the death itself. But every time these agents seek to eliminate the scandal of the superfluity of a certain concrete death (or at least to ascribe this superfluity to random factors that could not have been predicted or controlled), they reaffirm the very scandalousness of superfluous death. As these agents multiply, and as the means of representation and justification at their disposal become ever more sophisticated, the sense of scandal grows sharper. The cultural, economic, and mental effort invested in removing the superfluity of a concrete death merely testifies to the dimensions of the scandal that would have raged without it.

8.534 True, there are differences between deaths. Only limited efforts are invested in concealing slaughterhouses (in a culture such as ours), and almost no trouble at all is taken to justify the eating of meat — the scandal of killing animals is a small one in most cultures.[158] State-sanctioned killing is justified through complex and well-oiled ideological mechanisms, by law, and in keeping with the common public interest. However, at times, in war or in times of hardship, or when faced with a particularly inferior or hated enemy, less effort is made. For some people, death, even if it is superfluous, does not amount to a real scandal, at least under certain conditions. The sixteenth-century Spanish theologian Bartolomé de las Casas failed to make his countrymen feel the scandal of the massacre of Native Americans as he did.[159] Soldiers in every army tend to decrease the scandalousness of killing prisoners. Primo Levi (who deals with superfluous violence in general — I will return to this difference shortly) says of the violence that characterized Auschwitz (and in fact the Nazi universe in general, and the entire world of the camps) that it was blatantly superfluous, superfluous to the point where no one even took the trouble of trying to remove its superfluity, and this was precisely the climax of its scandalousness: the scandal reaches its heights when there is no longer any scandal.[160] These differences between kinds of deaths express differences in the threshold of moral sensibility that I've already discussed (from 7.104 on). They do not change the fact that in every culture a radical difference is formulated between permissible killing and superfluous killing, more radical than any other difference between what is permitted and what is superfluous (regarding the appropriation of property, for instance, or torture, or lying, or the denial of liberties). And this difference testifies, beyond all the intercultural differences of moral sensibility, to the scandalousness of superfluous death.

8.540 The question is why superfluous death is so scandalous. This question is more radical and more difficult than the question that should be asked again, too: under what conditions is it justified to annul the scandalousness of a superfluous death and to justify killing? The radical question is why causing death seems a more terrible act than most of the other acts causing evil, why murder seems to be a clear revelation of Evil, clearer than it is in most other atrocities. This question is radical because its very introduction opens up the alarming possibility that the scandalousness entwined in superfluous death is a cultural effect that may emerge as redundant and groundless at the end of a critical examination. This possibility should be thought, not rejected up front.

8.541 Is superfluous death scandalous because murder generates a superfluous irreparable loss? But this is true as well of many acts of destruction and vandalism. Is it because murder causes terrible suffering to those close to the victim? But there are quite a few acts of injustice and cruelty that are capable of causing equal suffering, the types of experiences that cause people undergoing them to say, "Better my death than this," or, "Let me die with the

Philistines." Is it because death causes the loss of one who can be interested in the loss and testify to it, and bear suffering and create life out of it? This seems like a description of what is lost, which doesn't answer the question but rather necessitates its reformulation: what is so scandalous about this loss? Is it that death reminds everyone of her own death, and because everyone sees her own death as the ultimate loss, everyone hopes with all her heart and soul that her death will not arrive a single moment before its necessary and inevitable time and sees every superfluous death as a mirror, of sorts, of her own superfluous death, which she seeks to prevent at any price? The last answer shifts the discussion onto a psychological-anthropological plane, removing it from the moral realm. The origin of the "supreme" moral command, "thou shalt not kill," is accordingly given an explanation or a pseudo explanation by an empirical hypothesis that it would be extremely difficult (though not logically impossible) to test, to corroborate, or to refute empirically. According to this hypothesis, the command originates not in morality but in the realm of self-care. Therefore, what creates the scandal cannot be relevant to moral judgment. And the question still stands. And perhaps it has no answer. If suffering and loss exclusively are taken into account, perhaps it is impossible to explain the scandal of superfluous death without relying on psychological-anthropological explanations, on the one hand, and a tradition of religious prohibitions, on the other, or, in other words, without leaving the realm of the moral. If the living for whom a certain death means suffering and loss are not taken into account, perhaps superfluous death cannot be calculated within the framework of the economy of evils. It's one thing to talk about superfluous violence, for torment belongs to the living; it's another to talk about a superfluous death, for this death belongs to the dead. And indeed, from the point of view of the economy of evils in general and that of superfluous evils in particular, it is impossible to take the dead into consideration. The dead are the disaster of the living. When the living whose disaster this death is die, the disaster ends. This is the terrible paradox of the loss named Auschwitz (9.130 on) and of the loss in every catastrophe of similar dimensions.

8.542 If so, why not kill solitary, completely kinless people in their sleep (if some enjoyment or use can result from this)? Because it is impossible to dismiss everything a solitary, kinless person stands to lose without first killing her, and until she is killed, it is prohibited to cause her superfluous loss. Why not kill one who has already lost everything and is not tormented by her death (if we assume ourselves capable of knowing this)? And why not put to death one whose death will cut short her torment? Because this loss is not yours to calculate, you don't bear this suffering, this life is not yours to take. You cannot judge the sufferer until you reach her place; you cannot know what more she stands to lose and for the sake of what she continues to suffer.[161] The annihilation of those parties who have an interest in a loss, the bearers of the suffering, is the limit of the rational calculation of the reduction of superfluous evils. It is impossible to take into account the removal of superfluous evils when the party with a direct interest in these evils is annihilated. And from the opposite direction, it is possible to take them into account only if the interested party is already as good as dead (not suffering any longer), but then she, too, is of no account. In other words, one can only justify murder after one has committed murder in thought; the only murder that can be legitimated is the murder of one who is as good as dead anyway. The conclusion of the act of murder begins in thought. Murder becomes permissible when someone is considered superfluous. But there is no justification for thought murder, for thinking a man or a woman to be superfluous, just as there is no way to ground the command "thou shalt not kill" from the dead person's point of view. Both leaps are equally absurd.

8.543 Killing, like suffering, torment, and loss, must be examined from the point of view of the living. Isn't this an opening for the justification of killing for the sake of the living, as indeed every regime, every culture, does? Doesn't it follow from this that the question "Under what conditions is it justified to annul the scandalousness of a superfluous death?" should be answered according to the degree of the death's comparative utility? No. Killing cannot be measured in terms of comparative utility, for it is the absolute loss of parties who are interested in what is useful and what is harmful, in pleasure and in torment. Killing is a total loss that can only be justified as a last resort in order to prevent another total loss, the death of others. Even then the justification is only possible from the point of view of a third party, seeking to protect an other whose life is in danger and seeking to prevent the disaster that his killing will bring on others. In the economy of evils, nothing justifies giving one's life in order to avoid taking a life. But neither does anything allow a broadening of the license to kill beyond instances of a certain and immediate threat to life. All other cases of seemingly permissible killing — of spies and traitors, of the enemy's soldiers when battles are not raging and they do not pose a real and deathly threat, of criminals and sinners — thus become superfluous.

8.544 Is the victim of violence who is first of all, and perhaps only, interested in saving her soul doing the proper deed when she struggles unto death against her assailant, her tormentor, or the one out to kill her? In the eyes of the witness, the moral account is relatively simple: if she has no other means at hand, the superfluous death of the aggressor, who puts his life on the line, is preferable to her superfluous death, for if she hadn't been assaulted, she would have threatened no one. Even when matters are more complicated and it is difficult to divide the world into hotheaded or ruthless aggressors and innocent victims, the moral judgment from the witness's point of view should be as closely attached as possible to the violence that could have been prevented: could she have defended herself without acting violently? Is he attacking her in order to prevent evils that can only be prevented violently? And with such horrendous violence? But how do matters look from her point of view? The closer the aggressor, the closer the victim is to sacrifice, to the terrible waste of surrender to an aggressor, who may not be worthy of having a thing surrendered to him. Is this waste proper? She alone knows. No one knows what she will lose when she harms him. And how will she know whether she is allowed to defend herself violently, in a fight to the death? She will only know if she adopts the point of view of the witness, the onlooker, who has a moral interest in her, but in her aggressor as well. She will know, if she is capable of finding the peace of mind for moral deliberation while fighting for her life, and usually only in hindsight, in an attempt to justify a done deed.

8.545 — In other words, you don't agree with Lévinas, who claims that responsibility for the other exceeds all measure, is not conditional on the actual power relations between the self and the other in a concrete situation, and is not invalidated even when the other tortures, persecutes, murders?

— Not necessarily. I agree that the responsibility is not invalidated, and, like Lévinas, I believe that it does not entail a duty to surrender to the torturer, the murderer (just as it doesn't entail anything else concrete). But Lévinas does not think through the differences between various moral situations and doesn't take a stand on the difference between permissible and superfluous killing.

— You do take a stand, and then it turns out that the one defending her life, like all of us, needs the point of view of the impartial spectator (Adam Smith) or of reason — the test of the categorical imperative (Kant).

— The regulative ideal of that impartial spectator will do. And she needs it, like all of us, only at the moment when answering the call, or in this case the threat, coming from an other threatens her directly. At that moment, in the struggle unto death, when care for the other is eliminated because the other is seeking to annihilate the self, the indignation of the self affirming itself can go on grasping the moral only through the point of view of an other other, an impartial other, who will know better how to decide between the two deaths. And if the victim ignores the moral interest—frightened, flooded with anxiety, hatred, or rage as she is— then her violent act will not be morally improper from the witness's point of view.

— Aren't you returning here to the classic frame in which moral law appears out of the suspension of the struggle unto death? Isn't this a return to morality's emergence from the state of nature and to the constitution of a social contract that subjects violence to the law?

— I don't think so, for a few reasons. What we're imagining here is not a state of nature but a concrete historical situation, which is sufficiently extreme, even if it is far too common. What applies to this situation does not necessarily apply to any other situation. There's no conclusion from the state of entrapment and struggle unto death that can be applied to any other state in which an individual has additional options for action besides the default option: kill or die. What appears in this situation is not a moral law but a form of moral judgment, an adoption of the impartial spectator's ideal point of view. This form of judgment should not be applied to any situation in which the victim of the violence can take a moral interest in the aggressor without this interest threatening to annihilate her.

— This refusal to determine an absolute, universal principle, this retreat, time and again, to pragmatic and fragmentary considerations—doesn't it amount to a willing surrender to anyone who seeks to present every confrontation of hers as a struggle unto death and every act of violence on her part as a proper response to this struggle? Every aggressor presents the death she causes as necessary and the death she is threatened with as superfluous.

— Rivals in a struggle use all the tools at their disposal, including rhetorical ones. This is certainly the case in a deadly struggle. Absolute, universal principles can be abused for purposes of false righteousness and fraud, no less than pragmatic considerations. My abstinence from absolute, universal principles has been justified here in several contexts, and these arguments are still valid when the moral situation gets complicated. The aggressor's fraud should be uncovered in any case; this should be done by using the conceptual tools at the disposal of moral inquiry, including the critique of ideology and discourse analysis. And this should be done regardless, with or without absolute principles for distinguishing between permissible and superfluous killing.

8.550 These times are steeped in agents of death that license blood, in advance and in retrospect. Justifying killing in thought, making man superfluous — this is the essence of totalitarian logic, in the words of Hannah Arendt. Totalitarianism has made man superfluous first of all in thinking, the thinking that preceded and legitimized mass murder. "Radical evil has emerged in connection with a system in which all men have become equally superfluous. The manipulators of this system believe in their own superfluousness as much as in that of all others, and the totalitarian murderers are all the more dangerous because they do not care if they themselves are alive or dead, if they ever lived or never were born."[162] The people who have become superfluous can be described as those whose end will cause no one any loss. The people declared superfluous are thus transformed into a mass of solitary people; because they themselves will lose each other, it is permissible to destroy them in masses. However, mass murder assumes systematic "superfluation," and totalitarian regimes are not the only ones that allow this. The Nazis systematically superfluated their victims, the Jews above all, long before annihilating them, but so did, and so do, most mass murderers — in America, in the Ottoman Empire, in Cambodia, in Rwanda. It is logically possible that a massacre would lead to a totalitarian regime's facilitating its containment rather than the opposite, and this may be a fair description of what happened in Cambodia (I will elaborate on this point in Chapter Nine).

8.551 Totalitarianism is the progeny of these times, and with all its uniqueness (whether or not one accepts Arendt's characterization) it has no monopoly over licensing bloodshed. The historical present identifiable as our present is an age in which superfluous killing is more permissible and more possible than ever before, an age in which more people in more parts of the globe are considered superfluous.[163] In these times, the technical capacity to manufacture death is growing exponentially, along with the technical capacity to manufacture everything else, as well as many things previously unknown. Our era is witnessing the swift multiplication and growing sophistication of the means of exterminating human beings, whether all at once or in masses, gradually, the whole of humanity, or selected parts of it.[164] There is a growing sophistication of the means of selecting those designated for extermination, of separating them from others so as to be rid of them and only them efficiently and neatly. There is a growing sophistication of the means of indiscriminately annihilating masses. The accelerated multiplication of the means of annihilation is accompanied by an enhanced development of forms of discourse that license thinking of human beings as superfluous and declaring them fair game. The frightening proliferation of the license to kill and of man's superfluity is one matter that makes a difference. To understand ourselves, our historical present, the era in which we live, what distinguishes it from other times, what distinguishes us from others before us and from others decisively different from us in ways that "make a difference," we must also, or first, understand this matter.

8.552 "This matter" is the appearance of being as completely and utterly superfluous, in both of the senses this concept begins to acquire here: the utter superfluity of masses of human beings; and the utter superfluity of the persecutions of masses of people until their annihilation. Only human beings can appear completely and utterly superfluous (animals are killed because they are required for food, or to fend off the damage they cause), and that is precisely why their annihilation is utterly superfluous. "This matter" is the unique, absolute form in which Evil appears in the twentieth century. Absolute, not because Evil is an absolute value or anti-value, or because there is any absolute value negating it. Evil is not a value. Absolute, because it concerns what is completely and utterly superfluous — what serves nothing other than doing evil, that is, than multiplying superfluity, which there is no possibility of justifying, of making intelligible, of assigning a reason or an end, for it appears as its own end (but never as its own cause) and provides a sense to the intentionality of others. This absolute Evil assigns a sense both to the actions of those who are prepared, either intentionally or inadvertently while performing other actions, to go back and create it time and again and to the actions of those seeking to disrupt its regularities, to dismantle its appearance as part of the order of things, and to deconstruct its naturalization as part of what is there.

8.553 "Absolute," "its own end," "giving a supreme sense," "a supreme object of intentionality" — no, the absolute form of Evil is not a new divine revelation. It is a simulation of the creation of absoluteness. The point is to try to understand how, after the death of God, man seeks to take his place and what the terrible results of this transgression are. The point is to understand how it is that after understanding that they had made God and were not made by him, after understanding God to be their most original creation, the act in which the origin itself was created, human beings have not ceased to manufacture simulations of the original act. The point is to understand how it is that before we have even finished ridding ourselves of the shadow of the dead God, new representatives for him appear everywhere, denying his death and purporting to represent — that is, to manufacture — both the old God and the new simulations of his creation by man, the most horrifying yet.

8.554 Simulations that always fail at the same point — the absolute Evil that appears as its own end is not a causa sui. This historical form of Evil is born of the contemporary historical configuration of human freedom, the one formed in the West that has gradually colonized the entire globe, creating the globalization of Evil (see 9.3). Because it is not its own cause, this form of Evil subjugates those created in the image that is not its own image, those created who are not its creatures, those created who create it, or the possibility of it, anew every day. It needs them utterly and completely. Without them, it will revert to nothingness, even if to a nothingness whose ghostly presence may not be eradicable until the end of memory. The creative action of a few human beings and the orderly, serial action of masses of human beings, with which creativity has always been combined, are the secrets of the existence of this form of Evil. But because it has appeared, it hardly needs acts of renewal; all it needs are acts of repetition and reaffirming. It will disappear if the possibility of repetition is foiled. Foiling the possibility of the repetition that allows the absolute form of Evil to appear — this is the absolute duty established by Evil in its absolute form.

8.555 Thinking the historical present at the end of the twentieth century means thinking the present from the point of view of absolute Evil. Thinking the present from the point of view of Evil means responding to the challenge that the humanity of "extremes," generating, carrying, and suffering this Evil in practice, poses to thought, the thought of all those kinds of humanities in "the middle" that haven't known how to prevent it. After all, we are the middle of these extremes; we are the progeny of their terror and are invariably placed at some point on a continuum that may lead to them.

CHAPTER NINE

These Times

9.0 *Sanctification of the Name*[1]

9.000 The humanity of extremes in the twentieth century has many names: Verdun, Musa Dagh, Colima, Stalingrad, Treblinka, Hiroshima, Kampuchea, Biafra, Rwanda, Sarajevo. Auschwitz. Just a partial list. Almost always of place-names. Sites of catastrophe. The place lends its name to the event, not the event to the place; and the name in turn suspends the place from its location and establishes it on many cultural maps that people can (and do) use without knowing a thing about the geographic site. Where is Rwanda? How do you get to Verdun? To Hiroshima? These names, which tell you a lot, tell you nothing about this. Until the tourist industry turned catastrophe sites into places of pilgrimage, the name was almost never used for asking that question. If you're not a tourist of catastrophe sites, that question has almost no importance. When the name is uttered, only very rarely does someone ask how to get there; the question is how to avoid going back there. The name of the place announces: this place should never be returned to.

9.001 The role played here by names is one granted them in very few other cultural contexts. At one and the same time, and almost completely explicitly, it denotes an unclosed complex, an event or a series of events that is difficult or impossible to fully exhaust or cover (as is the case with any event), and also the very impossibility of fully exhausting it. In other words, the name of the place denotes a finished event that has no closure, a past that is continuously present. At issue here are events (whose occurrence is always "there," very far from "here") in the course of which a catastrophe took place, the horror of which is unimaginable and inexpressible, which is probably the reason for the endless attempts to tell it. The name denotes a complex that extends far beyond the event itself. The complex already comprises the aftermath of the event, its ongoing presence in collective memory, the baggage of meanings and the meaning-giving potential it carries, and the cultural contexts in which the name has operated, in which people have been activated by and for the sake of the name. All these contexts are washed into the complex over time and accumulate within it.

9.002   The place that grants this complex its name plays a metonymic role, but not in the way that Paris symbolizes France as a segment of a broader geographic area or even as part of a whole social or political entity. The place is metonymic in relation to the un-closed complex within which the geographic space of the event that was and is no more merges in a single continuum into the realms of the memory in which the event continues both to be and to be made present. But this, too, is merely the tip of the ice-berg. The complex denoted by the name is broader yet. It in-cludes, and assembles in a single continuum of homogeneous and multidimensional space, both the vicinity of the catastrophe — all the dead-end roads that led to it, the regions of cumulative multi-layered memory, the repeatedly forking and intersecting paths of memory and remembering — and the future regions of the cata-strophe in the memory of generations to come. The labor of mourning brought into the world by the catastrophe, which is also denoted by the name, ensures that the place-name has an entire life ahead of it.

9.003   Still, this characterization, too, is merely partial. In the homoge-neous space covered by the catastrophe complex denoted by the place-name, all kinds of discourse seeking to give the horror form and image, to understand and interpret it, spread out in a single continuous weave, along with the endless margins of incompre-hension of the horror. And it is unclear whether the understand-ing (like the attempt to imagine what the catastrophe was) is the image arising from the background of incomprehension, or whether all attempts at interpreting and giving form are the back-ground on which the image of the incomprehensible appears, eternal and immovable, appears in an unbearable luminescence until it collects into, coalesces with, the sacred name.

9.004   The catastrophe place-name has magic power. Its mere enuncia-tion makes the complex present. Merely whispering it makes the entire complex echo in its unattainable presence, for the name instantaneously makes present both the complex and the impossi-bility of making the complex present. The name instantaneously says: "Here is that which cannot be spoken" and "Here is all there is left to say." Frequently, the name is said in a way announcing that it alone can and should suffice. Many utter it along with bodily or lingual gestures announcing that they are forgoing all the rest, because the rest is both impossible and superfluous, as well as both known to all and unknowable. The name is uttered in a way that announces it to be an unexchangeable substitute for the more or less exhaustive representations of the complex, for even if it were possible (which it isn't) to separate once and for all pre-sentation from re-presentation, what was and is no longer from its representations in memory, even in such a case it would be impossible to attain an exhaustive collection of representations. True, in principle, the name of a person who has died, or left forever, functions in a similar manner. But names like "Dudu," "Ruti," "Jimmy," "Dad," "Ben-Gurion," and "John Lennon" do not thematize a failure of representation. Even if the name is uttered with longing, yearningly, with great pining and wonder, these pertain to the inability to bring back, or to understand, what has been lost, not to the very inability to represent it prop-erly in discourse.

9.005 The catastrophe place-name is always shrouded in a kind of aura that is signaled in tone of voice, in body language, in punctuation, in the fragmentation of speech, which always mean the same thing: this is the place where the unspeakable should have been spoken. The aura signifies the inability to express the event according to the rules of a conventional truth game. In fact, this is an extreme form of a routine state of speech in which one speaks of what-is-there, using names of some or another thing that is around. As Lyotard demonstrates, in a routine state of speech a name denot-ing some real thing means that there is still a lot to say about the bearer of the name; in other words, there are many more state-ments bearing truth claims in which this name will be included like a peg on which senses are hung.[2] The name also means that what is said may be found invalid, and then it will be necessary to bid good riddance to whatever was hanging from the peg. In other words, reality is a "matter for the future," that is, a gamble on the correctness of a statement that from now on will undergo all kinds of tests of refutation, so that calling the name of some real thing always means there will be more to say on the matter, that talking about it isn't over.[3] But in addition, every reality is a mat-ter for the future, in which a rupture will occur in the boundaries of the utterance dictated by the rules of this or that discourse and something new will be said, something that cannot be repre-sented at present, under the rules of the prevailing discourse. "Every reality entails this exigency [to represent the unrepre-sentable] as it entails possible [yet] unknown senses." Therefore,

Lyotard can say, when speaking of Auschwitz, that it "is the most real of realities in this respect" and also that "its name marks the confines wherein historical knowledge sees its competence impugned." In this respect, the difference between the place-name of a catastrophe and just a name, a name of some real thing in the world, is the difference between figure and background, between emphasis and blurring. In the first case, the open, unstable future of what the name denotes is relegated to the background, overshadowed; its inability to represent whatever is to be represented is denied as far as possible, and it is employed as if its designation were stable and all the senses depending on it were already collected into an integrated, closed complex; when this name is used to indicate, the index finger doesn't tremble. In the second case, the name's open future derives directly from the ongoing presence of the past; its inability to represent announces itself, and it is used to signify an unstable designation, an open, incoherent complex of senses; when this name is used to indicate, the index finger trembles as if to promise it could go on trembling forever.

9.010   Many of the survivors, those who were "there," are bewitched by the memory. Sometimes the magical power of the name causes them terror; sometimes it calms them. There's no complaint to be made against them if they seek a name to distance the place of the catastrophe to "there," and to distance themselves from there, to act as a dividing curtain between them and the tormenting memory. There's also no berating them if they seek a name to separate them, those who were there, from all the others who were not: those who have collected all the documents, recorded all the stories, traced all the images they could lay their hands on, built libraries out of the representations of the catastrophe that they've assembled, and still understand nothing; those who will never understand, those who can only grasp with certainty a mere name. No complaints should be addressed to the survivors.

9.011   But those who weren't there and the survivors who seek to understand and to make sense for others, not just for themselves, and who avoid turning this understanding into an instrument for their personal salvation from the continuing horror, must not be ensnared by the name. The name must not be allowed to exert its magic powers; it must not be allowed to partition off those who seek to understand the catastrophe from the place and the event that the catastrophe was. I, who wasn't there, don't know in advance that it is impossible to understand, and I will never know if I don't try. On this matter, one shouldn't count on the survivors alone. Many of them, who were there, testify to themselves that they came back different people, that the mark of the catastrophe divides them forever from people like me. Therefore, perhaps they are also unable to imagine, to decide in advance, what I and the likes of me are capable of knowing, if we just seek to understand. Understanding in this context doesn't mean reconstructing the experience, or just analyzing the conditions that made it possible. It means grasping its novelty as a human experience that changes the historical conditions of being human (see 9.022).

9.012   Clearly, the experience itself can only be understood through the mediation of the survivors, and even then only by deduction, analogy, and hypothesis, for identification, in its literary sense, as an attempt to take the hero's place, is out of the question. It is impossible to identify with the victims of the catastrophe. While there are many "human" stories through which identification is possible, these almost always touch only the margins of the horror. For instance, the description of life in a concentration camp at the beginning of Robert Antelme's book is a description of an experience that a reader like me, who has gone through boot camp, compulsory military service, years of annual reserve duty, including brief terms on both sides of the bars of military prisons, is capable of understanding.[4] Not because the boot camp and the military prison were concentration camps but because it is possible to identify continuities of resemblance between the strange and the familiar: continuities of practices of isolation, distribution, monitoring and control, hierarchies, patterns of organizing gaze, management of space and time, the development of a special style of speech, the eradication of identities and of cultural heritage, humiliation of the intellect, and degradation of the body. Even Primo Levi says, "It seems evident to me that in many of its painful and absurd aspects the concentrationary world was only a version, an adaptation of German military procedures. The army of prisoners in the Lagers had to be an inglorious copy of the army proper."[5] But Antelme emphasizes that he did not experience the worst. He was not a Jew, he was not in Auschwitz, and his camp was not part of the Gulag. And Levi reiterates that witnesses like himself should not be trusted, for they are not representative, because they are the exceptions, because it was impossible to survive the catastrophe without being, in some sense, "prominent," relatively privileged.[6] From the inferno itself, and not just in Auschwitz, there are very few testimonies; the testimonies that exist come mainly from the antechambers. The catastrophe placename seeks to denote the inferno itself, to denote what it is that evades the continuities between the mechanisms creating the cat-astrophe and the familiar practices of army, imprisonment, pun-ishment, torture, and oppression. The sanctified names do not strive to denote the experiences of the new conscript, the pris-oner, the man sentenced to death, the deported person, or the refugee; all these terrible experiences are not terrible enough. At issue here is an experience in which continuities seem to have been completely erased. It is an experience of the limits of the human, an experience that occurred at the place where these lim-its were pushed to unimagined distance, which we, from our safe position at the heart of civilization, cannot even conceive of, be-cause we can no longer reconstruct the continuities.

9.013   Experiences at the places of catastrophe, both the victims' and the murderers' when it is possible to distinguish between them, are always experiences at the limits of the human. Neither superhu-man nor subhuman, neither God, nor animal, nor monster, but always simply additional kinds of humans: the bomb droppers, the capo, the body burners, the throat slashers, the exterminators in the forests, the scalpers, the guards, the architects of the camp, the physicians, the transport escorts, the oven lighters, the grave dig-gers, the engine drivers, all — types of human beings. Places of catastrophe generate new ways of being human, new or renewed types of the human mode of being. And this experience seems to be at the limits of the human only from our point of view — we, all who are already, or still, not there. In the meantime, we are somewhere in the middle, at a place where it is possible to ask the questions in such a way, out of our leisure and well-being, and without an urgent need to decide the mode of our partnership in all this. And it remains necessary to ask who, precisely, "we" are (see 9.304 on).

9.014   Nevertheless, one can and must ask whether reconstruction of the experience of the catastrophe truly poses difficulties different from those of the reconstruction of the experience of a very for-eign, very distant, by now extinct world. Are we "really" capable of understanding what the prophet "went through" at a time when prophecy was not just for fools? Or of understanding a medieval farmer at carnival time? Or the wife of an Athenian man in the time of Pericles? Or an oarsman chained to his bench on a Roman boat? Or a captive handmaid in the army of Genghis Khan? Is the curtain lowered by the catastrophe truly more impenetrable than the curtain of silence lowered by history on the people vanquished in battles and struggles for existence?[7] One must also remember that the mystical experience of prophetic enthusiasm is situated on or beyond the borders of language; the medieval farmer, the Athenian woman, the oarsman in the Roman boat, and the handmaid left hardly any interpretable traces, whereas the catastrophe — at least some modern catastrophes — is a subject of unending discussions that deploy entire archives. The vanquished did not leave sufficient traces for their experiences to be categorized, and relative to which continuities might be restored. However, attempts to express the experience of catastrophes, at least the modern-day catastrophes, are incessant. Saying "it is impossible to grasp" that thing, that it is beyond "any possibility of expression," is one way of speaking about the catastrophe. It is a rather common way, at least in my culture. There are others.

9.020 A literature (a literature of memory, a fictional literature, a historical literature) exists that seeks to overcome the chasm between those who live in places where it is possible to read literature and those who lived and perished in the border zones of humanity. One thing that can be said of this literature (without presuming to be exhaustive, and possibly even missing the main point) is that it attempts to transmit what can be transmitted without demanding identification. It situates itself in the border zones and from there seeks to reconstruct the continuities of resemblance and to locate the decisive lines of difference. But this is precisely the point at which reconstruction of the experience is relinquished, for it was a permanent experience of a breakdown of continuities, an experience of what, when it first appeared, was unlike anything familiar and which later, when it repeated itself hour after hour, day after day, erased the memory of what had once been familiar. This is the moment when one attempts to understand the general meaning of the experience, a meaning that one who wasn't there can share with one who was. The continuities that Levi tries to reconstruct in *The Drowned and the Saved* are a prominent, exemplary instance: the *Lager* is "an inglorious copy of the [German] army proper"; "the useless violence" of the concentration camp is a special addition, though not unfamiliar in itself, to the abhorrent violence of war, occupation, and tyranny; the labor of the prisoners in the *Lager* is similar to slavery in general (for it exploits without wage) and to the Gulag in particular (for it exterminates political adversaries), but it is distinguished by a unique component (extermination of the inferior races); between the "normal" or "regular" prisoners and the regular wardens there stretches a "gray area" crossed by a continuous line running from "privileged," through various functionaries, through collaborators with command authority and exceptional Nazis who dared to disobey orders.[8]

9.021 A distinction should be drawn — even if it is at times a fussy one — between reconstructing the experience of the event and understanding the meaning of the event. The latter attempts to reconstruct what the event was for those who experienced it but reaches far beyond that. Besides, the attempt to understand a catastrophe may sometimes require giving a smaller role to the accounts of those who went through the catastrophic experience. What use is there in understanding that particular moment, that very nano-second of experience, in the atomic death of 130,000 men, women, and children in Hiroshima (and in Nagasaki; but in a sense, the second name is already included in the first)? What use is an understanding of this experience to an understanding of what the event was for us? Just this: we now know that it is possible to destroy millions of human beings instantaneously, without their experience of their incumbent deaths having any significance at all, and almost without anyone experiencing their death as an onlooker or a mourner too powerless to help. Everyone close enough to see them died. It was a death from which the possibility of a witness experiencing it as the death of an other was eliminated.[9] In other words, the relative and absolute foreignness of experience in places of catastrophe is one of the elements constituting an understanding of its meaning. Understanding the meaning means, among other things, trying to bridge the distance of time and place and the chasm of total foreignness. This cannot be performed without uncovering, revealing, or hypothesizing and checking similarities between those involved in the catastrophe — its generators and its victims — and those seeking to understand. Forgoing the attempt to understand contributes to blurring the similarities, while refusing to recognize the similarities expels the catastrophe from his sphere of meaning, the sphere of what is meaningful for him.

9.022 To understand the meaning, one must desecrate the sacred name to a certain extent. It is necessary to spread out, layer upon layer, what is enfolded within the complex denoted by the name. That historians do this is taken for granted, it's their job; but usually they do it in order to tell the tale of the name of the place as one tells tales of renowned, name-bearing heroes, as one weaves reams of documents and testimonies into an amazing story. But even if the story is credible, and even if it is explanatory, its meaning still needs to be understood. The understanding I'm referring to seeks to give the catastrophe ontological meaning, not just to explain, in the manner of historians, the conditions that made it possible and the causes that generated it. The ontological meaning of the catastrophe has to take into account the very best of the scientific research of it — the place, the event, the processes that led to it, the conditions that enabled it, the memory, sanctification of the name — while keeping in mind that innovations are always to be expected in the area of historical knowledge, opening up space for, inviting, or necessitating new ontological thinking. It is impossible, though, to ground this thinking in historical narratives. It must begin from the place where the historical narrative ends, or from the place where it transcends itself, and turns into an analysis of the kind or kinds of human existence that appeared within, and out of, the catastrophe, those for whose appearance the catastrophe was a necessary condition. In other words, this thinking seeks to understand all at once what the new thing is that appears along with the catastrophe, and what this thing means from our point of view, for us, which new possibilities of existence it opens up, which possibilities it seals off. And above all, this thinking attempts to clarify whether there arises from the name of the place that call that everyone talks of ("never again," "we shall never forget!"). Is it indeed always the same call? And what is it that calls in this call, which posits us as its collective addressee? How is it that the terror and the horror (which are simply historical events), and the new possibilities of being human (which are simply forms of being) that they have revealed, can suddenly be transformed into authorized speakers in a moral discourse while transforming us into their addressees?

9.023 In any case, it is clear that such a meaning cannot make do with a mimetic representation of the catastrophe. The ontological thinking necessarily feeds on autobiographical, literary, and historical representations dealing with the catastrophe, but it should permanently suspect the mimetic facet of these representations. It must begin at precisely the point where the autobiography, the literature, and the history cease to represent and begin discussing the very problem of representing the catastrophe (even if this place is located on the very same page of text). It must situate itself at the distance between the reader and the represented world and be aware of the possibilities of, and the restrictions on, building bridges of understanding to a world at the limits of the human. In contrast to possible attempts to represent other, now extinct, worlds, these bridges must be built without assuming any act of identification or sympathy.[10]

9.030   Among all the sacred names of places of Evil in the twentieth century, there is in Western culture one name whose sacredness seems to surpass all the rest: "Auschwitz." Or so it seems at least from Tel Aviv and apparently also from Washington, Paris, or Rome, but it might look somewhat different from Tokyo or Phnom Penh or Kigali. The name "Auschwitz" overshadows all the others, placed as a luminescent backdrop on which they are supposed to appear, by the light of which they are supposedly to be measured. The aura surrounding them is too weak, and they are destined to be forgotten (because they are too distant or because the complex they symbolize is less horrific, or because Auschwitz is predetermined as a catastrophe unlike any other). In comparison to them, "Auschwitz" is a promise of eternal memory. Someone who thinks in Hebrew, or in any other Jewish tongue, cannot think the places of catastrophe without first thinking Auschwitz and through "Auschwitz." When he says the name of the other place, he knows that at one or another stage he will also have to utter (or say he has already uttered) the sacred, divine, and forbidden name — "Auschwitz."[11]

9.031   "Auschwitz" is sometimes uttered as the name of all these names combined. But more frequently it is uttered as the name of what none of the other names can denote. Then Auschwitz appears as an upside-down Sinai, a new focus of revelation that turns all the other sacred places into altars of idolatry.[12] And out of the sanctification and revelation a new "religion" emerges, with its centers of priesthood, knowledge, and belief, with its practices of ritual and pilgrimage, with the economic and political capital invested in nurturing religious institutions and in spreading faith.[13]

9.032   There are two main ways to sanctify something. Most seek to make unique what is sanctified. As monotheists, they perceive divinity as transcendental; they believe in the singularity of Auschwitz and the transcendence of the Evil whose place of revelation was Auschwitz. Others seek to generalize. As pantheists, they perceive each and every one of the multiple names of holiness as an expression of the totality of Evil, or as a manifestation of Evil as totality's mode of being; only the levels of clarity change among the different place-names. The smoke of the ovens seems clearer than any of these, in any case, and thus "Auschwitz" seems to be the name that can substitute for all the other manifestations of the totality and absoluteness of Evil.

9.033   But on the matter of Auschwitz, and after Auschwitz, we should under no circumstances succumb to temptations of sanctity and holiness. Auschwitz was of this world. Auschwitz was a place west of Cracow, south of Katowice, a community near the longitude of Prague and Frankfurt and the latitude of Budapest. It was the site of a plant deploying familiar technologies of space management, of the classification and management of human beings, of the processing of organic and inorganic materials. It was seemingly, but only seemingly, an impossible combination of slaughterhouse and distillery, prison camp and industrial plant, slave camp and mechanized meat-packing plant. Auschwitz must be thought through on all these continuities combined, even if it turns out that on each separate continuum Auschwitz is located at the extreme point, that it manifests an apex of what the continuum measures, and it is not yet possible to know that this will be the case.[14]

9.040 To speak about Auschwitz is hard, particularly in Hebrew. Even after — and there is no guarantee we can — we've rid ourselves of all the clichés. Even after we've rid ourselves of the hollow and sticky language and the cynicism that grows under the overload of horror (even when this horror proves freshly astonishing time and again), even then speaking is hard. And maybe then it's immensely harder. The trap of Zionist instrumentalization (or any other kind of instrumentalization) of the Holocaust lurks on one side; the trap of sanctification — Jewish, Christian, or humanist-universal — lurks on the other. And language constantly risks falling into both these traps.

9.041 In Israeli society, instrumentalization and sanctification feed into and intensify each other: the state and its ideologists are interested in sanctifying, in creating the type of religiosity that lies beyond the prevalent controversy between observant and secular; the priests of the new religion are interested in serving the state and wish to enlist in its ideological mechanism, if only to reach those audiences to which the state gives them access. This combination of interests has a long history.[15] In the past ten to fifteen years, it has resulted in wicked manifestations (for instance, in the denial, by various state institutions, of the Armenian genocide), in ludicrous manifestations (for example, the "Young People's Holocaust and Heroism Quiz" conducted in the 1980s), in blinding and hate-fanning ones (representation of the Arabs as the new Nazis; of Arafat or Saddam Hussein as Hitler; of the Israeli occupying army as a "Judeo-Nazi" army; of Rabin as an SS or *Judenrat* officer), and also in some dangerous ones ("never again" as a justification for every criminal act committed by, or in the name of, the state). Sometimes these manifestations are so obnoxiously objectionable that they lead to exhortations such as that of Professor

Yehuda Elkana, himself a survivor of Auschwitz, to stop remembering or, in other words, to stop transmitting "the memory of the Holocaust" through ideological state mechanisms.[16]

9.042 But silence about Auschwitz is both hard and forbidden. Hard, because of the unbearable ease with which the name "Auschwitz," which was supposed to substitute for the image of the image-less and patternless catastrophe, lends itself as an absolute criterion of Evil in a world in which all values are declared relative. Forbidden, because of the deniers and the abusers. The instrumentalization, by Zionists and others (mainly the mainstream of the American Jewish community), of the destruction of European Jewry is no reason to keep silent about Auschwitz, with the exception of the silence that accompanies thought or precedes new speech. The abuse of the forbidding name adds yet another challenge for those seeking to think Auschwitz, the place, the name, the name of the place, the sanctity of the place, and the sanctification of the name. This challenge cannot be responded to with cries of fury at the desecration every time someone utters the forbidding name at an improper moment or place. Such cries merely reproduce the structure of sanctity that encircles Auschwitz and strangles every thought, as if the meaning is clearly given already and the lesson known in advance. Responding to the challenge is possible only if one circumvents the sanctifying discourse and desecrates the name — first of all, through dismantling the sanctifying mechanism itself.[17]

9.050 When speaking of Auschwitz, one can assume that the main facts are known, but one should not presuppose any meaning, not even that Auschwitz was the worst of all horrors, absolute evil, and certainly not that it was a monstrous madness or a mad monstrosity, a total aberration of humanness. People kill in a systematic, industrialized way as a matter of routine, every day — killing animals for food (one should take into consideration the possibility, at the moment seemingly absurd, cynical, horrifying, or insane, that one day the three and a half years of Auschwitz will pale in the face of centuries of industrialized slaughter, the endless and superfluous taking of life by human beings). People kill other people by the hundreds of thousands, by the millions, in world wars, in colonial wars, in various forms of civil and ethnic wars. Peoples are systematically made extinct by other peoples, either more or less intentionally or inadvertently due to the conditions generated by their own regimes (8.532).[18] The historian Rudolph Rummel, comparing data from various sources, has reached a conservative estimate, with, he claims, a possible downward bias, according to which in the course of the twentieth century over 140 million people were killed by their governments or by gangs, underground groups, and rebel armies from their own peoples attempting to overthrow the rulers and take power. At least 45 million of these were killed in China, about 60 million in the USSR, over 20 million in the Europe of the Third Reich, about 2 million Cambodians by the Khmer Rouge, at least 1 million Armenians by the Turks, about 1 million Buddhists by the Chinese in Tibet, about 800,000 Tutsi by the Hutu in Rwanda. The list goes on and on, and even if Rummel is seriously exaggerating and doubling the true numbers, it is enough to establish a quantitative criterion for the destruction that was Auschwitz.[19] If Auschwitz is a "model,"[20] this is surely not because it established a new quantitative apex of killing and destruction, in either absolute or relative numbers. If Auschwitz is a model, perhaps this is because it was not a symbol of human distortion and perversion but a symbol of human excellence, a model in which killing was brought to a perfection of efficiency and precision.

9.051 It should also not be assumed that after we understand all there is to understand about Auschwitz, an unintelligible and unspeakable event will remain there, pointed to in the same way by all the efforts to bespeak it. Speaking of the unspeakable, or the unintelligible, has already become part of the routine expression when speaking of Auschwitz, a kind of aside emitted by the speaker in order to relieve himself of the duty to think, or to get rid of the need to rethink. There is obviously no reason to assume that every instance of such speech indicates the same "remainder" in the same way. And even if it were the "same" remainder, there's no reason to assume that we know how to distinguish it from other "remainders" in other experiences of other unspeakable events. As for the experience: are we capable of measuring and comparing what and how much remains inexpressible in the experience of the person sentenced to death, the witch to be burned at the stake, the slave in chains in the belly of a slave ship, the child dying at his father's side in the coal mines or on the endless marches of refugees through the jungles? And as for the event: Auschwitz may be a paradigmatic event as regards the inability to understand its meaning, but it is no more enigmatic or mysterious than other "great events," no description of which can exhaust them and no series of historical explanations for which can turn them into necessary (and therefore totally intelligible) occurrences. "Auschwitz" may be a model for the impossibility of expressing the real in any kind of discourse, as Lyotard presents it. "Every reality entails this exigency" — to listen attentively to what "cannot be phrased in the accepted idioms" — for every reality contains within it "possible unknown senses" that are inexpressible in a given hegemonic genre of discourse. This is the event that Auschwitz was that stays forever an unintelligible margin, as in every event, not Auschwitz as an event. Even if "Auschwitz is the most real of realities."[21]

9.052　Auschwitz amazes those who thought there was a limit to the human and that humanness is a limit to cruelty. Perhaps all the members of that generation thought so, and perhaps only the victims thought so. But since then we have collected the traces, the testimonies of the victims and the testimonies of the murderers and the generators of the massacre; since then we have witnessed many other acts of mass extermination, industries of death, and highly productive projects of cruelty; since then we have also contemplated more seriously those phenomena of cruelty and extermination in earlier generations that had been suppressed or forgotten. Therefore, we have no right to be amazed. Amazement in the face of Auschwitz is at worst a kind of self-righteousness and at best a case of ignorance. This does not mean that no types of horror make Auschwitz unique or that all is already understood about the issue of Auschwitz.

9.053　In a form of hyperbole, this entire work could be said to be an attempt to find a way of talking about Auschwitz without presupposing "the meaning of Auschwitz" and without presupposing Auschwitz to be some negative pole, an apotheosis, as it were, that every discussion of Evil has both to lead to and to end with, in a predetermined, teleological manner. I sought to think Evil outside the aura of its forbidding name, in a way as free as possible from the shadow cast by this aura, partly to better understand Auschwitz and the historical present that finds in it its exemplary symbol. No less than that, however, I sought to think Evil outside the shadow of Auschwitz in order to return to Auschwitz equipped with criteria for comparison, and to be able to think of other places of catastrophe without it, and in addition to be able not to return to it at all, ever. The conception of Auschwitz as the incomparable, the taboo prohibiting comparison, was from the outset a command to abandon thinking itself. Someone seemingly sought to cut off thinking in order to vacate space for sanctity. I moreover sought distance from that shadow in order to be able to determine it at the correct distance in time, without eliminating the fact of its continuing, present presence, without damaging the vitality of the continuing labor of mourning in advance, but also without becoming enslaved by it in advance. And finally, I sought thinking without Auschwitz in order to go back and think Auschwitz in relation to that Evil that perhaps never was and will never be as horrific as Auschwitz but is much more urgent to think, for predictable Evil may still be preventable, the Evil being produced right now under conditions that can still be repaired.

9.1 *Auschwitz*

9.100 Desecrating the name "Auschwitz" means trying to understand Auschwitz like any other place of catastrophe — or at least beginning to. Allowing what is novel, singular, to appear in the process of description itself. Not presupposing that a unique singularity will appear, or assuming in advance what it will be. Sticking to a description that is as distant, dry, and to the point as possible, in an attempt to reach, as swiftly as possible, the main issue: forms of existence and their novelty. Trying not to succumb to the temptation of pathos. Trying to understand the place of the catastrophe as a state of affairs, trying to reconstruct the internal logic of the production of loss and suffering, the rule-governed regularity of the movement of the horror's dispersion. Distancing oneself, at least at first, from intentions, from symbols, from gestures charged with meaning. Ignoring, at least at first, the interpreting consciousness of those who were part of the state of affairs, the tormenting imprint of the survivors' memory. Being willing in advance to risk erring, generalizing, misunderstanding, paying the price of distance, and asking forgiveness up front from those who may be hurt.

9.101 One must try to understand the catastrophe place as a place where an exceptional concentration and intensification of evil-producing mechanisms occurred. I have presented the production of evils as a production of loss and suffering, which I have tried to understand as an intensification of simple and more abstract ways of being-there — of appearance and presence. The phenomenological logic that has guided me since the beginning of this work was: to try to locate the moment of appearance of something new out of something else, simpler and more abstract than it (but not preceding it, either logically or temporally), in two parallel ways — when the thing accumulates to the point where it overburdens (presence → excitation → suffering); when someone's intentionality is added to it without changing the thing itself, "only" changing its meaning, its value for someone (when that someone appears as an interested party, in the transition from disappearance to loss, or when an exchange value is determined, in the transition from loss to damage). I assume it is possible to objectify loss and suffering, always at the price of reifying them within a given matrix of meaning and experience. I assume it is possible to develop systematic knowledge about the creation of loss and suffering, their mechanics and dynamics, their distribution across geographic space, and their enmeshing with various exchange systems in social space. I'm fully aware that the physics, the geography, and the economy of loss and suffering are future sciences. But I assume that what I have said about them so far is sufficient to signal the direction of the rest of this study.

9.110 "Suffering is caused in an encounter with casualties in which one refrains or is refrained from disengaging" (6.000). Long before the establishment of death camps, the Nazi regime created for the Jews under its jurisdiction a comprehensive system of continuous, intensive encounters with injuries and casualties of all kinds in all areas of life, under conditions in which it was more and more difficult, costly, or impossible to disengage. The impossibility of disengaging from encounters that generate loss and suffering was a structural characteristic of the Nazi regime. This characteristic applied to all its subjects, and especially to the Jews. For Jews sentenced to live under the Nazi regime, life itself became a prison barring free departure (6.403). From an early stage in the Nazi takeover of eastern Europe, the "exit toll" (6.4) collected from Jews rose steeply in almost every situation: torture or death for one who dared to try, along with death and torture for many additional Jews in his vicinity. Jews were driven from their homes and from their living areas to foreign places where exit was almost impossible. Others were concentrated in their own living areas, but their own living areas turned into zones subjected to increasingly tightened "closure." Anyone living under these conditions was sentenced to exist in a sphere of constant suffering without respite or rest, and a sphere of incessantly growing loss with no expression or compensation. (From the outbreak of the war, at the latest, Jews living under the Nazi regime could no longer translate what they had lost into damage suits, and every additional damage accelerated the whirlpool of loss and suffering.[22]) In no-exit conditions, every instance of suffering causes additional suffering, both to its immediate victim and to those around him, and every instance of loss is instantly doubled and tripled in a chain of losses — endless suffering and loss. When a ghetto is hermetically sealed, it turns into a "death-box."[23]

9.111   From the time the Nazis' eastern front began to deteriorate, in Slovakia and Hungary, and especially near the end of the war, there are a few known instances of Nazis' trading, or attempting to trade, in "exit options." They set a price for the possibility, which they were prepared to offer to a precious few, and attempted to obtain several kinds of goods in return — material resources, protection, and even a "good name," which was supposed to be at the disposal of the "benefactors" when they were tried by the Allies. Himmler's shipment of women from Auschwitz to Sweden (brokered by Count Bernadotte) and the deal between Eichmann and Kestner are two of the more well-known instances. The point is that few such instances exist. That such deals existed should come as no surprise. A regime that methodically creates suffering can at any moment — if it so wishes — turn the "right of exit" into a form of currency in its relations with those who have an interest in the destiny of the victims. The right to pardon prisoners, which is granted to the sovereign, both limits and facilitates the use of this currency. The same currency is used, always, in agreements on the exchange of prisoners of war; it was used in relation to permits to emigrate from the states of the Soviet bloc; and it is a legal and regular currency in the relations between the Israeli occupation regime and its Palestinian subjects (the common use by the Israeli army of cordons, blockades, enclosures, and sieges as forms of punishment and means of control of the Palestinian population; entry permits into the area within the "Green Line," issued by Israel to Palestinians in times of curfew and closure; and the permanent requirement to obtain travel permits in order to leave the country). The amazing thing about the Nazi regime is the small number of instances in which the right of exit turned into currency and became part of an exchange relation.[24] The closure of the Jews was actually hermetic. In the sealed world that was Europe under Nazi rule, the movement of suffering and loss was multiplied to infinity, like a ray of light in a chamber of mirrors. And it should be kept in mind that a hermetic closure under an occupying rule is sufficient for creating a *perpetuum mobile* of suffering.

9.112   Uprootings and transfers dealt a deathblow to Jews' capacity for exchange and conversion. The ghettos barred them from most channels of exchange with their non-Jewish surroundings and, gradually, also from most channels of exchange among themselves. The channels of conversion, too, were sealed off one by one in the ghetto. It became virtually impossible to share something with someone; it became virtually impossible to exist without the existence of someone willing to share, lending immediate, direct, and unrewarded support. The people of the Jewish councils who had a considerable influence on the distribution of evils produced by the Nazi regime became almost the only mediators who could still secure various mitigations in exchange for a great deal of capital and services, and through the capital they accumulated, many of them attempted to get themselves and their loved ones out, or to postpone the end as far as possible. Virtually every conversion was also an act of collaboration with the regime of extermination. In order to save someone, one almost always had to assist in managing the starvation or the destruction of many others (see 9.114). Solidarity became a rare commodity, but also a condition for survival.[25] In the absence of almost any access to exchange markets outside the sealed area, and due to the mortally damaged options for conversion (6.541–6.552), the movement of loss and suffering was swiftly accelerated. When there is no refuge from suffering, the suffering is annihilating; when there is no compensation, not even very partial compensation, for what has been lost, the loss means ruin. Without exchange and conversion, suffering and loss are exhaustive. They end in the way a fire subsides after it has devoured everything in the vicinity, suffocating after all has been destroyed. Unbearable suffering, loss of the means of living and protection, of a familiar human and cultural environment, and of the very capacity to give meaning to what is taking place, each of these sinks anyone who undergoes it, as well as his intimates (if any are left and if intimacy retains any meaning), to the bottom of his existence, squeezes him dry, physically, materially, spiritually. Even before the camps were established, the ghettos became places of catastrophe where disaster was methodically produced through relatively simple means: closure, disconnection from means of livelihood, confiscation of property, forced overcrowding and abandonment of the population to epidemics and illness, a prohibition of exchange, and a disruption of both the channels of conversion and the capacity to give without reward. When systematic extermination began, this long chain of plagues was joined by terror of personal and collective death and uncertainty concerning the "transports."

9.113   This dynamic of suffering and loss is common to the ghetto and the concentration camps, to the Gulag, and to refugee camps and prison camps in wartime. It can be produced through the relatively simple means of imprisonment, isolation, and supervision, internal division and hierarchy, total management of the time, space, and options for movement of the imprisoned individual, usually through the mediation of a group of prisoners who comply with the rulers' authority and fill policing roles themselves, thus broadening and deepening the circles of surveillance.[26] After an initial use of force that robs camp inmates of most of their resources, also completely eliminating their potential for armed resistance, the camp regime can continue to exist at a minimal investment of resources, through an efficient, thrifty, and routine application of force combined with policing, surveillance, and management. Under such conditions, endless occasions arise for a theater of cruelty produced as an end in itself, as a source of aesthetic or erotic pleasure for the torturers, as it were, devoid of any functional justification from the point of view of managing the sealed space.[27] This theater of cruelty can exist as long as it doesn't interfere with the camp's correct functioning and doesn't disrupt its familiar ordering rules. The economic and social vacuum generated by the sealed camp allows for the creation of an arena of cruelty exacting almost no price at all in economic or symbolic terms. This arena depends exclusively on the desires of each of those with power and authority, and on the manner he selects to realize these desires within the space left him by the camp's rules of order and discipline.

9.114 In the Jewish ghettos, a system of self-management existed that allowed for a relatively long time an entire fabric of social, cultural, and even political life. The moment the demand was made, this autonomy placed itself, along with the structure of authority that had evolved within it, at the disposal of the Nazi rulers, including their mechanism of extermination, and it evaporated the moment the Nazis decided it would do so.[28] There was no contradiction between the fact that Jewish self-rule in the ghettos was complicit with the Nazi mechanism producing evil, including that of extermination, and the fact that it succeeded for a relatively long time in maintaining a system of assistance that alleviated the suffering and distributed the loss more justly. These were merely two faces of the selfsame regime, the regime of the camps, of which the Jewish ghetto was one specialized form. Jewish self-rule managed the exchange and monitored the channels of conversion, thus allowing the Nazis efficient and cheap penetration of every corner of the Jewish lifeworld. At the same time, the self-management of the ghetto enabled the continuation of a certain space of human solidarity.[29] Even under the worst conditions in the *Lager*, there were still a few who had access to this or that channel of conversion, the simplest and the "cheapest" (6.542) being that of giving meaning. Giving meaning received its most

537

noble expression here, a last vestige of existence along with, be-side, and alongside others.[30] In the conditions of the camp, even giving meaning involved giving oneself and giving away. This kind of giving was the last remnant of social relations, of "mutual acknowledgment," reciprocal relations without reciprocation.

9.115 This type of inferno was peculiar to the Nazi camps where Jews were imprisoned and differentiated them, most of the time, from other ghettos and concentration camps, though it was not exclu-sive to them. It can be found in other camps, in the Gulag, in Japan or China. The similarities among different concentration camps are more important than the differences in the specific forms taken by the movement of loss and suffering, more important than the rulers' random or systematic intervention to alleviate or worsen conditions, or than the differences in inmates' relative autonomy in managing internal affairs. There were considerable differences among the various camps, within the Third Reich and outside it, as regards the character of the — military, political, or ideological — justifications for their existence, the goal whose realization the camp was a means of advancing, and the ways in which the various disciplinary instruments, already available, adopted, or newly invented, were mobilized for this or that political end. But at this stage, from the present point of view, which attempts a scrutiny of the presence of Evil as the catastrophe is taking place, all these differences, in justification, goal, and intention, make much less difference than the differences among forms of surveillance, among the internal regimes of the inmates, or among the degree of inmates' collaboration with their jailers. This is because from our point of view it is the order of evils that counts — the order of the production and distribution of suffering and loss — and not the "source" of these evils or their goal. In fact, from this point of view, justification, goal, and intention are always outside the sphere of Evil's being-there, preceding or following the super-fluity of being, or accompanying it from outside, without being part of its presence, subsistence, or persistence. The differences in justification, goal, and intention are only relevant if they have the potential for reducing the range of the superfluous being. There-fore, at this stage of the catastrophe, they make no difference at all. It doesn't matter for whose sake or to what end the regime produces a hell for such large masses of human beings, for at this point the justification of the goal and the justifying goal no longer have any justification. The superfluous suffering and loss are pro-duced in the camps in such quantities, at such speeds and such intensities, that nothing human — that is, the suffering and loss that the camps are supposed to prevent — can justify them, not even the other side's camps, if it has any. The camps are an exemplary case of the unjustifiable (7.121). However, from a certain stage in the process of consolidating "the final solution," it seems that the Jewish ghetto constituted a special case of the unjustifiable. It was a case of sheer unjustifiability. The ghetto was not only designed to isolate, to control and supervise, to exploit. It wasn't created for economic reasons or due to "security considerations" (even if these occasionally had a role in the rhetoric of its managers and in the survival tactics of the Jews living in it). The ghetto was intended, first and foremost, to methodically harm the condition of the Jews. Incessant increase of suffering and loss for the Jews was the name of the game. This is the moment when the intention of the ruling power organizing the ghetto as a regime for the production and distribution of loss and suffering appears as a parameter distinguishing one evil from another. Is this a difference of kind or of quantity? Does it allow a decision as to what is more horrific? Does a more terrible intention, resulting from the existence of a pure will to harm, necessarily generate a more terrible Evil? I will return to this matter later (9.221).

9.120 The ghetto was intended, first and foremost, to methodically harm the condition of the Jews. Systematic murder was not an issue yet, and until the summer of 1941 deportation was still an option.[31] The mortality rate in the ghetto was of course high, due to the weakening of the population, the denial of medical treatment, enforced starvation, and the deterioration of sanitary conditions, but, as stated, the ghetto was intended to harm, not to exterminate. At the end of 1941, the ghettos turned into stockyards through which people were led to the slaughter, in the *Aktionen* or in the death camps. I accept the view of historians who distinguish ghettoization of the Jews and creation of the labor camps (which were not necessarily intended for the Jews) from methodical murder, through shooting or gas, which was not a direct, planned, or necessary sequel to the Jews' isolation but which exploited the new conditions created by the camps and the ghettos in the new territories occupied by the Nazis.[32] The opposing view holds that the final goal had "already been conceived" when the war broke out and that ghettoization was a planned phase toward its achievement.[33] Even if this is true, the plans for methodical extermination were, as the war began, a secret known to very few, whereas ghettoization, deportations, and assorted types of persecutions were carried out by tens of thousands, and perhaps hundreds of thousands, of Germans, Ukrainians, Poles, Lithuanians, Latvians, Croats, and others. To fulfill his job, each of these had no need for imagining the final solution or, most certainly, for consenting to it. Even if a continuum of intent on the part of the Nazi leadership did exist, the decisive distinction — from the point of view of the accumulation of evils and the appearance of the unjustifiable — is located not on the level of intention but on that of the practices and technology of industrialized killing. The ghettos and camps facilitated methodical annihilation and turned overnight into part of its mechanism. Their internal logic did not generate methodical mass murder, but it did eliminate in advance almost any possibility of an effective resistance from inmates or jailers within this sealed world.

9.121 Concurrently, after the invasion of the USSR, *Aktionen* were conducted in areas along the eastern front, where extermination did not necessarily pass through the phase of concentration in ghettos. The areas in which the units known as *Einsatzgruppen* were active turned into disaster zones with lightning speed but also stopped functioning as such with equal speed when the area of operation became "Jew-free." A different regularity controlled the movement of suffering and loss there. Everything was swifter and briefer and led directly to the loss of the victims themselves. From here on, what remained was only the loss and suffering of the survivors, those who escaped in time to the east, those who escaped into the forests, the isolated individuals who hid for months and years in attics and cellars.

9.122 In the zone known as Auschwitz, all these apparatuses for the production of evils existed concurrently, in extreme forms, in relatively separate areas. The entire camp was hermetically sealed. The encounter with suffering and loss continued unceasingly, intensified without respite, without any possibility of disengagement. In the labor camps and in part of the death camp itself, those left alive were doomed because almost no channels of exchange or conversion were left unblocked, destitution was complete, and the mechanisms that produced suffering and loss methodically and efficiently worked without intermission. The death camp was ruled by the law of total, swift loss, quickly erasing its own traces: radical loss seeking to complete itself through the total extermination of loss itself.

9.123 In Auschwitz, death was industrialized. In contrast to extermination in *Aktionen*, this was an industrial revolution. In contrast to the intensity of destruction revealed in Hiroshima, this was an archaic cottage industry preceding the introduction of the steam engine. But nuclear intensity could destroy not only Jews (or Gypsies), a people dispersed among all other peoples. If Jews had all been assembled in one country, even in a single, limited part of Europe, it is doubtful that the Nazis would have wished to exterminate them; the myth of the Jew as a lethal germ polluting the Aryan race and endangering all of civilization is unlikely to have occurred to them. Jews were present everywhere, everywhere contaminating, everywhere weaving webs of conspiracy and usurpation of the new German man's society and soul. To be rid of them, one had first to collect them from all their diasporas throughout the expanding Reich. In principle, it would then be possible to get rid of them in more than one way. As is known, the Nazis tried deportation before they shifted to extermination, and tried "manual" extermination (the *Aktionen*) before and during the industrialized gassing. But these were technical solutions to technical problems created after the decision was made in principle to implement the ideological demand to be rid of the Jews, and in keeping with the creation of conditions in which the Jews of occupied Europe could be dealt with.[34]

9.124 Choosing industrialized death created its own problems. The industrialized process included living raw material, slated for extermination, and waste matter created in the course of the production process that in turn needed to be eliminated. The incoming raw material took up about the same volume as the waste matter left after the production of death. It was necessary to find an efficient way of getting rid of the bodies, that is, to solve another series of technical problems. The crematoriums were their answer. Various professionals were involved in this process: doctors, architects, chemists, construction engineers, train planners, clerks, and administrators. No one forced them to participate in solving the scientific and technical problems or in operating the mechanism and maintaining the routine operation of the death machines. There is sufficient testimony to the fact that anyone who wished to leave was able to do so.[35] But almost all of them fulfilled their duty and did their jobs faithfully. Almost none of them ever killed a living being. Together they annihilated a people. All this is well known.

9.125 "The process of murder cannot be placed . . . at the center, for that cannot serve as a topic for historical research, except to a rather limited degree. After we have learned how people were suffocated in Auschwitz, the process of suffocation is actually not a subject of study," states the Israeli historian Yehuda Bauer.[36] Because the fact of the murder is crystal clear and the technique is known, the historian should investigate other questions. What, then, should interest the Jewish historian (Bauer, speaking in 1971, expressly distinguishes between the role of the Jewish historian and the historian of some other descent)? Reproducing the "character of the Jews' life on the eve of, and during, the destruction."[37] This is so because, very simply, almost no one else is capable of, or interested in, doing this in his place. A simple matter of the distribution of labor. On the same basis — the logic of distributing the labor of research — and without going into the political meaning and ideological role of this distribution, I wish to state, almost three decades later: for two generations, an entire army of Jewish researchers has been reconstructing the character of Jewish life on the eve of, and during, the destruction. Jewish historians (at least in Israel) direct less of their attention to thinking about "the process of suffocation," its technological character, the cultural and political conditions that allowed an entire society to be enlisted in its service, caused this society to accept it, even when not actively participating in it.[38] Even fewer attempts have been made to understand these conditions as our own possibilities, as options already open to us, to the societies in which we live. The attempt to understand these things is not necessarily a matter for historians, and certainly not exclusively for Jewish historians, but a matter for every intellectual, every thinking person. Nonetheless, the children and the grandchildren of the survivors may have a special responsibility toward this catastrophe because of their predicament: they are heirs to its memories. A historical coincidence has turned their society, the society within which I am living and writing, into a terrible laboratory testing the response of the survivors and their offspring to the emergence of conditions that allow — with their full, partial, or tacit collaboration — both the industrial mass production of death and the precise and detailed selection of its victims (see 9.332).

9.130　As stated, the bodies were not the product of the production process but rather its refuse. The Nazis were not interested in the bodies, and all the things they extracted from the people going to their deaths that have become symbols of the annihilation — the piles of shoes, the false teeth — were insignificant and marginal to the main point. The main point was a product that took up no space or volume. The product was death, voidance. This death could not be weighed or packaged, although it was distributed and disseminated in a measured and precise way, according to the lists. The unique end product of the labor of Nazi Evil, the only prod-

uct that was neither a by-product nor a link in the chain of production, a means to some other end, was a totally nonmaterial,
hence spiritual product. What is superfluous here is not susceptible to expression in material terms; it is the nothingness itself,
whose superfluity is immeasurable. As the Nazis finally sought to
annihilate the Jews as well as the victims of the loss created by this
annihilation, the witnesses, the mourners, and also all traces of
the act of annihilation itself,[39] they in fact strove to annul the
materiality of Evil, strove toward a maximal reduction of the psychophysical presence of Evil. The final solution was an aspiration
toward the total spiritualization and idealization of Evil.

9.131 As the destruction generated by the Nazi power intensified, the
spiritual dimension of this Evil intensified, too, while its material
presence diminished: the traces of destruction were gradually
erased, masses of victims disappeared, and progressively fewer victims were left who could testify to what this Evil was. This
process, in which the material presence of Evil decreases as its
spiritual dimension intensifies, has a strange result. When it
reaches its apex, the point of view of the murderers converges
with that of the witnesses of the annihilation. If the Nazis had completed their task, the convergence would have become complete.
The Nazis, for whom the presence of the Jew was the actualization
of absolute Evil, and the witnesses, for whom the extermination of
the Jews was the actualization of absolute Evil, would have seen
only the space emptied of all Jews that was left behind by the project of annihilation — a Jew-free Europe.[40] If they had fully carried
out their plans, the Nazis, in contradiction to the principle of the
final solution, would most probably have needed an idea of the
Jew, who had in the past been absolute Evil, to affirm their victory
and determine their value. The Jews were not destined for annihilation alone; they were supposed to be transformed into a spiritual
idea with no material existence.

9.132 If the Nazi victory over the Jews had been completed, the witnesses of this annihilation, too, would have needed an idea of the
Jew. Without it, they could not have remembered the Jews or
understood and remembered the Nazi Evil, so as to determine it
as absolute. However, in order for the Jews to exist as an idea —
for the Nazis or for others — someone would have had to possess a
material memory of them, someone would have had to remind
others of them; the idea needs an image, a figure, something that
brings it to mind. As long as someone — whether a Nazi or a witness of the annihilation — remembers, anything material in the
Jew-free space can be revealed as a trace of the absence. The Jews

were supposed to be a signified devoid of presence, of which any material presence could be the signifier, a ghost of which the Nazis were prohibited from altogether ridding themselves and which the witnesses were prohibited from allowing to disappear forever.[41] This context allows an understanding of the establishment of the Jewish museum in Prague, diligently planned by Nazis along with representatives of the Jewish community, in 1943, and of the collection of libraries and art possessed by Jews, which were designated for use in the advanced school of National Socialism, according to a plan entrusted to Alfred Rosenberg. At the end of the day, the spirituality of Evil means that both the presence of Evil and the continuation of resistance totally depend on memory, within a consciousness that interprets the traces.

9.133　The last claim may seem to follow Heidegger as it opens and Derrida as it closes, and so I would like to make the following clarification: in diametric opposition to claims presented by Heidegger, I am not referring to a spirituality whose very appearance in the world generates evil — like a gust of whirling wind or a breaking storm. Nor am I referring to a metaphysical spirituality erroneously detached from its power relations and its material, earthly configurations.[42] The spirituality in question is not what generates Evil; it is rather a result of its outbreak. The outbreak of Evil is generated by a power that, like every social, cultural, and political power, is from the outset both material and spiritual, generating an Evil that becomes more spiritual as it becomes more intense, extensive, and efficient. But the spirituality to which I'm referring here is not of the power; it is the spirituality of the transmutation of life into an inanimate object, and the spirituality of emptying the given space. It should also be noted that the problem with Heidegger's "spiritual reading" of Nazism doesn't lie only in the fact that it failed to identify the meaning of the transition from a metaphysics of subjectivity to a metaphysics of race. Nor does it lie exclusively in the fact — as shown by Derrida — that it ignored the meaning of the radical, uncritical difference between spiritual and non-spiritual on which racist metaphysics is based, while also ignoring the actual Nazi deeds that drew on this metaphysics.[43] The problem with Heidegger's "spiritual reading" of Nazism is that it ascribes spirituality only to the ideology of Nazism and the metaphysics in which it is embedded while failing to discern the traces of spirituality in the results of the Nazi deeds themselves, the void that the Nazi whirlwind left in Europe.

9.134　The meaning of this spirituality is that both the continued presence of Evil and a continuing resistance to it totally depend on memory, within a consciousness that interprets the traces. The final solution sought to erase all traces, including the traces of the erasure itself. Had it been completed, the Nazi Evil, or the Jews who were — for the Nazis — Evil, would have become a totally abstract idea with no actual existence. The total spiritualization of Evil is the climax of Evil but also its culmination. This is the origin of one side of the paradox of elimination (9.142–9.143). The second side emanates from the simple fact that the materiality of Evil cannot be erased. Evil is the result of superfluous suffering and loss; both suffering and loss possess material, tangible, physical, and emotional presence that cannot be entirely erased (see 9.150–9.151).

9.140 The mechanism of destruction creates new forms of suffering: suffering en route to extermination. This suffering consists of the terror of death — in the sense of a total loss of personal life, of the lives of dear ones, and of the entire world of the living — but also of the very presence of loss, including the loss of any hope for giving meaning to death, and of the terror of one's presence at the death of the world in which one dies.[44] At times, added to these is the terrible torment of choosing, for those able to choose, between one death and another, between one's own death and the death of dear ones, or between the dear ones to be put to death immediately and with certainty and the ones apparently to be put to death a little later. And despite all this, many of those led to extinction suffered relatively little in comparison to the horrific suffering in the surrounding camps, sometimes just the days of the terrible train journey, and then they swiftly lost all they had and perished. However, in loss, both in the *Aktionen* and by gas, there are no compromises. The loss is absolute and includes the loss of name, of memory, of the traces of the personal death itself. Large parts of the collective memory are obliterated even before this, with the destruction of communities, synagogues, and all cultural institutions in which such memory had a material existence. Had they won, or even held on for a year or two longer, the Nazis would have completed their task and obliterated the extermination factories themselves, erased as best they could not only the traces of millions of cases of personal death but also the traces of collective death.

9.141 Millions of those exterminated are missed by no one. They were lost along with all of their families, friends, and acquaintances. Therefore, as early as the summer of 1945, and not just today at the end of the twentieth century, there was no one to miss them as concrete, specific individuals with names and addresses and entire lifeworlds; there was no one to experience the irreparable singularity of their loss. "The biggest loss is the loss of interested parties. A complete annihilation wishes to annihilate the movement of loss along with what is being lost: a loss multiplied, the loss of the ability of the disappeared to become lost, to exist as someone's problem" (2.231).

In this context, the words of the poet Itzhak Katzenelson on "the murdered Jewish people" are sounded to this day as a part of discourse that seeks to make present the loss that no longer has any witnesses by creating a collective subject to whose destruction every living Jew is obligated to bear witness.[45] Thus the unending labor of mourning, thus the obsessive attempt to remember and recall those who were not, and will never be, missed by anyone among those living "on the other side," to give them names, faces, addresses. Thus the need to provide those who lost nothing with images of what was lost, to create the masses of interested parties who lost some one and some thing that they never possessed. Thus the inevitable abstraction of the unknown victims and their transformation into anonymous representatives of a collective loss. Thus — and this is perhaps the most symptomatic and blatant expression — the etching out, in the discourse of memory, of the ideal figure of the loss: "six million," behind which all individual faces are obliterated. "Six million" as a figure, in the double sense of this word, integrating into itself at the drop of a word who knows how many more tens or hundreds of thousands. According to the calculations of experts, 5.8 million and we don't know precisely how many more perished. And, truth be told, every number cited is a closer or more distant approximation.[46] (This, too, is one sign of mass catastrophe, unlike a local disaster such as a car crash or a terrorist attack or even an earthquake, in which — in our culture — the dead are counted one by one, and their names known, none left out.) "Six million" that are one, a single subject, a single loss, capable of re-containing the memory of each of those who were lost, in the absence of sufficient concrete images and sufficient capacity to produce new interested parties in place of those lost.

9.142 The Nazi Evil isn't over. It exists to this very day, due to and by virtue of memory. This claim may sound perverse, but I can find no way to evade it: despite the suffering created by the mechanism of annihilation and despite the loss it creates, or perhaps precisely it creates such total loss, total annihilation annihilates the suffering of the victims and also their loss. Total annihilation is the evil that puts an end to all the evils. One should dare to think radically about the horror of the finitude of the final solution, the fact that the "solution" was designed not only to remove the traces of the loss along with its own traces but also to put an end to the horror, to exterminate itself and the horror that it was, at the end of the extermination. This context may also properly inform an interpretation of the Nazi talk of "clean" killing and even "humane" killing, as it were, as well as the perception apparently shared by many Nazis that death by gassing was a less cruel, not just a more efficient, way of killing.[47] All this should be taken into account, not only so as to understand what "the Jewish problem" was for the Nazis, or to understand the meaning of the final *solution* that they invented to this problem, but also to understand the meaning of the *final* solution in the framework of the Nazi economy of Evil at large.

9.143 Death is an end to suffering and loss. The perception of evils and Evil that I have presented here is based on the experience of superfluous evils, on the presence of evil (including the presence of loss) for a living victim. From the point of view of the economy of evils in general and of superfluous evils in particular, the dead cannot be taken into consideration. "The dead are the disaster of the living. When the living whose disaster this death is die, the disaster ends" (8.541). This finitude of death can be escaped only by positioning a witness to the loss. In order to rise up against total annihilation, in order to refuse to accept the extermination seeking to murder the possibility of mourning, one must create testimony to the loss. Testimony can be created by constituting a nonpersonal subject whose life is eternal or at least spans an entire history: the Jewish people, humanity, Europe, various types of "us." In a familiar and well-documented process, the victims became the alibi of this subject, needed by its spokespeople and representatives for other purposes altogether. Conversely, it is possible to create testimony within a culture that invites individuals within it to bear witness, each in his own way, man and woman. The duty to remember makes present once again the Nazis' victory over the Jews in order to go on fighting it even after it is over.

A familiar commandment appears here: in every generation, each individual is bound to regard himself as if he had personally survived Auschwitz, as if he had witnessed the revelation of Evil.[48] The total annihilation must be repeatedly, unendingly represented in order to affirm the absoluteness of the Evil that was there, at times to the point of its sanctification as the presence of a transcendental moment in history, as the symmetrical inversion of divine holiness.[49]

9.144 The commandment to affirm the absoluteness of Evil is also the commandment instructing that doubt be cast time and again, in the course of the very act of testimony, on the absoluteness of the destruction. This commandment has many faces, but it almost always involves an affirmation and a denial — an affirmation of the destruction, and a denial of its absoluteness. Therefore, it also always involves remembrance and forgetting: remembrance — of the uprising, of the surviving remnant, of the resurrection — allowing a denial of the absoluteness of the destruction; the overall, obvious affirmation of the absoluteness of Evil allowing a forgetting not only of individuals and details but also of processes, stages, conditions, and causes that might have complicated the story. In Israel, the dual commandment has turned into a central and vital element within a complex system of ritual and symbol, patterns of ceremony and discourse that have crystallized into a "state religion" of sorts.[50] The commandment is "passed on" day by day to the young through the educational system, from preschool through military academy; the public at large is exposed to concentrated doses of it on Holocaust Memorial Day and the periods before and after it. Similar patterns, relying on the state and its institutions or opposing them to various degrees, have evolved among many Jewish communities throughout the world.[51] In Israel, I'm referring, first of all, to mechanisms of public ritual that have been nationalized and that, for one day every year, turn the citizens of an entire state into hostages of memory, trapped in a sticky web of hollow hyperbole and sad tunes. These mechanisms are fed throughout the year by agents of culture, the producers and distributors of memory, narratives, and images. They tend to represent the Shoah, on the one hand, as a homogeneous fabric of horror and, on the other, as a collection of given "meanings" and "lessons" creating an impersonal subject — the Jewish people — whose life spans an entire history; to this subject is ascribed the already-reified loss — or sometimes this subject is just the narrator of this loss. The destruction and resurrection of the national subject have been intertwined over time as a single narrative-mythological continuum, concatenating the annihilation in Europe with the establishment of the state of Israel and the series of wars between the Jews and the Arabs in a single indivisible causal chain.[52] The Israelis' heroism and victories in these wars are represented time and again as evidence that "the Nazi persecutor failed to complete his task."

9.145 However, alongside, and against, the official and manipulative organization of the duty to remember are individuals who become, sometimes against their will, parties with an interest in the lost loss, bearers of a mission on behalf of themselves and future generations. The individual who makes himself a witness takes upon himself an infinite debt to a no-longer-utterable past and the infinite task of the labor of memory. He participates along with others in forming the memory with a relative openness to the paradoxes of affirmation and denial, remembrance and forgetting, and an awareness of the political uses and abuses of the religion of memory, seeking to take part in the struggles these involve.[53] Opposite the orthodoxy of the state religion, heterodox "communities of memory" arise. These take upon themselves the duty to remember without necessarily recognizing the high priests of official memorial institutions or accepting their pronouncing the name or their interpretations (historical, theological, ideological-political) of "what took place there."[54] An ambivalent and complex relation between remembrance and forgetting, preservation and denial, is inherent in every memorial project; regarding the annihilation of the Jews of Europe, the paradoxical character of this relation is intensified to the extreme due to the intention and the internal logic of the final solution and due to the infinite loss it generated. An awareness of the conflictual nature of memory and its political dimensions is a necessary (but naturally insufficient) condition for any clear-eyed examination of the fact that even in the case of the destruction of the Jews of Europe, there can be no remembrance or memorializing without forgetting. And here, too, there is a price to remembrance, not just to forgetting; it is possible to become enslaved to memory, to become its victim, not just the victim of a denial seeking to erase it.

9.150 The culture of counter-memory acts in a manner similar to that of prominent intellectuals in Europe who seek to posit the annihilation of the Jews — and not just "the camps" — as a matter urgent to their self-understanding. The cultural orthodoxy that they criticize is, in their view, responsible for attempts to subsume the narrative of the Jews' annihilation under the history of "Fascism," on the one hand, and under the tale of the Second World War, on the other. To them, such attempts are connected with the way in which the new regimes of postwar Europe have shaken off various continuities between themselves and preceding regimes, the Nazis and their collaborators. Vis-à-vis this orthodoxy, critical thinkers insist on both understanding the singularity of the Jewish catastrophe and uncovering the continuity between the civilization that produced it and their own. These intellectuals are usually self-appointed witnesses. A non-Jewish person doesn't become a witness to the lost loss just like that. The work of memory is never self-evident for him; he takes it upon himself as a mission. The act of bearing witness is a struggle conducted not only against Holocaust deniers but also against revisionist historians, public figures, and politicians who minimize the dimensions of the horror and also the burden of responsibility borne by their peoples so as to free them from the heavy yoke and presence of the past.[55] Conversely, in Israeli culture every Jewish child is educated as a witness, and the duty of remembrance is so taken for granted that almost no one dares to question it. In fact, there is no place from which to refuse the commandment of memory; there is debate about the nature of the memory, but no debate about the duty to remember itself.[56]

9.151 Be this as it may, the very imperative to be a witness testifies to the fact that the suffering has ended, that the loss is reaching its end (most of the survivors are dead), that there is nothing more to be said, that there is no one to say it to. The Evil of the extermination itself cannot be located in the suffering of those murdered or in the loss whose victims they were. Or perhaps I should say that it should be located there, too, but then, the swifter and "neater" the killing, the lesser the Evil, both in absolute terms and relative to the infinite suffering of those living in the ghettos and the labor camps. This seems to be the inescapable conclusion of the argument up to this point. It may be claimed that at just this moment, when no one is left to say, no one is left to say it to, and nothing is left to be said, the most horrific loss is created, the loss that there is no one to express, placing the heaviest burden on one who can be the witness of the *différend* in which such a loss is implanted. This is what Lyotard claims.[57] The strength of this claim is limited, though, for its range is enormous; it applies to all of history, all human life that has been lost without a trace, everything lost to culture without leaving any traces, or at least (if one adds a reservation that is not easy to justify) everything that has been destroyed, violently laid to ruins, and obliterated.[58] In other words, the labor of testimony not only repeatedly makes present yet again the Nazi victory over the Jews (as its raison d'être) but also paradoxically erases the singularity of this victory. Auschwitz turns from a private name into the family name of the victims of the West — the Native Americans, the Africans, the Japanese of Hiroshima, and all the rest.

9.152 Lyotard: "The name localizes the object within nominative networks ... the object of history arises from a world (which is a fairly stable complex of nominatives." "Reality entails the *différend*," and "Auschwitz is the most real of realities in this respect."[59] Therefore, the *différend* derived from the reality known as Auschwitz is the most distinct *différend*. Auschwitz becomes a metonym for the real; the *différend* of the memory of the extermination becomes a metonym for the *différend*; the problem of representing Auschwitz becomes a metonym for the representation of reality in general.[60]

9.153 In one obvious sense, this claim about the finality of the final solution pertains only to the loss of all those whose traces have been lost. It doesn't concern the innumerable ways in which that destruction continues to be present in the lives of the survivors, and no less in the lives of the second and third generations of their families and in the lives of those in their vicinity. Here, too, however, we must acknowledge the close relation between the continuing presence of the destruction, a presence mediated entirely by memory, and the labor of mourning and testimony seeking to undo the loss of the loss itself. Willing surrender to the memory of the destruction, like the organized subjection of memory to the destruction, turns memory into an unfailing source of new evils, which total forgetting would prevent. (And the possibility of total forgetting, at least here and there, should not be ruled out in advance. Not every forgetting is a repression and a disavowal, and not every repressed thing returns to take over the repressing psyche.[61])

9.154 The claim about the finality of the final solution accordingly concerns the living, too, for it is a claim about memory and forgetting. If total forgetting brings an end to a series of superfluous evils, then struggling against forgetting, the effort to remember and testify, preserves the final gusts of that terrible storm which, more than half a century ago, created the Jewish suffering, loss, and destruction. The attempt to become a witness so as to testify to the fact that that loss is not total, that the final solution was not finalized, time and again revives the ghosts of the final solution. It bars these ghosts from reaching a final resting place and bars the horror from reaching its end, though now only the finality of the "solution" can eliminate the continuing presence of the Evil it produced. On the other hand, the alternative offered by total forgetting means allowing Nazism to complete the act of destruction (not to continue the destruction to the last of the Jews but to complete what that destruction was).

9.155 Remembering means resisting the final solution but preserving a remnant of its power, keeping it as a ghost; forgetting means being resigned to the final solution and allowing the finalization of the solution. Remembering also means producing the continuity of the Jewish people, the people who were killed and the people who rose from the ashes; testifying to the fact that the final solution was not completed; turning the living into hostages of the dead; and turning revival into the direct continuation of the destruction. Continuation, that is, what came after it and goes on maintaining what was begun in the past. Forgetting also means disconnecting the genealogical continuity between the Jews alive today (and even only those who will live tomorrow, in another fifty or one hundred years, when the labor of forgetting is done) and the Jews who were destroyed — and paying the price of this denial for many generations. This satanic choice is the final victory of the Nazis over the Jews.

9.2 *The Uniqueness Question*

9.200 A "satanic choice." Does it make Auschwitz unique? Is this the locus of (or part of) the novel aspect of what is known as "Auschwitz"?[62] By definition, evil is an excessive burden, a superfluity of suffering and loss that has become too much, a superfluity no justification can contain. Was the intensification of the Evil-producing mechanism in Auschwitz — the site where superfluity itself became a principle of action — overflowing to the point of creating a new manner of being-there, a new form of being as Evil, a new form of superfluity transcending the very principle of the superfluity of Evil?

9.201 Is the satanic choice imposed on us by the memory of Auschwitz (after more than fifty years) any different from the choice imposed on the Armenians (after almost one hundred years) or the choice imposed on the indigenous peoples of North and South America (after four hundred years)?[63] Over time, what counts is not the intention to exterminate the group but the fact that the group was indeed exterminated, while the few survivors are trapped in the paradox between affirmation and denial, between memory and forgetting. Over time, there is no difference between the few survivors of an almost-final extermination and the many survivors of a terrible catastrophe that led the entire group toward extermination. In this sense, that satanic choice posed by the memory of the Jews' destruction does not differ from the choice facing the descendants of the Africans sold into slavery.[64] In this context, does the radical character of the final solution reveal something that is, in principle, absent in the dual relation described above: the paradoxical complicity between memory and loss and between forgetting and resignation (2.011–2.012 and 2.231)? Doesn't this reveal the tormenting and addictive character of memory, the comforting character of forgetting, and the capacity of both to function simultaneously in contradictory ways, to serve two masters locked in a fight unto death or, better yet, master and slave, victor and vanquished? The victors make their mark in the memory of the vanquished so as to torment them for many years after they, the victors, have disappeared from the arena. In order to evade the victors, the vanquished need forgetting, not only memory.

9.202 Indeed, forgetting benefits the victors. The vanquished seek in memory resources for resistance as well as hope and consolation. Until when? How long does memory endure before nothing is left of it but a myth whose effect is restricted to the heterotopic space-time of whatever ritual grants it existence?[65] And what happens when the victors are, in turn, vanquished, when there is no one left to benefit from the forgetting of the vanquished? What happens when the rescued vanquished become the victors in another war? When the victims die (and, with them, most of the murderers), memory — like forgetting — becomes complicit with the machinations of Evil and with the existing order of a ruling power that produces and distributes it.

9.203 And if we were to claim that the Americans in North America and the Spaniards in South America, the Turks in the Ottoman Empire, the Khmer Rouge in Cambodia, and even the Hutu in Rwanda weren't seeking a "final solution"? If we were to claim that they were trying to solve, through particularly cruel means, a political or ideological problem but were not attempting to remove the traces of the solution along with the traces of the loss, and were not seeking to bring the horror to completion and climax concurrently, by exterminating the final solution itself and exterminating the traces of the extermination after the process of extermination (a claim that is arguably untrue of the genocide in Rwanda)? Would this claim make any difference in understanding the Evil that was the methodical elimination (not the camps but the elimination machine that operated out of them)? Would this claim in any way lessen the weight of the decision to get rid of those declared superfluous, the one made in the past and the one still being made in some places (Cambodia, Rwanda, Bosnia, Kosovo)? When people are declared superfluous and turned into fair game, justifications make no difference anymore — at least not from the point of view of the superfluous ones. It makes no difference whether there was a real, not-imagined problem whose solution necessitated declaring them superfluous, such as the problem of the Tutsi's hegemony for the Hutu in Rwanda, perhaps, or such as the very presence of the Indians for the Americas' conquerors, perhaps. It makes no difference whether the problem seems to us today to be imagined or hugely exaggerated if it was real from the point of view of the murderers, as the problem of the peasantry must have been for Stalin and the "Jewish problem" must have been for certain Nazis. There's no need to deliberate over the question of who is authorized to determine what is reality here and what is merely imagined, or whether it is right in hindsight to project such a distinction, made from the historian's point of view, onto the consciousness of the torturers and murderers. Nor does it matter — for moral considerations — whether an entire group is declared superfluous or whether many different people who were declared superfluous become a group of people slated for destruction. This last typological difference — between intention to destroy those declared superfluous and intention to destroy an entire group defined as such — enables the historians Yehuda Bauer and Steven Katz to distinguish holocaust from genocide, and genocide from massacre. Intention to destroy the entire group is a necessary condition for "genocide," in Katz's terms, or for "holocaust," in Bauer's terms, and both of them find only a single instance under the category thus defined.[66] But as Katz himself clarifies explicitly, the meaning of this distinction is phenomenological, not moral.[67] The attempt to destroy part of a group may be more serious from a moral point of view than the attempt to destroy an entire group, depending on the relative sizes of the part and the group (and see 9.220). It is not the definition of a group declared superfluous that counts, but the fact of counting those defined as superfluous. This is what counts from a moral point of view: the moment superfluity becomes a characterization of one who suffers and not of the suffering, of the interested parties and not of the lost interest, everything goes. In Auschwitz, as in Rwanda; in Treblinka, as in Colima.

9.204 The decision to get rid of the superfluous ones, to the very last of them, was accompanied by a methodical mechanism of destruction. Perhaps this is the difference. The methodical character of the destruction, its industrialization, its mechanization, and its bureaucratization increased the likelihood of causing total loss, a loss of the loss, and of swiftly and intensively positing the paradoxes of memory and forgetting. But what difference does this methodical character make in moral terms? Total loss can be achieved through simpler means, with a narrower scope and at a slower rate. For the last few years, this has been proved in the jungles of Rwanda and Congo (Zaire) before the wondering, weary, or jaded eyes of the West. The paradoxes of memory and forgetting will appear in any case. And the obsession with surrendering to memory will always divert attention from the mechanisms creating new evils at present and from those preparing the possibility of the next destruction. Is the decisive matter not the amazing effectiveness of the production of Evil? Is it not the huge range it covered and spread through, that Evil branded on the bodies and souls of the survivors until it radiates throughout their surroundings many years after the ovens stopped burning and all the camps were dismantled? If so, it's important to note that this effectiveness concerns the complex of Auschwitz in its totality — the imprisonment, the enforced labor and conduct, the barring of exchange and conversion, the erasure of the civilized and political dimensions of human existence, the acceleration of all disaster factors, and the complete instrumentalization of slaughter — and it concerns everyone who was "treated" within this complex, not just the Jews. Even more important, it should be remembered that in terms of the efficiency of destruction, both the nuclear bomb in Hiroshima and the machetes in Rwanda were more efficient (about 80,000 human beings in a single moment in Hiroshima and about 50,000 in Nagasaki; 800,000 human beings in eight weeks in Rwanda).

9.205 Every one of the practices at Auschwitz intended to produce Evil existed separately and in various constellations in other cases of mass murder and in other instances of machines of Evil operated at historic dimensions, to this day. This is also true, of course, of extermination by gas. There was killing by gas both before and after Auschwitz, there were massacres of masses, there was methodical putting to death of people who belonged to particular groups, and there was also (in Rwanda, in Kurdistan or the Ottoman Empire, and, much earlier, in South and Central America) methodical putting to death of people just because they were born belonging to a particular human group. Auschwitz is, among other things, the specific combination of putting to death by gas, mass killing, and methodical and orderly extermination, which allowed the death machine to operate with such horrifying efficiency. When this machine is broken down into its component parts, one finds that its technologies and the practices maintaining it exist or are ready for operation in various combinations at the heart of Western society, not only far away beyond its borders, and that they are an inseparable part of the systems of domination and government in almost every contemporary democratic regime, and of the power relations within and outside these. This is the most important lesson in Arendt's analysis of totalitarian regimes, in Foucault's analysis of disciplinarian society, and in the studies of bureaucracy and rationality in the Evil-producing mechanisms of the Nazi regime (influenced by both the above sources) conducted by theorists such as Zygmunt Bauman and Alain Brossat and the historian Omer Bartov.[68] Auschwitz was an especially "successful" model of the combination of all these practices, but not the most successful attempted to date, in quantitative terms. The singularity of Auschwitz isn't located only in the methodical character of the extermination, in the special technique of putting to death, in the technological nature of the process, in the special form of management of life until death, or in the very killing. The singularity of Auschwitz lies in the special way in which all these elements were combined to create a death world, a world in which dying and putting to death became forms of existence, the continuing existence of death.[69] All the components of this combination are present separately, and at varying levels, in each instance of genocide in the twentieth century. There is no case of genocide from which rationality in one form or another is absent, playing no part in the classification, labeling, and location of the population defined as superfluous, or in which the extermination completely lacks methodical character or fails to deploy technologies that produce suffering and loss to the point of loss of the loss itself: technologies of arms, of the classification and management of human beings, of space management, of surveillance and detainment, of the erasure of identities and the cover-up of traces, and so forth.

9.210　And yet there is perhaps one sense in which Auschwitz is different from all the known historical forms of the production of Evil (until the genocide in Rwanda, it would seem): it is the first time that Evil appears in its most purified, distilled form as superfluity itself, superfluity without limits or measure, for Evil appears as its own end (8.552–8.554).[70] The ghettos and the labor camps were means of doing evil; the death camps were means of exterminating. Sometimes the goal was first to do evil, and then to exterminate; at other times, it was first to exterminate, and then to do evil to the remnant. Evil was produced with enormous intensiveness, fully intentionally, while enlisting considerable material resources, technical knowledge, and manpower equipped with various skills, part of which was specifically trained for carrying out the task. Numerous superfluous evils had definite addressees with precise addresses — people defined as Jews or Gypsies by religion or descent, or according to the bureaucratic decisions of the Nazi regime. The mechanisms producing systematic loss, suffering, and destruction had no goal other than harming them and eliminating them as individuals and as a people. They were not means toward achieving any other goal, military, political, or economic. On the contrary, near the end of the war, continued operations toward implementation of the final solution became a burden on the German forces in the various frontline areas and an obstacle to the efforts of various elements within the Nazi regime to improve their standing in the foreseeable encounter with the Allied forces. The death camps were not a secondary product of an economy of war; they were a burden to it. Nor were they a side effect of Nazi ideology; they were its realization. Their operation was the end and the raison d'être of many other institutions and actions (although it would not be right to ground all aspects of the Nazi regime in the final solution). When capital degrades human beings, exploits, alienates, and enslaves, robs masses of people of their shelter, their dignity, and their hope, it also produces riches. When tyrannical regimes torture and murder, and even exterminate entire populations of their subjects, they also produce, or attempt to produce, a social order and routine lives for their obedient citizens. When the Nazis destroyed the Jews and the Gypsies, they cleansed Europe of Jews and Gypsies, that is, destroyed Jews and Gypsies. Nazism allowed the revelation of Evil in its full superfluity, devoid of any utility, benefits, or enjoyment. Of course, very many — German, Ukrainian, Polish, Lithuanian, Latvian, French, Hungarian, and more — both benefited and gained some enjoyment from the destruction, in the process and in its aftermath. True, many economists, social scientists, and social planners have formulated proposals and justifications for the policy of extermination in economic terms, turning the "superfluity" of a population into a permissible category in their economic and social theories. But this "demographic superfluity" did not necessarily entail physical extermination and definitely did not entail extermination of the Jews or the Gypsies; moreover, this extermination was not born as an answer to questions posed by economists but the opposite: social scientists formulated their questions in terms of social superfluity as a response to Nazi ideology.[71] In more general terms, the mechanism of destruction did not operate just to provide those participating in it with either benefits or enjoyment, and it didn't come to a halt when these could no longer be provided. Moreover, it is reasonable to assume that most of the people who took part in the extermination found themselves working in the death industry without having intended it; they didn't choose to murder in order to attain something, but, usually, when they understood what their occupation was, they chose not to stop murdering in order not to lose something. The conditions in which it was sometimes possible to gain benefits from the extermination usually arose by the way, as a side effect of various phases of the effort to be rid of the Jews—ghettoization, deportation, and elimination (so, for instance, the confiscation of Jewish property was made possible as a result of the steps to get rid of the Jews but was not the reason for these steps). None of the stages of the Jews' "treatment" was intended from the outset to achieve any general use beyond a "solution" of the Jewish problem (or the Gypsy problem), even if it was often retrospectively given such instrumental justifications. In the case of the Jews, the matter was all the more distinct because of the special role played by the Jew in Nazi ideology (see 9.233 and 9.242). The need to get rid of the Jews—and perhaps also of the Gypsies—lay beyond the principles of pleasure and utility.[72] It was a need determined by a kind of superprinciple imposing restraints on the search for pleasure and utility and, in the final account, determining its permissible patterns. And the Nazis were almost always willing to sacrifice something of themselves, too, in order to exterminate their victims—making a sacrifice in the full sense of the term.[73]

9.211 What appears to us as the most purified case of Evil as an end in itself appears totally differently to the eyes of others. Some always saw just a segment of the destruction machine—the laborers of the death factories, the train drivers, the guards, the clerks responsible for the transports and the inventories, and also the neighbors, those who, in times of hardship and shortage, suddenly encountered an abundance of children's shoes for sale at reduced prices, those who saw the smoke, heard some of the voices, and recognized the smell. If they knew there was Evil there, it was—for them—a background, perhaps despicable or cursed or troubling, to their daily lives for a considerable period of time. But they didn't see it in its revelation, as it was, in its full superfluity. Others did their jobs, period. Still others fulfilled a mission there. Relatively few, but by no means only a handful, experienced the horror as the less noble part of a magnificent vision in the process of being realized. On what do we base our certainty that we see more rightly than they did? We have given up the presumption of overcoming the partiality of our point of view, of determining in advance, once and for all, its advantage over the points of view of others. Why do we insist on doing so here?

9.212 A misdirected question. We don't insist. We have no quarrel with the other points of view. For us, the points of view mentioned here — of the Nazi ideologist, of one who participated in the labor itself, of the bystanders — are part of the Evil revealed in Auschwitz, both part of the absolute superfluity itself and part of the conditions enabling it. These points of view can be objects of historical, philosophical, or psychological research. They cannot be the positions of speakers in a debate, for this is not a debate to be entered into. Turning these points of view into the positions of speakers in a debate means going back and producing the conditions of possibility for the appearance of the absolute form of Evil. Such positions are enemy positions in the fullest sense of the term (see from 9.235 on).

9.213 — So, again you take the place of absolute speech. The absoluteness you have attributed to the form of Evil that appeared in Auschwitz is contagious. Moreover, you contradict everything you've said about the impossibility of removing the *différend* from discourse. Here you are again seeking to say the last word in the debate.

— Not exactly. Last words are a privilege of the dead. No one has the last word in discourse, because no one can put an end to discourse. Labeling those positions as enemy positions means trying to draw boundaries to the debate, not putting an end to it. Every border, as you know, is a zone of struggle. And there are other positions. Some people see the appearance of Evil in Auschwitz as similar to its appearance in the Gulag or in Kampuchea and identify within it other characteristics, place it along other historical, political, and ideological continua. For some people, the Jewishness of the victims, or the intention to destroy all of them, overshadows the methodical character of the destruction. The debate continues here. Not only have I not said the last word in the debate; I haven't even said my own last word in the debate. There are things yet to be taken into account.

9.214 Before proceeding, we should contemplate the cultural-political meaning of the question itself. We should clarify who is interested, and who is willing (and there is of course a difference between "interested" and "willing"), and who even needs to singularize Auschwitz; and vice versa: who is interested or willing to

cancel the singularity. We should clarify what the cultural contexts are in which this debate takes place and what is at stake. Is
the unique singularity determined or denied in a context justifying the claim of the victims or the excuses of the victimizers? Is it
attributed to the Jews or the Germans as singular nations? Are
additional unique characteristics attributed to the singular nation
in the process, and what do they seek to justify? In these debates,
everyone usually agrees that every event is singular in some way,
that an event is unique in its very essence, and it is not this obvious singularity that is at issue. In these debates, everyone com-
pares, including those who claim that Auschwitz is beyond any
possibility of comparison, for without comparison, nothing can
be singularized. It is necessary to resort time and again to comparison, if only to reject the existence of a common ground. In
these debates, everyone seeks to employ memory for the purposes of the present. But the purposes of the present are contradictory, and they in turn give rise to contradictory uses of the
same memory while also generating contradictory memories enlisted for the same use.[74]

9.215 Jews and Germans are fused together in this debate, each inverted
relative to the other. A square of positions can be schematically
discerned in this linkage: (1) In Israeli culture, the consensual
position, basically shared by right and left, seeks to establish singularity. There is agreement both on the principle of singularity
(although not on its specific characteristics) and on the fact that
this principle entails the supreme political-moral command of the
Jewish state and the justification for the injustice involved in, and
still evolving from, its establishment, through its definition as a
Jewish state.[75] (2) In German culture, the demand for singularity
expresses a critical position. Singularity relates to the difference
between the annihilation of the Jews and other state crimes, chiefly Stalin's purges, but also to the particular responsibility of the
Germans of today for Germany's past crimes. The critical position seeks to derive from the special responsibility borne by Germans for the past the current supreme moral-political command
of the German nation.[76] (3) Concurrently, in Israeli culture the
critical position seeks to emphasize continuities, to dim singularity, in order to uncover the instrumentalization of the Holocaust
in Zionist ideology and Israeli secular religion, and the dangerous
points at which the victims' inheritors express positions and implement practices that are alarmingly reminiscent of the slippery
slope that led to "there." Because the effort to singularize often
serves to justify state crimes or to represent them in a way that

wards off criticism, critiques of the belief in singularity in fact call for a re-shouldering of responsibility for the way the loss is preserved. (4) The conservative German position seeks to annul the singularity as well as the demand for special German responsibility for and a special German commitment to the past. The continuities it seeks to forge, particularly between the crimes of Nazism and the crimes of Stalinism, are supposed to free today's Germans from the yoke of the past, which was undoubtedly horrific but not more specifically German than Soviet, Japanese, or American.

The present discussion seeks to take a position within this square without falling into any of its corners. The first step (in the previous section, "Auschwitz") sought to dim the singularity, but only to emphasize the singular problematic of memory. The second step (9.220–9.235) will attempt to emphasize the singular, but only so as to reinstate continuities and be precise on the matter of responsibility.

9.220   The historian Steven Katz conducted a monumental historical and comparative study of mass murders of the human race, on the basis of which he proposes a precise historical-phenomenological sense of the singularity of the extermination of European Jewry, the Shoah. The Shoah is a unique catastrophe, according to Katz: the Holocaust is phenomenologically unique "by virtue of the fact that never before has a state set out, as a matter of intentional principle and actualized policy, to annihilate physically every man, woman and child belonging to a specific people."[77] Katz proposes a reductive definition of genocide: a realized intent — regardless of its success — to physically destroy an entire social group.[78] He uses this definition to characterize the Shoah and also to claim that it is the sole instance of genocide. Any other sense of "genocide" misses the reason for the term's existence, for it was intended to characterize the Nazi annihilation of the Jews.[79] The singularity of the Shoah is accordingly qualitative rather than quantitative (either in absolute or in relative numbers, and even relative to catastrophes that have befallen the Jewish people).[80] This is a purely "phenomenological" singularity indicating the appearance of something new that has never before occurred, not of something that will not occur again and is not of the world. This characterization of the Shoah as a singular historical event is not given *a priori* and is not derived from a conceptual analysis. It is, rather, a result of "judgment based on reflexive examination and construction of distinct and defined phenomena" and their comparison with other phenomena. The type of difference that sets the Shoah apart is not unique itself but rather historical and analyzable (that is, it falls within categories of intent, state decisions, policy and its implementation, and the object of extermination). The unique event is, in principle, expressible in language, understandable and explainable, and above all comparable. The event is unique, even though not all its components are new; what is new and unique is the catastrophic combination of familiar and novel components. This phenomenological singularity should not be given a transcendental status; it should not be employed to derive theological meaning or a criterion for moral comparison; and it should not be used as grounds for claiming the privilege or precedence of Jews as interpreters of the Shoah, as those authorized to give it meaning.[81]

9.221 However, if the Shoah is characterized and singularized by historical-phenomenological categories while this singularity does not allow the derivation of theological or moral conclusions, what interest does it hold for a theory of morals? The historical typology of the catastrophe proposed by Katz is extremely valuable but does not necessarily bear on an understanding of the meaning of the Shoah from a moral perspective. In contrast to Katz, I believe that the moral irrelevance of his conception of the Shoah is not necessarily a result of the difficulty of quantifying evils and comparing different catastrophes or instances of suffering. The main problem, morally speaking, lies in his (and many others') attempt to anchor the massacre's singularity in the intent of its authors. The difference between the intention to exterminate an entire group and other destructive or wicked intentions is important to the historical explanation, and here, too, only when considering the structural conditions calling for and making possible the realization of this intention. As regards the moral meaning, the importance of intention is doubtful. The same superfluous evils, and perhaps even the same social order producing and distributing superfluous evils, could — in principle — have followed from a "realized intention" of total extermination (or a methodical worsening of the condition of the living, whose "natural" result is extermination [see 9.115–9.123]), but it could also have followed from an abstinence from actions capable of preventing an inadvertent extermination. What counts is the superfluity of the evils, and this is determined according to the possibility and the price of their prevention, not according to the intentions of the massacre's authors, collaborators, or bystanders.[82] If the Shoah has any moral singularity, it is not because it was the sole instance in history — until the massacre in Rwanda, it seems — when an intentional attempt was made to annihilate an entire human group, but because the evils the Nazis produced, which they intended first and foremost for the Jews, were of an unprecedented superfluity, absolute and superfluous in and of itself.

9.222 If one understands the singularity of Auschwitz in this way, it is obvious that this singularity does not necessarily entail a claim to being the sole historical instance of its kind, and it is clear that it is not novel in moral terms, save perhaps the fact that superfluous being appears there in and of itself for any intelligent person who is not deluded by the Nazi myth. Not everyone dares to look, and some deny what they see or might have seen and what clearly arises from all the testimonies. But one who looks, hears, and reads and doesn't see the embodiment of pure superfluity must — it turns out — be deluded by the Nazi myth.

9.223 The Jews were an ideal victim. At Auschwitz, in parallel with the spiritualization of Evil, there occurred an actualization of the idealization of being a victim. The Jews were a victim whose sacrifice was in vain, a sacrifice that atones for nothing and achieves nothing. The Jews didn't endanger anything Nazi — aside from the very legitimation of Nazism. But Nazism constituted the Jews as a threat to its legitimacy, for it constituted itself on the basis of a negation of the Jew. Nazism in its very appearance as the myth of the Nazi state made the Jew both superfluous and vitally necessary. The Jew was necessary as the Nazis' raison d'être and superfluous due to the end and sense of Nazi existence (as conceived from a Nazi point of view). The Jew was vital in his superfluity. In other words, when doing evil to Jews, Nazism didn't produce Evil in passing, almost inadvertently, or due to some internal logic yet inattentively, or as a means toward achieving some good, or even because this Evil was vital to its existence. Nazism produced Evil whose addressees were Jews because the production of such evil was a fundamental part of its being. Nazism was a machine for purifying, a cleansing that made people superfluous and removed them; Nazism was in fact purely a machine for the production of Evil. Every other thing that Nazism produced — order, law, a new cultural order, war, or (an always temporary) peace — was part of this machine, a means toward the cleansing operations, or was created contingently, as a by-product of these, or resulted from the state structure inherited by Nazism from the previous regime, or resulted coincidentally from developments on the battlefield. Both the state structure it inherited and the state structure it created, the military moves it initiated and its response to moves imposed on it, existed in the space left by the constrictions arising from the cleansing operation itself, which was always an act of self-cleansing, of the Self cleansing itself of the Other it discovers inside it. Therefore, it's no wonder that Nazism continued the annihilation of the Jews even when this was in contradiction to all military logic and impaired the Reich's chances of survival. The supreme end — producing Evil, annihilation — should not be presented as a means contingent on its serving some other end. The Nazi regime existed for the purpose of cleansing the race, not the other way around, and cleansing the race was the annihilation of the Jews (and of the invalids and the insane, and only then of the Gypsies and other non-Aryan elements). The state was the means. Thus the annihilation had to continue as long as the means were capable of operating, as long as the state was capable of destroying.[83]

9.224   In Nazi ideology, extermination of the Jews was a means toward creating a new man, ruthless and magnanimous, a new Reich, and a new world. From this point of view, the extermination was not superfluous. It was intended to better the lot of all the others, or at least of all those whose race made them worthy. We understand and accept that there is no supreme tribunal before which we can require a decision on the *différend* between the justification of the annihilation in Nazi discourse and ideology and its conviction in almost any other ideology. Nazi ideology is defeated not in debate but in war. The point is not to prove that the Nazis were "mistaken" in their view of Evil, as in so many other issues, but to understand which roles this "mistake" fulfilled in Nazi discourse. Nazism was a myth of self-constitution, the self-creation of a new human strain, a constitution that, according to the consistent logic of the act of constitution, necessitated radical differentiation from within, from an internal other, defining the new strain through negation. The new identity was seen as creation through negation and necessitated incessant creative motion, which accordingly meant an incessant negating motion. Racial differentiation, according to the Nazi theory of race, is not predetermined, ahistorical, as, for instance, in Plato's view of the three types of the human race, but is, rather, the result of a continuous historical process. Race is a dynamic essence that creates itself from itself. It does not find its other outside itself and does not need to protect its purity from external pollution. The other is the inferior something that the noble race needs to excrete from itself so as to be born. The other is sentenced to be excreted so as to allow the appearance of the new that departs from the old like a snake shedding its skin; it is the appearance of the pollution that separates from the pure solution in a process like the clearing of a distilled liquid. The process of self-creation is dynamic; excretion of the other leads, according to the internal logic of the act of constitution, from negation in principle to negation in practice, that is, to the act of extermination.

9.230 At first glance, there is an inversion and a distortion of the Hegelian dialectic between self and other, but also a fundamental preservation of its framework, at work here. In the Hegelian dialectic, the self reaches consciousness of itself, completes its evolution, and realizes itself through negation of the other; this becomes a surrender to and an immersion in the other, whom it finally swallows up. The other's otherness is superseded, that is, simultaneously annulled and preserved and granted its most refined, sophisticated expression within the developing totality of the self. The Nazi myth reduces the three moments of the dialectic to the single moment of annulment, removal, but without totally canceling the others. On the one hand, the process of the Jews' extermination realizes their image in the Nazi myth and finally leaves this image only as the truth of the Jew in a world without Jews — thus granting the otherness of the other its refined expression. On the other hand, to be born of the negation of the Jews, the Aryan race must continue to preserve the memory of Jewish otherness, even after the Jews have been completely excreted from the self-purifying body. Therefore, either the image of the Jew was intended for preservation at the heart of the myth (once again we may refer to the Jewish museum in Prague that would have filled this role), or the otherness of the Jew would shift to other others, positing them as the next candidates for extermination (see 9.232 and 9.242).

9.231 At second glance, two types of differentiations from the other can be discerned, as well as two types of negations of the other related to them. One type of differentiation is external: it is based on excluding the other or on distancing oneself from the other. The other is outside; even when he is inside, he is external in his foreignness. This other is almost never an impersonator; his otherness is inscribed on his face, is evident in the way he looks, is declared by his external appearance. If he has infiltrated and reached the inside, he must be banished; if he is threatening to infiltrate, he must be shut out. The exclusion is based on the differentiation, the differentiation on the exclusion. The two actions are in fact interdependent, and at issue is the creation of a border line between an internal zone (that of the same, of the one differentiating itself) and an external zone (that of the other, of the one from whom the same is striving to differ). Practices and discourse of this type of differentiation and exclusion play a central role in Judaism: shutting out the other in conditions of exile; symbolic and physical exclusion of the other in conditions of sovereignty. In contrast, the other type of differentiation is internal. The other is inside; even when he is outside, he stretches out tendrils and representatives, both visible and hidden, that penetrate the perimeter. This is a dark other, an other of conspiracies and shady plots, unfailingly adept at disguise and imposture. Biological racism conforms to this conception of otherness. Inborn marks of difference, carried in the blood (or the genes), are not necessarily manifested in the external appearance of a member of the inferior kind. What is "in the blood" may remain hidden. Biological discourse splits the individual between hidden racial essence and visible social conduct, therefore allowing imposture and necessitating a search for the racial, toward the racial, along the family tree of the race. Racialization becomes a major discursive practice of differentiation and self-assertion.

9.232 This distinction between two types of differentiations is historical-phenomenological, a distinction between emphases, not essences. It can easily be deconstructed; the logic of one form of differentiation can be shown to lead to the other. It can be shown that in the first case, the other, even when excluded, always leaves traces "inside" and that this "in" must repeatedly find the other so as to affirm its differentiation. Jewish-Zionist history can provide some interesting examples here.[84] Analogously, in the second case, the construction of self-identity involves unending location and banishment of the other. Prevalent anti-Semitic caricatures of the Jew with a distorted body, an excessively long nose, and a lustfully protruding mouth may be interpreted in this context, too. These are not mimetic representations of familiar types; perhaps they can be seen as a kind of guide to the identification of the Jew hiding among us, thus allowing a transformation of the Jew from an internal other to an other of the first kind, external and foreign, who is instantly identifiable by appearance. Nazism, which in principle demanded differentiation of the second type — that is, differentiation from the "internal" other — led the logic of the dialectical relation between these two types of differentiations to its culmination and to the culmination of the dialectic between self and other. Not only did it turn the internal into an external other; it transformed exclusion into total extermination. Within the dialectic in which everything is simultaneously denied and preserved, nothing is lost. Within the framework of the dialectic, it is impossible to exterminate the other. Extermination of the other is the end of the dialectic (and therefore cannot be contained by the dialectical logic).[85]

9.233 Nazism is a movement of differentiation from an internal other that is not satisfied with determining the other as separate from the self, as different from or even contradictory to it, but that insists on determining the other as superfluous, to be exterminated. Differentiation from the internal other involves a dual act of constitution and extermination: the radical otherness of the other is constituted within the internal zone of existence of the very self that reconstitutes its differentiated identity; ongoing in and to a large extent through this move of constitution is an incessant action to exterminate the other, who remains forever imprisoned within the zone of the self's interiority (within its *Lebensraum*, or living space). Before the war, at an early stage, when the Nazis designated the Jews for banishment but not yet for total extermination, this logic led them to create mechanisms whose role was to differentiate the Jew, to produce and enhance his otherness and reorganize the social map so as to facilitate his identification as other.[86] At the same time, this logic led to the extermination of "imperfect" Germans, disabled people and the mentally ill. Still later, exterminated before and along with the Jews were homosexuals, Gypsies, Communist commissars, Polish intelligentsia, and other "asocial" elements. The Nazi subject was propelled by a constant drive to take over every environment in which the other was located, in order to again be able to differentiate the self from the other at every site where he may have appeared. The same logic led the Nazis eastward when the drive to expand further, to conquer more territories, developed hand in hand with abstraction of the other, with a willingness to erase differences between groups of others, first and foremost between Jews and Bolsheviks, and with an extension of otherness to include not only "inferior elements" such as Jews, Gypsies, and Communists but also, gradually, all Slavic peoples (9.243).[87]

9.234 It can be claimed that among all the groups of others sentenced to excretion, the Jew was the ultimate other, both as a symbol of all otherness and in the consistency with which the conception of otherness was translated into practical terms and imposed on every man, woman, and child of Jewish descent. It is possible to overlook the fact that the Nazis exterminated many more non-Jews than Jews,[88] or to call on the entire religious, cultural, and political history of Europe at large and Germany in particular to explain why the Jews again became the chosen people.[89] This, however, is not the main point. As is well known, the fact that Jews were a persecuted other does not make Nazism unique. Anyone attempting to situate the Nazis' uniqueness in persecution of the Jews, rather than the character of the persecution, is missing the decisive issue.[90] To clarify further, I'll risk hyperbole and say that had there been no Jews in Europe, in the role of a "ready-made" persecuted other — a group whose degraded status and despised and threatening image preceded Nazism and were rooted in European anti-Semitism in general, which had its particular German strain — the Nazis would have had to invent such an other for themselves. In other words, Nazism or quasi Nazism can also grow in a place devoid of Jews, on the condition that it find that internal other intended for excretion. The main issue is that Nazism needed an other from whom to differentiate itself and to exterminate, and that this otherness was vital to its very existence. The main issue is that the Nazi myth was at one and the same time a myth of self-constitution and one of excreting the other in the self out of the self, a myth that, from the outset, established part of the subject bearing it — the German nation, the Aryan race, Europe — as differentiated and superfluous, a myth that posited the distillation of differentiation and the extermination of superfluity as the end of the historical motion that it generated and guided. Something in human, social, historical being was perceived as superfluous; the superfluous had to be removed.

9.235 Isn't the logic of resisting Evil revealed here? Couldn't Nazism be represented as a particular, and perhaps paradigmatic, instance of the conception equating Evil with superfluous being-there and of the general principle commanding the removal of this superfluity? If Evil involves irreparable superfluity that must be removed, how is it possible to explain a rejection of the Nazism identifying the Jew as superfluous and as the root of evil (without recourse to values that the theory of morals proposed here disallows relying on)? Doesn't this possibility of representing the Jew as a superfluity that must be removed and of seeing Jewishness as the root of evil confirm a suspicion that the reader must have been harboring for a long time now as to the total (not to say absolute) relativism and the destructive nihilism to which this theory of morals leads?

— That would be an utterly mistaken understanding of the main course of the argument so far. From a moral point of view, there are superfluous evils but not superfluous people. Jewishness can be identified as the root of evil, and the Jew can be identified as the very face of superfluity, only if one is situated thoroughly outside the moral. This can only be done at the price of complete indifference to the suffering and loss of the Jews, or any others. From a moral point of view, this can be done only at the price of a complete acceptance of the extremely sophisticated machine for the production of Evil established by Nazism.

9.240 Nazism is the opposite pole, the absolute, exact antipode, of the moral as such, of the moral as an area in which the constituting rule is non-indifference to the other's distress, or, in other words, a permanent willingness to be the addressee of a call to do something for the sake of the other. The absolute antipode is not indifference to the other; that can be found in philosophical thinking both implicitly and explicitly, both more and less systematically, and in practice at every street corner. The absolute antipode is a cultural and political mechanism that produces otherness in order to remove the others to whom it is attributed, an otherness that posits the individual as the addressee of a call to identify the superfluous as a certain type of other, and to locate the superfluous other in order to increase his distress to the point of his total extermination. For the Nazi, the presence of the Jew is a command to action whose end is the production of Evil. The Jew is both what interpellates the Nazi and the addressee of the act the Nazi is called upon to perform.

If there is an irreducible "relativism" here, it is rooted in the factuality of the *différend* between various, differentiated genres of discourse. The meaning of the *différend* is that it is impossible to justify the decision to be within the moral or to remain outside it, to respond to a call or to remain indifferent to it, just as it is impossible to justify the decision to conform to the rules of logic (see 9.244). Within the moral, at least in the presence of the Nazi, nothing is relative. From a moral point of view, Nazism is the final extermination of the moral. From a Nazi point of view, the moral point of view proposed here is the extermination of Nazism. Either-or. No dialectic can mediate or reconcile or propose a middle ground between these two points of view.

9.241 Nazism was the final extermination of the moral not because it exterminated the Jews but because it identified superfluity in specific groups of others ruled by it and posited these others as superfluous. Nazism conceived of Evil as a superfluous other, whom it then exterminated. Hannah Arendt identified this trait in totalitarian regimes in general:

> Totalitarianism strives not toward despotic rule over men, but toward a system in which men are superfluous.... As long as all

men have not been made equally superfluous — and this has been accomplished only in the concentration camp — the idea of totalitarian domination has not been achieved. Totalitarian states strive constantly, though never with complete success, to establish the superfluity of man, by the arbitrary selection of various groups for concentration camps, by constant purges of the ruling apparatus, by mass liquidation.[91]

I owe a great deal to this insight, but I wish to refine it. Arendt sees the production of superfluity as a principle of rule defining the essence of the totalitarian regime, which had, in her opinion, only two historical appearances, Nazism and Stalinism. This principle of rule, however, not only defines the common denominator of Stalinism and Nazism but also reveals a fundamental difference between them. In the Stalinist regime, superfluity was a principle of rule obliging the ruling group to redefine itself according to the way in which it was implemented. There was no knowing, ever, in advance, who would be declared superfluous by Stalinism; when a person or a group was declared superfluous, this superfluity was represented retrospectively as a result of the regime's self-definition, which had already been rewritten in light of the new policy of extermination. In the Nazi regime, the determination of superfluity served first of all to define the essence of the ruling group. The principle of extermination was implemented according to the self-definition rather than the other way around. Nazism — and this is one of the crucial ways in which it differed from Stalinism — defined and affirmed itself through attributing human superfluity to a single group of "inferior races." The contents of this group shifted from time to time, but the Jew always took the central role in it as the embodiment of ultimate superfluity. Nazism invented the superfluity of the concrete other in order to be able to identify Evil. Only then did it create an Evil of its own. Not every person reached the camps, only the superfluous ones. The need to produce superfluity preceded the camps; it was the reason for their establishment, or at least the reason for their particular organization and management. This is at the root of part of the difference between the various camps, the prison camps, the labor camps, and the death camps. The prison camps held enemy soldiers, not those who were superfluous. The enemy is not superfluous; he is part of the order of a world at war. The labor camps had others at varying levels of superfluity — Communists, anarchists, left-wing activists, clergymen who dared resist the regime, and regular criminals. All these were superfluous in principle, so it made no difference if they died; however, they were put to death not according to what they were but according to their deeds. They were exploited in forced labor, allowed to slowly starve or somehow survive — it made no difference as long as the work got done and the stock of superfluous people didn't run out. The Jews and the Gypsies intended for annihilation were superfluous according to what they were, not in principle and not in an abstract way, but *because* they were the embodiment of superfluity itself. They were super-fluous in their very presence, which became a threat, like the presence of bacteria, a presence that may exterminate the body-self. The familiar repertoire of zoological images is intended to express both the omnipresence of the foreign element, its capac-ity for integration into the living body, the threat to the body of the nation that it carries with it everywhere, and the vital need to be rid of it immediately.

9.242 From our point of view, the superfluous being identified as Evil always belongs to an other (who is concrete, this or that one); his superfluity is always a superfluity of the real suffering and loss that befall him. In the Nazi myth, the superfluity of the other con-cerns not necessarily the superfluous evils befalling someone else, but the very possibility of the self, of race as intensified I, as a transhistorical subject, appearing as what it is and becoming what it should properly be. Conversely, moral superfluity is the exces-sive being-there that the moral subject encounters or posits after he has been called upon, as an addresser of the call, as a source of the imperative that is always already there, when the moral state-ment appears. The superfluity articulated in the racist myth must be produced, must be created so that the self may be created out of it, must be constantly returned to and re-created. Due to its internal logic, Nazism had to label the other who was next in line and prepare for his excretion. If it were not for their defeat at war, if the final solution had reached its culmination, the mechanism of excretion would presumably have entered a new phase. If Hitler hadn't been defeated at the Russian front, it is likely that an anni-hilation of Slavic peoples would have commenced (9.230 and 9.233). But this would not have been surprising: the Slavs were labeled inferior in advance. If Hitler's rule over Europe had stabi-lized during longer periods of cease-fire, the "euthanasia" of disabled and mentally ill people might have resumed. Clearly, in such a case anti-Semitism alone would no longer have explained a thing. Anti-Semitism cannot explain the Nazi myth; it explains only the fact that the Jews were its first and principal victims.

And it should not be forgotten that from the outset, the cleansing also included non-Jews, whose extermination continued throughout the war, even after the "euthanasia" project. The race cannot rest on its laurels; the myth is incessant motion.[92] Pollution, flabbiness, weakness are always lurking around the corner; it is imperative to identify the parasites that threaten to destroy the healthy body. Internal destruction can end only with the collapse of the self — of the regime and the myth — that builds itself out of it. And indeed, this was how it ended.

9.243   Nazism defined itself through a superfluous other that it finally exterminated. Long before that, though, and already by virtue of its very definition of self, of its very constitution based on negation of an other predetermined as superfluous, Nazism exterminated the possibility of morality. In a Nazi regime — by definition — there is no space for the moral.

9.244   The decision whether to be within or outside the moral is not a moral decision, even if it can be given moral justifications in retrospect. Just as the decision whether to be within or outside the scientific is not a scientific decision, even if it can be given scientific justifications in retrospect. And so forth as regards every language game, every genre of discourse, with more or less distinct rules. The decision to enter or leave a game can only be justified in terms of the game within which one is already when making the decision (and one is always already within some discourse or another, within some language game, according to whose rules one acts, speaks, and thinks for the time being). Therefore, the decision to enter or leave the moral sphere can be justified with economic, emotional, political, or religious reasons (8.424). But from the moral point of view, all these justifications neither add nor subtract a thing. From the moral point of view, there is nothing to justify; the decision is always a leap. Accepting the constituting rule — non-indifference toward the distress of another — is the starting point. There is nowhere to retreat to from there. But this leap can be represented less dramatically than it might seem at first glance, without retreating all the way to Kierkegaard's absurd leap of faith. How can the decision to begin evaluating objects, actions, and people in terms of their market value be justified from an economic point of view? Can economic value be attributed to this decision, the very decision that allows the evaluation? And how can the decision to start playing chess or football be justified according to the rules of chess or football? And how can the rules of logic justify the decision to accept the conclusions of valid arguments whose premises are true?

9.245 Meanwhile, however, and perhaps unsurprisingly, a nonmoral justification emerges here for being within the moral: indifference to the distress of the other opens the gate to the slippery slope leading to acceptance of the other's superfluity. Just a small distance separates this indifference from resignation to the representation of the other as superfluous and to everything that produces the other as superfluous and allows one to put up with the other's removal. In other words, acquiescence in the superfluity of a certain other leads to acquiescence in that system of government, totalitarianism, in which a limited number of people attain complete rule over masses of people by making every person just as potentially superfluous as any other. As is well known, this acquiescence had dire consequences, not only for the groups of others declared superfluous, but also for the many millions whose superfluity was affirmed retrospectively, in the course of the Nazi war and occupation. There is, obviously, considerable reason for opposing Nazism. However, it turns out that only being within the moral rules out the possibility of coming to terms with the presence of Nazism under any circumstances — that is, in any such presence, including circumstances even remotely reminiscent of it (and unfortunately, such are the circumstances in which we are living today in Israel after thirty-five years of occupation). This is no light matter, though it may seem trivial, for what emerges here is a clear difference between moral objection to the Nazis and a resistance whose basis is political, economic, religious, or ideological. All the latter genres of discourse can, under certain circumstances, based on reasons conforming to all their rules, accept this or that collaboration with Nazism, or with neo-Nazi social forces, or with Nazi-like elements of domination and governance. There are innumerable examples, then and now, there and here, of such acceptance, even though in each case weighty arguments against the collaboration with the Nazis or the neo-Nazis could have been presented, too. If the account is economic or political — that is, instrumental and centered on the self — or even religious — that is, directed toward an abstract and transcendental other — the possibility always remains of circumstances in which acquiescence is preferable to resistance. For one who is already within the moral, who has already adopted the moral point of view, opposition and resistance to Nazism are absolute and uncompromising. Afterward it is possible, if one wishes, to enlist economic, political, religious, or ideological considerations as well, to explain or justify the resistance.

9.250 The superfluity produced by Nazism and the superfluity that the moral point of view finds before it are located at two contradictory poles. They are two poles of the same opposition. Superfluity is the common denominator. It is impossible to totally cancel out the continuum in the sphere of practice, as in the sphere of concepts. Philosophical discourse must identify the lines of continuity not only between itself and those philosophers who were willing to place their thinking at the service of Nazism, and not only between it and the philosophical residue that found its way into Nazi ideology. Philosophical discourse must identify its own dangerous capacity for patterns of thinking that are willing to accept Nazism; it must do so in order to be able to raise high the wall. At issue here is not just a fundamental resistance to the Nazis' demonizing and de-historicizing, two prevalent phenomena that are usually rejected, even if as mere lip service, by many of those who deal with Nazism and the annihilation of the Jews. I mean an attempt to identify elements in the cultural and spiritual climate, despite all the differences, that are common to "us" — no matter who the "we" in question may be — and "them." Such an effort characterizes several thinkers who studied Nazism as a cultural and intellectual (and not purely political) phenomenon, first and foremost Hannah Arendt, in her great work on the sources of totalitarianism and in her essay *Eichmann in Jerusalem*.[93] I wish to emphasize here one aspect of the structural similarity that Arendt reveals in that essay, without sufficiently lingering over it. Arendt presents an opposition between Eichmann's blind obedience of the Führer's command and the moral subject's noble obedience of the law of reason. This opposition can exist, however, only because the Nazi subject and the Kantian subject bear a disconcerting structural similarity. In both cases, the subject is subject to an unconditional imperative that must be adhered to above and beyond any principle of enjoyment or utility, as an end in itself — the command of the Führer or the command of reason. Eichmann, who in the course of his interrogation and trial demonstrated a reasonable knowledge of the principles of Kantian morality, preserves a sort of Kantian dichotomy between the empirical and the transcendent, between the demands of self-love and the absolute duty whose origin lies beyond the interests and desires of the individual. Eichmann did not even invert the traditional hierarchy in this dichotomy. He simply added the rational imperative to all the other temptations that may present themselves to the loyal subject of the Reich, one more desire one should know how to overcome, while placing the absolute command of the Führer, opposite all these, in the position of the categorical imperative.[94] The temptation to break the law is shifted from the particular moment to the universal moment (the universal moral law is a temptation to be overcome), while the absoluteness of the law is shifted from the universal moment to the particular one (the law is absolute because it is an expression of particularity — a particular chosen race, a singular Führer — that founds itself as an absolute value).

9.251 The command of the race, whose embodiment is the Führer's will, is not a negation of self-love, as it is in Kant, but rather an extension of the self that is to be loved — the race instead of the individual, and the race, as it were, as the ultimate place of the individual. The self-negation expressed by Kantian moral law is rejected disdainfully as a kind of degeneration. After the self has undergone a racist metamorphosis, self-love is positioned as the supreme law guiding every action. The satanic wish to act in diametric opposition to the moral law that is, Kant determined (naively? ironically? due to denial?), unsuited to human beings takes up residence in the hearts of human beings.[95] But it settles there — mediated by the Nazi myth — not as a satanic wish but as a wish to do what should be done according to the commands and instructions dictated by the ruling power. Eichmann usually intended not to do evil but rather to do what he was told to do, and sometimes also what he thought his superiors expected him to do. And what was expected of him was the realization, in practice, of the principle of the other's superfluity, that is, the extermination of the superfluous.

9.252 Nazism was the antipode of morality, for it produced superfluous otherness in order to create an imagined self instead of eliminating superfluity in order to save a real other. Superfluity is produced in a dual manner and in two stages. First the other is labeled superfluous; then the superfluous evils (from a moral point of view) are produced, the evils that will eventually lead to the elimination of what was originally identified as superfluous (according to the myth). The Nazi myth turns morality inside out, empties out what is inside and turns it upside down. In this sense, Nazism was a precise structural inversion of morality. Perhaps this precise inversion makes it unique among all other racist ideologies. Perhaps this is the singularity of Auschwitz from a moral point of view — that it was a progressively broadening zone of human superfluity, leading to the extermination of the superfluous ones and to the unending production of superfluous evils. Nazism annihilated the superfluous in order to cleanse itself and become transcendent, but this transcendence had no meaning beyond the excretion of the other, that is, his elimination. Destruction is not a means toward transcendence. It is transcendence itself. In other words, the Evil that is Nazism is an end in itself.

— This, though, is a doubtful singularity. In fact, it concerns not Auschwitz as an event but the plan that activated Auschwitz, the blueprint of the machine of annihilation. Other machines of annihilation operated according to other blueprints in the twentieth century, sometimes no less efficiently (9.204).

— You are absolutely right. There is, moreover, no reason to assume that the mythical blueprint lending uniqueness to Auschwitz or to the mechanism of implementation developed especially for the realization of this plan will remain exclusive to Auschwitz. The analysis I have proposed here allows the identification of Nazism as the antipode of morality without sanctifying any value and without predetermining the machine of destruction invented by Nazism as the absolute Evil. This discussion has assumed neither the absoluteness of the Evil created at Auschwitz nor its uniqueness; it does not use Auschwitz as a model against which the measure of Evil's horror is determined. It does not exclude the possibility that there have been (or will be) additional "Auschwitz instances," in which there have existed (or will exist) those characteristics making Auschwitz unique and differentiating it from Verdun, the Gulag, Cambodia, or Rwanda. And finally, whatever the singular traits of Auschwitz may be, they do not converge into the dogma of uniqueness and do not allow the sanctification of anything. On the contrary, they feed on a deconstructive analysis and continue the act of deconstruction.

9.253   European culture of the mid-twentieth century accepted the negation of morality and allowed an acceptance, in practice, of this negation. It allowed Evil to appear as is, as complete superfluity at the heart of being, and allowed the existence of Evil in and of itself, as an end in itself. The thinking interested in the historical present as the condition of its emergence and the horizon for its voyages, thinking that seeks — because this search is crucial for its self-reflection and self-understanding — the difference that is decisive to this present and to differentiate from its past, confronts Auschwitz in a wonderment reminiscent of the way philosophers at the turn of the eighteenth and throughout the nineteenth century confronted the French Revolution. They saw the Revolution as an arena for the revelation of liberty and a demonstration of its dangers, for the proof of progress, as a theater for demonstrating the dialectical relation between terror and reason; Kant even found in it signs for the possibility of the supreme Good itself (see 8.125). We look at Auschwitz and see in it an arena for the revelation of Evil as a category of being. But at this point, an unbridgeable chasm opens up between reason's two distinct "interests," the contemplative and the practical, that is, the moral. The contemplative interest, seeking to understand and formulate in a much clearer way the concept of Evil, examines Evil at the site where its appearance is as fully purified as possible, brilliant in the depth of its darkness. The moral interest seeks to identify Evil in the most mundane places, in the places where it is most successfully camouflaged, at the site where what is superfluous seems necessary and what is preventable seems natural. At this site, the road forks. The contemplative interest seeks to understand how this era has reached such a climax of clarity regarding the appearance of Evil. After all, it's not every day that an idea appears in history in its full-blown magnificence. The practical interest seeks to understand how so many people at this time can go on living alongside evils whose systematic production can always be assembled in a way that resembles the complex whose name was Auschwitz (as stated: hermetic closure, annulment of the possibilities of exchange and conversion, mechanisms of suffering and loss, methodical extermination — this list doesn't purport to be exhaustive). The practical interest will seek to understand how people go on participating in the production of these evils without taking part in the experience of "revelation" (too blind to see, too insensitive to marvel, or too overburdened with their own worries to pay attention). In addition, the practical interest will seek to understand the mechanisms of the production of Evil, a singular combination of which appeared at Auschwitz, in all the horrifying variety of their other combinations, paying meticulous attention to the continuities existing by virtue of these mechanisms between disaster areas and the most peaceful realms of civilization.

9.254　A pure machine for the production of Evil isn't necessarily the most powerful mechanism for the production of Evil. The two shouldn't be confused. On considering effects, products, and not just the "perfect" mechanism, the crystal-clear appearance of the principle of superfluity, one must admit that even if it was perfect in its superfluity, Auschwitz was not the worst possible occurrence, the most horrific evil of all. The absoluteness of Evil can also appear when a single human being is murdered for no reason, just because someone has declared him superfluous. Absoluteness is not a measure of size, not even of infinite size. A single moment in Hiroshima, on August 6, 1945, was as lethal as several weeks at Auschwitz during the previous summer. Can it be said that at that moment Hiroshima was a more terrible place of Evil? Can it be said that due to the "real" political interests served by the bombing of the city, due to the real struggle between Japan and the United States, due to the values that seemingly justified deployment of the bomb, that day was less terrible than those months of annihilation at Auschwitz? And what if a day in Hiroshima is compared to one month at Auschwitz? One week? One day? How many questions are needed in order to take *ad absurdum* the attempt to make this quantitative comparison?

9.255 This is the decisive matter: in the third decade of the twentieth century, there appeared in Europe a pure machine of Evil, a form of human existence based on annihilation. This was not merely the appearance of a wish or an intention to annihilate. It was the appearance of a human form in whose very being annihilation was a necessary component. In the autumn of 1941, this machine began operating at a formerly unknown scope and pace. In the spring of 1944, when thousands of Hungarian Jews were being exterminated each day in the death camps, and when in the camps surrounding the ovens tens of thousands awaited their deaths, nuclear scientists in the United States completed the prototype of a new tool for mass annihilation. They developed the technical capacity for a form of annihilation thousands of times more powerful than gassing or any other method of human slaughter known before. A year later, this potential was partially realized. Ever since, civilized and less civilized nations have continued to develop it, until the bombs lowered on Hiroshima and Nagasaki have become mini-toys in the atomic playing field. But as the Second World War ended, three facts were already clear, the combination of which we have not yet fully understood:

1. Humanity is capable of developing and maintaining forms of social organization whose end is the annihilation of defined parts of the population.

2. Some human beings have tools whose entire utility lies in their absolute and total capacity for destruction.

3. Certain human beings have the capacity to activate these tools and perhaps also a sufficient measure of desperate determination, cynicism, or mindless obedience to do so.

In other words, human beings are equipped today with both the technical ability and the social, cultural, and political practices allowing total annihilation of large groups of designated humans or of the entire human race. In all the horrors that have occurred since then, less sophisticated tools of destruction were used, and the will to annihilation was combined with political and economic struggles.[96] What has not yet happened since — in the meantime and perhaps miraculously — is a final convergence between the technological and the social, between the capacity for absolute destruction and the social form engendering the will to realize it. Or even less than such a will, for clearly two sides willing to risk annihilation would suffice, and perhaps even one such side. The rest will evolve independently. If history is any guide, such a convergence is merely a matter of time.

9.3 *The Whole World, the End of the World*

9.300 There is a period of time, astronomical perhaps but nevertheless finite, that separates us from the end of the world. This is what we are told by the scientists studying how planets are born and die and measuring the rate at which the sun is cooling. The end of the world, it would seem, at least at this stage of human knowledge, is both inevitable and meaningless, beyond the horizon of any human expectations. The whole of human history is a tiny speck on the continuum of astronomical time, but the astronomical end does not belong to historical time. One can speculate extensively on the meaning of this finitude of the world, assigning a precise, completely finite meaning to the finitude of man. But such speculations lie outside the realm of moral discussion.

9.301 Many religious doctrines, mystical and otherwise, promise or warn their believers that a finite and indefinite time span separates the present from the end of the world. The end of the world is perhaps the aim of human history, but it is not part of it, even if history leads to it according to some messianic or eschatological view. It doesn't belong to its rhythm or to the rhythm of cosmic time or to the rate of the deity's intervention in the world. Paradoxically perhaps, messianic, apocalyptic, millenarian, and other declarations of the end of the world actually confirm its infinitude, for "the end," that cosmic theatrical spectacle, is but one more chapter in the history of the intervention of the deity in the world, and after it salvation is ensured, at least for a few of those who predict the end. In other words, in contrast to the astronomical end, which is absolute and inevitable, the eschatological end is not a total end and in a sense is not inevitable either (for believers, for the pious, for the repentant).

9.302 A combination of political processes and technological developments currently posits a new possibility: the people who make

579

history may bring about its end. People can, in their actions, bring the end nearer and put an end to the world. They can do so gradually, as a result of a series of ecological catastrophes and a continuing disruption of the balance of world ecology; and they can do so all at once, through atomic holocaust. In both cases, the expected destruction combines two axes of time that were hitherto totally separate, the eschatological and the astronomical: the technological and the economic-political developments of Western societies position the end of the world on the visible horizon of human history. From the day the bomb was created, a historical time span, indefinite and unknown but finite, has separated us from the end of the world, the lifeworld of at least the most sophisticated life-forms. This, however, is not an inevitable end. Therefore, this end is (or should be) located at the heart of moral discourse, even if it often seems to be its most distinct un-thought.

9.303   On the other side of the finish line, once all is over, there will be no more life whose disaster this total death will be. Only sheer-winged creatures, distant angels or insects particularly resistant to radiation, will witness the loss. There will be nothing, not even Evil. But there is no thought on the other side of the finish line; thought exists only on this side. And on this side, the end seems very evil, the worst possible evil. The end of the world is total otherness, the most radical otherness conceivable. The radical otherness of the end of the world doesn't demand any sacrifice, isn't the addressee of any gift or submission, and is not a reason for or cause of any waste. One can't take an interest in it, care for it, or disengage from it, but can only reject it in advance, a rejection directed toward the future out of which it threatens to appear. The end of the world is total and inclusive nothingness. While it contains individual death, it is radically different from it. The transition to nothingness expected in individual death is a principle of individuation; the presence of death as what-will-come has an individuating and differentiating effect, and addressing it — at least if one concedes Heidegger's approach — is crucial for the constitution of self, as well as a test of its authenticity and singularity. However, the transition to nothingness expected in common death is a principle of commonality. The presence of this end as an end that may occur and can still be prevented or postponed has a connecting and cohesive effect, and addressing it can be an axis of social commonality and a test for the morality of such a commonality. The presence of the end of the world is a basis for the appearance of a common consciousness reflecting a common negation of a common otherness — a common destiny of those threatened with common obliteration at the end of the world. The collective self that this self-consciousness seeks to represent does not need to draw any limit to waste of any kind so as to affirm itself. The otherness on the basis of whose negation it appears imprisons the waste along with the interested, self-centered investment within a closed economy of threat and hope.

9.304 In the face of the catastrophe that threatens to bring the world to its end, it would no longer seem possible to separate moral waste from an investment that is in keeping with self-interest, or care for the other from self-care; in fact, in the shadow of ultimate otherness, the otherness of the common end, it is impossible to separate self from other and us from them at all. The delineating line does not disappear, though. It only shifts from the geopolitical space to the space of historical time. It may well be that we're now producing the tools and creating the conditions through which and due to which other people will bring an end to the world. We can remain indifferent to this destruction, because the end of the world is postponed somewhat and our deaths will still be individual, or we can turn it into a focus of moral intention, out of care for others who will be annihilated. In this context, it is difficult to disconnect the moral intention toward others from its ethical aspects — the care of individuals for the meaning of their lives and deaths in the face of the expected end of the world, the death of memory, the end of history, and the total annulment of every meaning. In this situation, it is difficult to distinguish between the ethical and the moral, just as it is difficult to distinguish between an interested investment and waste, and indeed there is really no point in trying. However, the more the presence of the expected end of the world is dimmed, the clearer the separation becomes: between us, who are conscious of the expected end of the world and can act to prevent it, most probably while impinging on various selfish interests, and others who will possibly experience it one day. "We" will signify here a voice seeking to represent that imagined subject who is supposed to appear out of the negation of the radical otherness of the end of the world, and out of care for the specific others whose end this may be. We: those who are progressing together toward the end of the world, leading toward it those who come after us, and who are capable of hastening or preventing the end. They: those whose individual end the end of the world will be, the whole of humanity at the moment human history comes to an end.

9.305 It may be that in the (very) end, we are merely part of them. From the point of view of the end of memory and the end of meaning,

the end of the very possibility of making sense and giving meaning, there is no distance separating us from them. Humanity as an
abstract universal idea, in which the difference between self and
other is overcome, appears only at the end of history. From a
moral point of view, too, the whole of humanity only appears as
the necessary object of moral interest at the end of history. The
end that may still be prevented is common, general, and inclusive;
the total loss is the loss of all and of everyone. But the moral point
of view preserves the difference between those who have a moral
interest ("us") and this interest's objects ("them"), distinguishing
those representing the panhuman from the general collective of
humanity that is represented, and those representing the duty to
act from those for whom the action is intended.

9.310 The whole world appears at the end of the world. "World history," "universality," appears truly for the first time along with
the expected end of history. But this end of history is not expected
to appear with the completion of the process of the rationalization
of reality and the realization of reason, as one can gather from
Hegel's writing, nor will it arrive with the appearance of the perfect political forms of the liberal West, as Francis Fukuyama
believes.[97] The end of history in question is the end of all those
making history. When this finitude reaches self-consciousness as
an actual possibility, perhaps soon approaching but preventable
and belonging equally to anyone making or seeking to make history, then history becomes truly universal, a "world history" in
the full sense.

9.311 In familiar Hegelian-Marxist terms, it could be said that human
history long ago became world history in itself but not for itself.
Human history has become a single world history as a function
of the imperialist phase of capitalism, the appearance of a global
market, and a series of international treaties born of two "world
wars." In this phase, there were several distinctly ideological attempts at partial representations of historical universality from a
one-sided point of view — that of Western civilization or one of
its facets — in an effort to present the part as the whole. But only
the appearance of the end of the world threatening the whole of
humanity, east and west, north and south, engenders the appearance of world history for itself, that is, the appearance of a history
conscious of itself as "truly" universal or the appearance of a self-
consciousness in which human history as a whole is posited as the
self. But even this is not enough. Even a world history that has
become universal, acquired self-consciousness, and appears for

itself needs representatives ("us"). Not everyone participates in this self-consciousness. Those directly threatened, here and now, by the globality of the world do not take part in it but resist it — if they can — and seek to deny it. Those threatened in this way seek not to prevent the nearing end of the world but to prevent the world from hastening their individual ends and the destruction of the group to which they belong. The members of tribes perishing through starvation, violence, and epidemics in Africa's rain forests; the workers selling their bodies and souls for a pittance and in slave-labor conditions in South America or Southeast Asia; the people of the inner-city ghettos in the megalopolises of the West, the homeless, the addicts, those degraded and rotting at the doorsteps of comfortable, peaceful citizens; those struggling under the collapsing ruins of the societies of the former Soviet bloc — all these need reprieve immediately, for their ruin is near. Their ruin is the result of a globality that hasn't reached self-consciousness, of a universal history stuck in the darkness of existence in itself. What solidarity can they— let's call them the abject of the earth, the inhabitants of "the planet of the drowning" — have with those capable of hastening or preventing the end of the world? At the present stage of history, those capable of hastening or preventing the end of the world are also those who benefit, day by day, hour by hour, from the ruin of those who are drowning.

9.312 History has become universal and the world has become one through the growth and dissemination of the two most potent power systems that have developed in the West: capitalist economy and the nation-state. These two are also by far the most powerful of the systems producing and distributing superfluous evils. The combination of the two generated colonial expansion, allowing and accelerating the globalization of both economy and war and, as a result, of culture at large. The United States and the industrialized countries of Europe methodically subjugated, exploited, plundered, and destroyed the peoples of the Third World in their colonial expansion, even while developing Third World countries and engendering the accelerated modernization of their cultures and regimes. These peoples were sucked into the global economy growing out of Europe. Today, they flood industrialized countries and disrupt their social and economic systems; they export revolutionary-religious terror, triggering the development of the destructive antibodies — nationalism, racism, neo-Fascism, and neo-Nazism — that threaten to destroy all in a furious rage, too blind to understand a thing. Weapons of mass destruction invented by the West, which had hoped to control them, are produced, distributed, and stockpiled by Third World countries. Conventional weapons serve acts of mass destruction (Rwanda), and the threat of unconventional weapons (Iraq) rekindles a willingness in the West to commit mass murder (for instance, threats to deploy "tactical" nuclear weapons during the Gulf War). Opposing the global linkage of capitalism and democracy are an Islamic fundamentalism whose revolutionary and terrorist forms threaten, or are perceived as threatening, to destroy democracy from the outside, and a Christian (and Jewish) fundamentalism threatening to destroy it from within. Both greatly intensify the repression of women and minorities in the states and communities under their rule; both arouse in the still largely secular West a sense of powerlessness, on the one hand, and a willingness to deploy the most extreme forms of violence, on the other.

9.313 Clearly, responsibility for all the world's woes cannot be ascribed to the West, to the world market, or to other aspects of the processes of globalization (8.040). Moreover, developments that are part of globalization in the realms of technology, transport, communications, health care in particular and life management in general, insurance, and financial accounting have brought about far-reaching changes in the capacity for giving aid and alleviating distress in every sphere: reducing suffering, preventing scarcity, curing, nursing, lengthening life expectancy, and ensuring compensation for loss (see 9.444). However, all these changes are merely one side of the coin of the revolutions in industrialization, information, and communications; the flip side can definitely be identified as those globalization processes responsible for the appearance of evils reaching a scope and range unprecedented in the whole of history. Here is a partial list:

- Globalization of the employment and capital markets and the possibilities for swiftly moving capital and means of production from one end of the earth to the other, where capital can remain totally disconnected from the producing-exploited society, allowing full exploitation of the work of the latter while totally ignoring it and abandoning it when necessary, without rechanneling back into it the profits of exploitation.
- A global arms market lacking efficient controls, allowing any regime to be provided swiftly and massively with varied and high-powered killing tools, which is thus capable of igniting a terrible blaze in every local conflict.
- A global drug market, into which Third World people are forcibly pushed to make relatively easy profits, and which works

to disintegrate entire layers of populations in the megalopolises of the First World, with the aid of a rigid, undifferentiated regime of criminalization of drugs of any kind.

- Processes of resistance to the economic and cultural imperialism of the West that accelerate the expansion of new, violent, repressive forms of religion and religious politics in both developing and developed societies.
- The constant erosion of state welfare mechanisms in the industrialized countries of the West due to the constrictions of the global market, impinging on the capacity to defend the market's casualties, the local unemployed and immigrants.
- The global networking of information, of communications channels, and of means of transporting people, goods, and messages, giving the privileged unprecedented advantages and accelerating the rate of wealth acquisition and of impoverishment.

These processes exist in every place where the production and distribution of evils is combined with the market system. Previous accumulation of capital is the main motive for additional accumulation of capital; the cause generating more suffering than any other is previous suffering; the cause generating more loss than any other is previous loss. The spread of evils intensifies the spread of evils. Can this whirlpool in which the postmodern world is caught come to a stop only through a total collapse of the global political and economic order?

9.314 Such a presentation of the processes of globalization and their role in the production and distribution of evils preserves one fundamental dichotomy: between rich and poor, between well fed and drowning, between those capable of defending themselves from evils and those sentenced to go from bad to worse. On the basis of such a view of the order of evils, there are probably those who dream of an Internationale of the "drowning," the oppressed of the world, who will one day make their reckoning with Western civilization in a terrible furious rage, drowning it in an insatiable lust for revenge, in a vein of "let me die with the Philistines." Others are willing to make do with small acts of sabotage, local acts of terror (the Jewish community building in Argentina, the Pan Am jet over Lockerbie, the federal building in Oklahoma City, the U.S. Embassy in Nairobi — a partial list), attempting to derail "the system" and almost always eventually increasing its power. Terror simply intensifies state surveillance and state invasion of the daily world (just as frequent strikes and successful labor-union struggles

are prone to lead to the relocation of factories and to the accelerated penetration of market mechanisms into a town struck by
unemployment). Universal history still appears in such a presentation of globalization processes as it exists in itself, without self-
consciousness, imprisoned in a collision between strong and weak
(north and south or west and east), the end of which is predetermined. We seek to overcome this rift through a common consciousness of finitude and a moral interest in the common fate of
humanity as a whole, appearing through the anticipation of the end
of the world. But from the point of view of the oppressed of the
whole world — if I am at all entitled to conjecture what it looks like
from there — every attempt to create a universal self-consciousness
and solidarity to overcome this conflict (and all the other local
conflicts contained within it or dimmed within its context), in the
name of the expected but preventable end of the world, is yet
another attempt to produce a false consciousness that blurs the
actual stakes and conflicts of interest.

9.315 Let's assume that we are very close to nuclear holocaust, that we
know it, that this can be demonstrated to others. Let's assume that
nature, which was always indifferent, rises in rebellion and joins
the campaign for the extermination of human civilization through
a series of environmental catastrophes: swift growth of the hole
in the ozone layer, accelerated intensification of the greenhouse
effect, melting glaciers, rapid spread of viral epidemics, and new
strains of bacteria that are resistant to existing antibiotics. In
short, let's assume that we're just a hairbreadth away from the end
of the world and that we have a certain idea of what can be done
to postpone it, to buy time, and then to find other ways of changing the course of world history. In that case, would solidarity and
common interest arise between "us," the well fed, and "them,"
the drowning? There's no knowing. From a certain depth of
despair, I suppose, one seeks to see how the end of the world will
look. From a certain stage of despair and physical and spiritual
want, one is willing, I suppose, to subject everything, even humanity's salvation from destruction, to a simple question: what
will the world look like afterward, will lifesavers for the drowning
appear in it? This is not an attempt to examine the conditions for
cooperation between the well fed and the drowning. It is an
attempt to imagine and illustrate the conflicts of interest.

9.320 The moral point of view is blind to conflicts of interest. This is
not only because of the different forms of the end of the world
that erase the dichotomy between self and other, or because the

interests of the abject of the world are hidden, or because the lack of self-consciousness prevents a grasp of how the culture out of which the moral interest grows benefits from exploitation and oppression, and from the growing gap between the well fed and the drowning. The moral point of view is blind to conflicts of interest because the self-interest of the contemplator possessed of moral interest lies outside its field of vision. The moral horizon opens up at the precise instant when self-interest is suspended, and is closed off at the precise instant when self-interest again dictates the guiding rules of action. From a moral point of view, the decisive difference is not between them and us, for it is only "them," the others, that interest "us," we "who are progressing together toward the end of the world . . . and . . . are capable of hastening or preventing the end" (9.304). The decisive difference is one of location on the slope leading from evil to more horrible evil. But we are already aware of at least three distinct slopes.

9.321   Evil unrolls on three slopes, each of which leads to an abyss of its own, in three heterogeneous spaces. The first space is that of world-historical time; the abyss at its end is the end of the world, the end of history. In Hiroshima, this abyss appeared for the first time as a real historical possibility rather than an eschatological one, that is, as a possibility stemming from human action rather than the intervention of the deity in historical time. The second space is that of governance and domination, of the possibilities available to the powers that be for harming their subjects in intentional and organized ways; this abyss is the methodical, controlled annihilation of a defined group that is part of the population, of a size as large as the regime may wish. The third space is the geopolitical space of globalization; the abyss yawning within this space has no name or place, and it is difficult to identify a distinct moment when it appeared in history.[98] The abyss in the third space is not an exceptional catastrophic event or a campaign of organized violence directed at a specific group within the population, but rather the daily routine of the entire population (with the exception of a thin layer of ruling elite). In fact, at issue is not an abyss but rather the gradual flooding of the world of life with irreparable evils that cause the general disintegration of the cultural and social fabric and drown entire parts of the population. On the planet of the drowning, encompassing at least half of the earth's populated area, the slope of Evil is simply the expansion of that environment which regularly and systematically produces suffering and loss, degradation and decay, in the form of closed, self-reproducing, and intensifying circles of evils. This is the environment of chronically disaster-stricken areas in which conditions are always ripe for the outburst of yet new catastrophes. This is also the environment into which regimes of catastrophe are absorbed with relative ease, regimes of the type characterizing the second slope: Cambodia, Burma, Uganda, Somalia, Rwanda, Zaire, Paraguay.

9.322 Three spaces: that of historical time, of the modern state, of geopolitics. Three forms of intersection: according to era, according to the type of regime, according to chronic disaster zones. Three slopes, three climaxes, three forms of end: the end of the world, the end of the political, the end of the human. In the current era, there are indications (on the first and third slopes) or actual appearances (on the second slope) of the lowest places that man can reach, three summits of Evil: nuclear holocaust or an ecological catastrophe generating the total and undifferentiated annihilation, either intentional or not, of all forms of sophisticated life; the appearance of a regime conducting an organized and methodical extermination of definite parts of the population; a combination of natural disasters, state and ethnic violence, economic, social, and cultural degeneration, creating environmental conditions that bring total ruin upon indefinite but chronically vulnerable and constantly growing groups of the earth's inhabitants.

9.323 The field of vision that opens up from the moral point of view does not allow the unification of these spaces or the combination of the three slopes within a single continuum. There are contingent relations between the different spaces and the different slopes, and they cannot be grounded upon each other. But there is also no reason to totally rule out a combination of circumstances in which the slide down one slope will accelerate the slide down the other two. The moral discourse guiding the gaze allows a discussion of them together, and an attempt to place every act on all three slopes simultaneously. Political regimes, economic and military policies, economic transactions, international agreements, institutions of punishment and discipline: each of these needs to stand a triple test according to its placement on each and all of the three slopes. Does it contribute to the hastening or the postponement of the end of the world, that is, of a nuclear or ecological holocaust; does it reproduce, strengthen, or sabotage the creation of conditions allowing a reappearance of concentration camps, forced-labor camps, and death camps (or some contemporary version of them); does it contribute to a further deterioration of living conditions in the various areas of the planet of the drowning, or contribute to stopping the circular processes accelerating the material and spiritual bankruptcy of these zones?

9.324 No one is free to decide, at any given moment, on what slope to be located or which slope may be ignored. At least no one among us, we the inhabitants of the planet of the well fed. On the one hand, it's impossible to merge the three spaces listed here — the historical, the political-ideological, and the geopolitical — and it's impossible to ground the slope opening onto an abyss in one space upon the one opening onto an abyss in another; on the other hand, the shifting relations between one slope and another cannot be severed, and it's impossible to ensure that slipping toward the abyss at the bottom of one slope will not lead as well to a slippage toward the others. In the present historical state of affairs, in the conditions of an interconnected world economy, in the processes of the globalization of the market, war, politics, communications, science, and the whole of culture, the moral point of view necessarily leads, at one and the same time, to both a local political interest in the globality of the world and a cosmopolitan interest in each of the "social forms of the political" within it. And vice versa: a serious attempt to understand a matter — political, economic, technological, military, or cultural — within its inclusive global context necessarily leads to the threshold of the moral point of view. The global analysis uncovers the borderless globality of vulnerability, of impending catastrophe and of responsibility for its prevention, of the all-pervasive presence of the final destruction (an end that has, as we've seen, at least three forms) and the worldwide nature of the state of being called upon to extend help at every moment, in principle, from everyone to everyone, from every place to every place.

9.325 I'm referring to the threshold of the moral point of view and not to the point of view itself, for it is always possible to prefer the particular interest and ignore the global implications of the actions guided by it, and indeed this is the usual preference. But this is a short-term, short-range particular interest. Sometimes the other whom one is prepared to ignore soon becomes the selfish interested party himself, in the foreseeable future, or he is situated outside one's spheres of belonging. As stated (9.304), the closer we draw to the end of the world, the harder it is to separate care of the self from care for the other. Thus, on the verge of the finish line, history achieves its "final end," approaches the Kantian "kingdom of ends," in which moral consideration precedes and dictates every matter. The "final end," however, is attained not due to man's transcendence but as a direct result of his fall, of his nearing destruction.

9.330 The abyss at the bottom of the first slope — whether a nuclear or an ecological holocaust, an outburst or a process — is a catastrophe whose possibility was born of technology and cannot be prevented without technological intervention. But technology isn't enough. Scaling the first slope also necessitates a new political form that allows people to regain control over technology. The abyss at the bottom of the second slope is a catastrophe whose possibility was born of the technologies of "governmentality," combining the control of a whole population with surveillance of each and every individual in it, and it cannot be prevented without governmental, military, and legal intervention.[99] But such intervention is not enough. Scaling the second slope also necessitates a new political form that allows more people to resist the colonization of their lifeworld by anonymous systems of power. The abyss at the bottom of the third slope is an incremental, ongoing destruction whose possibility was born of the very existence of global social systems and the intensification of globalization. It is unclear how this destruction can be prevented without bringing about the complete collapse of these social systems, for the expanding destruction is, it would seem, the underside of their proper functioning, and total destruction seems an expected, even if not unpreventable, sequel of the natural course of their development. In addition, there is a good chance that a collapse of the social systems will accelerate, not prevent, the destruction of the planet of the drowning.

9.331 The Nazis sought to annihilate one group but were prepared (and later dragged) to sacrifice millions of other people. The Americans sought to signal their destructive capacity through the "controlled" destruction of two cities but sparked a nuclear arms race that currently allows more and more regimes (and soon perhaps also those evading all regimes) to destroy everything. During colonial rule, every developed Western country was willing to profit from destroying broad layers of its subjects' societies and to ignore and even accelerate the destruction of entire cultures; together they triggered the processes that now threaten to drown large parts of Africa and entire regions in Asia and in Central and South America. There is no point in dealing with the motives of those who started the processes in question. The mechanisms and systems producing Evil are not ruled by any one center, and no change of motives or intentions can ensure a change in the patterns of the globalization of Evil. Moral thinking must be systemic and global. To counteract the abyss at the bottom of the first slope, a political form is required that will allow a renewed control of technology; the second slope requires new structures of association, of social and cultural networking, that will allow and support the spread of effective resistance to any regime willing to make people, not evils, superfluous; the third slope requires local and global systems of governance capable of balancing the destruction-accelerating factors embedded in processes of globalization. This is no more than very general talk, some blurred outlines that moral thinking must posit on the practical political horizon. The rest is a matter for new forms of practical reason: the interpretation of historical processes, a specialization in the analysis of the global systems at issue, and a capacity, which is difficult to attain, for creating a synthesis between different directions of study and areas of discussion. It is difficult to measure the success of such a theoretical-practical effort, and it is impossible to provide recipes for it; it is easy to point out the places where it is missing.

9.332 The state of Israel can serve as a paradigmatic example.

1. In their decision to produce nuclear weapons (or to attain the capacity for swiftly producing them — it makes no difference), very small groups of experts and politicians, operating in the name of the successive governments of Israel, accelerated the proliferation of nuclear arms. They sought to achieve deterrence against an attack threatening the very existence of the state of Israel, but they also made their own contribution to the processes increasing the likelihood of nuclear holocaust and hastening the end of the world.

2. Following the takeover of the West Bank and the Gaza Strip in the war of 1967, the denial of the civil rights of the Palestinian inhabitants, and the gradual colonization of these territories by Jewish settlers, Israel developed a singular form of repressive government and nationalist separatism (apartheid on a national, rather than racial, basis). This regime methodically deploys mechanisms of domination and control, practices of violence, ideological discourse, and technologies of "governmentality" that combine rule over the population and surveillance of each individual in it. It has instituted a broad spectrum of possibilities for harming Palestinian subjects (and in fact, any subject of the regime) through different forms of state violence. At the bottom of the gaping slope of this space is the methodical and controlled removal — either through transfer (as it is commonly called), deportation, or destruction — of a "superfluous" group that is part of the governed population.

3. Here it is enough to mention the way Israel has turned the whole of Palestinian territories into a chronic disaster zone. But

Israel is involved in the globalization of Evil in more than one way. In order to maintain an advanced and profitable arms industry and exploit the economic and diplomatic advantages opened up to it by the local arms race, Israel joined the world producers and distributors of armaments, engaged with the worst of world regimes, and — both directly and indirectly, usually in secrecy, and almost indiscriminately — supplied and continues to supply weapons to those who spread destruction throughout the planet of the drowning. At the same time, with much clamor in the media, Israel occasionally joins well-orchestrated short-term and short-range humanitarian gestures offering assistance to disaster-stricken zones at various corners of the world. Also, since the early 1990s, Israel has been part of the international labor market, absorbing immigrants from all over the world, exploiting their labor, abandoning them to all the crimes that threaten a migrant labor force, and slipping, along with them, down to those places where the capitalism of the nation-state verges on the depths of slavery.

And all this is still entrapped in the chains of the memory of that abyss at the heart of the culture in which the Nazi nightmare is still alive and well, borne in the minds of those who were rescued and those who grew up in the shadow of the survivors, and of all the others inundated by the unending verbalization that sanctified the destruction and set up Auschwitz in the blank space of God.

9.333 In Israel-Palestine — and this is but an example — all these matters are interconnected in various and shifting ways. In one direction, the globalization of the economy apparently makes a certain contribution to political and economic processes that may hasten the end of the occupation regime; perhaps the proliferation of nuclear arms will also contribute to that. In the other direction, the development of forms of control and domination that are based on and articulate nationalist separation, that oppress and deny the human rights of an entire people, alongside the growing prevalence of a nationalist ideology with distinctly racist and atavistic features, and close ties between elected governments and the settler groups implementing this ideology while deploying violence and enjoying free rein in the territories under occupation, may hasten the outbreak of war, encourage a seemingly limited use of "tactical" nuclear arms, further deteriorate the existing discrimination against immigrant workers, and strengthen opportunistic ties between Israel and the worst of world regimes. My intention here is not to present a detailed analysis of historical processes, just to point out the moral horizon of such an analysis, the vital importance of a global, multi-systemic framework of analysis, and the irreducible link between the moral and the global (9.324).

9.340 The global, multi-systemic view of moral interest proposed here has at least three complementary facets: (1) Certain "local" actions (that is, actions taken due to local or systemic considerations) have far-reaching global effects; people on one side of the earth are liable to cause very serious harm to the condition of people at the other side of the earth, usually without meaning to do so and sometimes without even retrospective knowledge of the connection between the actions and their results.[100] (2) No regime in the world is capable today of hiding for a prolonged period the horrors it produces; no catastrophe fails to become public knowledge, almost no disaster-stricken area fails to receive media exposure; reliable information about any place on earth in which evils systematically accumulate is sooner or later accessible (even if this information does not necessarily include an understanding of the mechanisms of Evil). (3) Not everyone is capable of offering aid, and not everyone is willing or able to pay the price of intervention, but there is no place on the face of the earth that cannot be reached in order to offer aid to those struck by disaster or persecuted by their regime or, conversely, in order to slowly lead people toward their annihilation, hypnotized by the magic flute of "market forces" or by the mind-numbing drumbeat of holy war declared in the name of some deity. The globality of moral interest is closely associated with three interconnected but not equivalent processes of globalization: a globalization of the market, war, and international relations; a globalization of information and the media; a globalization of the capacity for state intervention.

9.341 The industrialized countries of the First World have economic, technological, and military power and political patterns of action that allow them, in principle, to intervene at every moment, at every site, in order to aid disaster-stricken areas. The question of whether to intervene or abstain from intervention is a complex political and moral one. Interveners are frequently required to collaborate with murderous regimes in order to protect the latter's subjects or their neighbors from catastrophes that they themselves have brought about; the interveners thus strengthen wicked regimes and increase their chances of bringing about more and more disasters. Frequently, intervention is avoided due to fear of clashing with violent forces in the population of the disaster-stricken area and fear of possible casualties among the aid givers, which would almost always be vastly disproportionate to the number of victims destined to perish due to a lack of aid. Sometimes intervention can exact a high political, military, or economic price and may cause large numbers of victims — this was the case in Bosnia, in Chechnya — and is avoided even though the price of nonintervention is obviously higher, although the latter price is paid only by the population of the disaster-stricken area. Sometimes the intervention costs many casualties, and the moral principle guiding it is no more than a facade for distinct political and economic interests — this was the case during the Gulf War.[101]

9.342 The distinction between the moral and the political can be sharpened through a distinction between different intervention agencies. Governments and agencies representing governments, or organizations composed of member governments, restrict moral interest and determine their willingness to intervene according to economic and political considerations. At least some nongovernmental organizations, first among them humanitarian aid agencies, are guided by moral considerations; for them, in principle, the moral point of view is supposed to set limits to the interference of "other" considerations, economic, political, media, and so forth. Of course, in practice, these organizations are subject to the manipulation of governments and of powerful elements in economics and the media, and daily life within them is fraught with power struggles, as it is in any organization, but they are finally obliged to formulate the justification for their every action in moral terms.[102] The crucial question in every decision, action, or strategy of intervention is whether it brought about a maximal reduction of the evils produced and distributed throughout a given disaster zone. In this sense, international aid agencies are sometimes similar to a site of "sheer care for the other," the distinct place of the moral. Local volunteer organizations and lobbies are similar to them, in this aspect, in seeming to curb various political or economic actions in the name of care for others who are harmed by these actions (for instance, lobbies that promote the boycott of companies using sweatshop labor in the Third World, or the prohibition of the use of antipersonnel land mines or unconventional weapons). However, the difference between these two types of organizations is no less important. It is the difference between a local and a globalized care for the other.

9.343 The intervention of First World countries in the Third World is incessant, carried out through the market and the media, through the proliferation of arms, through humanitarian aid agencies, through bilateral and international contracts, treaties, and so forth, and is perceived as "natural" and legitimate, at least by the interveners. Intervention is not uniform in its aims and results, but it usually intensifies mechanisms for the production and distribution of evils on the planet of the drowning or at the very least allows them to go on unhindered. Only to a small extent does it contribute to reducing the power of these mechanisms, mainly through diplomatic pressure to extend human rights, the underside of which is pressure to liberalize and to accelerate the capacity of industrialized countries to penetrate the markets of Third World countries. Opposite this regular intervention, intervention in disaster-stricken areas is limited, almost always occurs after the fact, and concerns only the horrific results of the catastrophe, not its enabling conditions. Probably unknowingly and perhaps despite themselves, the NGOs providing aid often assist First World governments, and the market forces operating under the auspices of these government, to maintain a balance between disastrous methodical intervention and ad hoc intervention aiding disaster-stricken areas. In contrast to aid organizations, the lobbies and organizations struggling against one aspect of the intervening systems stand a chance of generating fundamental change in the patterns of the production and distribution of evils. It doesn't necessarily follow from this that the aid agencies make no difference or are even harmful; when catastrophes occur, they are irreplaceable. What does follow from this, however, is a consciousness of the fundamental limitation of their activity, of its structural ideological role, and of the need to improve on the pattern of seasonal flurries of activity in the face of the catastrophe when Evil breaks out and to develop political and organizational tools for efficiently confronting the ongoing, chronic presence of Evil in the times between catastrophes.

9.344 But should not the paupers of one's town come first? From the point of view of a luckily comfortable resident of New York, don't the blacks destined to poverty in the inner city come before the blacks being slaughtered in some distant jungle? From the point of view of an Israeli citizen living in Tel Aviv, don't 200,000 exploited and degraded foreign workers near his home come before the millions of their respective peoples denied even the chance of surrendering themselves to employers in slave-labor conditions just to survive? The answer can't follow from a direct calculation of the "volume of evils." It must emerge from an understanding of the mechanisms of the production and distribution of evils. What comes first is what is closer to the Achilles' heel of some such mechanism. An average resident of Tel Aviv has a better chance of alleviating the plight of the foreign workers in his city than of aiding the famine-stricken of Somalia. More important, the chances that anyone in his vicinity save him will take an interest in the latter are slim. His duty to aid the impoverished of his own town comes first not because these are his relatives but because his geographic, systemic proximity to them creates an opportunity that doesn't exist for more distant others. A systemic, near-holistic perception of the production of Evil casts the blame on all human beings but leaves very little hope for change. In planned, initiated activity, the issue is often side effects that no one intended, even if no one does a thing to prevent them, and from which many may benefit, after they have been created — a situation that hinders attempts to get rid of these side effects. Frequently at issue is the immanent, fundamental inability to control overly complex webs of mutual relations that lack control centers, given the impossibility of containing everything occurring in them under a single description. Often, all one can do is avoid complicity in systems of discourse and action that produce Evil, and only take part in local resistances. There's no knowing in advance what the side effects of such resistances will be or how much evil they, in turn, will produce. But because the systems producing Evil are never sealed and because they are always networks permeated by indeterminacy rather than permanent and ossifying structures, there's no ruling out hope, and there's no dropping out of the duty to resist. In principle, resistance that has a precise addressee comes before the expression of a general position, of moral gestures simply launched into air. As in every moral dilemma, what counts is the chance of reducing superfluous evils, and moral stances differ from each other according to the type of intervention they allow and its chances of reducing evils (7.412 and from 7.420 on). The distinction between "my town" and "other towns" belongs to the economy of selfhood and not to the rational account of waste; preference for those nearby follows from a particular perception of self and not from an essential willingness to give to another what ought to be given.

9.345 Moral interest cannot stop at any border, territorial, religious, tribal, or national; it must be directed simultaneously toward all members of the human race and toward every group within it (see 8.421 and its note). This is so not because moral considerations are guided by an idea of man or of universal humanity, but because the concrete historical conditions now posit the pan-human on the horizon of moral interest. Neither humanity nor the humanness in every human being is what creates the moral imperative; moral interest is that which, in the current historical conditions, identifies humanity on the horizon of its intentions. In the end, the same process may bring about (and in some communities has already brought about) a lowering, if not a full erasure, of the partition between the human and the inhuman. The end of the world is the loss of all complex forms of life, those to which we can ascribe suffering, on the one hand, and those who have an interest in what disappears, on the other.

9.350 The globalization of the economy, of war, of politics, and of culture produces the conditions allowing the appearance of humanity. But only the moral imperative actualizes it in practice. Not humanity as a biological kind, not humanity as a "moral community,"[103] and not humanity as an empty ideological abstraction, but humanity as all the victims to be taken into account when considering a political, economic, communicational, or scientific act. Humanity is posited both as the concrete ensemble joined by each and every individual in danger of suffering and loss and as the solidarity of each and every individual with all the rest in the concrete collective created by mechanisms of the globalization of evils. When the line between the human and the inhuman blurs, this is due not to loss of interest in people's destiny but, on the one hand, to an interest in the destiny of other kinds of animals as if they were human beings and, on the other, to a confrontation with the (human) creation of "inhuman" conditions, in which civilization itself becomes "inhuman."[104] On the one hand (the interest in animals), the inhuman is granted a measure of humanness;[105] on the other (the interest in inhuman conditions), a measure of inhumanness is ascribed to a distinct product of human civilization.

9.351 For Kant, humanity is an abstract idea located beyond the limits of experience. At issue is not the very existence of humankind but an *a priori* idea of moral judgment — the universalization of humanness as the rule guiding free will — and, through a regulative idea of aesthetic judgment, the counterfactual expectation for a panhuman common sense (*sensus communis*). The realization of this idea, the appearance of human life in which every human being treats every other human being as an end in itself and not just as a means, is one of the faces of supreme Good. Supreme Good is the end of history. Realization of the idea of humanness is posited as the end of history, while the idea itself directs moral action within history. In fact, humanity is an idea contained in the idea of freedom and is illuminated or signified with every activation of free will, but the activation of free will belongs to the inconceivable sphere of "the thing itself" (the "noumenal" sphere) and is recorded not as a phenomenon of the world but as a thought about human actions in the world. For Kant, humanity never transcends the sphere of thought, is never part of experience; it precedes morality and enables it.

9.352 For Marx, humanity is an abstract idea soon to be realized. Humanity appears and is realized thanks to the very worst of Evil, exploitation, and oppression, of capitalist alienation and decadence, arousing a proletariat with nothing to lose save its chains and engendering its self-consciousness. A proletariat that has reached self-consciousness recognizes itself as the representative and embodiment of what is human in general, above and beyond class, national, or tribal distinctions. It becomes the object, and the bearer, of the idea of humanity and finally the agent of its actualization in history, when the oppressed of the world are liberated and Communist society forms a worldwide pattern of social existence. In the Marxist view of history (and in fact already in Hegel, but for different reasons), humanity is an idea in a process of actualization, becoming a reality before our eyes. This is a necessary process. It is in our power to join it in solidarity and participate in its advancement, or to be ingested into it in one way or another. The appearance of humanity in the Marxist worldview amounts to "turning morality from duty to fact."[106]

9.353 For us, as stated, humanity is "all the victims to be taken into account" in every action and matter, "the concrete ensemble joined by each and every individual in danger of suffering and loss and . . . the concrete collective created by mechanisms of the globalization of evils" (9.350). Humanity is not contained within the idea of freedom and is not realized with its realization. It is not an idea that the processes of globalization turn into a reality but rather an upside-down reflection of them, which it is now high time to stand on its feet. Humanity is an "imagined subject who is supposed to appear out of the negation of the radical otherness of the end of the world" (9.304). Better, perhaps, humanity is an image appearing on the horizon in which this era perceives its extinction in three forms of end: the end of the world, the end of the political, the end of the human. Facing the horizon that is the finish line, humanity is the common general address of all the valid moral concerns appearing in the present era, and the precise individual address pertaining to the destructive capacity and to the forms of destruction institutionalized in the course of this era.

It doesn't precede morality but reaches self-consciousness through the mediation of the moral point of view; its appearance is not an expression of the transformation of morality from duty into fact, but an expression of fact that engenders duty. The fact in question is the "worldhood" of the world that has appeared in this era, and its not-inevitable, now-visible ends.

9.4 Critique of the Historical Present

9.400 At least since Kant, the philosophical effort toward self-under-standing has involved an understanding of the philosopher's historical present. Foucault proposes to see the philosophical interest in the historical present that first appears, in his view, in Kant as the beginning and the model for a sharp shift in modern thought in general and in the appearance of the historical present in particular.[107] In at least two canonical texts, Kant seeks to understand a "grand" historical event — the Enlightenment and the French Revolution — according to the event's implications for the state of reason. With the historical event, something new appears, and thinking seeks to discover in this novelty an essential difference concerning thinking itself, the cultural modes in which it takes place and its social roles. Philosophical thinking seeks to locate in the historical event a sign of the difference that differentiates the present era, which is also simultaneously a difference in its attitude to thinking itself. As such, this difference also posits a "philosophical task."[108] In Kant, as in Hegel or in Marx after him, the "philosophical task" that the historical event both engenders and enables fulfillment of is a deciphering of the historical status of freedom.

9.401 Liberation is possible, Kant says, we are at the height of it; criticism, the perfect implementation of rational liberty, has determined the borders of consciousness and freed space for belief; it is permissible to believe in the realization of the supreme Good. Liberation has been completed, Hegel says; nothing more should be expected of history; understanding the totality is the unending work of an eternally continuing present. Liberation is possible, Marx says; criticism should turn into a political struggle, and its violence should change shape and move from the texts into the streets and from there back into the texts; in some places, the time has already come, and in other places, even if it tarries, it will surely come. Kant views the French Revolution as a spectacle of moral progress; beyond the blood, fire, and smoking ashes, beyond the horror and the terror, one can already make out the signs (8.312). Hegel views the French Revolution as a spectacle

displaying to all the cruel struggle between the interiority of freedom, moral and pure of intention, and the horror and the terror
of its external realization, its transformation from potential to
reality. The death spread by terror is "without meaning" and
"contains nothing positive," a sacrifice with "nothing in return,"[109]
and this is precisely the reason and the moment for moving from
action to thinking, from history to the absolute spirit. Out of
his study of the French Revolution and the political upheaval in
Europe that came in its wake, Hegel reaches conclusions as to the
limits of the process of liberation in history, as to the distinct
supremacy of legal monarchy (of the type promoted by Napoleon,
which the Prussians instituted following him) over republican
democracy and absolute monarchy, and as to the necessary move
from history to "absolute spirit," that is, to the noble cultural
expressions of freedom in art, religion, and philosophy.[110] Marx
views the rebellions of the "Spring of Nations" as a failed prelude
to the true activity of revolution — conditions were not yet ripe,
preparation of consciousness had not yet been completed, but the
moment was drawing near: its ghost was already hovering over
Europe. Soon enough, freedom would appear in its true revolutionary attire and free the freedom immanent within every man as
a productive, producing being.

9.402   In the final analysis, criticism of the present is an implementation
of freedom that seeks to ensure the possibility of an end to the
project of freedom and a chance to succeed (Kant), to come to
terms with it and with the worst of its results (Hegel), or to complete it (Marx). Evil is present at the point from which philosophical reflection departs, as the reason for the existence of the
categorical imperative (in Kant),[111] or of the demand to change
the world and realize the idea of freedom (in Marx), or it appears
at a certain point in the course of this reflection (for instance, in
the chapter on the criminal and his punishment in Hegel's *Philosophy of Right*) but disappears long before the end of the play.
Even when unquestionably modern thinking immerses itself in an
attempt to understand the historical present, as in Hegel or Marx,
instead of grazing it at the margins of its discourse, as in Kant, it
doesn't linger on Evil except briefly. The modern philosophical
narrative has two protagonists that are actually one — reason and
freedom.[112] All other characters are secondary; their appearance is
supposed to serve the heroine who bears the plot and the plot that
constructs the heroine. Either they are derived from her figure
(the concept of rights, for instance, or of meaning, or of the end),
or they are swallowed up by her, over time (power, will, desires,

and interests). Evil belongs to the second group. It is difficult not to run into it in the course of the tale, at least to the extent that philosophy is truly interested in the historical present, and it is almost impossible to ignore it. Evil, in its horrific character, threatens freedom or tempts her; in its pointless superfluity, it contradicts reason. Therefore, it needs to be digested, to be annulled at least in theory if not in practice (Hegel), or secured as an element to be ingested and eliminated in due course (Kant, Marx). In any case, Evil is not perceived as an essential part of the difference the present makes from the point of view of reason or freedom. In the difference that modernity makes, in its principle of differentiation and in differentiation as its constituting principle, there is no evil.[113]

9.410 In "What Is Enlightenment?," his second lecture on Kant's essay, Foucault formulates two additional possibilities for understanding the relation of modern thinking, thinking that perceives itself as freedom, with its present. The first, constituting one is Baudelaire's:

> For the attitude of modernity, the high value of the present is indissociable from a desperate eagerness to imagine it, to imagine it otherwise than it is, and to transform it not by destroying it but by grasping it in what it is. Baudelairean modernity is an exercise in which extreme attention to what is real is confronted with the practice of a liberty that simultaneously respects this reality and violates it.

This possibility, Foucault adds, cannot exist except in art. The other possibility is that of Foucault himself, close to but not identical with Baudelaire's position:

> And this critique [of Enlightenment]... will separate out, from the contingency that has made us what we are, the possibility of no longer being, doing, or thinking what we are, do, or think. It is not seeking to make possible a metaphysics that has finally become a science; it is seeking to give new impetus, as far and wide as possible, to the undefined work of freedom.... I do not know whether it must be said today that the critical task still entails faith in Enlightenment; I continue to think that this task requires work on our limits, that is, a patient labor giving form to our impatience for liberty."[114]

As is well known, in the same period, in Foucault's attempt to develop an ethics, this impatience evolves into "self-care," into aesthetic work on the self as a model of resistance to the normalizing, liberty-denying forces of modernity.[115] What starts with freedom must end with freedom. What started with the subject ended with care of the self and aestheticization of individual existence. When freedom is the first category in the attempt at self-understanding and at an "ontology of the present," the presence of Evil and the care for others involved in it emerge, at best, as coincidental stops along the journey of thought and, at worst, as superfluous stops — luxuries of the rich.

9.411 The rebellion against Evil that we identified in Marx and Engels (7.211) is an exception demonstrating the rule. Kant's critical modernity can exist only up to the limit of obedience of the enlightened monarch and only at the margins of philosophical discourse.[116] Hegel's, in the last account, can exist only within philosophy. Nietzsche's or Baudelaire's can exist only within the framework of art, and in any case beyond Good and Evil. And in Foucault, the critical spirit is weary after the long and promising journey that started out with Europe's insane asylums and ended between its bedrooms and brothels; it retreats into the individual, wraps itself up in his bodily pleasures, the infinite plasticity of his life, ever at the mercy of his liberty, which forms and kneads it like clay.[117] Nothing is left of the great challenge to modernity emitted by *Madness and Civilization*, which evolved into the declaration of "the death of man" in *The Order of Things*, save "self-care." What is posited opposite all the forms of normalization and discipline of the modern individual, whose deconstructive genealogy was presented in *Discipline and Punish*, is an "aesthetic of existence." This aesthetic knowingly relinquishes historical consciousness and borrows its exemplary figures from a combination of Athens and San Francisco despite declaring this combination impossible. The presence of evil adorns these role models like the faint bluish halo in religious icons.

9.420 Before Foucault turned to study of the care of self in the ancient world, he displaced the concept of sovereignty, "beheaded the king"; unraveled the polarized, binary conception of the political; dispersed power throughout a complicated web of centerless relations; exchanged the metaphysical analysis of the subject for a genealogy of practices of "subjectification"; and uncovered the ideology of liberation as a strategy within a web of subject-producing apparatuses. The turn toward the nurturing of the self in ancient times was supposed to broaden a perception of the modern subject as a construct of subjectification processes and present him as a single, but not sole or necessary, possibility in the relation of individual to truth, others, and self. The self-care of ancient times expresses a possibility totally different from the modern one, which is intended to illustrate the contingency of the modern structure of subjectivity, the possibility of evading its constrictions and of positing alternatives to it. Foucault doesn't propose the ancient model as an alternative but uses it as a replacement, as it were, for utopia. While the ancient model is impossible today — there's no return to Greece — it signifies the very existence of another possibility. However, from the moment the turn is taken, what originally motivated it seems to be forgotten. The problematization of modernity developed by Foucault was never explicitly moral, though it was permeated from the outset by moral pathos; now this, too, disappears, and what remains is only an aesthetic interpretation of ethics as "self-care."

9.421   Foucault seeks to understand who "we" are as subjects of knowledge, of action, and of self-attentiveness. But also what that "we" is which is formed by and in turn distinguishes this era. The question of the present for the philosopher is the question "of his membership of a certain 'we,' a we corresponding to a cultural ensemble characteristic of his own contemporaneity. The philosopher's own singular state of adherence to this 'we' now begins to become an indispensable theme of reflection for the philosopher himself. Philosophy as the problematisation of a present-ness, the interrogation by philosophy of this present-ness of which it is part and relative to which it is obliged to locate itself: this may well be the characteristic trait of philosophy as a discourse of and upon modernity."[118] The critical genealogy of modernity proposed by Foucault is a necessary part of every attempt to answer these questions, but such an attempt cannot remain within the borders of this genealogy, for we are "those who are progressing together toward the end of the world, leading toward it those who come after us, and who are capable of hastening or preventing the end" (9.304). This progression, like these capabilities, transcends what we know and even what we presume to know, or what we intend to cause each other; the threat of the end of the world cannot be dealt with through a genealogy of modernity that focuses on the subject, retreats into the aesthetics of existence, and formulates itself in terms of self-care. In the present era, Evil has become global, and the manners of its production play a central role in the processes of the creation of the world as a single system; in this era, perfect and final Evil, like a final solution to the problem of Evil, is merely a question of time. Foucault's critical genealogy —

and in this matter he is no different from other critics of modernity or postmodernity such as Derrida, Deleuze, Baudrillard, and Lyotard — is not sufficient for thinking the Evil of the present and for thinking the present as the Evil that it is.

9.422 What is required to complete the genealogy of the present is a "genealogy of the end of the world," whose appearance on the tangible horizon of historical time is an event and a future with which this era is imprinted. Such a genealogy will probably include the processes of globalization, the ecological catastrophes and the appearance of environmental awareness, and of course the genealogy of the death industries that were the twentieth century, from the annihilation of the Armenians through the annihilation of the Jews and from the Siberian steppe through the hills of Rwanda. If one seeks to understand Auschwitz, Hiroshima, the Khmer Rouge, and Bosnia as historical events from the point of view of "the difference that differentiates the present era," it is impossible to presuppose that this will also be "a difference in [the] attitude to thinking itself" (9.400). Foucault's own analysis, reconstructing a continuum between the disciplinary regimes that developed at the heart of Western societies and the world of the camps,[119] indicates that from the point of view of reason there is in fact no crucial difference between the disciplinary regimes that emerged at the outset of modernity and the death camps that appeared at its end. All the principles allowing the extermination, the Gulag, or the bomb were already there before, when the Indians were annihilated in South America, when the Africans were hunted down like animals and forced into slavery, when universal conscription was allowed and declared. From the point of view of reason, it is all just "more of the same," at most taking on a new constellation of old components. The "difference that makes the difference" is to be sought not in some innovation in the state of reason, and certainly not in some turn in the genealogy of the subject, but in the new manners of producing Evil and the new configurations of its presence.

9.430 The first buds of the disciplinary institutions that Foucault describes appear in the seventeenth century, and, starting at the end of the eighteenth century, they become a main axis of the organization of society at large as a disciplinary society. But only in the twentieth century does there appear a society with a "carceral texture,"[120] of which prison is a "normal" and acceptable embodiment, taken for granted by the bourgeois mind, and of which the world of the camps, the *Lager*, and the Gulag, with its disciplines

and mechanisms of mass imprisonment and subjugation, of industrialized death production, is an intensified embodiment, which
the bourgeois mind cannot bear. Foucault claims — and on this
point he joins Adorno, Horkheimer, Marcuse, and other critics
of modernity — that there is a common plane encompassing the
eighteenth-century boys' boarding school and the SS officers'
training course, the Prussian officers' companies of Friedrich, the
enlightened monarch, and the companies of masses roaring "Heil
Hitler." He claims there is a common plane encompassing the politics of liberation and the politics of cleansing and, at the end of
the day, the industries of culture and the industries of death. Only
on the basis of understanding such a common plane is it possible
to locate the differences, to understand first what differentiates
and then what enables, for instance, the Gulag — that system of
imprisonment typical of Communist regimes — and so forth for
various other forms of domination, control, subjugation, and
annihilation. The core of these differences is in the specific configurations of the strategies of power and the mechanisms of
domination, subjugation, and extermination. The claim to a common plane rests on a reconstruction of the genealogy of the disciplined subject, an analysis of the manners of his production and
the sites at which he was produced, including the internal organization of the disciplinary site and the characteristic constellations
of knowledge/power evolving within these sites. However, in
order to point out the differences, one also needs to study what
these subjects produce, the ends succumbed to by people who
obey the orders of these practices, employing all the strategies
and wiles for speaking and acting that are allowed within them.
Do they succumb equally to the creation of meaning as they do
to destruction and extinction, to the production of riches as to
imposing hunger, to the production of exemplary state order or
mass death?

9.431 If all the oppositions mentioned are situated on a common plane,
then the market can and should be thought from the point of view
of imposing hunger; it isn't enough to think hunger from the
point of view of the market. The state should be thought from the
point of view of authorized killing and the legal forsaking of lives;
it isn't enough to think death from the point of view of the logic
of the state. And culture as a whole should properly be thought
from the point of view of the end of civilization. The various, differentiated areas of culture should also be thought in this way: science, technology, medicine, politics, bureaucracy, art. Each of
these was complicit, or may be found to be complicit, situated on

the same plane as the science and technology of the mass industrialized annihilation, as the politics and bureaucracy that enabled it, and as the culture that legitimated it or, at the very least, ignored it and continued to exist alongside it. All of these contain, at this very time, elements that collaborate with the powers dealing destruction on the planet of the drowning.

9.432 We will never understand this collaboration, we will never succeed in disclosing these continua and these correlations between the summits and the gutters of civilization, between liberation and slavery, culture and destruction, transcendence and annihilation, if we look at them solely through the prism offered by the category of freedom as it is thought through in modern philosophical tradition, from Kant through Hegel and Marx, through Sartre, Camus, Arendt, and Foucault.[121] Therefore, neither will we ever succeed in combating this collaboration if we make do with a critique of the damage to civil liberties and a struggle against the denial of rights. Freedom should be pushed to the background. More precisely, liberty should be freedom disconnected from the subject, even from his remainder as a self forming himself, and situated in the open space of the regularity of practices (8.343–8.354). Freedom is merely the difference between regularity and predetermined order, but this difference — presupposed and predetermined by us as irreducible and ineradicable — will not explain the character of the collaboration and what allows it while disclosing its possible cracks and weaknesses. That can only be provided by the historical, historicist, contingent character of the regularity itself.

9.433 Even less useful here is care of the self, the main category studied by Foucault at the end of his life. Self-care should be understood as Foucault's reaction against the practices of normalization and discipline of the modern disciplinary society. Our culture is flooded with various agents proposing innumerable practices of self-care, all of which are unfailingly "alternative," available to almost anybody on the well-fed side of the planet. These tempt the individual to discover himself and create his selfhood, allowing no distinction whatsoever between discovering and creating, hidden truth and invented truth, surrender to a foreign but nearby temptation, and following an inner but unfamiliar voice. In a culture such as ours, it is no longer possible to distinguish practices of normalization through which the forming of self is entrusted to more or less anonymous disciplinary institutions and practices of care in which the aesthetic formation of the individual is seemingly entrusted to the individual himself. In a culture such as ours, practices of self-care and of discipline, of treatment and of normalization, are inextricably interconnected, and together they are part of the very collaboration with the order of evils that we must understand and strive to undo. More important, self-care, and especially the Nietzschean aesthetics of existence proposed by Foucault, are situated, by definition, beyond good and evil. Self-care is blind to the presence of Evil, for even compassion or surrender to another in distress, and in general every form of waste, are controlled by the self and by a transcendence of self that is none other than an effort to create the self out of itself.

9.434   Within the framework of such a perception of self, the presence of Evil is at most a pretext for transcendence, an opportunity to call for a more authentic or freer self. If Evil can be ascribed to the "carceral" society and to all the forms of discipline and normalization that have evolved in it, this is obviously because it has produced subjects who have forgone the self's self-transcendence and subjects who have been denied the possibility of even dreaming of such transcendence. In the end, and perhaps only at the end of his life, Foucault rejoins the tradition that identifies Evil with the denial of freedom. The critique of the concept of liberation, on the one hand, and of disciplinary society, on the other, leaves the struggle against Evil within the boundaries of the self striving to preserve and broaden its liberties. The critique itself participates in this struggle, a form of self-care and self-governance ("the art of not being governed"[122]). The critique of our era, according to Foucault, is still a critique of enlightenment, inseparably intertwined with freedom, and it still necessitates giving "new impetus, as far and wide as possible, to the undefined work of freedom . . . [this] work on our limits, that is, a patient labor giving form to our impatience for liberty."[123] Because Evil (if one is at all interested in it) is identified with the denial of freedom and freedom retreats into the self seeking to form itself out of itself, it is no longer possible to see the critical changes in the presence of evil in modern times, or to uncover the role that particular practices of self-care play in these changes, and it is no longer possible to identify what it is that differentiates the modern era in terms of the Evil produced in it.

9.435   To respond to the "philosophical task" that the historical present poses for thinking, in keeping with Foucault's understanding of critical enlightenment, one should think the present through the characteristic regularities responsible for the production and distribution of evils and reconstruct their systematic reproduction. An attempt must be made to understand the processes of the globalization of patterns of production and distribution of evils, as well as the role these patterns play, in turn, in processes of globalization, and their contribution to both the globality of the world and the hastening of its end (9.422). This necessitates a genealogical study, after Foucault, and, even more, an application of his perception of power relations as actions that modify the actions of others.[124] However, if Evil is not posited explicitly at the center of this study, freedom will again encircle the self that cannot be its source and should not properly be its end. If evil is not posited explicitly at the center of the study, it will be possible neither to think the difference of "our" historical present (as well as "us," "we" whose horizons are determined out of and by this present) nor to think our historical present as a difference in being itself.

9.440　At the end of his life, Foucault admitted the influence of Heidegger's thinking. In one of his more Heideggerian passages, in the introduction to the second volume of *The History of Sexuality*, he redefines, apparently for the last time, his philosophical course as an attempt to write a "history of truth":

> Not a history that would be concerned with what might be true in the fields of learning, but an analysis of the "games of truth," the games of truth and error through which being (*être*) is historically constituted as experience, that is, as something that can and must be thought. What are the games of truth by which man proposes to think his own nature when he perceives himself to be mad; when he considers himself to be ill; when he conceives of himself as a living, speaking, laboring being; when he judges and punished himself as a criminal? What were the games of truth by which human beings came to see themselves as desiring individuals?[125]

There's no escaping the overt slant toward Heidegger's early work here, the work still positing the being-there of *Dasein* as a privileged site for ontological investigation. Foucault's interest is in the historical constitution of being as experience, that is, in the historical constitution of being as what appears through the gaze, speech, and action of a subject, as what depends on history and on the historicity of the constitution of subjectivity. In this sense, there is no difference between the discussion of a "history of truth" in the present context and the discussion of a genealogy of the subject in other contexts. And it is impossible to avoid wondering about the meaning of the return of the universal category of "man." Man is no longer the impossible duplication and combination of subject and object, as presented in *The Order of Things*; now man is a universal, metahistorical individual who undergoes subjectification. And opposite this process of subjectification the philosopher is positioned as an individual who knows how "to learn to what extent the effort to think one's own history can free thought from what it silently thinks, and so enable it to think differently."[126] Philosophy again appears as a liberator. Philosophy seeks to restore the individual to his being as a man capable of transcending subjective constrictions and being himself, that is, always becoming anew what he is. This is a central direction in Foucauldian thinking that I wish to reject.

9.441   A different interpretation can be offered for the Foucauldian project, including its relation to Heidegger, and, as a result, also for the task of thinking the historical present. Actually, I have already offered a sample of this possibility through several instances in the course of this discussion where I have employed the work of Foucault while placing emphases of other kinds on his words. I can now summarize.

The subject, and the truth games within which he is embedded, are not just a contingent and not-inevitable historicist configuration through which being appears (in the sense of things' being-there, the being of speakers who en-tongue them, and the being of that which manifests — or conceals — itself through appearance and its articulation). The subject and his truth games are also, perhaps first and foremost, a configuration — historical, contingent, and not-inevitable — of being-there, of relations between things and words, between things and things, and between words and words, existing in the spheres where people who have become subjects appear (people in general and perhaps only Western man, or only white Western man — important as these distinctions are, they make no difference for our present purposes). The genealogy of the subject is a genealogy of a single aspect, central perhaps but not the only one, of the forms of people's existence as human beings in Western civilization and in the form of being of things and the environments within which they live and act. Since the end of the nineteenth century, the family tree of this subject leads to changes that concern not only the appearance of being as a human experience but also the very forms of the appearance of being. Human beings who have become subjects cause other subjects to appear superfluous; human beings who have become subjects are complicit, knowingly and mainly unknowingly, in the creation of superfluous being, suffering, and loss; human beings are simultaneously complicit in the concealment of this superfluity as a means of organizing the relations between them and in the presentation of this same superfluity in public spectacles through which and around which other relations between them are organized (and sometimes the very same relations, for these require a degree of play between concealment and public spectacle); and above all, human beings who have become subjects are capable today of exterminating once and for all the entire human dimension of being, which means exterminating the very capacity of being to appear in and through language. And to the extent that this capacity is perceived as belonging to the essence of being (at least in the framework of Hegelian or Heideggerian thought),[127] what is in question is the actual possibility of a total change in the essence of being. Superfluous being within the boundaries of man's world leads not only to the extermination of human beings as superfluous; it threatens — and this is its immanent potential — to superfluate part of being itself, the entire world in which its appearance in and through language was enabled.

9.442 This formulation results not from an insane anthropomorphism but from the insanity of the late development of the *anthropos* himself. This insanity is the "difference that makes the difference," what differentiates the present era and makes it unique. It is impossible to think it if one stays within the boundaries of the self, of the subject, or of the history of truth as the history of being-cum-experience. Modern subjectification is at most a component of the conditions that allow the appearance of superfluity as a form of being that threatens to bring about the end of the world in which being appears. It is impossible to think this superfluity through the genealogy of the subject and his truth games; on the contrary, the subject and his truths, the self and its self-cares, should be thought through the superfluity that we have reconstructed here as the form of the presence of Evil.

9.443 The intensification of mechanisms for the production and distribution of evils and their global interweaving are also responsible for this: they have created new forms of care for the other, new truth games within which the distress of others, individuals and masses, lies in the balance, as well as new subject positions vis-à-vis this distress. Superfluous evils are objects that can be seen and shown; the regularity of their appearance can be described and intervened in. In the face of these evils, subjects are posited who take up positions in structured fields of discourse and action from which it is possible to en-tongue Evil and extend a hand to victims. Bodies of knowledge have developed that describe and predict the likelihood of the occurrence of accidents, the spread of hunger and epidemics, and the outbreak of disastrous natural forces, alongside bodies of knowledge that incessantly improve the means of protection against these and other evils. Bodies and organizations have been established to document distress and distribute information about it, to study its sources, and to struggle against the political, economic, military, and technological forces generating catastrophe, to amass resources and extend aid to the victim populations. Care for the other is not a slogan of bleeding-heart liberals but a complex of widespread practices anchored in the infrastructure of social commonality and woven into the cultural fabric of most countries (with the differences entailed by disparities in economic power, in the type of regime, and in the specific character of intervention in the production of evils).

9.444 Of course, the innovation isn't in the very willingness to help the other or in the mere institutionalization of such help. Part of it — but only part of it — is included in the modern form of government that Foucault called "bio-power," which combines a capacity for the rule and surveillance of an entire population with a capacity for locating, identifying, and characterizing every individual within it and treating him as a singular member of his group. At this point appears that dangerous continuum, pregnant with risks and prospects, between the welfare state and the totalitarian regime, and between the modern state's tools of oppression and its tools of aid. But it's impossible to understand the practices of care for another as just a facet of this new form of power over life. Since the mid-nineteenth century, the treatment of individuals and of entire populations has acquired a degree of autonomy from the state apparatuses that intervene in the lives of individuals and administer the conduct of entire populations. Only a single legitimate matter is supposed to be at stake in the implementation of these practices: the reduction of superfluous evils that befall others, individuals and masses. It is difficult to differentiate this matter from other matters, political, economic, and so forth, and it is impossible to cancel out the manipulation that such forces exert on moral actions (9.341). The manipulation is mutual, though, and it assumes a degree of autonomy in the agents manipulating each other. Parties with a moral interest use political and economic interests as others use the discourse and tools at their disposal. The innovation here is the degree of autonomy, of relative differentiation of the fields of discourse and action whose interest is distinctly moral, as well as the global scope of the action.

9.445 This innovation is not an expression of progress and does not testify to a happy change in the nature of man. More likely, it is a side effect of the globalization of the production and distribution of evils and of the slide down the three slopes described above (9.313 and 9.320–9.322). But it can be said that as a result of these processes, morality appears for the first time in the history of culture as a field (in Bourdieu's sense of the term) with a place of its own. The moral is no longer one more branch of religion or undefined aspect of education, of social convention, of the rules of etiquette or ritual; the moral is no longer one more interest of reason, a form of judgment, a genre of phrases (although all of these will be involved in it). The moral now appears — and this is the distinguishing mark of this era — as an area of culture that has borderlines, gateways and gatekeepers, rules of discourse, principles of exchange, experts, apprentices, patterns of certification, and above all distinct locations: disaster-stricken areas.[128] From now on, the rational calculation of waste has truth games of its own (7.311–7.312).

9.450 There is something seemingly paradoxical to this claim. Truth games are an arena of subjectification, whereas waste is the point of transcendence beyond the structure of subjectivity, from a given field of exchange relations, a given identity of self. If individuals shape themselves as generous and even as saints completely dedicated to others, then this is no longer care for others but a form of self-care, and the aid they extend to others in distress is not an end in itself but rather a pretext for the elevation of their own selves. To be rid of the shadow of this paradox, one must be precise and distinguish the subject position from self-care. One can care for himself without taking a subject position and can take a subject position without caring for himself. One can transcend his subject position (1.314) in order to care for himself, in order to form himself or to create himself out of himself (according to the aspiration-demand of Nietzsche and Foucault), and he can do so in order to care for another (when he "outdoes himself" or "bends over backward," or acts supererogatorily). The self is "the limit of prodigal waste ... a boundary line that one concern draws for another," and is first and foremost the boundary line of self-sacrifice (8.430); the position of the moral subject constituted by the relatively autonomous fields of discourse and action in the moral realm is characterized by its suspending the moment of the appearance of this limit and creating the conditions necessary for pushing it, to a greater or lesser extent, beyond the mark usually accepted in other fields of discourse and action (in addition to enlisting the selfish economic and political interests of morally indifferent others for the benefit of others in distress).

9.451 — We have not yet left the shadow of the paradox. You claimed that the new form of the appearance of the moral is the distinguishing mark of this era. But the discussion of "this era" being conducted here, after Foucault, given and despite all the reservations, as well as his presumption to criticize the present and its "ontology" presented or intimated here, is merely part of an attempt at self-understanding, a practice of criticism that, as stated, is a form of self-care (9.434). Moreover, "this era" is the current epoch that reaches self-consciousness, differentiating itself from other epochs. Such a concept would seem to necessitate an amplification of the extended I, of the "we" associated with a historical era, a perception of selfhood as substance, in some version of the "spirit of the times" that every self-consciousness takes part in and expresses in its own way, an I of a type requiring that a borderline be drawn between I and not-I, as a designation of otherness and a representation of historical time in units of a present present.[129] The attempt to understand this era is nothing but a form of self-constitution. If so, the identification of the new form of the moral, the new practices of care for the other, and the new truth games of sacrifice and waste that serve as distinguishing marks for this era may be an evasion of the challenge that the moral summons poses to the philosophy of the subject and the metaphysics of presence. "This era" that has reached self-consciousness (through philosophical discourse, of course) shifts the boundaries of selfhood unfailingly undermined by the summons to another from the individual to the era, thus transforming the new forms of summons and of answering a summons into a characterization of that same extended self, the new historical subject. — This claim, however, ignores the perception of the subject that I have presented here (see 1.3), including the distinction between taking a subject position and caring for oneself, and it misses the manner of this era's appearance to one who examines it from a moral point of view.

9.452 Subjectivity is a synthesis of gaze, expression, and touch allowing the presence of differentiated entities that can be seen and shown, talked about, touched, and acted upon, all in defined and periodically changing historical-cultural conditions (1.3). At the same time, this synthesis makes it possible to ignore non-presence, flux, and concealment, to ignore all that cannot be made present. A certain aspect of the "difference" characterizing this era is the appearance of a new subject position that allows individuals who take it to see and show superfluous evils, to describe and predict the regularity of their appearance and to intervene in it, "to en-tongue Evil and extend a hand to victims" (9.443). Such a position introduces practices of care for the other and postpones the moment of the appearance of self as the limit to waste necessitated by these practices. From such a position, the self, not the other, is what remains in its non-presence, concealed or suppressed, part of the flux. From the position of the moral subject, it is impossible to see in this self anything that can or should be differentiated and articulated in moral discourse, not to speak of being depended on to guide action. The above view of the critique of the present (9.451) seeks to use "this era" in order to return the self to the subject or the subject to itself, but it can do so only when it ignores the manner in which this era is revealed to the moral subject. From a moral point of view, at least from the one presented here, this era is differentiated and defines itself based not on what distinguishes it from its immediately adjacent past but on what distinguishes it from the future threatening to void it. The tangible appearance of this future on the horizon of human history blurs the border between the human and other forms of life (9.344–9.350), annuls the difference between care of the self and care for others, and signifies the possibility of a radical otherness that "imprisons the waste along with the interested, self-centered investment within a closed economy of threat and hope" (9.303). "We" who seek to represent this era appear out of "the negation of the radical otherness of the end of the world, and out of care for the specific others whose end this may be" (9.304). If there is a selfhood formed by taking part in this "we," it is clearly dictated by the nature of care for another. And if we seek to represent the whole of humanity here, this is not a humanity that determines the essence of self but rather the humanity that appears out of the changes occurring in this era in forms of care for the other (9.340–9.341), which also determine the forms of interestedness in that other.

9.453 Thinking the present in order to respond "to the challenge that the humanity of 'extremes'... poses... [because] we are the middle of these extremes; we are the progeny of their terror and are invariably placed at some point on a continuum that may lead to them" (8.555). Thinking the present in order to go back and extricate ourselves, along with Foucault, "from the contingency that has made us what we are, the possibility of no longer being, doing, or thinking what we are, do, or think" (9.410), but also in order to guard ourselves from the possibility of being no longer, a possibility now, and from here to eternity, embodied in our way of being.

9.5 *The End of an Era*

9.500 Modernity, according to the philosopher and historian of ideas Hans Blumenberg, is the first era to show an interest in its epochality, the first era in which self-understanding is mediated by an understanding of the historical present or even identified with it, and in which the historical present is differentiated as a separate, "new" period. Modernity is a perspective of self-understanding that shows an incessant interest in the intersecting lines that separate "the modern era" from previous periods, and it is out of this interest that the moderns differentiate themselves from their predecessors. Distinct boundaries, as well as a common essence unifying a variety of different phenomena manifested in its course, are attributed to this era. Such an attribution assumes a continuous temporality constituting a history whose duration is unitary and synthetic. But such a temporality is just one form of temporalization and historicization. There are others. Temporality can be split, unrolling in many different ways from different points in the present and the recent past to different points in the more distant past, while fragmentary, partial histories arrange themselves around the temporal continuity that links them, histories of sections of culture and society. The historicity of the science of nature from Newton through Einstein is different from the historicity of the writing of history from Vico through Foucault. The historicity of the European nation-state is different from the historicity of the prisons or schools under its rule; the university as a bureaucratic institution, for instance, belongs to an organization of time that differs from the one that governs some of the discourses that thrive within it. Television as a communication and information-distributing network temporalizes historical time in a manner that is totally different from that of some of the ideological texts that television distributes. In other words, and despite partial overlaps, the time of the prison is not the time of the state, the time of the state is not the time of capital, the time of capital is not the time of moral sensibility.[130]

9.501 There is no basis or last source available for the synthesis of historical time. There is no single unifying pattern of relation with the past that I/we belong to or that belongs to us. There is no single unbroken line connecting the present to the past; the present has more than one possible past, and there is no single normative, unified framework of intentionality toward the past that should properly be preserved and remembered or thrown off. In no area is there a body (corpus) of knowledge, of custom and convention, of moral norms or aesthetic values, passed from past to present as charged in advance with any obligating power relating to the present. Every moment of the present is an opportunity to reappropriate, drop, and grant new meaning to parts of the past. Every moment of the present is an opportunity to draw new lines of continuity between present and past, and alongside them lines of crucial difference dividing before and after. The epochality discussed by Blumenberg decomposes into components according to varied areas of the social space and loses its unifying organization.[131]

9.502 Every attempt at self-understanding and at constituting self-identity must pass through a knot of time continuities intersecting the present and connecting it to different areas of the past in many different forms of belonging and disconnection, acceptance and denial, approval and resistance. The historical present cut across in this way is not static and has no permanent and perpetual identity. It is a present penetrated by differentiations from all kinds of pasts that the present is no longer, and from all kinds of futures that may arrive at any moment. It is permeated by ties to all kinds of pasts that the present seeks to renew, preserve, and make present, and to all kinds of futures that this present seeks to anticipate or hasten. Incessant differentiation is the condition for the survival of all cultural merchandise within the wild, competitive market of exchanging fads, all of whose narratives condense into the "grand narrative" of capitalism. The present is sown with constant differentiations of the "now" from the "previously," from the past whose time has past; it is studded with voices declaring themselves innovations and declaring the crucial differences between them and what came before. Every such voice tends to swiftly undergo reification and is prone to turn, at any moment, into a commodity in the market of images and the culture industry, and to unknowingly serve an existing power structure. The instances of transcendence are quickly reproduced, turn overnight into norms, and are in turn deployed for the reproduction of the existing order — although sometimes such differentiation can also be a means of struggling under market conditions and a way of escaping the "grand narrative" dictated by the existing order.

9.510 In this era, culture's archive is losing its coherence and its internal organization, is splitting and dispersing. It stands open to the winds, lacking rigid hierarchical principles, accessible to anyone with sufficient means to wander through it and to build himself his own narrative of the past out of it (that is, almost only to those with sufficient financial means and only to those with some initial amount of cultural capital). Alongside the more or less official history of the state, religion, the nation, and class, there appear innumerable local histories, regional histories, histories of a field, family histories, histories of professions, and on and on. Israeli rock music, haute couture, the royal family, the family Abarbanel or Banai or Rabinowitz, molecular biology, the theory of evolution, the Zionist idea, Alsace-Lorraine, Jerusalem, the soccer team Manchester United, the Dome of the Rock, mountain climbing, journeys to the poles — every topic and its own history, for the moment some matter is differentiated and already has a history. And when interest in some matter grows and the parties interested in it multiply, the story of this matter's past becomes an arena of cultural struggle, and the narrated, written, and photographed histories proliferate and compete with each other. Within every field, too, there are multiple histories, intersecting each other and differentiating in different ways from each other and from the histories outside the field. In the field of cinema, for instance, there are histories of the entire field, histories of genres, of technologies of photography, of practices of photography and even of sites of photography, of movie studios and production companies, of the relations between capital and cinema, and of cinema as an ideological tool. The number of histories is as large as the number of possibilities of declaring a new beginning, a present differentiating itself from the past whose time is past and declaring the crucial difference by virtue of which someone claims recognition of the present moment as "other" or "different" or "new." And vice versa: everyone who seeks to differentiate himself tailors his own suit of history. Alongside these are innumerable attempts to "photograph" and map differentiated and defined moments in the present through opinion polls, statistical questionnaires, and various other measures; every two moments that are eternalized and measured in this way already foretell a "trend," a process, with its own pace and historicity, and when the third moment accumulates in the series, it is already possible to declare the novelty of the present and the new present while predicting the direction of future development. The future has traces in the archive, in advance, and the past has retrospective traces in the future, for the entire archive is an endless reservoir of fragments of yet to be written tales of history — the past of a pending future.

9.511 The archive is the incessantly growing inventory of all the items of meaning in the culture. But the archive is also the codex of rules for wandering among and bridging the shelves and for accessing the exhibits, rules that change constantly and in turn determine innumerable possibilities for narrating the past and differentiating the present. The state, the Zionist movement, the municipality, the labor movement, Husserl, Einstein — each of these historical subjects can be given an archive of its own; every such archive has a subject of its own, and the two grant each other unity and coherence in space and time. But the archive of this era has no subject of its own. The archive of the historical present is the medium for constituting and deconstructing subjects, the arena in which subjects are formed, the reservoir out of which new subjects take their pasts and into which the remnants whose time is past are cast. The archive is what is woven and unraveled, rebuilt and re-destroyed, underlined and erased continuously, with every appearance of a new subject forming his past out of it and redefining his contemporary differentiation as well as the present differentiating him. No wonder so many subject positions seek to supervise both access to and movement within the archive.

9.512 The archive is the structure of this era's self-consciousness, the form of its presence to itself. What is repressed, forgotten, is always on the surface; interested parties merely need to descend to the appropriate floor and open the right drawer. Everything present in the archive is a trace of something else that was and is no longer, and self-consciousness is always a play of traces. Every reflection is an intervention in the archive's organization, but this organization has no center, no set cohesive procedures, controlling all. There is no field of culture that is not occupied with constructing and reconstructing this archive, or its own archive, and with building out of the archive, but there are never clear boundaries among the different archives. Everyone obsessively documents his past and the pasts of others, trying to save memory from the abyss of obliteration and simultaneously, whether unnoticed or through visible effort, to bury other memories in it, as well as others' memories. Everyone obsessively summarizes — the millennium, the century, the decade, the year, the first hundred days — so as to differentiate the present and create a new center of self-identity and self-understanding, but in fact so as to constitute a self to be understood and a core of the past to be narrated.

9.513 This era has disintegrating margins that constantly recede, an empty center that every self seeks for itself; every one or thing that seeks to establish itself in it is swallowed up by it as if in a black hole, dragging with it representations like shifting sands. This era can no longer make itself present to itself as an era, because its past splinters into innumerable axes of time intersecting its present without any possibility of mutual synchronization, without any possibility of temporalization along a single time line, without any possibility of constituting a single self based on the splinters. It is even less possible to constitute on this basis a cohesive self, with clear boundaries and a known other, not to speak of the possibility of a self preceding historical temporalization and capable of assembling within it all the stories of the past. This era is made present to itself via negation, via innumerable borderlines without structure or order, always as what it is no longer — times past. The present era cannot attain presence for itself, for only the past era attains a present — in the archive — and reflection on the present is a constant intervention in the determination of its boundaries.

9.514   "There is no basis or last source available for the synthesis of historical time.... There is no single unbroken line connecting the present to the past" (9.501). In the same way, we should have said, there is no single unifying pattern of relation to a future for which we can reasonably hope or which we would be better off fearing. There is no single unbroken line leading the present to the future awaiting it; the present has more than one possible future, and there is no single normative, unifying framework of intentionality toward a future that should properly be reached or whose occurrence should properly be prevented. But this is not true. In the present time, the end of the world appears as the common horizon of the whole world that determines a common future for this era. This common horizon draws a limit to the fragmentation of self-understanding in the current era and offers a new roof under which it may be possible to unify all the borderlines running through and intersecting the scramble of differentiations incessantly being made. In the present era, the finish line offers a new structure of historicity and a basis for common self-consciousness. "This era is differentiated and defines itself based not on what distinguishes it from its immediately adjacent past but on what distinguishes it from the future threatening to void it" (9.452).

9.520   Solon, Montaigne, Hegel, and Heidegger all express differently the fundamental relations among self-understanding, finitude, and consciousness of the end. It can be determined that a man is happy, Solon said, only after his life has ended. The moment of death is the moment of truth. Obviously, the dying man will reveal his secrets and speak the truth about himself, Montaigne said in a similar spirit while granting the dead individual a rare moment of candor and with it the grace of understanding that Solon denies him, granting it only to others who witness his departure. Minerva's owl only appears at sunset, Hegel says, as darkness falls. Understanding comes at the end, when all has been completed, at the moment of closure, when the whole appears in its entirety — an era closing, global history drawing to its conclusion, or reality becoming transparent to itself in its totality.

9.521 Heidegger (the Heidegger of *Being and Time*) understood that the end need not occur as an event, that consciousness of the end is temporalized at every moment and temporalizes consciousness in its own way, cuts through it as an intentionality toward a nothingness-not-yet-there and as the voidance of the meaning of every intentionality toward what-is-no-longer. Self-understanding involves accepting finitude and anticipating it, not completing the finite, which always comes before its time. But this is the privilege of the individual who is going to die, the one who is always outside himself, transcending himself on the verge of dying. This is the moment when self-understanding is an understanding of the absence of essence and of the absence of the selfhood of self, an understanding of the self in its irreparable and groundless singularity. The individual understands himself as one who negates himself and as one who makes himself above and beyond whatever his world, his history, the environment, and the era into which he was cast have caused him to be, thrown and unbridled as an individual among many, all of whom were thrown and solitary like himself and all of whom were complete others. Being-toward-death is a form of being permeated by a historicity that overrides any historical positioning and any relation of social belonging. The consciousness of finitude disconnects the individual from his era and his environment, opening a window on an ontological, ahistorical understanding of historicity in general and of historical understanding in particular. From the point of view of the individual who finds himself the addressee of that content-less call arising from the presence of his personal end, there is no obligating relation between his personal historicity and some general and common historicity offered to him by his era and his culture. Heideggerian authenticity is ahistorical, just as it is amoral. It is indifferent to the historical present and the moral call arising from it, to the point where in the present era it becomes both antihistorical and immoral.[132]

9.522 The historicity of the present era is a historicity of an end, the moral call arising from humanity verging on the finish line. This end is a common one, and the presencing of the common finitude is the basis for a new, imposed universal association. Consciousness of historicity permeates existential consciousness, dismantles it from inside. The most private emerges as the most general; finitude is not what separates but what lays common ground. Retreating into the self hastens the common end, while committing to an other in a diversion of attention from self and a complete waste of self may emerge as a way of forming an "authentic" self, that is, a self simultaneously appropriate to the conditions of common existence and to the unique and singular structure of existence. In this era, the end of the world is present within the world, and every attempt at historical self-understanding necessitates anticipation of the end of the world in its various forms and an internalization of the immanent, nearing (even if not yet inevitable) end of universal history. In the present time, historical self-understanding has existential character (à la Heidegger), and existential self-understanding is submerged in the understanding of universal history (à la Hegel).

9.523 Modernity's self-perception is Hegelian at base. The modern consciousness of modernity includes not only the moment of the differentiation of "the modern era" from the outdated past preceding it but also a consciousness of the expected end of modernity as an era. It is impossible to avoid declaring this end, and at the same time it is impossible to avoid dismissing it in advance, re-internalizing the end itself into the complex evolving into infinity that is "the modern age." For over a hundred years now, it has been declared everywhere: the death of God, the end of art, the end of the novel, the death of man, the death of the author, the end of the social, the end of the political, the end of sovereignty. And everywhere it is declared, the end of the end itself is immediately revealed, the appearance of new forms of belief, of writing and authority, new forms of religiosity and sacredness, of the artistic, of the social and the political, and, more generally, new forms of the human, whose expressions these all are. Declaration of the end is necessary, just as its predictable failure is necessary. Those declaring the end are the harbingers of the postmodern era, but modernity seeks to reassemble within it all of the seeming "postmodernities" and to declare postmodernity an unripe moment, its own youthful mischief soon to be forgotten.

9.524 Postmodernity is included in modernity, a necessary outcome of its insular perception of understanding. But what postmodernity is, modernity cannot say. It purports to know only how to identify from within the negation growing out of it. Because modernity is capable of identifying the negativity that permeates postmodernity, its entire attitude toward the latter is imprinted with the mark of negation. On identifying postmodernity, modernity seeks to obliterate it, for in it, it identifies its end, and it seeks to go on being what it is — for itself: enlightened, rational, humane, or at least that which undergoes processes of enlightenment, rationalization, and humanization, progressing toward what it should be. The postmodern consciousness of modernity turns everything upside down. It knows that modernity needs the otherness it identifies as a total negation, which it can annul or even exterminate and from which it would differentiate itself so as to become what it is. The postmodern consciousness of modernity identifies the same otherness in ethno-geographic (or geopolitical) space and historical time, and it seeks, at the heart of modernity, a space common to the modern and the postmodern in which struggles of differentiation take place. This space is the archive of culture, or culture as an open-ended ensemble of overlapping archives.

9.525 The postmodern consciousness of postmodernity goes even further. It declares the present time the period after modernity that is unable to perceive itself as an epoch at all. It declares itself unable to accept modernity any longer while also unable to complete modernity, unable to bring it to a conclusion. This is not because postmodern consciousness has lost its sense of epochality, its belief in the grand narratives that periodize time into epochs and structured periods of time, but because modernity has generated a process in which its own end is not just the end of an epoch but also the end of the world. If postmodernity accepts modernity, brings it to its conclusion, it will be the end of the world. With postmodernity, the end of the world appeared within the world itself, and it is present not just in vain eschatological beliefs but in daily practices, networked within the global processes of information, armament and technological development, capitalization and mediatization. Here it is, pulsating from the screens, seeping through the smog fumes, bleeping from the detectors of radiation and pollution, assembling scientific conferences and diplomatic congresses — an end that one hears of already on the radio, whose traces are already visible on the evening news.

9.530 "The historicity of the present era is a historicity of an end" (9.522). We identified three forms of total end in three heterogeneous spaces — the space of historical time, the space of the political, and the geopolitical space of disaster-stricken areas, three slippery slopes down which Evil spreads in the present era: "the end of the world, the end of the political, the end of the human.... Three summits of Evil: nuclear holocaust or an eco-logical catastrophe generating the total and undifferentiated annihilation, either intentional or not, of all forms of sophisti-cated life; the appearance of a regime conducting an organized and methodical extermination of definite parts of the population; a combination of natural disasters, state and ethnic violence, eco-nomic, social, and cultural degeneration, creating environmental conditions that bring total ruin upon indefinite but chronically vulnerable and constantly growing groups of the earth's inhabi-tants" (9.322). If this era is postmodern, this is not because it comes after modernity, for no "era" will come after modernity, but because — perhaps only if — in the course of the postmodern era modernity has attained a consciousness of its finitude and it seeks to think — or cannot avoid thinking — about itself through the moment after.

9.531 The three forms of end belong to separate, heterogeneous spaces. A nuclear holocaust can occur even in the absence of any totalitar-ian regime crazed by delusions of a future better world. An eco-logical holocaust can occur even in the absence of any regime that knowingly hastens it. Regimes of mass extermination appear in areas that are technologically undeveloped as well, and they de-stroy masses even without weapons of mass destruction (the Otto-man Empire, Cambodia, Rwanda). Nazism was defeated, the ovens shut down, but mass destruction remains a widespread and famil-iar practice. The chronically disaster-stricken areas of the planet of the drowning may suddenly or gradually expand, regardless of types of regimes or of the willingness of technocratic-political elites to be involved in nuclear or ecological holocaust.

9.532 Not only is each of the three slopes situated in a different space; each of them also opens onto a different temporality: three forms of temporalization that are also heterogeneous and cannot be grounded in each other. The first is anchored in some future point, a definite point whose location is unknown — nuclear or ecological holocaust. The second is anchored in a definite past point — Auschwitz — that is returned to and re-presenced in the present, in an apparent attempt to magnetize forcefully all skeins of memory to it. The third temporality is linear, developmental, gradual, a temporality of predictable processes, of timetables con-structed and incessantly reconstructed according to changing assessments and calculations. The first temporality converges into an unknown future, the second converges into a very well-known past, and the third spreads out, like the present itself, on the axis of geophysical time along which the earth moves. Nonetheless, despite the fundamental heteronomy of these three forms of temporalization, they converge at a single common point at the limit of time itself — the end. In all three cases, self-consciousness is temporalized as a consciousness of immanent finitude that is not simply the finitude of one who is thinking it and of the group he belongs to but also the total finitude of thinking itself.

9.533   Thinking thinks itself through the minute after that is the end of thinking. All forms of the end are naturally forms of the end of thinking, but thinking will reach its end at the bottom of the slope even before the end itself arrives. If it doesn't obliterate all in an instant, the catastrophe fuses the individual with his being, when the sliding presence of suffering and loss is all there is and survival is all one can think of, if one can think at all. The world of the camps that abolished the social and political dimensions of human existence before it exterminated the people themselves provided many examples of the abolition of thinking before or during the extermination of the thinking bodies, sometimes without even needing to exterminate their life.[133]

9.534   Where it is still possible to think, it is still possible to resist Evil. Where it is impossible to resist Evil, it is already impossible to think. Thinking is not a condition for the possibility of resistance but a sign of it, whereas the possibility of resistance is a necessary but insufficient condition for thinking. If it is no longer possible to resist, a superfluous being appears, producing an unlimited superfluous being (whether through the systematic and planned "superfluation" of human beings in totalitarian regimes or through an abolition of the necessary conditions for human life). At a certain stage, the superfluous is all there is, until being is left with no one to testify to what there is. This is how it was in the past in the world of the camps, in Cambodia or Rwanda, in clearly defined, limited parts of the world. This is how it will predictably be the world over, if and when. The end is a being without witness. The end superfluates thinking. To the extent that it thinks itself through the end, thinking must understand the superfluity that threatens to void it; to the extent that it is resistance, thinking seeks to put an end to superfluity. In this era, thinking thinks the conditions for its possibility through the end of thinking, and thinks the end through the conditions for the very possibility of thinking.

9.540 Opposite the three forms of end according to which the present era is supposed to measure itself, there are three forms of denial and suppression. Attempts are made to view Auschwitz as a historical accident. Accidents are repeatable instances. It is therefore important to invest in memory and memorizing — so as to know how to identify the accident in the unthinkable event that it repeats itself. Attempts are made to represent Hiroshima as an uncondemnable necessity while forgetting and suppressing the possibilities it disclosed, behind partial treaties for reduction of the nuclear stockpiles in the hands of the superpowers, while also ignoring their proliferation in other countries. In the nuclear field, claim experts who have sold their souls to the bomb, the main fear is that irresponsible groups or individuals will get hold of the bomb — as if there were any states or regimes whose responsible conduct was a proven, self-evident fact from here to eternity. Therefore, the talk is of full control and of partial disarmament, of turning the means of control into mechanisms in the hands of "responsible" states for intervening with the "irresponsible" ones. Pushed out of memory in the process is the history of mass destruction in which those responsible states have been involved, alongside the facts that "responsible" states are capable of destroying the entire world in an instant and that they are as yet unable to control terror or corruption or to cope with the disintegration of state mechanisms that encourage "irresponsible" people to attain nuclear arms. In the meantime, the planet of the drowning is treated as "business as usual" — routine import and export of goods and manpower, of epidemics and aid, of arms and desire — as if the looming end were the exclusive future of the Third World.

9.541 There is poetry after Auschwitz, there is science after Hiroshima, there is ideology after the Gulag, and there is thinking that continues uninterrupted to the tune of the drowning of the drowning. Yet we are not just after Auschwitz, but always also before it, verging on it; not just after Hiroshima and Nagasaki, but also before the next bomb. The planet of the drowning is our planet. Therefore, if there are still poetry, science, and thinking, they should sound to us as the music played on board the *Titanic* would have sounded had the passengers only known how to see the iceberg.

9.542 We must never forget that we are located somewhere down the slope, on each one of the three slopes. We must never stop measuring the distance. No attempt at self-understanding should be accepted if it isn't formulated, at least partly, in terms of this distance, in terms of a projection (of the end) and of an absence (the conditions still missing for its appearance). This distance is historical, but it cannot be measured in units of time. Time itself is measured in terms of conditions, of tools, of removed restrictions, of interests that have arisen, of functioning and collapsing systems, in terms of the nature, the stability, and the expansion of webs of association and communication, the globality of their intertwining, the capacity to control what takes place in them, to intervene, to promote, to prevent. And all the time, time is measured relative to the bottom edge of the slope. The distance doesn't express any essence — common, present, manifested, intimated, signified, unifying — reconciling contradictions, bridging gaps, and enduring over time. It is a distance not from presence to presence, like two points situated in a common space, but from a present unable to presence itself to itself as an essence, to what is no longer there, and should be allowed to return, and to what is not yet there, and should not be allowed to come. It is the distance between traces of the past and traces of a future that always only appears through anticipation, hypothetically based on what is there and what is not, on what has disappeared and what appears. It is a distance that we should never stop trying to estimate through thinking, or to lengthen through action.

9.55 It's all we can do. We should do no less.

Notes

1. There is a certain debt to Marx here, and it will briefly be explored in later chapters.

2. The Hebrew word *inyan* has two meanings: "interest," and "subject matter" or "topic." I have used them according to the context, but both meanings should be kept in mind. — TRANS.

3. It is impossible to translate the Hebrew word *raooy* accurately, for it means "proper," "right" (but not in the legal sense), "ought," and "deserve." I use "proper" and "ought" according to the context, but all four meanings should be kept in mind. — TRANS.

4. I have developed this Heideggerian conception in "Evils, Evil, and the Question of Ethics," in Alan Schrift (ed.), *Modernity and the Problem of Evil* (Bloomington: Indiana University Press, forthcoming). There, however, for reasons related to Heidegger's text and its immanent critique, I used "the ethical" instead of "the moral" and for clarity's sake refrained from making the distinction between the two that is proposed in Chapter Eight below.

5. With two exceptions: a long digression in Chapter One on a systematic reconstruction of the concepts of discourse and subject, resulting from what I call the radical critique of modern philosophy, and a short digression on the "epochality" implied by the "post" of postmodernity in Chapter Nine.

6. See n.2.

7. I have started dealing with it elsewhere. See, for example, "Moral Technologies," *Theoria ve-Bikoret* 22 (2003), pp. 67–103 [in Hebrew].

8. Giorgio Agamben, *Homo Sacer: Sovereign Power and Bare Life*, trans. Daniel Heller-Roazen (Stanford, CA: Stanford University Press, 1998); *Remnants of Auschwitz*, trans. Daniel Heller-Roazen (New York: Zone Books, 1999); *Etat d'exception* (Paris: Seuil, 2003). See also my "Life Sacred and Forsaken: Introduction to *Homo Sacer*," in Shay Lavie (ed.), *Technologies of Justice* (Tel Aviv: Ramot, 2003), pp. 353–94 [in Hebrew].

1. Martin Heidegger, *Being and Time*, trans. John Macquarrie and Edward Robinson (New York: Harper and Row, 1962), p. 19; the quotation is from Plato, *Sophist* 244a. I kept to the language of Heidegger's translators, which differs slightly from that of Plato's canonical translators.

2. "Some thing," as opposed to "thing" or "something," so as to denote non-commitment to the permanence of being as a clear and distinct thing. See also 1.301.

3. The Hebrew word דיגוּש is an emphatic form of the more common רגש, which means emotion, sense, or affection.

CHAPTER ONE: DISAPPEARANCE

1. For convenience, each chapter will use either male or female pronouns for the length of the chapter, and successive chapters will alternate the use of male and female pronouns; see 1.321.

2. This invented term is an approximation of Ophir's invention, in the original Hebrew, of a verb, הלשׁן, denoting a thing that has been initiated into language. The original form, turning the Hebrew noun לשׁוּן ("tongue" in both its English meanings) into a verb, also refers to an act of informing to the authorities, "naming names" in the idiomatic sense. The English "en-tongue" and its subsequent variations lack this clear additional sense of the betrayal of some thing through its representation in language. — TRANS.

3. Deep Throat is the name of a well-known porn feature. It was a code name for the informer who betrayed White House secrets during Watergate.

4. "En-tonguing" was an attempt to say in Hebrew what Heidegger expresses when he says that "language is the house of being" (see also 1.131).

5. The arts work in the reverse direction as well, that is, to let that which has not yet been en-tongued — a visual phenomenon, an affection — appear.

6. Haim Nachman Bialik, "Zohar," in *The Complete Poems of H.N. Bialik* (Tel Aviv: Dvir, 1966), p. 115 [in Hebrew].

7. Emmanuel Lévinas, *Existence and Existents*, trans. Alphonso Lingis (The Hague: Nijhoff, 1978).

8. Emmanuel Lévinas, "Time and the Other," in Sean Hand (ed.), *The Lévinas Reader* (Oxford: Blackwell, 1989), p. 41.

9. G.W.F. Hegel, *Hegel's Logic*, pt. 1 of the *Encyclopaedia of the Philosophical Sciences*, trans. William Wallace (Oxford: Oxford University Press, 1978), nos. 86–88. At this early stage, the knowing subject, our witness, is still curled up within the womb of dialectical thinking in one of the postures of the "in-itself."

10. In just the same way, Hegel has to assume the temporality of perception for purposes of the first transition in *The Phenomenology of Spirit*, from the fullness of senses unquestionably perceiving something, "this and this, the particular thing," to the empty abstraction of "here" and "now" as inclusive. See G.W.F. Hegel, *The Phenomenology of Spirit*, trans. A.V. Miller (Oxford: Oxford University Press, 1977), nos. 90–110 ("Self-Certainty; or, The 'This' and 'Meaning'").

11. In Hebrew, Ophir uses the neologism *yeshnut* instead of the conventional *yeshut* to dissociate himself from any substantial sense of being and to allude to the relation of being to time. — TRANS.

12. Martin Heidegger, *Being and Time*, trans. John Macquarrie and Edward Robinson (New York: Harper and Row, 1962), for instance, pt. 1, 4, no. 27; and also Martin Heidegger, *An Introduction to Metaphysics*, trans. Ralph Manheim (New Haven, CT: Yale University Press, 1959).

13. Jean-François Lyotard, *The Differend: Phrases in Dispute*, trans. Georges Van Den Abbeele (Minneapolis: University of Minnesota Press, 1988), Kant Notice 1, pp. 61–65.

14. For instance, in Jean-Paul Sartre, *The Transcendence of the Ego*, trans. Forrest Williams and Robert Kirkpatrick (New York: Noonday Press, 1957), pp. 43–54.

15. Therefore, Derrida, who is thinking (through) the trace, the temporalized difference and the differentiating temporalization, is so intensively preoccupied with specters. The thinking of *différance* is a spectral business. See, for instance, Jacques Derrida, *Of Spirit: Heidegger and the Question*, trans. Geoffrey Bennington and Rachel Bowlby (Chicago: University of Chicago Press, 1989); *Specters of Marx*, trans. Peggy Kamuf (New York: Routledge, 1994).

16. I assume it's possible here to accept without discussion the claim ascribed to Wittgenstein against the possibility of a private language, against the possibility of a private testimony to sensation in particular (including a sensation of disappearance), and against the possibility of a seemingly private account of sensation that someone gives himself. However, I don't believe that this claim applies to the privacy of the sensation, too, the private testimony, the condition of being a witness of something. See Ludwig Wittgenstein, *Philosophical Investigations*, trans. G.E.M. Anscombe (New York: Macmillan, 1953), nos. 246ff.

17. This is a central theme in the work of Lyotard, who seeks to identify this motif in history (regarding the question of the representation of Auschwitz; see 9.050 and 9.143), in writing, in psychoanalysis, and in art. See, for instance, *Differend*, nos. 124, 128, 188; *The Postmodern Explained to Children*, ed. Julian Pefanis and Morgan Thomas (London: Turnaround, 1992), ch. 6; *Heidegger and "the Jews"*, trans. Andreas Michel and Mark S. Roberts (Minneapolis: University of Minnesota Press, 1990), ch. 8.

18. In Hebrew, "to recognize" and "to be present at" are denoted by the same word, *nokhach*. — TRANS.

19. The literal meaning of the idiom used by Ophir in Hebrew is "at the time of the act," while its idiomatic sense is linked with being caught in the act. — TRANS.

20. Giordano Bruno, *The Ash Wednesday Supper*, ed. and trans. Edward A. Gosselin and Lawrence S. Lerner (Hamden, CT: Archon Books, 1997), pp. 215–16.

21. *Ibid.*, p. 85.

22. Theophilos (the lover of God) is the main speaker in *The Ash Wednesday Supper*, which is written as a dialogue among four speakers. For a systematic analysis of the semiotic dimension in the work, see Rivka Feldhay and Adi Ophir, "Heresy and Hierarchy: The Authorization of Giordano Bruno," *Stanford Humanities Review* 1, no. 1 (Spring 1989), pp. 118–38.

23. The Hebrew that Ophir uses is more concise and its sense more open than what the English can afford: מי conveys both "he who" and "some one that"; מהש conveys both "that which" and "that something that." — TRANS.

24. On the stabilizing function of the name, see Lyotard, after Kripke and Wittgenstein, in *Differend*, ch. 2.

25. "Grant perfect [or proper] rest beneath the shadow of thy divine presence" is a phrase from the Jewish prayer El Malee Rachamim (God Full of Mercy), said at the grave site in the funeral ceremony. *The Authorised Daily Prayer Book*, new ed., trans. Rev. S. Singer (London: Eyre and Spottiswoode, 1962), p. 423.

26. "Gaze" will henceforth denote other types of sensual perception at a distance as well (hearing, smell), the principal differences between which will not occupy me here; expression that denotes any form of representation of what is sensed or perceived will be represented here by "speech"; "touch" will denote every excitation, internal or external, as well as any "action upon," including manipulations and actions from a distance. The inclusive speech about touch is intended to erase the dichotomized difference between internal and external, passive and active, indirect and direct touch. Such differences will always be relative to a particular positing, in particular conditions, of who is touching and what is touched.

27. Bertrand Russell, *The Problems of Philosophy* (Oxford: Oxford University Press, 1971), pp. 1–2. Russell's text, which is a popular presentation of classic philosophical problems, exemplifies the positing of an object through gaze, touch, and expression but does not deal with this; its topic is the distinction between phenomena and reality. The idea that positing an object is an act of coordination between what is seen and its lingual expression is already implicit in Kant's conception of a synthesis between the sensible and the conceptual. Heidegger places the encounter with the object in the linguistic, rather than the conceptual, context and adds touch (along with the spatial dimension that accompanies it) as a separate dimension of this encounter, manifested in his distinction between the being of entities as usable tools (*zuhanden*) and the being of objects with which one is presented in action-free contemplation (*vorhanden*) (*Being and Time*, nos. 16 and 22). For a more explicit discussion of the relation between the visible and the "sayable" (*énonçable*) in the context of Foucault's conception of discourse, see Gilles Deleuze, *Foucault* (Paris: Minuit, 1986), chs. 2–3.

28. For instance, Immanuel Kant, *Critique of Pure Reason*, trans. N.K. Smith (London: Macmillan, 1950), p. 152. See also Edmund Husserl, *Cartesian Meditations: An Introduction to Phenomenology*, trans. Dorion Cairns (The Hague: Nijhoff, 1960), nos. 17–18 and 30–34.

29. I use "position," in the sense assigned it by Bourdieu, as always linked with other positions in a given field of relations. See, for example, Pierre Bourdieu, *La Distinction: Critique sociale du jugement* (Paris: Minuit, 1979); *The Logic of Practice* (Stanford, CA: Stanford University Press, 1990); *Les Règles de l'art: Genèse et structure du champ littéraire* (Paris: Seuil, 1992). "Subject position" is a conceptual construct halfway between Descartes or Kant and Heidegger, Kant grounded and placed within a practical-material context, or Heidegger domesticated by Bourdieu and historicized by Foucault.

30. As Jean-Paul Sartre says of the anti-Semite in *Anti-Semite and Jew*, trans. G.J. Becker (New York: Schocken Books, 1948), p. 54.

31. Kant, *Critique of Pure Reason*, p. 152. Further into this section, Kant introduces his readers to the correct relation between the thinking I and the object posited by him: "Only in so far, therefore, as I can unite a manifold of

given representations in *one consciousness*, is it possible for me to represent to myself the *identity of the consciousness in [that is, throughout] these representations*. In other words, the *analytic* unity of apperception is possible only under the presupposition of a certain *synthetic* unity" (pp. 153–54). Yirmiahu Yovel presents this matter convincingly in his book *Kant and the Rehabilitation of Metaphysics* (Jerusalem: Bialik Institute, 1986), ch. 13 [in Hebrew].

32. My reference here is to Heidegger's distinction between some thing posited as an object and some thing that remains a tool ready for use, which has not necessarily been articulated linguistically, or identified explicitly as such and such, and whose features may not have been discerned and turned into linguistic attributes adjoined to an essence, which exists, as it were, beyond the thing's appearances and is denoted in descriptive language by a concept. See esp. *Being and Time*, pt. 1, ch. 3.

33. *Ibid.*, p. 32.

34. *Ibid.*, pt. 1, ch. 3, nos. 16 and 22; compare Ran Sigad, *Existentialism* (Jerusalem: Bialik Institute, 1975), pp. 141–45 [in Hebrew].

35. ου (on), "that is something"; τοδε τι (tode ti), "something that is such and such."

36. This notion of Deleuze and Guattari's is a necessary correction for and a reminder to anyone who takes the idea of structure or system too rigidly. See Gilles Deleuze and Félix Guattari, *A Thousand Plateaus*, trans. Brian Massumi (Minneapolis: University of Minnesota Press, 1987), pp. 9ff., 88–89, and elsewhere.

37. On this matter, see Ariella Azoulay, *Training for Art* (Tel Aviv: Hakibbutz Hameuchad, 1999), esp. ch. 4 [in Hebrew].

38. Michel Foucault, *Madness and Civilization: A History of Insanity in the Age of Reason*, trans. Richard Howard (New York: Pantheon, 1965); *The Birth of the Clinic: An Archaeology of Medical Perception*, trans. A.M. Sheridan Smith (New York: Random House, 1975); *The Order of Things: An Archaeology of the Human Sciences* (New York: Vintage Books, 1973); *Discipline and Punish: The Birth of the Prison*, trans. Alan Sheridan (New York: Pantheon, 1977); *The History of Sexuality*, vol. 1, *The Will to Knowledge*, trans. Robert Hurley (New York: Penguin, 1978).

39. This matter is even more prominent if one accepts Sigad's position that Socrates's love of wisdom amounts to overcoming oneself, to forbearance, to a suspension of surrendering to one's lover, and to a forgoing of erotic satisfaction intended to sustain love as a liminal state, an incessant transcendence. This transgressive drive doesn't allow Socrates to take any subject position fully, seriously — neither that of a lover, nor that of a citizen, nor that of a philosopher. And for that reason, he is the most tempting of lovers, the most loyal of citizens, and the wisest of philosophers. See Ran Sigad, *Philo-Sophia: On the Only Truth* (Jerusalem: Dvir, 1983), pp. 25–42 [in Hebrew].

40. Plato, *The Republic* 509b, trans. Allan Bloom (New York: Basic Books, 1968).

41. My main basis here is the early research of Jürgen Habermas, *The Structural Transformation of the Public Sphere: An Inquiry into a Category of Bourgeois*

Society, trans. Thomas Burger with Frederick Lawrence (Cambridge, MA: MIT Press, 1989). See also Azoulay, *Training for Art*, ch. 3; Adi Ophir, "Civil Society in a City That Never Sleeps," in Adi Ophir and Yoav Peled (eds.), *Israel: From Mobilized to Civil Society?* (Tel Aviv: Hakibbutz Hameuchad, 2001) [in Hebrew].

42. On the historical evolution from the concept of the subject as *subjectus* to the concept of the citizen and the appearance of the modern concept of subject, see Etienne Balibar, "Citizen/Subject," in Eduardo Cadava, Peter Connor, and Jean-Luc Nancy (eds.), *Who Comes After the Subject?* (New York: Routledge, 1991).

43. Lévinas, "Insomnia," in *Existence and Existents*.

44. Michel Foucault, *The Archaeology of Knowledge*, trans. A.M. Sheridan Smith (New York: Pantheon, 1972). On the subject position as a function of discourse, see pt. 2, ch. 4, and pt. 3, ch. 2.

45. Samuel Beckett, *The Beckett Trilogy: Molloy, Malone Dies, The Unnamable* (London: Pan Books, 1979).

46. Immanuel Kant, *Critique of the Power of Judgment*, ed. Paul Guyer, trans. Paul Guyer and Eric Matthews (New York: Cambridge University Press, 2000), pp. 90–91.

47. Scientific, historical, or legal discourse, artistic discourse, or the discourse of insurance assessors, every discursive regime has its special truth game. The expression is Foucault's.

48. Compare Foucault, *Archaeology of Knowledge*, pp. 88–92.

49. Foucault, *Order of Things*, pp. 145–57.

50. Gilles Deleuze, introduction to *Difference and Repetition*, trans. Paul Patton (New York: Columbia University Press, 1994).

CHAPTER TWO: LOSS

1. Jean-François Lyotard, *The Differend: Phrases in Dispute*, trans. Georges Van Den Abbeele (Minneapolis: University of Minnesota Press, 1988), no. 240; and see 6.551.

2. See Ariella Azoulay, "With Open Doors: Museums and Historical Narratives in Israel's Public Space," in Daniel J. Sherman and Irit Rogoff (eds.), *Museum Culture* (Minneapolis: University of Minnesota Press, 1994), pp. 109–85.

3. Epictetus, *The Golden Sayings* 11, in C.W. Eliot (ed.), *The Harvard Classics* (Danbury, CT: Grolier Enterprises, 1980), p. 120.

4. Ariella Azoulay, "The Black Box of the Occupation," in David Reeb and Ellen Ginton, *David Reeb: Paintings 1982–1944* (Tel Aviv: Tel Aviv Museum of Fine Arts, 1994).

5. Michel Foucault, *The Order of Things: An Archaeology of the Human Sciences* (New York: Vintage Books, 1973), pp. 386–87.

6. Plato, *The Republic* 605–606, trans. Allan Bloom (New York: Basic Books, 1968).

7. This claim was already implicit in the assertion "The ability to identify what was lost, to take an interest in it, and to express that interest is a principal component in the constitution of subjectivity" (2.023).

8. See, for example, Hannah Naveh, *Mourning in Modern Hebrew Literature*

(Tel Aviv: Hakibbutz Hameuchad, 1993); Yehudit Hendel, *The Mountain of Losses* (Tel Aviv: Hakibbutz Hameuchad, 1991) [both in Hebrew].

9. Israel Pinkas, "The Cold and the Heat" (4), *Lecture on Time* (Tel Aviv: Hakibbutz Hameuchad, 1991), p. 12 [in Hebrew].

10. In itself, longing is always for the absent, not necessarily for the lost, hence in this case the absent has to be posited as a loss.

11. Jean Baudrillard, *Seduction*, trans. Brian Singer (New York: St. Martin's Press, 1990), p. 11. For Baudrillard, seduction is the feminine, as opposed to desire and sexuality, which are primarily and essentially masculine. Since I will be using a few of Baudrillard's insights on seduction (see 4.530 on and 5.120), I would like to emphasize that the notion of seduction I shall present here will have no particular affiliation to femininity and will not be limited to the erotic.

12. As distinct from nostalgia, "nostomania" is a craze for the past, nostalgia that has lost its seductive dimension, the pleasure of deferring the absence of the desired, and turned it into an obsession with something that is desirable only because it is lost and is retained as lost in order to preserve the pleasure or benefit of displaying incorrigible longing.

13. *Ibid.*

14. Lyotard, *Differend*, nos. 82 and 88. For example: a new elementary particle is christened into reality when it is possible not only to give it a name and give it meaning (within a general theory of the structure of matter, say) but also to show it (only its traces in this case, and only in the lab, with the mediation of instruments and more theories). The question of the reality of this particle, as well as the question of its being at a particular place in a particular moment, is a moot point open to future proofs: perhaps there was a mistake in identifying the traces, in isolating the particle, in the calculation; perhaps the entire theory will be replaced one day with a simpler theory in which several particles identified as different will be shown to be different appearances of the same particle. Perhaps we can ascertain that it is impossible to determine both the time and the place of the particle; that is, it is impossible to show the particle itself, and we can only show the probability of there being groups of particles of its kind. What is true about the real presence (or the present reality) of a particle of matter is also true of the real presence of a man (is "Ivan the Terrible" from Treblinka dead or living in America under a false name? Perhaps we can still expect surprises), of an entire lifeworld (was there a city called Troy? And Atlantis?) and components within it, social relations, mental mechanisms, and so on.

15. René Descartes, *Meditations on First Philosophy*, trans. John Cottingham (Cambridge, UK: Cambridge University Press, 1986), 3rd Meditation.

16. *News from Within* 11, no. 6 (1995).

17. But that there are no "natural rights" or that "human rights" have no basis in human nature or in human essence is not a reason to abandon the concept of rights altogether. See 3.521 on.

18. For a brief discussion of this question, see 9.130–9.134.

19. This matter is somewhat reminiscent of Nicholas of Cusa's conception of infinity. According to the fifteenth-century philosopher, the absolute maximum and the absolute minimum unify in God, perceived as an undifferentiated

absolute, but also in infinite motion, which is also complete rest. See Jasper Hopkins, *Nicholas of Cusa on Learned Ignorance: A Translation and an Appraisal of "De docta ignorantia"* (Minneapolis: Arthur J. Banning Press, 1985).

20. On the principal incoherence of goals and values within an individual or a group discussed from a different perspective, see Isaiah Berlin, *The Crooked Timber of Humanity* (London: John Murray, 1990).

21. I am indebted to my friend Shalom Weinstein for this idea. He suggested the taxonomy of "insult groups," groups constituted on the basis of an offense of the kind that creates solidarity between everyone who was offended or could be offended by this kind of insult. But being insulted presupposes a loss, even if it is only the loss of self-respect. Speaking about insult also attributes, often unjustifiably, the bulk of responsibility for the creation of the group to the subjective perception of the indignant, who could have, allegedly, been indifferent toward the offense, or ironic, or condescending, "above all this."

22. I briefly discuss these differences in "Absolute Loss and Vacant Identities," in Laurence Silberstein (ed.), *Mapping Jewish Identities* (New York: New York University Press, 2000).

Chapter Three: Damage

1. Jean-François Lyotard, *The Differend: Phrases in Dispute*, trans. Georges Van Den Abbeele (Minneapolis: University of Minnesota Press, 1988), no. 38. My debt to Lyotard will emerge as this chapter progresses. I have also dealt with some of these issues elsewhere; see "Shifting the Ground of the Moral Domain: Reading Lyotard's *Differend*," *Constellations* 4, no. 2 (Oct. 1997), pp. 189–204.

2. On statements and signs, see Chapter Four, n.12.

3. Ferdinand de Saussure, *Course in General Linguistics*, trans. Wade Baskin (New York: Philosophical Library, 1959), pt. 1, ch. 1.

4. Walter Benjamin, "The Work of Art in the Age of Its Technological Reproducibility," in *Selected Writings*, ed. Howard Eiland and Michael W. Jennings (Cambridge, MA: Harvard University Press, 2002), vol. 3, pp. 101–33.

5. Ariella Azoulay claims that Benjamin not only refers to the loss of the aura but also describes how the aura is retrospectively created by modern art and the art history and aesthetics discourse that accompany it. See Ariella Azoulay, *Death's Showcase: The Power of Image in Contemporary Democracy*, trans. Ruvik Danieli (Cambridge, MA: MIT Press, 2001), ch. 1.

6. See, for example, Umberto Eco, *A Theory of Semiotics* (Bloomington: Indiana University Press, 1979), pp. 68–72.

7. Jacques Derrida, "Différance," in *Margins of Philosophy*, trans. Alan Bass (Chicago: University of Chicago Press, 1982), pp. 1–27.

8. Karl Marx, *Capital: A Critique of Political Economy*, vol. 1, trans. Ben Fowkes (New York: Penguin, 1976).

9. *Mishnah*, Nezikin, Baba Kamma, trans. Edward Levin (Jerusalem: Maor Wallach Press, 1994), ch. 1.4.

10. Ulrich Beck developed this theme and turned it into the cornerstone of his understanding of late modernity. See his *Risk Society: Towards a New Modernity*, trans. Mark Ritter (London: Sage Publications, 1992).

11. Plato, *The Republic* 546a–47b, trans. Allan Bloom (New York: Basic Books, 1968).

12. This genealogical view was clearly expressed by Foucault, who interprets and continues Nietzsche on the matter. See Michel Foucault, "Nietzsche, Genealogy, History," in Donald F. Bouchard (ed.), *Language, Counter-Memory, Practice: Selected Essays and Interviews* (Ithaca, NY: Cornell University Press, 1977). Many share the principles of this view, and not necessarily disciples of Nietzsche or Foucault. The historian of culture Norbert Elias, for instance, reconstructs a genealogy of cultural patterns, from table manners through royal protocol; the geographer and architect Bill Hillier analyzes a genealogy of ways of organizing social space; the sociologist Michael Mann reconstructs a genealogy of forms of power and patterns of ruling throughout history. See Norbert Elias, *The Civilizing Process* (New York: Urizen Books, 1978); Bill Hillier and Julienne Hanson, *The Social Logic of Space* (Cambridge, UK: Cambridge University Press, 1984); Michael Mann, *The Sources of Social Power*, 2 vols. (Cambridge, UK: Cambridge University Press, 1986, 1994).

13. Compare Lyotard, *Differend*, nos. 240–55.

14. As Hobbes already fully understood, in his famous chapter on representation in *Leviathan*: "For it is the *Unity* of the representer, not the *Unity* of the represented, that maketh the Person *One*" (Thomas Hobbes, *Leviathan*, ed. Richard Tuck [Cambridge, UK: Cambridge University Press, 1991], ch. 16, p. 114).

15. For a more detailed discussion of this matter, see Ophir, "Shifting the Ground of the Moral Domain."

16. Lyotard, *Differend*, nos. 12–13.

17. An analogy can be drawn here to Habermas's idea of a state of ideal communication. See Jürgen Habermas, *The Theory of Communicative Action*, trans. Thomas McCarthy (Boston: Beacon Press, 1984), vol. 1, pp. 279–337; *Moral Consciousness and Communicative Action*, trans. Christian Lenhardt and Shierry Weber Nicholsen (Cambridge, MA: MIT Press, 1990), pp. 43–116.

18. "Giving back what a man has taken from another" (Plato, *Republic* 331c).

19. Lyotard, *Differend*, nos. 7 and 9.

Chapter Four: Presence

1. As Sigad does when he reads Socrates in Plato's *Symposium* and then finds the structure in Spinoza, Fichte, Kierkegaard, and Nietzsche. Ran Sigad, *Philo-Sophia: On the Only Truth* (Jerusalem: Dvir, 1983) [in Hebrew].

2. The Hebrew verb *nachakh* (נבח) is an active form of a verb meaning both "to be present" and "to learn about" or "to become aware of." Thus Ophir's original Hebrew expresses a strong, immediate bond between the witness's act of presence and her act of coming to know, to see, her learning. The English translation has chosen to emphasize the immediacy of the bond between the witness's presence and her acquisition of new knowledge. In doing so, however, it has forfeited the sense of the witness's active performance of both. An alternative translation of this sentence, retaining the witness's active role, could read: "The presence of what-is-there is always a presence for someone who learns of this presence...." — Trans.

3. See, for example, Jacques Derrida, "Différance," in *Margins of Philosophy*, trans. Alan Bass (Chicago: University of Chicago Press, 1982), pp. 1–27.

4. "Presented with" and "learns that" are conveyed by a single word in Hebrew, *nochakhat* (נוכחת). See n.2 above. — TRANS.

5. Here, too, Ophir uses, and plays with, the same word, *le-nochakh* (לנוכח), which means both "before" and "opposite." — TRANS.

6. In this context, Heidegger wrote of "being-in" and of the spatialization of the primordial characteristics of the existence of *Dasein*. See *Being and Time*, trans. John Macquarrie and Edward Robinson (New York: Harper and Row, 1962), pt. 1, ch. 3, esp. nos. 23–24.

7. As Sartre demonstrated so well in his chapter on the gaze in *Being and Nothingness: An Essay in Phenomenological Ontology*, trans. Hazel E. Barnes (London: Methuen, 1957).

8. Heidegger, *Being and Time*, mainly pt. 1, ch. 3, "The Worldliness of the World."

9. Derrida emphasizes that every presence assumes inside-outside relations, the spatialization of being (and is therefore always already inscribed, written). See, for instance, Jacques Derrida, *Of Grammatology*, trans. Gayatri C. Spivak (Baltimore: Johns Hopkins University Press, 1976), pt. 1, ch. 2. But the opposite, too, should be noted: some thing needs to be present and some other thing absent in order for there to be inside-outside relations, in order for space to unfold (see 4.041–4.043).

10. The spatial imagery of the soul in Plato and of the regionality of Husserl's transcendental consciousness needs no evidence. Kant spoke of time as the space of the inner sense "in which alone is actuality of appearances possible at all" without going to the trouble of explaining where the space is within which the internal and the external are distinct and convergent. Immanuel Kant, *Critique of Pure Reason*, trans. N.K. Smith (London: Macmillan, 1950), pp. 67 and 75.

11. The simplest, sharpest formulation of the omnipresence of the sign is Eco's: not everything can be reduced to semiotic relations, but every thing can be studied as a semiotic phenomenon, "sub specie semiotika" (Umberto Eco, *A Theory of Semiotics* [Indianapolis: University of Indiana Press, 1979], pp. 27–28). Eco refers to the presence of signs, but this can equally be applied to his claim on the immanent spatiality of the sign: every sign can be described as "sub specie geometrica."

12. A "statement" as I wish to describe it below is a cross of sorts between Foucault's *énoncé* and Lyotard's *phrase* (these two Frenchmen were close to each other in space and time, but due to the marvelous ways of Parisian philosophical discourse never referred to each other in their writings). In *The Archaeology of Knowledge*, Foucault elaborates on the difference between the general function of the *énoncé* and the grammatical structure of the phrase, which he construes as a sentence in natural language, and the logical structure of the proposition (pt. 3, ch. 2). This distinction led to the widespread error identifying Foucault's *énoncé* with the speech act described by the school of linguistic pragmatism; see, for example, Hubert L. Dreyfus and Paul Rabinow, *Michel Foucault: Beyond*

Structuralism and Hermeneutics (Chicago: University of Chicago Press, 1983), ch. 4. Such an identification misses the *énoncé*'s dimension of visibility emphasized by Foucault: the *énoncé* as a relation to a "correlate" "space of appearance" that determines the conditions for possible appearance of the statement's reference (Foucault, *The Archaeology of Knowledge*, trans. A.M. Sheridan Smith [New York: Pantheon, 1972], pp. 88–92). Foucault's *énoncé* is always a function of a more or less structured discourse and can never appear independently of a series of other *énoncés* possessed of defined regularity (*ibid.*, p. 97). Lyotard's concept of the *phrase* differs from Foucault's *énoncé* in three main respects: the emphasis on the phrase as an event, the primacy given to the addressee among the phrase's four "instances" (addresser, addressee, meaning, and referent [nos. 18, 25, 91, 111]), and the conception of the phrase as a primary atomic unit from which discursive regularities are constructed — phrase regimen (*régimes de phrases*) and genres of discourse (Jean-François Lyotard, *The Differend: Phrases in Dispute*, trans. Georges Van Den Abbeele [Minneapolis: University of Minnesota Press, 1988]). The phrase is a unit that can wander from series to series and be recombined with different units in each case, in keeping with different regulating rules (*ibid.*, nos. 40 and 78–80). Also, Lyotard is interested less in the visual conditions of discourse and the en-tonguing of the visual than in describing a level of pre-linguistic sensation (visual and otherwise) that is already constructed through a series of liminal phrases in which every instance remains vacant except that of the addressee. In sensation, the addressee is called upon by a certain presencing about which she is still/no more capable of saying anything (*ibid.*, ch. 13, Presentation), but Lyotard blurs the phrase's "pure" semiotic component, the relation constituted by every phrase between signified and signifier. For more on the phrasing of presence, see 4.310ff.

13. In this section, the Hebrew term *leshoni* (לשוני), and its various derivations, will be translated as "lingual," along with respective (sometimes invented) derivations. The Hebrew term is directly evolved from the Hebrew word for tongue. While "tongual" doesn't exist in English, "lingual" is an analogous term, meaning pertaining to the tongue or some tonguelike part; pertaining to languages; articulated with the aid of the tongue, especially the tip of the tongue (*The Random House Dictionary of the English Language* [New York: Random House, 1981]). Ophir's use of the term in the Hebrew foregrounds the physical materiality of linguistic expression, along with its abstract semiotic aspect. The less habitual form "lingual," replacing the common "linguistic," is an attempt to alert readers to this dual meaning. — TRANS.

14. Even if the statement "the text has no outside" meant "all the world's a text" (and the two should not be seen as identical), and even if the latter could be (wrongly, I think) interpreted as analogous to "all the world's a stage," for instance, one would still have to concede that there are words and that words have presence for someone. Or, as Sartre says in the introduction to *Being and Nothingness*, the perception of being as a phenomenon (in Husserl's phenomenology) doesn't solve the problem of the being of phenomena (p. xlviii).

15. Ophir's Hebrew employs the verb *lehitakel* (להיתקל), which means both "to encounter" and "to stumble" and is hence widely associated in Hebrew usage

with a concrete physical impact, analogous to the literal meaning of the English "to run into" or "to stumble into." An English equivalent of this sense of encounter might better be conveyed by the expression "running smack into." Both the verb and the derivative noun *hitaklut* (היתקלות) are accordingly very commonly used to denote a military clash or skirmish. Ophir's Hebrew distinctly retains both senses: of unexpectedly perceiving and of a startling physical impact. — TRANS.

16. Deleuze discusses the impossibility of reducing the visible to the sayable (*dicible*). He interprets Foucault's early work as based on the metaphysical assumption of an irreducible gap between the space of things' appearance and the space of discourse in which they are expressed. Despite the precedence assigned to language, the visible is not derived from the sayable (Deleuze doesn't refer to the other senses, but the visible is no different in this aspect from what is sensed in general through touch, hearing, taste, and smell). In each of his "archaeological" studies, Foucault deals with the reconstruction of different systems of relations between these spaces. See Gilles Deleuze, *Foucault*, trans. and ed. Seán Hand (Minneapolis: University of Minnesota Press, 1988), pp. 47–69.

17. In Ophir's original, the Hebrew expression used here is *lenatek maga* (לנתק מגע) — literally, "to cut off contact." The expression is commonly used both in the general sense of "disengage" or "cut off communication" and in the specifically military sense of "retreat." — TRANS.

18. Plato, *The Republic* 439d, trans. Allan Bloom (New York: Basic Books, 1968).

19. After Heidegger's distinction between the presence of a posited "object," which is that of an extending entity, *res extensa*, and the presence of a tool ready to hand (*zuhanden*) and ready for use. In fact, the tool ready to hand cannot even be said to be present, for according to Heidegger presence presupposes *res extensa* (Heidegger, *Being and Time*, pt. 1, ch. 3). The concept of presence I'm trying to develop here, of course, seeks to shed the remnants of the Cartesian view of subject-object relations criticized by Heidegger, and it allows me to speak of the presence of the tool, or of a "toolish" presence, as well.

20. Emmanuel Lévinas, *Existence and Existents*, trans. Alphonso Lingis (The Hague: Nijhoff, 1978), intro. and "Insomnia."

21. See Harold Schimmel, "Treatise on Memory," *Teoria ve-Bikoret* 4 (1993), pp. 9–22 [in Hebrew].

22. *Mishnah*, Nezikin, Baba Kamma, trans. Edward Levin (Jerusalem: Maor Wallach Press, 1994), ch. 8.1.

23. Or consciousness in the face of being, a subject in the face of an object — but each of these terms is too loaded and charges the experience with more than it necessarily contains. So better "some one" in the face of "some thing."

24. On the four "instances" of the "phrase" (in Lyotard's terminology) or "positions" of the "statement" (in our terminology), see n.12.

25. Lyotard, *Differend*, ch. 3, Presentation.

26. One of Foucault's greatest contributions was explaining how discourse enables and conditions this process in the context of the human sciences and disciplinary institutions.

27. As shown in various ways by Gadamer, Derrida, and Foucault. For instance, Hans Georg Gadamer, *Truth and Method* (New York: Continuum, 1975); Jacques Derrida, *Writing and Difference*, trans. Alan Bass (London: Routledge and Kegan Paul, 1978); Derrida, *Of Grammatology*, pt. 1, esp. ch. 2; Michel Foucault, "The Order of Discourse," in Robert Young (ed.), *Untying the Text* (London: Routledge and Kegan Paul, 1981).

28. On the "space of appearance" as one constitutive parameter of the order of discourse in general and of scientific discourse in particular, see Michel Foucault, *The Birth of the Clinic: An Archaeology of Medical Perception*, trans. A.M. Sheridan Smith (New York: Random House, 1975), pp. 3–16, and *Archaeology of Knowledge*, pt. 3, ch. 2.

29. Sartre, *Being and Nothingness*, "The Look," pt. 3, ch. 1, sec. 4, pp. 252–302; "First Attitude Toward Others: Love, Language, Masochism," pt. 3, ch. 3, sec. 1, pp. 364–78. It is no coincidence that in Sartre the discussion of the gaze and the discussion of love are in close proximity, and that both are part of the chapter about the other person.

30. I will use "an other" to denote any one else, and not only one who is posited as my other or the other of the social group I belong to, or one relative to whom I am posited as the other.

31. "*They were there*"; "*Every photograph is a certificate of presence*" (Roland Barthes, *Camera Lucida: Reflections on Photography*, trans. Richard Howard [New York: Hill and Wang, 1981], pp. 82 and 87).

32. Susan Sontag, *On Photography* (New York: Dell, 1980), pp. 6–7.

33. "If you know these things well, you'll see at once that nature is free, no slave to masters proud; That nature by herself all things performs by her own will without the aid of gods; For — by the gods who in their tranquil peace live ever quiet in a life serene — Who has the strength to rule the sum of things ... At all times present and in every place" (Lucretius, *On the Nature of the Universe*, trans. Sir Ronald Melville [Oxford: Clarendon Press, 1997], bk. 2, 1090–1110, p. 67).

34. Compare Jean-François Lyotard, *Peregrinations: Law, Form, Event* (New York: Columbia University Press, 1988), p. 18.

35. It is impossible to distinguish between "temptation" and "seduction" in Hebrew. Despite Ophir's explicit reliance on Baudrillard's *Seduction*, I preferred to translate the Hebrew *pitouui* (and the related verb *lephatot*) as "temptation," because in most of its occurrences in the text the sexual connotations are marginal or nonexistent. — TRANS.

36. See Jean Baudrillard, "The Ironic Strategy of the Seducer," in *Seduction*, trans. Brian Singer (New York: St. Martin's Press, 1990), pp. 98–118.

37. *Ibid.*

CHAPTER FIVE: EXCITATION

1. The connotation of "excitation" overlaps that of "stimulus," "passion," "emotion," and "affection." The difference between these terms is a matter more of a lexicon and a jargon than of essence. An attempt to fix the meaning of the term used here will unfold below.

2. Jean-Paul Sartre, *Sketch for a Theory of the Emotions*, trans. Philip Mairet (London: Methuen, 1962), pp. 81–82.

3. Thomas Hobbes, *Leviathan*, ed. Richard Tuck (Cambridge, UK: Cambridge University Press, 1991), pt. 1, ch. 6.

4. Friedrich Nietzsche, *Beyond Good and Evil*, trans. Walter Kaufmann (New York: Vintage Books, 1966), no. 230, p. 159.

5. Hobbes, *Leviathan*, p. 38.

6. Immanuel Kant, *Critique of the Power of Judgment*, ed. Paul Guyer, trans. Paul Guyer and Eric Matthews (New York: Cambridge University Press, 2000), bk. 2, nos. 23 and 27.

7. Sartre, *Sketch for a Theory of the Emotions*, p. 63.

8. Kant, *Critique of the Power of Judgment*, bk. 1, no. 2, p. 91.

9. Emmanuel Lévinas, "Interiority and Economy," in *Totality and Infinity*, trans. Alphonso Lingis (Pittsburgh: Duquesne University Press, 1969).

10. See, for instance, two early texts by Derrida dedicated to a critical reading of Husserl: *Edmund Husserl's Origin of Geometry*, trans. John P. Leavey Jr. (Stony Book, NY: N. Hays, 1978); *Speech and Phenomena*, trans. David B. Allison (Evanston, IL: Northwestern University Press, 1973).

11. Compare 1.210 and n.20 there.

12. Jean-François Lyotard, *The Differend: Phrases in Dispute*, trans. Georges Van Den Abbeele (Minneapolis: University of Minnesota Press, 1988), no. 153, Hegel Notice.

13. Avraham Ben Yitzhak, "Untitled," in *Collected Poems*, ed. Hannan Hever, trans. Peter Cole (Jerusalem: Ibis Editions, 2003), p. 42.

14. Martin Heidegger, "The Origin of the Work of Art," in *Basic Writings*, 2nd. ed., ed. David Farrell Krell, trans. Albert Hofstadter (New York: Harper-Collins, 1993), p. 181; see also Hans Georg Gadamer, *Truth and Method* (New York: Continuum, 1975), chs. 1 and 2, especially concerning the concept of the play (pp. 91–99) and the discussion in "The Ontological Value of the Picture" (pp. 119–27). In Benjamin's concept of the aura, there is also a component that can be interpreted as the power of a work of art to intensify presence: even the most perfect reproduction of a work of art lacks "the here and now of the work of art — its unique existence in a particular place." See Walter Benjamin, "The Work of Art in the Age of Its Technological Reproducibility," in *Selected Writings*, ed. Howard Eiland and Michael W. Jennings (Cambridge, MA: Harvard University Press, 2002), p. 103. Unlike Heidegger and Gadamer, Benjamin addresses the historic conditions for the appearance and the disappearance of the aura of a work of art and the historicity of the aura's role in art's social function.

15. See Ariella Azoulay, *Training for Art* (Tel Aviv: Hakibbutz Hameuchad, 1999), ch. 3 [in Hebrew]; "Learning to See (Art)," *Studies in Education* 3, no. 2 (1997), pp. 77–92.

16. Ludwig Wittgenstein, *Philosophical Investigations*, trans. G.E.M. Anscombe (New York: Macmillan, 1953), no. 142.

17. Friedrich Nietzsche, *The Birth of Tragedy and The Case of Wagner*, trans. Walter Kaufmann (New York: Vintage Books, 1967), no. 7, pp. 59–60.

18. Baudrillard believes that this principle no longer holds after the appear-

ance of "exorbital" forces, such as nuclear arms and the growing debt of developing countries traded in the market and distributed among states and corporations. Here, the action of power, power's act of making itself present, the cessation of its suspension, and the realization of the threat mean the end of the game. See Jean Baudrillard, *The Transparency of Evil*, trans. James Benedict (London: Verso, 1993), pp. 26–35.

19. This is a Hebrew term adopted from Israeli military discourse and widely used in contemporary Hebrew. It refers to the act of "absorbing" blows, usually in a physical position intended to minimize the damage without responding, and to endure the assault. — TRANS.

20. In the background of this section is the chapter on the master and the slave in Hegel's *Phenomenology of Spirit*, as well as the analysis of the reciprocal relations between power and its representation in Louis Marin's introduction to his *Portrait of the King*, which can be read as an exceptional interpretation of Hegel's dialectic of the master and the slave. See Louis Marin, *The Portrait of the King*, trans. Martha Houle (Minneapolis: University of Minnesota Press, 1988), pp. 3–16.

21. Ra'hel, *Flowers of Perhaps: Selected Poems of Ra'hel*, trans. Robert Friend with Shimon Sandbank (London: Menard Press, 1995), p. 31.

22. This claim requires further evidence.

23. Kant, *Critique of the Power of Judgment*, no. 26, p. 138.

24. Lyotard, *Differend*, Kant Notice 4; Jean-François Lyotard, *Lessons on the Analytic of the Sublime*, trans. Elizabeth Rottenberg (Stanford, CA: Stanford University Press, 1994), esp. chs. 5 and 6.

25. It is similarly possible to intersect the opposing values of all of philosophical tradition from Plato (good and bad, knowledge and ignorance) through Heidegger (authenticity and everydayness), as well as opposing emotions such as sorrow and happiness, shame and pride, with the contradiction between the repleteness of the excitation and the voidness of all feeling. The result will always be a multiplication of oppositions, as in a mirror image.

26. This concept was formulated by Foucault in the introduction to *The Order of Things*, and also in a short lecture on heterotopic spaces: Michel Foucault, "Of Other Spaces," *Diacritics* 16 (1986), pp. 22–27. On places of knowledge as heterotopic spaces, see Adi Ophir and Steven Shapin, "The Place of Knowledge: A Methodological Survey," *Science in Context* 4, no. 1 (Spring 1991), pp. 13–21; and Adi Ophir, "The Cartography of Knowledge and Power: Foucault Reconsidered," in Hugh J. Silverman (ed.), *Cultural Semiosis: Tracing the Signifier* (London: Routledge, 1998), pp. 193–97. On the museum as a heterotopic space, see Azoulay, *Training for Art*, ch. 4.

27. Sartre, *Sketch for a Theory of the Emotions*, p. 65.

28. On the production of excitation in candid-camera films, see Haim Lapid, "Flat on Its Back: A Scholarly Study of Israeli Hidden-Camera Movies," *Theory and Criticism* 2 (Summer 1992), pp. 25–52 [in Hebrew].

29. Immanuel Kant, *Critique of Pure Reason*, trans. N.K. Smith (London: Macmillan, 1950), no. 16.

30. Lévinas does not distinguish between these three moments, and accord-

ingly he arrives directly at the most intensive one, without pausing over the others. See Emmanuel Lévinas, *Existence and Existents*, trans. Alphonso Lingis (The Hague: Nijhoff, 1978), p. 121.

31. G.W.F. Hegel, "Independence and Dependence of Self-Consciousness: Lordship and Bondage," in *The Phenomenology of Mind*, trans. J.B. Baillie (New York: Harper and Row, 1967).

32. Jean-Jacques Rousseau, "Discourse on the Origin and Foundations of Inequality," in *The First and Second Discourses*, trans. Roger D. Masters and Judith R. Masters (New York: St. Martin's Press, 1964), p. 95.

33. *Ibid.*, pp. 130–32. In this section, Rousseau presents examples of pity among animals: "the repugnance of horses to trample a living body underfoot"; the "uneasiness" an animal expresses when "passing near a dead animal of its species," and even a behavior that can be interpreted as erecting a "sepulcher" for the dead beast; as well as "the sad lowing of cattle entering a slaughterhouse" as they are stricken by the "horrible sight" that they suddenly behold. A view of animals as capable of pity is not exclusive to Rousseau. Pity was perceived not just as an excitation identified in animals but even as a fundamentally "animal" excitation, which civilized humans are supposed to overcome (see 7.411).

34. *Ibid.*, p. 133.

35. *Ibid.*, p. 131.

36. Bernard Mandeville, *The Fable of the Bees; or, Private Vices, Publick Benefits*, ed. F.B. Kaye (Oxford: Clarendon Press, 1924).

37. Rousseau, *First and Second Discourses*, pp. 130–31.

38. Nietzsche, *Beyond Good and Evil*, nos. 55 and 225; *Thus Spoke Zarathustra*, trans. Walter Kaufmann (New York: Vintage Books, 1965), pt. 4.

39. Elias Canetti, *Crowds and Power*, trans. Carol Stewart (Harmondsworth, UK: Penguin, 1981).

40. On the notion of a "display of presence," see Ariella Azoulay, "The Place of Art," *Studio* 40 (1993), pp. 9–11 [in Hebrew].

41. A passage from the "General Remark on the First Section of the Analytic" in Kant's *Critique of the Power of Judgment* demonstrates this matter well: "All stiff regularity (whatever approaches mathematical regularity) is of itself contrary to taste: the consideration of it affords no lasting entertainment, but rather, insofar as it does not expressly have cognition or determinate practical end as its aim, it induces boredom. By contrast, that with which the imagination can play in an unstudied and purposive way is always new for us, and we are never tired of looking at it. In his description of Sumatra, Marsden remarks that the free beauties of nature everywhere surround the observer there and hence have little attraction for him any more; by contrast, a pepper garden where the stakes on which the plants were trained formed parallel rows had much charm for him when he encountered it in the middle of a forest" (p. 126).

CHAPTER SIX: SUFFERING

1. Ophir's irony is lost in the translation. The Hebrew idiom is a quotation from a Hebrew song commonly sung at memorial ceremonies, the prayer-like lyrics of which were written by Hannah Senesh, an émigré from Hungary to

Palestine who was tortured and died in a Nazi prison after parachuting into Nazi-occupied territory on a resistance mission. — TRANS.

2. See, for example, Hobbes's definition in *Leviathan*: "This Endeavour, when it is towards something which causes it, is called APPETITE, or DESIRE.... And when the Endeavour is fromward something, it is generally called AVERSION" (*Leviathan*, ed. Richard Tuck [Cambridge, UK: Cambridge University Press, 1991], ch. 6, p. 38).

3. Emmanuel Lévinas, *Time and the Other*, trans. Richard A. Cohen (Pittsburgh: Duquesne University Press, 1987), p. 69. See also Lévinas, *Totality and Infinity*, trans. Alphonso Lingis (Pittsburgh: Duquesne University Press, 1969), pp. 236–40. And from another direction, Simone Weil says similar things: "There is a point in affliction where we are no longer able to bear either that it should go on or that we will be delivered from it" (Simone Weil, *Gravity and Grace*, trans. Emma Craufurd [London: Routledge and Kegan Paul, 1952], p. 73). That is, you cannot annihilate the presence of the increasing excitation in order to escape it, but the loss that causes the excitation is so horrific that the idea that there may come a moment at which one will be able to tolerate it is unbearable as well.

4. Marcus Aurelius says after Epicurus, "On pain: what we cannot bear removes us from life; what lasts can be borne" (Marcus Aurelius, *Meditations*, trans. A.S.L. Farquharson [Germany: Everyman's Library, 1946]). He treats the "unbearable" literally, and in this greatly confines the ability to distinguish between excitations, whereas I wish to understand the "unbearable" as a form of amplified excitation.

5. Friedrich Nietzsche, *Beyond Good and Evil*, trans. Walter Kaufmann (New York: Vintage Books, 1966), no. 55.

6. The distinction between diffuse and focused suffering has a wider context with relation to excitation in general: like the difference between a numb headache and a burn, between a continuous, tender longing and a flooding yearning, between gaiety and a surge of happiness, between erotic pleasure and the rapture of an orgasm.

7. Jean-Jacques Rousseau, "Discourse on the Origin and Foundations of Inequality," in *The First and Second Discourses*, trans. Roger D. Masters and Judith R. Masters (New York: St. Martin's Press, 1964), p. 122.

8. *Ibid.*

9. The Hebrew term for "pretend" — *leha'amid panim* — means literally to put up a face, to place the face as a barrier between the internal and the external. — TRANS.

10. Rousseau, "Discourse on the Origin and Foundations of Inequality," p. 54; see also 5.333 above.

11. Umberto Eco, *A Theory of Semiotics* (Indianapolis: University of Indiana Press, 1979), p. 7.

12. Emmanuel Lévinas, "Useless Suffering," in Robert Bernasconi and David Wood (eds.), *The Provocation of Levinas* (London: Routledge, 1988), pp. 156–57.

13. *Ibid.*, p. 164.

14. *Ibid.*, p. 333; see also 7.201 on.

15. Weil, *Gravity and Grace*, pp. 73–74.

16. "This is a chronicle from the Planet Auschwitz. Time there was not what time is on Earth. There, each fraction of a minute timed on cogwheels of that other time. The inhabitants of that planet had no names. Had no children. Dressed not the way people dress here. Were not born nor gave birth. Breathed according to laws of a different nature and neither lived nor died by the regulations of the world that is here." From Ka-tzetnick's evidence at the Eichmann trial in Jerusalem, cited in Ka-tzetnick, *Star of Ashes*, trans. H. Zeldes and N. De-Nur (Tel Aviv: Hamenora Publishing House, 1967).

17. Jean-Paul Sartre, *Sketch for a Theory of the Emotions*, trans. Philip Mairet (London: Methuen, 1962), p. 66.

18. Genesis 35 and 37.

19. "He that goeth forth and weepeth, bearing precious seed" (Psalms 126.6).

20. Exodus 2.23–24.

21. Psalms 118.5; Lamentations 3.56.

22. *High Holyday Prayer Book*, Yom Kippur, trans. and annotated by Philip Birnbaum (New York: Hebrew Publishing Company, 1960), pp. 553–59.

23. *Mishnah*, Nezikin, Baba Kamma, trans. Edward Levin (Jerusalem: Maor Wallach Press, 1994), ch. 1.8.

24. Sartre, *Sketch for a Theory of the Emotions*, p. 63.

25. Weil, *Gravity and Grace*, p. 5.

26. Hannah Arendt, *The Origins of Totalitarianism*, 2nd ed. (New York: Meridian, 1958).

27. Hannah Arendt, *Eichmann in Jerusalem: A Report on the Banality of Evil* (New York: Viking Press, 1963). On the same issue, see also Zygmunt Bauman, *Modernity and the Holocaust* (Ithaca, NY: Cornell University Press, 1989).

28. Foucault made this claim in detail, in the context of sexual liberation, in his criticism of the "repressive hypothesis" (Michel Foucault, *The History of Sexuality*, vol. 1, *The Will to Knowledge*, trans. Robert Hurley [London: Penguin, 1990], pt. 2). This critique may serve as a model for criticizing other kinds of liberation discourse.

29. For more on the morality of liberation, see below, "Freedom" (8.3), in particular 8.330.

30. See Luc Boltanski, *Distant Suffering: Morality, Media, and Politics*, trans. Graham Burchell (Cambridge, UK: Cambridge University Press, 1999).

31. B'Tselem is the Israeli Information Center for Human Rights in the Occupied Territories.

32. The differences between the photographer or reporter whose only interest is another "news item" and the photographer or reporter who rushes to the disaster area with a sense of mission, sent by some aid organization, are differences of nuance on a single continuum, between cooperating with the causes of disaster and struggling against them. For more on the ambivalence embedded in the position of the photographer in the face of the horror of the suffering of others, see, for example, Rony Brauman and René Backmann, *Les Médias et l'humanitaire: Ethique de l'information ou charité-spectacle* (Paris: CFPJ, 1996); and Ariella Azoulay, *Death's Showcase: The Power of Image in Contemporary Democracy*, Ruvik Danieli (Cambridge, MA: MIT Press, 2001), ch. 8.

33. Michael Walzer, *Spheres of Justice* (New York: Basic Books, 1983), p. 19.

34. Jean-François Lyotard, *The Differend: Phrases in Dispute*, trans. Georges Van Den Abbeele (Minneapolis: University of Minnesota Press, 1988), no. 240.

35. Discourse is also an exchange mechanism — between the seen and the spoken that describes it, between statements that describe "the same thing," and between speakers who exchange one statement for another, for authority, or for speaking or gazing positions.

ASIDE

1. Plato, *Phaedrus* 265e–266a, trans. H. N. Fowler (Cambridge, MA: Harvard University Press, 1914).

2. Jacques Carelman, *Catalogue d'objets introuvables* (Paris: Balland 1980).

CHAPTER SEVEN: EVILS

1. Karl Marx, "The German Ideology," in *The Marx Reader*, ed. Christopher Pierson (Cambridge, UK: Polity, 1997), p. 104.

2. Three contemporary examples from different contexts will suffice: for a description of social evil in terms of pathology, see Axel Honneth, *The Struggle for Recognition* (Cambridge, MA: MIT Press, 1996); on social correction as therapy, see Nancy Fraser, "From Redistribution to Recognition? Dilemmas of Justice in a Post-socialist Age," *New Left Review*, July/Aug. 1995, pp. 68–93, and Jean-Luc Nancy, "Entretien sur le mal," *Apertura: Collection de recherche psychoanalytique* 5 (1995), pp. 27–32.

3. Ludwig Wittgenstein, *Philosophical Investigations*, trans. G.E.M. Anscombe (New York: Macmillan, 1953), nos. 459–60; Jean-François Lyotard, *The Differend: Phrases in Dispute*, trans. Georges Van Den Abbeele (Minneapolis: University of Minnesota Press, 1988), no. 43.

4. See 3.544 and 6.555. Lyotard defines a wrong as a damage that cannot be proved and therefore has no expression in the discourse of the claimant (*Differend*, nos. 7 and 9). But in light of the discussion here, it is obvious that the definition should be extended to include suffering, that is, evils in general.

5. This theme is extensively discussed by Zygmunt Bauman in his *Postmodern Ethics* (Oxford: Blackwell, 1993) and *Life in Fragments: Essays in Postmodern Morality* (Oxford: Blackwell, 1995).

6. *Yalkut Shimoni*, Tract Beshalach, 233.

7. See, for example, Tzvetan Todorov, *The Conquest of America: The Question of the Other*, trans. Richard Howard (New York: Harper and Row, 1984), esp. ch. 3; David E. Stannard, *American Holocaust: Columbus and the Conquest of the New World* (New York: Oxford University Press, 1992).

8. Adi Ophir, "Beyond Good-Evil: A Plea for Hermeneutic Ethics," *Philosophical Forum* 21, nos. 1–2 (1989–90), pp. 94–121.

9. On Foucault's conception of the historical *a priori*, see Michel Foucault, *The Archaeology of Knowledge*, trans. A.M Sheridan Smith (New York: Pantheon, 1972), pt. 3, ch. 5.

10. Michel Foucault, *The Order of Things: An Archaeology of the Human Sciences* (New York: Vintage Books, 1973).

11. For the purposes of this discussion, "liberal," "feminist," and such will appear here as familiar stereotypes, at the cost of any attempt to outline differences and nuances within and among these general types.

12. "As for the metalanguage at play in 'my' phrases here, it has no logical status, its function is not to fix the sense of a term. It calls upon the capacity of ordinary language to refer to itself" (Lyotard, *Differend*, no. 108). And see above, "Aside," pp. 311–19. I take for granted here that there is no metalanguage.

13. Engels was not the first, of course. He was preceded by researchers of poverty such as Eugène Buret in France and James Kay-Shuttleworth in England, who pointed out the horrific living conditions of the lower classes, especially in the crowded areas of big cities, as the cause of the poor's susceptibility to plagues, lack of moral stamina, and tendency toward crime and delinquency. But unlike some of his contemporaries, Engels regarded the environmental conditions of the poor not as an explanatory factor but as a result that had to be explained. He spoke of the working class, not of the poor, and systematically attributed the totality of the working class's hardships, including their living conditions, to their working conditions. See Friedrich Engels, *The Condition of the Working Class in England* (New York: Oxford University Press, 1993); James Kay-Shuttleworth, *The Moral and Physical Condition of the Working Classes Employed in the Cotton Manufacture in Manchester* (London: James Ridgway, 1832); Eugène Buret, *De la misère des classes laborieuses en Angleterre et en France* (Paris, 1840). Also see Mitchell Dean, *The Constitution of Poverty: Toward a Genealogy of Liberal Governance* (London: Routledge, 1991), ch. 11.

14. Karl Marx, *Economic and Philosophic Manuscripts of 1844* (Moscow: Progress Press, 1977); and "The Working Day," in *Capital: A Critique of Political Economy*, vol. 1, trans. Ben Fowkes (New York: Penguin, 1976).

15. There were exceptions to this rule. Prince Kropotkin, for example, lists socialism as one of the three new movements within ethics that appeared in the nineteenth century (together with positivism and evolutionism). Among the socialist thinkers who contributed to ethical thought, Kropotkin enumerates Charles Fourier, Robert Owen, Pierre-Joseph Proudhon, Mikhail Bakunin, and of course Marx and Engels. See Petr Alekseevich Kropotkin, *Ethics: Origin and Development*, trans. Louis S. Friedland and Joseph R. Piroshnikoff (New York: Dial Press, 1934), pp. 231 and 266ff.

16. John Rawls, *A Theory of Justice* (Cambridge, MA: Harvard University Press, 1971); Jürgen Habermas, *Moral Consciousness and Communicative Action*, trans. Christian Lenhardt and Shierry Weber Nicholsen (Cambridge, MA: MIT Press, 1990). For a comparative analysis of both, see Kenneth Baynes, *The Normative Grounds of Social Criticism* (Albany: State University of New York Press, 1992), and also the debate between the two: Jürgen Habermas, "Reconciliation Through the Public Use of Reason: Remarks on John Rawls' Political Liberalism," and John Rawls, "Reply to Habermas," *Journal of Philosophy* 92, no. 3 (March 1995).

17. Compare Adi Ophir, "Shifting the Ground of the Moral Domain: Reading Lyotard's *Differend*," *Constellations* 4, no. 2 (Oct. 1997), pp. 191–92.

18. Lyotard, *Differend*, nos. 7 and 9; see also 3.554 and 6.555.

19. Ophir, "Shifting the Ground of the Moral Domain," p. 191.

20. Gayatri C. Spivak, "Can the Subaltern Speak?" in Cary Nelson and Lawrence Grossberg (eds.), *Marxism and the Interpretation of Culture* (Urbana: University of Illinois Press, 1988).

21. Hybrid situations are the center of critical postcolonial theory. See, for example, Homi K. Bhabha, *The Location of Culture* (London: Routledge, 1994).

22. Hannah Arendt, *The Human Condition* (Chicago: University of Chicago Press, 1958), p. 241.

23. *Ibid.*, p. 241. This conception of radical evil did not guide Arendt when she came to observe the Eichmann trial a few years later. Despite her criticism of the Israeli authorities, Arendt thought that both trying Eichmann and his death sentence were justified. See 9.250. I discuss this contradiction in Arendt's position in Adi Ophir, "Between Kant and Eichmann: Thinking on Evil After Arendt," *History and Memory* 8, no. 2 (1996), pp. 89–136.

24. Ophir, "Beyond Good-Evil," pp. 45–49.

25. Michael Walzer, *Spheres of Justice* (New York: Basic Books, 1983).

26. The primary intuition here comes from Nietzsche, who portrays the noble man as extremely generous. See, for example, Friedrich Nietzsche, "On Generosity," in *Thus Spoke Zarathustra*, trans. Walter Kaufmann (New York: Vintage Books, 1965). Under Nietzsche's influence, and that of the anthropologist Marcel Mauss's research of the concept of the gift, Georges Bataille develops the category of excess as the main axis in his explanation of human action in ritual and religion, aesthetics and sexuality, and as a key to his concept of sovereignty (*La Part maudite, précédé de la Notion de dépense* [Paris: Minuit, 1967]). Derrida, a careful reader of Bataille, and even more so of Lévinas, has lately discussed extensively the act of giving, and the (im)possibility of gratuitous giving, and made these a key issue in his ethical reflections. See Jacques Derrida, *Donner le temps* (Paris: Galilée, 1991); "Donner la mort," in Jean-Michel Rabaté and Michael Wetzel (eds.), *L'Ethique du don: Jacques Derrida et la pensée du don* (Paris: Métailié-Transition, 1992). My own discussion will often move in lines parallel to these but in a course of its own, failing to draw similarities and differences, as it should have done. I would therefore like to acknowledge my debt to these authors for everything I took from them, both knowingly and unknowingly, without explicit acknowledgment.

27. David Hume, *Enquiries Concerning the Human Understanding and Concerning the Principles of Morals* (Westport, CT: Greenwood Press, 1980), p. 172.

28. Adam Smith, *The Theory of Moral Sentiments* (Indianapolis: Liberty Fund, 1974), p. 9.

29. Ophir, "Shifting the Ground of the Moral Domain," p. 192.

30. Despite the appearance of applied ethics. See 7.433.

31. In Kant, these are two separate and autonomous systems; in Hegel, morality is a moment in the development of law, which is seen as a more developed totality. On the distinction between the two categories, see Immanuel Kant, "Introduction to the Metaphysics of Morals," in *The Metaphysics of Morals*, trans. Mary Gregor (Cambridge, UK: Cambridge University Press, 1996), pp. 20ff. G.W.F. Hegel, *Elements of the Philosophy of Right*, trans. H.R. Nisbet (Cambridge, UK: Cambridge University Press, 1991), nos. 30, 113, 213.

32. More generally, moral arguments tend to fill gaps in the logic of different social systems in a way that exposes the inherent fragility and ideological function of moral rhetoric.

33. I am aware that this formulation leaves at least three questions open: Who is the one offering the demarcation principle? In what way and from which discourse can this principle be argued for? And who is authorized to institutionalize it *de facto*? The first two questions will be partially answered (Chapter Eight, "The Limit of Waste," "Unto Death"). The third question opens up research into the genealogy of the care for the other in Western culture that cannot be contained in the present work.

34. Immanuel Kant, "Analytics of Practical Reason," in *The Critique of Practical Reason*, ed. and trans. Mary Gregor (Cambridge, UK: Cambridge University Press, 1997).

35. Like the handsome, wicked protagonist of Stanley Kubrick's *Clockwork Orange*, for example. It is harder to see how this wickedness passes the universalization test of the categorical imperative. See also 7.412–7.413.

36. Judith Shklar, *Ordinary Vices* (Cambridge, MA: Harvard University Press, 1984).

37. This is Lyotard's definition of wrong (*Differend*, no. 7), except that Lyotard uses "damage" instead of "evil."

38. Heinrich von Kleist, *Michael Kohlhaas, from an Old Chronicle*, trans. James Kirkup (London: Blackie, 1967).

39. Adi Ophir, "Damage, Suffering, and the Limit of Moral Discourse After Lyotard," *Iyuun* 45 (1996), p. 181 [in Hebrew].

40. *Ibid.*

41. *Ibid.*, p. 182.

42. Hannah Arendt, *Eichmann in Jerusalem: A Report on the Banality of Evil* (New York: Viking Press, 1963), pp. 105–106.

43. Compare Derrida's analysis of the first aporia (pp. 22–24) of moral judgment in "Force of Law: The Mystical Foundation of Authority," in Drucilla Cornell, Michel Rosenfeld, and David Carlson (eds.), *Deconstruction and the Possibility of Justice* (New York: Routledge, 1992), pp. 3–67; and 7.512 below.

44. Ophir, "Shifting the Ground of the Moral Domain," pp. 192–93.

45. *Ibid.*, p. 193.

46. See, for example, Jean-François Lyotard, *Peregrinations: Law, Form, Event* (New York: Columbia University Press, 1988).

47. Plato, *Apology* 31a, in *Plato's Complete Works*, ed. John M. Cooper (Indianapolis: Hackett, 1997).

48. Derrida, "Force of Law," pp. 22–29.

49. Friedrich Nietzsche, *Beyond Good and Evil*, trans. Walter Kaufmann (New York: Vintage Books, 1966), sec. 2.

50. Ecclesiastes 3.16.

51. For example: *The History of Sexuality*, vol. 2, *The Use of Pleasure*, trans. Robert Hurley (London: Penguin, 1987); "From the Classical Self to the Modern Subject," in Paul Rabinow (ed.), *The Foucault Reader* (New York: Pantheon, 1984), pp. 359–72.

52. Ophir, "Shifting the Ground of the Moral Domain," pp. 187–90. It is (just about) possible to interpret Kantian morality as a limit case of this rule. The Kantian subject is required to respect absolutely and unconditionally the moral law, which posits the subject as an addressee of a call that has no source. The sourceless law is an abstract other but also an absolute other in relation to the interested subject. The moral law or "the principle of morality" is in "direct opposition" to the care of the self, "the principle of private happiness," in the language of Immanuel Kant. "So distinctly and sharply drawn are the boundaries of morality and self-love that even the most common eye cannot fail to distinguish whether something belongs to the one or the other" (Kant, *Critique of Practical Reason*, pt. 1, ch. 8, remark 2). "Respect for the law" can be interpreted accordingly as a kind of interest in a non-concrete other. See also 8.517–8.518.

53. Richard Rorty, *Contingency, Irony, Solidarity* (Cambridge, UK: Cambridge University Press, 1989), ch. 4; Shklar, *Ordinary Vices*, ch. 2.

54. Nietzsche, *Beyond Good and Evil*, nos. 55 and 229.

55. Michel Foucault, *Discipline and Punish: The Birth of the Prison*, trans. Alan Sheridan (New York: Pantheon, 1977), pt. 1, ch. 1. Foucault exposes there, among other things, the way in which humanism, which forbade the attainment of pleasure from blatant physical suffering, channeled cruelty from the colorful arena of the execution to the depressing grayness of prison cells and classrooms.

CHAPTER EIGHT: EVIL

1. There are significant differences among these three thinkers regarding many fundamental issues, but these are irrelevant to the present discussion. For Arendt, such webs exist in the public space of "the political"; for Foucault, such webs of power relations are the only form in which power exists; for Nancy, "being-together" is always an infinite activity of tying and untying connections with and among others. I have elaborated elsewhere on the discussion about webs of association and communication. See Adi Ophir, "Civil Society in a City That Never Sleeps," in Adi Ophir and Yoav Peled (eds.), *Israel: From Mobilized to Civil Society?* (Tel Aviv: Hakibbutz Hameuchad, 2001), pp. 113–80 [in Hebrew]; Michel Foucault, *The History of Sexuality*, vol. 2, *The Use of Pleasure*, trans. Robert Hurley (London: Penguin, 1987); Hannah Arendt, *The Human Condition* (Chicago: University of Chicago Press, 1958), chs. 6 and 24–28; Jean-Luc Nancy, *The Sense of the World*, trans. Jeffrey S. Libert (Minneapolis: University of Minnesota Press, 1997), pp. 34–45 and 103–17; Jean-Luc Nancy, *Being Singular Plural*, trans. Robert D. Richardson and Anne E. O'Byrne (Stanford: Stanford University Press, 2000), chs. 9–11.

2. It is not enough for God to be causa sui in order for him to be necessary. If necessity is limited to God's self-creation, then the world he created and the act of creation might be contingent and perhaps even superfluous, at least from God's point of view. That would mean that at least some of God's deeds or being would not be necessary. Therefore, God, an absolute necessity in rationalist thinking, must be equated with, or somehow responsible for, the totality of being, and this ontology tends to (and perhaps must, from a strictly logical point of view) end in pantheism.

3. On the difference between an ethics and a theory of morals, see from 8.515 on.

4. See, for instance, the preface to *Totality and Infinity*: "Without substituting eschatology for philosophy, without philosophically 'demonstrating' eschatological 'truths,' we can proceed from the experience of totality back to a situation where totality breaks up, a situation that conditions the totality itself. Such a situation is the gleam of exteriority of, or transcendence in, the face of the Other" (Emmanuel Lévinas, *Totality and Infinity*, trans. Alphonso Lingis [Pittsburgh: Duquesne University Press, 1969], p. 24).

5. Compare Nancy, *The Sense of the World*, pp. 103–17; Nancy, *Being Singular Plural*, chs. 9–11. Michael Mann, *The Sources of Social Power* (Cambridge, UK: Cambridge University Press, 1986), vol. 1, ch. 1.

6. Karl Marx, *Capital: A Critique of Political Economy*, vol. 1, trans. Ben Fowkes (New York: Penguin, 1976), ch. 1.

7. The analogy between the capitalist system and the system of evils is far from perfect. For example, I have drawn distinctions not between different historical stages in the economy of Evil — although this may be possible — but rather between different phenomenological dimensions of it.

8. Compare Jean Baudrillard, *Fatal Strategies*, trans. Philip Beitchman and W.G.J. Niesluchowski (New York: Semiotext(e), 1990), pp. 7–24; Jean Baudrillard, *The Transparency of Evil*, trans. James Benedict (London: Verso, 1993), pt. 1; Bruno Latour, *Aramis; or, The Love of Technology*, trans. Catherine Porter (Cambridge, MA: Harvard University Press, 1996), ch. 1.

9. This section and the following two are originally from Ophir, "Civil Society in a City That Never Sleeps."

10. Gilles Deleuze and Félix Guattari, introduction to *A Thousand Plateaus*, trans. Brian Massumi (Minneapolis: University of Minnesota Press, 1987).

11. See Baudrillard, *Transparency of Evil*, pp. 51–74.

12. Michel Foucault, *Discipline and Punish: The Birth of the Prison*, trans. Alan Sheridan (New York: Pantheon, 1977), pp. 224–28 and 231–56.

13. On the production of "deviations" as the correct and normal condition of state systems under occupation, see Adi Ophir, "The Dreyfus Affair and Other Political Schools," *Theoria ve-Bikoret* 6 (1995), pp. 161–76 [in Hebrew].

14. For a Foucauldian analysis of the welfare state, see François Ewald, *L'Etat providence* (Paris: Grasset, 1986). On the continuum connecting an occupying regime and a well-functioning liberal regime, see Ophir, "Dreyfus Affair."

15. The expression is Habermas's, but I have added the media as a third steering system. See Jürgen Habermas, *The Theory of Communicative Action*, trans. Thomas McCarthy (Boston: Beacon Press, 1984), vol. 2, ch. 6; Ophir, "Civil Society in a City That Never Sleeps," pp. 133–35.

16. See, for instance, Rony Brauman and René Backmann, *Les Médias et l'humanitaire: Ethique de l'information ou charité-spectacle* (Paris: CFPJ, 1996); Myriam Tsikounas, ed., *Les Ambiguïtés de l'humanitaire* (Paris: Seuil, 1996); Raimo Väyrynen, *The Age of Humanitarian Emergencies* (Helsinki: UNU/WIDER, 1996). I discovered the abundant literature concerning these issues and learned much more about them after publication of this book in Hebrew. See

Adi Ophir, "Moral Technologies: Managing Disaster and Forsaking Life," *Theoria ve-Bikoret* 22 (Spring 2003), pp. 67–103 [in Hebrew].

17. See, for instance, Jean-Luc Nancy, *L'Impérative catégorique* (Paris: Flammarion, 1983), pp. 12–13.

18. Jacques Derrida, *Specters of Marx*, trans. Peggy Kamuf (New York: Routledge, 1994), pp. 77–78.

19. The title of the second essay of the treatise *The Contest of the Faculties*: Immanuel Kant, "A Renewed Attempt to Answer the Question: Is the Human Race Continually Improving," in *Kant: Political Writings*, ed. Hans Reiss, trans. H.B. Nisbet (Cambridge, UK: Cambridge University Press, 1991), pp. 177–90.

20. From a purely logical — that is, divine — perspective, there is a clear difference between these two formulations. But the logical distinction between the worst possibility within this world and the worst of all possible worlds makes no difference for humans, who are capable of transforming their world but not of creating or discovering others (for creation and discovery, as well as anything created or discovered, are always already part of the human world).

21. Happiness is not the absence of suffering, Lévinas justly claims, but he adds, unjustly, that suffering is a failure of happiness (*Totality and Infinity*, p. 115). Suffering and happiness do not rule each other out, either logically or existentially. People may be happy in their suffering and suffer in the course of their happy excitation.

22. The Hebrew word *deaga* designates care for and about something, concern for something as well as worry about something. "Care," "concern," and "worry" could be alternately used here according to context, but the reader should bear in mind that all these terms stand for the single Hebrew notion. — TRANS.

23. Suffering, loss, and deprivation may indeed multiply worries and foil every possibility of being happy, so their removal may often be (or be perceived as) a condition for happiness. But a wise resignation to the order of things and their manner of occurrence may reduce the worry of suffering and loss, as both Stoics and Epicureans believed. The Stoics saw happiness as a state resulting from the removal of worry and other types of concerns through wise resignation to the order of things (see, for instance, A.A. Long, "Stoic Eudaimonism," in *Stoic Studies* [Cambridge, UK: Cambridge University Press, 1996]), pp. 179–201). The Epicureans grounded happiness in *ataraxia*, a worry-free enjoyment, and believed the removal of worry and concerns, and first and foremost the fear of death, to be the result of an avoidance of groundless beliefs and superstitions. See, for instance, Epicurus, "Letter to Menoeceus," in *Epicurus: The Extant Remains* (bilingual ed.), trans. Cyril Bailey (Oxford: Oxford University Press, 1970), pp. 83–93. In this respect, they came close to the stance of skeptics such as Sextus Empiricus, who sought to teach the *epoché*, the self-acquired attitude of suspending judgment, and viewed it as a way of overcoming concerns and worries following from mistaken evaluations of deeds and a mistaken interpretation of their consequences (Sextus Empiricus, *Outlines of Pyrrhonism* [New York: Prometheus Books, 1990]), nos. 235–38). This brief note obviously cannot do justice to the complexity of the ancient Greeks' perception

of happiness, worry, or enjoyment. On this, see, for instance, Julia Annas, *The Morality of Happiness* (Oxford: Oxford University Press, 1993), chs. 15–19.

24. The Greeks spoke of *eudaimonia*, which interpreters caution us is not exactly happiness, first of all because the Greeks usually talked about a comprehensive state, an entire life cycle, not about an excitation. "One swallow does not make a summer, nor does one day, or a short time, make a man blessed and happy," Aristotle said in his *Nicomachean Ethics* (1.1098a20, trans. W.D. Ross, in *The Basic Works of Aristotle*, ed. Richard McKeon [New York: Random House, 1941]), and Solon believed that only a dead man's happiness could be assessed (*ibid.*, 10.1100a). But in structural terms, the similarity is greater than the difference, and the latter lies in the fact that the others considered by the Greeks in the context of the concept of happiness, those whose company arouses this sense of cheering sufficiency, were gods. Being "blessed by the gods," *eudaimon*, meant not only being the favorite of the gods but also being alongside them without fearing them or their jealousy and without conflicting with them, without being jealous of them or jealous of others on their account, feeling sufficiency in their company.

25. Benedict de Spinoza, *The Ethics*, pt. 5, props. 32 and 33.

26. Aristotle, *Nicomachean Ethics* 1.1095a15–25.

27. This *différend* is multiplied, of course, if one takes into account the unconscious character of desire as well as the unconscious profits and damages that accompany enjoyment. But here as elsewhere in the present work, the (personal) unconscious will remain completely consciously repressed.

28. In this context, I'm thinking first and foremost of Nietzsche and Foucault. Nietzsche was perhaps the first to contemplate the moral problematization of desires in Christianity and in classical philosophy; Foucault studied the problematization of desire in the first volume of *The History of Sexuality* (*The Will to Knowledge*), in which he dealt with the emergence of sexuality (to be distinguished from sex) in modern fields of discourse as a site of truth and an arena of the intervention of various social forces that impose discipline on the individual and give his experiences meaning; and, on the other hand, in the latter volumes of *The History of Sexuality* (especially in the second, *The Use of Pleasure*), Foucault turns to classical culture and reconstructs "the moral problematization of pleasure."

29. See 8.512–8.515; Michel Foucault, *The History of Sexuality*, vol. 3, *The Care of the Self*, trans. Robert Hurley (London: Penguin, 1990).

30. Ἡδονή (*hedone*) or ηδος (*hedos*). The distinction between pleasure and enjoyment is phenomenological and analytic and should not be projected onto earlier forms of moral discourse, certainly not onto the Greeks, who never made such a distinction.

31. Adi Ophir, *Plato's Invisible Cities: Discourse and Power in the Republic* (London: Routledge, 1991), pp. 31–34.

32. Plato, *The Republic* 509c–d, trans. Allan Bloom (New York: Basic Books, 1968).

33. For instance, Immanuel Kant, *Critique of the Power of Judgment*, ed. Paul Guyer, trans. Paul Guyer and Eric Matthews (New York: Cambridge University Press, 2000), no. 83, p. 300.

34. The Hebrew *raooy* has this double meaning: the proper thing to do, and being worthy of or deserving something. — TRANS.

35. Immanuel Kant, *Critique of Practical Reason*, ed. and trans. Mary Gregor (Cambridge, UK: Cambridge University Press, 1997), pt. 2, ch. 2, pp. 231–36; Kant, *Critique of the Power of Judgment*, no. 87, p. 315; Immanuel Kant, *Religion Within the Boundaries of Mere Reason*, trans. and ed. Allen W. Wood and George Di Giovanni (Cambridge, UK: Cambridge University Press, 1998), pt. 3, div. 1, II–IV, pp. 108–12; and many other passages. Compare Yirmiyahu Yovel, *Kant and the Philosophy of History* (Princeton, NJ: Princeton University Press, 1980), pp. 61–64.

36. Kant, *Critique of the Power of Judgment*, no. 87, p. 314n.

37. Kant, "Renewed Attempt," no. 6; "Perpetual Peace: A Philosophical Sketch," in *Kant: Political Writings*, pp. 93–130.

38. Kant, "Renewed Attempt," no. 6.

39. Immanuel Kant, "Conjectural Beginning of Human History," in *Kant: Political Writings*, pp. 231–32.

40. Kant, *Religion Within the Boundaries of Mere Reason*, pt. 1, sec. 3, p. 57n.

41. Arendt, *Human Condition*, ch. 32.

42. A literal translation of a common Hebrew proverb. — TRANS.

43. Though this knowledge, too, is uncertain, for only the one who suffers can be certain (4.030; from 4.230 on; 6.045).

44. Plato, *Republic* 509c-d.

45. "Goodness is transcendence itself" (Lévinas, *Totality and Infinity*, p. 305).

46. On the face, see *ibid.*, pt. 3.

47. This sentence is of course an allusion to the title of Lévinas's book *Autrement qu'être; ou, Au-delà de l'essence* (The Hague: Nijhoff, 1974).

48. Martin Heidegger, *Being and Time*, trans. John Macquarrie and Edward Robinson (New York: Harper and Row, 1962), pp. 32–33.

49. Derrida, "Violence and Metaphysics," in *Writing and Difference*, trans. Alan Bass (London: Routledge and Kegan Paul, 1978).

50. Lévinas, *Totality and Infinity*, pp. 21–24.

51. *Ibid.*, p. 29.

52. Genesis 9.12–17.

53. Francis Wolff, "Le Mal," in Denis Kambouchner (ed.), *Notions de philosophie: Tome III* (Paris: Gallimard, 1995), pp. 184–85.

54. Friedrich Nietzsche, *The Gay Science*, ed. Bernard Williams, trans. Josefine Nauckhoff (Cambridge, UK: Cambridge University Press, 2001), no. 125, pp. 119–20.

55. Plato, *Republic* 614–21. From the first attempt to define justice (*ibid.* 331e) until its full definition (*ibid.* 443d–444a), the Platonic discussion of justice turns on questions concerning the disruption and restoration of balance in the parallel systems of relations within the soul and within the city.

56. *Ibid.* 509b.

57. *Ibid.*

58. Compare Plato, *Timaeus* 29a-30a.

59. Augustine, *Confessions VII*, 11; Thomas Aquinas, *Summa theologica I*, question 48, art. 2; compare Wolff, "Le Mal," pp. 190–92.

60. Spinoza, *Ethics*, pt. 3, prop. 39n.; pt. 4, definitions 1–2, props. 8 and 14.

61. See Benedict de Spinoza, *On the Improvement of the Understanding*, trans. R.H.M. Elwes (New York: Dover, 1977), nos. 1–12, esp. pp. 3–6.

62. For example, Nietzsche, *Gay Science*, no. 278.

63. *Ibid.*, no. 276.

64. René Descartes, *Meditations on First Philosophy*, in *The Philosophical Writings of Descartes*, trans. John Cottingham, Robert Stoothoff, and Dugald Murdoch (Cambridge, UK: Cambridge University Press, 1984), 4th Meditation, vol. 2, pp. 37–43. See also the discussion by Francis Wolff, to whom I owe some of the formulations of the present section: "Le Mal," pp. 193–94.

65. Rousseau distinguishes between "amour propre" and "amour de soi." The first is "a relative sentiment, artificial and born of society, which inclines each individual to have a greater esteem for himself than for anyone else, inspires in men all the harm they do to one another." The second is merely care for oneself, "a natural sentiment which inclines every animal to watch over its own preservation." When reason "directs" this feeling and mercy "modifies" it, it becomes a "source of humanity and virtue" (Jean-Jacques Rousseau, "Discourse on the Origin and Foundations of Inequality," in *The First and Second Discourses*, trans. Roger D. Masters and Judith R. Masters [New York: St. Martin's Press, 1964], n. O, pp. 221–22n).

66. "The direct opposite of the principle of morality is the principle of one's own happiness made the determining ground of the will" (Kant, *Critique of Practical Reason*, bk. 1, ch. 1, no. 8, theorem 4, remark 2, p. 168).

67. Kant, *Religion Within the Boundaries of Mere Reason*, pt. 1, secs. 3 and 4, pp. 55–56, 59, 66n.

68. G.W.F. Hegel, *Elements of the Philosophy of Right*, ed. Allen W. Wood, trans. H.B. Nisbet (Cambridge, UK: Cambridge University Press, 1991), nos. 139–40. F.W.J. Schelling, *Philosophical Inquiries into the Nature of Human Freedom* (La Salle, IL: Open Court, 1936), pp. 39ff.; see also 8.313–8.314 below.

69. Kant, "Concerning the Origin of Evil in Human Nature," in *Religion Within the Boundaries of Mere Reason*, pt. 1, sec. 4, pp. 61–73.

70. On the temptation to do evil, see *ibid.*, pp. 65–66. What remains mysterious, and "surpasses every concept of ours," is not just the temptation to do evil but also, equally, the capacity to overcome it (*ibid.*).

71. "The rational origin, however, of this disharmony in our power of choice..., i.e. this propensity to evil, remains inexplicable to us...evil can have originated only from moral evil (not just from the limitations of our nature)...there is no conceivable ground for us, therefore, from which moral evil could first have come in us" (*ibid.*, p. 64). See also Myriam Revault d'Allonnes, "Kant et l'idée du mal radical," *Lignes*, no. 22 (June 1994).

72. Kant describes the action against the inborn drive to do evil as "incessant laboring and becoming"; "constant *progress* from bad to better"; "ever-continuing striving for the better"; he says it "directly counters the innate propensity [to do evil]" (*Religion Within the Boundaries of Mere Reason*, pp. 68–70).

73. *Ibid.*, p. 59.

74. *Ibid.*, p. 58.

75. *Ibid.*, pt. 4, pp. 179–80. See also Jacob Rogozinski, "Ça nous donne tort," in *Kanten* (Paris: Kimé, 1996).

76. Kant, *Religion Within the Boundaries of Mere Reason*, pp. 56–57.

77. *Ibid.*, pp. 65–66 and 68.

78. *Ibid.*, pp. 68–69.

79. Kant, "Conjectural Beginning of Human History," pp. 231–32. See also *Critique of the Power of Judgment*, no. 83.

80. In another instance, Kant says that there is an evil greater than war, for war isn't "so incurably evil as the grave of universal despotism" (*Religion Within the Boundaries of Mere Reason*, p. 57n.). The difference, it would seem, is not in the force of the evils but in the state of freedom. A despotic regime means the systematic annihilation of freedom, whereas war is the "scourge of the human race" that spurs on the development of culture and leads to the development of more sophisticated forms of political freedom. See also 8.332 below.

81. *Ibid.*, pp. 56–57.

82. Kant, "Renewed Attempt," p. 182.

83. Compare Jean-François Lyotard, "The Sign of History," in *The Differend: Phrases in Dispute*, trans. Georges Van Den Abbeele (Minneapolis: University of Minnesota Press, 1988).

84. Kant, *Religion Within the Boundaries of Mere Reason*, p. 57n.

85. For instance, *ibid.*, intro. to the 1st ed. On the historical imperative and its relation to the formal categorical imperative, see Yovel, *Kant and the Philosophy of History*, ch. 1. Yovel discusses the problem presented here and attempts to settle the contradiction between "the cunning of nature" as responsible for moral progress and the moral obligation to act to advance supreme Good (ch. 3), but he presents it, finally, as Kant's "historical antinomy" (epilogue). The expression "the cunning of nature," an explicit paraphrase of Hegel's "cunning of history," is borrowed from Eric Weil, *Problèmes kantiens* (Paris: J. Vrin, 1963).

86. On the crooked tree, see Immanuel Kant, "Idea for a Universal History with a Cosmopolitan Purpose," in *Kant: Political Writings*, pp. 41–53, and *Religion Within the Boundaries of Mere Reason*, p. 66.

87. Although a subject who doesn't understand the principle of sovereignty may imagine such a gap and complain incessantly. See Thomas Hobbes, *Leviathan*, ed. Richard Tuck (Cambridge, UK: Cambridge University Press, 1991), ch. 21, pp. 148–49.

88. *Ibid.*, ch. 21, pp. 151–54.

89. *Ibid.*, ch. 13, p. 89; see also p. 90.

90. *Ibid.* The fundamental equality of power among individuals is based on the following simple claim: "The weakest has strength enough to kill the strongest" (*ibid.*, p. 87).

91. *Ibid.*, p. 90; ch. 17, pp. 120–21; ch. 21, pp. 145–48.

92. This theme was elaborated on at length by Leo Strauss, *The Political Philosophy of Hobbes* (Chicago: University of Chicago Press, 1963).

93. Jean-Jacques Rousseau, *The Social Contract*, in *The Social Contract and*

Other Later Political Writings, ed. and trans. Victor Gourevitch (Cambridge, UK: Cambridge University Press, 1997), bk. 1, ch. 7, pp. 52–53.

94. *Ibid.*, bk. 1, ch. 4.

95. *Ibid.*, bk. 1, ch. 6, pp. 50–51.

96. Immanuel Kant, *The Metaphysics of Morals*, trans. Mary Gregor (Cambridge, UK: Cambridge University Press, 1996), "Public Right," general remark A.

97. Hegel, *Elements of the Philosophy of Right*, no. 139, p. 167. See also the discussion in the chapter "The Beautiful Soul, Evil, and Forgiveness," in Hegel, *The Phenomenology of Spirit*, trans. A.V. Miller (Oxford: Oxford University Press, 1977), pp. 383ff.

98. Hegel, *Elements of the Philosophy of Right*, no. 140, p. 182.

99. *Ibid.*, no. 139, p. 167.

100. Hegel, "The Revealed Religion," in *Phenomenology of Spirit*, p. 472; compare Rogozinski, *Kanten*, pp. 28–30.

101. Kant, *Religion Within the Boundaries of Mere Reason*, p. 57n.

102. And indeed "the frontier zones of humankind," that is, the cultures of the savages of the New World, are mentioned time and again in traditional discussions of the state of nature. See, for instance, Hobbes, *Leviathan*, ch. 13, p. 89; John Locke, "Second Treatise," in *Two Treatises of Government*, ed. Peter Laslett (Cambridge, UK: Cambridge University Press, 1988), ch. 2, nos. 14–15, ch. 5, no. 42; Kant, *Religion Within the Boundaries of Mere Reason*, p. 56.

103. Aristotle, *Nicomachean Ethics*, bk. 5.

104. Plato, *Republic* 8–9. Plato takes actual measurements but also ridicules the attempt to measure what has no agreed-on measurement in a famous passage about the distance between the tyranny and the tyrant and the just constitution and the righteous man (576d–588a). Marx made no attempt at explicit comparison between good and evil, or evil and even worse evil, but such comparisons are to be found in Marxist discourse of various shades. They are manifested in folk wisdom, as it were, in aphorisms such as "when you fell trees, some chips are bound to fly" (that is, some evils are necessary for the progress of the revolution) or "it will get worse before it gets better" (that is, the level of humiliation and oppression has not reached its worst depths — those that will ignite the fire of revolution and bring about a turn for the better).

105. Niccolò Machiavelli, *The Prince*, ed. Quentin Skinner, trans. Russell Price (Cambridge, UK: Cambridge University Press, 1988), ch. 25, p. 85.

106. Yemima Ben-Menahem, "Historical Contingency," *Ratio* 10, no. 2 (Sept. 1997), pp. 99–107.

107. *Ibid.*, p. 102.

108. For instance, Friedrich Nietzsche, *Beyond Good and Evil*, trans. Walter Kaufmann (New York: Vintage Books, 1966), no. 19.

109. "Animals have not waited for man to teach them their playing. We can safely assert, even, that human civilization has added no essential feature to the general idea of play. Animals play just like men. We have only to watch young dogs to see that all the essentials of human play are present in their merry gambols" (Johan Huizinga, *Homo Ludens: A Study of the Play-Element in Culture*, trans. R.F.C. Hull [London: Routledge and Kegan Paul, 1949], p. 1).

110. Claude Lefort, *Democracy and Political Theory*, trans. David Macey (Cambridge, UK: Polity, 1988), p. 17.

111. This conception of freedom and the metaphors of space and spacing are borrowed from the work of Jean-Luc Nancy. See Jean-Luc Nancy, *The Experience of Freedom* (Stanford, CA: Stanford University Press, 1993), ch. 7; and *The Sense of the World*, pp. 163–82.

112. Even in the most extreme situations, in concentration camps, there are sufficient testimonies to the capacity of the same people, victims and hangmen alike, in similar or proximate situations, to do both bad and good, to be both cruel and compassionate. For more on this matter, see, for instance, Tzvetan Todorov, *Facing the Extreme*, trans. Arthur Denner and Abigail Pollak (New York: Metropolitan Books, 1996), pp. 141–78.

113. The brief discussion of duty presented here is clearly indebted to the chapter "Obligation" in Lyotard's *Differend* and to the readings of Lévinas and Kant he proposes there, but his conclusions are totally different. The "ethical genre" of discourse, according to Lyotard, is "the one whose rule is to admit no rule but that of obligation without conditions," and in this aspect it is "akin to the philosophical genre" (no. 175). The (moral) obligation is merely a kind of prescription characterized by its lack of a definite source (addresser), while the demand it addresses to the addressee is unconditional. I'm claiming that moral duty is not a statement (or phrase, in Lyotard's terms) but a passage from a descriptive to a prescriptive genre, and that this passage is always conditional upon the contents of the descriptive phrase, upon the knowledge allowing a decision on what is more urgent, what the price of the required action is, and so forth (see 8.424). It can be claimed that this duty is the general and unconditional duty to reach out to others in distress and not be indifferent to their suffering. But moral duty does not have the status of such a general phrase. The obligation to respond to others in distress neither precedes nor entails the concrete call of an other. It can only be formulated as a general prescription retrospectively, once the boundary line has been crossed, once the indifference to the fate of a concrete other emerges as the underside of not responding to a call for help.

114. Martha C. Nussbaum recently re-aroused the debate between cosmopolitan morality and a morality whose basis or horizon is limited by a community, a nation, or some other context of "local" belonging. Nussbaum, arguing for "world citizenship" and Kantian universalism, claims in an answer to her critics that "to relate to people as morally equal means to relate to nationality, ethnicity, religion, class, race, and gender as morally irrelevant, irrelevant for equal status" (Martha C. Nussbaum with respondents, *For Love of Country: Debating the Limits of Patriotism*, ed. Joshua Cohen [Boston: Beacon Press, 1996], p. 133). I would like to rephrase this claim: it is not the morally equal value of different local contexts of belonging — which Nussbaum claims *a priori* on the basis of a Kantian anthropology — that determines their moral irrelevance. It is, rather, their irrelevance — because they all concern the self and not the other in distress — that constitutes their morally equal value. Nussbaum's point of departure and her mode of argumentation are different from

mine, but the identity in conclusions is clear. See also contributions to the same debate by Anthony Appiah, Michael Walzer, Immanuel Wallerstein, and Amartya Sen; and also below from 9.350 on.

115. See 9.3. I cannot elaborate further on this matter here. The basis for such an association, I have claimed elsewhere and in a different context, is the sharing of place, position, and status within various systems for the distribution of evils in society. See Ophir, "Civil Society in a City That Never Sleeps."

116. Here I wish to elaborate on a matter I presented earlier in another aspect; see 7.254–7.300 and 7.320–7.321.

117. This position should be clearly distinguished from Bataille's, despite the centrality given here to the notion of waste or expenditure and the obvious debt to Bataille on this point. See, for instance, Georges Bataille, *The Accursed Share: An Essay on General Economy*, trans. Robert Hurley (New York: Zone Books, 1988); *Theory of Religion*, trans. Robert Hurley (New York: Zone Books, 1989). For Bataille, expenditure (*dépense*) to the point of self-sacrifice is an ultimate expression of individual sovereignty. The negation of the self unto death is paradoxically the highest moment of self-assertion and its simultaneous negation of the other. More precisely, for Bataille waste and sacrifice are linked with the closed economy of the self and with submerging oneself in the "immanence of life" that seeks to erase the differentiation of individuals — the self, the others, and the natural and objectified environment surrounding them — to overcome the rigid "order of things" and succumb to the abundant flow and the brilliantly illuminating and dimming outbursts of "the intimate order," a sort of Dionysian-Nietzschean world rich with strong appetite and creativity, violence and magnanimity. According to such a view, distress, suffering, and loss are moments of transgression. This transgression is a leap out of an order of things that reifies the flow of life, freezes it into forms, and restrains it within straps of careful, measured calculations based on what is instrumental for a given individuum, into the intimate order completely freeing it from any calculation and accountability. For Bataille, violence toward the other, ignoring or taking pleasure in his suffering and loss, can be a moment of transgression, just like self-directed violence. Opposite this Dionysian metaphysics I wish to speak only of a waste focused on superfluous suffering and loss with the aim of soothing, reducing, and preventing them. I note this with considerable trepidation. I'm not sure I have understood Bataille.

118. Compare Nancy, *The Sense of the World*, "Politics II," esp. "(K) not, Tying, Seizure of a Speech"; *Being Singular Plural*, esp. pp. 28–41.

119. "The domain of morality begins where the individual who states the abstract rule goes on to apply it to him- or herself," says Todorov. He distinguishes, in the moral realm, between a morality of principles and a morality of sympathy, and between "heroic" and "ordinary" virtues according to the receiver of the moral act: a hero acting for the sake of abstract values; ordinary virtues directed toward concrete, identified people (Todorov, *Facing the Extreme*, pp. 107–10). Todorov rejects the claim that a morality of sympathy is the only proper kind and argues that the two types conform with, and finally complement, each other: care for an other is the implementation of the morality of principles (p. 118). Todorov's argument is correct — but trivial — in one case

only: when the abstract principle dictates care for concrete others. In all other cases, the abstract principles can injure concrete others, and care for an other can contradict abstract principles.

120. The other in whom a self submerges, or from whom a self disconnects distractedly, or relative to whom a self individuates upon appearing, need not be another subject, someone else. I can submerge my self in writing, as I am doing at the moment, or in playing music, or in listening to music. My small daughter can submerge her self in playing with a doll or in following a dung beetle. Anything that a self can be submerged in can be an object of care and waste, and the background out of which the self is individuated, which draws their limits. But moral interest appears only when this otherness emits a call concerning superfluous loss or suffering. Anything that can suffer, or have an interest in its losses, is a possible object for moral concern.

121. Foucault, *Discipline and Punish*, pp. 90–92.

122. Compare Nancy, *The Sense of the World*, pp. 103–17.

123. The concept of *tzimtzum* is kabbalistic, but transposing it from a theological into a purely political and earthly context brings me, once again, into a tense proximity to the ideas of Bataille and in diametric opposition to the progression of his thinking—if I've rightly understood it. "Life beyond utility is the domain of sovereignty," says Bataille, a domain "to which the beggar can sometimes be as close as the great nobleman" (*Sovereignty*, vol. 3 of *The Accursed Share* [New York: Zone Books, 1991], pp. 197–98). Bataille, however, is talking about a sovereign person and means one "who gives nothing a second thought" and is prepared to sacrifice all, everyone included, through which he aggrandizes himself. And yet sovereignty itself starts for Bataille the moment someone begins to waste. For Bataille, putting an end to the waste means succumbing to a competing principle of usefulness and losing rather than relinquishing sovereignty. On the other hand, I'm referring to one who relinquishes sovereignty from the outset and doesn't give himself a second thought, abstains from calculating his own personal account, and sacrifices for the sake of others. This relinquishment does not testify to someone's losing or forfeiting his sovereignty. The relinquishment can be understood in two ways: a forgoing of selfhood itself, of the actualization of a self in relation to which depreciation can be evaluated; the forgoing self is so powerful that it can reduce itself, undergo *tzimtzum* (like God in Jewish Kabbalah), and vacate space for an other. Sovereignty will appear as the principle that puts a stop to this waste but that, out of the same power enabling it to draw a boundary line, can also transgress this boundary line, reduce the scope of self-accounting and enlarge the scope of waste.

124. Schmitt's concept of sovereignty is displaced from the realm of the political to morality and attributed to every individual. This is a possible reading of Derrida's "Force of Law" and his analysis of moral judgment. See Carl Schmitt, *Political Theology: Four Chapters on the Concept of Sovereignty* (Cambridge, MA: MIT Press, 1985); and *The Concept of the Political* (New Brunswick, NJ: Rutgers University Press, 1976).

125. Here Ophir uses a single word, *revach*, that in Hebrew signifies both benefit and space (or interval). — TRANS.

126. On the distinction between the ethical and the moral, see 8.511.

127. A sentence of Hegel's quoted above (8.325) can be reread here: "Evil in general is self-centered being-for-self, and Goodness is what is simple and without self" ("Revealed Religion," p. 472). Hegel, like the rest of the tradition of German idealism, equates Evil with self-love and places the self in opposition to the moral, so much so that Good demands the annulment of self. But in Hegel this is a one-sided perception of morality. The self will be not annulled but "sublated" in a dialectical *Aufhebung* and will turn out to be one moment of the benevolent, total subject, a moment whose negation is a condition for the latter.

128. Albert Camus, *The Myth of Sisyphus*, trans. Justin O'Brien (Harmondsworth, UK: Penguin, 1975).

129. The relation between the I and its body may be different. For example, maybe it is "I" who is bearing it, and maybe this body is precisely what I am now. In either case, the question of the continuity and persistence of the self remains open.

130. Foucault, *History of Sexuality*, vol. 2, *The Use of Pleasure*, and vol. 3, *The Care of the Self*; "Technologies of the Self," in Luther H. Martin, Huck Gutman, and Patrick H. Hutton (eds.), *Technologies of the Self* (Amherst: University of Massachusetts Press, 1988); "On the Genealogy of Ethics: An Overview of a Work in Progress," in Paul Rabinow (ed.), *The Foucault Reader* (New York: Pantheon, 1984).

131. The forming of self can involve reproofs and painful torments, and this dimension is preserved in the Hebrew term for morality, *musar* (מוסר), derived from the root *ysr* (יסר [torment] in many of its biblical occurrences [compare Deuteronomy 11.2; Jeremiah 2.30 and 32.33; Ezekiel 5.16; Proverbs 1.2 and 8, 4.1, 5.12, 22.15, 23.13; Job 5.17]). Despite a partial overlap in the meanings of the terms, "morality" (מוסר) is not an appropriate Hebrew translation for "ethics." It should be kept in mind that in Hellenistic and Roman culture, care of the self was first and foremost the business of the individual, whereas in ancient Jewish culture it was entrusted completely to the father, the elder ("My son, hear the instruction [*musar*] of thy father" [Proverbs 1.8]). In the former, care of the self was primarily an aesthetic matter, whereas in the latter it was a matter of piety and purification, of one's relation to God and to the sacred.

132. Plato, *Phaedo* 67c–68b.

133. Compare Etienne Balibar, "A Note on Consciousness/Conscience in the Ethics," *Studia Spinoza* 8 (1992), pp. 37–53.

134. Spinoza, *On the Improvement of the Understanding*, p. 5.

135. See the development of this theme in Ran Sigad, *Philo-Sophia: On the Only Truth* (Jerusalem: Dvir, 1983), pp. 24 and 40–48 [in Hebrew].

136. People who deal with ethics (in the sense I have outlined here) write about the good life for an audience of readers, but this leads to the conclusion not that their interest is in others, but only that they have a need for others' interest in them, in their thinking, in the example they set through their lives and their writing. The good life seems to them to depend to some extent on others' recognition, presence, and cooperation, but their interest in others is always guided by their interest in the self.

137. Lévinas, however, uses the term "ethics" for what I am calling here a

theory of morals — "the essential of ethics is in its transcendental intention [toward a transcendent other]" (*Totality and Infinity*, p. 29 and elsewhere) — and the term "economy" for the realm of care of the self that I am calling ethics (*ibid.*, sec. 2, "Interiority and Economy," pp. 109ff.).

138. Sigad interprets this as an expression of Socrates's love of wisdom, which is none other than his total surrender to the law of contradiction. According to Sigad, this infatuation and surrender cause Socrates to prefer withstanding wrong over doing wrong. In other words, while it is true that Socrates doesn't care for others, he is interested not in himself but in wisdom, or in the one truth (Sigad, *Philo-Sophia*, pp. 42–55). But Socrates is not just a tormented lover. He is in love not only with wisdom but also with his own love of wisdom. Even if he wishes to transcend his self through his love of wisdom, this is but another way of dealing with self.

139. This is the essence of that famous episode in the *Republic* where, after the discussion at long last reaches the question what Good itself is, Socrates avoids telling the frustrated participants what he knows of the matter (506–507). See Ophir, *Plato's Invisible Cities*, ch. 5.

140. Aristotle, *Nicomachean Ethics*, bk. 10, ch. 7. Perhaps this was why Aristotle sensed a need to speak about friendship and to show how extensively it, too, involves self-love, before he returns to his discussion of the happiness of contemplative life, seemingly seeking to dim this tension somewhat (bk. 9).

141. This is a literal translation from Hebrew. The word *mida* designates quantitative measures of all sorts, but also moral qualities, both virtue and vice, since one may "have" or "possess" both good or noble measures (*midot tovot, naalot*) and bad or lewd measures (*midot raot, megunot*). *Torat hamidot* (theory of measures) was the common medieval and early-modern term for moral philosophy, ethics, or more generally for any moral doctrine. — TRANS.

142. This passage plays with Hegel's analysis of the concept of measure in his *Science of Logic*, trans. A.V. Miller (Atlantic Highlands, NJ: Humanities Press International, 1969), nos. 107–10. But instead of reconstructing the seemingly dialectical relation between the two types of immeasurable measures, I wish here to separate them, attributing them to two different regimes of discourse, ethics and the theory of morals, between which there are shifting connections in different historical periods but no logically necessary link.

143. Lévinas: "We name this calling into question of my spontaneity by the presence of the Other ethics" (*Totality and Infinity*, p. 43). In order to avoid misunderstandings, I wish to note again that what Lévinas calls "ethics" forms part of what I call a "theory of morals," and that what I call "ethics" here belongs to the philosophical tradition which for Lévinas is the antithesis of what he calls "ethics." In this tradition, against which Lévinas argues, being is thought in terms of self, subject, and totality, and otherness appears as a moment in the development of the self, in the acquisition of self-consciousness or of an understanding of the totality of being. There is no controversy here but rather a confusing lack of fit in terminology. Needless to say, the above definitions are not historical, even if a certain history echoes through them. They seek to utilize a certain semantic range, a certain possible use of each of the three terms, in order to

determine a difference that cuts through the entire length of the history of thinking, but not necessarily under the same terms.

144. This section includes a play on phonetic affinities at the expense of etymology. The word *musar* (morals, morality), whose root is *ysr*, is linked to a group of words deriving from the root *msr*: *moser* (gives, transmits), *mesira* (transmission), *masoret* (tradition), and *hitmasrut* (giving oneself, devoting or dedicating oneself). — TRANS.

145. Kant, *Critique of Practical Reason*, bk. 1, ch. 1, no. 7, p. 164.

146. *Ibid.*, no. 7, corollary, p. 165. Sittengesetz was rendered in Hebrew as "the law of measures [*midot*]." — TRANS.

147. There must certainly be an unbridgeable gap, a *differend*, between that which the self is to itself and the self formulated as a maxim of the will. But as long as what is at stake is just the maxim of a will free from a general law, it is possible to try to fit the rule's formulation to the selfhood that this rule is supposed to represent, without any need of explicitly identifying a moment of otherness as the opposite of the self in question. Such a moment is already embodied in language itself. "The relation between the same and the other ... is language ... the relation between the same and the other, metaphysics, is primordially enacted as conversation [*discours*], where the same, gathered up in its ipseity as an 'I,' as a particular existent unique and autochthonous, leaves itself " (Lévinas, *Totality and Infinity*, p. 39).

148. Kant, *Critique of Practical Reason*, bk. 1, ch. 1, no. 7, remark, p. 166.

149. *Ibid.*, p. 165.

150. Lévinas, *Totality and Infinity*, p. 84.

151. Kant, *Critique of Practical Reason*, bk. 1, ch. 3, p. 203.

152. Making a sacrifice, says Bataille, restores the sacrificial object from the world of things, which man can only know from outside and which is in fact sealed to him, to the intimate world, which he knows immanently (through eating, through erotic relations, through mystical relations). Making a sacrifice is only intended to remove the objectivity of the sacrifice, its status as a thing apart and possessed of real relations to other things, and through this removal the one making the sacrifice seeks to return, himself, to the intimate world or to the intimacy of an undifferentiated world. From the sacrificer's point of view, sacrifice is the elimination of something useful that overcomes the logic of utility which determines him, too, as a thing, while what is sacrificed is simply the useful thingness that must be eliminated from the thing before him (Bataille, *Theory of Religion*, pt. 1, ch. 3). In the realm of the sacred, the sacrifice is a waste devoid of use that cannot be intended for utilization by any real creature or for any real interest. In this view, the nonmaterial other to whom the sacrifice is offered as a gift ensures the uselessness of the sacrifice through its nonmateriality, even if making the sacrifice is represented as a religious duty (*mitzvah*) that will be rewarded. More precisely, a representation of the sacrifice as part of the exchange relations between God and the believers expecting reward for their sacrifice makes the sacrifice meaningless, as was well understood by the prophets of Israel who frequently criticized sacrificial rituals. And indeed, after the discontinuation of these rituals following the destruction of the Second Temple, Jewish law retained

only a single sacrifice as a *mitzvah* without reward: the self-sacrifice of life in an instance of the duty of sanctifying the Name. The Name commanding the duty to sanctify it is the ultimate principle of waste. Such a relatively rare case merely clarifies the difference between giving oneself to a concrete other, so as to alleviate his suffering, and giving oneself to an abstract other, so as to glorify his name.

153. Todorov proposes an interesting comparison between the values commanding sacrifice during the 1944 Polish rebellion against the Nazis in Warsaw and those guiding the Jewish rebels in the Warsaw Ghetto a year earlier. The first were guided by amoral and nonethical values, such as the honor of the homeland and national pride. The latter sought to give meaning and form to their deaths, to control, at the very least, the manner in which they would be put to death. The values guiding them were from the realm of ethics in the Foucauldian sense assigned to it here, of an aesthetics of existence. Neither uprising was guided by moral considerations, and in both cases the act of rebellion itself remained morally ambiguous (Todorov, *Facing the Extreme*, pp. 5–30; see also 9.114 below and *ibid.* n.28).

154. "You don't sacrifice life for a symbol." Thus, simply, Marek Edelman, deputy commander of the Warsaw Ghetto uprising in a conversation with Hanna Krall, referring to the suicide of Mordechai Anielewicz and his comrades. See Hanna Krall, *Shielding the Flame: An Intimate Conversation with Dr. Marek Edelman, the Last Surviving Leader of the Warsaw Ghetto Uprising*, trans. Joanna Stasinska and Lawrence Weschler (New York: Henry Holt and Co., Jewish Publication Society, 1986), p. 6.

155. Todorov, *Facing the Extreme*, pp. 71–90. Todorov also notes the opposite fact there: in extreme situations, the individual finds more internal strength when he is preoccupied with aiding another than when he is preoccupied with himself alone (pp. 98ff.).

156. Genesis 9.6. This is one of the commands to the sons of Noah defined as part of the covenant of the rainbow, immediately after the flood and shortly before the destruction of Sodom and Gomorrah, two particularly successful projects of mass destruction to which God sentenced humankind in his efforts to raise a better kind of man. In the same context, permission was also given to kill animals and eat both animals and plants, alongside the prohibition of eating the blood before the departure of the soul: "But flesh with life thereof, which is the blood thereof, shall ye not eat" (Genesis 9.4).

157. "Thou shalt not kill" (Exodus 20.13); "He that smiteth a man, so that he die, shall be surely put to death.... If a man come presumptuously upon his neighbour, to slay him with guile; thou shalt take him from mine altar, that he may die. And he that smiteth his father, or his mother, shall be surely put to death. And he that stealeth a man, and selleth him, or if he be found in his hand, he shall surely be put to death. And he that curseth his father or his mother, shall surely be put to death" (Exodus 21.12–17).

158. Derrida claims that throughout the entire tradition of Western philosophy up to and including Heidegger, the killing of animals is an unaccounted limit of "the subject." A challenge to this limit, according to Derrida, is part of what follows from a rethinking of the concept of the subject and is a necessary part of

the attempt to form other concepts that might take its place. See the conversation between Jacques Derrida and Jean-Luc Nancy, "Eating Well, or the Calculation of the Subject," in Eduardo Cadava, Peter Connor, and Jean-Luc Nancy (eds.), *Who Comes After the Subject?* (New York: Routledge, 1991), pp. 96–119.

159. See Tzvetan Todorov, *The Conquest of America: The Question of the Other*, trans. Richard Howard (New York: Harper and Row, 1984), ch. 3.

160. Primo Levi, *The Drowned and the Saved*, trans. Raymond Rosenthal (New York: Summit Books, 1988), ch. 5; see also 9.113 below.

161. I'm not dealing here with the question of assisting a person in full possession of his faculties in putting an end to his suffering. From the logic of my discussion up to this point, it will be clear that in extreme cases where the only way to put an end to suffering is death, and subject to the reservations necessitated by the shortsightedness of the one suffering and the one called on to assist, such assistance is a proper deed. Is a sufferer wishing to die doing the proper deed? This is essentially a question of ethics pertaining to the "beautiful death," to the individual's control over his death as a continuation or climax of his efforts to form his life himself.

162. Hannah Arendt, *The Origins of Totalitarianism*, 2nd ed. (New York: Meridian, 1958), pt. 3, p. 157.

163. "The danger of the corpse factories and the holes of oblivion is that today, with populations and homelessness everywhere on the increase, masses of people are continuously rendered superfluous if we continue to think of our world in utilitarian terms. Political, social, and economic events everywhere are in a silent conspiracy with totalitarian instruments devised for making men superfluous" (*ibid.*). Note Arendt's tacit distinction between a totalitarian regime and totalitarian instruments. The latter may serve other regimes, including democracies, and hence deconstruct the too-easy opposition between democracy and totalitarianism.

164. Here are a few scattered figures: between 1750 and 1970, eighty-five million people were killed in wars, of these over ten million in the First World War and thirty-eight million in the Second World War. In the First World War, 5 percent of those killed were civilians; in the Second World War, 48 percent of those killed were civilians; in the Korean War, civilians accounted for 84 percent of those killed. See Jean Berthier, "Penser Hiroshima," *Lignes*, no. 26 (Oct. 1995), pp. 34–47. And see 9.050 below, including n.18.

Chapter Nine: These Times

1. In the Hebrew of observant Jews, both "the Name" (*hashem*) and "the Place" (*hamakom*) are used to refer to God, while "the name of the place" (*shem hamokom*) is used to refer to God's name, emphasizing that merely uttering the sacred name is taboo. Associated with this almost automatically, and equally taboo, is seeing God ("Thou canst not see my face: for there shall no man see me, and live" [Exodus 33.20]). The combined import of these allusions resonates throughout the following sections, where Ophir discusses the use of "the name of the place" (in the literal rather than the religious sense) to refer to the inscrutable aspect, and denote the inscrutability, of man-made catastrophes, and particularly those elements that "no man see[s] and live[s]." — Trans.

2. All the quotations in this section are from sections of Jean-François Lyotard's *Differend: Phrases in Dispute*, trans. Georges Van Den Abbeele (Minneapolis: University of Minnesota Press, 1988), from the chapter "The Referent: The Name." According to the order of their appearance in the text, they are quoted from pages 50, 53, 57–58. Here, as throughout the book, I am using the term "statement" where Lyotard uses "phrase."

3. This is equally true for names such as "Othello," "Hamlet," and "Venus" when they are perceived to represent some textual reality, a segment of discourse that once took place or is still going on at present, rather than denoting figures in some insular fictional world in which all has already been said, because the text has been sealed and the play has ended.

4. Robert Antelme, *The Human Race*, trans. Jeffrey Haight and Annie Mahler (Marlboro, VT: Marlboro Press, 1992).

5. Primo Levi, *The Drowned and the Saved*, trans. Raymond Rosenthal (New York: Summit Books, 1988), p. 116. Similar things can be said about Jean Améry; see Jean Améry, *At the Mind's Limits: Contemplations by a Survivor on Auschwitz and its Realities*, trans. Sidney Rosenfeld and Stella P. Rosenfeld (Bloomington: Indiana University Press, 1980).

6. Levi, *The Drowned and the Saved*, pp. 17 and 40–41.

7. Hayden White raises a similar question, to which he gives a carefully argued negative answer. Hayden White, "Historical Emplotment and the Problem of Truth," in Saul Friedlander (ed.), *Probing the Limits of Representation: Nazism and the Final Solution* (Cambridge, MA: Harvard University Press, 1992), pp. 37–53. See also Yehuda Bauer, *The Holocaust in Historical Perspective* (Seattle: University of Washington Press, 1978), pp. 30–50; and Steven Katz's discussion of the Holocaust as a historical phenomenon, *The Holocaust in Historical Context* (Oxford: Oxford University Press, 1994), vol. 1, ch. 1.

8. Levi, *The Drowned and the Saved*, ch. 2. As stated, this is an exemplary instance, which is nevertheless only an example. Within the scope of the present work, I cannot go into a real discussion of the literature of catastrophe. See n.10 below.

9. Jean Berthier, "Penser Hiroshima," *Lignes*, no. 26 (Oct. 1995), pp. 34–47.

10. The question of representation of the Holocaust in literature and in historical studies has recently preoccupied many researchers. The following is a limited and nonrepresentative selection of instances: Friedlander, ed., *Probing the Limits of Representation*; Lawrence L. Langer, *Holocaust Testimonies: The Ruins of Memory* (New Haven, CT: Yale University Press, 1991); Lawrence L. Langer, *Admitting the Holocaust* (Oxford: Oxford University Press, 1995); Sidra deKoven Ezrahi, *By Words Alone: The Holocaust in Literature* (Chicago: University of Chicago Press, 1980); Dominick LaCapra, *Representing the Holocaust* (Ithaca, NY: Cornell University Press, 1994); Omer Bartov, *Murder in Our Midst: The Holocaust, Industrial Killing, and Representation* (New York: Oxford University Press, 1996). Ezrahi distinguishes between two orientations in the literary representation of the Holocaust — the perception of Auschwitz as a "black hole," emphasizing the "unrepresentable," and the attempt to circumvent this problematic through the description of "more human" alternative sites on the memory map

(Sidra deKoven Ezrahi, "Representing Auschwitz," *History & Memory* 7, no. 2 [1996], pp. 121–54). From our point of view, it is impossible to make do with the alternative sites. It is imperative to see them as a transit station on the way to Auschwitz, in an attempt to en-tongue that place.

11. Ophir writes "hashem hameforash," literally, "the explicit name," a term usually referring to the name of God, *yhva*, which Jews are forbidden to utter or write. — TRANS.

12. The most explicit systematic expression of this conception in Jewish thinking was formulated by Fackenheim. See, for instance, Emil Fackenheim, *To Mend the World: Foundations of Future Jewish Thought* (New York: Schocken Books, 1982). For a similar attempt in Protestant theology, striving to give Auschwitz the status of a quasi revelation, see Alice L. Eckardt and A. Roy Eckardt, *Long Night's Journey into Day: A Revised Retrospective on the Holocaust* (Detroit: Wayne State University Press, 1988). For additional voices in Jewish thinking seeking a dimension of sanctity among the ruins, even if only by a process of elimination, see, for instance, Richard Rubenstein, *After Auschwitz: Radical Theology and Contemporary Judaism* (Indianapolis: Indiana University Press, 1966); Elie Wiesel, "A Plea for the Dead," in *Legends of Our Time* (New York: Holt, Rinehart, and Winston, 1968), pp. 134–97; Arthur A. Cohen, *The Tremendum: A Theological Interpretation of the Holocaust* (New York: Crossroad, 1981).

13. See 9.143–9.144. For more on the place of the quasi-religious dimension of the "Holocaust culture" in Israeli society, see Charles Liebman and Eliezer Don-Yehiya, *Civil Religion in Israel: Traditional Judaism and Political Culture in the Jewish State* (Berkeley: University of California Press, 1983), pp. 100–107 and 137–53; Adi Ophir, "On Sanctifying the Holocaust: An Anti-theological Treatise," *Tikkun* 2, no. 1 (1987), pp. 61–67; Adi Ophir, "On Inexpressible Feelings and Indubitable Lessons," in *Working for the Present* (Tel Aviv: Hakibbutz Hameuchad, 2001), pp. 22–28 [in Hebrew].

14. For a detailed description of the shaping process of the architectural and functional identity of the camp, see Robert-Jan Van Pelt, "A Site in Search of a Mission," in Israel Gutman and Michael Berenbaum (eds.), *Anatomy of the Auschwitz Death Camp* (Bloomington: Indiana University Press in association with the U.S. Holocaust Memorial Museum, 1994), pp. 93–156.

15. Tom Segev describes major segments of it in *The Seventh Million: The Israelis and the Holocaust*, trans. Haim Watzman (New York: Hill and Wang, 1993). Idith Zertal elaborates especially on instrumentalization of the Holocaust in the Eichmann trial and on the verge of the Six-Day War (Idith Zertal, "From the People's Hall to the Wailing Wall: A Study in Memory, Fear, and War," *Representations* [Winter 2000]). Moshe Zuckermann discusses the instrumentalization of the Holocaust in Israeli culture and analyzes one of its chapters at length — the Gulf War period — in his *Shoah in the Sealed Room: The "Holocaust" in the Israeli Press During the Gulf War* (Tel Aviv: M. Zuckermann, 1993) [in Hebrew].

16. Yehuda Elkana, "A Plea to Forget," *Haaretz*, March 2, 1988 [in Hebrew].

17. Criticism of the theological role played by Auschwitz in Jewish culture is no longer a rarity among Jews both in and outside Israel. See, for instance, Jacob

Neusner, *Stranger at Home: The Holocaust, Zionism, and American Judaism* (Chicago: University of Chicago Press, 1981); Yehuda Bauer, "The Significance of the Final Solution," in David Cesarani (ed.), *The Final Solution: Origins and Implementation* (New York: Routledge, 1994). See also my works cited in n.13 above.

18. In terms of dimensions, the most enormous catastrophe occurred as a result of the meeting between the Spanish conquerors and the indigenous communities on the American continent. At the end of the fifteenth century, 112 million indigenous people lived in America. Only some 4 to 5 million were left there at the end of the sixteenth century. But even if one accepts the view shared by many scholars that most of this population drop was caused by the unprecedented spread of epidemics due to exposure to the Europeans, millions were nevertheless directly put to death by the conquerors, and millions more died preventable deaths. See David E. Stannard, *American Holocaust: Columbus and the Conquest of the New World* (New York: Oxford University Press, 1992); Steven T. Katz, *The Holocaust in Historical Context* (Oxford: Oxford University Press, 1994).

19. Rudolph J. Rummel, *Lethal Politics: Soviet Genocide and Mass Murder Since 1917* (New Brunswick, NJ: Transaction Publishers, 1990); *China's Bloody Century: Genocide and Mass Murder Since 1900* (New Brunswick, NJ: Transaction Publishers, 1991); *Democide: Nazi Genocide and Mass Murder* (New Brunswick, NJ: Transaction Publishers, 1992). All these data are naturally debated, and some of them are denied by various regimes (the most prominent case is the Turks' denial of the Armenian genocide). I don't know how the dead are counted, and I am willing to assume, for the sake of argument, that Rummel exaggerated considerably. Instead of 140 million victims of murder, let the number be 100 million. Well? Does that alter the inconceivability of these figures? There is also considerable controversy about the level of direct government responsibility for the mass deaths, chiefly with regard to the USSR under Stalin. But even if the mass starvation in the collectivization period was not an intentional policy of extermination, it is completely clear that there was also no policy — or any attempt at all in fact — to save the millions of starving farmers from dying of hunger. Unlike the epidemics that ravaged the indigenous peoples of the Americas in the sixteenth century, most of the catastrophes that caused mass dying in the twentieth century were preventable, or at least greatly reducible. On the development of industrialized killing in the twentieth century, see also Bartov, *Murder in Our Midst*; Richard Rubenstein, "Modernization and the Politics of Extermination," in Michael Berenbaum (ed.), *A Mosaic of Victims* (New York: New York University Press, 1990).

20. Lyotard is reading Adorno's famous text on Auschwitz here ("After Auschwitz") and stressing that this text appears in the third part of the *Negative Dialectics*, titled "Models" (Lyotard, *Differend*, nos. 152–54); Theodor W. Adorno, *Negative Dialectics*, trans. E.B. Ashton (New York: Continuum, 1973).

21. Lyotard, *Differend*, no. 93; Adi Ophir, "Shifting the Ground of the Moral Domain: Reading Lyotard's *Differend*," *Constellations* 4, no. 2 (Oct. 1997), pp. 189–204.

22. Compare Zygmunt Bauman, "Sealing Off the Victims," in *Modernity and the Holocaust* (Ithaca, NY: Cornell University Press, 1989), pp. 122ff.

23. The expression was coined by Goebbels. The Germans definitely perceived the ghetto as an apparatus of extermination only after the final-solution policy had been formulated. See, for instance, "Ghetto," in *Encyclopedia of the Holocaust*, Israel Gutman (editor in chief), Geoffrey Wigoder (editor of the English ed.) (New York: Macmillan, 1990), vol. 2, pp. 579–82. The Lodz ghetto was hermetically sealed as early as May 1940. We know that Chaim M. Romkovsky, "king of the ghetto," sought to use the ghetto's "productivity" as a guarantee against physical extermination. He thought he could trade in the Jewish work force, provide efficient labor, and attain decent living conditions and security. But the Jews were barred from all circuits of exchange. The Germans exploited the energy of the labor force to the last drop, provided living conditions that were insufficient for the reproduction of this force from one day to the next, and turned the very gap between the labor force and the living conditions into an exterminating apparatus — hunger weakened people, keeping them away from work, without which they could not afford to buy the food rations provided by the Germans at a trickle; hunger weakened them still more, eroding social ties along with emotional and mental stamina, until it killed. On loss and suffering in the ghetto, see, for instance, Leni Yahil, *The Holocaust: The Fate of European Jewry, 1932–1945*, trans. Ina Friedman and Haya Galai (New York: Oxford University Press, 1991), pp. 210–14.

24. I have not found any presentation of, or attempt to answer, this question in the research literature, which deals mainly with the reconstruction of several famous cases involving the Jews of Slovakia and Hungary. See, for instance, Haim Barlas, *Rescue in Days of Holocaust(?)* (Lochamei Hagettaot: Lochamei Hagettaot and Hakibbutz Hameuchad, 1975), ch. 8 [in Hebrew]; Bauer, *The Holocaust in Historical Perspective*, ch. 4; Randolph L. Braham, "The Rescue of the Jews of Hungary in Historical Perspective," in *The Historiography of the Holocaust Period: Proceedings of the Fifth Yad Vashem International Historical Conference, Jerusalem, March 1983* (Jerusalem: Yad Vashem, 1988), pp. 447–66. Of course, there were cases — the number of which is inaccessible — in which various SS personnel, Nazi guards, policemen, and clerks extended some aid in return for bribes, but I know of no place in which a trade in escape routes was developed and institutionalized beyond the isolated, local instance. Most of the other cases of flight from the sealed Jewish zone resulted from collaboration with various forces opposing the regime, from the Church through partisan groups, and not from direct negotiations with the Nazis. It should be kept in mind that Jewish organizations usually adopted policies opposing solutions of individual escape, which were perceived as an abandonment of the community.

25. See, for instance, Zygmunt Bauman, *Modernity and the Holocaust*, ch. 5; Tzvetan Todorov, "Caring," in *Facing the Extreme*, trans. Arthur Denner and Abigail Pollak (New York: Metropolitan Books, 1996), pp. 71–90, and the wide array of testimonies quoted there.

26. This is the fundamental logic of the camp, described by Foucault as regards the early practices of military camps in the seventeenth century (Foucault, *Discipline and Punish: The Birth of Prison*, trans. Alan Sheridan [New York: Pantheon, 1977], pp. 135–41). The first concentration camps were erected by

the Spanish government in order to incarcerate the indigenous population during the rebellion in Cuba in 1895, and by the British in the course of the Boer
War in South Africa (1899–1902) in order to incarcerate citizens residing in the
republic of Transvaal and the Cape Colony. The model was soon replicated in
other countries, first by the Communists in the Union of Soviet Socialist Repub-
lics and later by Hitler in the European territories occupied by Germany. The
Americans, too, as is well known, had their own camps, in which they incarcer-
ated Japanese citizens during the Second World War.

27. This was the cruelty referred to by Primo Levi when he spoke of "useless violence" and attempted to distinguish between the violence necessary for
the proper functioning of the *Lager* and the violence that it creates as a kind of
"surplus value": "One is truly led to think that, in the Third Reich, the best
choice, the choice imposed from above, was the one that entailed the greatest
affliction, the *greatest waste*, the greatest physical and moral suffering" (*The
Drowned and the Saved*, p. 120; my emphasis).

28. The manifestations of resistance involved in maintaining this autonomy
and the heroism involved in such resistance made no difference at all when the
Nazis decided on the final eradication of the ghetto. When the Nazis wished to
do so, they turned the apparatuses of Jewish self-management into apparatuses
operating toward Jewish annihilation. The rare cases in which the Nazis were
called on to exert added force in order to exterminate the manifestations of
Jewish autonomy and together with the remaining Jews — of which the most
well known was the Warsaw Ghetto uprising — merely reveal the fundamental
fact of mutual relations between the bodies of Jewish self-management and the
organs of the Nazi regime. Among other things, the uprising was a relinquishment of the space that remained for self-rule of the ghetto subject to the Nazi
regime. More than anything else, it was a struggle to determine the form of
death. The rebels sought to wrest from the hands of the Nazis their right to
choose the form of their deaths; they sought a "good death" for themselves. In
the ghetto conditions, then, the decision to rebel fell into the realm of ethics,
not that of morality. (See 8.521–8.522 and *ibid.*, n.153.)

29. The uniqueness of Primo Levi's *If This Is a Man*, its invincible optimism,
lies, among other things, in its descriptions of the small pockets of solidarity and
exchange channels existing, despite all else, in the inferno (*If This Is a Man*,
trans. Stuart Woolf [London: Orion Press, 1959]). In *The Drowned and the Saved*,
written many years later, with incomparable lucidity and clear-sightedness, Levi
situates these pockets of solidarity on a continuum of thefts from dear ones and
distant ones, betrayals of near and distant ones, and collaboration: "Preferably
the worst survived, the selfish, the violent, the insensitive, the collaborators of
the 'gray zone,' the spies" (p. 82).

30. An exemplary instance of this matter is provided, again, by Levi, in the
description of his attempt to teach his friend "Piccolo" segments of Dante's
Inferno en route to fetching the daily pot of soup (Levi, *If This Is a Man*, pp.
127–34). And also Victor E. Frankl, *Man's Search for Meaning: An Introduction to
Logotherapy*, trans. Ilse Lasch (Boston: Beacon Press, 1962).

31. Browning and Bauer argue convincingly that this was a real option until

the summer of 1941, and that the Allied forces, which prevented Jews' entry into their territories and failed to come to their aid in any other way, bear responsibility for the fact that the Nazis finally chose extermination over deportation as a final solution to the question of the Jews. See Bauer, *The Holocaust in Historical Perspective*, p. 139; Christopher R. Browning, *Fateful Months: Essays on the Emergence of the Final Solution, 1941–1942* (New York: Holmes and Meier, 1985).

32. See, for instance, Bauer, *The Holocaust in Historical Perspective*, pp. 135ff.; Christopher R. Browning, *The Path to Genocide: Essays on Launching the Final Solution* (Cambridge, UK: Cambridge University Press, 1992), ch. 5.

33. For instance, Lucy S. Dawidowicz, *The War Against the Jews, 1933–1945* (Harmondsworth, UK: Penguin, 1987), ch. 6.

34. These conditions also included the conduct of local governments and of the civilian public at large in the German-occupied countries and the Axis-pact countries. These places had considerable freedom of action, the limits of which went virtually unmonitored. In some, it allowed a resistance sufficient for postponing the Jews' annihilation, or reducing its scope, for sabotaging the extermination apparatus, or even — in Bulgaria and on one small Greek island, Zakynthos — for preventing it altogether.

35. See, for instance, Browning, *Path to Genocide*, ch. 8.

36. Yehuda Bauer, "The Implications of Holocaust Study for Our Historical Consciousness," lecture to the Group for Study of the Jewish Nation in the Diaspora at the President's House (Hebrew University, Jerusalem: Institute for Contemporary Judaism, Shprintzak Section, 1972), p. 13.

37. *Ibid.*

38. Two exceptions on this matter are prominent among Israeli historians: Omer Bartov and recently Boaz Neumann. See, for instance, Omer Bartov, *Hitler's Army: Soldiers, Nazis, and War in the Third Reich* (New York: Oxford University Press, 1991); Bartov, *Murder in Our Midst*; Boaz Neumann, "How People Died in Auschwitz? Death in Auschwitz as an 'Ugly Death'" (master's thesis, Tel Aviv University, 1997) [in Hebrew]; Boaz Neumann, *The Nazi Weltanschauung: Space, Body, Language* (Haifa and Tel Aviv: Haifa University Press and Ma'ariv Library, 2002) [in Hebrew].

39. On this issue, see, for example, Shoshana Felman, "The Return of the Voice: Claude Lanzmann's *Shoah*," in Shoshana Felman and Dori Laub, *Testimony: Crises of Witnessing in Literature, Psychoanalysis, and History* (New York: Routledge, 1992), pp. 204–32; Lyotard, *Differend*, esp. nos. 1–28 and 88–93.

40. The internal logic of the final-solution plan necessitated the annihilation of all the witnesses, including those who escaped from Nazi-occupied territories. If the Nazis had won the war in Europe and the victory had led to a new status quo, it is reasonable to assume that the Nazis would have continued to persecute Jews even outside the areas under their rule. Steps toward the expulsion of Jews and a tolerance toward Jews' escape were characteristic of the period before formulation of the final solution. The willingness of Nazis such as Himmler to use Jews as hostages for exchange in the course of negotiations with the Allies, near the end of the war, signified an acceptance of imminent defeat and a recognition that the final solution would not attain finality.

41. I am indebted here to Derrida's analysis of spectrality. See, for example, *Specters of Marx*, trans. Peggy Kamuf (New York: Routledge, 1994), esp. ch. 2.

42. A formulation of the first view may be found, for instance, in Martin Heidegger, *Schelling's Treatise on the Essence of Human Freedom*, trans. Joan Stambaugh (Athens: Ohio University Press, 1985). The second formulation relates to Heidegger's self-criticism for his metaphysical naïveté from 1929 to 1934, as expressed in his rector address and in other texts from that period. The late Heidegger criticizes any attempt to distinguish between spirituality and material power, claiming that destruction and violence are spiritual events preceding language and moral responsibility and that they are not external to the spirit.

43. According to the reading suggested by Derrida, Heidegger in his rector address both supports Nazism and proposes its vindication through a metaphysical gesture, while he later regrets not his support for Nazism per se or for the Nazis as a historical catastrophe, but mainly his metaphysical slip, which he viewed as preventing him from understanding Nazism to be a failed metaphysical expression of spirituality. In Derrida's view, this reservation of Heidegger's is also stuck in an anthropocentric position that nevertheless employs the — still metaphysical — concept of spirituality in order to distinguish between the human and the bestial (which may be eaten) and between the spiritual and the non-spiritual (which may be exterminated or, at the very least, relinquished). See Jacques Derrida, *Of Spirit: Heidegger and the Question*, trans. Geoffrey Bennington and Rachel Bowlby (Chicago: University of Chicago Press, 1989); and see the interpretation of Michal Ben-Naftali, "On Different Mobilizations 'Of Spirit': Derrida on Heidegger's Politics," *Iyyun: The Jerusalem Philosophical Quarterly* 44 (Oct. 1995), pp. 371–98 [in Hebrew].

44. This is the loss of the "beautiful death" discussed by Adorno (in *Negative Dialectics*, in the chapter "After Auschwitz") and others who followed him (Lyotard, *Differend*, nos. 153–57; see n.20 above). But the "beautiful death" is just one facet of the total loss involved in the industry of death in Auschwitz.

45. Itzhak Katzenelson, *The Song of the Murdered Jewish People*, trans. and annotated by Noah H. Rosenbloom (Beit Lohamei Hagettaot: Hakibbutz Hameuchad, 1980).

46. See, for instance, Martin Gilbert's estimate: between September 1939 and May 1945, slightly over 5.75 million Jews were murdered, not including thousands of infants who were exterminated in the autumn of 1941, before their births could be registered, as well as thousands of unregistered inhabitants of distant villages who were added to the deportation trains leaving the larger communities (*A History of the Holocaust* [London: HarperCollinsIllustrated in association with the Imperial War Museum, 2000]). For additional estimates based on fairly precise, up-to-date research (including Nazi lists) and reaching similar figures, see *Encyclopedia of the Holocaust*, vol. 4, Statistical Appendix; Wolfgang Benz, ed., *Dimension des Völkermords* (Munich: Oldenbourg, 1991).

47. The right-wing cultural critic Gerhard Hoffmann, known by his pseudonym, Ernest Mann, expressed the main substance of this view as early as 1922: "Suffering can be removed only through the painless extermination of the sufferer" (Ernest Mann, *Die Erlösung der Menschheit von Elend* [Weimar: F. Fink,

1922], p. 3). Eugenic views of society prevalent among the Nazis and their fore-runners, like the medicalization of politics under the Nazi regime (in *Mein Kampf*, Hitler already spoke of "the most modern of medical means" for putting to death for the sake of purifying the race), rendered the idea acceptable in broad circles. Hannah Arendt relates an episode that seems to me to provide sufficient evidence: "'The Russians will never get us,' says a woman in a town already besieged by the Red Army, and no one protests: The Führer will never permit it. Much sooner he will gas us" (*Eichmann in Jerusalem: A Report on the Banality of Evil* [New York: Viking Press, 1963], p. 111). The concept of "med-ical killing" as cleaner and more respectable was also widely accepted regard-ing the annihilation of the Jews (Dawidowicz, *War Against the Jews*, p. 136). Researchers unanimously agree that the technique of gassing was duplicated and improved on from the experience accumulated in the period of "mercy killings" of mentally retarded and mentally ill people. On these, see, for instance, Robert Jay Lifton, *The Nazi Doctors: Medical Killing and the Psychology of Genocide* (New York: Basic Books, 1986), also the source of the above quotation from Ernest Mann (p. 44). The fact that in practice the Nazi killing machine was immeasur-ably "dirty" and cruel, and that this cruelty was characteristic of all the units that "handled" Jews, does not contradict the effort in certain circles to fit a "humane" face to the annihilation. On the contrary, it may be that the "humane killing" discourse succeeded in diverting the attention of those who might have been shocked had they known the full details of the reality and practices of the killing. On the fundamental political aspect of developing techniques for "ratio-nal" killing and on the political-medical discourse in which they were rooted in Germany during the Weimar Republic and later in the Nazi regime, see Giorgio Agamben, *Homo Sacer: Sovereign Power and Bare Life*, trans. Daniel Heller-Roazen (Stanford, CA: Stanford University Press, 1998), pt. 3, chs. 3–5.

48. This statement is a paraphrase of a famous saying from the Passover rit-ual that commemorates Jewish liberation from slavery under the pharaohs of Egypt: "In every generation, each individual is bound to regard himself as if he personally had gone forth from Egypt." — TRANS.

49. I have elaborated on this issue at length in two essays mentioned above: "On Sanctifying the Holocaust" and "On Inexpressible Feelings."

50. See n.13 above. See also Don Handelman's discussion of the space of state ritual, *Models and Mirrors: Towards an Anthropology of Public Events* (Cam-bridge, UK: Cambridge University Press, 1990), ch. 9.

51. In the United States (and recently in Canada, too), the Jewish commu-nity has enlisted state mechanisms and various public authorities in the remem-brance project. However, the difference between the Jewish-American and the Jewish-Israeli case is crucial: in America, the authorities respond to initiatives and demands coming out of the Jewish sector of civil society; in Israel, the authorities monopolize the remembrance project, while grassroots initiatives growing out of various sectors of Jewish civil society — and recently out of the Palestinian-Israeli public as well — are forced to adapt to the already-institution-alized system of commemoration patterns and remembrance practices, blazing their independent trails through these with extreme difficulty.

52. Of course, the justificational relation preceded the causal one; it appeared in Zionist discourse on the eve of the state's foundation and was canonized in the Israeli Declaration of Independence. The perception of a causal relation developed gradually in public discourse, also receiving various manifestations in the historiographical discourse. Over time, however, both relations merged inseparably in Israeli public discourse. On the development of the perception of a causal relation between the Holocaust and the establishment of the Jewish state in the study of the Holocaust and the public discourse surrounding it, see Dan Michman, "From Shoah to Revival," *Iyunim Bitkumat Israel: Studies in Zionism, the Yishuv, and the State of Israel* 10 (2000), pp. 234–58 [in Hebrew].

53. The most prominent example of this in the Israeli cultural context is possibly the group of actors, Jews and Arabs, led by David Maayan, that staged the play *Arbeit macht frei* in Acre in the early 1990s. For an analysis of the play that emphasizes this aspect, see Freddy Rokem, "*Arbeit macht frei*," *Theoria ve-Bikoret* 12–13 (1998), pp. 389–400 [in Hebrew]. Other instances are the performance of the artist Ori Dromer and his rock group Duralex Sadlex at the Auschwitz death camp toward the end of the 1980s, or the Holocaust Memorial Day ceremony held at the Kedma School in the Tel Aviv Hatikva quarter, initiated, written, and to a large extent "staged" by the school principal, Sammi Shalom Chitrit (see Tamar Barkai and Gal Levi, "The Kedma School," *Theoria ve-Bikoret* 12–13 [1998], pp. 440–43 [in Hebrew]). I have focused on this issue at length in my article "The Finitude of the Solution and the Infinity of the Loss," in Dan Michman (ed.), *The Holocaust in Jewish History* (Jerusalem: Yad Vashem, forthcoming). Several excerpts from this article are included verbatim in the present discussion. An earlier, English version appeared in Laurence Silberstein (ed.), *Mapping Jewish Identities* (New York: New York University Press, 2000), pp. 174–200.

54. The most blatant and distinctive instance of such a confrontation is the debate over the Jewish orthodox representation of the Holocaust and the Jewish secular representation of Jewish orthodoxy in the Holocaust. See, for example, Dan Michman, "The Influence of the Holocaust on Religious Jewry," in Israel Gutman (ed.), *Major Changes Within the Jewish People in the Wake of the Holocaust* (Jerusalem: Yad Vashem, 1996), pp. 613–56; Kimi Kaplan, "Were Many Lies Accumulated in the History Books?" *Yad-Vashem: A Collection of Studies* 29 (2001), pp. 249–92 [in Hebrew]; Amos Goldberg, "The Holocaust in Orthodox Newspapers: Between Memory and Repression," *Contemporary Judaism* 11–12 (1998), pp. 155–206.

55. Here are a few prominent examples that do not come close to exhausting a vast, heterogeneous literary field: Jürgen Habermas, *The New Conservatism: Cultural Criticism and the Historians' Debate*, ed. and trans. Shierry Weber Nicholsen (Cambridge, MA: MIT Press, 1989); Lyotard, *Differend* and *Heidegger and "the Jews"*, trans. Andreas Michel and Mark S. Roberts (Minneapolis: University of Minnesota Press, 1990); Jean-Luc Nancy and Philippe Lacoue-Labarthe, *Le Mythe nazi* (La Tour: L'Aube, 1991).

56. Yehuda Elkana was, as far as I know, the only thinker who explicitly exhorted forgetting, in a short article he published during the first Palestinian

uprising (intifada), in the course of the Demjanjuk trial ("A Plea to Forget"), and in response to these two events. However, discernible even in Elkana's provocative piece is not just a call to forget but also a discussion of the character of memory. Elkana challenges the wisdom of trying to turn every Israeli Jew into a witness who is unable to view the present without an overlay of the Auschwitz perspective. But he doesn't totally reject the need for testimony itself.

57. Lyotard, *Differend*, no. 93; see also *Heidegger and "the Jews,"* ch. 8.

58. This is the logic on which Benjamin's antihistorical memory work is based in "Theses on the Philosophy of History," in Walter Benjamin, *Illuminations*, ed. Hannah Arendt, trans. Harry Zohn (London: Cape, 1970), pp. 255–66. It sometimes seems that Lyotard is simply applying Benjamin's pan-historical labor of mourning to the individual case of the annihilation of the Jews, of which Benjamin himself was a victim.

59. Lyotard, *Differend*, nos. 81, 92, 93.

60. Thus the whole historical singularity of Jewish existence is erased as well when the term "the Jews" is presented in Western culture as a synonym for erasure of the loss, for denial of what cannot be represented (Lyotard, *Heidegger and "the Jews,"* chs. 1–14). And see a similar complaint from the Boyarin brothers, who criticize Lyotard's allegorization of the Jew: Daniel Boyarin and Jonathan Boyarin, "Diaspora: Generation and the Ground of Jewish Identity," *Critical Inquiry* 19, no. 4 (1993), pp. 693–725. I believe the Boyarin brothers to be mistaken on one marginal point: at issue here is not an allegory but a metonym, for the Jew remains part of what he symbolizes, just as Auschwitz remains part of the reality for which it serves as a distinct model.

61. "He who forgets the past is doomed to repeat it" goes a familiar slogan of those who oppose the extreme right in Europe, referring, among other things, to the attempts to deny and forget the annihilation of the Jews. Like any well-known aphorism concerning repetition in history, this one has nothing to support it, and if it testifies to anything, it is not to the predictable progress of history but rather to the speaker's position in the struggle over memory.

62. "Auschwitz" here expressly as a metonymic signifier of the annihilation of Jews in Europe. For an exhaustive survey of the extensive research and polemic dealing with the singularity of this annihilation, see Katz, *The Holocaust in Historical Context*, vol. 1, ch. 1, esp. pp. 27–30. See also Alan S. Rosenbaum, ed., *Is the Holocaust Unique? Perspectives on Comparative Genocide* (Boulder, CO: Westview Press, 1996). The singularity I shall discuss will concern not just the characteristics of Auschwitz as a historical phenomenon but also its characteristics as a moral phenomenon (see 9.220).

63. As stated, about 100 million Native Americans perished in the course of the sixteenth century due to massacres and, mainly, epidemics caused by the encounter with the Spanish conquerors. According to conservative estimates, the Turks massacred at least one million Armenians in the course of the First World War, about 40 percent of the Armenian community at the time, a percentage similar to that of the Jews annihilated during the Second World War. For estimates of the Indian casualties and of (the distinctly different case of) the Armenian casualties, see nn.18 and 19 above.

64. In her singular style, Toni Morrison gives lucid expression to this dilemma, most directly in her book *Beloved* (New York: New American Library, 1987), which deals with the ghosts of the African-American past and expresses the inability to choose between the labor of mourning and resignation to the finitude of the catastrophe that black slavery was, on the one hand, and resignation to this catastrophe through severing the bonds of memory, on the other.

65. How long will the Palestinians continue to be slaves to the memory of their catastrophe of 1948? And the peoples of the states of the former Yugoslavia, to the memory of their catastrophe in the 1990s? And we, the Jews, who, besides Auschwitz, still drag with us two thousand years of destruction and persecution? The same question acquires a totally different meaning depending on whether it is voiced by the victors and bystanders or by the vanquished.

66. Bauer, *The Holocaust in Historical Perspective*, ch. 2; Katz, *The Holocaust in Historical Context*, vol. 1, p. 131; and also 9.220 below. It seems to me that following the events in the spring of 1994 in Rwanda, a second case can be added, even according to their reductive definition. See, for instance, Gérard Prunier, *The Rwanda Crisis, 1959–1994: History of a Genocide* (London: Hurst and Co., 1995); Alain Destexhe, *Rwanda and Genocide in the Twentieth Century*, trans. Alison Marschner (London: Pluto Press, 1995); Philip Gourevitch, *We Wish to Inform You That Tomorrow We Will Be Killed with Our Families* (New York: Farrar, Straus and Giroux, 1998).

67. Katz, *The Holocaust in Historical Context*, vol. 1, pp. 31–35.

68. Hannah Arendt, *The Origins of Totalitarianism*, 2nd ed. (New York: Meridian, 1958), pt. 3, and *Eichmann in Jerusalem*; Foucault, *Discipline and Punish*, and *The History of Sexuality*, vol. 1, *The Will to Knowledge*, trans. Robert Hurley (London: Penguin, 1990); Bauman, *Modernity and the Holocaust*; Alain Brossat, *L'Epreuve du désastre: Le XXe Siècle et les camps* (Paris: Albin Michel, 1996); Bartov, *Murder in Our Midst*. See also Rubenstein, "Modernization and the Politics of Extermination."

69. Giorgio Agamben develops this theme in a thoughtful way in his *Remnants of Auschwitz*, trans. Daniel Heller-Roazen (New York: Zone Books, 1999). I came to read Agamben's trilogy *Homo Sacer* (of which *Remnants* is the last part) only after completing my book. Regrettably, I can neither give it its proper due nor come to terms and argue with some of its claims.

70. My saying that it is the "first time" is a historical claim open to refutation. There may have been similar instances of which I am unaware. My Jewish-Western bias in this discussion is self-evident. I hope to balance it as far as possible at the end of the work.

71. Here, I'm adopting the gist of the conclusions of critics who have rejected the claims of the German historians Heim and Aly, according to which the final solution can be explained on grounds of economic motives. These claims were based, first and foremost, on an economic conception viewing adjustment of the size and makeup of the population to the productive power as a supreme planning objective. See Susanne Heim and Götz Aly, "The Holocaust and Population Policy: Remarks on the Decision on the 'Final Solution,'" in Aharon Weiss (ed.), *Yad Vashem Studies 24* (Jerusalem: Yad Vashem, 1994), pp.

45–70; Dan Diner, "Rationalization and Method: Critique of a New Approach in Understanding the 'Final Solution,'" *ibid.*, pp. 71–108; David Bankier, "On Modernization and the Rationality of Extermination," *ibid.*, pp. 109–30; Browning, *Path to Genocide*, ch. 3. The claim presented here echoes Browning's closing sentence: "Where they [Heim and Aly] see economic calculation as the prime mover of the Final Solution, I see the Final Solution as a policy carried out in spite of its economic irrationality" (p. 76).

72. I'm not seeking to take a position in the controversy regarding the degree of similarity between the annihilation of the Gypsies and the annihilation of the Jews, or on the question of whether the Nazis intended to exterminate the Gypsies as a nation, that is, to exterminate all the Gypsies in Europe. Even if one accepts the positions of historians such as Katz and Bauer on this issue (Katz, *The Holocaust in Historical Context*, vol. 1, p. 24; Bauer, *The Holocaust in Historical Perspective*, ch. 2), I don't see how this reservation makes any difference from a moral point of view, or what the difference is between the Evil suffered by Jews and the Evil suffered by part of the Gypsy community. The difference between the two groups has more to do with the justifying ideology and less with the practicalities of the extermination and makes no difference to an understanding of the essence of the Evil involved. On the annihilation of the Gypsies, see, for instance, Donald Kenrick and Grattan Puxon, *The Destiny of Europe's Gypsies* (New York: Basic Books, 1972); Ian Hancock, "Responses to the Porrajmos: The Romani Holocaust," in Rosenbaum (ed.), *Is the Holocaust Unique?*

73. The main effort to exterminate the Jews of Poland, which occurred between the spring of 1942 and the spring of 1943, was largely conducted in the shadow of the collapse of the eastern front and necessitated an extensive allocation of economic and military resources, at least part of which might have been channeled into the war effort (see, for instance, Browning, *Path to Genocide*, pp. 169–70). The exceptional case of the Lodz ghetto reveals the desire to be rid of the Jews as a super-principle. The final eradication of the ghetto was delayed until August 1944 because the Jews were of evident use to the war effort, and a controversy developed in different branches of the Nazi regime between those (mainly the head of the SS) demanding eradication despite the ghetto's usefulness and those (Hans Biebow, head of ghetto administration, and local officials, as well as Albert Speer) demanding the exploitation of the ghetto despite the ideological imperative of eradication. See, for instance, Israel Gutman, "The Uniqueness of Lodz Ghetto," in Michal Unger (ed.), *The Last Ghetto* (Jerusalem: Yad Vashem, 1995). In fact, though, up to a certain point, there was no clash of interests. When the first exterminations of Jews began in the Chelmno ghetto, in the winter of 1942, they suited the economic logic of productive ghettoization: superfluous Jews were annihilated, population density decreased, there were fewer mouths to feed, and the conditions of the productive Jews allowed continued production (Browning, *Path to Genocide*, ch. 6). A distinct example of the supremacy of the desire to annihilate the Jews can be found in the special effort invested in the annihilation of the Jews of Hungary in May–July 1944, and in the death march of the Jews of Budapest in November of the same year, despite a clear awareness of the pending damage to the collaps-

676

ing German war machine. The same goes for the deportation of twenty-two hundred Jews from Rhodes to Auschwitz in June 1944, transported instead of valuable military equipment left on the island by the retreating Germans (Diner, "Rationalization and Method," pp. 88–89).

74. Katz proposes to distinguish between historians who approach the study of the Holocaust from a paradigm of similarity for purposes of comparing (and proving the horror of the cases in which they are the witnesses of loss — Armenians, Gypsies, homosexuals, and so forth) and historians who approach the study of the Holocaust from a paradigm of difference for purposes of singularizing (mainly Zionist Jews and Christian theologues). According to Katz, these two paradigms share no common criterion (*The Holocaust in Historical Context*, p. 57, n.96). But most of the scholars mentioned by Katz in this context share the assumption that the Holocaust is an absolute criterion for absolute Evil. In fact, their polarized positions are enabled by a common cultural and intellectual field (in Bourdieu's sense of the term) responsible for the difference in paradigms and for the semblance of no shared criterion (see 9.250). The struggle in this field is over the use of the memory of the Holocaust in order to justify or demand, on the one hand, privileges for the victims of acts of mass murder and, on the other, a decrease or increase in the historical debt owed by the perpetrators of acts of mass murder. Katz is a participant in this field despite himself, and his monumental study is a veritable treasure for all the other participants. Predictably, despite his vehement statements that no moral or theological demand of any kind can be derived from his position, the parties involved will interpret his work *malgré lui*, each according to the interests dictating his position in the field, and will most probably attempt to use this work to redetermine outlines of similarity and singularity.

75. However, the extreme right wing and the liberal left seek to derive contradictory conclusions from the singularity: a particularist conclusion on the right (we will never allow this to happen to *us* again); a universalist conclusion on the left (we will never allow this to happen to *anyone* again). Compare Elkana, "A Plea to Forget."

76. See Moshe Zuckermann, *Zweierlei Holocaust: Der Holocaust in den politischen Kulturen Israels und Deutschlands* (Göttingen: Wallstein, 1998).

77. Katz, *The Holocaust in Historical Context*, vol. 1, pp. 28 and 58.

78. *Ibid.*, vol. 1, pp. 128–30. It's important to note that Katz does not restrict the character of the group in advance (and hence is prepared, in principle, to include a grouping based on gender, political, or economic features). Nor does he restrict the annihilating party in advance, and hence he takes into account the possibility that annihilation will not be conducted by the state or necessarily result from a centralized or totalitarian regime, but will result rather from a lack of a central government strong enough to prevent the massacre.

79. And therefore, there is no point, in Katz's view, in the distinction between holocaust and genocide proposed by Yehuda Bauer, according to the scope of the planned extermination: "genocide" as a term designating mass murder aimed at exterminating part of the group (but as, and because it is, a part of the group singled out for extermination) and "holocaust" as a term designating

mass murder aimed at exterminating the entire group (*ibid.*, p. 131; Bauer, *The Holocaust in Historical Perspective*, ch. 2; see also 9.203). The Holocaust is a unique event, according to Bauer, for the same reasons presented by Katz, and the debate between them actually concerns not the Holocaust but other cases of genocide. Bauer, for instance, insists that the massacre of the Armenians by the Turks was genocide; without disputing the facts, Katz believes it wasn't.

80. Katz, *The Holocaust in Historical Context*, vol. 1, ch. 2.

81. *Ibid.*, vol. 1, ch. 1.

82. In previous sections of the present work, I have tried to show that it is definitely possible to compare different social, political, economic, and cultural conditions according to their contributions to the production and distribution of evils, yet without hoping for some scale that would allow a measurement of what is measureless. Katz is of course right to oppose a moral judgment based on a positivist quantification of "the facts," but mistaken when he attempts to draw a sharp distinction between the victims of direct extermination and the victims of those conditions of catastrophe that cannot be attributed to a guiding hand. And see David E. Stannard's criticism in "Uniqueness as Denial: The Politics of Genocide Scholarship," in Rosenbaum (ed.), *Is the Holocaust Unique?*, pp. 163–208.

83. In this section and the following ones dedicated to Nazism, I relied on the works of Philippe Lacoue-Labarthe and Jean-Luc Nancy: Lacoue-Labarthe, *Heidegger, Art, and Politics: The Fiction of the Political*, trans. Chris Turner (Oxford, UK: Basil Blackwell, 1990); Lacoue-Labarthe and Nancy, "The Nazi Myth," trans. Brian Holmes, *Critical Inquiry* 16, no. 2 (Winter 1990), pp. 291–312.

84. I've dealt with this question in two different pieces: "We Were at Auschwitz, We Weren't at Mt. Sinai," *Davar*, June 2, 1987; and "From Pharaoh to Saddam Hussein: Deconstruction of the Passover Haggadah," in Laurence Silberstein and Robert Cohn (eds.), *The Other in Jewish Thought and History* (New York: New York University Press, 1994), pp. 139–57.

85. This is the argument presented by Lyotard so convincingly in the sections that deal with the reconstruction of the pragmatics of Hegelian dialectics (Lyotard, *Differend*, Hegel Notice, pp. 91–97).

86. Saul Friedlander elaborated extensively on these processes in the first volume of his book *Nazi Germany and the Jews* (New York: HarperCollins, 1997).

87. As early as the 1930s, there was talk of prohibiting reproduction among Slavic peoples. For testimonies regarding the plans for "handling" the non-Aryan population of Eastern Europe, from sterilization through annihilation, see, for instance, Uriel Tal, *Political Theology and the Third Reich* (Tel Aviv: Sifiriat Poalim and Tel Aviv University, 1991), pp. 197–200 [in Hebrew]. On the treatment of the Slavic population within the framework of Nazi population policies, see Heim and Aly, "The Holocaust and Population Policy."

88. Far more than double the number, according to Rummel's count in *Democide*. See also Berenbaum, *Mosaic of Victims*.

89. A somewhat simplistic expression of this approach can be found in two pieces by Rivka Schechter, *The Theological Roots of the Third Reich* (Tel Aviv: Ministry of Defense, 1990) [in Hebrew]; *Auschwitz, Faust-Kingdom* (Jerusalem:

Achshav, 1986) [in Hebrew]. The latest, even if not fully original and still simplistic, manifestation of this trend is Daniel Jonah Goldhagen's *Hitler's Willing
Executioners: Ordinary Germans and the Holocaust* (New York: Knopf, 1996). In
order to explain the choice of the Jews, Goldhagen attempts to "singularize" the
Germans and ascribes to them a collective mentality (formed in the modern era
and altered all at once after the defeat of the Reich), one of whose main components is a deep-rooted anti-Semitism, exceptional in its intensity and character,
as well as a willingness to employ violence. Even if Goldhagen's historical arguments were flawless, no national or emotional "essence" can explain what
allowed the institutionalization of practices of mass extermination, and even less
what these mean to us. On the contrary, any attempt to singularize the German
soul or character and cast the blame on it distances the annihilation of the Jews
of Europe as our problem and damages attempts to give it meaning in terms of
contemporary reality. Numerous and severe historiographical fallacies in Goldhagen's work have been discussed at length by many historians, and the truly
interesting point is the gap between the way his book was received by the public
at large and the way it was received by "professionals." A selection of critiques of
the book and a historiographical discussion of causal explanations for the final
solution can be found at the Web site http://www.h-net.msu.edu and via the
links listed there.

90. This is so even if one — justly — assigns some weight to the fact that the
Nazis accepted the image of the Jews as the chosen people and sought to invert
it so as to place themselves as the chosen people of a new civil religion. This
argument is, for instance, mentioned by Vidal-Naquet, who draws on the work
of Michael Kater and Alain Besançon (Pierre Vidal-Naquet, *Assassins of Memory:
Essays on the Denial of the Holocaust*, trans. Jeffrey Mehlman [New York: Columbia University Press, 1992], pp. 122–23 and nn.96–97).

91. Arendt, *Origins of Totalitarianism*, pt. 3, pp. 154–55.

92. Compare Lacoue-Labarthe and Nancy, *Le Mythe nazi*, pp. 50ff.

93. This effort is also characteristic of some of the thinkers influenced by
Arendt, for instance, Claude Lefort, *The Political Forms of Modern Society* (Lon-
don: Polity, 1986), and Brossat, *L'Epreuve du désastre*. The question of the cultural
motives common to "us" and "them" is a central one that preoccupies both
Lacoue-Labarthe and Derrida and guides their contributions to the debate on
Heidegger's relations to the Nazi party, regime, and ideology. See Lacoue-
Labarthe, *La Fiction du politique*; Derrida, *Of Spirit*; and see also the above-men-
tioned discussion by Ben-Naftali, "On Different Mobilizations 'Of Spirit'"; and
Tal, *Political Theology and the Third Reich*, pt. 5.

94. Arendt, *Eichmann in Jerusalem*, p. 136. See also Adi Ophir, "Between
Kant and Eichmann: Thinking on Evil After Arendt," *History and Memory*, 8 no.
2 (1996), pp. 108–14.

95. Immanuel Kant, *Religion Within the Boundaries of Mere Reason*, trans.
and ed. Allen W. Wood and George Di Giovanni (Cambridge, UK: Cambridge
University Press, 1998), pt. 1, ch. 3, p. 58.

96. Particularly prominent is the genocide in Rwanda in the spring of 1994,
which took place with lightning swiftness and great sophistication and was

highly systematic, but was carried out using extremely simple murder weapons: in two months, about 800,000 members of the Tutsi tribe were massacred by thousands of members of the Hutu, both soldiers and civilians, armed with machetes, rifles, and hand grenades. On the course of the genocide and its social background, see the sources in n.66.

97. Francis Fukuyama, *The End of History and the Last Man* (New York: Free Press, 1992). This view is also echoed in the work of a contemporary philosopher as respected as Richard Rorty: "Indeed, my hunch is that Western social and political thought may have had the last conceptual revolution it needs. J.S. Mill's suggestion that governments devote themselves to optimizing the balance between leaving people's private lives alone and preventing suffering seems to me pretty much the last word." In the note to this section, Rorty adds, "This is, of course, not to say that the world has had the last political revolution it needs. It is hard to imagine the diminution of cruelty in countries like South Africa, Paraguay and Albania without violent revolution. But in such countries, raw courage is the relevant virtue, not the sort of reflective acumen which makes contributions to social theory" (Richard Rorty, *Contingency, Irony, and Solidarity* [Cambridge, UK: Cambridge University Press, 1989], p. 63 and n.21).

98. In different times, in different cultures, in the framework of different views of "the world" and "globality," this abyss took on changing forms and names. What is decisive in this context is what they share: terrible destruction caused by the very globality of the world, that is, by the globalization of the means of causing evil.

99. Michel Foucault coined the term *gouvernementalité* to describe the special forms of power/knowledge that have developed in the West since the nineteenth century and combine the collection of information on, the classification of, the surveillance over, and the intervention in various aspects of the lives of individuals, groups, and entire populations (*History of Sexuality*, vol. 1, *The Will to Knowledge*, pt. 5). In this context, Foucault's analysis conforms with and strengthens the critique of modernism presented by the Frankfurt school. I'm referring, especially, to Marcuse (*One-Dimensional Man*), to Adorno and Horkheimer (*Dialectic of Enlightenment*), and even more to Habermas, who describes the colonization of the lifeworld and its depletion by social systems in *The Theory of Communicative Action*, trans. Thomas McCarthy (Boston: Beacon Press, 1987), vol. 2, chs. 6 and 8.

100. On breaking off the connection between intention, action, and results in complex bureaucratic systems as an enabling condition for the production of atrocities under the Nazi regime, see Bauman, *Modernity and the Holocaust*, ch. 4, esp. pp. 98–111.

101. This is not always the case, but one should always be suspicious that it might be. No innocence can be assumed here. A comparison between Bosnia and the Gulf War is instructive: in the first case, moral interest entailed political attention, but political attention severely restricted the possibilities of moral intervention; in the second case, economic and political interests were formulated through moral rhetoric (defending liberty, respect for the principle of self-determination), but the acts of intervention were never guided or restricted by

moral considerations. Nevertheless, during the Gulf War there was one instance of intervention that was guided first and foremost by moral considerations and would not have been possible without military intervention — this was the aid extended to the Kurdish refugees in northern Iraq, in an area declared a "free zone" in the course of the war, and the protection of these refugees from the Iraqi army and the Turkish army. On humanitarian aid to the free zone in northern Iraq, see Rony Brauman and René Backmann, *Les Médias et l'humanitaire: Ethique de l'information ou charité-spectacle* (Paris: CFPJ, 1996), pp. 141–44. More generally, on the problematic nature of humanitarian aid, see, for instance, Graham Hancock, *Lords of Poverty: The Power, Prestige, and Corruption of the International Aid Business* (New York: Atlantic Monthly Press, 1992); Thomas G. Weiss and Cindy Collins, *Humanitarian Challenges and Intervention: World Politics and the Dilemmas of Help* (Boulder, CO: Westview Press, 1996).

102. Brauman and Backmann, *Les Médias et l'humanitaire*, pp. 116–19.

103. Compare Lyotard, *Differend*, Kant Notice 2 and 5.

104. In some cases, this "inhumanity" is referred to as bestiality, but this is only due to ignorance of the animal world and to a mistaken identification of the otherness of inhumanity with the otherness of animals.

105. But only a certain measure of humanness, that allowing the appearance of compassion. Humanness here is limited to the capacity of the one arousing compassion to suffer and to take an interest in what has disappeared, (almost) without any capacity to be a witness to the loss and suffering, (almost) without any capacity to be the addressee of a call for help, and without demanding of the one arousing compassion any gratitude or recognition of the humanness of the one who feels compassion (see 5.332–5.341).

106. As formulated by Sartre in one of his last conversations with Benny Lévy, regarding what he saw as worth preserving in Jewish messianism. I'm grateful to Menachem Brinker for bringing my attention to this aphorism of Sartre's: Jean-Paul Sartre and Benny Lévy, *Hope Now: The 1980 Interviews*, trans. Adrian van den Hoven (Chicago: University of Chicago Press, 1996).

107. Foucault gave three lectures dealing with the interest that Kant showed in the questions of the age, particularly in relation to its self-understanding as "enlightenment" and concerning the French Revolution. The entire discussion presented here is a variation of sorts on parts of the two later versions of Foucault's lecture on enlightenment: Michel Foucault, "What Is Enlightenment?" in Paul Rabinow (ed.), *The Foucault Reader* (New York: Pantheon, 1984), pp. 35–50; "Qu'est-ce que les Lumières?" *Magazine littéraire*, May 1984, pp. 35–39. The two texts appeared in Michel Foucault, *Dits et écrits*, ed. Daniel Defert and François Ewald (Paris: Gallimard, 1994), vol. 4, pp. 562–78 and 679–88. On this matter, see the excellent discussion by James Schmidt and Thomas E. Wartenberg, "Foucault's Enlightenment: Critique, Revolution, and the Fashioning of the Self," in Michael Kelly (ed.), *Critique and Power* (Cambridge, MA: MIT Press, 1994), pp. 283–314, which includes an English translation of the third lecture.

108. Foucault, "Qu'est-ce que les Lumières?" in *Dits et écrits*, vol. 4, p. 568.

109. On the widely accepted assumption that the chapter "Absolute Freedom and Terror" in *The Phenomenology of Spirit* (no. 594) indeed concerns the

French Revolution. For Hegel, liberty is not a possibility within the reach of the masses or of any of the individuals in them — not when those masses are led by republican revolutionaries and not when they are led by national "liberators" of various kinds. In a letter to a friend he comments, "I am ready to fall down on my knees if I see one liberated person" (Hegel to Niethammer, Dec. 23, 1813), cited in Shlomo Avineri, *Hegel's Theory of the Modern State* (Cambridge, UK: Cambridge University Press, 1972), p. 70, n.33.

110. G.W.F. Hegel, *Elements of the Philosophy of Right*, trans. H.R. Nisbet (Cambridge, UK: Cambridge University Press, 1991), no. 359.

111. Compare Jean-Luc Nancy, *L'Impérative catégorique* (Paris: Flammarion, 1983), pp. 12ff.

112. Unless these are two versions of the same story. See Jean-François Lyotard, *The Postmodern Condition: A Report on Knowledge*, trans. Geoff Bennington and Brian Massumi (Minneapolis: University of Minnesota Press, 1984), ch. 9.

113. On the differentiation of modernity as an epoch, see Hans Blumenberg, *The Legitimacy of the Modern Age* (Cambridge, MA: MIT Press, 1983), pt. 4, ch. 1. I have dealt with this issue elsewhere: Adi Ophir, "Postmodernism: A Philosophical Stance," in Ilan Gur Zeev (ed.), *Education in the Age of Postmodern Discourse* (Jerusalem: Magnes, 1996), pp. 135–63 [in Hebrew].

114. Foucault, "What Is Enlightenment?," pp. 41, 46, 50.

115. Michel Foucault, *The History of Sexuality*, vol. 2, *The Use of Pleasure*, trans. Robert Hurley (London: Penguin, 1992); *The History of Sexuality*, vol. 3, *The Care of the Self*, trans. Robert Hurley (London: Penguin, 1990); "Ethique de souci de soi comme pratique de la liberté," interview in *Concordia* no. 6 (1984), pp. 99–116.

116. "*Argue* as much as you like and about whatever you like, *but obey!*" (Immanuel Kant, "An Answer to the Question: *What Is Enlightenment?*" in *Kant: Political Writings*, ed. Hans Reiss, trans. H.B. Nisbet [Cambridge, UK: Cambridge University Press, 1991], p. 55).

117. This journey is steeped in pathos and reveals a permanent interest in the distress of the other, but both this pathos and this interest accompany Foucauldian thought from the outside and cannot be accounted for in its own terms.

118. Michel Foucault, "Kant on Enlightenment and Revolution," *Economy and Society* 15, no. 1 (1986), p. 89. A translation by Colin Gordon of "Un Cours inédit," *Magazine littéraire*, May 1984, pp. 35–39.

119. See, for instance, Michel Foucault, "Power and Strategies," in Colin Gordon (ed.), *Power/Knowledge: Selected Interviews and Writings, 1972–1977* (New York: Pantheon, 1980), pp. 134–45.

120. Foucault, *Discipline and Punish*, p. 304; and see the last chapter in its entirety.

121. When Foucault speaks of freedom, he is Sartrean in spite of himself. The ubiquity of power is also the ubiquity of freedom, about which Foucault often prefers to speak in terms of "resistance." Freedom cannot be derived from power relations and cannot be removed by them, for where there is no freedom, there is no meaning to the deployment of power; power relations assume the irreducible existence of freedom: "Resistances ... are the odd term in relations

of power; they are inscribed in the latter as an irreducible opposite" (Foucault, *History of Sexuality*, vol. 1, *The Will to Knowledge*, p. 96).

122. Michel Foucault, "What Is Critique?," trans. Kevin Paul Geiman, in James Schmidt (ed.), *What Is Enlightenment? Eighteenth-Century Answers and Twentieth-Century Questions* (Berkeley: University of California Press, 1996), pp. 382–98.

123. Foucault, "What Is Enlightenment?," p. 50 (see 9.410 and n.114). See also Foucault's comments on philosophy as "work on our limits, as essay, as withstanding the test necessitated by thinking differently, which means an effort of the thinking self to be different" (introduction to *History of Sexuality*, vol. 2, *The Use of Pleasure*).

124. Foucault, *History of Sexuality*, vol. 1, *The Will to Knowledge*, pp. 92–102; and even more explicitly: Michel Foucault, "The Subject and Power," in Hubert L. Dreyfus and Paul Rabinow, *Michel Foucault: Beyond Structuralism and Hermeneutics* (Chicago: University of Chicago Press, 1983), pp. 208–26.

125. Foucault, *History of Sexuality*, vol. 2, *The Use of Pleasure*, p. 13. Foucault refers here to each of his books of research in chronological order: *Madness and Civilization, The Birth of the Clinic, The Order of Things, Discipline and Punish*, and *The History of Sexuality*.

126. *Ibid.*, p. 9.

127. G.W.F. Hegel, *Hegel's Logic*, pt. 1 of the *Encyclopaedia of the Philosophical Sciences*, trans. William Wallace (Oxford: Oxford University Press, 1978), no. 131; Martin Heidegger, *Being and Time*, trans. John Macquarrie and Edward Robinson (New York: Harper and Row, 1962), nos. 5–7; Martin Heidegger, "Being and Appearance," in *An Introduction to Metaphysics*, trans. Ralph Manheim (New Haven, CT: Yale University Press, 1959), pp. 98–115.

128. By natural or man-made disaster — it makes no difference — for it is always the case that some evils could and should be prevented, the damage minimized, the loss reduced, and the suffering alleviated.

129. See from 9.500 on, following Blumenberg, *Legitimacy of the Modern Age*, pt. 4, ch. 1.

130. This view of historical time is a prominent characteristic of postmodernism in philosophy in particular and in culture at large. I have discussed this in "Postmodernism: A Philosophical Stance," pp. 151–53.

131. The modernist seeking to locate the watershed that sets apart the "new" era is constantly preoccupied with the line itself. He usually seeks to determine the decisive difference between the modern present and the premodern past, from the point of view of reason, in its relation to the sources of religious authority (the Reformation and the separation of religion from science), or to empirical experience (the growth of experimental natural science as an autonomous field), or to the development of the means of production (the rise of capitalism and instrumental rationalization). In any case, at issue is the moment of reason's liberation from any foreign authority, the emergence of a court of reason — pure and abstract, or practical and embedded in social and economic institutions — as a supreme tribunal pronouncing its own judgments. In the modern view, the historicity of reason is circumscribed: a historicity of the

appearance of the autonomous principle, of its internalization in the consciousness of the people of the West, of its dissemination and its political institutionalization, but not a historicity of the principle itself.

132. As is well known, Heidegger did not follow the logic of his authentic
existence. He did listen to the call arising from the historical present. The result
was catastrophic. One wishes that he had stuck to his amoral conception of
authentic existence rather than opting for a historicist conception of Nazism as
the common horizon and vocation of the historical present.

133. Compare Améry, *At the Mind's Limits*, ch. 1.

Index

Zone Books series design by Bruce Mau
Typesetting by Archetype
Printed and bound by Maple-Vail on Sebago acid-free paper